W9-BHM-724

INFORMATION SYSTEMS

A PROBLEM-SOLVING APPROACH

THIRD EDITION

INFORMATION SYSTEMS

A PROBLEM-SOLVING APPROACH

THIRD EDITION

KENNETH C. LAUDON
New York University

JANE PRICE LAUDON
Azimuth Corporation

THE DRYDEN PRESS
Harcourt Brace College Publishers

Fort Worth   Philadelphia   San Diego   New York   Orlando   Austin   San Antonio
Toronto   Montreal   London   Sydney   Tokyo

Executive Editor: *Richard J. Bonacci*
Developmental Editor: *Lisa A. Toftemark Rittby*
Project Editors: *Michele Tomiak/Nancy Weaver*
Art Directors: *Beverly Baker/Brian Salisbury*
Production Manager: *Ann Coburn*
Product Manager: *Scott Timian*
Marketing Assistant: *Kathleen Sharp*
Director of Editing, Design, and Production: *Diane Southworth*
Publisher: *Elizabeth Widdicombe*

Copy Editor: *Elaine Eldridge*
Permissions Editor: *Elizabeth Banks*
Photo Researcher: *Avery Hallowell*
Indexer: *Edwin Durbin*
Compositor: *Weimer Graphics, Inc.*
Text Type: *10/12 Adobe Garamond*

Cover photo: © *Nick Meers*
Part Openers: © 1995 *Rob Atkins/Image Bank*
Copyright © 1995, 1993, 1991 by The Dryden Press

All rights reserved. No part of this publication may be reproduced or transmitted in any form or by any means, electronic or mechanical, including photocopy, recording, or any information storage and retrieval system, without permission in writing from the publisher.

Requests for permission to make copies of any part of the work should be mailed to: Permissions Department, Harcourt Brace & Company, 6277 Sea Harbor Drive, Orlando, Florida 32887-6777.

Address for orders:
The Dryden Press
6277 Sea Harbor Drive
Orlando, FL 32887
1-800-782-4479 or 1-800-433-0001 (in Florida)

Address for editorial correspondence:
The Dryden Press
301 Commerce Street, Suite 3700
Fort Worth, TX 76102

ISBN: 0-03-002068-9

Library of Congress Catalog Card Number: 94-69391

Printed in the United States of America

6 7 8 9 0 1 2 3 048 9 8 7 6 5 4

The Dryden Press
Harcourt Brace College Publishers

The Dryden Press Series in Information Systems

Parker
Understanding Computers & Information Processing:
Today and Tomorrow
Fifth Edition

Parker
Understanding Computers & Information Processing: Today and
Tomorrow with BASIC
Fifth Edition

Robertson and Robertson
Microcomputer Applications and Programming: A Complete
Computer Course with DOS, WordPerfect 5.1, Lotus 1-2-3,
dBASE III PLUS (or dBASE IV) and BASIC

Robertson and Robertson
Using Microcomputer Applications (A Series of Computer
Lab Manuals)

Simpson and Tesch
Introductory COBOL: A Transaction-Oriented Approach

Sullivan
The New Computer User

Swafford and Haff
dBASE III PLUS

Thommes and Carey
An Introduction to CASE Tools with Visible Analyst (DOS)
Using CASE Tools with Visible Analyst (Windows)

Electronic Learning Facilitators, Inc.
    The DOS Book
    The Lotus 1-2-3 Book
    Stepping Through Excel 4.0 for Windows
    Stepping Through Windows 3.1
    Stepping Through Word 2.0 for Windows
    Up and Running with Harvard Graphics 1.03 for Windows
    Up and Running with PageMaker 5.0 for Windows
    Up and Running with WordPerfect 5.2 for Windows
    Up and Running with Quattro Pro 1.0 for Windows
    Up and Running with Microsoft Works 2.0 for Windows
    Up and Running with Lotus 1-2-3 Release 4 for Windows
    Up and Running with Paradox 4.5 for Windows
    Up and Running with DOS 6.0
    Up and Running with Paradox 4.0 for DOS
    Up and Running with Microsoft Works 3.0 for Windows
    Up and Running with Excel 4.0 for the Macintosh
    Up and Running with Word 5.1 for the Macintosh
    Up and Running with PageMaker 5.0 for the Macintosh
    Up and Running with Windows 4.0
    Up and Running with WordPerfect 6.0 for Windows
    Up and Running with Access 2.0 for Windows
    Up and Running with Microsoft Works 3.0 for Windows
    Up and Running with Excel 5.0 for Windows
    Working Smarter with DOS 5.0
    Working with WordPerfect 5.0
    Working with WordPerfect 5.1

Martin and Parker
Mastering Today's Software Series
Texts available in any combination of the following:
    Microcomputer Concepts
    Extended Microcomputer Concepts
    Disk Operating System 5.0 (DOS 5.0)
    Disk Operating System 6.0 (DOS 6.0)
    Windows 3.1
    Word Processing with WordPerfect 5.1
    Word Processing with WordPerfect 5.2 for Windows
    Word Processing with WordPerfect 6.0 for DOS
    Word Processing with WordPerfect 6.0 for Windows
    Spreadsheets with Lotus 1-2-3 (2.2/2.3)
    Spreadsheets with Lotus 1-2-3 (2.4)
    Spreadsheets with Lotus 1-2-3 for Windows (4.01)
    Spreadsheets with Quattro Pro 4.0
    Spreadsheets with Quattro Pro 6.0 for Windows
    Database Management with dBASE III PLUS
    Database Management with dBASE IV (1.5/2.0)
    Database Management with Paradox 4.0
    Database Management with Paradox 5.0 for Windows

Martin, Series Editor
Productivity Software Guide Lab Manual Series
    Disk Operating System (DOS)
    Windows 3.1
    Word Processing with WordPerfect 5.1
    Word Processing with WordPerfect 5.2 for Windows
    Word Processing with WordPerfect 6.0 for Windows
    Spreadsheets with Lotus 1-2-3
    Spreadsheets with Lotus 1-2-3 for Windows (4.01)
    Spreadsheets with Quattro Pro 4.0
    Spreadsheets with Quattro Pro 6.0 for Windows
    Database Management with dBASE III PLUS
    Database Management with dBASE IV
    Database Management with Paradox 4.0
    Database Management with Paradox 5.0 for Windows
    A Beginner's Guide to BASIC

THE HARCOURT BRACE COLLEGE OUTLINE SERIES

Kreitzberg
Introduction to BASIC

Kreitzberg
Introduction to Fortran

Pierson
Introduction to Business Information Systems

Veklerov and Pekelny
Computer Language C

About the Authors

KENNETH C. LAUDON is Professor of Information Systems at New York University's Stern Graduate School of Business. Ken has played an important role in defining new content, teaching materials, and techniques for business students throughout the United States. He holds a B.A. in economics and philosophy from Stanford University and a Ph.D. from Columbia University.

Ken has written seven books and numerous articles in academic journals about the organizational and societal impacts of information technology. He has testified before Congress on many occasions and has worked as a consultant to the Office of Technology Assessment (United States Congress), the Office of the President, several executive branch agencies, and congressional committees.

Ken's current research deals with the planning and management of very large-scale systems, multimedia learning technology, and knowledge work systems. This research is funded by the National Science Foundation and private corporations.

JANE PRICE LAUDON is a management consultant in the information systems area and a professional writer. She has written seven books. Her special interests include systems analysis and design, software evaluation, and teaching business professionals how to design and use information systems. She has taught at the New York University Stern Graduate School of Business and at Columbia University. She received her B.A. from Barnard College, her M.A. from Harvard University, and her Ph.D. from Columbia University. For the past ten years, Jane has been an information systems consultant for leading *Fortune* 500 companies. She and her husband, Ken, have two daughters, Erica and Elisabeth.

Information Systems: A Problem-Solving Approach is the second book the Laudons have written together. It reflects the Laudons' personal belief that undergraduate information systems textbooks must include a multidimensional perspective involving people, technology, and organizations, and that such books must be, above all, readable, enjoyable, and informative.

⇸ Preface ⇽

Information Systems: A Problem-Solving Approach is based on the premise that virtually all college graduates will be employed in computerized organizations by the twenty-first century. Regardless of their occupations, college graduates will be expected by employers to understand, use, and possibly design computer-based information systems.

Accordingly, we wrote this book for nontechnical undergraduate students in business, information systems, and the liberal arts who will find a knowledge of information systems and technology vital for professional success. This book also provides a broad foundation and understanding for students who are MIS majors.

Increasingly, many colleges, universities, and business employers are finding that students cannot apply computer technology effectively unless they understand more about organizations—the important features of businesses and other organizations and how organizations use information and information systems. They realize that students cannot appreciate the full potential of information technology unless they can see how it is used in real-world settings. Moreover, information technology has changed so rapidly that using computer hardware and software effectively requires considerably less technical knowledge than in the past. Both businesses and educators are finding that the major stumbling block to using computers effectively is not insufficient knowledge of the nuts and bolts of computers but *the need for greater understanding of the role of information technology in organizations and how it can be applied to solve business problems.*

Equally important, the educational and business worlds are both calling for students to hone their critical-thinking and problem-solving skills. To remain competitive, productive, and prosperous, we need to educate people not only with specialized skills but also with the broader knowledge required to solve new problems they will encounter in the future. Our responsibility does not end with teaching students about information systems. We must teach students how to apply what they have learned. This is essential for leaders and problem solvers in a world where the knowledge base and business environment are constantly changing. Our textbook was designed to address these challenges and the American Assembly of Collegiate Schools of Business (AACSB) recommendation for more skill building in the business curriculum.

•UNIQUE THRUSTS OF THE BOOK

Information Systems: A Problem-Solving Approach departs from other textbooks in several ways. It treats information systems as more than simply computers. Instead, we view information systems as composed of information technologies, organizations, and people. We emphasize the broader concepts of information systems rather than computer systems and information systems literacy rather than computer literacy. By information systems literacy, we mean a full understanding of organizations and individuals from a behavioral perspective combined with knowledge of information technology. From this point of view, a firm's procedures, values, and plans, as well as the training it provides its employees, are equally as important as its technologies.

One solid discovery of the past five years is that information technology alone is not sufficient to bring about changes in productivity or personal effectiveness. We need to redesign organizations, create new roles for people, and develop new ideas about how to use information technology wisely in order to achieve higher levels of productivity.

In today's systems environment, the computer is one of many technical elements in a network of devices that may include "smart" printers, facsimile machines, personal digital communicators, and a host of other devices. Data processing is only one of many functions that such networks perform. Hosts of new functions have appeared: multimedia, image processing, graphics, desktop publishing, communications, and group support, to name only a few. Therefore, this book will shift from a singular focus on the "computer in the box" toward an understanding of the many information technologies used in computer-based networks.

Our textbook further departs from textbooks of the past by employing an explicit problem-solving and critical-thinking perspective. It shows how businesses, nonprofit organizations, and individuals can design and use information systems to solve organizational problems, and it emphasizes the teaching of critical-thinking and problem-solving skills. Students will learn how to analyze and define a business problem and how to design an appropriate solution. In many cases the solution requires students to visualize a new information system application.

Avoiding a simple "hands-on" approach, our book seeks a broader understanding of the behavioral and organizational setting of systems. Mere computer literacy or hands-on training will not suffice as the basis of an enduring professional education; knowing how to strike keys on the keyboard is insufficient preparation for the twenty-first century. It is more important for students to know why and how an information system might solve a business problem, how to evaluate software and hardware, and what organizational changes are required to make systems work for a business. Knowing the difference between an organizational problem, a people problem, and a technology problem is central to this understanding.

INTERACTIVE MULTIMEDIA EDITION

This text also stands apart from others by offering an interactive multimedia edition on CD-ROM. It is the first introductory information systems book in this exciting new form. The Multimedia Edition provides all the features and content of the full 16 chapters of the printed text plus features unique to this interactive medium: 16 additional videos explaining key concepts, audio clips, animations and three-dimensional simulations of technology concepts, and interactive projects and exercises. Voice guides walk the student through key concepts and provide chapter introductions. The multimedia edition can be used independently of the hard-cover version or in conjunction with it as an interactive study guide. All supplements for the printed version may be used with the Multimedia Edition.

• HOW THIS BOOK PREPARES YOU FOR THE TWENTY-FIRST CENTURY

Now and in the foreseeable future, the success of a business—whether it becomes the market leader in design and quality, the low-cost producer, or the successful innovator—will increasingly depend on the quality of its information systems and technologies. In turn, the quality of a business's systems and technologies will depend largely on you—the professional who works in the firm. You will be expected to perform the following functions: suggest new uses for information systems; participate in the design of systems; purchase information systems equipment, solve problems using information technology; and understand the limitations of information technology. These new roles and expectations for college graduates require a much deeper understanding of information and information systems than ever before.

Whether you work in business, science, education, or government, you will be expected to assimilate information about a dizzying array of new hardware, software, and telecommunications developments. To keep up with the rapid pace of change tomorrow, you will need a firm foundation today. All your reading, analysis, writing, and problem-solving skills will be required.

To prepare you for the twenty-first century, this book aims to accomplish three goals:

- Show you how to envision, design, and evaluate computer-based solutions to problems found in business and other organizations

- Teach you how to use contemporary and emerging hardware and software tools

- Provide enduring concepts for understanding information systems that you can apply in your future careers or information systems courses

The features of the book accomplish these objectives in a variety of ways.

• PROVIDING CRITICAL-THINKING AND PROBLEM-SOLVING SKILLS

Computers cannot solve a problem unless people can first understand the problem, describe it, and then design a solution. Accordingly, Part 3 of this book (Problem Solving with Information Systems) is devoted to this topic. Earlier chapters introduce problem solving by providing a framework for analyzing organizational problems in terms of people, organizations, and technologies.

How we define a problem fundamentally shapes the solutions we devise. Some problems can be solved by changing organizational structure, management, or procedures. Others require a solution that changes the way an existing information system works or that provides an entirely new one. Thus, problem solving in the information systems world requires a methodology that considers technology, people, and organizations. This methodology, accompanied by real-world case studies depicting alternative solutions, is presented in two core chapters of the text. It appears in many of the other chapters as well.

This edition of the textbook puts even more emphasis on critical thinking and problem solving than earlier editions. It encourages students to learn more actively by providing them with numerous cases, problems, and projects in which they can synthesize the material provided in each chapter and apply the concepts they learn to new situations. Each chapter includes at least one project or exercise that is suitable for group work and presentation, and each is replete with opportunities for students to sharpen and integrate their analytical, writing, and oral-presentation skills. We have added hands-on software exercises to each chapter, in which students can select appropriate software and use spreadsheet and database software skills to develop small real-world applications.

•PROBLEM SOLVING WITH INFORMATION TECHNOLOGIES

Information Systems: A Problem-Solving Approach offers an unparalleled package of both internal and supplementary hands-on materials that makes it relatively easy to learn how to use contemporary information technology to solve business problems.

Parts 2 and 4—Foundations of Information Technologies and Overview of Information System Applications—provide an overview and in-depth understanding of information technologies using real-world examples. Because microcomputers are important tools of individual workers, entrepreneurs, and large corporations, many examples relating to microcomputer hardware, software, and applications are included. Yet mainframes, minicomputers, long-distance telecommunications networks, and large corporate information systems also receive full discussion. The focus of the text is the entire array of contemporary information technologies.

Internal software case studies in key chapters provide the opportunity to use spreadsheet and database software to solve real business problems. These cases are generic in the sense that they can be used with any available software on your campus or in your home.

Hands-on software exercises have played an important role in introductory information systems courses because they have enormous potential for teaching information systems concepts. In competing books, the primary emphasis has been on learning commands and keystrokes to gain facility with various software packages. In this book, software exercises are problem driven. Emphasis is placed on developing concepts and skills for applying software to problem solving.

•PROVIDING AN ENDURING SENSE OF UNDERSTANDING

Most of the hardware and software you use now is at least five years old. Much of it will be gone in five to ten years, replaced by better hardware and software. Hence, some of what you learn today will no longer be relevant five years after your graduation. What will be relevant?

We believe critical-thinking and problem-solving skills will last a lifetime. In addition, many underlying principles of information systems—the structure of computer hardware and software and ways of using this technology intelligently—will not change.

For instance, the basic principles of how computer hardware and software work will not have changed a great deal by the year 2000. Some radically new principles of computing may, indeed, be discovered, but full implementation of totally new computing concepts usually takes a long time. Similarly, the basic professional, financial, and management knowledge base will change slowly over the years. The basic skills that enable you first to understand a problem and then to solve it will not change.

In addition to enhancing your knowledge of contemporary information systems, this textbook develops a more fundamental understanding of technology, organizations, and human beings. We believe this understanding is necessary to cope with a rapidly changing technological base.

We hope *Information Systems: A Problem-Solving Approach* will help you become effective leaders and analysts who can innovate and use information systems to help businesses and other organizations manage change.

•OVERVIEW OF THE BOOK

Part 1 describes the major themes of the book and explores the role of information systems in contemporary businesses. These chapters are especially important for describing the major challenges that we all face in applying information technology effectively. Part 1 raises several major questions: What is an information system? What is an organization? What is a business? How much do I need to know about information systems and why? How can information systems help businesses become more competitive domestically and abroad? What broader ethical and social concerns are raised by information systems in organizations?

Part 2 provides the technical foundation for understanding information and telecommunications technologies. It answers two questions: How do information technologies work? How are they likely to change in the near future? Students with no prior background in computing will find Part 2 very helpful because it provides a basic foundation for computing and systems literacy. More advanced students will find that these chapters considerably extend and update their knowledge of contemporary systems.

Part 3 describes how to use the knowledge gained in Parts 1 and 2 to analyze and design solutions to problems faced by businesses and other organizations. This part focuses on the question: How can information systems be used to solve an organizational problem? Two entire chapters in Part 3 are devoted to critical thinking and problem solving. Chapter 9 describes an overall methodology for analyzing organizational problems. Chapter 10 puts this methodology to work. The emphasis throughout is on a broad understanding of how organizations, technologies, and people must work together. Chapter 11 examines various ways of building systems using basic problem-solving methods and alternative systems development methodologies, while Chapter 12 describes the issues that must be addressed to build information systems that are accurate, reliable, and secure.

Part 4 provides a more extensive introduction to real-world information systems in organizations. It answers two major questions: How do contemporary businesses and other organizations use information systems? How can systems be used to improve management decision making and distribute organizational knowledge? The emphasis here is on real-life examples and how these systems fit into the larger world of business, science, education, and government.

Some of the new themes covered in this book are given complete chapter-length treatment. Among these unique chapters are Information Systems: Challenges and Opportunities (Chapter 3); Knowledge Work: Systems for Offices and Professionals (Chapter 14); Problem Analysis: Critical Thinking Skills (Chapter 9); and Designing Information System Solutions (Chapter 10).

•BOOK DESIGN FEATURES

The following design features reflect the authors' concern for providing a comprehensive understanding of issues and a highly readable text that students and professors will appreciate.

Focus Boxes: In each chapter you will find examples of the four highlighted Focus boxes. The purpose of these boxes is to present contemporary examples of the conceptual foundation, design, use, and management of information technology and systems. Focus box themes are:

Technology	Hardware, software, telecommunications, and data and information storage.
Organizations	Histories, activities, and plans of organizations using information systems.
People	Careers and experiences of individuals working with systems.
Problem solving	Examples of successful and unsuccessful solutions to problems encountered by organizations and their consequences.

Each Focus box features several questions that challenge students to think creatively and apply chapter concepts to the real-world material in the box.

Real-World Examples: Only real-world examples are used throughout the text for cases and Focus boxes. More than 200 American and foreign corporations are discussed in chapter cases, Focus boxes, and the body of the text itself (see the Organization Index).

Problem-Solving Exercises: Each chapter concludes with exercises or projects based on the material covered in the chapter. All these exercises are designed to sharpen problem-solving skills and can be used with any available software or paper and pencil. The problem-solving exercises encourage students to answer a question, think about a problem, work with a group of students to define a solution to a problem, or outline the pros and cons of an issue. Each chapter contains at least one problem-solving exercise designed for group work and presentation and one hands-on software exercise.

Chapter Cases: Thirty-two real-world business cases are included in the text—one at the beginning and one at the end of each chapter. The chapter-opening cases introduce or illustrate the major theme of each chapter. Typically, they focus on how a real-world organization uses a technology (or fails to use it) to solve a problem. The chapter-ending cases, called Problem-Solving Cases, help students review the material covered in each chapter and apply this new knowledge to specific problems.

Leading-Edge Technology Section: Many chapters contain an illustration of leading-edge information technology that is related to chapter topics.

•CHAPTER FORMAT

We have made every effort to ensure that each chapter is lively, informative, and often provocative of further debate, discussion, and thought. Each chapter employs the following format:

A detailed outline at the beginning to provide an overview of chapter contents

A list of chapter learning objectives

A chapter-opening case

A summary that identifies key themes, terms, and topics introduced in the chapter

A list of key terms for students to review

A set of review questions for student use in reading

A set of discussion questions for the instructor and students to use in class discussion or individual study

Problem-solving exercises at the end, consisting of both group and individual projects and hands-on software exercises

A problem-solving case at the end

Notes with references to provide students with guidance for additional research or term papers

•CHANGES TO THE THIRD EDITION

More attention to the ethical, global, strategic, and quality dimensions of information systems: An entirely new chapter on the challenges of information systems describes the leading issues that information systems must deal with today: the ethical and social impact of systems; using systems for competitive advantage; the information system requirements of a global business environment; using systems to promote quality; and reengineering and organizational change. Throughout the text, the authors show how critical thinking and problem solving can help students deal with these issues, with special attention to human and ethical problems such as privacy, software copying, employee monitoring, and employee health and safety.

Expanded coverage of non-business uses of information systems: The book expands coverage of non-business uses of information systems to solve problems in science, art, health care, and the environment, while maintaining its thorough treatment of business applications of information systems. We show how information systems can be used to solve all kinds of problems in everyday life.

Broader international coverage: Many more cases, Focus boxes, and examples emphasizing the global nature of business and information systems have been added to this edition. Three chapter ending cases, 20 Focus boxes and opening vignettes, and two part-ending cases plus numerous other in-text examples are drawn from organizations in Canada, Europe, Africa, South America, and Asia.

Leading-edge coverage of new technical and business developments: The text features extensive treatment of such leading-edge technical and business developments as:

> The Internet and the Information Superhighway
> Redesigning organizations with reengineering
> Case-based reasoning
> Object-oriented programming and databases
> Client/server computing
> Multimedia
> Group decision support systems
> Fuzzy logic

More attention to active student learning and to developing problem-solving skills that students can use throughout their careers: Students can use the projects, problems, and exercises in the text to create portfolios of their work to demonstrate what they have accomplished in the course. These projects and exercises replicate the types of problems students are likely to encounter in their future careers. They can be used to create a structured portfolio demonstrating the student's mastery of analytical, writing, presentation, and software skills that would be of great interest to prospective employers. Exercises and projects suitable for inclusion in the portfolio are highlighted in the text. The *Building Your Portfolio* appendix describes how students can construct a portfolio for future use in job hunting.

New pedagogical aids further promote student critical thinking and activist problem solving:

Interactive learning: The CD-ROM version provides an interactive, computer-managed instruction component that lets students learn at their own pace. They can review key terms with on-line glossaries and access material using electronic indexes. Each text chapter contains a bulleted summary of the key points for immediate on-line access and review. Videos and audio clips for each chapter illustrate real-world applications of key concepts. Students can create and move objects and text as they work through on-line projects that apply text concepts and problem-solving skills. The output of these projects can be used to create digital portfolios of their work. An interactive test bank provides helpful question-and-answer sessions, which can be automatically graded and handed to the professor.

Hands-on problem-solving exercises have been added for use with software of the student's choice. Students must decide whether to use spreadsheet or database software to complete each exercise and then use the software to develop a simple application. The problems are based on real-world businesses and public organizations.

Videos on real-world organizations discussed in the text illustrate important concepts and can be used for class discussion or written projects. Florida Power Corporation, McKesson, and Chrysler Corporation are among the video subjects.

New running case and illustrated cases for student problem solving: An ongoing case about Macy's lets students see critical thinking and problem solving in action, as this retailing giant grapples with declining sales, pressure from competitors, and opportunities to use new information technologies. Four episodes let students apply the concepts they've learned to an unfolding real-life business problem. Illustrated essays on the Internet, Seagram's information system strategy, CASE tools, and the reengineering of Cigna concluding each of the four major sections of the book provide additional case studies to apply concepts and sharpen problem-solving skills.

Diagrams to reinforce the people, organization, and technology framework for analyzing information systems and solving information system problems. A diagram accompanies each chapter-opening vignette, showing how people, organization, and technology work together to solve the problem discussed in the vignette.

•INSTRUCTIONAL SUPPORT MATERIALS

Many additional resources available with this text will assist students in learning more about information systems.

VIDEOS

The Dryden Press 1995 Information Systems Video Series has been developed in response to a need for real business cases tailored to the educational market. Instead of borrowing corporate training tapes or using industry promotional videos, this series has been custom-developed, from the ground up, specifically for classroom use.

The video segments range from 8 to 14 minutes in length, depending on the topic. They were all filmed on location and contain interviews with each organization's key information systems executives, managers, and system users. Most of the video segments highlight a specific use of information technology as it supports the business enterprise; others present different types of technologies in more general context. All the segments are informative, thought provoking, and enjoyable to watch.

The series is accompanied by a detailed instructor's guide. For each video segment, the guide contains a brief description about the video's content, its length, a list of topics discussed in the video, additional background information relevant to the video material, and several discussion questions to stimulate classroom interaction after viewing.

SOFTWARE

In our experience teaching this course, we have found that a strong computer-based learning package can be vital to strengthening student understanding. A software problem-solving supplement called *Solve it!* is available to support the text. Prepared by Ken and Jane Laudon and Peter Weill, *Solve it!* consists of spreadsheet and database cases based on real-world business problems. *Solve it!* is available through Dryden custom publishing or it can be obtained directly from Azimuth Corporation, 124 Penfield Avenue, Croton-on-Hudson, NY 10520. Contact your Dryden/Harcourt Brace sales representative for additional information.

SOFTWARE APPLICATION MANUALS

A wide variety of current software application manuals is also available from The Dryden Press and can be packaged with this textbook as part of the EXACT custom-publishing program. Please contact your local Dryden/Harcourt Brace representative for the latest offering of manuals and to arrange for your custom product.

INSTRUCTOR'S MANUAL

The Instructor's Manual, written by Jane and Ken Laudon and Laurette Poulos Simmons of Loyola College, has been extensively revised for the third edition. It provides additional material to support your classroom preparation and lecture presentation. For each chapter of the text, the Instructor's Manual includes a chapter summary, learning objectives, key terms, lecture outline, answers to review questions, answers to discussion questions, answers to case questions, answers to Focus questions, and completely new transparency masters. The manual highlights where each transparency acetate and transparency master is used in a lecture. The Instructor's Manual is also available on disk.

TEST BANK

The Test Bank, extensively revised for the third edition by Susan Helms at Metropolitan State College, contains more than 2,100 test items, including multiple-choice, true/false, matching, vocabulary application, and short-answer questions as well as problem-solving applications. Questions are keyed to the relevant page number in the text and include an answer key noting the question level and cognitive type. The revision to the test bank was carefully prepared to ensure that language and vocabulary were appropriate for introductory students.

The Test Bank is also available on the ExaMaster Computerized Test Bank in IBM 5.25, 3.5, Windows, and Macintosh versions. The electronic versions allow instructors to easily preview, edit, or delete questions as well as to add their own questions, print scrambled forms of tests, and print answer keys.

TRANSPARENCY ACETATES

A set of approximately 100 full-color transparency acetates, completely revised for the third edition, is available to illustrate and explain key concepts. The acetates feature both selected text diagrams and new pieces of art. Teaching notes for each transparency are included.

•ACKNOWLEDGMENTS

This book was developed over a ten-year period of teaching information systems courses at the Leonard N. Stern School of Business, New York University. We thank the more than 3,000 students who have helped us learn how to teach this material in an engaging manner. We also thank our colleagues at NYU for encouraging us to rethink the curriculum in information systems. At current rates of technological change, this appears to be a biannual process.

Many persons were very helpful in shaping the content and style of this book. We are especially grateful for the comments and insights provided by William H. Starbuck of the Stern School of Business, New York University; Edward Roche of Seton Hall University; Jiri Rodovsky; and Russell Polo. We thank the following people for their helpful suggestions and reviews of all three editions:

Beverly Amer, *University of Florida*
Gary Armstrong, *Shippensburg University*
Robert Behling, *Bryant College*
Thomas Blaskovics, *West Virginia University*
Bill Burrows, *University of Washington*
Thomas Case, *Georgia Southern University*
Sergio Davalos, *Pima Community College*
Patsy Dickey-Olson, *Western Illinois University*
Glenn Dietrich, *University of Texas at San Antonio*
James Divoky, *University of Akron*
Marianne D'Onofrio, *Florida International University*
Jim Dutt, *Bloomsburg University*
David Farwell, *Metropolitan State College*
Dan Flynn, *Shoreline Community College*
Carroll Frenzel, *University of Colorado*
Myron T. Greene, *Georgia State University*
Tom Harris, *Ball State University*
Bill Harrison, *Oregon State University*
Susan Helms, *Metropolitan State College*
Al Kagan, *North Dakota State University*
Milan Kaldenberg, *Northwest Nazarene College*
David Letcher, *Trenton State College*

Cheryl F. Lou, *University of Washington*
Kenneth L. Marr, *Hofstra University*
Ian McKillop, *Wilfrid Laurier University*
John Melrose, *University of Wisconsin—Eau Claire*
Marilyn Moore, *Purdue University—Calumet*
Denise Nitterhouse, *DePaul University*
Jim Payne, *Kellogg Community College*
Shailendra Palvia, *Babson College*
Eugene Rathswohl, *University of San Diego*
Bill Richmond, *George Mason University*
Nick Robak, *St. Joseph's University*
Arline Sachs, *Northern Virginia Community College*
Bruce Saulnier, *Quinnipiac College*
Ronald Schwartz, *Wayne State University*
Irmtraud Seeborg, *Ball State University*
Maung Sein, *Florida International University*
Shashi Shah, *Seton Hall University*
Laurette Poulos Simmons, *Loyola College in Maryland*
Jeff Smith, *Georgetown University*
Charles Snyder, *Auburn University*
Hung-Lian Tang, *Western Michigan University*
Mohan Tanniru, *Syracuse University*
John Tarjan, *California State University—Bakersfield*
David Van Over, *University of Georgia*
Ronald Vaughn, *Western Illinois University*
Randy Weinberg, *St. Cloud State University*
Jacqueline Wyatt, *Middle Tennessee State University*
Judy Wynekoop, *University of Texas at San Antonio*

We are deeply indebted to Marshall R. Kaplan for his assistance with preparation of new Focus boxes, problem-solving cases, and updated text material.

Special thanks to Susan Helms for her extensive work on the Test Bank and to Laurette Poulos Simmons for her splendid revision of the Instructor's Manual.

We also thank our editors at The Dryden Press for insisting on a high-quality text and for encouraging first-rate designs and graphics. Special thanks to Richard J. Bonacci, our acquisitions editor, Lisa Toftemark Rittby, developmental editor, Michele Tomiak, our project editor, Ann Coburn, production manager, and Beverly Baker and Brian Salisbury, art directors, for superb project development, management, coordination, and design. We are grateful, also, to our first-edition editors at The Dryden Press, who launched with great enthusiasm this successful title.

Finally, we want to dedicate this book to our children—Erica and Elisabeth—and to our families for putting up with a couple of writers through yet another project.

Kenneth C. Laudon
Jane Price Laudon
January 1995

Brief Contents

Contents

PART 1   THE WORLD OF INFORMATION SYSTEMS   1

INFORMATION SYSTEMS

A PROBLEM-SOLVING APPROACH

THIRD EDITION

THE WORLD OF INFORMATION SYSTEMS

Chapter

⇾ O N E ⇽

INTRODUCTION TO INFORMATION SYSTEMS

LEARNING OBJECTIVES

After reading and studying this chapter, you will:

1. Be able to define an information system.
2. Understand the basic components of information systems: organizations, people, and technology.
3. Know how knowledge, information, and data differ.
4. Know what skills are required for information systems literacy.
5. Be aware of the information system challenges ahead of you.

*W*ith the world's fish supply dwindling and competition from foreign fisheries mounting, the simple life of a fisherman is disappearing rapidly. Staying in the fishing business today takes insight, creativity, and the use of information systems.

Lund's, the Cape May fishery, started placing computers in its office 12 years ago. Since then, it has started to use information systems in all aspects of the business, from its front office to its freezing operations. Even Lund's fishing boats off the Atlantic coast use computers to plot courses and regulate the placement of their nets, tracking schools of fish with on-board sonar and depth gauges.

Computerization has increased Lund's efficiency and enabled the company to expand worldwide. Lund's now ships between 7,000 and 10,000 tons of mackerel, squid, herring, butterfish, and other catches to over a dozen countries, including Spain, Portugal, China, and Scandinavian nations. It transmits orders, inquiries, quotes, price changes, and invoices to its customers using two desktop computer–based fax machines. Using optical character recognition software, Lund's converts fax documents into data that can be incorporated directly into its office systems. There is no need to rekey in the information.

Although large, multinational companies can maintain offices in many countries, many small businesses such as Lund's do not have the necessary resources to do so. Thirty-five years ago, if you wanted to do business abroad as an individual entrepreneur, you were doomed to a life of airplane travel. Now you can perform most operations right from your desk or even *from a fishing boat. With today's information systems, even a small firm on a shoestring budget can communicate with customers, suppliers, and partners overseas.*

Not everything has changed. Some aspects of a business still can't be managed from an armchair. Lund's, as well as other firms with global business, have found that information technology has not eliminated the need to travel. But Jeff Reichle, Lund's president, needs to take to the airways only once or twice a year to improve service and products. He believes that the face-to-face part of doing business doesn't go away.

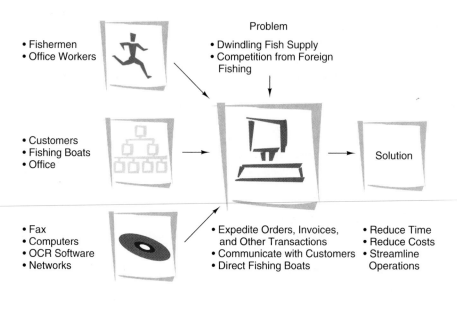

- Fishermen
- Office Workers

Problem
- Dwindling Fish Supply
- Competition from Foreign Fishing

- Customers
- Fishing Boats
- Office

Solution

- Fax
- Computers
- OCR Software
- Networks

- Expedite Orders, Invoices, and Other Transactions
- Communicate with Customers
- Direct Fishing Boats

- Reduce Time
- Reduce Costs
- Streamline Operations

SOURCE: Michael Finley, "Hooking Up Planet Earth," *Profit*, July/August 1993.

Lund's fishery is typical of many organizations today that find information systems essential to their day-to-day operations and long-term survival. Regardless of size, organizations increasingly need information systems to respond to the problems and opportunities of today's competitive global business environment. Information systems are transforming the way work is conducted, the products and services that are produced or provided, and who is producing or providing them. Information systems are also giving individuals new tools for improving their lives and their communities. This chapter starts our discussion of information systems by explaining how an information system works and how it uses people, organization, and technology elements to solve problems.

1.1 INTRODUCTION

Why should you be concerned about information systems? Isn't that the job of technical people? After all, no one asks that you take a course on the "telephone system." The example of Lund's fishery above provides at least three reasons why you should understand how information systems work.

As a society, we are engaged in a global economic competition for resources, markets, and incomes with other nations in both Europe and Asia. For Adam Smith, the eighteenth-century Scottish economist who initiated the modern study of economics with his book *The Wealth of Nations*, the income of a nation depended on how well that society organized production in its domestic factories. Now, in the 1990s, it is clear that our society will have to organize global markets, international corporations, and multinational work forces if we are to maintain and enhance our standard of living. We will need information systems to do this effectively and successfully.

Second, we will need a thorough understanding of information systems to achieve higher levels of productivity and effectiveness within our domestic factories and offices. Without higher levels of productivity in domestic businesses, we will lose the international competition for incomes and resources. This translates directly into lower real incomes for us all. It simply will be impossible to operate even a small business efficiently without significant systems investments. Those of you who want to become entrepreneurs should note that almost half of all new businesses in the 1990s will involve computer-based services or products.

More forces are causing businesses to rethink what they are doing and change and adapt. The challenges posed by new customers, competitors, technology, political relations, economic conditions, government regulations, and labor force characteristics call for many kinds of changes, such as improved production techniques, new products and services, new administrative systems, and new employee skills. As an individual entrepreneur or as an intrapreneur sponsoring change from within a business organization, you must know how to identify problems and opportunities and how to use information systems to help businesses manage change.

Finally, your effectiveness as a professional or entrepreneur—indeed, your career and income—will in part depend on how well you apply yourself to the task of understanding information systems. Whether you want to be a graphic artist, professional musician, lawyer, business manager, or small business owner, you will be working with and through information systems. The conclusion is inescapable: you will have to be information systems literate.

Before we explore the growing role of information systems in business, we must first define an information system and its basic components.

INFORMATION SYSTEMS IN ORGANIZATIONS

An **information system (IS)** can be defined as a set of interrelated components working together to collect, retrieve, process, store, and disseminate information for the purpose of facilitating planning, control, coordination, analysis, and decision making in businesses and other organizations (see Figure 1.1). Information systems contain information on significant people, places, and things in an organization's surrounding environment and within the organization itself. Information systems essentially transform information into a form usable for coordinating the flow of work in a firm, helping employees or managers make decisions, analyzing and visualizing complex subjects, and solving other kinds of problems. Information systems accomplish this through a cycle of three basic activities: input, processing, and output.

Input entails capturing or collecting raw data resources from within the organization or from its external environment. **Processing** entails converting this raw input into a more appropriate and useful form. **Output** entails transferring the processed information to the people or activities that will use it. Information systems also store information, in various forms of completeness, until it is needed for processing or output. **Feedback** is output that is returned to appropriate members of the organization to help them refine or correct the input phase.

Information system

A set of interrelated components working together to collect, retrieve, process, store, and disseminate information for the purpose of facilitating planning, control, coordination, analysis, and decision making in business and other organizations.

Input

The capture or collection of raw data resources from within an organization or from its external environment.

Processing

The conversion of raw input into a more appropriate and useful form.

Output

The transfer of processed information to the people or activities that will use it.

Feedback

Output that is returned to appropriate members of the organization to help them refine or correct the input phase.

FIGURE 1.1

Activities of Information Systems: Input, Processing, and Output

An information system operates in cycles of three steps each. In the first step, input, the system collects data from within the organization or from the organization's environment. The next step, processing, involves converting the raw input data into a form that is more useful and understandable. Finally, the output information is transferred to people or activities that can use it. Feedback is output that is "fed back" to appropriate people or activities; it can be used to evaluate and refine the input stage.

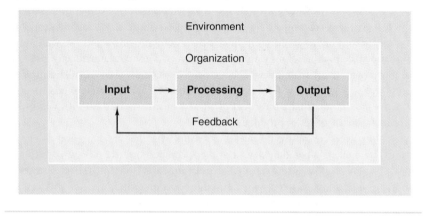

Computerized information systems capture data from either inside or outside an organization by recording them on paper forms or by entering them directly into a computer system using a keyboard or other device. Input activities, such as recording, coding, classifying, and editing, focus on ensuring that the required data are correct and complete. During processing, the data are organized, analyzed, and manipulated through calculations, comparisons, summarization, and sorting into a more meaningful and useful form. Output activities transmit the results of processing to where they will be used for decision making, design, innovation, coordination, or control. The output of information systems takes various forms—printed reports, graphic displays,

By using a computerized reservation system, the Hilton hotel chain can instantaneously book and keep track of individual and group reservations made for Hilton's hotels all over the world. Hotel salespeople can enter reservation data and view reservation information directly from their desktop workstations.

SOURCE: Courtesy of Hilton Hotels Corporation.

video displays, sound, or data to feed other information systems. The information system must also store data and information in an organized fashion so that they can be easily accessed for processing or for output. Computerized information systems are essential in today's work environment because they can help people analyze problems, visualize complex subjects, create new products, communicate, make decisions, coordinate, and control.

For example, the Hilton Hotel chain uses an information system called Answer*Net to book and keep track of travel reservations for group bookings and conventions. Approximately 600 Hilton salespeople enter client data into the system using desktop computer workstations (input). The data are transmitted to a large computer center in Texas for updating Hilton's reservation and client records (processing) and for storage. The system produces bookings forms; site availability, sales lead, and market reports; and forecasts (output). Figure 1.2 illustrates the input, processing, output, and feedback functions of this system.

We need to clarify our definition further by saying that we are concerned exclusively in this book with formal, organizational, computer-based information systems (CBIS). Each of these words deserves some comment. The CBIS we describe in this book are **formal systems**, which rely on mutually accepted and relatively fixed definitions of data and procedures for collecting, storing, processing, and disseminating information. For instance, a manual file of customer names and addresses, or an alphabetical card catalog in a library, is a formal information system because it is established by an organization and conforms to organizational rules and procedures; this means that each entry in the system has the same format of information and the same content.

Formal systems

Information systems that rely on mutually accepted and relatively fixed definitions of data and procedures for collecting, storing, processing, and disseminating information.

FIGURE 1.2

Input/Processing/Output Model Applied to the Hilton Answer*Net System

This diagram of the Hilton Answer*Net reservations system illustrates the input, processing, and output functions of a typical information system. About 600 Hilton salespeople from all over the United States enter raw data into the system via desktop computer workstations. The central computer center in Texas processes the data by updating records and storing necessary information. The output includes bookings forms; site availability, sales lead, and market reports; and market forecasts. These are sent to appropriate staff members, whose feedback can have an impact on how future input data are collected.

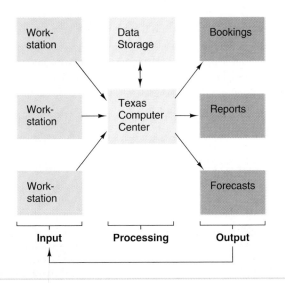

FIGURE 1.3

An Information System: Not Just a Computer
Throughout this book we emphasize a sociotechnical approach to information systems. A successful system has organizational and people dimensions in addition to technical components. It exists to answer organizational needs. The organization, in turn, is shaped by its external environment, which includes political, demographic, economic, and social trends.

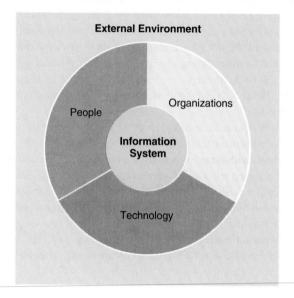

Informal systems, by contrast, do not have these features. For instance, students inevitably form small groups of friends, and these groups usually have information systems. In these informal information systems, there is no agreement on what information is, how it will be stored, and what will be stored or processed. Like office gossip networks, groups of friends freely share information on a large and constantly changing set of objects, topics, and personalities. These open, informal systems are very important—indeed, they are very powerful and flexible—but they are not the direct subject of this book.

CBIS are built for the purpose of solving significant problems as they are perceived in organizations. This insight—that systems exist to solve business and other problems—will be used often throughout this book. We can use this insight to understand not only the systems that exist now (and why) but also the way to build systems in the future and the skills you will need to have.

COMPONENTS OF INFORMATION SYSTEMS

CBIS use computer technology to perform some portions of the processing functions of an information system and some of the input and output functions as well. It would be a mistake, however, to describe an information system in terms of the computer alone. An information system is an integral part of an organization and is a product of three components: technology, organizations, and people (see Figure 1.3). One cannot understand or use information systems effectively in business without knowledge of their organizational and people dimensions as well as their technical dimensions.

Organizations   Organizations shape information systems in several obvious ways. Business firms are formal organizations. They consist of specialized units with a clear-cut division of labor and experts employed and trained for different business functions such as sales, manufacturing, human resources, and finance. Organizations are hierarchical and structured. Employees in a business firm are arranged in rising levels of authority in which each person is accountable to someone above him or her. The upper levels of the hierarchy consist of management, and the lower levels consist of non-managerial employees. Formal procedures, or rules for accomplishing tasks, are used to coordinate specialized groups in the firm so they will complete their work in an acceptable manner. Some of these procedures, such as how to write up a purchase order or how to correct an erroneous bill, are incorporated into information systems. Each organization has a unique culture, or bedrock assumptions, values, and ways of doing things that have been accepted by most members of the firm.

Different levels and different specialties in an organization in turn create different interests in the organization and different points of view, which often conflict. Out of these conflicts, politics, and eventual compromises come information systems. Organizations need to build these systems to solve problems created both by these internal factors and by external environmental factors, such as changes in government regulations or market conditions.

People   People use information from computer-based systems in their jobs, integrating it into the work environment. People are required to input data into the system, either by entering data into the system themselves or by putting the data on a medium that can be read by a computer.

Personal computer training classes take place at Rockwell International's Newport Beach, California, plant. In all companies, proper training is essential to the effective use of information systems.

SOURCE: Courtesy of Rockwell International.

Employees require special training to perform their jobs or to use information systems effectively. Their attitudes about their jobs, employers, or computer technology can have a powerful effect on their ability to use information systems productively. Ergonomics refers to the interaction of humans and machines in the work environment; it includes the design of jobs, health issues, and the way in which people interact with information systems, and it has a strong bearing on employees' morale, productivity, and receptiveness to information systems. The user interface, or portions of an information system that people must interact with, such as reports or video displays, also has a strong bearing on employees' efficiency and productivity.

Technology   The technology is the means by which data are transformed and organized for human use. An information system can be an entirely **manual system**, using only paper and pencil technology. (An example would be a professor's file folder containing course records and grades.) Computers, however, have replaced manual technology for processing large volumes of data or for complex processing work. Computers can execute millions and even hundreds of millions of instructions per second. A processing task that might take years to perform manually can be performed by a computer in a matter of seconds. Computers can also perform consistently and reliably over a longer period of time than a human being can. The information systems described in this text are computer based; that is, they rely on some form of computer technology for input, output, processing, and storage.

Computer hardware is the physical equipment used for the input, processing, and output work in an information system. It consists of the computer processing unit itself and various input, output, and storage devices plus physical media to link these devices together.

Input hardware collects data and converts them into a form that the computer can process. The most common computer input device is the computer keyboard, but others will be described in subsequent chapters. Processing hardware transforms input to output based on instructions supplied to the computer through software. A special processing unit in the computer itself, called the central processing unit, is primarily responsible for this task. Output hardware delivers the output of an information system to its user and commonly consists of printers or video display terminals. Chapters 4 and 5 discuss computer hardware in greater detail.

Computer software consists of preprogrammed instructions that coordinate the work of computer hardware components to perform the processes required by each information system. Without software, computer hardware would not know what to do and how and when to do it. Software consists of related programs, each of which is a group of instructions for performing specific processing tasks. Chapter 6 treats computer software in more detail.

The storage technology for organizing and storing the data used by a business is a powerful determinant of the data's usefulness and availability. **Storage technology** includes both the physical media for storing data, such as magnetic or optical disk or tape, and also the software governing the organization of data on these physical media. Storage media are discussed in Chapter 5, and data organization and access methods are treated in Chapter 7.

Telecommunications technology is used to link different pieces of hardware and to transfer data from one location to another. Telecommunications involves both physical media and software that support communication by electronic means, usually over some distance. Chapter 8 covers telecommunications.

Let's return to the Hilton Answer*Net reservation system and see where each of these components fits in. The technology consists of a large central computer linked via

---

Manual system

An information system that uses only paper and pencil technology and does not rely on computers.

Computer hardware

The physical equipment used for the input, processing, and output work in an information system.

Computer software

Preprogrammed instructions that coordinate the work of computer hardware components to perform the processes required by each information system.

Storage technology

Physical media for storing data (e.g., magnetic and optical disks or tapes) and the software governing the organization of data on these media.

Telecommunications technology

Physical media and software that support communication by electronic means, usually over some distance.

telecommunications to desktop workstations and technology for storing reservation and client data. By using a computer, Answer*Net can process hundreds of thousands, even millions, of reservation requests each day. The people component requires training the sales staff to enter and receive bookings, to use the sales and site availability reports to attract more reservations, and to use the workstations as well as designing an appropriate user interface for these tasks. The organization component anchors the Answer*Net system in Hilton's sales and marketing function; it identifies specific procedures for booking reservations (i.e., obtaining customer identification, confirming the reservation, securing the reservation with a deposit or credit card number) and provides reports and forecasts for sales staff and higher levels of management. How might hotels use information system technology in the future? This topic is explored in the Focus on Technology.

Review the diagram at the beginning of this chapter. It shows how people, organization, and technology elements work together to create an information system solution to a problem. We begin each chapter of the text with a similar diagram to help you analyze the opening vignette and other systems you will encounter.

1.2 APPROACHES TO STUDYING INFORMATION SYSTEMS

You have probably already gathered that our emphasis in this book will be on how information systems work, not just on computers. Most people think that computers and information systems are the same thing. They also think that computer literacy and information systems literacy are identical. Although this may have been true in the early days of computing and systems, it is no longer true today.

DIFFERENCES BETWEEN COMPUTERS AND INFORMATION SYSTEMS

We will draw a sharp distinction in this text between a computer, a computer program, and an information system. Computers—and other information technologies—are the technical foundations or the tools of information systems. Computers and telecommunications equipment store, process, disseminate, and communicate information. Computer programs, or software, are the sets of instructions that direct computer processing.

Information systems are much broader in scope. They encompass the technologies, organizational procedures, practices, and policies that generate information as well as the people who work with that information.

COMPUTER LITERACY AND INFORMATION SYSTEMS LITERACY

Computer literacy means knowing how to use information technology. It involves a knowledge of hardware, software, telecommunications, and information storage techniques. In general, computer literacy focuses on what goes inside the box called a computer—how disk drives work, how a random access memory works, and so forth. Computer literacy is an important part of designing solutions to problems, but it is just the first step.

Computer literacy
Knowledge about the use of information technology; it involves knowing about hardware, software, telecommunications, and information storage techniques.

FOCUS ON TECHNOLOGY

THE HOTEL OF THE FUTURE: IT'S HERE

When you arrive at the hotel you introduce yourself by slipping your smart card into a doorway slot. The smart card looks like a credit card, but its tiny embedded circuitry can store and record information such as a person's name, purchase transactions, and bank account. Forget about the check-in desk. You can go straight to your room, which was assigned earlier by computer. The door to your room opens when you say your name. After you unpack, you punch in channel 143 on the TV and hold a videoconference with your colleagues 2,000 miles away in Seattle. After the meeting you switch to another channel to shop for a gift. Just before turning in, you use the videophone to see how the family is doing while you are on the road.

This "future" scene will be commonplace soon because companies like the Marriott hotel chain are finding new ways to use information system technology to please their customers. According to Steven P. Weisz, Marriott's senior vice-president of sales and marketing, Marriott doesn't just want to satisfy its customers—it wants to delight them.

Hotel guests habitually complain about the amount of time required to check in. Marriott listened. The hotel chain launched a program called 1st 10 that virtually eliminates the front desk. When a guest makes a reservation, an information system collects pertinent information such as the credit card number and time of arrival, reducing check-in time from an average of three minutes (even more at large convention hotels) to 1½ minutes. With smart card technology Marriott hopes eventually to reduce check-in time to seconds.

Marriott will install videophones so that guests can visually communicate with family, colleagues, and clients. And information system technology will help Marriott to personalize customer service in new ways. Rapid advances in computer hardware and software make customer service easier—and more fun. Voice recognition technology will allow customers to speak into a computer when opening a room at the hotel of the future instead of pushing buttons or typing. This technology has matured and is predicted to be widespread by the year 2000, in use at banks, restaurants, hotels, libraries, and mail-order houses.

Voice recognition technology will be able to provide a wide array of services. AT&T's Universal credit card service plans to use voice recognition technology to create a "personal servant" for its 17 million cardholders. The cardholder will be able to use a telephone or computer to instruct the "personal servant" to make hotel reservations, balance the checkbook, and do various mundane chores. The cardholder may even be able to design the voice and personality of the "personal servant" to mimic Marilyn Monroe, Madonna, Sir John Gielgud, or anyone he or she chooses.

FOCUS Questions:
What new information system technologies are being used in this case? How could they be used to change the way the Hilton Answer*Net system works?

SOURCE: Faye Rice, "The New Rules of Superlative Service," *Fortune: The Tough New Consumer*, Autumn/Winter 1993.

As we saw earlier, an information system involves not just technology, but people and organizations as well. Thus, to develop information systems literacy, you need more than just computer literacy. You also need to understand the nature of problems

FIGURE 1.4

Information Systems Literacy: More Than Just Using a Computer
Because an information system involves people and organizations as well as technology, it follows that information systems literacy is more than just knowing how to program. To be information literate, you must develop skills in analyzing and solving problems and in dealing effectively with people at both the individual and organizational levels. Think of this course as the center of this diagram, with the three skill areas comprising the major themes of the course. This also gives you an idea of what you will study if you major in Information Systems. Generally, an IS major will take classes in all three skill areas.

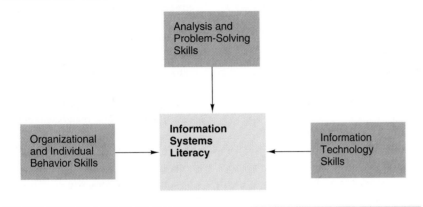

faced by organizations: Where do they come from? How can systems be designed to solve them? Who else is involved in building system solutions? How can the work be coordinated? These issues involve design, organization, and people.

Thus **information systems literacy** consists of three elements:

- A knowledge and hands-on facility with information technologies.

- A broadly based understanding of organizations and individuals from a behavioral perspective.

- A broadly based understanding of how to analyze and solve problems.

Figure 1.4 illustrates the three components of information systems literacy. Generally, students who major in information systems take courses in these three areas.

A house provides a good analogy for the difference between computer and information systems literacy. Houses are built with nails, hammers, wood, and plaster. But these alone do not make a house. Also involved in a good house are design, location, setting, landscaping, and hundreds of other features. These other considerations are crucial to the essential problem: putting a roof over one's head.

So it is with information systems: information technologies are the tools—the hammers, nails, and materials. But to understand the systems, you need to understand the problems they were designed to solve, the proposed architectural and aesthetic solutions, and the organizational process that leads to systems.

Information systems literacy
Knowledge and hands-on facility with information technologies, a broadly based understanding of organizations and individuals from a behavioral perspective, and a similar understanding of how to analyze and solve problems.

DIFFERENCES AMONG DATA, INFORMATION, AND KNOWLEDGE

Philosophers have for centuries been struggling to define data or facts, information, and knowledge. A small library could easily be filled with their results. To arrive at some operational definitions, we can start with Plato (c. 428–348 B.C.), an ancient Greek philosopher whom you will no doubt read while in college. For Plato, pure data were a

FOCUS ON PROBLEM SOLVING

THE NEW LIBRARY: NO BOOKS

Every day, teenaged workers at the Chicago–Kent School of Law at Illinois Institute of Technology take books off library shelves, slit open their bindings, tear out the pages, and throw the books away. But these are no acts of vandalism. The teenagers are creating the library of the future.

How can this be a library if there are no books? The answer lies in new computer technology. A computer scans the pages of each book and stores them in digital form so that they can be retrieved by computer. The card catalog is gone, too. Instead, patrons can search for book titles, authors, and subjects on the computer.

The advent of electronic libraries will transform knowledge acquisition and research. When people "go to the library" they won't have to go anywhere. With new communications technologies, the library will come to them via a desktop computer. People will be able to sit at home browsing catalogs and shelves. To obtain original documents from Harvard or Oxford Universities, tap in a request and the material you want will appear on your screen–text, pictures, graphs. You will even be able to hear oral history collections through earphones. All of these features make computerized libraries more accessible, particularly for the disabled.

Searching for a book electronically can be easier and more efficient than traditional methods. Many library systems let users ask questions in English and furnish a list of documents related to the question. A researcher at a computerized library terminal could type in the terms "child abuse and child pornography" and receive a list of 50 documents on subjects such as child labor, family violence, or child pornography. When the researcher highlights two paragraphs as being close to what she or he wants, the system refines the list of documents.

Computerized libraries eliminate redundant effort. If computerized information could be sent cheaply from one library to another, there would be little need for libraries to maintain the same collection of books, articles, or documents. If Harvard University kept the electronic copy of all the Nuremberg trial information, there would be no need for Columbia or other universities to keep their own copies. Libraries would no longer have to keep dozens of copies of items on reserve for large classes, since many students could read them simultaneously on the computer.

Without the need to shelve hundreds of thousands of books, it is likely that electronic libraries will be much smaller than those of today. It may take decades before all libraries are electronic, but the move is on—many libraries are running out of space. Columbia University's law library cancelled a plan to build a $20 million addition to store new books, opting instead to scan and store 10,000 deteriorating old books each year on a $1.5 million supercomputer. This frees up enough shelf space for all the new copyrighted material the library acquires yearly—at far less cost than new buildings and bookshelves.

The electronic catalog of the Bibliotheque de France, France's new grand national library, will be able to hold up to 15 million entries. It can be used by readers on-site and in other locations to request documents and services and will start out by communicating with a digitized library of 300,000 documents. While the books in the collection themselves have not been fully digitized, the automated system will make it much easier to locate and transmit information, even from remote areas.

But there are obstacles. Publishers and authors worry about rampant copying of electronic material. Researchers may resent paying for data delivered by networks over phone lines when they are accustomed to obtaining most of it for free.

FOCUS Questions: What problems are solved by using electronic libraries? How can these new electronic libraries benefit businesses and society in general? What are the disadvantages? As libraries become electronic, how will the role of the library change?

SOURCES: William M. Bulkeley, "Libraries Shift from Books to Computers," *The Wall Street Journal,* January 8, 1993, and Marsha W. Johnston, "C'est Magnifique," *InformationWEEK,* August 24, 1992.

shadowy reflection on a wall of all the things going on in the world.[1] Thus **data** can be considered the raw facts, the infinite stream of things that are happening now and have happened in the past.

Information comes from the Latin word *informare*, meaning "to give form or shape." Most philosophers believe that it is the human mind that gives shape and form to data in order to create meaningful "information" and knowledge. Plato and other Greek philosophers originated this concept of a world of meaning, intention, and knowledge created by human beings. These ideas are at the heart of Western culture.

We will define **information** as data that have been given shape and form by human beings to make them meaningful and useful. **Knowledge** is the stock of conceptual tools and categories used by humans to create, collect, store, and share information. Knowledge can be stored as an artifact in a library—as a book, for instance—or in a computer program as a set of instructions that gives shape to otherwise meaningless streams of data.

Human beings have a long history of developing systems for the purpose of giving shape to data, as well as recording, storing, and sharing information and knowledge. Libraries, tabloids, writing, language, art, and mathematics are all examples of information systems. The focus of this text, and much of the course, will be on how CBIS store, collect, and share information and knowledge in organizations.

The Focus on Problem Solving shows how one of our fundamental information systems, the library, is being transformed by computer technology and how such changes affect the acquisition of information and knowledge.

A SOCIOTECHNICAL PERSPECTIVE ON INFORMATION SYSTEMS

The view we adopt in this book is that information systems and information technologies are sociotechnical systems that involve the coordination of technology, organizations, and people. The information architecture of the firm—the computers, networks, and software—rests on these three pillars.

In the past the study of information systems was regarded as a technical subject, of interest primarily to computer science students. By the 1970s, however, there was a growing recognition that a purely technical approach to information technology failed to take into account organizational and individual factors. The most advanced computing technology is essentially worthless unless businesses can make use of the technology and unless individuals feel comfortable using it.

In the **sociotechnical perspective**, information technology, organizations, and individuals go through a process of mutual adjustment and discovery as systems are developed. Figure 1.5 illustrates what happens over time as information systems are built. In many instances, the technology must be altered to fit the unique needs of each organization. Almost always, organizational changes must be invented and then implemented. And, of course, a considerable amount of retraining of employees must take place to develop a successful, useful system.

1.3 PURPOSE OF STUDYING INFORMATION SYSTEMS

You don't have to know how a car engine works in order to drive a car, so you shouldn't have to learn about how information systems or computers work if all you want to do is use them.

Data
Raw facts that can be shaped and formed to create information.

Information
Data that have been shaped or formed by humans into a meaningful and useful form.

Knowledge
The stock of conceptual tools and categories used by humans to create, collect, store, and share information.

Sociotechnical perspective
An approach to information systems that involves the coordination of technology, organizations, and people; in this approach, information technology, organizations, and individuals go through a process of mutual adjustment and discovery as systems are developed.

FIGURE 1.5

A Sociotechnical View of Information Systems

In a system, technology, organizations, and people must cooperate and support one another to optimize the performance of the entire system. The three elements adjust as they move from planning to actual operation and continue to change over time, not always improving but sometimes degrading until they must be corrected or entirely replaced.

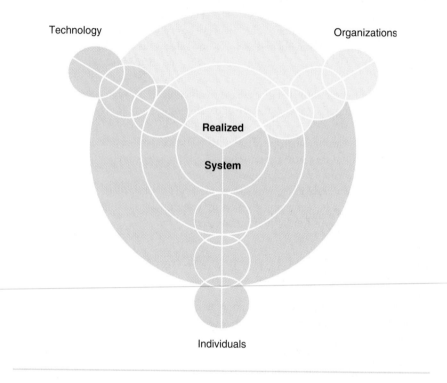

Technology   Organizations

Realized

System

Individuals

There is some truth to this statement, but it has clear limitations as well. If you want to buy a car, especially a used car, you might want to know something about how a car engine works—at least what a healthy engine sounds like. If you want to fix a car, you surely will need to know something about cars. When you are stranded on the highway in a rain storm, you might wish you knew a little more about your own car engine. Certainly, if someone told you to go out and put a car together in order to save the business (or your job), you would really need to know something about how a car works.

As we pointed out earlier, the chances are very high that your employer will in fact ask you to go out and find some sort of system solution to a business problem. The intent of this book is to prepare you for that eventuality.

But what do you really need to know about computers and information systems to succeed in today's and tomorrow's job markets? Do you have to know how a computer processes bits of data, how to program a computer in some esoteric language, how to wire together a microcomputer workstation and a printer, how electrons behave on the surface of a chip, how a disk drive works, or how a business uses information systems for competitive advantage? Do you have to know everything about computers? These are difficult questions with which educators themselves struggle.

INTERSECTING SKILLS

Given the broad sociotechnical perspective on systems described above, it is clear that no one person has all the expertise needed to put together successful information systems that can solve business problems. Even technical professionals acknowledge that no one person has a complete technical understanding of all there is to know about, say, an IBM or an Apple Macintosh microcomputer. As it turns out, information systems are inherently a group effort involving different people with different technical, business, and analytic skills.

So one answer to how much you need to know is that there are three skills to consider: technical, organizational, and analytic/problem-solving abilities. Some people will excel in one or two areas; most people will not excel in all three.

CAREER PATHS AND CRUCIAL SKILLS

Some of you will want to pursue a career in the information systems profession either as a technical person or as a manager of projects and systems. Others will choose a career

Helping business people make decisions, producing original works of art, and generating weather maps are but some of the many uses of computers today. Information systems literacy is becoming essential for careers in business, science, and the arts.

SOURCES: Courtesy of International Business Machines Corporation, Computer Associates International, Inc., and © John Bowden Uniphoto Picture Agency.

FIGURE 1.6

The Importance of Sociotechnical Skills in Your Career

Whether you're interested in a technical or nontechnical career, sociotechnical skills are crucial. Note that analysis and problem solving are important abilities for all four of the career paths shown. Managers—whether in IS or some other business function—need to develop their behavior and communications skills, and technical skills are important even for non-IS professionals. As the graph shows, all of these career paths demand at least some expertise in all three skill areas.

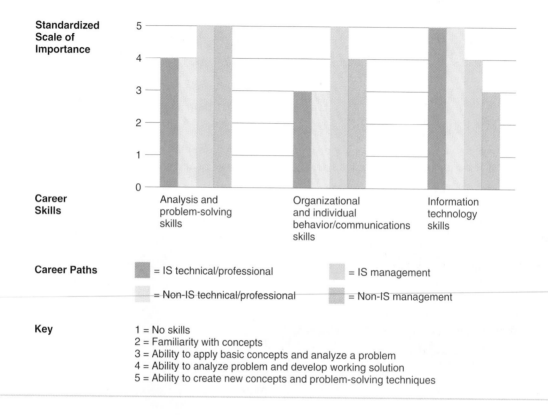

path outside information systems, either in a technical area like engineering or biology or in a business field such as management, marketing, accounting, finance, or sales. But life and careers are unpredictable. Many current managers of information systems divisions, even entire computer companies, had little or no background in computers or systems. Hence, you will have to be prepared for several possible futures.

Depending on what kind of career path you want to pursue, you can obtain some idea of the skills you will need from Figure 1.6. There we have ranked the importance of specific skills on a scale from 1 to 5 with 1 indicating that no knowledge is required and 5 indicating that extensive training is needed.

RELATED COURSES

Figure 1.7 lists specific interpersonal and on-the-job abilities that are part of these skills. It also shows courses in related disciplines that will help you develop these crucial skills. You can use this table to plan your undergraduate career and to see the relationships between diverse courses. You might wonder, for instance, what possible relevance a philosophy course has to information systems. Philosophy courses teach you about the differences among data, information, and knowledge, and they can help you understand how to conceptualize systems and how to proceed with problem solving. Psychology classes can help you understand the dynamics of individual change, interpersonal conflict, and learning. Sociology courses are useful for understanding organizational structure, change, and decision making, while economics courses provide you with the concepts needed to evaluate the return on investment in information systems and productivity.

As these figures show, information systems are no longer islands isolated from the mainstream of the corporation, staffed by technical experts. A person must have a very broad background in the liberal arts, behavioral sciences, and technology to really excel in an information systems world. Communication skills—being able to read, write, speak, and think clearly—will be more important in the information economy of the 1990s and the twenty-first century than at any time in history. Therefore, you should see this course in relation to other courses in your college career and plan accordingly.

1.4 USING INFORMATION SYSTEMS WISELY: THE ROAD AHEAD

You might think from listening to advertisements or reading the newspaper that most of the significant problems with computers and information systems have been solved

FIGURE 1.7

Courses that Will Help You Develop Important Career Skills
Each of the skill areas shown in Figure 1.6 involves an ability to perform specific organizational tasks. Here we break down each skill area into some of the particular skills that it includes. The third row lists relevant courses that will help you develop your abilities in this area. Note that even nontechnical courses are important for developing information systems literacy.

Career Skill	Analysis/Problem Solving	Behavior and Communication Skills	Technology Skills
Specific Skills	Analytic framework Functional requirements Physical design Implementation Systems development	Organizational strategy Structure Culture Making decisions Business procedures and functions	Hardware Software Telecommunications Database
Relevant Courses	Philosophy English literature History Behavioral sciences Mathematics	Psychology Sociology Economics English literature Languages Speech	MIS Database Telecommunications Advanced software

and that all we have to do is rely on cheaper, more powerful technology to solve our pressing productivity, quality, national wealth, and competitive problems in world markets. Nothing could be further from the truth. In fact, we are just beginning to learn how to use the currently available technology wisely, not to mention the new technology being tested in the lab.

Every technology has a development path, and it often takes almost two generations (30–40 years) before the full potential of a technology even begins to be exploited. For example, most experts would agree that although automobiles were invented in 1890, it was not until the 1920s, or even the 1930s, that the modern, mass-produced, consciously engineered automobile appeared. For a considerable period, the auto was simply a "horseless carriage" with a tiller rather than a steering wheel.

With computers and information systems we are still facing many difficult problems. Here are four issues for you to think about as you read this book. You might want to discuss and debate these issues with your classmates or professor.

TECHNOLOGY

Briefly stated, we face two related technology problems: (1) computing hardware is advancing far more rapidly than our ability to write useful software, and (2) both are changing much faster than the ability of our organizations to understand and apply the hardware and software (see Figure 1.8). Moreover, information systems must not only perform the well-defined tasks for which they have traditionally been used, but they must also provide resources that will enable people to do their jobs more efficiently and effectively.

An appropriate analogy might be your college library. Once the library has installed and mastered the card index system and students have learned the mechanics of working with card catalogs, the college dean, president, and professors must answer a more challenging question: What else is needed at the library to raise the quality of student research, thinking, and education? This is a far more complex problem than the mere mechanics of storing and accessing information. Similarly, information technology must address the broader concern of changing the way people work and think so that they will be able to take full advantage of the technology.

As we will discuss in greater detail in Chapters 4-6, while computing hardware is growing exponentially in power, and prices are falling about as fast, software—the set of instructions that controls information systems—is growing in power linearly. In contrast, the rate at which people learn is relatively constant, and the rate of change in the absorption and application of new knowledge in factories and offices is no greater than the annual rate of productivity increase (about 2 percent per year).

No one wants (or knows how) to slow down the growth of technology because it is potentially beneficial. Therefore, we must find a way to increase the rate of growth in the power of software and reduce its cost. And we must also increase the rate at which individuals absorb and understand information technology knowledge.

One possibility is to make writing software applications as simple as, say, using pen and ink to write an essay. In Chapter 6 we talk about new developments in programming and applications development that might make this possible.

But how can we increase the rate at which individuals in business firms increase their stock of knowledge and learn new technologies and techniques? What do we do about senior and middle managers who do not want to learn? What about other employees?

FIGURE 1.8

The Productivity Problem: Why Can't We Get Better Faster?

Since 1950 the power of software has steadily improved; it doubles approximately every eight years. The power of hardware has soared; it grows by a factor of ten every five years. Meanwhile, the average rate at which people (and organizations) learn and apply new information and knowledge in the workplace grows very slowly—an average increase in productivity of 2 percent per year. As we move into the twenty-first century, the United States must learn how to become more productive in order to compete economically with other countries.

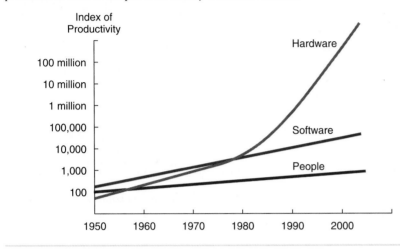

PRODUCTIVITY

Although the United States has invested more in computers than any other country, there is an enormous—and still expanding—gap between the growth in computing power and the annual increase in productivity in the United States (see Figure 1.8 for an illustration). Why is this so? How can the power of hardware grow so fast, while software and ultimate productivity in offices and factories grow so slowly? One central challenge of this course is to learn how to bend the productivity curve upward so it will be more in line with the growing power of the technology.

Finding a solution to this problem is essential because the United States is losing the competition for economic resources, and indeed wealth itself, to economies that not only save and invest more but also apply information technology more wisely. The United States saves much less than other countries, it invests in new businesses and technology at a lower rate, and, consequently, its productivity suffers. Japan (our major competitor) and most other industrialized countries save much more. Higher savings translate into higher investment, which leads to higher productivity. It is not surprising, then, that since 1950, the productivity of Japan and other countries has grown at up to twice the rate of the United States. This gap may continue unless the United States can find a way to use the growth in computing power to increase productivity.

STRATEGIC BUSINESS ISSUES

As you learn more about business organizations in Chapter 2, you will discover that successful businesses become very good at doing certain things relentlessly, repetitively, and

FOCUS ON ORGANIZATIONS

THE BANK BECOMES A HIGH-TECH BOUTIQUE

Banks have been traditional and conservative institutions, but they too have been swept by the winds of change. Securities and mutual fund firms are luring away their customers. How can banks win them back? It takes a new vision of the banking business and the selling skills of successful retailers like Nordstrom and The Limited.

Citibank knew it had to innovate and change to survive, so it redesigned its concept of how a bank branch should look and what it should do. In September 1993 it unveiled its branch of the future on Park Avenue and 53rd Street in Manhattan. The branch of the future represents the best ideas from Citibank's far-flung branch system and will serve as a model for the 1,400 other Citibank branches in 14 countries.

The branch of the future has a new look: Posters in the window have been replaced by free-standing triangular advertising kiosks. The walls are smudge resistant. Tellers, the traditional staple of bank branches, are still present, but there are 8 positions instead of 19, and 20 automated teller machines instead of 8. Salespeople are more numerous. Greeters at the door direct customers to personal bankers who open new accounts, answer questions, and sell products.

The staff includes investment counselors who are licensed to sell securities and mutual funds. To meet federal regulations they are housed in glass enclosures separated from the main banking floor. Kiosks highlight various investment products, displaying returns from mutual funds available through Citibank that in recent years have been much higher than those from bank deposits. One Citibank customer, attracted by the new signs and marquee over the entrance, remarked that the branch of the future looked more like a store or sales outlet than just a place to make a deposit.

John C. Ryan, head of a consulting firm that advises companies such as The Limited about how to design their retail stores, observed that banks have a valuable selling outlet in their branches because they are visited by large numbers of people. What banks frequently lack, because historically there has been no need, are the desire and ability to sell.

Citibank believes that it can create an effective sales staff at its branches through training and a new information system. The system can rapidly provide customer records and print out application forms and issue bank cards within minutes. With this new system, customers with a credit card problem no longer have to call the Citibank affiliate in South Dakota that issues the card. The new system also lets tellers balance their books within minutes at the end of the business day, a process that previously had taken an hour or more. Citibank used the time saved to expand branch hours. Eventually the bank expects the new technology to do away with deposit slips.

Rather than trying to improve profits by cutting costs, Citibank chose to spend to improve customer service and increase its client base and therefore its revenues. Its management hopes that the new design will keep the bank in a leading position in the New York City area and that it will increase profits from its global consumer business of credit cards, branch banking, and private banking for wealthy individuals.

FOCUS Questions:
What is the role of information systems in the bank branch of the future? What people, organization, and technology elements had to be changed to create the branch of the future?

SOURCE: Michael Quint, "Bank Branch as High-Tech Boutique," *The New York Times*, September 16, 1993.

routinely, which permits them to make a great deal of money. What happens when a major change occurs in a firm's external environments, such as a change in technology or markets? How fast can a business change to take advantage of the new technology (before its competitors do)? How fast can a business change its routine procedures to make new products or deliver new services?

Many expert observers believe we must redesign, rethink, and reconceptualize how we produce and deliver products and services in order to achieve breakthroughs in productivity. As the Focus on Organizations explains, this is how Citibank is using information technology to gain a competitive edge.

PEOPLE

Yet another problem we face involves the interrelationship of technology and humans. Individuals and businesses must adjust to rapid changes in technology and to the need to design systems individuals can control, understand, and use responsibly. The estimated half-life of information systems knowledge is about five years. That means that roughly half of what you learn in this book will be outdated in five years! This is true of most other technical fields as well. Therefore, to stay current, individuals will have to invest more of their own time in retraining themselves. Obviously, business firms will have to contribute, facilitate, and even lead in this process. How much retraining a firm should undertake and how much it should invest in this process are critical questions raised throughout this book.

An important dimension of the people issue involves the need to design appropriate interfaces between human beings and machines. We must learn to design information systems—and other control systems—that permit and encourage humans to control the process and that function according to design and intentions. To understand the difficulties in designing systems that individuals can control and understand, consider the situation of the USS *Vincennes* when it mistakenly shot down an Iranian civilian airliner on a routine flight.

On July 3, 1988, at 6:47ZULU (Greenwich mean time), Iran Air Flight 655 took off from Bandar Abbas Joint Military Civilian Airport destined for Dubai.[2] Flight 655 was a routine, on-time, international air flight using commercial airway Amber 59. At the same moment, the USS *Vincennes*, cruising 47 miles offshore, picked up Flight 655 on AEGIS, the world's most sophisticated air combat control system. The AEGIS display system consists of four screens, each 42 inches square, which display the tactical information contained in the command and decision computers that keep track of all air and surface combatants.

At 3 minutes and 20 seconds after takeoff, Flight 655 was identified by the *Vincennes*'s officers as a "potential threat." At 6:54 A.M., 7 minutes and 8 seconds after takeoff, the ship's captain turned the firing key, and two SM-2 Blk II missiles left the launch rails and destroyed Flight 655 at a range of eight miles and an altitude of 13,500 feet. Two hundred and ninety civilians died in the Airbus 300 plane.

Subsequent investigations by the Joint Chiefs of Staff and Department of Defense concluded that the AEGIS system worked perfectly, and that neither the captain nor the crew were at fault or made material mistakes. The investigation showed that the AEGIS system accurately reported the bearing and location of Flight 655. Unfortunately, however, system operators mistakenly perceived the plane to be descending, in an attack mode, against the *Vincennes*. These mistaken perceptions occurred despite the fact that Flight 655 was continuously transmitting a civilian aircraft radio signal.

In the last three minutes, AEGIS operators sent numerous messages to what they believed was a plane at 7,000 feet. Flight 655 was at 13,500 feet, and the plane's captain had no reason to respond to signals that appeared to be directed to some other plane, perhaps a military plane. Hence Flight 655 did not respond to any messages sent by the *Vincennes.*

Navy psychiatrists and psychologists were called in to explain how a well-trained crew could misinterpret the AEGIS output, which was completely correct. They concluded that "stress, task fixation, and unconscious distortion of data may have played a major role in this incident."

Both the tactical information coordinator (TIC) and the identification supervisor (IS) became convinced that Flight 655 was a hostile Iranian F-14 when the IS received

People in this control room monitor key system functions. Companies must take great care in designing the apparatus with which people interact to ensure that human beings can control and understand the information from computerized systems.

SOURCE: © John Zoiner, Uniphoto Picture Agency.

a report that the plane was squawking a military identification signal. The IS had momentarily forgotten to move the electronic marker for Flight 655 from Bandar Abbas airport to its current location. This 90-second error may have permitted an Iranian military jet issuing a military identification signal from Bandar Abbas to become confused on the TIC's screen with Flight 655. This mistake may have been critical.

Once the mistaken identification of Flight 655 occurred, "the TIC appears to have distorted data flow in an unconscious attempt to make available evidence fit a preconceived scenario ('scenario fulfillment')."

In briefings that followed, Defense Secretary Carlucci and the Chairman of the Joint Chiefs of Staff, Admiral William J. Crowe, Jr., concluded that given the heat of battle, the large number of things that the captain had to keep track of, the time compression, and the setting, no one was at fault.

In a separate report on crew training for the AEGIS system, the General Accounting Office—a congressional watchdog agency that monitors government spending and performance—concluded that the crew using AEGIS had not been trained in settings that even approached combat conditions.

Every day we rely more and more on semiautomated activities, which, if they fail or are poorly used, have extremely harmful consequences. Control rooms where controls do not work, where people do not understand and are not trained to understand the system, where instruments give false signals, where time is compressed, and where mistakes are costly, perhaps deadly, are all invitations to disaster in the computer age.

The Focus on People shows that these disasters do not have to occur. By carefully considering the people aspects of information systems, we can design systems that can be used safely and effectively. This issue will be addressed throughout the book.

Another dimension of the people problem is the ethical issues posed by the proliferation of information systems: How do we design and use information systems in a morally as well as socially responsible and accountable manner? Should information systems be used to monitor employees? What should be done when an information system designed to increase efficiency and productivity eliminates people's jobs?

These problems of technology, productivity, business organization, and people—while daunting—also suggest that there are great opportunities for applying information technology in new and powerful ways that have not yet been discovered.

1.5 ORGANIZING CONCEPTS OF THE BOOK

There are four key organizing concepts in this book that are reflected in each chapter. We have already alluded to these concepts earlier in the chapter, but we want to emphasize them before you go further. In general, if you understand these four concepts and their implications, you will have mastered the book. We briefly review each concept in the following sections.

KNOWLEDGE AND INFORMATION VERSUS DATA

Our focus in this book is on how to deliver information and knowledge to professionals who are engaged in problem solving and analysis. This is not a data processing book focused primarily on how data are input and output by computers or on the growing power of information processing technology. Although we do cover this technical material, it is always with an eye to what difference it will make to the success (or failure) of an organization, or to your success as a professional.

FOCUS ON PEOPLE

PEOPLE-FRIENDLY SYSTEMS

Information systems can make your company more efficient and productive, but not if your workers aren't comfortable with them. According to Mitchell Fromstein, CEO of Manpower, Inc., the largest temporary services firm in the United States, almost every white-collar job in America requires some level of familiarity with computers, as do 75 percent of manufacturing jobs. Employers need to understand what enables workers at any skill level to master computers and use them effectively.

When Paine Webber decided on a new $75 million trading and information system for its stockbrokers, it carefully studied their needs and wants. The system was to provide 5,200 brokers in 264 offices across the country with state-of-the-art microcomputer desktop workstations with independent computing capabilities that could also receive continuous updates of stock and bond prices through a network. The new machines replaced "dumb" Quotron terminals that merely delivered securities pricing data and had no independent computing power of their own. The new system was designed to provide brokers with easy access to more information about accounts and investment options so that they could provide better financial advice to clients.

The new system gave brokers more power and control. They could use any financial software to analyze data for customers as well as maintain their own data. But Paine Webber found the brokers had different needs. A third of the brokers were happy with the old system, while others wanted a varying array of new capabilities. So Paine Webber designed the new system to incorporate features of the old system, which allows individual brokers to determine what features they will use. They can work exclusively with features from the old system or use as many new capabilities as they feel comfortable with. Paine Webber even had special keyboards built with green keys for the old Quotron features and keys of different colors for other new specialized applications and capabilities.

Designed in this manner, the system lets brokers learn and grow. Francis Keegan, a 27-year Paine Webber veteran in the firm's Iselin, New Jersey, office, considers himself a dinosaur when it comes to computers. He finds that using the old Quotron features lets him swim without sinking as he gradually learns to use the new capabilities. Keegan's office neighbor, Steve Rothman, who never owned a computer, uses many of the new features and even saved a big account by providing detailed records of unrealized gains and losses. Rothman enthusiastically bought a microcomputer to use at home.

To handle the boom in mutual fund investing, many leading mutual fund companies have had to modify their systems to respond to surging numbers of customer transactions and telephone calls. Besides installing voice response systems and systems to reroute telephone calls to available telephone representatives in different regional centers, these companies have made their systems easier to use. For instance, Kemper Service Company, which handles back office functions for Kemper funds and other mutual fund companies, introduced a more user friendly system that reduces by 60 percent the number of keystrokes required to open a new account. After the client's street number is keyed in, the system automatically provides the zip code and state name or indicates that the address doesn't exist. Telephone representatives don't need to memorize the myriad rules that each state requires for transactions when an investor marries, divorces, or dies, because these are embedded in the system. The system guides the representative through the entire process and remembers everything the shareholder asked the fund company to do. Kemper recently redesigned its customer statements to reflect the total returns on investments over different time periods and to compute taxes, tasks that shareholders formerly had to ask their accountants to complete.

FOCUS Questions:
Why is it important to design systems that are easy for people to use? What would happen if the systems described here did not have user friendly features?

SOURCES: "Making It All Worker-Friendly," *Fortune: Making High Tech Work for You*, Autumn 1993 special issue, and Ivy Schmerken, "All Ears at Mutual Funds," *Wall Street & Technology*, April 1992.

ANALYSIS AND PROBLEM SOLVING VERSUS TECHNOLOGY

Some people think choosing the right technology for a system is a difficult problem. Actually, the most difficult part of designing an effective information system is understanding the problem it is intended to solve. Information systems and technologies are useful tools only when they are used wisely.

Therefore we start with the strategic needs of the organization, the needs of work groups, and the needs of individual professionals. Once we have developed a broadly based analysis of a business situation, we can begin to talk about how to solve problems. Only then can we begin to talk about technology.

A SOCIOTECHNICAL PERSPECTIVE

Our approach throughout is to think of information systems as composed of three mutually adjusting entities: technologies, organizations, and people. A broadly based set of skills is required to understand systems; the subject is inherently multidisciplinary, involving teams of people working together.

SYSTEMS ARE NETWORKS OF INFORMATION TECHNOLOGIES

The technical foundations of information systems today are much broader than in the past. Whereas most attention in the past focused on the computer itself, our focus will be on a wide variety of information technologies that share some principles but are very different. We will consider telecommunications and networking technology, multimedia, and various software issues.

SUMMARY

- An information system is a set of interrelated components designed to collect, process, store, and disseminate information to facilitate coordination, control, analysis, visualization, and decision making.

- Input, processing, and output are the three basic activities of an information system; through these activities, raw data are transformed into useful information.

- The purpose of building information systems is to solve a variety of organizational problems. This insight can be used to describe existing systems and to develop new systems.

- An information system consists of three components: people, technology, and organizations.

- The people dimension of information systems involves issues such as training, job attitudes, ergonomics, and the user interface.

- The technology dimension of information systems consists of computer hardware, software, storage, and telecommunications technology.

- The organization dimension of information systems involves issues such as the organization's hierarchy, functional specialties, business procedures, culture, and political interest groups.

- Computers and information systems and computer literacy and information systems literacy are different. Information systems literacy involves understanding the people and organizational dimensions of information systems as well as information technology.

- Knowledge, information, and data are different. Information is created from streams of data through the application of knowledge. The purpose of information systems is to create and disseminate useful information and knowledge in a manner designed to solve some organizational problem.

- A sociotechnical approach to information systems combines three areas of study: information technology, organizational and individual behavior, and analytic problem-solving skills.

- You do not need to know everything about information systems to know a great deal, perhaps enough. Skills in three areas are important: technical skills, business and organizational skills, and analytic problem-solving skills. Many courses in your college—both information systems courses and liberal arts and math courses—can be helpful. The specific mix of skills you need depends on what you want to become.

- This book describes four problems in using systems wisely. The technology is changing very rapidly, faster than software or people. Productivity—at least in the United States—has not yet responded to massive investments in information technology. Organizations do not change easily, even though they must to make optimal use of new technology. And people often must work with awkward systems, under duress, in situations that have not been anticipated or tested by designers or that need clearer moral guidelines.

KEY TERMS

Information system	Storage technology
Input	Telecommunications technology
Processing	Computer literacy
Output	Information systems literacy
Feedback	Data
Formal systems	Information
Manual system	Knowledge
Computer hardware	Sociotechnical perspective
Computer software	

REVIEW QUESTIONS

1. Define an information system.
2. How do an information system, a computer program, and a computer differ?
3. What are the three basic activities of information systems?

4. What role is played by feedback in an information system?

5. What are the three components of an information system? Describe each of them.

6. What role does the surrounding environment play in shaping a business organization's information systems?

7. What is the basic flow of information in an information system?

8. What is the organizational basis of information systems?

9. Distinguish between computer literacy and information systems literacy.

10. How do knowledge, information, and data differ?

11. What are the major reasons why you should study information systems?

12. What problems and opportunities are posed by information systems?

DISCUSSION QUESTIONS

1. Some people argue that information systems should be designed and built by technical specialists, persons trained in computer science and engineering. Discuss and comment.

2. With faster and better computers, most of the problems we currently experience with information systems will disappear. Comment and discuss.

PROBLEM-SOLVING EXERCISES

1. *Group exercise:* Divide into groups and have each group find a description of a business information system in a business or computer magazine. Have each group describe the system in terms of its inputs, processes, and outputs. What are the people components of the system? The technical components? The organizational components? Consider having each group illustrate its system in a manner similar to Figure 1.2 and present its findings.

2. The Yamaha Motor Corporation, one of the world's largest motorcycle manufacturers, uses a CBIS for supplying its dealers with parts. The system stores data about the quantity, price, and location of the parts in Yamaha's inventory. Each dealer has a terminal connected to Yamaha's central computer in Atlanta. When a part is needed, the dealer uses a menu on the terminal screen to select the correct parts, specifying each part with a 12-digit part number. At the end of the order, a shipping/packing list prints out on the dealer's printer. The shipping/packing list states where each part will come from and indicates back-ordered parts, retail and dealer value, and preferred freight route. Describe the inputs, outputs, and processes of this information system and its people, organizational, and technical components.

3. *Hands-on exercise:* Carole Stavis stayed two nights at West Vista Hotel. The room fee was $125 per night. Carole made a telephone call that cost $4.50 and ordered a meal for $16 through room service. Hotel bills must include a 5 percent state tax on hotel services. Use appropriate software to design, calculate, and produce a bill for Carole. Identify the inputs, processes, and outputs of your application.

NOTES

1. Plato, *The Republic.*

2. "Formal Investigation into the Circumstances Surrounding the Downing of Iran Air Flight 655 on 3 July 1988," Department of Defense, July 28, 1988.

PROBLEM-SOLVING CASE

SPEEDING JUSTICE IN MILAN

Over the past few years, Italy has waged a fierce struggle against political extortion and organized crime. In May 1993 car bombs injured almost 100 people and damaged the prized Uffizi art gallery in Florence. The following month, Italian authorities in Rome charged executives from French computer giant Cie. des Machines Bull and Dutch electronics leader Phillips Electronics NV with corruption. Former Prime Minister Giulio Andreotti has been brought to trial. The extent of criminal activity remains undetermined, but investigators have successfully uncovered wrongdoers. They have benefitted both from hard-nosed police work and from the aggressive use of new information systems that speed the search for political and organized crime.

Mafia investigations last ten to 15 years. No single police official can remember all the details that might be helpful in an investigation today. So Antonio Di Petro, chief magistrate in Milan, created a system that provided a repository for all the information on each person under investigation for political bribery. Tax statements, records of personal assets, transcripts of interviews with informants, and news articles have been digitized and stored electronically. This information can be easily extracted and combined with other information from five national databases on judicial sentences, investigations in progress, the tax rolls of the Ministry of Finance, Department of Motor Vehicle registrations, and legal decisions from the Italian supreme court. Information from Italy's prison administration on cell availability and prisoner rosters will eventually be included as well.

Magistrates can use the system to extract and combine information and have it delivered to them directly over a computer network. The system is currently in place in Milan, but there is great demand for it elsewhere. One problem delaying national implementation is that the information systems in various Italian prosecutor divisions cannot easily exchange information with each other. Another problem is that all information of this sort remains confidential with the individual prosecutor until a suspect has been served official notice of investigation. Making even preliminary investigation data available to other prosecutors runs counter to Italian investigators' strong instinct for privacy.

The computer crime division of the state police has provided investigators with a system of archived data from all its Mafia investigations since 1984. The system provides investigators with a "super memory" of Mafia activities and makes certain connections the user might overlook. If an investigator keys in a name or license plate number, for example, the system will remind the investigator that the suspect was seen three years ago with someone in a given town.

Italian state police also use other capabilities recommended by the United States FBI to track cellular telephone calls, and can isolate the exact second of a call. Two telephones using the same number means that one phone has been illegally cloned. The registration number of the cloned phone is altered to correspond to another person's legitimately registered telephone. This disguises the true source of calls. When authorities discover two telephones using the same number they interview the registered subscriber to determine whether all the calls were legitimate. If not, the registered phone is replaced with another and the police continue to monitor the illicit phone traffic without the user's knowledge. Using such cellular surveillance techniques, police investigators located Nitto Santapaola, considered one of the most important military bosses in organized crime.

The central role played by information systems in major organized crime investigations was underscored in this newspaper headline: "New 007s, Carrying Tie and Computer."

SOURCE: Marsha Johnston, "Organized Justice," *InformationWEEK*, June 21, 1993.

CASE STUDY QUESTIONS

1.   What problems can be solved by the systems described in this case? What problems can't be addressed by these systems?

2.   What are the people components of these systems? The organizational components? The technology components?

3.   Analyze one of these systems in terms of inputs, processing, and outputs.

Chapter
→ T W O ←

HOW BUSINESS FIRMS USE INFORMATION SYSTEMS

LEARNING OBJECTIVES

After reading and studying this chapter, you will:

1. Be able to define a business organization.
2. Understand the major functions performed by businesses.
3. Know why business organizations need information systems.
4. Understand how the core business information systems support the manufacturing and production, finance and accounting, sales and marketing, and human resources functions.

WHAT IS OUR BUSINESS?

Two years ago, Ethel Dufbaeck's job seemed like a big headache. As inventory control manager for the European affiliates of Becton, Dickinson & Co., a $2.3 billion manufacturer of medical supplies and diagnostic equipment, she makes sure there is enough overseas inventory on hand to meet customer demand. That requires timely information from the firm's Franklin Lakes, New Jersey, headquarters. But Dufbaeck is based in Meylan, France, and until recently, that information was hard to come by.

Dufbaeck had to call, fax, and otherwise scour the distribution chain for clues about when shipments might arrive at Becton's Belgian distribution center. Between telephone tag and time zone differences, two or three days could elapse before she found the needed information. Shipping errors, warehouse delays, and foreign customs' bureaucracies could further delay product deliveries. Dufbaeck often overstocked key items or used expensive air delivery, only to learn that a critical shipment had already arrived.

Tom McDonnell, an information systems analyst, is on the management team of Becton, Dickinson's International Distribution Services Division. He works to ensure that information systems meet the needs of the business. In strategic meetings he learned of the logistic hurdles faced by Dufbaeck and her counterparts around the world. He knew the time was ripe to pull together data from disparate sources into a single system that could provide information instantaneously on a computer display terminal. With McDonnell as project manager, Becton, Dickinson decided to solve these problems by implementing a new Worldwide Inter-Company Logistics

Information System (WILIS), which shows exactly which items have been shipped and when they can be expected to arrive. The system can even show the container number for each order, so that when a shipment arrives at customs, Dufbaeck knows how to prioritize unloading and distribution.

WILIS is an example of an information system that has become virtually indispensable to businesses around the world. It is also an example of what can be done when information technology is combined with business knowledge. Becton, Dickinson & Co. can build successful business information systems because it treats information and information technology as integral parts of the company's business. In effective companies, ideas for information systems come from business managers, factory workers, and clerks as well as from information systems staff. WILIS was implemented only after a thorough consideration of Becton, Dickinson's goals, products, and business challenges. Without Dufbaeck's input, McDonnell could not have designed an effective information system.

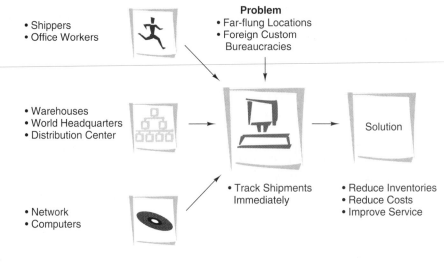

SOURCE: Alice LaPlante, "Expedite!" *Computerworld*, September 13, 1993.

The experience of Becton, Dickinson & Co. illustrates how effective information systems can be if they are deliberately designed to fit business needs. To do this, both business and technical specialists must have a clear understanding of the nature of the business in which they work and how information systems can be used to make that business more productive and competitive. Business people need to become more aware of the potential offered by information systems, and computer and information technology experts need to become more aware of the business environment. This chapter explains what businesses are and how they use information systems.

2.1 COMPONENTS OF BUSINESS

A **business organization** is a complex, formal organization whose aim is to produce products or services for a profit—that is, to sell products at a price greater than the cost of producing the product. Customers are willing to pay a price greater than the cost of production because they believe they receive a value equal to or greater than the sale price. Of course, there are nonprofit firms (the Society for the Blind produces goods but does not aim to make a profit), nonprofit organizations (like churches and public interest groups), and government agencies, all of which are complex formal organizations that do not operate to produce a profit. In general, the information systems found in non-profit organizations are remarkably similar to those found in private industry.[1]

Business organization
A complex, formal organization established for the purpose of producing products or services for a profit.

ORGANIZING A BUSINESS

Imagine that you wanted to set up your own business. Just deciding to go into business, of course, would be the most important decision, but next would come the question of what product or service you would produce. The decision of what product or service to produce is called a strategic choice because it will determine the kinds of employees you need, the production methods, the marketing themes, and a host of other factors.

Once you answer these questions, what kind of an organization would you need? First, you would have to design some sort of production division—an arrangement of people, machines, and procedures to be followed to produce the product (which could be a service). Second, you would need a sales and marketing group or division whose principal job would be to sell the product or service at a profitable price. Third, you would need a finance and accounting group. These people would seek out sources of credit or funds and would keep track of current financial transactions such as orders,

The human resources group at The Travelers Corporation conducts training sessions for employees, encouraging them to share ideas and expertise. In organizing a business, vital functions like human resources cannot be neglected.

SOURCE: © R. J. Muna.

FIGURE 2.1

The Four Major Functions of a Business

Every business, regardless of its size, must perform these four functions to succeed. It must *produce* something, whether a physical product or a service, and it must *market and sell* the product. The firm must perform *finance and accounting* tasks to manage its financial assets and fund flows, and it must also focus on *human resources* issues. In large corporations these functions are split into separate divisions or departments; in a one-person company the business owner must perform all these tasks.

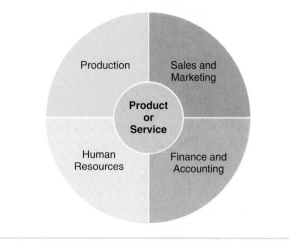

purchases, disbursements, and payroll. Finally, you would want a group of people to focus on recruiting, hiring, training, and retaining people to work for you. In other words, you would want a human resources group (see Figure 2.1).

Of course, if your business was very small with only a few employees, you would not need, nor would you have the resources, to create specialized groups or divisions to perform these tasks. You would be doing all the work yourself with the assistance of one or two others. But your business would still entail the **business functions** of production, marketing, finance and accounting, and human resources activities.

How would you go about actually organizing a business? Most organizations go through several stages. First, work is divided among a large number of employees, which permits **specialization**: each employee focuses on a specific task and becomes adept at it. Next, a **hierarchy** of reporting and authority relationships is developed to assure that the work is completed. Over time, an **informal structure** emerges in a formal organization as people get to know one another. Birthday parties, births, new hires, and retirements are all occasions for informal relationships to grow and for a culture to emerge. An organization needs both informal relationships and culture to help coordinate work and to provide meaning to work. In general, organizing is never completed but is instead an ongoing process driven by constant environmental changes and changing perceptions within the organization.

MAJOR BUSINESS FUNCTIONS AND STRUCTURE

Like your hypothetical business, most business organizations typically perform four specific functions. A specialized department or division is usually created for each function shown in Figure 2.1 (e.g., the Marketing Department, the Production Division, and so on).

Business functions

The various tasks performed in a business organization—for example, manufacturing and production, sales and marketing, finance and accounting, and human resources activities.

Specialization

The division of work in an organization so that each employee focuses on a specific task.

Hierarchy

The arrangement of people in an organization according to rank and authority; people at the bottom of the hierarchy report to those on the next level who have more authority, who in turn report to the next level, and so on, up to senior management.

Informal structure

A network of personal relationships within an organization.

LEVELS IN A BUSINESS ORGANIZATION

Like all organizations, business firms coordinate the work of employees through a hierarchy in which authority is largely concentrated in the top. The hierarchy is typically composed of a **senior management** group, which makes long-range decisions about what products and services to produce; a general or **middle management** group organized into specialized divisions, which carries out the programs and plans of senior management by supervising employees; a group we call **knowledge and data workers**, who design the product or service (such as engineers) and administer the paper work associated with a business (such as clerical workers); and, finally, **production** or service **workers**, who actually produce the products or services of the firm (see Figure 2.2).

Organizations differ in terms of how much authority is concentrated in each layer. Some organizations are "flat" with a small group of senior managers and a single layer of middle management, followed immediately by production workers. Other organizations are much more bureaucratic and may have as many as 7 to 15 layers of management between the senior group and the production worker. Never, however, is all authority concentrated solely at the top. Indeed, production workers can often stop production entirely; hence what they do and feel is quite important to the firm. Perhaps the most important strategic business decision employees make every day is the decision to come to work.

As you can see, a business firm is a complicated entity that requires many different kinds of skills and people, who must be organized rather tightly to enable the firm to operate efficiently and make a profit. Imagine, then, how difficult it is to start a new business and make it successful.

Senior management

The people at the top of the hierarchy in an organization; they have the most authority and make long-range decisions for the organization.

Middle management

The people in the middle of the hierarchy in an organization; they carry out the programs and plans of senior management by supervising employees.

Knowledge and data workers

The employees in an organization who create and/or use knowledge (e.g., engineers) or data (e.g., clerical workers) to solve problems.

Production workers

The employees in a business organization who actually produce the firm's products or services.

FIGURE 2.2

The Organizational Pyramid: Levels in a Firm

All business organizations are hierarchies consisting of four principal levels: senior management, general or middle management, knowledge and data workers, and production and service workers. Each level of employees specializes in performing an important organizational role. Senior managers make long-term decisions about the future of the firm; middle managers implement these plans and programs. Knowledge and data workers design the firm's product or service and do much of the paperwork that running a business involves. Production and service workers are responsible for producing what the firm sells, whether a tangible product or an intangible service.

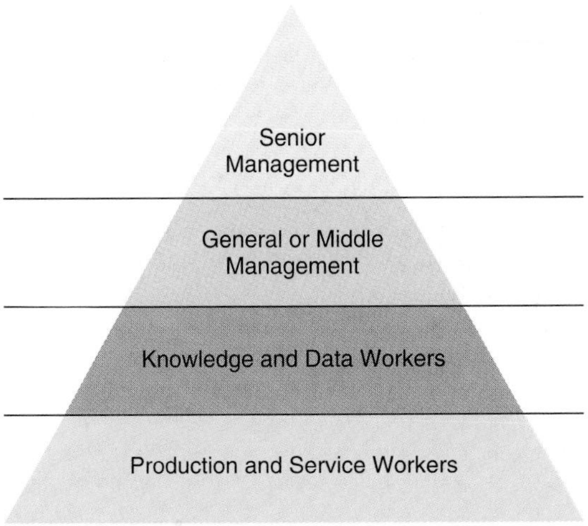

Senior
Management

General or Middle
Management

Knowledge and Data Workers

Production and Service Workers

Business environment

The aggregate conditions in which a business organization operates; the general environment includes government regulations, economic and political conditions, and technological developments, while the task environment includes people or entities with which the firm is more directly involved, such as customers, suppliers, and competitors.

THE BUSINESS ENVIRONMENT

So far we have considered business firms as if they existed in a vacuum. Actually, organizations depend heavily on their surrounding **business environment** to supply resources like capital and labor, to supply symbolic support or legitimacy (which helps in getting capital and labor), to provide protection, and, usually, to provide new technology, techniques, and education. Most importantly, the environment provides customers to the business, for without customers the business would fail.

The business environment can be divided into two components: a general environment and a specific task environment (see Figure 2.3). The general environment encompasses the political, economic, and technological conditions within which the business must operate. To stay in business, organizations must monitor changes in their general environment. A business, for instance, must comply with government directives and

FIGURE 2.3

The Complex Environment of a Business

The environment of a business firm has two elements: a general environment and a task environment. The task environment involves specific groups with which the business must deal directly, such as customers, suppliers, and competitors. Beyond this is the broader general environment: socioeconomic trends, political conditions, technological innovations, and global events. To be successful, an organization must constantly monitor and respond to—or even anticipate—developments in both areas.

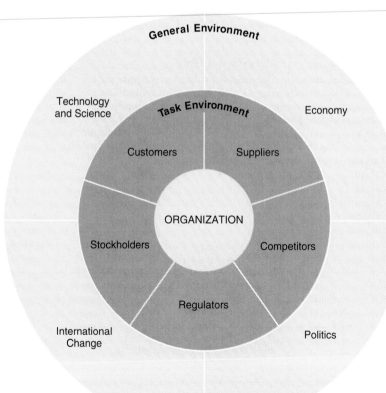

laws, respond to changing economic and political conditions, and continually watch for new technologies. In addition to having this broad view, businesses must also keep track of important groups with which they are directly involved. This is the task environment, which includes customers, suppliers, competitors, regulators, and stockholders.

Environments are always changing and fluid: new technology, economic trends, political developments, or regulations that affect businesses emerge constantly. When capital and labor can move freely, competitors are always present to take away customers. In general, when businesses fail, it is because they have neglected to respond adequately to their changing environments.

HOW WILL WE WORK IN THE YEAR 2000?

Some of these environmental changes are leading to smaller, more flexible companies that will reshape the way many people work. In the United States, the average number of employees per company has been decreasing since 1970. Many large companies will still be large—but they will be much smaller than they are today. IBM now employs 302,000 people, down from 406,000 in 1985. Caterpillar Inc., a world-leading heavy equipment manufacturer, today produces the same total product output that it did in 1979, but with 40,000 fewer employees (see the problem-solving case at the end of this chapter). In the future the average company will be smaller and will employ fewer people. More people will be in business for themselves.

Computerized information systems contribute to these changes by progressively automating more types of work, from guiding machines to transmitting information within the organization. "Coordinating" activities, such as processing orders or keeping track of inventory, can be performed with far fewer clerks and managers. Many firms will find it cheaper to acquire a product or service from an external contractor than to produce it in-house.

Some organizations, such as consulting firms or law firms, will become network organizations in which authority will rest more on knowledge and competence rather than formal position. Such network organizations will be much flatter than traditional large companies, with fewer levels of management. They will be mainly composed of highly trained specialists who do not need daily management from a hierarchical superior. Even in conventional manufacturing firms fewer organizational levels will be needed because the firms can communicate directly with customers and suppliers using information technology.

The workday will expand beyond the traditional hours of eight-to-five. The eight-to-five workday made sense when labor could only be performed and evaluated in the factory or office and was necessarily left there when the workday was over. Many people will work at home or use information systems to bring work home with them. Armed with laptop computers, cellular phones, and modems, insurance agents, sales representatives, or advertising account representatives can do much, if not *all*, of their work at home or on the road. Today, many types of work can be done any time or any place, regardless of physical location.

Five trends will redefine the workplace:

- The traditional large corporate hierarchy will still exist, but there will be proportionately more small organizations and a greater variety of organizational forms, with more organizations operating as networks of specialists.

- The primary focus of business will shift from making a product to providing a service. Service businesses account for three fourths of the gross domestic product (GDP) in the United States today and a still larger share of jobs.

Desktop computers and communications devices such as cellular phones, modems, and fax machines make it possible for people to run small businesses such as Pete Harris Worldwide, Inc. entirely from their homes. In the twenty-first century, more and more people will use information systems to work at home or in nontraditional settings.

SOURCE: © Chuck Savage, Uniphoto Picture Agency

- As the focus of business shifts, what we do on the job will change. Trained technicians such as copier repairmen, computer programmers, and radiation therapists will replace blue collar workers, who traditionally have been the backbone of manufacturing.

- What constitutes "work" will require more higher order thinking and constant learning and less eight-to-five mentality. Decisions passed on to workers by machines will require literacy, numeracy, and the capacity for critical thinking and innovation.

- Employment and pay will be regulated less by a person's position in the organizational hierarchy and more by the changing market value of his or her skills. Almost everyone will feel pressure to either specialize or to package themselves as a marketable portfolio of skills.

Throughout this text, we explore the role played by information systems in these trends. Clearly, this new environment calls for most organizations to make significant changes—some may have to rebuild themselves completely—just to stay in business. Businesses will increasingly seek people who are flexible and creative and who understand both business and information systems. The Focus on People explains what these trends mean for you and your career.

2.2 PLACEMENT OF INFORMATION SYSTEMS IN A BUSINESS

Until now we have not mentioned information systems or described their place in the organizational structure because we wanted to introduce the traditional business organization, structure, and environment. Now let's bring systems into the picture.

FOCUS ON PEOPLE

WANTED: THE EVERYTHING EXPERT

The job market is tighter than ever. If you listen to corporate recruiters and read the want ads, you may conclude that employers want the impossible person: "under 25, ten years experience in programming, with strong demonstrated management skills." Organizations not only want technical prowess in new employees but business and management savvy as well. Businesses are looking beyond the typical computer science and data processing major. They want more students with liberal arts, financing, marketing, and human resources skills. And they want technical skills as well—all in the same person.

People with strong communications and people skills are especially valued. A recent study by the New York–based Open Users Recommended Solutions (OURS) group and the Gartner Group, a Stamford, Connecticut, consulting firm, found an overwhelming need for "soft" skills, such as listening, sensitivity, and team building. In many leading-edge companies, information systems departments are moving toward a reporting structure in which information systems specialists are held accountable not only to information systems management but also to management within the business units, such as sales, finance, or manufacturing. In such instances, communication skills are indispensable.

Employment experts agree that soft skills are even more important to an information systems career than technical ability. Because the direction of both business and technology changes so rapidly, the individual must be able to master new technologies while using soft skills to stay in touch with the needs of the business and the direction of the marketplace.

Many believe that business effectiveness is enhanced when an information systems specialist can take a tour of duty into business operations to see how the technology is applied, and, equally, when a business specialist has experience with information systems. Combining perspectives helps both specialists spot ways of using information technology to improve the business. In fact, a significant number of top information systems executives began their careers in other business departments; most have a broad base of experience in other areas. For instance, Al Hyland, director of worldwide systems for the Polaroid Corporation in Waltham, Massachusetts, started out in research. Linda George, director of corporate information systems at Gencorp, Inc., in Akron, Ohio, studied to be a mathematics teacher.

FOCUS Question:
What skills should the "everything person" have? Why? Why are soft skills so important?

SOURCES: John P. McPartlin, "Generation Exasperated," *InformationWEEK*, October 25, 1993, and Katie Crane, "Take Chances and Diversify on Your Journey to Upper Ranks," *Computerworld*, November 4, 1991.

PURPOSES OF INFORMATION SYSTEMS

All businesses face two generic problems: how to manage the internal forces and groups that produce their products and services and how to deal with customers, government agencies, competitors, and general socioeconomic trends in their surrounding environment. The most powerful explanation of why businesses build systems, then, is to solve organizational problems and to respond to a changing environment.

Businesses build systems to respond to competitors, customers, suppliers, and vendors in a dynamic and fluid environment. As external forces and organizational problems change, new systems are required and old systems must be modified. Consider, for example, the impact of new federal regulations on the natural gas industry. The Focus on Organizations looks at the way businesses have to change their information systems to respond.

No single system governs all the activities of an entire business. Businesses have different kinds of information systems to address different levels of problems and different business functions. Since a firm's information systems tend to be specialized, changes in one area do not always spill over into other areas.

FOCUS ON ORGANIZATIONS

NEW REGULATIONS SHAKE UP THE NATURAL GAS INDUSTRY

For many years the natural gas industry was remarkably predictable. Pipeline companies bought natural gas from the producers and sold both the gas and its transportation service as bundled contracts to local utilities. These contracts typically lasted for as long as 20 years, with a leisurely 3-month business cycle for order, delivery, and billing. Then new federal regulations ended this leisurely and predictable way of doing business.

To increase competition and market efficiency, Federal Energy Regulatory Commission (FERC) Order 636 calls for U.S. pipeline companies to unbundle their services, leaving the purchase of natural gas to the utilities themselves. The utilities thus incur the financial risk of buying the gas and also face the possibility that their industrial customers and pools of residential customers might buy gas directly from the producer. In that case, the utility would only be used for transportation services. To ensure open access to all parties, Order 636 calls for the utilities' excess pipeline and storage capacity to be bought and sold as electronic transactions.

These new regulations require that pipeline companies radically change the way they handle information. Most pipeline companies responded by revamping their information systems, which had been designed to support bundled services. Gas management was traditionally handled by departments that never shared information. Now, systems and departments need to be integrated. Instead of a handful of long-term contracts, the pipeline companies are likely to have thousands of customers. Business transactions will be much more frequent as customers take advantage of price fluctuations in a more competitive marketplace. The pipeline companies will have to manage products and services for many more customers, and they will have to know costs on a micro level.

Panhandle Eastern Corp., a Houston-based pipeline company, responded to Order 636 with Link, a system that can be accessed on a dial-up basis from customer terminals. Link, a bulletin-board service, can be used for many different business needs, such as contracts and billing. Tenneco Gas Transportation, also Houston-based, has a similar customer bulletin board system called Tenn-Speed 2. Tenneco and Transco Energy Co., another Houston-based firm, teamed up to offer one-stop shopping through a system called Planet, which allows customers to dial in once and then toggle between Tenneco's and Transco's automated bulletin boards. Although Transco and Tenneco are competitors, they teamed up because customers demand the ability to switch from one company to the other in the same session at the computer. Panhandle, Tenneco, and others are even marketing the software they developed to comply with Order 636 to other firms.

Utility companies had to change their information systems as well. Colonial Gas, a Lowell, Massachusetts, utility with 120,000 customers, responded by building a new gas accounting system that is integrated with customer service applications. The system was designed to manage the risk involved in purchasing gas directly and to handle a diverse customer base that ranges from traditional full-service clients to customers who merely need support because they buy their own gas and transportation. With the new system, Colonial can manage more than 50 supply, transportation, and storage contracts. It could manage only 10 supply contracts before the system was installed.

What's coming down the pipeline next? No one is sure, but technology has become an important competitive factor.

FOCUS Question:
Experts have said that if a company in the natural gas industry hasn't already begun building flexible and responsive information systems, it may be too late. Why?

SOURCES: Doug Bartholomew, "A Small Utility Thinks Big," *InformationWEEK,* May 16, 1994, and Bruce Caldwell, "A Fossil No More," *InformationWEEK,* October 11, 1993.

Businesses also build systems to track materials, people, and activities inside the firm and to manage their internal problems, such as the production of goods and services or the tracking of parts, inventories, and employees. Some information systems deal with purely internal problems, some with purely external issues, and some with both internal and external phenomena. Typically, systems are categorized by the functional specialty they serve and by the type of problem they address.

FIGURE 2.4

An Integrated View of the Role of Information Systems within a Firm

Information systems can perform different functional specialties, depending on the organizational level that uses them. Strategic-level systems help senior managers plan the firm's long-term course of action. Tactical systems help middle managers supervise and coordinate day-to-day business activities. Knowledge and data workers use knowledge systems to design products, streamline services, and cope with paperwork, while operational systems deal with day-to-day production and service activities.

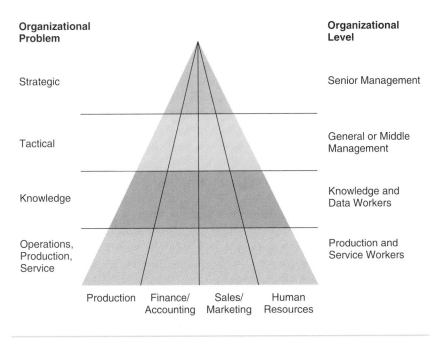

FUNCTIONAL BUSINESS SYSTEMS

Figure 2.4 provides a single integrated view of the role of information systems in business firms. Here you can see that business firms do not have one huge system but, instead, many different specialized systems. Each functional area of a firm develops systems: there are manufacturing and production systems, finance and accounting systems, sales and marketing systems, and human resources systems. The systems also serve different levels: strategic-level systems help senior managers plan; middle management systems help control an organization's day-to-day activities; knowledge systems assist engineers and office workers; and operational systems are used in manufacturing and service delivery.

Systems can be classified according to the type of organizational problem they solve. This usually corresponds to the level in the corporation that the system serves. For instance, some problems are clearly strategic because they involve questions of organizational goals, products, services, and long-term survival. Such problems in organizations are typically handled by senior management, and often **strategic-level systems** and applications are developed. Strategic-level systems might be used in deciding whether to introduce new products, invest in new technology, or move to a new location. Other problems in an organization are clearly tactical because they involve questions of how to achieve goals and how to control and evaluate the process of achieving goals. These problems are the province of middle management and typically involve the development

Strategic-level systems
Information systems used in solving a business organization's long-range, or strategic, problems.

Tactical systems

Information systems used in solving a business organization's short-term, or tactical, problems, such as how to achieve goals and how to evaluate the process of achieving goals.

Knowledge systems

Information systems used by knowledge workers in business organizations to solve questions requiring knowledge and technical expertise.

Operational systems

Information systems used in monitoring the day-to-day activities of a business organization.

of **tactical**, or management support, **systems**. Tactical systems might be used in such applications as monitoring sales to see if annual or quarterly targets were met or reviewing departmental budgets to make sure the firm is not wasting its resources.

A very different set of newly recognized problems faced by organizations involves questions of knowledge and technical expertise. Knowledge problems encompass a very wide range of questions: What is the optimal production mix? Where should factories be located? How should a bolt assembly be designed? How should training be performed? and What kind of information technologies should be employed? Knowledge problems are the province of knowledge and data workers, who create, distribute, and use knowledge and information on behalf of the firm. **Knowledge systems** are used in applications that serve these groups and solve this class of problem. In general, knowledge workers hold university degrees and often are professionals such as engineers, doctors, lawyers, or scientists. Data workers have primarily clerical skills and backgrounds.

Finally, **operational systems** are used to solve problems related to operations, services, and production: How fast should machines be operated? How should today's letters be produced? How many orders were shipped out today? How can an angry queue of customers best be handled? These problems are the province of technical, production, service, and operations workers and involve monitoring the day-to-day activities of the firm.

2.3 EXAMPLES OF BUSINESS INFORMATION SYSTEMS

Next, we discuss how organizations use information systems (from a functional perspective) to solve problems in specific functional areas. The examples of systems in this chapter provide an overview. More detail on how various types of information systems in the firm deal specifically with operational, tactical, knowledge, and strategic problems can be found in Chapters 13–16.

Businesses large and small use information systems to solve organizational problems and to respond to changing environments. Information systems help Boise Cascade engineers take part in a quality audit to ensure that Baily Control's Ohio plant meets specified quality standards.

SOURCE: © John Madere

FIGURE 2.5

Stages of the Production Process
The manufacturing or production process typically has three stages: inbound logistics, production, and outbound logistics.

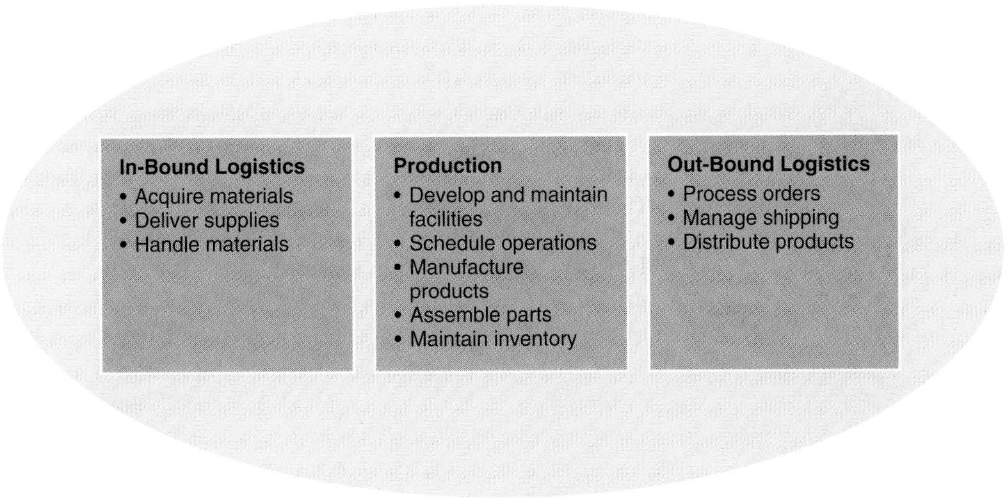

In-Bound Logistics	Production	Out-Bound Logistics
• Acquire materials • Deliver supplies • Handle materials	• Develop and maintain facilities • Schedule operations • Manufacture products • Assemble parts • Maintain inventory	• Process orders • Manage shipping • Distribute products

MANUFACTURING AND PRODUCTION SYSTEMS

Goods-producing organizations typically develop a **manufacturing and production function**, with a division or department of manufacturing that specializes in the production of the goods or services that the firm produces for the environment (customers). In service industries these departments are called "operations" or "production" functions rather than "manufacturing."

The typical production process can be divided into three stages: inbound logistics, production, and outbound logistics (see Figure 2.5).

To support this production process, a number of key strategic, management, knowledge, and operational systems are required. Manufacturing and production systems deal with the planning, development, and maintenance of production facilities; the establishment of production goals; the acquisition, storage, and availability of production materials; and the scheduling of equipment, facilities, materials, and labor required to fashion finished products (see the Focus on Problem Solving).

Manufacturing and production systems help provide answers to the following questions: What production technology will be used? What production plan will produce the required quantity of products and services within the required time frame and budget? How will parts and operations be designed and tested? How will the flow of production be controlled?

Table 2.1 shows some typical manufacturing and production information systems arranged by the organizational level of the problem. Strategic-level manufacturing systems deal with the firm's long-term manufacturing goals, such as where to locate new plants or whether to invest in new manufacturing technology. Tactical manufacturing and production systems deal with the management and control of manufacturing and

Manufacturing and production function

The division of a business organization that produces the firm's goods or services.

production costs and resources. Knowledge manufacturing and production systems create and distribute design knowledge or expertise to drive the production process, and operational manufacturing and production systems deal with the status of production tasks.

FOCUS ON PROBLEM SOLVING

JIT SYSTEMS HELP BRITISH FIRMS COMPETE JUST IN TIME

Faced with recession and mounting competition, British manufacturers have focused on ways to lower inventories, reduce work in progress, and increase cash flow. To make this happen, they needed new types of information systems. Many manufacturers used older material requirements planning (MRP) systems that could not handle stock and shop floor control and were especially ill-suited for manufacturers with a wide range of products. MRP systems produce a production master schedule—the long-range forecast that determines the ordering of parts and raw materials required to produce various items for the years ahead. But they are insufficient for controlling the short-term flow of supply and demand.

MK Electric, a major British electric wiring products company based in London, buys materials from numerous sources. It then cuts, molds, and welds them into more than 4,000 different products. Hundreds of thousands of units are produced and placed in a finished goods warehouse to be sold to distributors, who in turn sell them to building contractors and home repair shops.

The sheer number of MK's products resulted in abysmally slow production. Only one-third of its top product lines was delivered within the target schedule of ten days. Another third took over a month. MK developed a dismal reputation for customer service and was in danger of losing its market-leading position to aggressive competitors. These production and delivery delays were often caused by poor planning.

This problem was especially serious in MK's molding shop, where lack of synchronization caused serious bottlenecks. Due to a shortage of skilled personnel, it sometimes took up to three days to get molding machines and computerized, numerically controlled machine tools ready to produce the right items at the right time. If something went wrong, the level of goods in production soared.

The existing MRP system could not handle extremely variable set-up times for machinery. MK employed two full-time clerks to prepare a bar chart to regulate the deployment of machines and staff. But the bar chart was so inflexible that it could be thrown off by a small change in plans. Then the clerks had to start all over again.

The problem was solved with the help of a new optimized production technology (OPT) information system based on software from Scheduling Technology Group (STG) in London. OPT can completely recalculate the production schedule in about 1 and 1/2 hours. The system can also calculate the latest possible time that work can be started to meet a promised delivery date. The average work in progress

on the factory floor has been cut by approximately 80 percent. By using OPT, MK increased the number of deliveries filled under ten days from 30 percent to an average of 80 percent. The value of goods in production or in stock dropped from $30 million to $20 million.

The new system is similar to the just-in-time (JIT) production system made popular by the Japanese. The JIT system supplies needed parts to the production line on a last-minute basis, keeping inventory levels and production costs to a minimum.

Although strongly favored by finance directors anxious to trim costs, JIT is not always welcomed by production directors, who fear that if the technology is not used correctly, parts might not be received on time to meet delivery schedules. Suppliers resist JIT because they are concerned that they will be unable to meet customers' needs within the required period of time. But manufacturers have increasingly come to view JIT as providing control over the shop floor that can complement the planned purchasing promoted by MRP systems. Production managers adopting JIT have found they can get a clearer picture of their timetables because they can distinguish between production and waiting time.

FOCUS Questions: What are the advantages and disadvantages of material requirements planning and just-in-time systems? What problems can they solve? What people, organization, and technology issues are addressed by JIT systems?

SOURCE: George Black, "U.K. Manufacturers Adopting JIT Technology Just in Time," *Software Magazine*, October 1993.

TABLE 2.1

Manufacturing and Production Information Systems

Strategic-Level Systems
Production technology scanning applications
Facilities location applications
Competitor scanning and intelligence

Tactical Systems
Manufacturing resource planning
Computer-integrated manufacturing
Inventory control systems
Cost accounting systems
Capacity planning
Labor-costing systems
Production scheduling

Knowledge Systems
Computer-aided design systems (CAD)
Computer-aided manufacturing systems
  (CAM)
Engineering workstations
Numerically controlled machine tools
Robotics

Operational Systems
Purchase/receiving systems
Shipping systems
Labor-costing systems
Materials systems
Equipment maintenance systems
Quality control systems

One of the most popular uses of computers in manufacturing is to keep track of the location and number of component parts and finished products held in inventory by firms. By tracking exactly what items are in stock and where they are located, inventory control systems enable businesses to keep just the right number of parts and products on hand to fill orders.

SOURCE: © Oscar Palmquist, Lightwave

An example of a manufacturing and production system would be a bill-of-materials system, which is typically found in most factories today (see Figure 2.6). A bill-of-materials system provides managers and factory supervisors with a list of all the manufactured items that require a specific part—in this case, a six-foot power cord used in home and industrial air fan assemblies. The list can be "hard copy" (on paper) or on a computer screen.

As the figure indicates, the system itself is quite simple. Key data elements (pieces of information) in the system include the component description, cost, unit, and component part number. The system must also keep track of the item code of the end product that uses the part, a description of the end product, the quantity needed for each product produced, and the extended cost (unit times cost).

The component in the report shown is the "Triple S power cord," which is a three-conductor, six-foot long, grounded cable with a plug at one end and soldered lugs at the other and which attaches to the fan motor. This component costs $0.47 a foot and is used in three different fans, each of which requires a single unit (quantity = 1.0), with an extended cost of $2.82.

A bill-of-materials system has several uses. In the event of a part shortage or failure, factory supervisors can look on the screen to see immediately which ultimate end products may be affected and change delivery schedules accordingly. Perhaps most important, the bill-of-materials system can feed directly into the firm's tactical systems that coordinate orders, available parts, cost, and delivery dates.

Many firms are trying to create a seamless manufacturing process by integrating the various types of automated manufacturing systems using computers and communication technology. The data produced in one system are immediately available to be used by other systems.

Leading-edge applications are even using the data from computer-generated designs to drive the actual fabrication and assembly of products. For instance, the Northrup Corp. used computer-generated design data to simulate three-dimensional images of each component of the F/A-18 E/F bomber and to guide the robotic machine tools that cut materials for components of the aircraft. Traditionally, design engineers drafted plans and then handed them over to experts in manufacturing. The Focus on Technology illustrates another advanced application in which computerized simulation techniques can be used to test the consequences of design decisions before products are built, sharply reducing the amount of time required to develop a new product.

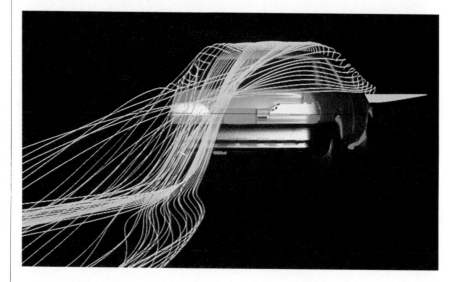

Ford Motor Company's computer-aided design (CAD) system can provide three-dimensional simulations of its automobile designs. Because sophisticated CAD systems allow many aspects of a design to be tested on computer screens before physical prototypes are built, companies like Ford can save considerable time and money developing new products.

SOURCE: Courtesy of Ford Motor Co.

FIGURE 2.6

A Bill-of-Materials System

A common example of a manufacturing/production system is the bill-of-materials system, which helps staff keep track of all products that require a particular part. One output from this particular system is a report on a Triple S power cord, which is readable both on paper (hard copy) and on a computer screen. A bill-of-materials system is useful for determining costs, coordinating orders, and managing inventory.

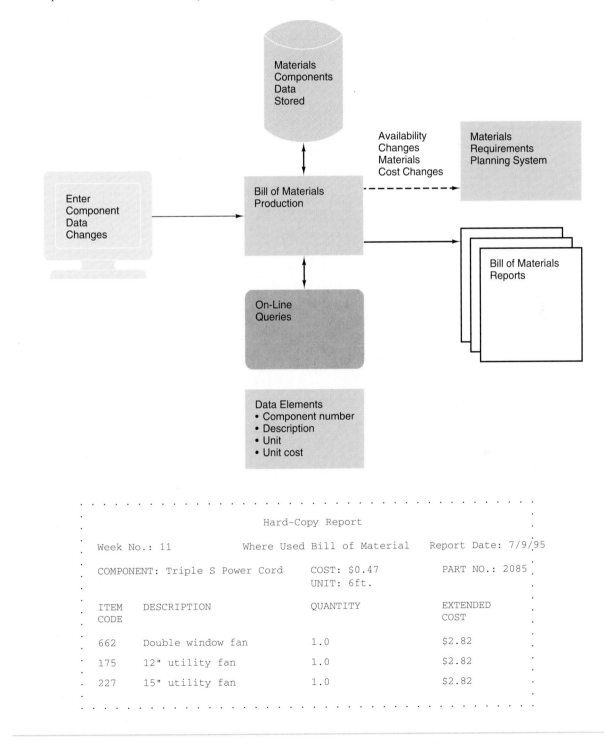

```
. . . . . . . . . . . . . . . . . . . . . . . . . . . . . . . . . . . . . . .
.                          Hard-Copy Report                                 .
.                                                                           .
.    Week No.: 11          Where Used Bill of Material   Report Date: 7/9/95 .
.                                                                           .
.    COMPONENT: Triple S Power Cord     COST: $0.47        PART NO.: 2085    .
.                                       UNIT: 6ft.                           .
.                                                                           .
.    ITEM    DESCRIPTION               QUANTITY           EXTENDED          .
.    CODE                                                 COST              .
.                                                                           .
.    662     Double window fan         1.0               $2.82             .
.                                                                           .
.    175     12" utility fan           1.0               $2.82             .
.                                                                           .
.    227     15" utility fan           1.0               $2.82             .
.                                                                           .
. . . . . . . . . . . . . . . . . . . . . . . . . . . . . . . . . . . . . . .
```

FOCUS ON TECHNOLOGY

3-D COMPUTING BRINGS INFORMATION TO LIFE

You've designed a beautifully styled new telephone casing that is sure to be popular. But will it break when dropped? Now you can find out by sitting in front of your computer. A $5,000 desktop computer equipped with an Autodesk "cyberspace development kit" allows designers to assign physical properties such as mass, density, springiness, and roughness to images they create. Before any physical prototype is built the designer can test the new casing by "dropping" it on a concrete floor.

Such computerized simulations are so accurate and economical that many automobile makers now perform most of their crash tests without real cars. A Cray supercomputer and software from Mecalog of Paris were used to model a broadside collision between two Opel sedans. The crash unfolds in slow motion, the cars appearing like ghostly X-ray images on the screen. The engineers can freeze the action at any point to study the effect of the impact on the key internal parts, the body work, and the passengers. This "accident" produces detailed results at a cost of $5,000 per crash; using real cars, the price would be $1 million.

The development of powerful desktop computers and workstations in the 1980s made it possible to apply visualization to manufacturing. Using computer-aided design (CAD) systems, engineers could create product designs on their screens and test them before building a physical prototype. They could also send the design specifications to computerized manufacturing systems to electronically direct the machines that build the products.

Bath Iron Works Inc. in Bath, Maine, uses CAD workstations with three-dimensional solid modeling capabilities to help build naval destroyers, which are considered among the most complex pieces of equipment that can be manufactured. Up to 2,000 design engineers must collectively decide the locations for massive quantities of cables, plumbing equipment, and other structures inside the cramped confines of a destroyer. The CAD system can identify and correct an object placed by one engineer that might interfere with one placed by another before the ship is built. In the past, when designers relied solely on manual drafting, engineers could not detect such problems until the ship was under construction.

Other uses for three-dimensional computing abound in science, architecture, medicine, oil exploration, and air-traffic control. Three-dimensional computer visualization is a powerful means of bringing designs to life. Design consequences and total effect can be seen and modified as needed. Almost half of the human brain is devoted to processing what the eyes see: People can grasp data presented as a three-dimensional object much more quickly than they can interpret columns of numbers or flat two-dimensional charts.

FOCUS Questions: What are the advantages of using this kind of software? Describe two other problems that could benefit from the use of three-dimensional visualization software.

SOURCE: Gene Bylinsky, "The Payoff from 3-D Computing," *Fortune: Making High Tech Work for You,* Autumn 1993 special issue.

Although we describe some of these systems in greater detail in later chapters, you should also be aware that production systems and problems are discussed in courses on Operations Management, or Production Management, in most business schools. If you are interested in a more detailed view of production systems, you should be sure to take one of these courses.[2]

SALES AND MARKETING SYSTEMS

The basic purpose of the **sales and marketing function** is to sell the product or service to customers willing to pay the asking price. While this sounds simple enough, to accomplish these goals, you will have to identify the customers, their needs, how to create awareness and need for your product, how to contact the customers, what channels of distribution to use, how to record and track sales, how to physically distribute the product, how to finance marketing, and how to evaluate the results (see Figure 2.7).

Information systems are used in marketing in a number of ways. Strategic-level sales and marketing systems monitor trends affecting new products and sales opportunities, support planning for new products and services and monitor the performance of competitors. Tactical-level sales and marketing systems support market research, advertising and promotional campaigns, and pricing decisions and analyze sales performance and the performance of the sales staff. Knowledge-level sales and marketing systems support marketing analysis workstations, and operational-level sales and marketing systems assist in locating and contacting prospective customers, tracking sales, processing orders, and providing customer service support (see Table 2.2).

Sales and marketing function
The division of a business organization that sells the firm's product or service.

FIGURE 2.7

The Sales and Marketing Process

There are three basic steps involved in sales and marketing: identifying and creating a market, developing it, and maintaining it. This can be more difficult than it sounds. Identifying market needs, locating potential customers, and satisfying those customers require a great deal of information that must be effectively analyzed and applied. Table 2.2 lists several ways in which information systems help firms become more effective marketers.

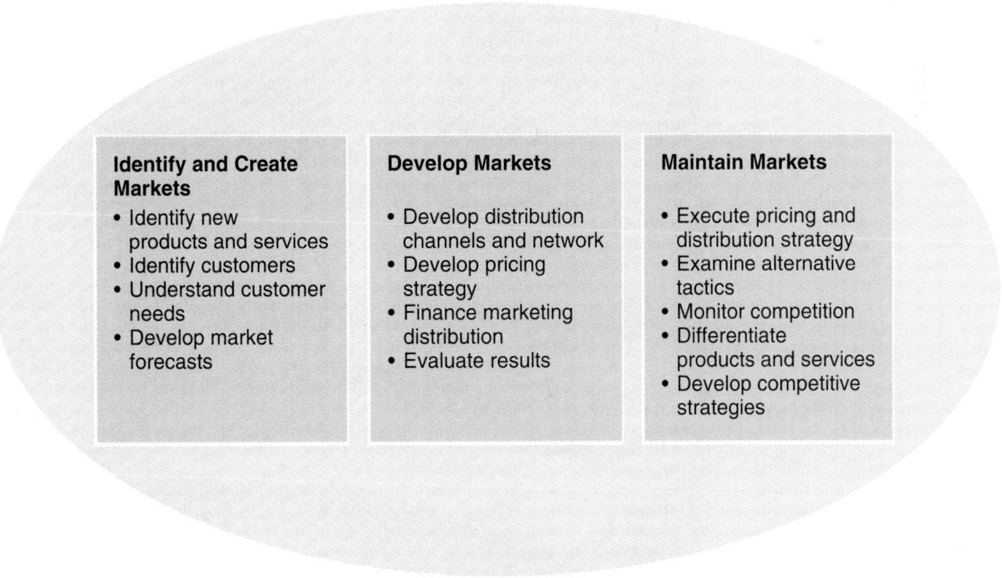

Identify and Create Markets
- Identify new products and services
- Identify customers
- Understand customer needs
- Develop market forecasts

Develop Markets
- Develop distribution channels and network
- Develop pricing strategy
- Finance marketing distribution
- Evaluate results

Maintain Markets
- Execute pricing and distribution strategy
- Examine alternative tactics
- Monitor competition
- Differentiate products and services
- Develop competitive strategies

TABLE 2.2

Sales and Marketing Information Systems

Strategic-Level Systems	*Knowledge Systems*
Demographic market forecasting systems	Marketing workstations
Economic forecasts	*Operational Systems*
Competitor scanning applications	Salesperson support systems
Tactical Systems	Order entry systems
Sales management systems	Point-of-sale systems (POS)
Pricing strategy decision support systems	Telemarketing systems
Sales personnel management systems	Credit information systems
Marketing data analysis	

One straightforward example of a sales information system (see Figure 2.8) is used by business firms like The Limited, The Gap, and many other retailers. In this Sales Analysis and Reporting System, data are captured from point-of-sale devices (typically hand-held scanners), which record each sale by item and item identification code. This sales information is recorded immediately in some systems, permitting precise and timely analysis of inventory levels, market trends, advertising effectiveness ("Did the television campaign really work?"), and sales targets.

FINANCE AND ACCOUNTING SYSTEMS

In most firms, finance and accounting are a single division even though they are relatively distinct functions (see Figure 2.9). Finance involves the proper management of a firm's financial assets: cash on hand, securities, stocks, bonds, and the like. The purpose of finance is to maximize the return on the firm's financial assets and to manage the capitalization of the firm (i.e., find new financial assets in stocks, bonds, or other

This scanning gun captures data about each item of clothing sold, such as style, size, and color, as the purchase passes the checkout counter. Sales information systems use this data to determine which items are in inventory, which items need to be restocked, and which items are selling well.

SOURCE: Courtesy of International Business Machines Corporation.

forms of debt). In many large manufacturing concerns, these financial assets are so large that the financial function is a significant contributor to the firm's profits. Hence finance has grown in importance from a mere support activity to a "primary" activity in many firms.

The accounting function involves the management of financial records—receipts, disbursements, depreciation, payroll, and so forth. The purpose of accounting is to

FIGURE 2.8

A Sales Information System
A sales information system can capture data about sales by having people key these data into the computer or by using point-of-sale devices such as cash registers or hand-held scanners, which capture sales data for the computer at the moment the sale takes place. The report displayed here compares sales figures for various items with the figures for the same items one week or one year ago as a means of pinpointing sales trends and identifying popular and unpopular items.

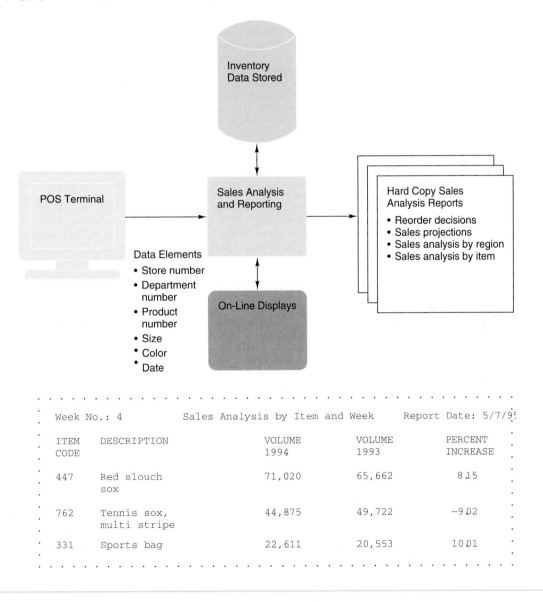

Week No.: 4	Sales Analysis by Item and Week		Report Date: 5/7/95

ITEM CODE	DESCRIPTION	VOLUME 1994	VOLUME 1993	PERCENT INCREASE
447	Red slouch sox	71,020	65,662	8.15
762	Tennis sox, multi stripe	44,875	49,722	−9.02
331	Sports bag	22,611	20,553	10.01

FIGURE 2.9

The Finance and Accounting Process

Many firms place finance and accounting in the same department, although they are actually separate processes. Finance is the function of managing a firm's financial assets; the accounting process manages financial records. While these can often be supported by separate systems, a great deal of information flows between the two.

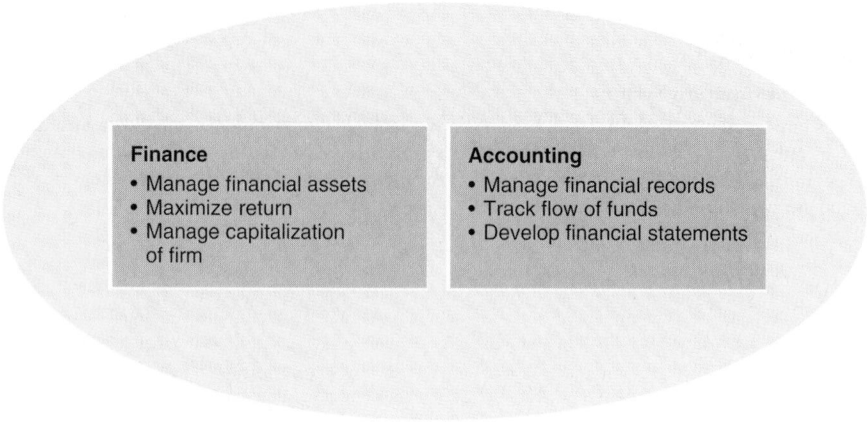

Finance
- Manage financial assets
- Maximize return
- Manage capitalization of firm

Accounting
- Manage financial records
- Track flow of funds
- Develop financial statements

Finance and accounting function

The division of a business organization that manages the firm's financial assets (finance) and maintains the firm's financial records (accounting).

"account" for the flow of funds in a firm. Both the **finance and accounting functions** share related problems: how to keep track of a firm's financial assets and fund flows. What is the current inventory of financial assets? What records do we have for disbursements, receipts, payroll, and other fund flows?

The finance function must obtain a considerable amount of information from sources external to the business. Finance ultimately must answer the question, "Are we getting the best return on our investments?" This can only be answered by obtaining a steady flow of daily financial information from outside the firm.

Table 2.3 shows some of the leading finance and accounting systems found in a typical large organization. Strategic-level systems for the finance and accounting function establish long-term investment goals for the firm and provide long-range forecasts of the firm's financial performance. Tactical financial information systems help managers oversee and control the firm's financial resources. Knowledge systems support finance

TABLE 2.3

Finance and Accounting Information Systems

Strategic-Level Systems	*Knowledge Systems*
Financial and securities market data analysis	Financial management workstations
Economic and demographic forecasting systems	Portfolio analysis systems
	Security analysis systems
Budget forecasting systems	Trader workstations
Tactical Systems	*Operational Systems*
Fixed assets accounting	Accounts payable/receivable
Cost accounting systems	General ledger
Budgeting systems	Payroll

MACY'S THRIVES ON SALES

Founded in 1858, the R.H. Macy Co. was the first department store in the United States. It was a large open-floor building with a wide variety of goods for sale. From its home store at Herald Square, Macy's expanded to over 114 locations, making it one of America's biggest department store chains. The flagship store at Herald Square was considered the largest department store in the world.

Macy's thrives on sales—if there's no sale, there's no business. Macy's still stocks a wide array of goods—clothing for men, women, and children, jewelry, dishes, appliances, linens, television sets. Some items feature nationally known brand names such as Polo by Ralph Lauren. Others are private-label items that are produced and marketed as a Macy's brand name. The merchandise mix for each store varies depending on geographic location and the tastes of the clientele. In some stores, brand-name items may be more popular than in others. Some stores do better selling brand-name housewares or expensive designer-label fashions; others have customers who look for value and lower prices. Stores in Texas and Minnesota need to stock larger sizes than stores in New York. A key problem for Macy's is determining which items to stock in which stores. Continuing success depends on stocking merchandise the customers want—the right items and styles in the right colors and sizes.

Merchandise buyers play a powerful role in determining what items each Macy's store will carry. At one time, Macy's had 425 buyers. The buyers select the items that will be sold—which brand of dresses, shoes, lipstick, or dinnerware. The buyers plan advertising and promotions, call on suppliers, order, and allocate merchandise to the stores. Until recently, stores called the buyers directly to ask for merchandise. The buyer for women's purses, for example, could get calls from more than 50 stores in his or her division. Buyers had to juggle all of these responsibilities and worry about whether they were making their sales targets. Often they could not return calls for several days.

Macy's management training program taught young buyers and executives the "more is always better than less" theory of inventory management. The idea was to make sure that the stores were well-stocked, because stocking desirable merchandise would increase Macy's chances of selling more and make sales more profitable. To make sure no customer went away empty-handed, Macy's buyers filled the stores with many more goods than were actually sold, carrying both best-selling items and goods that were difficult to move off the shelves. Macy's, the world's largest department store, became one of the world's most fully-stocked department stores as well.

SOURCE: Stephanie Strom, "A Key for a Macy Comeback," *The New York Times*, November 1, 1992.

RUNNING CASE Questions

1. How important is the sales function at a store such as Macy's? Why?
2. What role do merchandise buyers play in the sales and marketing process at Macy's?
3. What pieces of information do merchandise buyers need to do their job effectively?
4. How could a point-of-sale system such as the one illustrated in this chapter help a Macy's merchandise buyer?
5. How do decisions made by merchandise buyers affect the other business functions at Macy's?

FIGURE 2.10

An Accounts Receivable System

Every organization that collects payment from customers has an accounts receivable system. The system tracks and stores important customer data such as payment history, credit rating, and billing history. Input to the system includes payment and invoice data; answers and information can arrive both on paper and on a screen. As with all other accounting systems within a firm, the accounts receivable system is linked to the general ledger system, which tracks all of the firm's cash flows.

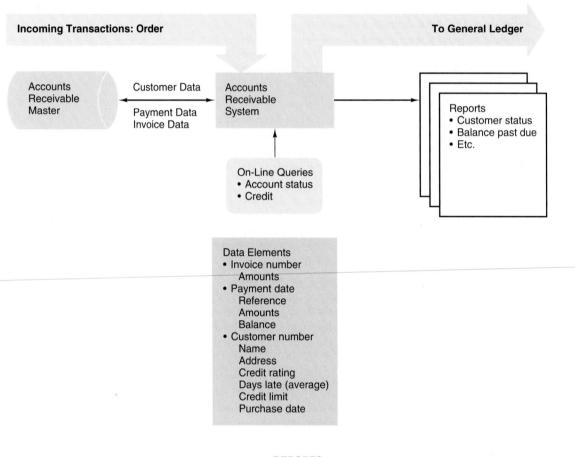

REPORTS

Customer Status

CUSTOMER NUMBER	CUSTOMER NAME	CREDIT RATING	CREDIT LIMIT	CURRENT BALANCE	AMOUNT RECEIVED	TOTAL BALANCE
61298	Nelligan Co.	2	4,500.00	2,000.00	0	2,000.00

Aged Accounts Receivable

CUSTOMER NUMBER	CUSTOMER NAME	CURRENT BALANCE	1–30 DAYS PAST DUE	31–60 DAYS PAST DUE	60+ DAYS PAST DUE	TOTAL BALANCE
61298	Nelligan Co.	0		2,000.00		2,000.00

FIGURE 2.11

The Human Resources Process
The role of the firm's human resources function is to attract, develop, and maintain an effective labor force. This includes locating and hiring new employees, measuring and improving the performance of current employees, and maintaining an appropriate and competitive staff over time.

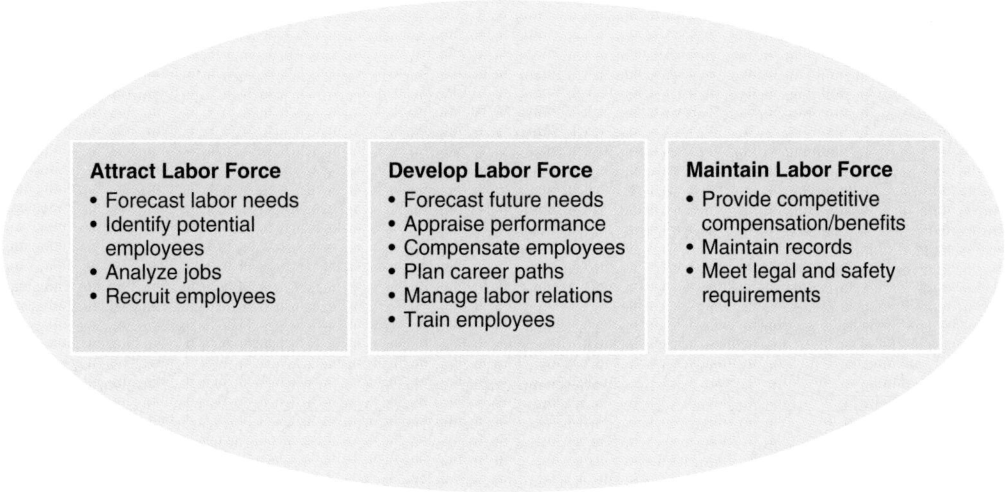

Attract Labor Force
- Forecast labor needs
- Identify potential employees
- Analyze jobs
- Recruit employees

Develop Labor Force
- Forecast future needs
- Appraise performance
- Compensate employees
- Plan career paths
- Manage labor relations
- Train employees

Maintain Labor Force
- Provide competitive compensation/benefits
- Maintain records
- Meet legal and safety requirements

and accounting by providing analytical tools and workstations for evaluating the firm's financial performance. Operational systems in finance and accounting track the flow of funds in the firm through transactions such as paychecks, payments to vendors, stock reports, and receipts.

A simple but powerful example of a finance and accounting system that is found in all businesses is an accounts receivable system (see Figure 2.10). An accounts receivable system keeps track of every customer invoice: each invoice generates an "account receivable"—that is, the customer owes the firm money. Some customers pay immediately in cash, and others are granted credit. As the business owner, you must decide if you wish to grant credit (some people really don't pay their bills).

The accounts receivable system records each invoice in a master file that also contains information on each customer, including credit rating. As the business goes on day after day, the system also keeps track of all the bills outstanding and can produce a variety of output reports, both on paper and on computer screens, to help the business collect bills. The system also answers queries regarding a customer's payment history and credit rating.

Note, however, that although this system is important on its own, it is connected directly to the general ledger system, which tracks all cash flows of the firm. We describe more extensive financial systems in later chapters.

HUMAN RESOURCES SYSTEMS

The purpose of the **human resources function** is to attract, develop, and maintain a stable, effective, and appropriately trained labor force (see Figure 2.11). Crucial to this mission are the identification of potential employees, the maintenance of complete records on existing employees, and the creation of training programs.

Human resources function
The division of a business organization that concentrates on attracting and maintaining a stable work force for the firm; it identifies potential employees, maintains records on existing employees, and creates training programs.

FIGURE 2.12

A Typical Personnel Record-Keeping System

All businesses need to keep records of their employees to satisfy government regulations as well as their own internal requirements. A typical personnel record-keeping system maintains data on the firm's employees, identifying those who have been newly hired or terminated. Human resources specialists can view employee data directly on their terminal screens or they can obtain hard copy reports such as the sample report displayed here.

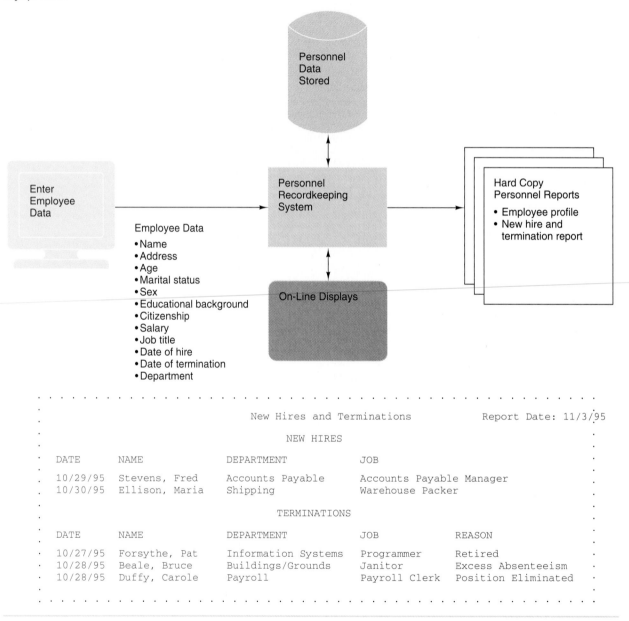

```
                              New Hires and Terminations              Report Date: 11/3/95

                                        NEW HIRES

    DATE        NAME              DEPARTMENT            JOB
    10/29/95    Stevens, Fred     Accounts Payable      Accounts Payable Manager
    10/30/95    Ellison, Maria    Shipping              Warehouse Packer

                                       TERMINATIONS

    DATE        NAME              DEPARTMENT            JOB            REASON
    10/27/95    Forsythe, Pat     Information Systems    Programmer     Retired
    10/28/95    Beale, Bruce      Buildings/Grounds      Janitor        Excess Absenteeism
    10/28/95    Duffy, Carole     Payroll                Payroll Clerk  Position Eliminated
```

Human resources managers use many types of human resources systems to solve problems. In some cases these "systems" are specific applications that can run on a small desktop computer (for instance, a small desktop-based system can help managers plan for the succession of key managers). In other instances, such as employee compensation and benefits, a major commitment of organizational resources is required to build very large systems.

TABLE 2.4	

Human Resources Information Systems

Strategic-Level Systems	*Knowledge Systems*
Human resources planning	Career path systems
Labor force forecasting systems	Training systems
Demographic analyses	Human resources workstations
Succession planning systems	*Operational Systems*
Tactical Systems	Personnel record keeping
Labor force budgeting systems	Applicant tracking
Positions control systems	Benefit systems
Compensation and job analysis systems	Training and skills inventory systems
Contract cost and labor relations systems	Positions tracking
Equal employment opportunity (EEO) compliance systems	

As we have done for the other organizational functions, let's examine some human resources information systems by type and level. Strategic-level human resources systems identify the manpower requirements (skills, educational level, types of positions, number of positions, and cost) for meeting the firm's long-term business plans. At the tactical level, human resources systems help managers monitor and analyze the recruitment, allocation, and compensation of employees. Knowledge systems for human resources support analysis activities related to job design, training, and the modeling of employee career paths and reporting relationships. Human resources operational systems track the recruitment and placement of the firm's employees (see Table 2.4).

A typical human resources system for personnel record keeping maintains basic employee data, such as the employee's name, age, sex, marital status, address, educational background, citizenship, salary, job title, date of hire, and date of termination (see Figure 2.12). The screen in the figure shows a report on newly hired and recently terminated employees. Another output of the system might be a "profile" of data on each individual employee, such as that illustrated in Figure 11.3 in Chapter 11.

SUMMARY

- To understand business systems, you need to know what a business is and how business firms operate.

- A business firm is a formal, complex organization that seeks to maximize profits.

- The major business functions are manufacturing and production, sales and marketing, finance and accounting, and human resources.

- Business organizations are arranged hierarchically in levels composed of senior management, middle management, knowledge and data workers, and production workers.

- Businesses develop information systems to deal with internal organizational problems and to ensure their survival in a changing external environment.

- Information systems can usefully be seen in two perspectives. First, information systems serve specific functional areas of the firm. Second, different kinds of systems are designed to solve different kinds of problems at different levels of the business.

- Manufacturing and production systems solve problems related to production technology, planning for production, design of products and operations, and controlling the flow of production.

- Sales and marketing systems help businesses promote products, contact customers, physically distribute products, and track sales.
- Finance and accounting systems keep track of the firm's financial assets and fund flows.
- Human resources systems develop staffing requirements; identify potential employees; maintain records of the firm's employees; track employee training, skills, and job performance; and help managers devise appropriate plans for compensating employees and developing career paths.

KEY TERMS

Business organization	Business environment
Business functions	Strategic-level systems
Specialization	Tactical systems
Hierarchy	Knowledge systems
Informal structure	Operational systems
Senior management	Manufacturing and production function
Middle management	Sales and marketing function
Knowledge and data workers	Finance and accounting function
Production workers	Human resources function

REVIEW QUESTIONS

1. How would you define a business organization?
2. What are the major steps you would go through in organizing a business?
3. What are the major business functions typically found in all business firms?
4. What are the levels of a business firm?
5. Why are external environments important for understanding a business?
6. How will organizations and jobs change as we move into the twenty-first century?
7. Why do business organizations develop information systems?
8. What are the major functional information systems of businesses? Give some examples of each.
9. What are the different levels of information systems in a firm? Give some examples of each.

DISCUSSION QUESTIONS

1.   Some people argue that computers will reduce the need for managers in an organization. They believe fewer managers will be required because employees using computers will supervise themselves. The results of their work will be monitored by computer and passed directly to senior management without the need for middle managers. Discuss and comment.

2.   How would the framework for describing business information systems introduced in this chapter have to be adjusted for a small business such as a drug store consisting of an owner and several sales clerks?

PROBLEM-SOLVING EXERCISES

1.   *Group exercise:* Divide into groups and have each group obtain an annual report of a business or find an article describing a business in *Business Week, Fortune*, or another publication. Have the group use the information provided to describe the kinds of information systems one might find in that business. Have each group present its findings to the class.

2.   Describe an operational process that you think can be radically improved by the introduction of information systems. You could focus on your college or university bookstore, cafeteria, or registrar's office or a local delicatessen.

3.   *Hands-on exercise:* Select appropriate software that could produce the new hires and terminations report illustrated in Figure 2.12. Design an input transaction that would capture this information, enter the information, and produce the report.

NOTES

1. Kenneth C. Laudon, "Information Technology and Non-Profit Organizations: A Concepts Paper" (Teaneck, N.J.: Reference Point Incorporated, an online public information utility for the nonprofit sector, 1989).

2. An excellent text, likely to be found in most university libraries, is Roger G. Schroeder, *Operations Management: Decision Making in the Operations Function* (New York: McGraw-Hill, 1992). In this text, as well as in others, you will find useful descriptions of the manufacturing and operations process as well as many examples of where information systems are and could be used.

PROBLEM-SOLVING CASE

CATERPILLAR MOVES MOUNTAINS WITH NEW INFORMATION SYSTEMS

Caterpillar Inc., based in Peoria, Illinois, is the largest construction equipment maker in the world and for years was a world market leader. But in 1982, sales tumbled by almost 30 percent. Losses continued to mount as Caterpillar grappled with Japanese competition, a downturn in the construction trade, and rising manufacturing costs.

Caterpillar management initially responded to the downturn in the usual way, by closing plants, laying off workers, and cutting expenses. But the usual ways were not enough to overcome Caterpillar's inefficient factories and excessively bureaucratic management. Management decided to pursue new production and business solutions using information systems.

In 1985 Caterpillar began a remarkable turnaround by launching a $1.85 billion program to modernize its factories and improve customer satisfaction. The goal was to increase product quality and plant flexibility while slashing inventories and production time. Caterpillar's "Plant with a Future" program was designed to eliminate wasted motion, excess inventory, and superfluous labor by simplifying, consolidating, and automating various tasks.

Here's an example of how the new program works. Caterpillar's Aurora, Illinois, plant makes earthmoving vehicles. It used to build several different models on only two assembly lines, which required frequent and lengthy set-up changes. Caterpillar redesigned its manufacturing process, spending $250 million on new information systems and equipment. Now, as vehicles move down its assembly line, automatically guided cranes and a monorail system deliver parts as needed from one of 500 or more storage locations next to the factory floor. The redesigned factory can run eight shorter, more specialized assembly lines.

At Caterpillar's plant in East Peoria, Illinois, partially assembled tractors move along the assembly line on air-driven dollies. Instead of continually moving units along an assembly line, the system holds a unit steady while parts and subassemblies are mounted. This means that workers can alter the pace of assembly to resolve any quality problems that might arise. Overhead monorails deliver major subassemblies such as radiator housings or the cab unit.

Networked computer terminals on the factory floor require workers to alert the system at key stages of the assembly process. Components are automatically replenished by having workers respond to computer queries, often with a single keystroke. The system monitors parts consumption, automatically transmitting reorders to suppliers and information on inventory levels and finished products to the financial tracking system at Caterpillar headquarters in Peoria. The integrated materials handling system has cut inventories of tens of thousands of components by nearly 40 percent. The company has reduced the time it takes to produce equipment such as wheel-loaders, which scoop, carry, and dump materials such as sand or gravel, from 16 days to only five days. On-time deliveries to customers have risen by 70 percent. Customers benefit from faster delivery, lower prices, and a defect rate that is 50 percent lower than before.

Caterpillar sells nearly all its tractors, loaders, and bulldozers through dealers. Seventy dealers run more than 300 outlets in the United States alone. Since the dealers are the firm's only direct link with the customers, Caterpillar wants to make it easy for dealers to do business with them. New information systems help by linking dealers' local computers to Caterpillar's central computers. A Dealer Business System enables dealers to access product and repair data from the central computers. Another system, Antares, allows dealers to order parts and process invoices and warranties from their local computers; parts can be obtained by 6:30 A.M. the day after an order is placed. A Service Information System electronically delivers catalogs of Caterpillar's engine parts to the dealers. The system provides a graphical diagnostic tool that dealers can use to identify and repair problems with Caterpillar machines or parts. Caterpillar's equipment commonly stays in use for 15 years or more, so dealers and field technicians have an ongoing need for parts data.

These systems eliminate time and paperwork because dealers don't have to call different people to obtain copies of invoices or information on customers and parts; they can now obtain this information directly from the computer. The systems expedite order fulfillment by allowing the immediate transmission of parts orders to Caterpillar's manufacturing and production systems. Thus, managers have an easier time scheduling production.

For instance, when a customer places an order with a Caterpillar dealer for six new bulldozers, the dealer first tries to fill the order from stock. If the equipment has to be built, the dealer places the order directly to Peoria through his or her computer. The order is transmitted immediately to Caterpillar's planning system, where it is matched against a master production forecast plan and given a slot on a master production schedule. Caterpillar then transmits the order to the plants that will produce the parts and assemble the machines through a global telecommunications network that connects 23 warehouses in 11 countries as well as the main supply hub in Morton, Illinois.

This process contrasts with traditional manufacturing, in which companies manufactured large volumes of parts and items for stock based on sales forecasts. The new "pull" approach lets a customer's order trigger a series of actions throughout the plant, ultimately generating an order to suppliers. Production is more closely tied to actual sales.

An executive information system built by Caterpillar's corporate information systems group lets business units project the profitability of various activities by performing "what if" scenarios. For example, a manager in the engine division can extract warranty information to identify the dealers who spend an unusual amount on customer warranty claims. An activity-based cost information system helps managers calculate each plant's contribution to the production cost of a particular product.

Caterpillar has cut the amount of time required to develop a new product and bring it to market by using a computer-aided design system with vehicle simulation software. By using the system to simulate products, engineers can eliminate up to 90 percent of the unworkable design ideas before even building a physical prototype. Time to market for new designs, which used to be six to eight years, is now two to four years. Caterpillar broadcasts a monthly "CAT TV" program to dealers, informing them of new offerings, product changes, and service-related announcements. This "business television" consists of a one-way video service with two-way audio. Communication with dealers and integration of Caterpillar headquarters, warehouses, and plants depends on the firm's global telecommunications network. The network provides more than 180 Caterpillar dealers in more than 1,000 locations with voice, data, and video, including electronic mail and electronic exchange of transactions between dealers and suppliers.

Caterpillar's business redesign had another goal: to help employees keep their jobs. Although slightly more than half of Caterpillar's products are sold abroad, three-fourths of these products are made in the United States. Nearly three out of four Caterpillar employees work on U.S. soil. Instead of cutting costs by farming out production to foreign plants, Caterpillar chose an information system plan that would preserve jobs at home. Since Caterpillar strengthened its market leadership, cheaper labor is no longer the most pressing issue. Instead, by concentrating on service, quality, mass customization, and lead time, Caterpillar is the world market leader once again.

Yet Caterpillar has been plagued by poor labor relations. While management made a sustained effort to keep jobs in the United States, it still had to find ways to rein in costs. Caterpillar management threatened to break a 163-day United Auto Workers strike by hiring nonunion workers to replace the 12,000 Caterpillar employees who walked off the job. Since 48,000 people applied for work during the strike, Caterpillar workers agreed to return to work without a contract. The matter has not yet been fully resolved.

SOURCES: Doug Bartholomew, "Caterpillar Digs In," *InformationWEEK*, June 7, 1993; "How to Bolster the Bottom Line," *Fortune: Making Information Technology Work for You*, Autumn 1993 special issue; and Bob Violino, "Unearthing a New Approach," *InformationWEEK*, April 13, 1992.

CASE STUDY QUESTIONS

1. What were Caterpillar's problems? What people, organization, and technology factors helped create these problems?

2. What role did Caterpillar's systems play in solving these problems? How successful were they?

3. What business functions are supported by Caterpillar's information systems?

4. What levels of the business do Caterpillar's systems support?

Chapter
→ T H R E E ←

INFORMATION SYSTEMS: CHALLENGES AND OPPORTUNITIES

LEARNING OBJECTIVES

After reading and studying this chapter, you will:

1. Know how businesses can use information systems for competitive advantage.

2. Be aware of the challenges to the development of information systems that support businesses on a global scale.

3. Understand how information systems can be used to promote quality in organizations.

4. Understand how organizations can be redesigned through reengineering to maximize the benefits of information technology.

5. Be aware of information system ethics and the major social and organizational effects that computer-based systems have had on advanced societies.

*I*magine that you work all semester on a tough term paper, one that requires you to spend hours in the library and more hours in the computer lab and at home preparing the document. On the day you hand in the paper you discover that several students have obtained copies of your paper and have already handed them in. Moreover, the professor announces that she will give full credit for the papers, even though she knows they were stolen from you! Something like this happens thousands of times a day whenever a copyrighted piece of computer software is illegally copied and often resold. Commonly called "software piracy," lawyers call this practice what it is— theft of intellectual property.

Just as widespread theft of term papers might discourage students from ever creating original term papers, so also does theft of computer software discourage business firms from creating new software. Consider the experience of Sirish Patel, a civil engineer in Bombay. Patel created an architectural engineering program that automatically calculated costs of construction materials and labor based on architectural drawings. His software speeded up the architectural bidding process. He set up a software company to sell the product to other engineering firms in India. After initial market success, sales dropped steeply. Sirish discovered that his software was being widely copied and distributed throughout Indian architectural engineering firms. He soon abandoned the software business and formed the Indian Federation Against Software Theft (InFAST). InFAST encourages Indian courts to enforce existing copyright laws and to impose stiff penalties. Managers convicted of producing or possessing pirated software could face a day's imprisonment and a fine of 100 times the cost of the software.

India is one of many countries with weak protections for intellectual property and a strong cultural tradition of copying software obtained from the U.S. While this tradition harms global sales of U.S.-produced software, it has destroyed the domestic Indian software industry. Ninety percent of U.S.-produced microcomputer software in Taiwan, China, and South Korea is believed to be pirated; 80% of the PC software used in Italy has been illegally copied, and even in the U.S. 40 percent of PC software is copied, resulting in an estimated $2.5 billion loss annually. As the largest exporter of software in the world, the U.S. government attempts to protect American software from pirating through international agreements, but success has been limited.

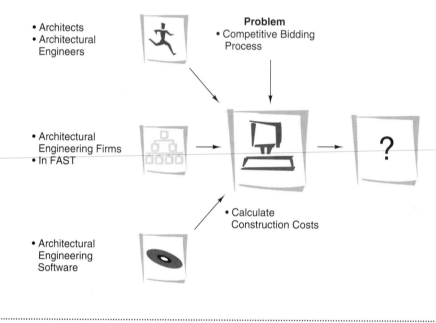

- Architects
- Architectural Engineers

Problem
- Competitive Bidding Process

- Architectural Engineering Firms
- In FAST

- Calculate Construction Costs

?

- Architectural Engineering Software

SOURCE: Suzanne P. Wiesband and Seymour E. Goodman, "Subduing Software Pirates," *Technology Review,* October 1993.

The globalization of trade offers new opportunities and threats for business firms, and for computer-based firms in particular. Globalization means larger markets, lower production costs, and greater profits. But global trade can cause clashes among nations over differing laws, ethical standards, and business practices that can eradicate many of the benefits of information systems.

Information systems cannot be used effectively without addressing these and other challenges posed by today's competitive global environment. These challenges include the drive toward competitive advantage; the need to understand the requirements for competing on a global scale; the need to ensure quality of products and services; the need to redesign organizations to make them more efficient; and the responsibility to ensure that information systems are used in an ethically and socially responsible manner. This chapter describes each of these challenges and the opportunities they have created for information systems.

3.1 ACHIEVING COMPETITIVE ADVANTAGE WITH INFORMATION SYSTEMS

A new role for information systems has been their application to problems concerning the firm's competitive advantage. Such systems are considered **strategic information systems** because they focus on solving problems related to the firm's long-term prosperity and survival. Such problems may entail creating new products and services, forging new relationships with customers and suppliers, or finding more efficient and effective ways of managing the firm's internal activities. The objective of such systems is to provide solutions that will enable firms to defeat and frustrate their competition. You will find many examples of information systems used strategically throughout this book.

    Although any information system application is "important" in the sense that it solves some important business problem, a strategic information system is one that places the firm at a competitive advantage. Strategic impact systems are far-reaching and deeply rooted; they fundamentally change the firm's goals, products, services, or internal and external relationships.

Strategic information systems
Information systems used in solving a business organization's long-range, or strategic, problems.

COUNTERING COMPETITIVE FORCES

To stay in business, almost all firms must worry about their competitive advantage—that is, their ability to compete with other firms. This competitive advantage is shaped by a series of competitive forces, such as substitute products and services, the bargaining power of customers and suppliers, and the threat of new competitors entering the market. These forces, in turn, affect the balance of power between the firm and its traditional competitors in the industry. Figure 3.1 illustrates how these competitive forces would affect the position of a cable television company.

    There are four basic strategies that firms can pursue to counter these competitive forces; these are summarized in Table 3.1.[1]

Low-cost leadership: produce products and services at a lower price than competitors.

Focus on market niche: create new market niches by pinpointing a target market for a product or service that the firm can provide better than its competitors.

Product differentiation: develop unique new products or services.

Linkage: develop tight linkages to customers and suppliers that "lock" customers into the firm's products and suppliers into the price structure and delivery timetable determined by the purchasing firm.

    Firms can use information systems to support each of the four competitive strategies. Information systems can create unique products or services that cannot easily be duplicated so that competitors cannot respond. Information systems can also target marketing campaigns more precisely or "lock in" customers and suppliers, making switching to competitors too costly and inconvenient to be worthwhile. Finally, information systems can have a strategic effect if they enable firms to do what they have been doing in a more efficient, cost-effective manner and to offer their goods and services at higher quality or lower prices than competitors. The following examples illustrate how leading U.S. and foreign firms have used strategic impact systems for competitive advantage.

FIGURE 3.1

Competitive Forces in the Cable Television Industry

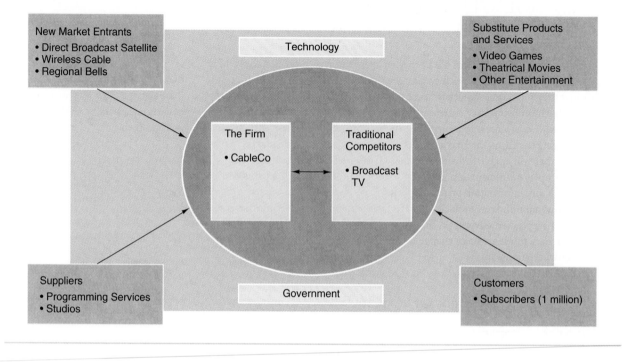

New Marketing Strategies   Powerful new sales and marketing information systems enable firms to "mine" existing information as a resource to increase profitability and market penetration. Firms can use this information to identify and target products for a particular market or product niche, or they may use it to determine ways to serve specific market segments more effectively.

Many companies mine their sales and customer data for marketing information. The Avon Corp. issues 15 million product brochures every 2 weeks for use in direct marketing. Avon's sales campaign management group uses information captured from invoices to plan the brochures. Invoice information is also employed to link the special offers in the brochures, such as a necklace offered for $6.99 when accompanied by a perfume purchase. Avon thus can link its promotions more effectively to a range of objectives—profitability, movement of inventory, or giveaways to boost customer service. Its order distribution facility in Newark, Delaware, is one of the most automated in the country.

The Hilton Answer*Net system described in Chapter 1 is also strategically mined for marketing information. The Answer*Net system includes historical data about every client's previous stays in Hilton hotels. These data provide sales staff with information about the client's personal preferences, such as parking facilities or high-security needs, that might be useful when trying to persuade the client to book a Hilton hotel for upcoming business meetings. (About half the Hilton chain's business comes from meetings and corporate travel.)

Companies can also examine customer service data to target sales campaigns and improve the quality of their products. The Whirlpool Corp. searches its customer-call data early in the life of its washing machine, dryer, and refrigerator models to identify

TABLE 3.1

Four Basic Competitive Strategies

Strategy	Problem to be Solved	Solution
1. Low-cost leadership	Competition from firms with comparable products and services at the same cost is taking away customers.	Produce products and services at a lower price than competitors without sacrificing quality and level of service.
2. Focus on market niche	Multiple firms are competing for the same market.	Identify a specific focal point for a product or service. The firm can serve this narrow target area better than competitors and attract a specific buyer group more easily.
3. Product differentiation	Customers have no brand loyalty, and competitors can lure them away with lower prices.	Create brand loyalty by developing unique new products that are distinct from competitors' products.
4. Linkage	Customers can easily switch to another firm. Suppliers deliver late or at unfavorable prices.	"Lock in" customers and suppliers, making it difficult for customers to switch and tying suppliers into a price structure and delivery timetable shaped by the firm.

faulty parts. Analysis of the data lets Whirlpool identify the customers who have purchased the machines so that mechanics can be dispatched to replace any defective parts before more complaints surface and customers become unhappy. Whirlpool also uses customer service data to target customers who might want to purchase warranty services or new appliances.

Customer service representatives can collect valuable information for the firm when they respond to customer complaints or questions. Information systems can analyze the data they gather about customer purchases and problems with products to identify problem products, expedite repairs, and target customers that might be interested in purchasing warranty services or additional items.

SOURCE: Courtesy of Whirpool Corporation

New Products and Services   Information systems have been used to create appealing new products and services that cannot easily be replicated by competitors. Many of these new products and services have been created for the financial industry. Classic examples are the bank debit card and automatic teller machine (ATM) systems, which were first developed by Citicorp in 1977. Citicorp's ATMs were so successful that other banks formed their own ATM networks, such as NYCE (The New York Cash Exchange) in the Northeast, Yankee 24 in New England, and the Star System in California. NYCE and Yankee 24 merged in late 1993 to offer new services such as bill payments by telephone or personal computer and the use of bank cards to make purchases in stores. Citicorp is trying to maintain its lead by allying with Ameritech to provide banking services by telephone. Citicorp customers will be supplied with advanced telephones with large calculator-like screens to check account balances, transfer money, make payments, and trade securities.

Solidifying Relationships with Customers and Suppliers   Information systems have also been used to "lock in" customers, making it costly or inconvenient for customers to switch to a competitor. The Federal Express Corp. has compiled a list of more than 20,000 steady customers. To prevent them from defecting to rivals like the United Parcel Service, FedEx installed free personal computers linked to its Memphis headquarters. Shippers using FedEx can use the machines to check the status of the packages they send each day. Even customers that are not large enough to qualify for free computers can receive free FedEx Tracking Software to use with their own PCs for this purpose.

Information systems can also create new relationships with suppliers that maximize the firm's purchasing power. For example, the Chrysler Corp. and all the major U.S. auto companies have established electronic links with major suppliers. The Budd Co.

The Federal Express Corporation supplies its steady customers with free software that they can use themselves to track the status of their Federal Express shipments anywhere in the world. The ease and convenience of using FedEx's package tracking system encourages customers to choose Federal Express over competitors.

SOURCE: Courtesy of Federal Express Corporation

Point-of-sale systems capture data about purchases at the moment a sale takes place, often using bar code scanners and computerized cash registers. Firms can use this data to determine what items in inventory need restocking and to send orders for new merchandise directly to suppliers. Sales data are also a valuable strategic resource because they can reveal buying patterns and sales trends that help firms target their products more effectively.

SOURCE: Courtesy of International Business Machines Corporation.

of Rochester, Michigan, a leading supplier of sheet metal parts, wheel products, and frames, receives manufacturing releases directly from Chrysler terminals installed in all its work areas. Chrysler achieves savings from strict delivery requirements that specify parts to be supplied on the day they are needed.

Improved Operations and Internal Management   Companies can also gain competitive advantage by performing their business tasks more efficiently and by improving productivity, reducing costs, or enhancing the quality of products or service. Basic business systems (such as those described in Chapter 13) that cut administrative costs, reduce costs from excess inventory, or speed production can be strategic if they help a firm become the low-cost leader in its field.

For example, Wal-Mart Stores Inc. rose to the top of the U.S. retail business by keeping its prices low and its stores well-stocked and by minimizing inventories. It uses a legendary inventory replenishment system triggered by point-of-sales purchases that is considered the best in the industry. The "continuous replenishment system" sends orders for new merchandise directly to suppliers as soon as consumers pay for their purchases at the cash register. Point-of-sale terminals record the bar code of each item passing the checkout counter and send a purchase transaction directly to a central computer at Wal-Mart headquarters. The computer collects all the orders and transmits them to suppliers. Because the system can replenish inventory so rapidly, Wal-Mart does not need to spend much money on maintaining large inventories of goods in its own warehouses. The system also allows Wal-Mart to adjust purchases of store items to meet customer demands. Competitors such as Sears spend nearly 30 percent of each dollar in sales to pay for overhead (i.e., expenses for salaries, advertising, warehousing, and building upkeep). Kmart spends 21 percent of its sales dollars on overhead. But by using information systems to keep operating costs low, Wal-Mart pays only 15 percent of sales revenue for overhead. By focusing on ways to maximize sales while minimizing inventory costs, Wal-Mart has become larger than Kmart and Sears combined and nearly as big as the entire U.S. department store industry.

The Hilton Answer*Net system described in Chapter 1 also provides strategic benefits by expediting reservations and sales reporting. It automatically provides to local, regional, and national sales offices information that used to take a week to obtain. Salespeople no longer have to take the time to prepare status reports for managers. When they need to verify whether rooms are available or whether reservations have been processed, they can key into the system. Answer*Net is also cheaper to operate than Hilton's previous system.

THE VALUE CHAIN

Value chain

The viewing of a business firm as a series of basic activities that add value to the firm's products or services.

The concept of the value chain can be used to identify the specific activities in each organization for which information systems can be used most effectively to enhance the firm's competitive position. The **value chain** views the firm as a series or "chain" of basic activities that add value to a firm's products or services. These activities can be categorized as either primary activities or support activities.

Primary activities include inbound logistics, operations, outbound logistics, sales and marketing, and service. The first four of these primary activities are described in the discussions of the manufacturing and production and sales and marketing processes in Chapter 2. The service activity involves maintenance and repair of the firm's goods and services. Support activities make the delivery of the primary activities possible and consist of administration and management, human resources, technology, and procurement.

FIGURE 3.2

Examples of Strategic Information Systems in the Value Chain
Systems can be built to support each of the activities in the value chain. For activities that add the most value to the firm's products and services, such systems can provide a competitive advantage.

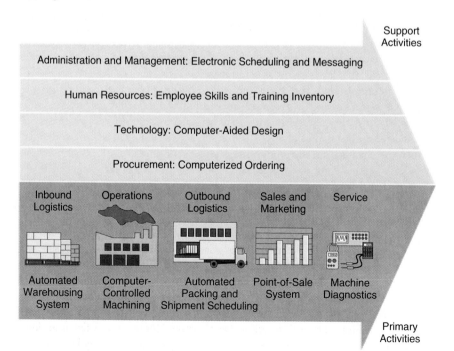

An information system could provide strategic impact if it helped the firm perform its value activities at a lower cost than competitors or if it provided the firm's customers with added value or service. Figure 3.2 illustrates the value chain and provides examples of strategic information systems that could be developed for each of the value activities. For instance, an automated warehouse system that identified and assigned warehouse locations for incoming goods could support inbound logistics. Operations could be supported by computer-controlled machine tools that cut materials into various shapes, and outbound logistics could be supported by a system that automatically generated packing lists and scheduled shipments. A system to diagnose problems with machine tools would support the service activity. A system that scheduled meetings electronically and sent messages from one employee's desktop to another would support administration and management. A system that inventoried the training and skills of employees would support the human resources activity. A computer-aided design system similar to the applications described in Focus on Technology in Chapter 2 would support the technology activity. Wal-Mart's continuous replenishment system supports both the sales and marketing activity and the procurement activity. The precise activities that add the most value to products and services depend on the specific features of each firm. Businesses should develop strategic information systems for the value activities that add the most value to their particular firm.

3.2 COMPETING ON A GLOBAL SCALE

Look closely at your jeans or sneakers. Even if they have a U.S. label, they were probably designed in California and stitched together in Hong Kong or Guatemala using materials from China or India. Many of the items we use every day come from other countries or have foreign components; the firm where you work probably engages in business abroad as well. Foreign trade now accounts for over 25 percent of the goods and services produced in the U.S. and even more in Germany and Japan. Today, and even more in the future, the success of many firms will depend on their ability to compete internationally.

Globalization has created new opportunities for using information systems to coordinate the work of different parts of the company and to communicate with customers and suppliers. It would be extremely difficult, for instance, for Lund's Fishery, described at the beginning of Chapter 1, to track its shipments of fish to various countries and to communicate orders, invoices, and price changes to customers at far-flung locations without its networked information systems. Information systems help large firms like Becton, Dickson (see the Chapter 2 opening vignette) coordinate ordering and inventory operations that span several continents. But building and using information systems on an international scale creates new challenges. In this section, we describe both the challenges and opportunities created by global information systems.

GLOBAL OPPORTUNITIES

While hundreds of thousands of small companies like Lund's Fishery conduct business abroad from a single domestic location, larger corporations often have factories, design centers, sales headquarters, and retail outlets in foreign countries. Very large corporations, like General Motors or Pepsico, have entire subsidiaries for each major country in which they do business, each with its own products, production facilities, and information systems based on national boundaries.

Quaker Oats, the food products company with headquarters in Chicago, Illinois, used to market its products on a country-by-country basis. The products used the Quaker Oats logo but had country-specific brand names. Quaker Oats organized its information systems around each country and the unique products in that country. Quaker used a **multinational** approach to organizing its business: financial management and control were maintained out of a central home office while production, sales, and marketing were distributed to units in other countries. After the creation of the European Community, which seeks to eliminate trade barriers and tariffs between countries and to create a single unified market, Quaker Oats began to develop more products like Gatorade, which is marketed under the same brand name in Italy, Canada, and Germany. Quaker Oats hopes to take advantage of the changes in Europe to restructure its operations and systems to span many countries and serve large economic blocks. The company will have to rebuild its systems to support common products sold to large geographic regions. The firm is moving from a multinational toward a **transnational** business organization in which sales and production activities are managed from a global perspective without reference to national borders.

Figure 3.3 illustrates how the Ford Motor Co. reorganized along transnational lines. In order to compete more effectively in emerging car and truck markets in Asia and in established European and North American markets, Ford created a single worldwide automotive organization called Ford Automotive Operations. Ford has plants in 30 countries and more than 322,000 employees worldwide. Ford's consolidation into a single global operating unit will eliminate redundant engineering and production activities and reduce the cost of materials so that the firm can cheaply and rapidly produce a wider variety of cars and trucks for diverse markets from Michigan to Malaysia. Instead of organizing its operations country by country, Ford will have five global vehicle development centers, each dedicated to specific types of vehicles that Ford will sell worldwide. For instance, the European center, composed of Dunton, England, and Merkenich, Germany, will develop small, front-wheel drive cars like the Escort for sale in Europe, America, and Asia. Ford's objective is to create a "world car" that can be sold in large numbers around the globe, with modifications for local tastes in styling and performance and local pollution regulations.

THE CHALLENGE OF BUILDING INTERNATIONAL INFORMATION SYSTEMS

What would it take to create information systems that could support Ford's new global organization or that could provide the management of Quaker Oats in Chicago with reliable information on the profitability of Gatorade in Germany and Italy? Systems spanning international boundaries pose special people, organization, and technology challenges.

People Challenges   Cultural and linguistic differences are a powerful impediment to building common international systems that can be used by business units in different countries.[2] If the user interface of a system is written in English, how can it be understood and used by other employees in Greece, Turkey, Spain, Italy, or France? Not all workers in international companies are fluent in English. To make the system work across national boundaries, special data entry screens, output forms, reports, and handbooks explaining how the system works will need to be created in the language of each country where the system will be used. The educational levels in some nations are lower than

---

Multinational

Approach to organizing a business in which financial management and control are maintained out of a central home office while production, sales, and marketing operations are located in other countries.

Transnational

Approach to organizing a business in which sales and production activities are managed from a global perspective without reference to national borders.

FIGURE 3.3

Ford Revamps with Eye on the Globe

Ford Motor Company will create a single automotive operation worldwide with five vehicle development centers. Four centers in the United States will focus on larger cars, trucks, and sport utility vehicles. The fifth center will be split between Ford's existing design centers in Dunton, England, and Merkenich, Germany. The idea is to develop specific types of cars that Ford will sell worldwide.

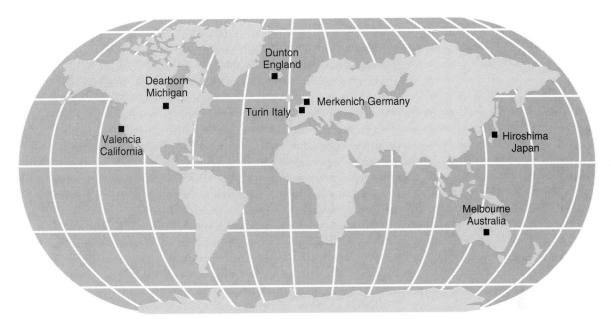

Ford's Existing Design Centers

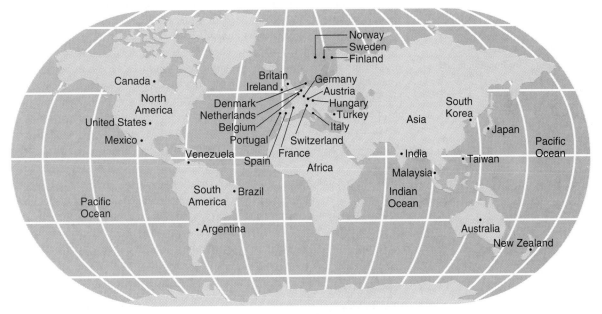

Where Ford Has Plants

others, making it more difficult to assemble an educated workforce that can easily acquire computer and information system skills.

Organization Challenges   Cultural and political differences have a profound effect on the way people work and on organizational procedures. For example, it is standard practice among Hong Kong garment manufacturers for the shop sewing the garment to handle the final steps of finishing and washing. In the U.S., in contrast, the individual steps are contracted out to different parties.

National laws and traditions have created disparate accounting practices in various countries that affect the way profits and losses are analyzed. German companies generally do not recognize the profit from a venture until the project is completely finished and they have been paid. British firms, on the other hand, begin posting profits before a project is completed when they are reasonably certain they will get the money.

These accounting practices are tightly intertwined with each country's legal system, business philosophy, and tax code. British, U.S., and Dutch firms share a predominantly Anglo-Saxon outlook that separates tax calculations from reports to shareholders to focus on showing shareholders how fast profits are growing. Continental European accounting practices are less oriented toward impressing investors, focusing instead on demonstrating compliance with strict rules and minimizing tax liabilities. How can an organization have an accounting system that serves two countries with different practices and goals? And how can a large international company with units in ten different countries obtain consistent data to monitor its performance? If a company wants to use the same information system in several countries, it may have to create special software that can take each country's tax laws into account.

The use of diverse national currencies and currency fluctuations offer further complications. A product that appears profitable in France may suddenly produce a loss because of changes in foreign exchange rates.

It is also difficult to understand how units of the business operate in different countries when they use disparate conventions for naming and identifying essential pieces of business data. A sale may be called an "order produced" in France, an "order scheduled" in Germany, and an "order booked" in the United Kingdom.

Transborder data flow

The movement of information in any form from one country to another.

Countries have different laws governing **transborder data flow,** the movement of information in any form from one country to another. Some European nations, for instance, prohibit the transmission of information about employees to foreign countries. The European Commission, which is the highest planning body for the integration of Europe, is considering measures to restrict the flow of personal information to countries such as the United States that do not conform to Europe's strict requirements governing the transmission of personal information.

Technology Challenges   To transfer data effortlessly from a business unit in one country to other units in other countries requires special hardware, software, and telecommunications capabilities. Often different divisions or operating units of an organization use different brands and models of computer hardware that are largely incompatible with each other. Information systems based on one computer cannot automatically be used on another computer. For instance, operating units that use IBM computers would not be able to transfer the data and software in their systems to Digital Equipment Corp. (DEC) computers, nor would all models of IBM computers be able to run the same information system applications automatically.

Telecommunications services are handled differently from country to country. The telecommunications systems in some countries cannot fulfill even the most basic business needs, such as providing reliable circuits (telecommunications lines in southern and eastern Europe and underdeveloped countries in Africa, Asia, and South America are notoriously unreliable), issuing bills in a common currency, or coordinating among different telecommunications carriers and the regional telecommunications authority. Europe's efforts to create a unified economic community have been thwarted by a hodge-podge of disparate national technical standards for telecommunications technology and levels of service.

Special software is required to translate between different brands of computer hardware and different telecommunications standards. Although standards for connecting networks, computers, and diverse pieces of software are starting to be developed, there are no universal standards that all businesses or countries have agreed upon. For instance, many different standards are used to transfer funds electronically from one organization's computer to another. In Europe, banks use the SWIFT (Society for Worldwide Interbank Financial Telecommunications) standard, while automobile companies and food producers use special standards developed for their respective industries for this purpose. Organizations skirt this problem when they have to by developing special software to translate between one system and another, but this process is very costly, especially if an organization needs to develop such software for all its information systems. We describe some of the software challenges in Chapters 6 and 8.

The Focus on Technology illustrates how the Ford Motor Co. overcame these challenges when it built a global design organization for its world car.

The rest of this text will provide you with the understanding of information system technology and problem solving to help you meet these and other people, organization, and technology challenges.

3.3 PROMOTING QUALITY WITH INFORMATION SYSTEMS

During the last decade of the twentieth century, quality has developed from a business buzzword into a growing and very serious goal for many businesses. The imperative of becoming and remaining globally competitive is the primary cause for this trend. Information systems have a major contribution to make in this drive for quality. After briefly defining quality, we will examine some of the ways information systems can help.

WHAT IS QUALITY?

A number of definitions exist for quality. One very common one is conformance to specifications (or the absence of variations). This definition is a producer view of quality rather than a consumer view. Using this definition, one can easily measure quality by first establishing specifications and then checking the product (or service) to make certain it meets those specifications. In an information system, for example, one specification for an online corporate payroll might be a 3-second response time 90 percent of the time when no more than 20 clerks are using the system. A simple statistical tracking of the system will allow those involved to determine whether the system is conforming to the specification. Similarly, the specifications for a telephone might include one that states the strength of the phone should be such that it will not be dented or otherwise damaged by a drop from a 4-foot height onto a wooden floor. Again, a simple test will allow this

FOCUS ON TECHNOLOGY

FORD DESIGNS FOR ITS WORLD CAR

The striking 1994 Ford Mustang represents a revolution in the way Ford designs cars. Thanks to powerful computer-aided design (CAD) tools and global networking, Ford transformed a collection of design studios scattered all over the world into a single global design organization.

In the past, automobile design was a slow, step-by-step effort in which artists carved clay models from design drawings (each costing $100,000 and a great deal of time); design changes were then made, new designs were drawn, and new models were created. This process was repeated many times until management was satisfied. Production engineers then took over; inevitably the production process forced additional design changes. Design and development consumed 60 months or more.

CAD created an automobile design revolution. Starting in Japan, more and more design work has been done on powerful workstations. Work progresses more quickly and efficiently because sophisticated CAD software can identify many design flaws while simultaneously allowing designers to "see" the actual product without carving expensive models at each step. Ford designed its 1994

Mustang in 35 months; Jack Telnack, Ford's design chief, believes design time can be reduced to 24 months.

Hardware technology developments have been partially responsible for these improvements. For example, three-dimensional graphics designs with photograph-like reality that can be rotated and viewed from all sides require enormous quantities of data and processing power. CAD workstations able to handle this processing are now readily available. Today a workstation can "crunch" more numbers per second than a person working nonstop could deal with in 2,400 years.

The newest wrinkle in technology support of automobile design is termed "virtual co-location"—designers scattered throughout the world working together as if they were in one location. A typical, transmittable CAD automobile design file now takes about 7.5 minutes to transmit on a network. Prior to satellite transmission and fiber optics, the transmission of such gigantic files was so slow as to be impractical.

Why the need for virtual co-location? Ford designers work in offices in the United States, Europe, Japan, and Australia. Each location has unique knowledge workers and equipment with specialties not available elsewhere. The original designs are usually created in Dunton, England. They are then transmitted to Dearborn, Michigan, where they are modified. Dearborn and Dunton designers work together on networked computers to make modifications, even rotating the three-dimensional images to view them from all sides. When the model is

acceptable to all, designers and engineers in Turin, Italy take over, using the data files transmitted from Dearborn to drive a computerized milling machine to turn out full-size, styrofoam clay models. Production engineers at scattered production sites also participate during the design process.

Ford believes its investment in this technology has brought a 50 percent reduction in design costs alone. More significant, Telnack estimates that about 40 percent of all past development costs resulted from design or production problems that only surfaced once actual automobile production began. He believes that the ability of CAD to catch design flaws early, along with production engineer involvement during product design, will eliminate many design and production mistakes before a vehicle goes into production, thus saving Ford hundreds of millions of dollars. S.I. Gilman, Ford's information systems chief executive, sums it up this way: "If we get only a 50 percent return on our investment, we'll have failed. With the new technology, we can change our product-development process."

FOCUS Questions: Both General Motors and Nissan Motors have explicitly rejected the virtual co-location approach to product development because of the national cultural differences of designers. What organizational, technical, and cultural problems do you think virtual co-location design might create for Ford or other users?

SOURCES: Julie Edelson Halpert, "One Car, Worldwide, With Strings Pulled From Michigan," *The New York Times,* November 6, 1993, and Ricardo Sookdeo, "Ford: Global Integration," *Fortune Information Technology Special Report,* Autumn 1993.

specification to be measured. For this producer perspective on quality to pay off, the organization must be willing to take the action needed to bring its products up to specifications when they fall short.

Today, as the quality movement in business progresses, the definition of quality is increasingly from the perspective of the customer. Customers are concerned with get-

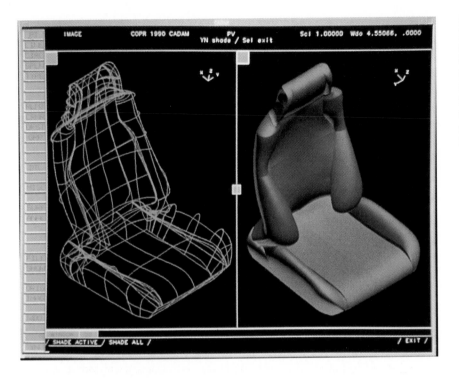

Networked computer-aided design (CAD) systems allow automobile design engineers in different locations to work on the same design simultaneously. Once the original design is created, it can be viewed from all sides and revised by many people.

SOURCE: Courtesy of International Business Machines Corporation.

ting value for their dollar and product fitness, performance, durability, and product support. A story from Perstorp Components, an auto noise–insulation sheet producer in Bloomfield Hills, Michigan, helps to demonstrate the emphasis on customer perspective. Art Mulwitz, vice-president for operations at Perstorp, was told by a production equipment maintenance worker that he considered 80 to 85 percent uptime for his equipment to be acceptable. Mulwitz responded, "What uptime do you expect from your Chevy Blazer?" Uptime quickly rose to between 94 and 97 percent.

Consumers define quality from three aspects. The first is the physical materials: the ease of installation and use of the product; product safety, reliability, serviceability, and durability; and the style and appearance of the product. Quality of service is a second aspect: truth in advertising; billing statement accuracy; responsiveness to expressed or implied warranties; support of product. Finally, psychological impressions are a significant aspect of consumer-defined quality: staff appearance, courtesy and sympathy; staff knowledge of their products and their job; and brand name reputation.[3]

The consumer definition of quality has become important for two reasons. Studies and experience have shown that lower quality is actually costly. For example, if a furniture manufacturer produces a folding chair with a defect rate of 8 percent, that means eight of every 100 chairs shipped are defective. It has long been obvious that returning a product can cost a great deal in extra shipping costs, spare parts, and staff time for repair as well as in customer loyalty. A list of some of the costs arising from producing those eight defective chairs includes:

- Cost of materials for eight chairs

- Labor to build eight defective chairs

- Production machinery wear-and-tear resulting in maintenance and replacement 8 percent more often

- Higher work-in-process inventory costs

- Higher storage costs due to the need to warehouse 8 percent more raw materials, work-in-process, and finished goods

- An 8 percent larger inspection staff to inspect the extra chairs

- Increased insurance liability costs and even legal defense costs due to harm caused by the defective chairs

A second reason firms now focus more on customer definitions of quality is the need to survive in an increasingly competitive market. Consumer preferences have changed. Customers have shown in recent years that they are willing to pay more to receive quality. The low-price, lower-quality producer or retailer often cannot remain in business.

Total quality management
Concept that makes quality improvement the responsibility of all members of an organization.

Total quality management (TQM), a concept made popular in Japan, has become the central approach to quality. TQM makes quality the responsibility of everyone within an organization. Everyone must improve quality, from the typist who reduces typing errors to the line worker who spots product defects, the engineer who eliminates design errors, and the sales person who sells only what the firm can deliver. With TQM quality is not achieved by eliminating defective products. Rather, whenever possible, quality is built in at the source; that is, the defect never happens. Some TQM companies adopt a goal of zero defects. Manchester Stamping, a Manchester, Michigan, producer of automobile door latches and other small metal stampings, relies on quality ratings issued by automobile manufacturers to sell its products. In 1991 they shipped about two million parts to Honda. During the entire year a single defective part was shipped, yielding a quality rate of 99.9999995. However, even this rate was high enough to endanger Stamping's top-quality rating with Honda.

HOW INFORMATION SYSTEMS CAN ENHANCE QUALITY

How can information systems contribute to the enhancement of a company's products or services? Many ways exist, but the answer will depend on the individual company, its business, its competitive environment, and its current needs. Let us examine some of the ways companies face the challenge of improving quality to see how information systems can be part of the process.

Simplify the product and/or the production process   One way to achieve quality is to reduce the number of steps in any process and the number of parts in any product, thus reducing "opportunities" for problems. Pitney Bowes, the $3.3 billion manufacturer of postage meters and mailing machines, decided to redesign its entire production process in response to a drop in market share. They held 88 percent of the market, but considering that historically they had almost no competition, this was a clear indication of trouble. They decided

- to reduce manufacturing costs, allowing them to either lower the price or increase quality for the same price (either way becoming more competitive and giving the customer more quality for the dollar); and

- to simplify their products, thus reducing opportunities for production errors and allowing the firm to establish higher quality standards.

Pitney Bowes used several computer software packages, including the Advanced Planning System (APS), a simulation software package from Carp Systems of Lexington, Massachusetts, and computer-aided design (CAD) engineering design software. First Pitney Bowes redesigned its products, switching from metal castings and mechanical parts

Pitney Bowes used simulation and computer-aided design (CAD) software to redesign its production process, reducing the number of moving parts and the number of steps required to create its business equipment products while consolidating production facilities. Information systems can help firms achieve higher levels of quality by facilitating advanced planning and simplifying the production process.

SOURCE: Courtesy of Pitney Bowes. Photo by Bill Freeman.

to plastics and electronics, thus reducing not only the weight but also the number of moving parts. Their engineers were able to cut the total number of parts per product in half, thus simplifying the production process. Next, using simulation, they redesigned their production facilities, enabling them to consolidate previously scattered factories into one facility. They also moved production steps closer to each other. This combination of changes simplified the production process, resulting in an improved ability to control product quality. The process redesign also increased their output per square foot by 50 percent while making them much more efficient.

Benchmarking   One way to improve quality is to benchmark—to statistically measure your products and activities and compare the results against your own high standards or external industry standards. As described in the Focus on Problem Solving, when Florida Power and Light decided to benchmark outages, customer complaints, customer time without power, and causes for power interruptions, they required a great deal of information. With the aid of their information systems groups, they collected and distributed the needed information. As a result, they improved customer service while reducing other serious problems such as downtime due to lightning strikes.

Direct the product or service toward customer demands   For example, improving customer service will improve quality, as demonstrated both by the Pitney Bowes and the Florida Power and Light projects. In both cases, information systems played a central role.

Reduce cycle time   Studies have shown that probably the best single way to reduce quality problems is to reduce cycle time (the amount of time from the beginning of a process to its end). Shorter cycle times mean that problems are caught earlier in the process, often before the production of the defective product is completed, saving some of the hidden costs of producing it. Moreover, because a shorter cycle time is easier to grasp and understand than a longer cycle time, employees are less likely to make mistakes. Finally, finding ways to reduce cycle time often means finding ways to simplify production steps, as in the case of Pitney Bowes. Information systems can contribute by eliminating critical time delays, as Rockwell International discovered. The Downey, California defense contractor found that slow communication between their manufacturing plant in Palmdale, California, other Rockwell design facilities, and the

FOCUS ON PROBLEM SOLVING

MEASURING FOR QUALITY

Florida Power and Light (FPL), with about $5 billion in revenues, provides electrical power to over three million Floridians, including residents of Miami, Sarasota, and Jacksonville. When FPL instituted its quality program, the Florida Public Power Commission was receiving about 2,100 complaints annually about FPL's service and billing, and FPL's average customer time without service after an outage report was 100 minutes. During the first 5 years of their Quality Improvement Program (QIP), complaints fell at an average rate of 15 percent per year and were down to just 900 per year, an even more impressive gain in the light of a customer-base growth of 3.5 percent per year. Customer electrical outage time dropped during the same period to 48 minutes, a reduction of 52 percent. The central methodology of FPL's quality program was to measure as much as possible and use benchmarks to set target goals. Extensive measuring also allowed FPL to identify and control problems at an early stage. As Al Horner, manager of information planning, systems, and programming, put it, "There are ways to measure everything."

IS played a central role in FPL's achievements by extracting data from existing systems whenever possible and by building new systems to measure activities when necessary. IS then collected all the data and made them available for everyone who needed them. A key to the IS contribution was its decision to make the data available in an easy-to-read graphics format so users could effortlessly spot deviations early enough to prevent serious problems from developing. IS built three systems to support FPL's QIP.

The Divisions Management Information System (DMIS) collects and analyzes customer survey and check-sheet data in 101 categories from all divisions. With this data users can measure their performance against benchmarks and also analyze the source of problems in more detail in search of a solution. For example, data from this system helped FPL to realize that many of its outages were caused when improperly grounded transformers were hit by lightning (Florida has the highest lightning rate in the U.S.). DMIS data from all five FPL divisions are available to all the divisions. Thus, if the Eastern Division has a particular problem and sees from the DMIS report that the Southern Division does not experience the same problem, staff members of the Eastern Division can analyze Southern's data or consult with its staff.

The Trouble Call Management System (TCMS) aids customer service personnel in locating electrical trouble and outages from customer service complaints and automatically notifies repair crews of the nature and location of the problem, thus significantly reducing response time. The same data are also used by technicians to analyze past problems in order to predict where future problems are likely to occur. TCMS is partly responsible for the 52 percent drop in outage response time and the resulting reduction in customer complaints.

The Distribution Construction Management System (DCMS) combines data from FPL's more than 400 locations to enable FPL users to estimate labor and material costs for the 150,000 work orders the utility processes every year. The system also supports and improves work-crew scheduling.

In 1989, FPL became the first U.S. company to win Japan's prestigious W. E. Deming prize for quality. The company has continued to improve its approach to quality with more emphasis today on cost reduction. Capitalizing on its quality improvement achievements, FPL launched its own quality consulting business. With 52 consultants and annual revenues of more than $13 million, FPL's Qualtec Quality Services, Inc. serves more than 100 clients worldwide.

FOCUS Questions: What aspects of quality was Florida Power and Light concerned about? How did information systems help the firm improve quality?

SOURCES: Daniel Greising, "Selling a Bright Idea," *Business Week*, August 8, 1994 and Alan J. Ryan, "Where Quality Takes Command," *Computerworld*, December 11, 1989.

Kennedy Space Center in Florida was causing errors to be made or to go undetected as the Space Center staff was preparing for a space shuttle launching. To correct the problem, the Rockwell IS department installed an automated imaging system and networked it to all relevant sites. Now engineers can transmit design changes instantaneously to wherever they are needed or review problems at the space center immediately.

Rockwell International's networked imaging system allows engineers to transmit design changes immediately between its manufacturing plant and other design facilities so that errors can be identified and corrected before space shuttle launchings take place. Information systems can promote quality by helping organizations detect problems early in the production cycle.

SOURCE: © David Perry, Courtesy of Rockwell International.

Improve design quality and precision   CAD software has made a major contribution to quality improvement in many companies, from producers of automobiles to producers of razor blades. One typical but interesting example of CAD's contributions to quality is Alan R. Burns' use of it to design a newly invented product, a modular tire. Burns, a Perth, Australia, mining engineer, developed the idea of a tire made of a series of removable, replaceable tread segments. The modules are not pneumatic and so cannot go flat, but they can be damaged. If that occurs, the damaged segment can simply and easily be replaced. Burns started a company, Airboss, and quickly found a major outlet for his product in the heavy equipment vehicle market, which manufactures equipment such as tractors and earth movers. He first established tire and tire usage quality criteria for the modules, such as speed, load, temperature, surface characteristics, wear life, and traction. Then, after entering this data into the CAD software, he iteratively designed, modified, and tested the product on the computer until he was satisfied with the results. Only late in the process did he have to develop an actual working model. By using CAD software, Burns was able to test with such precision that he produced a much higher quality product than would have been possible had he been able to test only by making repeated, manually tested models.

Improve production precision and tighten production tolerances   CAD software has been a major boon in designing improved production processes. Many CAD software systems include the capability of using the product design specifications to design production tooling and the actual production process. The user of this software is able to design a more precise production system, a system with tighter tolerances, than could ever be done manually. Burns used his CAD software to do just this. In testing the production process through the CAD software, he identified in advance such problems as uneven cooling. In addition, his design cycle time was short, thus saving money and allowing him to meet changing customer demands more quickly.

Reduce opportunities for human error   Usually this requires either reducing the number of steps or automating steps. With Airboss, for example, Burns did not need to enter data for design of the production process into the computer. Instead, he used the data developed within the CAD system for the process design step. Florida Power and Light used its TCMS system data to automatically notify repair crews of problems called in by customers. The data did not need to be reentered into a separate system.

Many of these efforts to promote quality were also successful because they were based on teamwork. The McKesson case study concluding this chapter is an excellent example of the value of such teamwork.

3.4 TRANSFORMING ORGANIZATIONS: REENGINEERING

Technology alone is often not enough to make organizations more competitive, efficient, or quality oriented. The organization itself may need to be changed to take advantage of the power of information systems. Our sociotechnical perspective on information systems suggests that organizations and people need to change in order to make information technology work properly. Sometimes these changes can be accomplished by adjusting and streamlining procedures; often the organization itself must be redesigned. The organization may need to rethink its goals, its relationships to customers and suppliers, and its fundamental operating procedures.

REENGINEERING BUSINESS PROCESSES

Reengineering
The rethinking and radical redesign of business processes to significantly improve cost, quality, service, and speed and to maximize the benefits of information technology.
Business process
A set of related activities performed to achieve a defined outcome, such as the processing of a sales order.

One way that organizations can maximize the benefits of information system technology is by redesigning their business processes. **Reengineering** is the rethinking and radical redesign of business processes to achieve dramatic improvements in cost, quality, service, and speed. A **business process** is a set of related activities performed to achieve a defined outcome, such as the development of a new product or the processing of a sales order. In reengineering, the steps required to accomplish a particular task are combined to cut waste, reduce paperwork, and eliminate repetitive or redundant work. Often this means breaking down the traditional divisions among functional areas, such as sales, marketing, manufacturing, and finance, and redeploying workers in multifunctional teams. Thus, instead of processing an order by passing the order from sales to manufacturing to warehousing to inventory to billing, a streamlined, reengineered ordering process might combine representatives from all these departments to work on order fulfillment simultaneously.

EXAMPLES OF REENGINEERING

To reengineer successfully, the organization must ask basic questions: Why do we do what we do? Why do we do it in the way we do? If we could start from scratch, what would we do now, and how would we do it? The organization needs to examine the tacit rules and assumptions underlying its standard operating procedures and the way it conducts business. Then it needs to reinvent these processes anew, without regard to traditional responsibilities of work groups, departments, or divisions.

The product development process is one area in which many companies have successfully used information systems to reengineer, as illustrated in the Focus on Organizations.

Here's how reengineering worked at IBM Credit Corp., a large subsidiary of IBM that provides financing for the computers, software, and services that IBM sells. In the past, when an IBM field sales representative called with a request for financing, the call was logged by 1 of 14 people sitting at a conference room table in Greenwich, Connecticut. The person taking the call wrote the financing request on a piece of paper (step 1).

The paper was then taken upstairs to the credit department, where a specialist entered the application into a computer system to check the potential borrower's credit worthiness (step 2).

The credit specialist wrote the results of the credit check on the piece of paper and sent it to the business practices department, which used its own computer system to modify IBM's standard loan terms in response to the customer request (step 3). A business practices department member would attach the special terms to the request form.

Next the request went to a pricer, who entered the data into a microcomputer spreadsheet to determine the appropriate interest rate to charge the customer. The pricer wrote the interest rate on another piece of paper (step 4) that was delivered with the other paperwork to a clerical group.

An administrator in the clerical group combined all the information into a quote letter for delivery to the field sales representative using Federal Express (step 5). An average of 6 days—sometimes up to 2 weeks—elapsed before the entire process was complete. The sales reps were dissatisfied because within those 6 days, customers could find another source of financing or turn to another computer vendor.

Two senior managers at IBM Credit learned that the actual work required to process a financing request took only 90 minutes. The work was primarily clerical—finding a credit rating, plugging numbers into a standard model, pulling standard "boilerplate" clauses from a file. Most of the 6 days was taken up by moving the form from one department to another. So IBM Credit restructured the process itself, replacing its credit checkers, pricers, and other specialists with generalists. Instead of sending a financing application from office to office, one person (called a deal structurer) processes the entire application from beginning to end. IBM Credit developed a new information system to support the deal structurers that provides access to all the required data and tools. Only in complicated credit situations does the deal structurer need to turn elsewhere. IBM Credit still maintains a small pool of real specialists in credit checking, pricing, and so forth to work with the structurers as a team.[4] Even under these special circumstances, the process has been reduced to a single step. Figure 3.4 compares the finance application process before and after reengineering.

3.5 PROMOTING ETHICAL AND SOCIAL RESPONSIBILITY

Building global, competitive organizations are significant information systems challenges. But information systems and technologies have ethical, social, and political dimensions

FOCUS ON ORGANIZATIONS

KODAK REENGINEERS PRODUCT DEVELOPMENT

The Eastman Kodak Company has long been a world market leader in photographic films, supplies, and equipment. In 1987, Fuji PhotoFilm, its archrival, announced it had developed a new single-use 35-mm camera. A single use camera is pre-loaded with film. The customer uses the camera once and returns it to the manufacturer, which processes the film and reuses the camera parts. At that time Kodak had no competitive offering, nor even one in the works. It would have taken 70 weeks for Kodak to produce a rival to Fuji's throw-away camera using its traditional product development process, which was mainly sequential. Camera body designers would do their work and pass the results to shutter designers, then to film advance mechanism designers. Manufacturing engineers did not begin their work until after the product designers had finished. If there was a change, it would have to go back to the other departments for rework. The time delay would have given Fuji an enormous head start and advantage in a new market.

To slash its time-to-market, Kodak reengineered its product development process. It creatively applied CAD/CAM (Computer Aided Design/Computer Aided Manufacturing) technology, which allows engineers to design at computer workstations and

captures the design data into an integrated product design database. The database is available to everyone on the design team. Every morning, all of the participating design groups inspect the database for changes and resolve problems immediately, instead of in weeks or months. Manufacturing engineers are involved before product design is completed so that they can contribute ideas that will make the design more easily and inexpensively manufactured.

In 1988, Kodak rolled out the Fling, its first disposable camera, just 38 weeks after the start of design work. It

had cut product development time nearly in half and had reduced tooling and manufacturing costs by 25 percent. Kodak now uses this process, called concurrent engineering, to develop its other products. The aerospace, automotive, and consumer goods industries have adopted concurrent engineering as well.

FOCUS Question: What people, organization, and technology factors did Kodak have to address in order to reengineer its product development process?

SOURCES: Julia King, "Re-Engineering Repercussions," *Computerworld,* June 28, 1993 and Michael Hammer and James Champy, *Reengineering the Corporation* (New York: HarperCollins, 1993).

FIGURE 3.4

Reengineering the Finance Application Process at IBM Credit Corporation
By reengineering, IBM Credit Corporation drastically reduced the number of steps required to obtain financing.

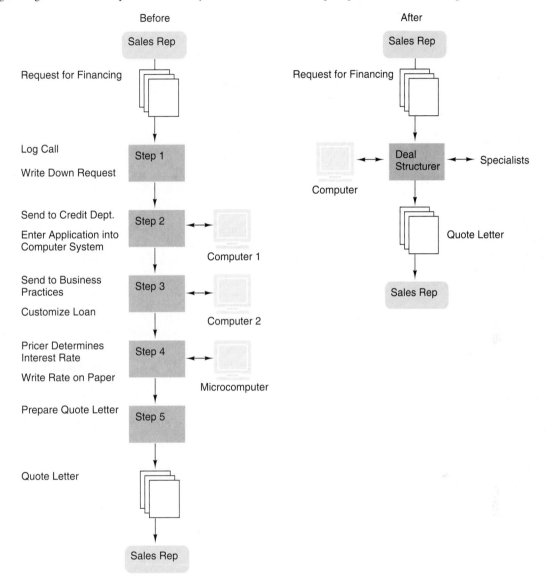

as well. A central challenge facing us all—and discussed throughout this book—is how to build powerful and effective systems and organizations that are socially and ethically responsible. What ethical objectives can we expect organizations to pursue? When faced with a choice between building a system that affords a strategic competitive advantage to your organization, but costs the jobs of hundreds of loyal employees, versus the alternative of building a system that is less effective but preserves existing jobs, what is the correct course of action? What new alternatives should you seek?

Ethics

Principles of right and wrong that can be used to guide the behavior of free moral agents who make choices.

Ethics refers to the principles of right and wrong that can be used to guide the behavior of free moral agents who make choices: What should I do in this situation? What principles of right and wrong apply? Information systems present an array of ethical issues because they involve so many ways in which an individual's actions can affect other people. For example:

- Firms such as airlines or telephone companies may routinely monitor the telephone conversations of reservation agents or operators in the interest of improving productivity or customer service. This monitoring may violate the agents' expectations of privacy and create resentment even as it improves the quality of agent responses.

- A software project to develop a new customer billing system will take longer to complete than originally planned. To deliver the system on time and within the original budget specified by management, the project leaders eliminate some safeguards, such as error correction and detection, and reduce the testing of the system. Safeguards and the finer details of testing will take place after the system is in production.

- A firm under intense competitive pressure to reduce costs in order to stay in business installs a new streamlined, state-of-the art, on-line order-entry system that is expected to eliminate the jobs of 50 order-entry clerks.

None of these situations involves violating a law, but in each situation different principles and sets of interests may be at odds. For instance, a firm might have to balance its need to reduce costs in order to stay in business against its responsibility toward the welfare of its employees. Monitoring employees' telephone conversations or electronic mail to make sure they are using the firm's telephone or electronic-mail facilities only for work-related purposes could run counter to the need to respect employee privacy.

THE RELATIONSHIP BETWEEN INFORMATION TECHNOLOGY AND ORGANIZATIONS

Computers themselves can't change society. Whatever good or evil comes from computers can be traced to some key design decisions about how they will be used by organizations and people. Behind all computing equipment (hardware and software) are engineers and designers who made conscious decisions about how the technology will perform in a technical sense. Once the equipment leaves the factory, systems analysts, programmers, managers, and end-users—people like you—determine how the computing equipment will actually perform its tasks. Through their decisions, these same people, sometimes unconsciously or unintentionally, determine how computer-based systems will change jobs, organizations, and people's lives. There is a long chain of decisions and decision makers in the journey from a simple "computer" to the "social impacts of computers."

Responsibility

The idea that individuals, organizations, and societies are free moral agents who act willfully and with intentions, goals, and ideas; consequently, they can be held accountable for their actions.

BASIC ETHICAL CONCEPTS: RESPONSIBILITY, ACCOUNTABILITY, AND LIABILITY

In this chapter we want to emphasize the concepts of ethical moral responsibility, organizational accountability, and legal liability. There can be no ethics without these concepts. The concept of moral **responsibility** is based on the idea that individuals, organizations, and societies are free moral agents who act willfully and with intentions, goals, and ideas. Because individuals, organizations, and societies are free moral agents, they are morally responsible for their actions. Organizational **accountability** means that actions can be traced throughout an organization to identify responsible individuals who can be held accountable by their fellow citizens and other governments and societies. These "higher authorities" can morally exact a payment for any harm done.

    Liability extends the ideas of responsibility and accountability to the law. Liability is the legal obligation of someone who has engaged in proscribed behavior to make a payment to those they have harmed; liability is established by laws that set out legal remedies for proscribed behavior. In societies governed by laws, individuals, organizations, and even governments are legally liable for their actions. No social actors are above the law.

    These considerations of responsibility and liability are important for understanding the ethical implications of using computers. Changes "caused" by computers cannot occur without human intervention. People and organizations who use computers in such a way that harm comes to others are morally responsible and can be held accountable just as the operators of motor vehicles can be held accountable for their actions. In some instances, specific laws govern the use of computers. Because computers are relatively new, however, the legal framework governing their use is still evolving.

Accountability
The ability to trace actions to identify individuals responsible for making the decisions to take those actions.

Liability
The idea that people may be obligated by law to compensate those they have injured in some way; liability is established by laws that set out legal remedies for proscribed behavior.

LEADING SOCIAL AND ETHICAL IMPACT AREAS

The concerns raised about the effects of computers are actually not about computers but about traditional, long-standing issues of an industrial society. For instance, people are concerned about how computers affect freedom, creativity, and education because these are important, enduring human concerns. Computers are important because they potentially affect long-standing social issues like autonomy, creativity, liberty, vulnerability, and morality. We can classify the impact of computers into five major areas: information rights, property, accountability, system quality, and quality of life (see Figure 3.5).

    The personal issues involve your deciding on the proper course of action: what should you do in situations in which the law is unclear? The organizational issues involve developing business policies to govern the behavior of employees: what should the policy of our firm be? Below we discuss each of these social impact areas and point out some of the personal and organizational choices in each area.

FIGURE 3.5

Computer Impact Areas

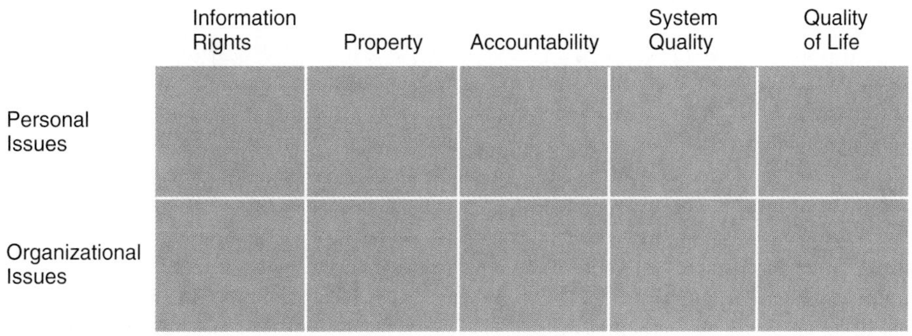

	Information Rights	Property	Accountability	System Quality	Quality of Life
Personal Issues					
Organizational Issues					

Information rights   In George Orwell's 1947 novel entitled *1984,* a centralized, machine-based surveillance system referred to as "Big Brother" controls the society through fear, punishment, and close surveillance of personal lives. Big Brother keeps track of the minute details of what people say, what they purchase, whom they speak with, and what materials they read. Perhaps no single image of the modern computer-based information system has had such a lasting effect. Orwell's best-selling novel raises many questions central to the modern computer-based age: How much should government snoop on its citizens? What rights do citizens have to be free from government surveillance? Do citizens have a right to keep personal information from private industries such as banks, credit bureaus, and retailers? Should schools, other citizens, and even foreign governments be given access to any or all of a person's personal files and records, purchase patterns, medical records, and telephone records? If France has stronger privacy laws than the United States, should any data on French citizens be processed in the United States? These problems existed before computers. Indeed, some of the world's most notorious dictatorships existed long before computers. But with computer-based information systems, huge private and government databases that contain detailed personal information on citizens can be created inexpensively and efficiently. What information is available on you, and where does it come from? Table 3.2 lists the kinds of information about you that is available to just about any business (or individuals in business) and government in the United States.

Most of this information originates with you through the process of borrowing money, participating in a government program, or purchasing goods. Consumers and borrowers—that's all of us—routinely give information voluntarily to retailers and creditors so we can purchase goods on credit. At least once a month, millions of banks, retailers, credit card companies, and mail-order houses send computer tapes or other electronic files detailing their customers' purchases and payment activities to credit bureaus. These files contain detailed personal information on bank balances, credit history, income, family makeup, employment, driving record, and the like for nearly every consumer in the United States and many foreign countries as well. The three largest national credit bureaus (TRW, Inc., Trans Union, and Equifax, which together have 500 million records on Americans) resell this information either as ordinary credit reports or as lists of names to marketing companies who want to know about you. In addition

---

TABLE 3.2

Information on Individuals Available to Businesses

- Credit records
- Income
- Debts and payment history
- Personal data (e.g., Social Security number, age, birth date, family history, ethnicity)
- Reading materials, including magazines and book clubs
- Listening materials, including record clubs
- Motor vehicle information
- Driver license information, including infractions
- Federal and state loans
- Telephone calls
- Medical records
- Insurance records
- School records
- Employment history
- Legal judgments, hearings, and related data
- Marital history

---

to these national bureaus, there are more than 200 "superbureaus" that serve small businesses in local and state regions. Credit reports cost about $10 to $50, depending on the detail requested. A list of names and addresses showing, for instance, all the college students in the San Francisco metropolitan area who purchased computer software in 1994 would cost about 10 to 20 cents a name. TRW Credit Data has a new product: it will sell you your own credit record for $10!

Federal, state, and local governments are a second major source of personal information about you. Citizens routinely and voluntarily provide a large amount of personal information to obtain college loans, small business loans, or other government benefits.

Why does the existence of huge, computerized, national information systems threaten freedom, privacy, and due process? **Privacy** is the right of individuals and organizations to be left alone and to be secure in their personal papers. Consider that both government and private industry have used information from computer-based data files to intimidate their opponents. As a result, these institutions have had what the courts call a "chilling effect" on political debate and have interfered with the exercise of political freedoms. For instance, if you take a public position against a corporation or a state agency, damaging information may be found about you in national data files and released to the press in order to destroy your credibility. Have you ever visited a mental health professional? Have you ever had a medical condition that you would not like to be made public? Have you ever committed an infraction of a law, statute, or regulation? Does your record include frank and critical comments by teachers or others? If you fall into any of these categories—and most of us have something negative on our many records—then you can be potentially embarrassed or even neutralized politically. You may not have done anything wrong or illegal, but chances are you have done something embarrassing that is filed on a national record system somewhere.

Second, consider whether the information is accurate. Have you inspected the information held about you in national files? What if it is used to make decisions about you but is not really accurate or true, or is no longer true? This raises the issue of due process. The right to **due process** is the right to be treated fairly in accordance with a set of published legal procedures, including such things as the right to appeal and the right to an attorney.

What can you, your business firm, and society do about these issues of privacy, freedom, access to information, and due process? The U.S. Congress and all state legislatures have passed many significant laws that attempt to govern record keeping in American society. European countries and Canada have even stronger legislation. These laws are described in Table 3.3.

Despite a number of laws seeking to protect privacy, the pressure of commercial interests to obtain access to personal information, coupled with powerful new technologies, has served to weaken existing laws. Nevertheless, the principles laid out by Congress in its preamble to the **Privacy Act of 1974** can be useful in extending legislation to cope with the age of electronic networks, personal computers, and huge, easily accessed private databases. (Note: Material in brackets is the authors'.)

The Privacy Act of 1974
Public Law 93-579

Be it enacted by the Senate and House of Representatives of the United States of America in Congress assembled, That this Act may be cited as the "Privacy Act of 1974." Sec. 2.

(a) The Congress finds that—

(1) the privacy of an individual is directly affected by the collection, maintenance, use, and dissemination of personal information by Federal agencies;

Privacy
The right of individuals and organizations to be left alone and to be secure in their personal papers.

Due process
The right to be treated fairly in accordance with established legal procedures, including such things as the right to appeal and the right to an attorney.

Privacy Act of 1974
A federal statute that defines citizens' rights in regard to federal government records and management's responsibilities for them; sets out some of the principles for regulating computer technology in order to protect people's privacy.

TABLE 3.3

Major U.S. Privacy Legislation

Freedom of Information Act (1966): This statute gives citizens and all organizations the right to inspect information about themselves held in government files and gives individuals and organizations the right to request disclosure of government records. This legislation has been the single most powerful information legislation in American history, giving individuals, writers, reporters, and even private corporations unprecedented access to unclassified government records.

Fair Credit Reporting Act (1970): Under this statute, credit agencies cannot share credit information with anyone but authorized customers; the act also gives citizens the right to inspect their records and be notified of their use for employment or credit. The law is easily circumvented because access is given to anyone with "a reasonable business need."

Privacy Act (1974): This law defines citizens' rights and management's responsibilities for federal government records. The law has had little effect because its language is vague and the Office of Management and Budget (the president's budget agency) does not enforce the law vigorously.

Family Educational Rights and Privacy Act (1974): This law requires schools and colleges to give students and parents access to student records and the right to challenge and correct those records.

Right to Financial Privacy Act (1978): This statute limits federal government searches of your bank records. State and local governments are not covered.

Cable Communications Policy Act (1984): This law regulates the cable industry's collection and disclosure of information on subscriber viewing habits.

Electronic Communications Privacy Act (1986); Computer Fraud and Abuse Act (as amended in 1986); Computer Security Act (1987): These laws protect the confidentiality of personal electronic communications and computer-based digital files against government and/or private abuse and intrusion. The Communications Privacy Act protects the privacy of electronic messages sent on public networks only against government surveillance (not against private surveillance) and does not cover internal corporate E-mail networks.

Video Privacy Protection Act (1988): Under this act, video rental records cannot be sold or released without a court order or consent of the person renting the video.

Computer Matching and Privacy Act (1988): This statute regulates computer matching of computer files in different agencies to verify eligibility for federal programs and to identify delinquent debtors. The law does nothing about law enforcement and tax-matching programs, and it has many other loopholes.

---

(2) the increasing use of computers and sophisticated information technology, while essential to the efficient operations of the Government, has greatly magnified the harm to individual privacy that can occur from any collection, maintenance, use, or dissemination of personal information;

(3) the opportunities for an individual to secure employment, insurance, and credit and his right to due process, and other legal protections are endangered by the misuse of certain information systems;

(4) the right to privacy is a personal and fundamental right protected by the Constitution of the United States; and

(5) in order to protect the privacy of individuals identified in information systems maintained by Federal agencies, it is necessary and proper for the Congress to regulate the collection, maintenance, use, and dissemination of information by such agencies.

(b) The purpose of this Act is to provide certain safeguards for an individual against an invasion of personal privacy by requiring Federal agencies, except as otherwise provided by law, to—

(1) permit an individual to determine what records pertaining to him are collected, maintained, used, or disseminated by such agencies;

[No secret records or record systems]

(2) permit an individual to prevent records pertaining to him obtained by such agencies for a particular purpose from being used or made available for another purpose without his consent;
[Informed consent]

(3) permit an individual to gain access to information pertaining to him in Federal agency records, to have a copy made of all or any portion thereof, and to correct or amend such records;
[Right of inspection]

(4) collect, maintain, use, or disseminate any record of identifiable personal information in a manner that assures that such action is for a necessary and lawful purpose, that the information is current and accurate for its intended use, and that adequate safeguards are provided to prevent misuse of such information;
[No record systems without statutory authority and the principle of management responsibility]

(5) permit exemptions from the requirements with respect to records provided in this Act only in those cases where there is an important public policy need for such exemption as has been determined by specific statutory authority; and
[Exemptions only by law]

(6) be subject to civil suit **for any damages which occur as a result of willful or intentional action which violates any individual's rights under this Act.** (Emphasis added.)
[Civil liability for damages]

Sections 3 and 4 of the Act define the key terms of the above preamble and the mechanisms for enforcing and administering the Act.

Note that Congress did not claim computers were the cause of privacy problems. Rather it is the use of computers by the federal government and private organizations that constitutes the threat.

The personal ethical issue is: under what conditions will you as an individual invade the privacy of others, with or without the use of computers? How can you use computer-based systems to protect your privacy and that of others? The organizational ethical issue is: does your firm have a privacy policy in place that informs employees about the kinds of surveillance and privacy invasion practiced by the firm? Many organizations handle information rights questions by developing formal policies and informing their employees about these policies. These are called an "informed consent" policy.

Property   Who owns the information that is so readily available in computerized information systems or on networks? How can that ownership be established when computerized information is so easily copied, distributed on networks, or accessed from a computer system? Information technology has made it difficult to protect intellectual property and other types of intangible property created by individuals and organizations.

There are three existing legal mechanisms for protecting intellectual property: trade secrets, copyright, and patent laws. Based on state law, trade secrets are any intellectual work product like a device, pattern, or compilation of data used in business provided such works are not in the public domain. Trade secret laws protect businesses so that they can develop unique formulas, recipes, and designs to sustain their profits. In general, computer software is rarely protected in this way because most of the ideas expressed in software are in the public domain. For instance, the concept of "windows"—computer screens that visually frame other screen objects—fell into the public domain as soon as it was publicly demonstrated in the 1960s!

Copyright laws are the most frequently used protection for computer software. A copyright protects the creator of intellectual property against copying by others for a commercial purpose for up to 28 years. The intent of Congress has been to reward the creators of books, music, artwork, and motion pictures. Unfortunately, copyright law does not protect the ideas behind a work, but only the work itself. The literal copying of software is illegal, but developing a software program that produces similar or exactly similar results is not illegal. Congress passed the Computer Software Copyright Act of 1980 to strengthen the protection of software.

Patents are sometimes used to protect software when the creators can show that the underlying ideas are novel, original, and nonobvious. These are stringent criteria that most software developers cannot meet.

The personal ethical issue is: how will you protect the property rights of others? What will you do when handed a piece of software that has obviously been copied? If your colleagues at work copy software, and the management tolerates this copying, what action should you take? The organizational ethical issue is to devise a business policy to ensure that employees observe the law and protect the property rights of vendors who provide the firm with software and other services. This involves writing a corporate policy that clearly establishes who owns what software, prohibits loading illegally copied software on corporate machines, and specifies penalties for infraction of copying rules.

One way to test your feelings about property is to consider the Focus On People, which describes the case of a student who made copyrighted software available on the worldwide Internet network. Would you have downloaded some "free" software if you could have?

Accountability and Liability   Who is responsible for the personal damages caused by a computer-controlled X-ray machine that occasionally administers lethal doses of radiation to patients undergoing radiation therapy for cancer? The software vendor, the hardware manufacturer, or the hospital that administers the test? Should Prodigy be held liable for pornographic messages posted to electronic bulletin boards and sent to customers' E-mail addresses? If a student puts copyrighted software programs on the Internet, who is liable for the damages done to the software company? The university (or other Internet provider) that provided the student access to the Internet, or the student, or all those who read the bulletin board and downloaded the software to their computers? But if the Internet cannot trace who downloaded the illegal software, can the Internet be held accountable? If not, should it be shut down until such accountability is in place?

These are just a few of the accountability problems raised by information technology and systems. Accountability is a basic prerequisite for an ethically responsible system: it is a system in which the actions and consequences of individual behavior can be traced, a system in which actors can be held responsible. Liability extends this idea to include the legal recovery of damages: if someone harms you, you can recover damages done to you.

Generally, existing legal protections for liability apply only to products, and not to services or intellectual products like books, magazines, and software. If software is considered part of a machine, then warranty, negligence, and strict liability can apply. In most instances, the software is claimed to be merely a service or an intellectual product like a book. Courts have refused to hold publishers of books, magazines, or newspapers liable for their contents except under unusual circumstances in order to protect First Amendment rights to freedom of speech. Hence, software and its creator are rarely held liable.

But software is different from books: we are more critically dependent on software; it is difficult to perceive errors in software until they happen; and people come to believe that software is infallible. We can expect that in the future courts will extend lia-

FOCUS ON PEOPLE

THEFT BY INTERNET

If you could copy a $500 spreadsheet program like Microsoft's Excel from your campus network, would you do it? How about WordPerfect, Lotus 1-2-3, and popular entertainment programs like Sim City? Several thousand people did in fact copy a wide range of programs from an Internet bulletin board in one of the largest software piracy cases in U.S. history. The Internet is a network primarily composed of university and research institution networks around the world. About 30 million individuals use the Internet worldwide from about 24,000 separate sites. Just about any user can create an electronic bulletin board on which other users—if they know the password—can leave messages or digital copies of software.

David LaMacchia, a 20-year-old electrical engineering and computer science student at the Massachusetts Institute of Technology, is charged by the U.S. Attorney in Boston with distributing more than $1 million worth of copyrighted software. LaMacchia is not charged with personally copying software, or placing software on the Internet, or selling software. Instead LaMacchia is charged with operating a bulletin board, distributing the bulletin board address and password, and letting others "avail themselves of the opportunity to copy . . . software and computer files." The U.S. Attorney is charging LaMacchia under the federal Computer Software Copyright Act of 1980 (amended in 1992).

LaMacchia created the bulletin board and then sent coded messages to potential users using a codename like "John Gaunt,sysop" seeking specific software products like WordPerfect. A few Internet users who received these messages would then send copies of the requested software via the Internet to an anonymous remailer service in Finland. The remailer service is used to strip the sender's name from the message, adding the remailer name, thus protecting the privacy of the sender. If you are going to steal, why advertise your name? People who wanted to copy the software would send their requests through the remailer service in Finland. The use of a remailer service makes it difficult (but not impossible) for authorities to discover who is placing stolen software on the Internet and who is making copies.

LaMacchia faces a prison term plus a $250,000 fine. Defenders of LaMacchia, many of them avid Internet users, claim that the First Amendment protections of freedom of speech should apply. They argue that AT&T is not liable for criminal conspiracies being discussed over its phone lines, and newspapers are not liable for gambling activities that rely on accurate sports page reporting, so why should a bulletin board operator be held liable for criminal activities that take place over his or her bulletin board? These defenders also claim that a successful federal suit could stifle the free flow of information on the national data highway.

FOCUS Questions: Should LaMacchia be prosecuted? Why? Are there any circumstances in which software copying is justified?

SOURCES: Peter H. Lewis, "Student Accused of Running Network for Pirated Software," *The New York Times,* April 9, 1994; William M. Bulkeley, "Two Face Computer-Fraud Allegations Over Software Piracy on the Internet," *The Wall Street Journal,* April 11, 1994.

bility protections to software in order to hold software manufacturers, sellers, and users liable for the damages they produce through the use of software.

The personal ethical issue is to decide the extent to which you are responsible for the consequences of the software that you create or use. For example, if you prepare a spreadsheet projecting business cash flow for the next year, are you personally liable for the accuracy and integrity of the spreadsheet? The organizational ethical issue is to understand the liabilities your business firm incurs to customers and employees through the use of software. Firms should carefully examine their responsibilities to customers, including implied warranties of fitness for consumption and reliability.

System Quality   Automatic Data Processing Inc. is one of the U.S.'s largest data processing service firms. ADP handles about 70 percent of all corporate proxy votes at annual and special meetings of shareholders. A software bug in its programs resulted in a 4 percent undercount at the annual shareholder meeting of CPC International, a 16 percent undercount at Martin Marietta, and the loss of 200,000 votes submitted by the

During the Persian Gulf War, a Patriot missile defense system in Dharan, Saudi Arabia, failed to track and intercept an incoming Scud missile launched by Iraq because of a software error in the system's weapons control computer. Twenty-five American soldiers were killed. Systems riddled with errors or performance problems can have catastrophic and tragic results.

SOURCE: AP/Wide World Photos.

Telecommuting

Working at home on a computer tied into corporate networks.

Connecticut Office of the Treasurer to one corporate election. In some instances these software errors and poor data quality practices resulted in decisions that otherwise might not have been taken.[5]

What level of quality is adequate for systems to achieve? Is a systems error rate on the order of 1 in 100,000 transactions acceptable? How about software program errors—is an error of 1 in 1,000,000 acceptable or morally unacceptable? If you fail to edit data input into a computer system and accept poor data quality, are you responsible for the errors produced? What if lives depended on these decisions? The main sources of poor system quality are software bugs and errors, hardware and equipment failures (often due to natural disasters—so-called "acts of God"), and poor input data quality. We discuss these sources of poor system quality in Chapter 12 in greater detail.

The challenge facing managers today is to build systems that achieve the highest levels of system quality within the firm's technological and economic resources. For instance, it is impossible to achieve zero defects in software code in large programs because all the paths through the program cannot be tested. Moreover, at some point testing must stop because of the cost of testing and the growing infrequency of error detection. But at what point should testing be stopped? No definitive standards have been established.

The most common source of system failure is much simpler: poor data quality. For example, 5 to 12 percent of bar code sales at supermarkets and retail stores are believed to be erroneous. Most organizations do not have a clear idea of the level of data quality in their systems, nor do they understand the sources of errors. Generally, budgets are inadequate to study data quality problems, and organizations rely on users to call in when they detect errors.

The personal ethical issue is to decide at what point you have exhausted the technological and economic resources available to you to deliver systems of high quality. What levels of error, and what consequences of errors, are you willing to live with? The organizational ethical issue is to investigate and gather data on the quality and performance of your systems, and then to develop policies and benchmarks for improving system quality. These policies are discussed in Chapter 12.

Quality of Life   Aside from concerns of privacy and freedom of information, computers are associated with a number of other broad social and organizational impacts (see Table 3.4). Social impacts include the changes in the location of work brought about by computers (telecommuting), dependence on computers, the speed of social change, the erosion of boundaries between work and family life, and the growth of computer crime (described in Chapter 12). Organizational impacts include computer-generated changes in the quality of work life and organizational structure and the role of middle managers in downsizing organizations.

Telecommuting

One area of social concern is how computers affect the distribution of workers, jobs, and businesses. The traditional distribution is changing as **telecommuting,** the ability to work for a company from one's home by using a telephone and networked computer, increases in the United States. While in 1985 about 17 million people (about 15 percent of the labor force) worked at home, in 1991 about 20 million people (about 18% of the labor force) did so.

Telecommuting was predicted to have several benefits: fuel consumption would decline dramatically as commuters abandoned the highways for home offices; working parents would be able to spend more time with their families; and efficiency would increase as workers no longer struggled just to get to work each day. Several negative effects were also predicted: urban areas would be abandoned for suburbs and exurbs (com-

TABLE 3.4

Quality of Life Issues and Computers

Few would deny that computers have had a large impact on social and organizational life. One way to classify these impacts is to distinguish between broad social impacts and more narrow organizational impacts.

Social Impacts	*Organizational Impacts*
Telecommuting	Quality of work life
Dependence	Change in structure
Speed of change	Reduced employment
Erosion of boundaries	
Computer crime	

munities even farther from central cities than suburbs); poor people who needed jobs would live in cities with declining employment; and the isolated workers at home would tend to be women and minorities who would miss out on promotion opportunities at central headquarters. It is too early to tell if computers are creating faster growth of suburbs or exurbs or the extent to which telecommuting is producing benefits or drawbacks.

Dependence on computers

A second broad area of social concern involves computer dependence—the fact that we as a society increasingly depend on computers to provide vital services. If computer hardware or software malfunctions, people are not merely inconvenienced, as they would have been a few years ago; instead, their lives may be in jeopardy. If the telephone system's

Telecommuting with computers makes it possible for people to work at home for a company located elsewhere. While telecommuting eliminates the need to travel to work, the "do anything anywhere" computing environment can blur the traditional boundaries between work, home, and leisure time.

SOURCE: Courtesy of International Business Machines Corporation.

computerized switches break down for only a few minutes entire industries (from mail-order retailing to data communications) can lose revenues amounting to hundreds of millions of dollars. As our dependence on computer hardware and software grows, so does our vulnerability. In general, information technology is advancing much faster than our ability to develop related moral principles and legal doctrines. The choices are not easy to make.

Speed of social change

Have you met people in the last year who said they were having a hard time keeping up with all the work they have to do? While we tend to dismiss these complaints as commonplace, many experts believe that fax machines, electronic mail, portable phones, cellular phones, and portable computing have all resulted in an acceleration of social change that many people find hard to cope with. The workloads of middle managers have expanded as their colleagues were laid off and they were expected to pick up the slack. Generally, professionals and other knowledge workers face the most extreme pressures, and the still-employed middle managers who must accomplish the work of their laid-off colleagues also are under stress.

Erosion of boundaries

Families are social units that provide a powerful bulwark against the demands of society, employers, and the state. Historically, the family has played a central role in training children, developing social values, encouraging original and radical thought, and nurturing emotions that cannot be expressed anywhere else. The digital revolution means, among other things, that more and more people will be working (at home, on vacation, on the weekend) when they should be communicating with their families and loved ones. This will erode traditional boundaries that separate work from play and family.

Computer crime

Almost every new technology—electricity, telephones, automobiles—has created opportunities for criminal behavior. For instance, automobiles greatly enhanced the mobility of bank robbers, making it more difficult for authorities to apprehend them. Likewise with computers: criminals will use computers to commit traditional and perhaps new kinds of crime. We discuss this topic in greater depth in Chapter 12.

Quality of work life

Although the use of computers raises significant issues at the social level, it is in the workplace, where computers are primarily used, that their effects first become apparent. The organizational impact of computers has affected the quality of work life, organizational structure, and employment.

Next to "Big Brother," the most common and long-standing fear of computer-based information systems is that they will degrade the quality of work by removing skill and craftsmanship, increase the authority of superiors by tightening surveillance, and reduce the training of workers as machines take on more and more sophisticated tasks. Other concerns center around the impact of computers on the **quality of work life**—the degree to which jobs are interesting, satisfying, and physically safe and comfortable. Table 3.5 summarizes the major aspects of work potentially affected by computerization.

Some have predicted that the mental and physical health of workers will decline as they are exposed to high-pressure jobs paced by a computer that requires them to use small muscle groups in the hands, arms, and eyes, leading to strain and fatigue (see the Focus on People in Chapter 5). Research has found that in some instances, computer-

Quality of work life
The degree to which jobs are interesting, satisfying, and physically safe and comfortable.

TABLE 3.5

Aspects of Work Potentially Affected by Computerization

Nature of work	Quality of employment
• Productivity	• Job satisfaction
• Frequency of tasks	• Job quality
• Ease of tasks	Variety
• Quality of training	Satisfaction with work group
• Quality of service and product	Autonomy
	Challenge
	Ability to see results of work
	• Pressure
	• Mental health
	• Quality of management

based systems do indeed result in significantly negative changes in the quality of working life. At the same time, many other instances have been documented in which systems had positive effects on work: in these cases, work was upgraded and made more interesting and self-paced. Systems can boost workers' productivity as well. Much depends on the kinds of jobs examined, the kinds of management involved, and the history and culture of the company. Researchers now believe that the effects "produced" by computers result from management decision making and the designs of systems developers.

For instance, in the largest and most sophisticated study to date of the impact of computerization on clerical work, researchers closely observed 485 service representatives for a large utility who worked in ten offices in six cities. The utility was changing from a microfiche- and paper-based customer record system to a computer-based system. The office layout and architecture were changed as well by replacing the open-floor offices of the past with cubicles in which workers could work undisturbed. The major goal of the changes was to reduce the costs of responding to customer complaints.

The researchers discovered that the technology made doing simple things easier, but also made it harder to perform complicated tasks (see Figure 3.6).[6] Job pressure declined, happiness increased, and mental health improved. On the down side, skills were lost because jobs were less complex, interesting, and challenging; previous training was made irrelevant; and there was decreased involvement with other workers. The researchers also found the effects of the technology depended on the quality of management. In offices with better management, the negative consequences were decreased.

It is important to remember that this study looked only at office clerical workers and did not look at sales personnel or highly educated professional and technical workers. Computers have tended to have far more positive effects on professional and knowledge workers: their skills are amplified by computing equipment, and they tend to have more control over their work. Computers have also tended to enhance most qualities of work in factories. In general, most researchers have found that information technologies have enhanced the cognitive skills of the labor force.[7]

These kinds of changes and efficiencies in the manufacturing sector will be more common in the future. The Bureau of Labor Statistics reports that by the year 2000, factory jobs will decline from 19 million to 18.2 million. At the same time, the kinds of jobs available in factories are expected to change radically. There will be several hundred thousand new jobs for engineers, technicians, managers, and computer scientists, but there will be hundreds of thousands of fewer jobs for assemblers, laborers, and machine setters—the traditional blue-collar jobs.

FIGURE 3.6

How Computerization Affected Clerical Employees at One Company
The chart illustrates that automation does not always affect people's jobs in a totally negative way. It became easier for workers to perform common tasks, for instance, and employees' mental health improved. Computerization exerted some negative effects as well: the variety and challenge of tasks declined. The mixed results indicate that simple models of "computer impacts" are often unrealistic.

SOURCE: Robert Kraut, Susan Dumais, and Susan Koch, "Computerization, Productivity and Quality of Work-Life," *Communications of the ACM* 32, no. 2 (February 1989): 226.

Changes in organizational structure

While work and supervision are affected almost immediately when new computer systems are installed, over longer periods of time the structure of organizations can change as well. By **organizational structure** we mean the number of different levels in an organization, the type of work and workers involved, and the distribution of incomes and power. Computers have helped some organizations become "flatter" by reducing the number of middle managers, making organizations more efficient and productive. Computers also automate tasks that formerly were performed by people, so that organizations can increase the output of their products and services with a smaller labor force to manage. Computers may empower lower level workers to take over supervisory tasks previously

Organizational structure

The number of different levels, the type of work, and the distribution of power in an organization.

done by managers. But there is no data to show that computers will necessarily produce these changes in all organizations.

Reduced employment

Computers have generally been seen as a major potential source of long-term unemployment in advanced economies. Since commercial computers first began to be widely used in the late 1950s, there has been a persistent fear that computers would reduce the need for all kinds of workers and lead to much higher levels of unemployment. The number of secretaries would decline radically, so it was thought, because computers would reduce paper work. The number of blue-collar factory workers would decline because robots would take over their jobs. Advanced to the mid-1990s, the argument is that because of business "reengineering" and enormous investments in information technology to create extensive telecommunications and computing facilities, organizations no longer need a large labor force of managers and specialists. Instead, business firms can rely on external contractors in an electronic marketplace to do the work, supervising them electronically and accepting or rejecting their work on a contract basis.

On the whole, only anecdotal evidence exists to support these arguments, and there are many counter trends. In 1993–94, for instance, the media announced that Fortune 1000 firms were laying off 1.1 million workers. Was the labor force shrinking, and were large firms in particular growing smaller? Hardly. In fact, during the same period more than 2.4 million net new jobs were created.[8] While some industries shrank (airlines, aircraft production, railroads, highway construction, construction, manufacturing) others expanded (retailing, health care, restaurants, finance, security, information technology).

While computers have proved useful for producing letters, quickly calculating spreadsheets, and printing lists of customers, this use has not led to any wholesale decrease in white-collar jobs. Contrary to the negative predictions, jobs for secretaries, middle managers, and accountants have been the fastest-growing occupations in the entire labor force since 1960! Employers have taken advantage of the higher efficiencies created by computers in selected tasks to assign additional kinds of work to secretaries, accountants, and managers. Instead of firing accountants who used to manually calculate a few spreadsheets a week, employers have retrained accountants to use computers to produce hundreds of spreadsheets a week, analyze many different scenarios by using the new software, supervise expenditures more closely, and achieve higher quality work. Instead of firing large numbers of secretaries, employers have tended to retain or even hire more secretaries to put out more letters to achieve more sales and greater market penetration. In fact, computers have tended to increase—not decrease—the amount of paperwork in advanced economies.

The personal ethical issue in these quality of life issues is to decide how you as an individual will use information technology. To what end will you put the new technology? What price are you personally willing to pay to make full use of the new possibilities? Likewise at the organizational level: you and your colleagues will have to decide what ends your organization serves and how it will use the technology to pursue those ends. Often there will be no clearly defined right or wrong answers. But whatever you decide, you will be held accountable for the results.

ETHICAL GUIDELINES

In searching for ethical principles to guide you and your colleagues through difficult decisions, there are many sources. First, know the law, because it is a synthesis of what your society believes is the minimal level of ethical behavior. Second, look for corporate ethics codes, published by nearly all Fortune 500 firms, or ethical guidelines published by

TABLE 3.6

The Ten Commandments of Computer Ethics

1. Thou shalt not use a computer to harm other people.
2. Thou shalt not interfere with other people's computer work.
3. Thou shalt not snoop around in other people's computer files.
4. Thou shalt not use a computer to steal.
5. Thou shalt not use a computer to bear false witness.
6. Thou shalt not copy or use proprietary software for which you have not paid.
7. Thou shalt not use other people's computer resources without authorization or proper compensation.
8. Thou shalt not use other people's intellectual output.
9. Thou shalt think about the social consequences of the program you are writing or the system you are designing.
10. Thou shalt always use a computer in ways that demonstrate consideration and respect for your fellow humans.

SOURCE: Computer Ethics Institute, Washington, D.C.

various professional associations (see Table 3.6). These corporate codes guide employees in diverse situations for which laws may not exist, from personal harassment behavior to sharing computer disks and corporate information. Third, look to various religious and philosophical treatises to discover general principles of ethical conduct. Some principles are well known, like the Golden Rule (do unto others as you would have them do unto you) and the Utilitarian principle (select the action that produces the greatest good for the greatest number). There are many others that you should discuss with your friends and professors.

SUMMARY

• Information systems can be used to gain a strategic competitive advantage over rival firms. Information systems can be used to develop new market niches, lock in customers and suppliers, differentiate products and services, and lower operational costs.

• The value chain can be used to identify business activities that offer opportunities to use systems with strategic impact.

• Information systems can help companies operate internationally by supporting coordination of geographically dispersed units of the company and by supporting communication with distant customers and suppliers.

• Disparate linguistic and cultural traditions, organizational procedures, and computer hardware, software, and telecommunications standards are obstacles to building international information systems.

• Quality can be defined from both a producer viewpoint (conformance to specifications) and from a consumer viewpoint (physical materials, quality of service, and psychological impressions). Total quality management (TQM) makes quality the responsibility of everyone in the organization.

• Information systems can enhance quality by simplifying a product or service; supporting benchmarking; reducing product development cycle time; improving quality and precision in design and production; and reducing opportunities for human error.

• Organizations may maximize the benefits of information system technology by redesigning their business processes. The rethinking and radical redesign of business processes to achieve dramatic improvements in cost, quality, service, and speed is called reengineering.

- The five major areas in which computers have social and ethical impacts are information rights, property, accountability, system quality, and quality of life.

- Privacy has been threatened by the ease with which computerized information systems can collect, process, and store vast quantities of detailed data about individuals. The U.S. Congress has passed many pieces of legislation to promote privacy, including the Privacy Act of 1974.

- The major effects of computers on the quality of life in society have been the growth of telecommuting, computer dependence, accelerated change, erosion of boundaries between work and family, and computer crime.

- Computers have both positively and negatively affected the quality of work life, organizational structure, and employment. Computer effects depend on the nature of management and the organization.

KEY TERMS

Strategic information systems	Responsibility
Value chain	Accountability
Multinational	Liability
Transnational	Privacy
Transborder data flow	Due process
Total quality management (TQM)	Privacy Act of 1974
Reengineering	Telecommuting
Business process	Quality of work life
Ethics	Organizational structure

REVIEW QUESTIONS

1. Give examples of how information systems can support each of the four competitive strategies.
2. What is the value chain? How can it be used to identify opportunities for strategic information systems?
3. List and describe some of the obstacles to creating global information systems.
4. What is quality from a producer perspective? From a consumer perspective? What is total quality management?
5. How can information systems help organizations enhance quality?
6. What is reengineering? How can information systems aid this process? How can reengineering make information systems more powerful?
7. Define accountability, responsibility, and liability. How are they related to ethics?
8. Define and describe the five major areas in which information systems have social and ethical impacts.
9. What is privacy? Why is it endangered by information systems?

10. Name and describe three laws enacted by Congress to protect privacy.

11. How can trade secret, copyright, and patent protection be used to protect property rights to information technologies?

12. Why is it difficult to hold providers of software and software services liable for failure or injury?

13. Why is system quality important? What are the common sources of system quality problems?

14. List and describe those aspects of society in which computers have affected the quality of life.

15. List and describe those aspects of organizations in which computers have affected the quality of work life.

DISCUSSION QUESTIONS

1.　Reengineering not only eliminates redundant work and excess paperwork but may also eliminate excess jobs. Should employers care about the unemployment caused by reengineering?

2.　Is it acceptable to copy software used on your job so you can continue your work at home?

PROBLEM-SOLVING EXERCISES

1.　*Group exercise:* Divide into groups. Have each group develop an information system code of ethics for your university. Prepare a report describing the issues that should be addressed by the code and the recommended standard of conduct. Present your reports to the class.

2.　Obtain an annual report of a business or find an article describing a business in *Business Week, Fortune,* or another publication. Analyze the business in terms of the value chain to suggest strategic information systems for that business.

3.　*Hands-on exercise:* Pacific Value Co. is a growing San Diego firm that sells low-cost computer and office equipment and supplies. It has six sales representatives, who are paid on a straight commission basis. Steven Ricciardi, the firm's owner, would like to pay his staff well to reward them for their efforts and to motivate them to sell more. On the other hand, the firm's competitive advantage lies in keeping operating costs, including employee expenses, low. Ricciardi has guaranteed his sales representatives a minimum of 15 percent commission on the sales they make. He is thinking of raising commissions to 16 percent or 17 percent. Use appropriate software and the data in the following report to analyze the impact of paying 15 percent, 16 percent, and 17 percent commissions to Pacific Value's sales reps.

Pacific Value Co.
1994 Salesperson Annual Sales Report

Salesperson Name	Sales
Carl Arneson	$203,000
Delia Baker	$265,000
Albert Giordano	$259,000
Michael Hubbard	$271,000
Alice Lerner	$276,000
Paula Townsend	$234,000

NOTES

1. Michael Porter, *Competitive Strategy* (New York: Free Press, 1980). See also Kenneth Laudon and Jon Turner, eds., *Information Technology and Management Strategy* (Englewood Cliffs, NJ: Prentice-Hall, 1989).

2. Paul John Steinbart and Ravinder Nath, "Problems and Issues in the Management of International Data Networks," *MIS Quarterly* 16, No. 1 (March 1992).

3. For an excellent discussion of quality control and management, see Lee J. Krajewski and Larry P. Ritzman, *Operations Management,* 3rd ed. (Reading, MA: Addison-Wesley, 1993).

4. Michael Hammer and James Champy, *Reengineering the Corporation* (New York: HarperCollins, 1993).

5. Elizabeth Lesly, "A Number-Cruncher Gets an 'E' for Errors," *Business Week,* May 24, 1993.

6. Robert Kraut, Susan Dumais, and Susan Koch, "Compensation, Productivity, and Quality of Work-Life," *Communications of the ACM* 32, No. 2 (February 1989).

7. D. R. Howell and E. N. Wolff, "Changes in the Information Intensity of the U.S. Workplace Since 1950: Has Information Technology Made a Difference?" Starr Center for Applied Economics, New York University, No. 93-08. 1993.

8. Louis Uchitelle, "Job Losses Don't Let Up Even as Hard Times Ease," *The New York Times,* March 22, 1994.

PROBLEM-SOLVING CASE

McKESSON DRUG COMPANY REDESIGNS FOR QUALITY

McKesson Drug Co. of San Francisco, California, is a $10 billion wholesaler and distributor of pharmaceuticals and other goods used in drugstores. McKesson's 45 warehouses nationwide stock 20,000 items, including aspirin, antacids, hair conditioners, and dozens of other personal-use products. McKesson has managed to obtain an impressive 28 percent of market share amid extreme competition that has reduced everyone's profit margins.

McKesson has been a pioneer in the use of computerized ordering and bar coding. It installed a system called Economost in its customers' stores that enables druggists to order products with essentially no typing. An Economost customer places orders by using a laser scanner to read product bar codes, noting which items on its shelves need reordering. The item numbers are transmitted to the system, which enters the order, automatically entering the usual quantity. Only if the quantity is not "normal" does the druggist need to type, and then only the new quantity. Thus, order quality is improved because typing errors are all but eliminated. The order is instantaneously transmitted to McKesson's central computer in Rancho Cordova, California. The computer captures the orders and relays them to a minicomputer in one of the company's regional distribution centers. The minicomputer assigns the orders to several pickers, who walk through the warehouse pushing totes on rollers to fill the orders. The warehouses are designed so that their shelves correspond to pharmacy departments. A minicomputer in the distribution center issues invoices, bar code order identification labels, price tags, and pick lists.

Approximately 99 percent of McKesson's pharmaceutical items and 93 percent of its over-the-counter items are delivered the next day. The orders are delivered in cartons that match the aisle arrangements and departments in the drugstore. With this reliable next-day service, many pharmacies have eliminated inventory other than shelf stock. However, this system did not address the issue of picking errors.

Picking orders in warehouses accurately and quickly has been a problem. As McKesson spokesperson Jim Cohune puts it, "It's a business of 'oneseys' and 'twoseys' and things can get confused." Cohune estimates that every mispick costs McKesson about $80 in lost time and shipping costs, not to mention customer dissatisfaction when the wrong product arrives. McKesson has used information technology to attack the problem with signs of genuine success.

Because picking a few of this and a few of that easily leads to wrong items or quantities being picked, McKesson developed a bar code reader for the pickers to carry. Before picking each product, the pickers would use the reader to read the product bar code to verify that they were choosing the correct item. However, the system did not work well. The pistol-shaped scanner had to be unholstered for each product, requiring the use of both hands. The pickers, who use both hands to pick, found the scanner gun very inconvenient and slow. Most simply did not use it. McKesson's senior vice-president of distribution services summarized the problem this way. "The warehouse employee must be able to electronically read bar codes to verify the incoming order against the purchasing order, while keeping both hands free to lift and move shipping containers"—a tall order indeed.

The solution was a genuine innovation called AcuMax. It was developed jointly by McKesson and Electronic Data Systems, a leading information systems consulting firm. McKesson had learned a critical lesson in the previous failure—involve the line workers, the pickers, in designing and implementing a solution. McKesson established a team that included technicians, managers, and line workers.

AcuMax is a computer with an attached laser bar code reader. It straps onto one arm, weighs only about three-quarters of a pound, and is in constant radio communication with the warehouse's minicomputer. The computer first plans the most efficient route for the picker to follow through the giant warehouse, thus reducing picking time. The AcuMax screen lists the first items and displays the route to that item. When the picker arrives, he or she points an index finger at the item's bar-coded shelf label. As the pointing finger is lifted, it throws a switch that activates the laser bar code reader. The bar code is fed into AcuMax, which compares the bar code to the stored purchase order product number to determine if the picker is pointing at the desired product. Assuming the item is correct, the arm-borne computer transmits the information to the warehouse computer, which instantly updates both the warehouse inventory file and the customer's bill. The arm-borne computer then displays the next product and the path to it, and the process is repeated until the order is filled. AcuMax has proven very effective. McKesson

Strapped onto one arm, McKesson's AcuMax computer lets warehouse pickers scan in bar code data about items selected to fulfill orders while freeing both hands to lift and move shipping containers. By using a team approach that includes line workers to design and implement a system, companies like McKesson have been able to raise quality and productivity.

SOURCE: Courtesy of McKesson Corp.

estimates that order picking errors have been reduced by 70 percent, while the productivity of the pickers has risen dramatically.

How does the new system rate in McKesson's drive for quality? From the perspective of the producer, it has achieved a 70 percent reduction in errors. From the consumer perspective, the system gives the buyer greater value for the dollar, less work in ordering, minimal bother with returns and problems with the order, and overall improved service. The productivity of the pickers has increased sharply. Given what has been learned over the past several decades about ways to improve quality, it is no surprise that the improvement was partly the result of teamwork that involved both line workers and managers.

The AcuMax project raised a major ethical issue for McKesson's management. One of their goals was productivity. If successful, McKesson's management realized, order processing data entry jobs and warehouse picking jobs would be eliminated (including a reduction in billing work as fewer errors would need manual correction). Thus, new technology would improve the profit position of the company by eliminating jobs. However, McKesson management also saw another side to the issue. McKesson needed the cooperation and input of the very workers whose jobs were threatened in order for the project to be successful. Management thought they had addressed the picking problem when they installed the pistol laser reader system, but that project failed precisely because the line workers were not involved.

This time several managers spent a few days working as clerks. When a preliminary version of the new picking system was developed, workers in the distribution center were asked to try it out. Management told the workers that the new hand-held computers were a tool to do their jobs better and asked them what they thought. Using worker feedback, EDS made more than 50 modifications to the device. For instance, moving the thumb to trigger the laser scanners gave some people sore hands. The device was redesigned so that workers activate the laser by pointing at the item and tapping a button with their index finger. Management learned its lesson—line workers were essential to the design process. Management took the obvious and ethical step, promising that no one would lose their job as a result of this project. The result was a successful project for McKesson and for its staff.

SOURCES: James Daly, "What Happens When 'Close Enough' Isn't Close Enough Anymore," *Computerworld,* December 12, 1993, and "McKesson Drug Curing Inaccuracy of Warehouse Labor with Wearable PCs," *Computerworld,* May 11, 1992; "Making It All Worker-Friendly," *Fortune Special Issue: Making High Tech Work for You,* Autumn 1993; and Myron Magnet, "Who's Winning the Information Revolution," *Fortune,* November 30, 1992.

CASE STUDY QUESTIONS

1.   Use the three perspectives of people, organization, and technology to categorize and analyze the problems faced by McKesson.

2.   How strategic was the Economost system? Why? Use the perspective of competitive strategies and the value chain to analyze its strategic benefits. What do you think McKesson needs to do to maintain its advantage over competitors?

3.   Analyze the McKesson quality program in terms of the eight ways to improve quality listed in this chapter. Did they use any other methods, and if so, what? How did information systems help McKesson improve quality?

4.   How ethical was the solution McKesson developed? Should McKesson have promised no job losses if management believed that line worker involvement was not critical in designing the solution? How would you justify your position to corporate management?

⋆ILLUSTRATED CASE⋆

INFORMATION SYSTEMS HELP SEAGRAM STAY ON TOP

With 1992 sales of $6 billion and operating profits of $754 million (12.6 percent of sales), Seagram Co. currently sits atop the liquor business; however the liquor business is declining. How can Seagram use information systems to help them thrive in a troubled industry?

Joseph E. Seagram & Sons, Inc. was founded in 1933 and currently has major offices in 36 countries on six continents. The list of leading brands Seagram markets includes Chivas Regal scotch, Perrier-Jouet champagne, Crown Royal Canadian Whiskey, Martell Cognacs, and Tropicana orange juice. In late 1993 they added Absolut vodka to the list. With such an excellent product portfolio and such high profits, what industry problems could possibly concern Seagram management?

The liquor industry is focusing its main efforts on premium brands, betting that consumers will maintain product

Seagram's distillery in Keith, Scotland, is one of the firm's facilities for producing high-quality, top-of-the-line spirits. Seagram's global business strategy has focused on promoting premium brands and on increasing sales abroad in emerging markets such as China and Eastern Europe.

SOURCE: Courtesy of Joseph E. Seagram and Sons, Inc.

Jack Cooper, Chief Information Officer, says that the Open Document Management System should enable Seagram sites around the world to have "boundary-less document access."

loyalty. The strategy is to create value for premium brands and increase marketing efforts focused on brand name. While this strategy has been successful, it has also created an opening for cheap brands and private labels that have recently gained a larger share of the market. If this trend continues, it will put serious downward pressure on premium product prices.

Seagram has followed the premium brand strategy by selling off such lower-priced labels as Lord Calvert Canadian Whiskey and Wolfschmidt Vodka and acquiring rights to market Absolut. In addition, they are pursuing a global strategy, seeking growth in the emerging markets of Eastern Europe and China; analysts cite this strategy as the primary reason for Seagram's obtaining the marketing rights to Absolut. Edgar Bronfman, Jr., CEO of Seagram, predicts that the proportion of Absolut's sales outside the United States will double from its current 25 percent by 1999.

Part of Seagram's response to these challenges is its worldwide multimedia document management system. According to Seagram's Chief Information Officer, Jack Cooper, the Open Document Management System (ODMS) is meant to achieve "boundary-less document access anywhere in the world." Using this system a document created in Hong Kong can be reviewed in the United States and stored in London. The documents are multimedia—they can contain video, voice, and graphics as well as text. For example, Seagram may use ODMS to store its company-wide, operational procedure manuals, use a video clip to illustrate a new procedure, or allow users to send and receive faxes from their desktop computers.

ODMS uses a worldwide network to connect Seagram's various sites, not only its larger offices but its staff members who work outside of established offices but who need to be linked with the rest of the company.

The first Seagram department to make use of the system was Accounts Payable, located in White Plains, New York. Prior to ODMS, invoices were hand sorted by type of bill and then delivered to the appropriate specialist (such as a phone specialist). The invoices were then passed from processor to processor in a time-consuming serial, paper-based work flow. Once the original processing was completed, the document was sent to be microfilmed for permanent storage, a process that took as long as two weeks. With an average of 450 invoices per day, the procedure was time-consuming and expensive. It was also a headache for suppliers. Supplier

inquiries were directed to one of the 18 specialists handling the supplier's area. To answer the supplier's question, the specialist hunted through a stack of bills until the appropriate one was found. Suppliers' phone hold time could be long while their patience could become short. In addition to these billing and supplier problems, when staff in California needed access to documents, they had to be located in the White Plains office and then faxed to California.

The new system changes all that. Incoming bills are now scanned directly into ODMS upon receipt, making them immediately available to the accounts payable processors. Managers can add voice annotation to documents; for example, a specific processor can be instructed to give a designated invoice special handling. Now, no matter which specialist answers the phone, he or she will be able to answer a supplier's questions quickly by on-line accessing of document information. Seagram staff time is saved while suppliers are not kept waiting. Accounts Payable is also redesigning its work flow by eliminating the traditional slow, serial, manual processing. They will institute a more efficient approach that will give various processors simultaneous access to the same document. Microfilming is obsolete. Finally, because the system is networked, California staff will have direct access to needed data.

Accounts Payable productivity benefited in still other ways from ODMS. Managers can now track the productivity

The Seagram headquarters in New York City oversees operations in 36 countries on six continents. Global information systems such a Seagram's Open Document Management System (ODMS) help companies coordinate the work of offices and staff members and communicate with customers and suppliers in many different parts of the world.

SOURCE: © Arlene Collins, Monkmeyer Press Photos.

of both the accounts payable process and of individual employees. Perhaps even more significant, Accounts Payable Supervisor Candice Puleo says that ODMS is a "real time-saver" for auditing, a critical aspect of the accounts payable function. No longer will auditors need to spend long hours digging through old microfilm or paper to find needed documentation (Puleo remembers once waiting four months to obtain 400 boxes of paper need for an Internal Revenue Service audit).

With Accounts Payable now on board, Cooper plans to sell the system to other departments. His hope is that three new groups will implement the system each month.

How does ODMS contribute to Seagram's strategy for survival in a declining market? In several ways. First, if sales fall and competition from lower-priced products increases, one classic response is to lower costs through improved productivity. ODMS contributed significantly to reducing costs in Accounts Payable. It can probably do the same throughout the company by allowing departments to redesign their work flow, reduce manual labor costs, and improve relations with suppliers and customers. In that way, the system will likely make a major contribution to survival.

Seagram's experience in developing this information system application also leaves the firm poised to take competitive advantage of the ongoing developments in computer and telecommunications technology. Seagram will be able to upgrade their technology both at minimal cost and with minimal disturbance if they find a competitive value in doing so.

Ultimately, to make the most significant contribution to the future of a company, an information system must be aligned with the company's business strategy. ODMS, a global system, is definitely strategic for Seagram. With the ODMS worldwide telecommunications system in place, Seagram can support its planned global expansion. More efficient departments and instant communications around the world should also allow the company to respond more rapidly to customer orders and to solve customer problems as needed. Finally, the network technology not only gives corporate management access to critical, worldwide data, but it also puts the local data where needed in a global market, on the desktop of the local clerk, manager, or executive.

SOURCES: Johanna Ambrosio, "High Spirits at SEAGRAM," *Computerworld Client/Server Journal,* August 11, 1993, and Julia Flynn and Laura Zinn, "Absolut Pandemonium," *Business Week,* November 8, 1993.

CASE QUESTIONS

1. What problems did Seagram face?

2. How did Seagram use information systems to deal with its problems? What people, organization, and technology factors did they address?

3. How did Seagram deal with the major information system challenges described in this section?

4. Assuming Seagram is able to gain maximum benefit from ODMS and other systems meant to lower costs and globalize the company, do you think these information systems are an adequate base for a successful strategy of survival in a declining market?

Part 2

FOUNDATIONS
OF
INFORMATION
TECHNOLOGIES

Chapter

→ F O U R ←

COMPUTER PROCESSING TECHNOLOGY

LEARNING OBJECTIVES

After reading and studying this chapter, you will:

1. Know the components of a computer and how they work.
2. Understand how a computer represents and processes data.
3. Be able to distinguish among mainframes, minicomputers, microcomputers, supercomputers, and workstations.
4. Know how to measure computer speed, storage capacity, and processing power.
5. Be aware of past and future information technology trends.

Nevada has an abundance of lights, and not just the neon signs of Las Vegas. As one of the fastest growing regions in the United States, its electric power consumption is rapidly increasing. With its customer base growing by 8–10 percent each year, the Nevada Power Co. is struggling to keep costs down while meeting surging electricity demands.

Although its electricity rates are among the lowest in the nation, utility deregulation has forced Nevada Power to work diligently to retain its customers. Without a monopoly, the company must compete with other power companies. Nevada Power met this challenge by keeping its information systems budget flat while using systems more effectively to provide greater economies and service. As Sherry Jackson, Nevada Power's information center manager noted, the only companies that survive when industry deregulation occurs are those with faster, cheaper information.

To more efficiently use its information systems, Nevada Power used new software productivity tools that can create new information systems more flexibly in a shorter amount of time. It carefully selected computer hardware, examining cost, processing power, and reliability. It increased its computer processing capacity by upgrading its IBM Enterprise System/9000 Model 320 mainframe to a more powerful Model 521 mainframe. Mainframe processing capacity was also increased by reallocating some engineering and resource planning modeling applications to distributed IBM RISC System 6000 workstations. Some applications remained on the mainframe because mainframe technology is so reliable.

Before these improvements in hardware capacity, the development of long-range planning models for predicting power requirements, based on factors such as water availability and weather patterns, took up to two hours on the IBM Model 320 mainframe computer. The same modeling problem can be performed on the RS/6000 workstation in less than ten minutes at a much lower cost. By moving some applications off the mainframe, Nevada Power uses 20 percent fewer processing resources on the mainframe and saves $100,000 per year.

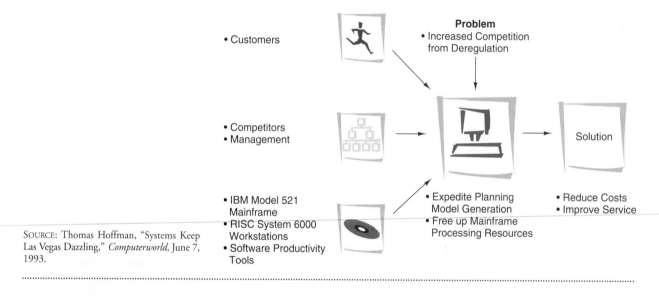

SOURCE: Thomas Hoffman, "Systems Keep Las Vegas Dazzling," *Computerworld,* June 7, 1993.

Like many organizations, Nevada Power found that to maintain a competitive edge, its computers needed appropriate processing capability. The company had to understand how much computer processing capacity was required by the business and it had to be able to evaluate the performance capabilities of various types of computers. It had to know why mainframes and workstations were appropriate processing hardware for its needs.

This chapter describes how a computer processes information, how to measure storage capacity and processing power, and how to evaluate the capabilities of the various categories of computers. We also examine important trends in computer processing technology.

4.1 INTRODUCTION: A VARIETY OF INFORMATION TECHNOLOGIES

Traditionally, information systems courses have treated the computer as the focal point of contemporary information technology. To some extent this is no longer appropriate. The problem-solving technologies in use today range far beyond the computer alone and include telecommunications networks, fax machines, "smart" printers and copiers, workstations, image processing, graphics, desktop publishing, multimedia, and video communications. Increasingly, problems will be solved not by an isolated mainframe or personal computer but by an array of digital devices networked together.

Likewise, the problems solved by this array of information technologies will no longer be limited to data processing. Design, visualization, communications, and group support are some of the new kinds of problems information technologies can solve. Therefore, instead of focusing exclusively on the computer, all of today's information technologies must work together.

Nevertheless, the electronic computer remains at the core of this digital revolution. And to understand today's array of information technologies and the way they can work together, you must still understand how a computer represents and processes information. Hence, this chapter focuses primarily on computer processing, and the following chapter deals with computer input, output, and storage devices. Other chapters in this section treat related information technologies—software, telecommunications, and files and databases. Throughout, the emphasis is on how all these technologies interact and work together.

4.2 COMPUTER CONCEPTS AND COMPONENTS

At the most general level, a computer is any device that takes an input from its environment, processes this input in some logical or mathematical manner, and produces a resulting output to the environment. More specifically, a modern **computer** is a physical device that takes data as an input, transforms these data by executing a stored program, and outputs information to a number of devices. Key words here are *input, process, output,* and, of course, *stored program* or *software.* The speed, capacity, and processing features of computers determine the role they can play in problem solving.

As Figure 4.1 illustrates, a contemporary computer system consists of a **central processing unit (CPU)**, primary storage, input devices, output devices, secondary storage, and communications devices. The characteristics of the central processing unit and primary storage largely determine a computer's speed and capacity to solve problems. The CPU manipulates raw data into a more useful form and controls the other parts of the computer system, while primary storage temporarily stores data and program instructions during processing. Input devices, such as keyboards, optical scanners, and computer mice, convert data into electronic form for input into the computer. Output devices, such as printers and video display terminals, convert electronic data produced by the computer into forms intelligible to humans. Secondary storage devices store data and program instructions when they are not being used in processing. Communications devices allow the computer to be connected to communications networks. Buses are paths for transmitting data and signals among the various parts of the computer system.

Computer

A physical device that takes data as an input, transforms these data by executing a stored program, and outputs information to a number of devices.

Central processing unit (CPU)

A hardware component of a computer system that processes raw data and controls other parts of the computer system.

THE CENTRAL PROCESSING UNIT AND PRIMARY STORAGE

The CPU is responsible for the manipulation of symbols, numbers, and letters and also controls the other parts of the computer system. As Figure 4.2 shows, the central processing unit consists of a control unit and an arithmetic-logic unit. The central processing

FIGURE 4.1

Components of a Computer System

A contemporary computer system consists of a central processing unit, primary storage, secondary storage, and input/output and communications devices. Buses are the pathways or connections that data and signals travel along between the central processing unit, primary storage, and the other components of the computer system.

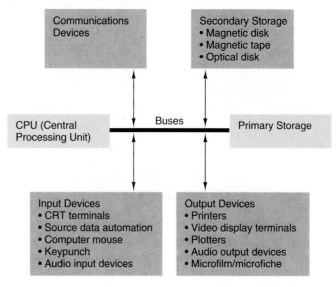

Semiconductor chip

A silicon chip upon which hundreds of thousands or millions of circuit elements can be etched.

Primary storage

The component of the computer system that temporarily stores program instructions and the data being used by these instructions.

Byte

A single character of data made up of a combination of bits that a computer processes or stores as a unit; the unit in which computer storage capacity is measured.

Address

The particular location in primary storage where data or program instructions are stored in a byte.

unit is often contained on an individual **semiconductor chip** (a silicon chip on which hundreds of thousands or even millions of circuit elements can be etched) with semiconductor chips for primary storage located nearby.

Primary Storage   **Primary storage** (also called main memory or primary memory) stores program instructions and the data being used by those instructions. Data and programs are placed in primary storage before processing, between processing steps, and after processing has terminated before being released as output. Once the computer is finished with specific pieces of data and program instructions, they are overwritten by new incoming data or program instructions, released as output, or returned to secondary storage.

Whenever data or program instructions are placed in primary storage, they are assigned to storage locations called **bytes**. Each byte stores only a single character of data and has a unique **address** so it can be located when needed. A byte may be compared to a mailbox, with its number being the address. As Figure 4.2 shows, primary storage contains many bytes.

Figure 4.2 also shows that there are three kinds of buses that connect the CPU, primary storage, and other devices in the computer system. The address bus carries signals used to locate a given address in primary storage. The data bus carries data to and from primary storage. The control bus carries signals indicating whether to "read" or "write" data to, or from, the address specified in primary storage and to, or from, input or output devices. The system clock helps regulate the pace of operations in the computer system.

FIGURE 4.2

Closeup of the Central Processing Unit and Primary Storage

Primary storage temporarily stores data, instructions, intermediate results, and output. Each byte in primary storage has a unique address. The central processing unit contains a control unit and an arithmetic-logic unit. The control unit coordinates the transfer of data between the central processing unit, primary storage, and input/output devices. The arithmetic-logic unit performs calculations and logical operations on data. The data bus, the address bus, and the control bus transfer signals between the central processing unit, primary storage, and other devices in the computer system. The system clock helps pace the sequence of events occurring in the system.

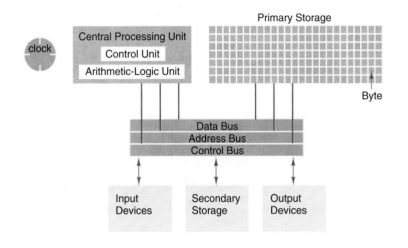

The Arithmetic-Logic Unit   The **arithmetic-logic unit (ALU)** performs arithmetic and logical operations on data. It adds, subtracts, multiplies, divides, and determines whether a number is positive, negative, or zero. The ALU can make logical comparisons of two numbers to determine whether one is greater than, less than, or equal to the other. The ALU can also perform logical operations on letters or words.

The Control Unit   The **control unit** controls and coordinates the other components of the computer. It reads stored program instructions one at a time, and based on what the program tells it to do, the control unit directs other components of the computer system to perform the required tasks. For example, it might specify which data should be placed in primary storage, which operation the ALU should perform on the data, and where the results should be stored. It might also direct the result to an appropriate output device, such as a printer. After each instruction is executed, the control unit proceeds to the next instruction.

The Basic Machine Cycle   The control unit is a key element in the most basic and fundamental CPU operation, called a **machine cycle**. As you will see, a machine cycle has two parts. One part is called the **instruction cycle (I-cycle)**, in which an instruction is retrieved from primary storage and decoded. A second part is called the **execution cycle (E-cycle)**, in which the required data are located, the instruction executed, and the results stored.

Arithmetic-logic unit (ALU)
The component of the CPU that performs arithmetic and logical operations on data.

Control unit
The component of the CPU that controls and coordinates the other components of the computer.

Machine cycle
The series of operations involved in executing a single instruction.

Instruction cycle
The portion of a machine cycle in which an instruction is retrieved from primary storage and decoded.

Execution cycle
The portion of a machine cycle in which the required data are located, the instruction is executed, and the results are stored.

FIGURE 4.3

A Machine Cycle

Each machine cycle consists of two smaller cycles: the instruction cycle (I-cycle) and the execution cycle (E-cycle). These involve a series of steps in which instructions are retrieved from a software program, decoded, and performed. Running even a simple software program involves thousands of machine cycles.

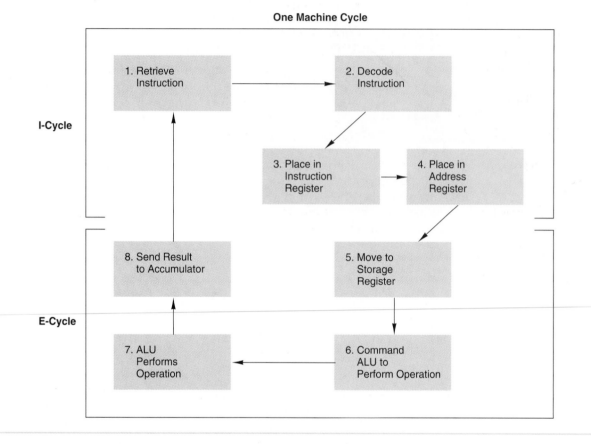

One Machine Cycle

Register

A storage location in the ALU or control unit; it may be an instruction register, an address register, or a storage register, depending on what is stored in it.

RAM

A memory device used for the short-term storage of data or program instructions; stands for random-access memory.

Figure 4.3 shows in greater detail how the machine cycle works. The control unit fetches an instruction from the program stored in primary storage, decodes the instruction, and places it in a special instruction **register.** Registers are special storage locations in the ALU and the control unit that act like high-speed staging areas. There are several different kinds of registers. The control unit breaks each instruction into two parts. The part of the instruction telling the ALU what to do next is placed in an instruction register. The part of the instruction specifying the address of the data to be used in the operation is moved to an address register. A storage register is used to store any data that have been retrieved from primary storage. Last, an accumulator is used to store the results of an operation.

In this manner, the modern digital computer methodically reads through a computer program and executes the program one instruction at a time, in sequential order. There may be millions, or hundreds of millions, of such machine cycles to perform in a program. However, because the machine works very fast—processing millions of instructions per second—extremely large programs can be executed in a few moments.

Memory Devices   There are several different kinds of semiconductor memory chips used in primary storage. Each serves a different purpose. **RAM,** or random-access memory, is used for short-term storage of data or program instructions. RAM is located in RAM chips physically close to the CPU. The sole purpose of these chips is to store digital data. The contents of RAM can be read and changed when required. RAM is **volatile:** this means that if the computer's electric supply is disrupted or the computer is turned off, its contents will be lost.

Another kind of memory found in a computer is **ROM,** or read-only memory, which stores important program instructions permanently. For example, in the IBM Personal System/2 microcomputer workstation, ROM permanently stores instructions concerning the display screen, keyboard, and printer. ROM is **nonvolatile,** meaning that its contents will not be lost if electric power is disrupted or the computer is turned off. Nor can it be destroyed if someone tries to write over the instructions.

There are several other categories of nonvolatile memory chips. **PROM,** or programmable read-only memory, is similar to ROM in that it can only be read from and cannot be changed once the chips have been programmed. Initially, however, PROM chips contain no program instructions. These are entered by the purchaser, usually a manufacturer, who programs the chips and implants them in manufactured products in which they serve as control devices. For example, instead of fabricating a specialized chip to control small motors, a manufacturer can program a PROM chip with the control instructions. **EPROM** (erasable programmable read-only memory) chips are also nonvolatile. Unlike PROM chips, however, EPROM chips can be erased and reprogrammed. Consequently, they are used in robots and other devices in which the program may have to be changed periodically.

MEASURING TIME, SIZE, AND PROCESSING POWER

How can we determine whether a given computer will help us with problem solving? How can we determine which model or size of computer to use? Assuming the problem lends itself to automation (see Chapters 9–11), we need to know how fast a computer can work, how much data it can store, and whether it can store the data required to solve our problem. Therefore, knowing the measures of computer speed and processing capacity is essential.

Very slow computers will measure machine cycle times in **milliseconds** (thousandths of a second). More powerful machines will use measures of **microseconds** (millionths of a second) or **nanoseconds** (billionths of a second). A few very powerful computers measure machine cycles in **picoseconds** (trillionths of a second). The largest business computers (such as IBM mainframes in the ES/9000 series) have a machine cycle time of less than 10 nanoseconds. Thus such computers can execute over 200 million instructions per second. MIPS, or millions of instructions per second, is a common benchmark for measuring the speed of larger computers.

Computer storage capacity is measured in terms of bytes. A thousand bytes (actually 1,024 or 2^{10} storage positions) are a **kilobyte.** The kilobyte is the typical measure of microcomputer storage capacity. Thus, when someone speaks of a microcomputer with a 640K memory, this means that the machine has an internal RAM capacity of 640 kilobytes. Larger machines have storage capacities in the **megabyte** (over 1 million bytes) or **gigabyte** (over 1 billion bytes) range. External computer storage devices can store trillions of bytes (**terabytes**) of data. Table 4.1 summarizes the key measures of computer time and storage capacity.

Volatile
Property of memory that means that its contents will be lost if electric power is disrupted or the computer is turned off.

ROM
A memory device used for the permanent storage of program instructions; stands for read-only memory.

Nonvolatile
Property of memory that means that its contents will not be lost if electric power is disrupted or the computer is turned off.

PROM
A memory device in which the memory chips can only be programmed once and are used to store instructions entered by the purchaser; stands for programmable read-only memory.

EPROM
A memory device in which the memory chips can be erased and reprogrammed with new instructions; stands for erasable programmable read-only memory.

Millisecond
A measure of machine cycle time; equals one one-thousandth of a second.

Microsecond
A measure of machine cycle time; equals one one-millionth of a second.

Nanosecond
A measure of machine cycle time; equals one one-billionth of a second.

Picosecond
A measure of machine cycle time; equals one one-trillionth of a second.

Kilobyte
The usual measure of microcomputer storage capacity; approximately 1,000 bytes.

Megabyte
A measure of computer storage capacity; approximately 1 million bytes.

Gigabyte
A measure of computer storage capacity; approximately 1 billion bytes.

Terabyte
A measure of computer storage capacity; approximately 1 trillion bytes.

TABLE 4.1

Key Measures of Computer Time and Storage Capacity

Time		Storage Capacity	
Millisecond	1/1000 second	Kilobyte	1,000 (2^{10}) storage positions
Microsecond	1/1,000,000 second	Megabyte	1,000,000 (2^{20}) storage positions
Nanosecond	1/1,000,000,000 second	Gigabyte	1,000,000,000 (2^{30}) storage positions
Picosecond	1/1,000,000,000,000 second	Terabyte	1,000,000,000,000 (2^{40}) storage positions

HOW COMPUTERS REPRESENT DATA

A computer represents data by reducing all symbols, pictures, or words into a string of binary digits. Binary means having two states, and each binary digit can have only one of two states or conditions, based on the presence or absence of electronic or magnetic signals. A conducting state in a semiconductor circuit represents a one; a nonconducting state represents a zero. In magnetic media, a magnetized spot represents a one when a magnetic field is in one direction and represents a zero when the magnetism is in the other direction.

Bit

A binary digit that can have only one of two states, representing zero or one.

A binary digit is called a **bit** and represents either a zero or a one. The binary number system, or base 2 system, can express all numbers as groups of zeros and ones. As in the decimal (base 10) system, which we ordinarily use, the value of each number depends on the place of each digit in a string of digits. Figure 4.4 illustrates how the decimal system works. Each digit has been broken down according to its place value to show how numbers are created. In Figure 4.5 we apply the same approach to show how to

FIGURE 4.4

Converting a Decimal Number to Its Decimal Components
The value of a number depends on the place of each digit within a series of digits. In the decimal (or base 10) number system, each number can be expressed as a power of the number 10.

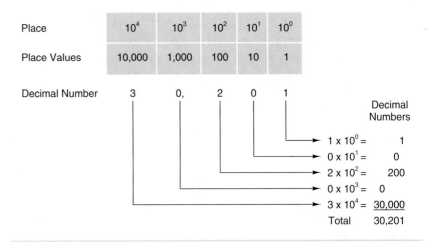

Place	10^4	10^3	10^2	10^1	10^0
Place Values	10,000	1,000	100	10	1
Decimal Number	3	0,	2	0	1

Decimal Numbers

$1 \times 10^0 =$ 1
$0 \times 10^1 =$ 0
$2 \times 10^2 =$ 200
$0 \times 10^3 =$ 0
$3 \times 10^4 =$ 30,000

Total   30,201

FIGURE 4.5

Converting a Binary Number to Its Decimal Equivalent

In the binary, or base 2, number system, each number can be expressed as a power of the number 2.

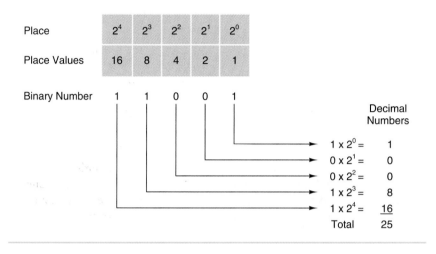

convert a binary number to its decimal equivalent. Any number in the decimal system can be expressed as a binary number and vice versa. For example, the decimal number 25 would be represented as 11001 in the binary system; the decimal number 27 would be the binary number 11011.

What about letters and symbols such as $ and &? These can also be represented in binary form using special coding schemes. The two most popular binary coding schemes are EBCDIC (Extended Binary Coded Decimal Interchange Code) and ASCII (American Standard Code for Information Interchange). **EBCDIC** (pronounced ib-si-dick) was developed by IBM in the 1950s and is used in IBM and other mainframe computers. **ASCII** was developed by the American National Standards Institute (ANSI) as a standard code that could be used by many different computer manufacturers to make their machines compatible. ASCII is used in data transmission, in microcomputers, and in some larger computers.

EBCDIC is an 8-bit coding scheme; that is, 8 bits are grouped together to form a byte. Each byte represents a single letter, symbol, or number and consists of a unique combination of bits. For example, the decimal digit 8 is represented by the EBCDIC code as 11111000. An A is represented in EBCDIC as 11000001. ASCII was originally designed as a 7-bit code, but most computers use 8-bit versions of ASCII. Table 4.2 compares the EBCDIC and ASCII 8-bit coding schemes.

EBCDIC and ASCII also contain an extra bit position called a parity bit. This bit is automatically set to zero or one to make all the bits in a byte add up to an even or odd number. Computers are constructed to have either even or odd parity. An even parity machine expects the number of "on" bits in a byte to add up to an even number. An odd parity machine expects the number of "on" bits in a byte to be odd. If the number of "on" bits in a byte is even in an odd parity machine, the parity bit will be turned on to make the total number of "on" bits odd. Figure 4.6 shows both valid and invalid representations of a character in an odd parity computer. Parity bits are used to detect errors caused by environmental disturbances or garbled data transmission.

EBCDIC

An 8-bit binary coding scheme used in IBM and other mainframe computers; stands for Extended Binary Coded Decimal Interchange Code.

ASCII

A 7- or 8-bit binary coding scheme used in data transmission, microcomputers, and some larger computers; stands for American Standard Code for Information Interchange.

TABLE 4.2

EBCDIC and ASCII Coding Systems

Character	EBCDIC Binary	ASCII-8 Binary
A	1100 0001	1010 0001
B	1100 0010	1010 0010
C	1100 0011	1010 0011
D	1100 0100	1010 0100
E	1100 0101	1010 0101
F	1100 0110	1010 0110
G	1100 0111	1010 0111
H	1100 1000	1010 1000
I	1100 1001	1010 1001
J	1101 0001	1010 1010
K	1101 0010	1010 1011
L	1101 0011	1010 1100
M	1101 0100	1010 1101
N	1101 0101	1010 1110
O	1101 0110	1010 1111
P	1101 0111	1011 0000
Q	1101 1000	1011 0001
R	1101 1001	1011 0010
S	1110 0010	1011 0011
T	1110 0011	1011 0100
U	1110 0100	1011 0101
V	1110 0101	1011 0110
W	1110 0110	1011 0111
X	1110 0111	1011 1000
Y	1110 1000	1011 1001
Z	1110 1001	1011 1010
0	1111 0000	0101 0000
1	1111 0001	0101 0001
2	1111 0010	0101 0010
3	1111 0011	0101 0011
4	1111 0100	0101 0100
5	1111 0101	0101 0101
6	1111 0110	0101 0110
7	1111 0111	0101 0111
8	1111 1000	0101 1000
9	1111 1001	0101 1001

FIGURE 4.6

Detecting Errors with a Parity Check, Using Odd Parity

With odd parity, the correct representation will involve an odd number of "on" bits. If there is an even number of "on" bits, this alerts the computer that an error has occurred.

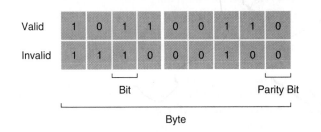

GENERATIONS OF COMPUTER HARDWARE

Computer hardware has undergone a series of transitions, each of which has widened the range of problems computers can solve. Each stage, or generation, in the history of computing has used a different technology for the computer's logic elements, the electronic components used in the computer's processing work. Each new logic element has dramatically boosted computer processing power and storage capabilities while lowering costs. Generational changes in computer hardware have been accompanied by generational changes in computer software (see Chapter 6). From an exclusive and esoteric toy of a handful of scientists and researchers, computers have become a major tool for solving problems in the business and commercial world.

Vacuum tubes permitted computers such as the IBM 701 to calculate thousands of times faster than did their electro-mechanical forerunners. Despite their enormous physical size, these computers had less processing power than today's IBM PCs.

SOURCE: Courtesy of International Business Machines Corporation.

The First Generation (1951–1958): Vacuum-Tube Technology   The first generation of computers used vacuum tubes to store and process information. These tubes were not very satisfactory: they consumed large quantities of electric power, generated a great deal of heat, and had short lives. First-generation computers were colossal in size, yet they had very limited memories and processing capacity. The maximum memory size was only about 2 kilobytes, with a speed of 10 kilo instructions per second. Rotating magnetic drums were used for internal storage, and punched cards were used for external storage. Jobs such as running programs or printing output had to be coordinated manually.

All in all, first-generation computers were so costly, unwieldy, and difficult to program that their problem-solving capabilities were very restricted. Consequently, these machines were used primarily for very limited scientific and engineering problems.

The Second Generation (1959–1963): Transistor Technology   Second-generation computers were based on transistor technology, with individual transistors wired into printed circuit boards. Not only were transistors smaller, cheaper, and more reliable than vacuum tubes, but they also generated far less heat and consumed less power. Memory size expanded to 32 kilobytes of RAM, and speeds reached 200,000–300,000 instructions per second. Internal storage used magnetic cores (small doughnut-shaped devices strung together on racks within the computer, which have much faster access speeds than magnetic drums). Magnetic tape and disks started to be used for external storage.

Second-generation computers saw more widespread use for scientific and business problems because of their greatly increased processing power, which supported easier-to-use software. Businesses started using computers to automate accounting and clerical tasks such as payroll and billing.

The Third Generation (1964–1979): Integrated Circuit Technology   Third-generation computers relied on integrated circuits, which printed thousands of tiny transistors onto small silicon chips. Computers thus could expand to 2 megabytes of RAM and accelerate processing speed to as much as 5 MIPS. Third-generation machines also supported software that was even closer to the English language and easier to use. This meant that persons without a technical background could use these machines and associated software without having to rely on specialists.

Increased capacity and processing power made it possible to use sophisticated operating systems—special software that automated the running of programs and communication between the CPU, printers, and other devices. Moreover, these operating systems could work on several programs or tasks simultaneously, whereas first- and second-generation computers could only handle one program at a time. Section 6.2 (Chapter 6) treats operating systems in detail.

A silicon wafer

A side view of an etched wafer

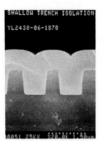

CVD over an etched wafer

A top view of a wafer after multilayer processing

Patterned wafer following fabrication process

Microprocessor

A silicon chip containing an entire CPU; used in microcomputers.

A chip begins with a wafer of silicon. A layer of high-quality, single-crystal silicon is deposited on the wafer's surface. Circuit structures are defined by a mask of photosensitive materials. Etching removes unwanted portions of the deposited layers not covered by the mask. Conductive and insulating materials are layered on the wafer in a process called chemical vapor deposition (CVD). In the implant process, electrically charged impurities are bombarded into the silicon wafer to increase electrical conductivity in selected regions on the circuit.

SOURCE: Jacobs/Fulton Design Group; Paper Sculpture by Pat Allen, © Applied Materials, Inc.

The Fourth Generation (1980–Present): Very-Large-Scale Integrated Circuit Technology   Fourth-generation computers use very-large-scale integrated circuits (VLSIC), which contain from 200,000 to over 3 million circuits per chip. More circuits can be packed into increasingly less space, so hundreds of thousands of circuits can be accommodated on a silicon chip the size of a fingernail. Fourth-generation technology has enabled conventional mainframes to achieve memory sizes over 500 megabytes and speeds over 200 MIPS. Supercomputers exceed these capacities and speeds.

Another feature of fourth-generation hardware is the **microprocessor.** A microprocessor actually consists of an entire CPU on a single silicon chip. Microcomputers and "intelligent" features in automobiles, watches, toys, and other items are based on microprocessor technology. Microminiaturization has produced computers that are so small, fast, and cheap that they have become ubiquitous in daily life. Software for such computers is becoming increasingly easy to use, so nontechnical specialists can use microcomputers to solve problems on their own. The Focus on Problem Solving illustrates the kinds of problems that can arise when organizations use outdated computer technology from an earlier generation.

4.3 MAINFRAMES, MINICOMPUTERS, MICROCOMPUTERS, WORKSTATIONS, AND SUPERCOMPUTERS

Computers are typically classified as mainframes, minicomputers, microcomputers, workstations, or supercomputers based on their size and processing speed. Because of continuing advances in computing technology, these definitions change constantly. Today's microcomputers have the computing power of mainframes from the 1980s, for example, and can perform many tasks that formerly were limited to larger computers. We discuss the effect of these changes in the next section. Here we describe each category of computer and the microprocessor technology they use.

FOCUS ON PROBLEM SOLVING

DEADLINES OR DEAD LINES?

Finishing a news article represents only half the battle for a reporter trying to get a story in on time. Sending it to the next step in the production process can pose just as large a challenge if editing and production are hampered by outdated computer hardware. Worse, any slowdown in the editing stage usually slows the rest of the production process. Ultimately, the paper's subscribers might not receive a paper in time to scan with their first cup of coffee.

For the past 8 years, the 320 reporters and editors at the *Dallas Morning News* have routed their stories among each other using a Digital Equipment Corporation (DEC) PDP 1184, a third-generation vintage minicomputer. On evenings with special news, such as the Persian Gulf War

bombings, the system's 500 available queues, or electronic "in-out" baskets, became so overloaded that newspaper production was alarmingly slowed. As a stopgap measure, the newspaper asked reporters to file their stories 15 minutes earlier than the usual deadline. Nevertheless, many stories were backed up and production was still delayed because of shortages in available computer space. The reporters were doing their jobs, but the paper's computer technology was failing.

Even on less hectic days, the technology was not up to the job. Bonnie Rogers, news systems manager, would rush around the newsroom asking if people were gone so she could delete their work queues. Sometimes the newspaper faced not only shortages of queues but also of terminals on which the reporters could write their stories.

The outdated PDP system was congested every day. When the paper acquired the assets of the rival *Dallas Times Herald*, the system could no longer function. The computer simply could not handle the increased circulation, reporters, pages, and

across-the-board operations. The *News* finally had to switch to new, more powerful computers manufactured by Tandem Computers, Inc. of Sacramento, California. Eight Tandem computers, four of which are for backup in case of hardware failures, work with 149 terminals and microcomputers to provide enhanced editing capabilities. The new system can automatically replicate the final look of a page (the old DEC system could provide only "galley" layouts that showed the text in columns but had to be manipulated into a page design) and can receive more wire services than the old system. With this new technology, the *Dallas Morning News* is now relieved of its worst nightmare—not being able to get the paper out.

FOCUS Questions:
What people and organization problems were created by outdated technology? How did the newspaper try to solve them before introducing more powerful computers?

SOURCE: Mark Halper, "Acquisition Speeds System Upgrade," *Computerworld*, February 1, 1993.

MAINFRAMES, MINIS, AND MICROS: WHAT'S THE DIFFERENCE?

Generally speaking, a **mainframe** is the largest computer, a powerhouse of a machine with huge memory and extremely rapid processing power. Mainframes are typically used for solving very large commercial, scientific, or military problems for which a computer must handle massive amounts of data or many complicated processes. A **minicomputer** is a mid-range computer, about the size of an office desk; minicomputers are often used in universities, factories, or research laboratories. A **microcomputer** is small enough that it can be placed on a desktop or carried from room to room. (Small laptop and notebook versions of microcomputers are fully portable, weighing less than 6 pounds.) Organizations use microcomputers for solving problems, but they are also widely used as personal machines (they were originally designed for nontechnical specialists).

Mainframes can be classified as having 50 megabytes to over 1 gigabyte of RAM; minicomputers, 10–650 megabytes of RAM; and microcomputers, 640 kilobytes to 64 megabytes of RAM. These distinctions are becoming less meaningful, however, because

Mainframe
A large computer, generally having 50 megabytes to over 1 gigabyte of RAM.
Minicomputer
A medium-sized computer, generally having 10 to 650 megabytes of RAM.
Microcomputer
A small, desktop or portable computer, generally having 640 kilobytes to 64 megabytes of RAM.

the capacity of computer hardware changes constantly and the computing power of micro-computers continues to soar. Mainframes and minicomputers can still perform many more tasks simultaneously than microcomputers and can be used more easily by large numbers of people at the same time.

WORKSTATIONS, SUPERCOMPUTERS, AND PARALLEL PROCESSING

Workstations are desktop machines with powerful graphics and mathematical processing capabilities plus the ability to perform several tasks at once. They are typically used by scientists, engineers, designers, and other knowledge workers. Their graphics and CPU capacity allows them to present fully rendered, multiple views of a physical object, such as an airplane wing; rotate the object three dimensionally; give its physical parameters, such as dimensions and weight; and provide its design history and cost factors. Workstations can easily integrate text and graphics, displaying multiple tools, applications, and types of data simultaneously. They are used increasingly in the financial industry, in which powerhouse desktop machines simultaneously provide financial data and news services, analyze portfolios, and process securities and commodities trades.[1]

Low-cost workstations and microcomputers are becoming harder to distinguish. Some of the more sophisticated personal computers have workstation-like features, and as microcomputers become more powerful and graphics oriented, the distinction is likely to blur further. Distinctions based on price (the purchase price of an inexpensive workstation starts at $4,000; a high-end microcomputer can cost $5,000) are also evaporating, although the most sophisticated workstations can cost hundreds of thousands of dollars.

A **supercomputer** is a sophisticated and powerful computer used for problems requiring extremely rapid and complex computations with hundreds or thousands of variable factors. Because supercomputers are extremely expensive, they have been used mainly for military and scientific applications, although business firms are starting to use them. For example, Dow Jones & Co. uses two supercomputers to handle its customer information requests and extra database services. Typically, however, super-computers are used for highly classified weapons research, weather forecasting, and petroleum and engineering applications, which involve complex mathematical models and simulations.

Supercomputers perform complex and massive computations much faster than conventional computers because they process up to 64 bits in less than 1 nanosecond—many times faster than the largest mainframes. Supercomputers do not process one instruction at a time but instead rely on **parallel processing.** In parallel processing, the computer processes more than one instruction at a time by dividing a problem into smaller parts and parceling out the parts to multiple processors. (In contrast, conventional computers use sequential or serial processing, in which the CPU executes only one instruction at a time in sequential order.) Figure 4.7 illustrates parallel processing for a hypothetical problem involving four parts (A–D). The problem is divided into smaller parts and assigned to multiple processing units, which work on it simultaneously. Some supercomputers have hundreds and thousands of microprocessors all working simultaneously.

Some supercomputer capabilities can be found in high-end workstations. Very fast workstations have speeds of over 100 million megaflops, and supercomputer speeds can exceed 9,000 megaflops. A **flop** is an acronym for floating point operations per second. A floating point operation is a basic computer arithmetic operation, such as addition, on numbers that include a decimal point. A department at the Lawrence

Workstation

Desktop computer with powerful graphics and mathematical processing capabilities and the ability to perform several tasks at once.

Supercomputer

A very sophisticated and powerful computer that can perform complex computations very rapidly.

Parallel processing

A type of processing in which more than one instruction is processed at a time using multiple processors; used in supercomputers.

Flop

Stands for *floating point operations per second.* A floating point operation is a basic arithmetic operation on numbers that include a decimal point.

FIGURE 4.7

Parallel Processing: An Important Ingredient in Supercomputers
Supercomputers can perform complex calculations much faster than even a mainframe can. This is possible in part due to parallel processing, in which multiple CPUs break down a problem into smaller portions and work on them simultaneously.

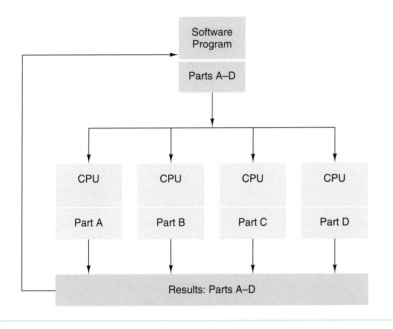

Livermore National Laboratory replaced its 10-year-old Cray X-MP supercomputer model with an advanced IBM RS6000 workstation to perform its computing-intensive scientific work. British Petroleum Co.'s Alaska production and exploration facility moved applications to model the flow of oil in reservoirs from its Cray supercomputer to IBM RS6000 workstations. However, only supercomputers can perform the billions of mathematical calculations per second required for the most complex problems.

MICROPROCESSOR TECHNOLOGY: THE CHIPS BEHIND THE MACHINES

The processing capabilities of computers depend heavily on the speed and performance of the microprocessor on which they are based. They can be affected by word length, bus width, and clock speed.

Microcomputers are typically labeled as 8-bit, 16-bit, or 32-bit machines according to their **word length**. A word is the number of bits that may be processed together as a unit. An 8-bit chip can retrieve or process 8 bits in a single machine cycle; a 32-bit machine, 32 bits. Thus, the bigger the word size, the more data and instructions the computer can handle at one time and the greater its speed. A 32-bit chip can process four 8-bit bytes at once.

Another factor affecting performance is **bus width**. The width of the data bus affects how much data can be moved at one time between the central processing unit, primary storage, and other devices in the computer system. The 8088 chip used in the original IBM Personal Computer, for example, had a 16-bit word length but only an

Word length
The number of bits that a computer can process or store together as a unit.

Bus width
The number of bits that can be moved at one time between the CPU and the other devices of a computer.

8-bit data bus width. This meant that data were processed within the CPU chip itself in 16-bit chunks but could be moved only 8 bits at a time between the CPU, primary storage, and external devices.

The width of the address bus determines the maximum size of memory. The 20-bit address bus width on the 8088 meant that the computer could address only 1 megabyte of memory at a time. On the other hand, the 80386DX chip and the 80486 chip used in the more powerful IBM Personal System/2 microcomputers have 32-bit word lengths and 32-bit data bus and address bus widths.

Cycle speed also affects speed and performance. An internal system clock sets the pace for sequencing events in the computer by emitting millions of electronic pulses per second. This clock speed is measured in **megahertz** (MHz), or millions of cycles per second. Each type of chip is equipped to handle clock speeds within a certain range. For example, the Intel 8088 microprocessor, which was the foundation for the early IBM personal computers, operates at 4.7 MHz, or 4.7 million cycles per second. The more recent Intel 80386 microprocessor operates at 16–40 MHz, and the Intel 80486 microprocessor, at 25–66 MHz.

Intel's 80486 chip and the Motorola 68040 are 32-bit chips that are three times faster than their predecessors. In fact, Intel's 80486 chip, which contains more than 1 million transistors on a thumbtack-sized silicon sliver, has been described as a "veritable mainframe-on-a-chip" with the number-crunching power of a low-end IBM 3090 mainframe. While microcomputers based on Intel's 80386 chip can perform a handful of tasks simultaneously, the 80486 can perform many more, each much larger and more sophisticated than anything being done previously.

Even more powerful are Intel's Pentium chip, Digital Equipment's Alpha chip, and the PowerPC chip developed jointly by IBM and Apple Computer Corp. The following section describes the capabilities of these and other "superchips." Table 4.3 compares the capabilities of the leading microcomputer chips.

REDUCED INSTRUCTION SET COMPUTING

Megahertz (MHz)
A measure of clock speed, or the pacing of events in a computer; stands for 1 million cycles per second.

Reduced instruction set computing (RISC)
Technology for increasing microprocessor speed by embedding only the most frequently used instructions on a chip.

Microprocessor speed and performance can also be enhanced by using **reduced instruction set computing (RISC)**, which drastically simplifies computer design. Conventional chips, which are based on complex instruction set computing, have many internal instructions built into their circuitry and take several clock cycles to execute an instruction. However, only 20 percent of these instructions are needed for 80 percent of the computer's tasks. The most frequently used instructions are the simple operations that can be performed at peak efficiency.

RISC chips, on the other hand, have only the most frequently used instructions embedded in them. With pared-down circuit design, a RISC CPU can execute most of its instructions in one cycle and may be able to execute many instructions at the same time. A feature called pipelining further enhances RISC processing by allowing instructions to be decoded while another instruction is being executed. RISC chips can be incredibly powerful. The Alpha chip (described in the following section) is a 64-bit RISC microprocessor that can reach speeds of 200 MHz, which gives it the performance of a small supercomputer.

RISC is most appropriate for scientific and workstation computing, which requires repetitive arithmetical and logical operations on data and sometimes three-dimensional image rendering. RISC technology is unlikely to be used for all microprocessors, since software written for conventional processors cannot automatically run on RISC computers; new software is required. Conventional microprocessors are being enhanced and streamlined to keep pace with most kinds of applications.

TABLE 4.3

Generations of Microprocessors

Microprocessor Chip	Manufacturer	Word Length	Bus Width	Clock Speed (MH$_z$)	Microcomputers Used in
8088	Intel	16	8	4.7–8	IBM PC and XT
80286	Intel	16	16	8–28	IBM AT AT&T PC 6300 Plus
80386	Intel	32	32	16–40	IBM Personal System/2 COMPAQ 386
68020	Motorola	32	32	12.5–32	Macintosh II
68030	Motorola	32	32	16–40	Macintosh IIx, IIcx Sun workstations Apollo workstations
80486	Intel	32	32	25–66	IBM microcomputers and workstations
68040	Motorola	32	32	25	High-end workstations
Pentium	Intel	32	64	60–100	High-end workstations and microcomputers
Power PC601	IBM, Apple, and Motorola	32	64	66	High-end laptops and workstations

4.4 INFORMATION TECHNOLOGY TRENDS

The microcomputer has emerged as one of the most powerful problem-solving tools in use today. Although microcomputers were originally designed for individuals working alone, they have become so powerful that they are no longer confined to personal information systems. Indeed, the micros of the 1990s have the same computing power as the mainframes of the 1980s plus new graphic and interactive capabilities. Microcomputers can also be applied to group and organization-wide problem solving, performing tasks that previously were reserved for minicomputers and mainframes.

With a small handheld computer, sales representatives and other business people can access data or transmit orders directly from the sales floor. Computers have become so portable and easy to use that they can be taken wherever the job requires.

SOURCE: Courtesy of Apple Computer Co.

Micros can be used either as individual stand-alone machines with their own processing power, stored data, and software or as part of a departmental or company-wide network. As stand-alone processing devices, micros have turned desktops into powerful personal workstations. Lightweight, portable laptop micros make it possible to use computers in many locations—at home, on the train, or on an airplane. No longer must business problem solving take place within the physical confines of the office. Laptop computers are proving especially valuable in areas such as sales force automation.

DISTRIBUTED PROCESSING

Distributed processing

The distribution of processing among multiple computers linked by a communications network.

Microcomputers can be linked in networks with other micros, printers, "intelligent" copy machines, and telephones; this enables the micros to provide processing power to coordinate the flow of documents and work without having to rely on mainframes. Such networks are discussed in Chapter 8. Micros can also be linked to minicomputers and mainframes, forming company-wide information networks that share hardware, software, and data resources. The use of multiple computers connected by a communication network for processing is called **distributed processing**. Instead of relying exclusively on a large central mainframe computer or several independent computers, processing work is distributed among the various microcomputers, minicomputers, and mainframes linked together. The network can be simple, as shown in Figure 4.8, or it can involve hundreds or thousands of separate computers.

Microcomputers can be linked to mainframes in a variety of ways. Special software can make microcomputers emulate ordinary mainframe terminals. Such terminals are called "dumb" terminals because they do not make use of their internal processing

FIGURE 4.8

Distributed Processing Linking a Computer Network
The network can include various combinations of mainframes, minicomputers, and microcomputers.

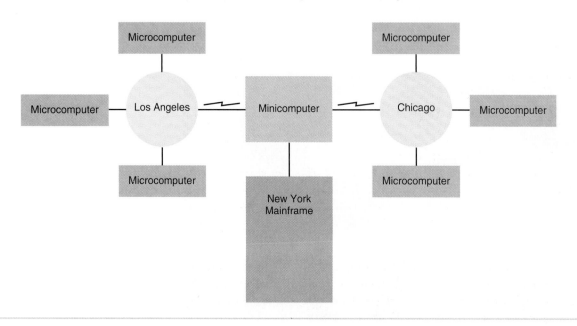

capacity. Special file-transfer software can be used to extract data from mainframes, reformat it, and place it in the microcomputer. This is called **downloading**. A typical problem solved by downloading might involve extracting corporate data from a mainframe system and downloading them to a microcomputer where they can be manipulated by spreadsheet software for next year's budget projections (see Section 6.4 on spreadsheets).

DOWNSIZING AND COOPERATIVE PROCESSING

Because microcomputers can now perform many problem-solving tasks that were formerly reserved for much larger machines, many organizations are **downsizing**, or shifting problem-solving applications from large computers to smaller ones. Computer industry reports show a fundamental shift in purchasing patterns away from giant mainframes toward lower-cost desktop machines. As firms replace mainframes and minicomputers with microcomputers, the microcomputers are often networked to share data and communication with each other (see Chapter 8).

Downsizing can lead to substantial cost savings for firms. Every MIPS on a mainframe costs about one hundred times more than on a microcomputer. A megabyte of primary memory on a mainframe runs about ten times the cost of equivalent memory on a micro, and mainframe disk storage runs about twice as much. Fewer technical specialists are required to run and maintain microcomputers compared with mainframes. For instance, the Turner Corp., a $3-billion international construction firm, saved over $1 million per year by replacing its mainframe with personal computer networks. The case study at the end of the chapter examines the pros and cons of downsizing in more detail.

Another computing pattern divides processing work for a particular application between mainframes and microcomputers. They communicate with each other on a network, and each type is assigned the functions it performs best. For example, the microcomputer might be used for data entry and validation, while the mainframe would be responsible for processing the input data and handling data stored by the system. This division of labor is called **cooperative processing**. Microcomputers are used because they can provide the same processing power much more cheaply than a mainframe.

THE FUTURE OF THE MAINFRAME

Will computers on a chip turn mainframes into technological dinosaurs? This is unlikely. The remaining chapters of this book help to explain why. Firms have invested too much effort and expense in mainframes to quickly shift to desktop technology for their problem-solving needs. Building information systems is too complex and costly for firms to redesign for smaller machines, at least in the short run of 3 to 5 years. Moreover, some functions in an organization are best handled by a central mainframe. For instance, firms in the year 2000 will still have to consolidate the operating incomes of all their divisions and subsidiaries. This information may be collected and transmitted by microcomputers, but it will probably be consolidated and stored on a central mainframe. Mainframes are also necessary when thousands of users must work with the same machine.

Desktop machines will likely be the technology of choice for solving new problems in the next decade, not only because of their low cost but because desktop technology has proven easier to use and more innovative than mainframe technology. The role of the mainframe will change from being the focal point of corporate computing to being one element in an intelligent network.

Downloading
The process of extracting data from mainframes, reformatting them, and placing them in a microcomputer.

Downsizing
The process of moving software applications from large computers, such as mainframes or minicomputers, to smaller computers, such as microcomputers.

Cooperative processing
The division of processing work for applications among mainframes and microcomputers.

FOCUS ON ORGANIZATIONS

PARALLEL PROCESSING FOR THE MASSES

Supercomputers were once an elite technology restricted to sophisticated scientific, military, and engineering work. Businesses settled for mainframes for even their most data-intensive work because supercomputers were too expensive. Today, thanks to massively parallel processing technology, that's no longer true. Supercomputers are moving into business.

Although businesses have traditionally used mainframes for their heavy-load processing work, there are some data-intensive business problems that mainframes cannot solve. For instance, point-of-sale systems in department stores, supermarkets, and automobile showrooms supply a wealth of information about buying patterns—but businesses must find a way to analyze it. While sifting through such mountains of accumulated data can cripple a mainframe, massively parallel processing permits pattern analysis of huge pools of data. Kmart Corp., Wal-Mart Stores, Inc., and Hallmark Cards, Inc. use massively parallel computers to analyze large volumes of point-of-sale data to create short-term sales forecasts that they can use to shape their order and delivery schedules.

Several large banks in the United States and Europe use massively parallel computers to access information contained in millions of customer records. ING Bank in Amsterdam, one of the top 80 banks in the world, chose a pair of massively parallel computers from Ncube Corp. of Foster City, California. The Ncube computers, which assign separate tasks to multiple processors, can handle many parts of a computing operation simultaneously. They are a cost-effective way of manipulating huge volumes of data.

ING Bank's stock-and-bond trading group managers were the first to use the new machines. Then 3,000 managers in the bank's Dutch branches began to use the system to obtain information from as many as 10 million customer records. The records contain background data about individual customers as well as data on the bank's regional and companywide performance. In the past, when managers used the bank's nine IBM mainframes to obtain this information, they had to wait up to 2 days. Now they can get answers in 30 minutes or less. Up to 30 users can extract information from the massively parallel system, an impossible feat with a mainframe.

With the improved decision making provided by the parallel system, financial managers can produce performance reviews for divisions or regions of the bank, and traders have immediate access to trading data and data about issuers of securities. The bank can react more quickly to changes in the market. Bank branch employees can rapidly obtain customer deposit and loan information to formulate marketing and customer service strategies. Information that previously took up to 12 hours to obtain can be provided in minutes. The bank expects to recoup its $3 million investment in parallel processing hardware in less than 2 years.

Financial institutions in the United States are also using massively parallel processing. BankAmerica Corp., the second-largest bank in the United States, uses a Teradata DBC 1012 Model 4 computer for loan portfolio analysis and marketing. The Teradata machine analyzes trends in the bank's relationships with customers to determine which customers are likely to purchase a particular bank product or service. These customers can then be targeted for promotional mailings. Bank of America also uses the massively parallel system to analyze potential acquisitions because the system can quickly compute the value of takeover candidates by integrating these companies' massive volumes of operational data into Bank of America's investment analysis format. It would be impossible to perform these computing tasks with any other type of computer.

FOCUS Question:
What people, organization, and technology factors should be considered when deciding whether to use massively parallel computers?

SOURCE: Doug Bartholomew, "Banking's New Payoff: Speed," *InformationWEEK,* January 17, 1994.

How important an element will the mainframe be? Will it be merely another machine connected to microcomputers, minicomputers, workstations, and communications devices? Mainframe manufacturers such as IBM want it to be the central hub that anchors the entire network, storing all the firm's data in one repository and distributing the data for processing on smaller machines. Microcomputer manufacturers claim, on the other hand, that new, more powerful desktop machines will accomplish most jobs in the future, while the mainframe will be relegated to a central library where it will simply store and transfer information at the behest of microcomputers.

A FIFTH GENERATION

Conventional computers are based on what is called the Von Neumann architecture, which processes information serially, one instruction at a time. John Von Neumann, an influential mathematician at Princeton University, sketched out the design elements of digital computers in the early 1940s. The Von Neumann design, in which a computer works through a list of instructions one at a time, has been the basis for virtually all conventional digital computing. In contrast, "fifth-generation computers" are supercomputers designed to function like the human brain in the sense that they carry out multiple streams of activity at once.

In the future, more computers will use parallel and massively parallel processing to work on many parts of a problem at the same time, producing solutions ten to 100 times faster than the most powerful sequential processors. **Massively parallel processing** harnesses very large numbers of processor chips interwoven in complex ways to solve a problem simultaneously. In contrast to parallel processing, which uses a small number of expensive specialized microprocessor chips working together, massively parallel processing chains hundreds and even thousands of inexpensive, commonly used chips to work on a single computing problem. Massively parallel systems can achieve supercomputer speeds at as little as one-tenth to one-twentieth the cost of conventional parallel computers. (See the Focus on Organizations.)

While contemporary supercomputers can perform hundreds of billions of calculations per second, massively parallel technology will make it possible to create super-supercomputers that can perform more than a trillion mathematical calculations

Massively parallel processing
Computer processing in which a very large number of inexpensive processor chips are chained together to work on a single computing problem simultaneously.

The Intel Pentium microprocessor contains more than 3 million transistors and possesses supercomputing processing capabilities. Powerful chips will continue to advance information technology.

SOURCE: Courtesy of Intel Corporation

FOCUS ON TECHNOLOGY

THE NEW CHIP WARS

Another epic battle is taking shape in the computer world. This time the struggle centers on the microprocessors that will form the heart of tomorrow's computers. For years, the lead has been held by Intel, whose microprocessors were the foundation for IBM and IBM-compatible microcomputers. Intel produced 85 percent of the microprocessors used in microcomputers in the United States. Now other computer manufacturers are challenging Intel with powerful, sophisticated microprocessors for handling the computing needs of the twenty-first century.

Intel has tried to maintain its lead by introducing the Pentium, a fifth generation of its "86" series chip. The Pentium microprocessor, introduced in March 1993, packs over three million transistors onto a single 2.16-square-inch silicon chip. The Pentium has a 64-bit data bus width, a 32-bit word length, and clock speeds of up to 150 MHz. It can operate at up to 112 MIPS.

Digital Equipment Corp. (DEC) has developed an Alpha series of microprocessors based on RISC architecture with clock speeds ranging from 50 to 200 MHz and potential processing speeds of up to 300 MIPS. Alpha chips have 64-bit buses and 64-bit word lengths. The fastest Alpha chip has the same peak performance as a small supercomputer. DEC uses Alpha chips in an entire series of machines ranging from handheld computers to minicomputers and supercomputers that it believes will provide the performance of larger, more expensive machines at lower cost. Since Alpha can run software written for DEC's earlier line of VAX computers, Alpha machines will be useful for business applications as well as for scientific and engineering work. However, observers point out that many of the performance features of Alpha chips can be found at the same price in the workstations of competing manufacturers.

The main challenger to Intel dominance appears to be the PowerPC series of microprocessors, developed jointly by Apple Computer Corp., IBM, and Motorola Inc. PowerPC chips, which use RISC architecture, are not only extremely powerful but can also run software developed for different brands of computer hardware. For instance, a Macintosh microcomputer equipped with a PowerPC chip can run software developed to run on an Intel microprocessor (on which IBM and IBM-type microcomputers are based) as well as software developed for the Macintosh. The consortium hopes that with such power and versatility, PowerPC microprocessors will create a new standard for microcomputers. Apple and IBM are both manufacturing computers that use PowerPC chips. The PowerPC 601 chip, first in the series, has a 64-bit data bus width, a 32-bit word length, and a clock speed of 66 MHz. It costs less to make than the Pentium chip because it has 2.8 million transistors on a die that is half the size of the die for the Pentium. In general, the bigger the die, the lower the yield of workable parts. The smaller die of the PowerPC chip also requires half the power and generates less heat than the Pentium, making it more suitable for small portable laptop and notebook computers.

Which chips will win out? The answer lies with how quickly new software can be written to take advantage of each chip's speed.

FOCUS Questions: If you were buying a computer, how would you select among machines with Pentium, Alpha, or PowerPC chips? What people, organization, and technology factors would you consider?

SOURCES: Jim Carlton and Laurie Hays, "New Computer Chip Hits Desktop Market with Intel in Its Sights," *The Wall Street Journal,* March 9, 1994; "Does IS Want the PowerPC?" *Datamation,* November 1, 1993; "Can Digital Sustain Alpha's Edge?" *Datamation,* March 1, 1993; and Andy Reinhardt, "Pentium Changes the PC," *Byte,* July 1993.

each second—a teraflop. The term *teraflop* comes from the Greek *teras,* which for mathematicians means one trillion, and flop, an acronym for floating point operations per second. Teraflop machines will help scientific researchers in the twenty-first century to map the surface of planets, design new computers, and simulate the mechanisms of biological brains. Future supercomputers could be used to test the aerodynamics of a supersonic airplane with speeds more than five times the speed of sound. Building a physical wind tunnel to generate winds more than five times the speed of sound would be impossible, but designers could use a supercomputer to calculate the flow of air over the plane's surface. Trillions of calculations would be required for engineers to recast their models to test different designs.[2]

SUPERCHIPS

Much of the progress in information technology will continue to be based on advances in semiconductor chips, which can now contain well over three million transistors on a tiny wafer. For the past 30 years, each decade has seen computing power increase by a factor of 100 while costs have dropped by a factor of 10. Advances in science, technology, and manufacturing will enable this momentum to continue. The future will see even more "intelligence" built into everyday devices, with mainframe-like computing power packed into a device the size of a shirt pocket or notebook.

The most powerful microprocessor chips, such as Intel's 80486 and Pentium chips, Digital Equipment's Alpha, and the PowerPC, developed jointly by IBM, Motorola Inc., and Apple Computer Corp., can provide the computing power of a mainframe or super-computer. We described the capabilities of the 80486 microprocessor in section 4.3. The Focus on Technology describes the capabilities of the most powerful microprocessors that are coming into common use for workstations and high-end microcomputers for applications such as graphics, CAD/CAM, multimedia (see the following chapter), modeling, and visualization.

Computers on a chip will guide automobiles, military weaponry, robots, and everyday household items as well as large and small computers and will allow computers and related information technologies to blend data, images, and sound and send them coursing through vast networks with equal ease.[3] The Focus on People examines one effect of microminiaturization—the growing use of smart cards and the move toward a cashless society. Subsequent chapters examine other aspects of these changes and their social and business implications.

Smart cards are being used to collect tolls electronically and have become popular alternatives to coins in public telephone booths. By embedding microprocessors and memory chips that can process and store data about account balances, these plastic cards may replace cash for many kinds of payment transactions.

SOURCE: Courtesy of AT&T.

FOCUS ON PEOPLE

THE ELECTRONIC WALLET

Very soon you'll be able to fill your car with gas, pay a highway toll, park in a metered lot, eat lunch at a fast-food restaurant, shop for groceries, rent a video, and buy snacks from a vending machine without ever taking a dollar or coin from your pocket. How? The answer is debit cards and smart cards. Thanks to powerful chips and networking advances, the necessary technology already exists.

Debit cards automatically draw funds from users' bank accounts to pay for goods and services. They are being used for growing numbers of point-of-sale applications. For instance, the Safeway supermarket chain has debit card systems in all of its stores. About 100 million people currently use such cards.

Smart cards can also provide "electronic money." Smart cards look like credit cards but contain embedded microprocessors and memory chips capable of storing data, such as bank account balances or phone numbers. Sophisticated cards have over 8 kilobytes of memory. Smart cards have been popular in France, where entire communities have their own smart cards for everything from mass transportation to vacation resorts. The French smart cards, or *telecartes,* have virtually eliminated coin-operated telephone booths. When inserted into the telephone, the chip automatically deducts the cost of the call from the card until the value of the card is reduced to zero. Similar cards are catching on in the United States and other countries because they have become less costly to produce. Microprocessor technology has become so inexpensive that a company can produce a very sophisticated smart card for less than $5.00.

At Loyola University in Baltimore, Maryland, students, faculty, and staff use smart cards to pay for various items including textbooks, parking, and dining hall meals. The U.S. Marines pays soldiers at its Parris Island boot camp in South Carolina with smart cards that they can use to make purchases on base. The New York City Transit Authority uses smart cards instead of subway and bus tokens and for toll collection on its highways and bridges. Smart cards are being used to help recipients of federal aid programs to receive benefits from food stamps, Social Security, and other programs and may be used to store individuals' medical records and authorize payments for health care services.

Smart cards can be valuable for emergency medical treatment when a patient is unconscious or incoherent and family members are too distraught to provide information about medical conditions, allergies, and prescription drugs. The ambulance service and six area hospitals in Midwest City, Oklahoma, use smart card technology to provide emergency personnel with instant patient data. Local residents can purchase smart cards to store their medical data for $30. When an ambulance crew arrives at the scene of a medical emergency, responders insert patients' smart cards into handheld computers that read the smart cards to obtain data critical to split-second treatment decisions. The smart cards can also be read by desktop computers installed in the six hospitals' emergency rooms and in eight local pharmacies. Information from the smart cards can be transmitted directly to clinical and billing systems, reducing data entry errors and paperwork.

What if someone steals your smart card? Smart cards are considered more secure than conventional credit cards because the magnetic strip on a credit card can be easily copied, but some fraud will be inevitable. When people first started using smart cards to pay their fares on the New York City subway, many were double-billed because they could not swipe the cards correctly through turnstile slots. Using these cards may require a little training.

FOCUS Questions:
Suggest some other applications for smart card technology. Can smart cards and debit cards ever fully replace cash?

SOURCES: Ronald Sullivan, "Used Incorrectly, Cards Bill Subway Riders Double Fare," *The New York Times,* April 22, 1994; Bob Violino, "The Cashless Society," *InformationWEEK,* October 11, 1993; and Mitch Betts, "Smart-Card Technology Used in Lifesaving Work," *Computerworld,* December 6, 1993.

SUMMARY

- The physical hardware components of a contemporary computer system are a central processing unit, primary storage, secondary storage devices, input devices, output devices, and communications devices.

- The central processing unit, where the computer manipulates symbols, letters, and numbers, consists of an arithmetic-logic unit and a control unit. The arithmetic-logic unit performs the arithmetic and logical operations on data. The control unit controls and coordinates the other components of a computer.

- Primary storage stores program instructions and data being used by those instructions. Primary storage locations are called bytes. Each byte has a unique address in primary storage.

- Primary storage includes RAM (random-access memory) for short-term storage of data and program instructions and ROM (read-only memory) for permanent storage of important instructions. Other memory devices include PROM (programmable read-only memory) and EPROM (erasable programmable read-only memory).

- A computer represents data as a string of binary digits. Two popular binary coding standards are ASCII and EBCDIC.

- The generations of computer hardware evolution can be classified by the technology used for the computer's processing work. First-generation computers used vacuum-tube technology; second-generation, transistor technology; third-generation, integrated circuit technology; and fourth-generation, very-large-scale integrated circuit technology.

- Contemporary computers rely on very-large-scale integrated circuits and microprocessors that can accommodate an entire CPU on a single silicon chip.

- Computers can be classified as mainframes, minicomputers, and microcomputers, with special distinctions made for supercomputers and workstations.

- The capabilities of microcomputers depend on the nature of their specific microprocessors and can be gauged by their word length, bus width, and clock speed.

- RISC (Reduced Instruction Set Computing) microprocessors can achieve great speeds because they have fewer internal instructions built into their circuitry.

- Instead of relying on a central mainframe or several independent computers for processing, distributed processing distributes the processing work among multiple computers connected by a communications network.

- Microcomputers perform much of the work formerly limited to mainframes as firms switch to downsizing and cooperative processing.

- Advances in microprocessor design and parallel processing technology will produce desktop microcomputers, workstations, and supercomputers that will eclipse today's mainframes in the near future.

KEY TERMS

Computer	Machine cycle
Central processing unit (CPU)	Instruction cycle
Semiconductor chip	Execution cycle
Primary storage	Register
Byte	RAM
Address	Volatile
Arithmetic-logic unit	ROM
Control unit	Nonvolatile

PROM	Minicomputer
EPROM	Microcomputer
Millisecond	Workstation
Microsecond	Supercomputer
Nanosecond	Parallel processing
Picosecond	Flop
Kilobyte	Word length
Megabyte	Bus width
Gigabyte	Megahertz
Terabyte	RISC
Bit	Distributed processing
EBCDIC	Downloading
ASCII	Downsizing
Microprocessor	Cooperative processing
Mainframe	Massively parallel processing

REVIEW QUESTIONS

1. Name the components of a contemporary computer system and describe the function of each.
2. Name the major components of the CPU and the function of each.
3. What is the difference between RAM, ROM, PROM, and EPROM?
4. What takes place during a machine cycle?
5. Name and define the principal measures of computer time and storage capacity.
6. How are data represented in a computer?
7. Distinguish between a bit and a byte.
8. Define ASCII and EBCDIC. Why are they used?
9. List the major generations of computers and the characteristics of each.
10. Define downloading, cooperative processing, and downsizing.
11. Name and describe the factors affecting the speed and performance of a micro-processor.
12. What is reduced instruction set computing (RISC)?
13. Distinguish between serial and parallel processing.
14. Name and describe three information technology trends.

DISCUSSION QUESTIONS

1.   What is the difference between a mainframe, a minicomputer, and a micro-computer? Between a mainframe and a supercomputer? Between a microcomputer and a workstation? Are these distinctions disappearing?

2.   How will various jobs and occupations change with the growing availability and power of microprocessor technology?

PROBLEM-SOLVING EXERCISES

1.   *Group exercise:* Divide the class into groups. Assign each group to find a writeup or review of an IBM Personal System/2 microcomputer or of one of the models of the Macintosh computer. Have each group use the information in that article to write a description of its features and analyze its computing capabilities. Have each group present its findings in class.

2.   You have been asked to purchase a microcomputer for your college work. Briefly describe and analyze the criteria you would use in selecting a microcomputer.

3.   *Hands-on exercise:* The New Age Computer Outlet is a mail-order service selling many different brands of both new and used microcomputers at discount prices. Sales representatives take orders on the telephone and respond to customer inquiries about the features of the computers for sale. They often are asked questions about the microprocessors in these computers. Using the data in Table 4.3 and appropriate software, develop a small application that a sales representative could use to provide instant information about microprocessors to inquiring customers. The application should be able to provide relevant data about all microprocessors having a specified word length, bus width, clock speed, manufacturer, or combination of these features. It should also be able to list the microprocessors used in IBM and Macintosh microcomputers.

NOTES

1. "Workstation Technology Comes to Information Services," *I/S Analyzer* 31, no. 2 (February 1993).
2. Gordon Bell, "Ultracomputers: A Teraflop Before Its Time," *Communications of the ACM* 35, no. 8 (August 1992).
3. Nicholas Negroponte, "Machine Dreams," *Technology Review,* January 1992.

PROBLEM-SOLVING CASE
THE DOWNSIZING DILEMMA

Banks absolutely must use mainframe computers. Supporting hundreds of thousands and even millions of daily deposits, withdrawals, and ATM transactions requires rapid response time, reliability, and massive processing power. Yet Richmond Savings of Richmond, British Columbia, a full-service bank with over 1.1 billion Canadian dollars in assets, has no mainframes. It has no minicomputers. It has used nothing but networked microcomputers for the past seven years. Not too long ago, this would have been unthinkable.

    Now, companies ranging from paper-products conglomerates to motorcycle makers are discarding their mainframes in favor of minicomputers or networked microcomputers. United Grain Growers of Canada, a $750 million agricultural conglomerate, had been relying on an IBM mainframe system at its Winnipeg, Manitoba, headquarters and on Digital Equipment Corp. minicomputers at its 270 storage sites in three provinces. The hardware was aging. United Grain Growers wanted to give its customers better service. The company downsized to Hewlett-Packard computers as central data repositories and microcomputers with 486 microprocessors in the field. Now United Grain Growers information systems run on networks of microcomputers and minicomputers.

To cut costs, Harley-Davidson, the Milwaukee, Wisconsin, motorcycle manufacturer, shut down its National Advanced Systems mainframes, moving from a highly centralized computing environment to one of microcomputers networked with IBM AS/400 minicomputers. Observes William Bluestein, a senior analyst at Forrester Research, Inc., in Cambridge, Massachusetts, "The monopoly the mainframe had as the core processor is gone." Because microcomputers and workstations can provide so much processing horsepower at a fraction of mainframe cost, many other companies now believe that discarding mainframes will substantially lower their operating costs, too.

But there are obvious costs to replacing mainframes, such as buying microcomputers, software, and networking equipment, not to mention sizable training expenses. Software written to run on mainframes often won't run on smaller machines without extensive modification, or it may have to be completely rewritten. Over the years, hundreds of software programs have been written to help companies run critical functions on mainframes, but relatively little is available to help companies that want to run the same applications on smaller machines.

Workers accustomed to large central mainframes may require extra time and training to feel comfortable with the freedom and powerful capabilities of their desktops. When Cleveland-based TRW, Inc., eliminated the mainframe from corporate headquarters in 1991, it found that the cost of training time per employee rose from 2 percent to 6 percent of annual income. Information systems specialists may be uncomfortable working in business units with end users after spending 20 years sequestered in a centralized mainframe computer center. A poll conducted by Forrester Research found that the two most common problems in downsizing were training end users and retraining information systems specialists.

The cost of eliminating mainframe dependence may be much higher at less technologically advanced firms that use old information systems that haven't been upgraded for many years. In such cases, eliminating the mainframe could require tearing apart business operations and building a new technology foundation from scratch. Harley-Davidson, for example, had a difficult time re-educating users. The firm had not spent much on information systems during the 1980s, and employees were accustomed to small changes or none at all. When the move away from mainframes occurred, both the information systems department and business users had to re-examine the way they did business. Both groups required extensive retraining before they could use desktop systems. Harley-Davidson had initially estimated that downsizing would cut computer costs by 50 percent, but for the first few years these savings failed to materialize. Fear of such post-mainframe trauma has kept many other firms from attempting drastic downsizing.

If not managed carefully, downsizing can create another problem: inadequate computing power. Keyport Life Insurance Co. in Boston, Massachusetts, moved its insurance policy and other applications from two mainframe computers to networked microcomputers. Although the firm reported savings of $1.3 million from its annual $5 million information systems budget, it found that the machines with 386 microprocessors, which were the main computing engines of the new network, weren't powerful enough to manage their large policy load of 180,000 policies. Subsequently, Keyport had to find more powerful hardware for their network.

SOURCES: Joe Celko, "Everything You Know is Wrong," *Datamation,* January 21, 1994; Scott Leibs, "Mastering the Migration Maze," *InformationWEEK,* November 29, 1993; Bob Violino and Thomas Hoffman, "From Big Iron to Scrap Metal," *InformationWEEK,* February 10, 1992.

CASE STUDY QUESTIONS

1. What are the advantages and disadvantages of downsizing?

2. What people, organization, and technology factors must be considered when downsizing computer hardware?

3. Why is downsizing computers more than just a technical change process?

4. What kind of business firm is most likely to benefit from downsizing?

5. Some information system executives believe there will always be a place for mainframes. Do you agree?

STORAGE, INPUT, AND OUTPUT TECHNOLOGIES

LEARNING OBJECTIVES

After reading and studying this chapter, you will:

1. Know the major secondary storage technologies and be able to describe how they work.
2. Be familiar with how the major input technologies work.
3. Understand how the major output technologies work.
4. Know which storage, input, and output technology is best suited to solve certain types of problems.

*U*nited Parcel Service (UPS), the world's largest air and ground package distribution company, began in 1907 with a promise of "best service and lowest rates." UPS still strives to fulfill that promise, providing both traditional and overnight delivery of close to 3 billion parcels and documents each year to any address in the United States and to more than 180 countries and territories. How can UPS manage this immense volume of packages with such efficiency and speed? The answer lies in advanced information systems technology, with special attention to technologies for input and output.

UPS links its 1,750 offices with a network of 31,200 microcomputers connected to five mainframe computers located in its Paramus and Mahwah, New Jersey, data centers. The microcomputers are located in UPS customer service telephone centers, which take calls from customers requesting that a package be picked up or traced.

UPS replaced its familiar driver's clipboard with a hand-held, battery-powered Delivery Information Acquisition Device (DIAD). The DIAD captures customers' signatures, scans bar code tags to identify packages and their destinations, and displays the day's delivery route. It stores such input until the end of the day and then transfers the information to UPS's computer network. A Delivery Information Automated Lookup System (DIALS) stores the information entered into the DIAD, which can then be retrieved to trace a shipment or to provide proof of delivery to the customer. Previously, UPS had to track ground deliveries manually. With these technologies, UPS hopes to entirely remove paper documents—delivery records, COD slips, even time cards—from the domestic delivery process.

Related systems allow packages to be monitored at various points in the delivery process. A Package Tracking System (PTS) uses shipping information contained on the package label that is scanned with a bar code device at various points in the delivery process and fed into a central mainframe computer. Customer service representatives can then use their microcomputers to access information on the status of packages and respond immediately to customer inquiries. An Advanced Label Imaging System (ALIS) scans data from UPS Next Day Air and 2nd Day Air labels. When a customer calls, a UPS customer service representative can bring up the image of the airbill on a screen in seconds. The on-line image is exactly as it appeared when the driver recorded it on the air label. UPS's International Shipments Processing System (ISPS) supports UPS package delivery services abroad by transmitting package information directly to customs prior to the arrival of shipments, thereby expediting customs clearance.

UPS customers can even ship and track their packages themselves using systems called Maxiship and Maxitrac. These systems use a 386 microcomputer, bar-code printers for scannable labels and reports, devices to link the microcomputer to the UPS network, and an electronic scale. Customers can enter recipients' addresses into the system, print their own shipping labels, track packages, order supplies, and send complaints to top executives on their own without calling UPS for service.

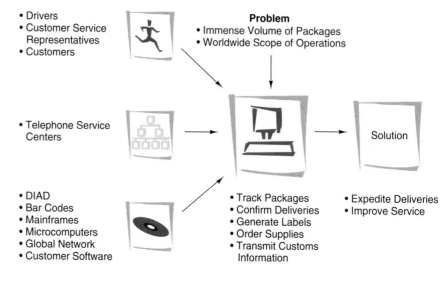

- Drivers
- Customer Service Representatives
- Customers

Problem
- Immense Volume of Packages
- Worldwide Scope of Operations

- Telephone Service Centers

Solution

- DIAD
- Bar Codes
- Mainframes
- Microcomputers
- Global Network
- Customer Software

- Track Packages
- Confirm Deliveries
- Generate Labels
- Order Supplies
- Transmit Customs Information

- Expedite Deliveries
- Improve Service

SOURCES: Lynda Radosevich, "When Overnight Isn't Good Enough," *Computerworld*, May 31, 1993, and *UPS Public Relations*, "High Tech Advances Lead UPS into the Paperless Age," April 1992.

UPS's use of bar coding, scanning, and pen-based input technology illustrates how organizations can become more efficient and competitive by using the proper input technology. Storage and output technology can play a similar role in enhancing organizational performance. In this chapter we examine the various input, storage, and output technologies and the kinds of problems they can help solve.

5.1 INTRODUCTION

Input and output devices make it possible for human beings to interact with computers. Input devices convert data, programs, or images into a form that can be processed by a computer. After the computer processes this input, output devices convert the resulting data into a form that humans can understand and use. Consequently, the speed, capacity, and ease of use of input and output devices have a direct bearing on the computer's usefulness in problem solving.

The speed and capacity of the central processing unit (CPU) differ enormously from those of the input or output devices. For instance, the CPU operates at the microsecond and nanosecond level, whereas some printers may be able to output only 40 characters per second. This means the CPU is thousands of times faster than the printer. Since the CPU processes information much faster than it can be printed out, the flow of information must be arranged in stages. (See the discussion of operating systems in Chapter 6.) Additional memory and storage devices must be placed between the CPU and the output media so that the CPU is not held back.

Storage technology is similarly important because it affects how quickly and flexibly data can be accessed and used by the CPU. Although the manner in which information is organized on storage devices will be discussed in Chapter 7, this chapter examines the major physical storage technologies themselves.

5.2 INFORMATION STORAGE TECHNOLOGY

Section 4.2 introduced the concept of primary storage, where data and program instructions are stored for immediate processing. Even in the biggest mainframes, however, the amount of data that can be kept in primary storage is very limited, and the cost of storing information there is high. Moreover, data stored in primary storage can easily be lost or destroyed if the electric power is disrupted. Therefore, unless information is needed at this very instant, it usually is stored outside primary storage.

CHARACTERISTICS OF SECONDARY STORAGE

Secondary storage refers to the relatively long-term storage of data outside the CPU and primary storage. Secondary storage is nonvolatile; that is, it will retain data even if the electric power is turned off. Secondary storage is slower than primary storage because it uses a number of electromechanical components, whereas primary storage is electronic and occurs nearly at the speed of light. Nevertheless, secondary storage media must still be able to transfer large bodies of data rapidly to primary storage. The principal secondary storage technologies are magnetic tape, magnetic disk, and optical disk.

Secondary storage
The relatively long-term storage of data outside the CPU.

MAGNETIC TAPE

Magnetic tape is the oldest of the secondary storage technologies and one of the least expensive. It is used primarily in older computer systems or when large amounts of data must be stored at very low cost. A magnetic tape is much like a tape cassette for storing music, in that records are stored in sequential order, from beginning to end.

Magnetic tape
A secondary storage medium in which data are stored by means of magnetized and nonmagnetized spots on tape; it is inexpensive and relatively stable but also is relatively slow and can only store information sequentially.

FIGURE 5.1

How a Magnetic Tape Stores Data

The number 6 is stored on magnetic tape using a unique combination of magnetized and non-magnetized spots. Each magnetized area represents a "one" bit (a 1 in EBCDIC binary code); non-magnetized areas correspond to zeros in binary representation. There is an additional parity track, containing a parity bit, for checking transmission errors.

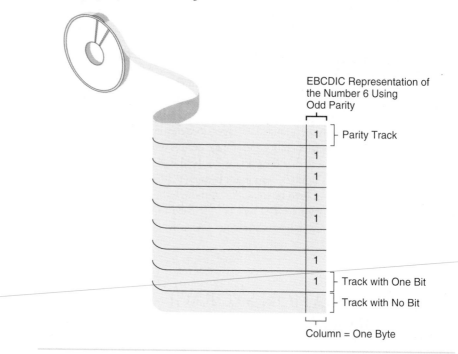

Magnetic tape comes in reels up to 14 inches in diameter with tape approximately one-half inch wide and up to 3,600 feet long (or in cartridges with ¼-inch-wide tape). Figure 5.1 shows how the number 6 is represented on magnetic tape using the EBCDIC coding scheme. Each byte of data uses one column on the tape. Each column consists of 8 bits plus a parity bit. Magnetic tapes have a range of densities for storing data, measured in bytes per inch (bpi). A low-density tape has 1,600 bpi, and a high-density tape has 6,250 bpi. A 10½-inch high-density tape reel can store up to 200–250 megabytes of data. A tape cartridge with 1,000 feet of high-density tape could store as much as 1.35 gigabytes.

The principal advantages of magnetic tape are that it is very low in cost and is a relatively stable storage medium (although the tape can age and crack over time and the environment in which it is stored must be carefully controlled). Magnetic tape is also reusable; its contents can be erased so that it can be used for storing new information. Magnetic tape is most appropriate for storing large amounts of data in a relatively stable form and when a large number of records must be processed in sequential order. It is often used as a "backup" storage medium for data in more volatile and expensive storage media like hard disks.

The disadvantages of magnetic tape are that it can only store information sequentially and that it is relatively slow. To find an individual record on magnetic tape, such as your Social Security earnings history, the tape must be read from beginning to end, one record at a time, until the desired record has been located. Magnetic tape is also very labor-intensive to mount and dismount. If a problem requires frequent access to only a few records (as opposed to accessing all or most of the records on a tape reel) and continual mounting and dismounting of tapes, it may be more cost-effective and more efficient to store information in another way, such as on magnetic disk. For example, before converting to disk technology, the Social Security Administration had 50 full-time employees who did nothing but mount and dismount more than 500,000 reels of tape. Much of the time, only a few pieces of information were accessed from each tape reel because most of the agency's work consisted of answering individual citizen's questions about their accounts.

Magnetic tape is clearly inappropriate for problems that call for rapid data access and an immediate response, such as booking airline reservations. Since information systems increasingly require immediate and direct access to data, and other mass storage alternatives have become available, conventional tape storage is a fading technology. On the other hand, magnetic tape may find new uses in the data-intense computing environment of the twenty-first century.

Microcomputers, which rely on floppy and hard disks as their principal secondary storage medium, use magnetic tape primarily to back up large volumes of data. Magnetic tape for micros comes in small cassettes similar to home recording cassettes, and the drive units (called "streaming tape" systems) can be mounted either internally or externally.

MAGNETIC DISK

The most popular and important secondary storage medium today is the **magnetic disk**. Disk technology permits direct and immediate access to data. The computer can proceed immediately to a specific record or piece of data on the disk instead of reading through records one by one. For this reason, disk technology is often referred to as **direct-access storage devices (DASD)**. There are two kinds of magnetic disks: hard disks and floppy disks.

Hard Disks   Magnetic **hard disks** are thin metallic platters—large ones are about the size of phonograph records—with an iron oxide coating. Several disks may be mounted together on a vertical shaft, where they rotate at speeds of approximately 3,500 revolutions per minute. Electromagnetic **read/write heads** are mounted on access arms. The heads fly over the spinning disks and read or write data on concentric circles called **tracks**. Data are recorded on tracks as tiny magnetized spots forming binary digits. Each track can store thousands of bytes. In most disk systems each track contains the same number of bytes with the data packed together more closely on the inner tracks. The read/write head never actually touches the disk but hovers a few thousandths or millionths of an inch above it. A smoke particle or human hair on the disk surface would cause the head to crash into the disk.

Disk storage capacity depends on the type, quantity, and arrangement of disks in a unit. Individual disk packs or fixed disk drives may have storage capacities ranging from several megabytes to several gigabytes. Microcomputer hard disks can store over 300 megabytes, but the most common sizes are 80- and 120-megabyte units.

Two popular kinds of hard disk systems are removable-pack disk systems, used with larger computers, and Winchester disk systems, used with microcomputers and minicomputers.

Removable-pack disk systems consist of hard disks stacked into a pack or indivisible unit that can be mounted and removed as a unit. They are typically found on

Magnetic disk
The most popular secondary storage medium; data are stored by means of magnetized spots on hard or floppy disks.

Direct-access storage device (DASD)
Magnetic disks, including both hard and floppy disks; called *direct access* because in this technology the computer can proceed immediately to a specific record without having to read all the preceding records.

Hard disk
Type of magnetic disk resembling a thin steel platter about the size of a phonograph record with an iron oxide coating; generally several are mounted together on a vertical shaft.

Read/write head
An electromagnetic device that reads or writes the data stored on magnetic disks.

Track
A concentric circle on a magnetic disk on which data are stored as magnetized spots; each track can store thousands of bytes.

Removable-pack disk system
Hard disks stacked into an indivisible unit called a pack that can be mounted and removed as a unit.

FIGURE 5.2

Side and Top Views of a Removable-Pack Disk System

Currently the most popular secondary storage medium, magnetic disks are an important direct-access storage device (DASD). A typical removable-pack system contains 11 two-sided disks. (There are actually only 20 surfaces in the pack on which data can be recorded, however; the top and bottom surfaces are not used since they can be damaged more easily.) Each disk contains concentric tracks; the 20 tracks located on the same vertical line form a cylinder. Data are stored in records, each of which has a unique location, or address, which references the specific cylinder, recording surface, and data record number.

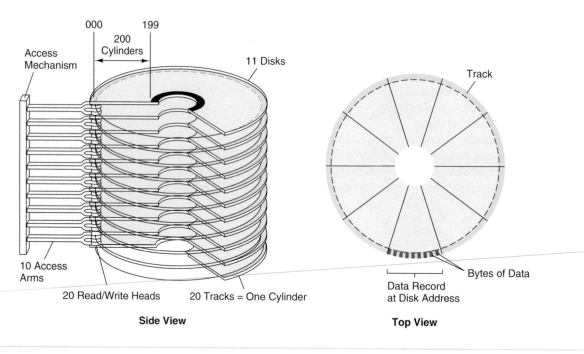

Side View   **Top View**

Cylinder

Represents circular tracks on the same vertical line within a disk pack.

Winchester disk system

A hermetically sealed unit of hard disks that cannot be removed from the disk drive.

mainframe and minicomputer systems, but some smaller units are available for microcomputers as well. A typical commercial removable disk pack has 11 disks, each with 2 surfaces (see Figure 5.2). Only 20 surfaces on the disk pack can be used for recording data, however, because the top and bottom surfaces are not used for this purpose. Each surface area, in turn, is divided into tracks where data are recorded. A **cylinder** consists of 20 circular tracks located at one position of the read/write access arms; they are on the same vertical line, one above the other. Read/write heads are directed to a specific record using a disk address consisting of the cylinder number, the recording surface number, and the data record number.

　　　Winchester disk systems do not differ in principle from removable-pack disk systems. The primary difference is that Winchester disks are hermetically sealed units that cannot be removed from the disk drive. They are typically used in microcomputers. Because they are hermetically sealed from dust in the environment, Winchester disks can achieve very high rotation speeds and smaller distances between the disks and the read/write heads. These advantages translate into high-speed access times: many Winchester disk units can retrieve information in 15 to 25 milliseconds (thousandths of a second). At the same time, because they are sealed, Winchester disks cannot be replaced with an empty disk once they are full. Instead, the user must transfer the information to some other storage device, such as a backup tape or floppy disk, or write over the existing disk. In recent years, high-speed, high-capacity fixed disk drives have been used for mainframe systems as well. A disk technology called **RAID (Redundant Array of Inexpensive Disks)** is also providing a high-performance alternative to fixed disk drives. RAID devices package more than 100 small 5¼-inch disk drives, a controller chip, and specialized software in one large unit. In contrast to traditional disk drives, which deliver data from the disk drive along a single path, RAID technology delivers data over multiple paths simultaneously to produce a faster disk access time. If one RAID drive fails, other drives are available to deliver data, making the technology potentially more reliable than traditional disk drives.

Disk access time refers to the speed at which data can be located on the disks and loaded into primary storage or written onto a disk device. It is determined by three factors: (1) the access motion time, which is the time required to position the read/write head on the cylinder where the required data are stored; (2) the rotational delay, which is the time required for the disk to rotate so that the read/write head is positioned where the required data are stored; and (3) the data transfer rate, which is the time needed to read the data from the disk and transfer them to primary storage (or transfer them from the computer to the disk). Sophisticated commercial disks have access times of 1–10 milliseconds, but typical microcomputer hard disks require 15–20 milliseconds. The data transfer rate ranges from 200,000 to 4 million bytes per second, depending on the speed of the disk and other factors.

Magnetic disks offer several advantages. Individual records can be accessed directly within milliseconds because they have a precise disk address. Thus disk technology permits solutions to problems requiring immediate access to data, such as airline reservation systems or customer information systems. Moreover, as we discuss in Chapter 7, disk storage permits records and pieces of related data to be organized and combined easily.

The principal drawbacks of disk technology are the need for backup, susceptibility to environmental disturbances, and cost. In disk technology there is only one copy of the information because the old record on the disk is written over if the record is changed. In contrast, record or file changes on magnetic tape are made on a different reel of tape, so the old version of the tape can be retained (and recovered). Disk technology also requires a pure and stable environment, since smoke or other particles can cause a disk pack to "crash." Technical advances have boosted disk storage capacity while reducing cost, but it is still much more expensive than magnetic tape.

Floppy Disks   Floppy disks are used primarily with microcomputers. These disks, which are round, flexible, and very inexpensive, are an ideal medium for storing data and programs that are not in constant use or for transporting data and programs. Floppy disks are available in 5¼ and 3½ inches (see Figure 5.3). The 5¼-inch disk used to be the most popular, but the 3½-inch disk has become the standard.

Floppy disks use a **sector method for storing data.** The disk surface is divided into eight or nine wedges like a pie; the actual number depends on the disk system used (see Figure 5.4). In most disks, each sector has the same storage capacity, since data are recorded more densely on the inner disk tracks. Each sector is assigned a unique number. Data can be located by using an address consisting of the sector number and an individual data record number.

The Apple Macintosh disk system varies the number of sectors on a single disk by adding sectors to the outer tracks so that all sectors take up the same space over the entire disk surface. This has increased the storage capacity on Apple's 3½-inch floppy disk by over 40 percent compared with earlier Macintosh disks.

Floppy disk storage capacities vary, depending on whether the disk stores data on only one side (these are called **single-sided disks**) or on both sides (**double-sided disks**), the disk's data-recording density, the track density, and whether the disk drive

RAID (Redundant Array of Inexpensive Disks)
High-performance disk storage technology that can deliver data over multiple paths simultaneously by packaging more than 100 smaller disk drives with a controller chip and specialized software in a single large box.

Disk access time
The speed at which data can be located on magnetic disks and loaded into primary storage or written onto a disk device.

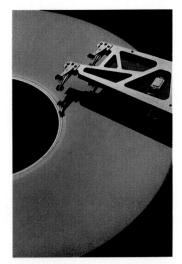

The read/write head of a hard disk flies over the spinning disk, never touching it.
Source: Courtesy of Amdahl Corporation.

Floppy disks
Flexible, inexpensive magnetic disks used as a secondary storage medium; primarily used with microcomputers.

Sector method for storing data
A method of storing data on floppy disks in which the disk is divided into pie-shaped pieces, or sectors; each sector has a unique number that becomes part of the address.

Single-sided disk
A floppy disk on which data can be stored on only one side.

Double-sided disk
A floppy disk on which data can be stored on both sides.

FIGURE 5.3

5¼-Inch and 3½-Inch Floppy Disks

Floppy disks (so called because they are flexible) are usually used with microcomputers. Each disk is encased in a protective plastic jacket pierced by an opening. The computer's read/write head "reads" the data on the disk through this opening. The 5¼-inch size is still in use, but it has been overtaken by its 3½-inch counterpart. The smaller disks can actually store more information (see Table 5.1), and their more durable construction protects the data better.

(a) 5 1/4" Disk

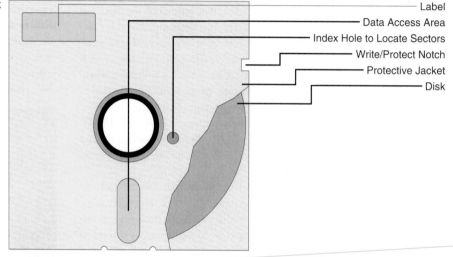

- Label
- Data Access Area
- Index Hole to Locate Sectors
- Write/Protect Notch
- Protective Jacket
- Disk

(b) 3 1/2" Disk

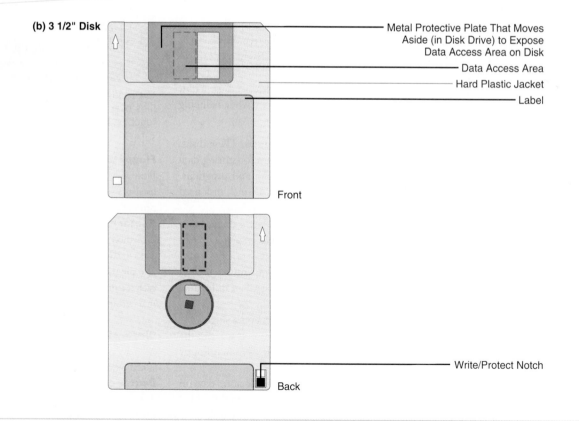

- Metal Protective Plate That Moves Aside (in Disk Drive) to Expose Data Access Area on Disk
- Data Access Area
- Hard Plastic Jacket
- Label

Front

Write/Protect Notch

Back

FIGURE 5.4

The Sector Method: How a Floppy Disk Stores Data

Like hard disks, floppy disks contain concentric tracks where data are stored as magnetized bits. In addition, the disk surface is divided into triangular sectors, each of which has a unique number. Data can be accessed directly by using an address that includes the sector and data record number. Some manufacturers divide disks into nine sectors, as shown here; others divide them into eight.

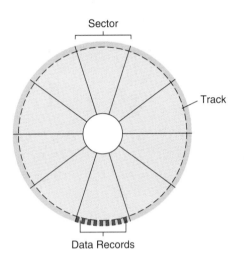

has read/write heads for the top and bottom surfaces of the disk. **Recording density** refers to the number of bits per inch that can be written on the surface of the disk; disks are characterized as single density, double density, and quad-density. The 3½-inch disk, for example, can store more data than the 5¼-inch disk and is more portable and durable. Table 5.1 shows the range of storage capacities for the various floppy disk sizes.

OPTICAL DISK TECHNOLOGY

Using a laser device that records data by burning microscopic pits in a spiral track, **optical disks** (also called compact disks or laser optical disks) store data at densities much greater than those of magnetic disks. There are two basic ways in which information is placed on an optical disk. The most common way is by using a small laser to burn permanent pits into the surface of the plastic optical disk (called an ablative technique). The resulting pattern of pits and clear surface is used to define a single bit of information. A pit can be defined as a "0" and a clear area as a "1." A small reading laser is used to read the pattern of bits. (See Figure 5.5.)

Recording density
The number of bits per inch that can be written on the surface of a magnetic disk.

Optical disk
A disk on which data are recorded and read by laser beams rather than by magnetic means; such disks can store data at densities much greater than magnetic disks.

TABLE 5.1

Floppy Disk Storage Capacities

Disk Size	Storage Capacity
3½ inch	720 K to 2.8 megabytes
5¼ inch	360K to 1.2 megabytes

FIGURE 5.5

How a WORM Drive Works

To write data on a Write Once, Read Many (WORM) optical disk drive, a high-power laser beam (panel a) heats the disk substrate, leaving a permanent pit on its surface for a binary 0 and leaving the disk surface smooth and reflective for a binary 1. A low-power laser (panel b) is used to read the data. The laser reflects from areas with no pits to read a binary 1. The pits diffuse the laser, creating no reflection, to read a binary 0.

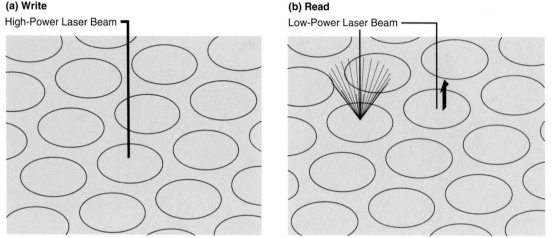

(a) Write
High-Power Laser Beam

(b) Read
Low-Power Laser Beam

Massive quantities of data can be stored in a highly compact form on optical disks. For example, a 4.75-inch optical disk can store up to 660 megabytes, equivalent to the storage capacity of 300 high-density floppy disks. Consequently, optical disks are most appropriate for problems requiring enormous quantities of data to be stored compactly for easy retrieval.

The second technique, used for rewritable optical disks, employs a laser and a magnetic field to melt and magnetize tiny areas on the surface of an optical disk. The magneto-optical disk consists of layers of magnetic film deposited on a rotating disk substrate. A strong laser beam strikes the disk as it rotates, heating a microscopic spot and causing atoms in the recording layer of the disk to form into a magnetized zone representing one bit of data. The size of each spot determines whether it represents a 0 or a 1. To read the disk, a weaker laser beam scans the magnetized spots. This beam is reflected to a photodetector that converts the variations in spot size into binary data.

CD-ROM

An optical disk system used with microcomputers; it is a form of read-only storage in that data can only be read from it, not written to it; stands for Compact Disk/Read-Only Memory.

The optical disk system most often used with microcomputers is called **CD-ROM** (**Compact Disk/Read-Only Memory**). CD-ROM is read-only storage, which means that no new data can be written to it; it can only be read. CD-ROM has been most widely used for reference materials with massive amounts of data, such as encyclopedias, directories, and large databases. For example, financial data from Quotron, Dun & Bradstreet, and Dow Jones are available on CD-ROM, as are titles such as *Street Atlas U.S.A.*, which provides street-level maps for every square mile of the United States. Microsoft's Bookshelf places eight reference books, including the *American Heritage Dictionary, The Columbia Dictionary of Quotations*, and *The Original Roget's Thesaurus*, on one CD-ROM. CD-ROM is also becoming popular for storing images (described in later chapters) and for interactive entertainment and multimedia (see Section 5.5).[1]

WORM

An optical disk system in which data can be recorded only once on the disk by users and cannot be erased; stands for Write Once, Read Many.

WORM (**Write Once, Read Many**) optical disk systems allow users to record data only once on an optical disk. Once written, the data cannot be erased, but they can be read indefinitely. WORM has been used as an alternative to microfilm for archiving digitized document images. For instance, California's Department of Motor Vehicles used

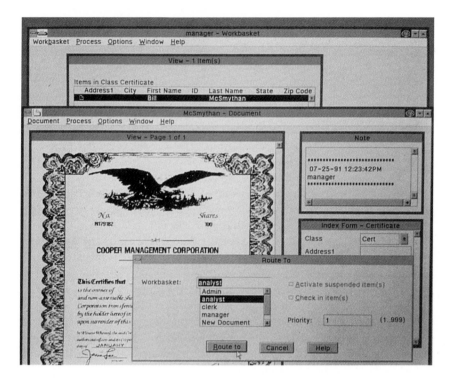

Documents with text, images, and color illustrations can be stored on a CD-ROM and easily retrieved. Because a single CD-ROM can store vast quantities of data, the technology is often used for storing books, encyclopedias, and reference manuals and for interactive multimedia applications.

SOURCE: Courtesy of International Business Machines Corporation.

WORM media to store pictures, signatures, and fingerprints so that no one could tamper with permanent information.

Erasable, rewritable optical disks are becoming faster and cheaper than tape storage. Optical disk drives operate at around 200 to 500 milliseconds, much faster than the 60 seconds required for a person to mount a tape and up to 30 minutes to read an entire tape. Erasable optical disks can also be more reliable than magnetic disks. Since they use laser beams instead of mechanical read/write heads to read and record data, they are immune to "head crashes." They also are not as easily affected as magnetic disks by stray magnetic fields (which can alter data). Magneto-optical disks are the most popular erasable optical disk technology.

Through special software with electronic search features and techniques for organizing data on CD-ROM, individual pieces of information become easy to retrieve (see the discussion of files and databases in Chapter 7). Herein lies another advantage of optical disk technology: it makes information more accessible for problem solving. In seconds, one can wade through vast amounts of data to find the right quotation or zip code or the correct meaning of a term.

5.3 INPUT TECHNOLOGY

As the opening vignette of this chapter illustrates, the nature of input technology affects processing and the way an entire information system can perform. The input technologies discussed here support several alternative approaches to data input. In selecting an input technology, an organization must decide not only how it wants to capture data for input but when and how it wants to process and use the data it has entered.

BATCH VERSUS ON-LINE INPUT AND PROCESSING

The manner in which data are collected for input is closely tied to processing. In **batch input and processing**, data are collected in the form of source documents such as orders or payroll time cards; these are accumulated and stored for a period of time in groups called batches. Then the batches of documents are keyed into the computer and stored in computer-usable form as a transaction file until they are needed for processing; that may be a few hours or a few weeks or even months later. Finally, the batch is processed as a group in a computer job (see Figure 5.6). The output is created only when new batches are processed. This was the earliest approach to input and processing and is still used today for processing payrolls and utility bills.

In contrast, with **on-line input**, data are immediately captured for computer processing instead of being collected and stored on source documents. In **on-line real-time processing,** the data are processed immediately upon input into the system. There is no waiting, and output and information stored by the system are always up-to-date. Airline reservation systems, which must respond immediately to new data, require an on-line real-time approach.

In on-line input with delayed processing, data are directly translated into computer-usable form, but they are not processed immediately. Instead, the data are held in temporary storage until scheduled processing occurs. For instance, some merchandise catalog sales firms input orders directly into terminals as the orders are taken over the telephone. The computer holds the orders in a transaction file until the end of the day, when they are all processed together.

TRADITIONAL DATA ENTRY

Traditionally, data have been input through a keyboard. In the past, data entry clerks used a **keypunch** machine to code their data onto 80-column punched cards; each character was identified by a unique punch in a specific location on the card. Another alternative was a **key-to-tape** or **key-to-disk** machine that allowed data to be keyed directly onto a magnetic tape or magnetic disk for computer processing. Such methods are being discarded in favor of more direct methods of entering data. Data can now be entered directly into a computer system by using a keyboard and computer terminal or by using new interactive tools such as touch screens, digitizing tablets, the computer mouse, pen-based input, and voice input.

TOUCH SCREENS

Touch screens allow limited amounts of data to be entered by touching the surface of a sensitized video display monitor with a finger or a pointer. The operator makes selections by touching specified parts of the screen. Although the applications of touch screens are limited at present, they are easy to use and appeal to persons who are not familiar with a keyboard. Stores, banks, restaurants, and some offices use them.

DIGITIZING TABLETS

Digitizing tablets are frequently used for graphics work and computer-aided design. They allow people to write, draw, and trace designs on a pressure-sensitive tablet using an electronic stylus or a puck (a hand-held pointing device with a small glass window and intersecting crosshairs).

Batch input and processing

An approach to input and processing in which data are grouped together as source documents before being input; once they are input, they are stored as a transaction file before processing, which occurs some time later.

On-line input

An input approach in which data are input into the computer as they become available rather than being grouped as source documents.

On-line real-time processing

A type of processing in which data are processed as soon as they are input into the system rather than being stored for later processing.

Keypunch

An early form of inputting data in which data were coded onto 80-column cards, with each location on the card representing a character.

Key-to-tape/key-to-disk

A form of inputting in which data are keyed directly onto magnetic tape or magnetic disk.

Touch screen

A sensitized video display screen that allows data to be input by touching the screen surface with a finger or pointer.

Digitizing tablet

Input device that allows people to write, draw, or trace designs on a pressure-sensitive tablet using an electronic stylus or puck. Used for graphics work and computer-aided design.

FIGURE 5.6

Three Different Approaches to Input and Processing

When choosing an input technology, a firm must also decide how it wants to process the input data and how up-to-date the output and data stored in the system must be. The oldest approach is batch processing, in which source documents are collected and entered into the computer as a batch, or group. There they are stored in a transaction file, and eventually the entire batch will be processed together. Thus the system is only updated when each batch is completed. With another option, on-line real-time processing, data are processed immediately as they are entered, so the system is constantly updated. A third approach combines the first two: data are entered immediately but are stored temporarily in a transaction file. At scheduled intervals the computer processes the new input.

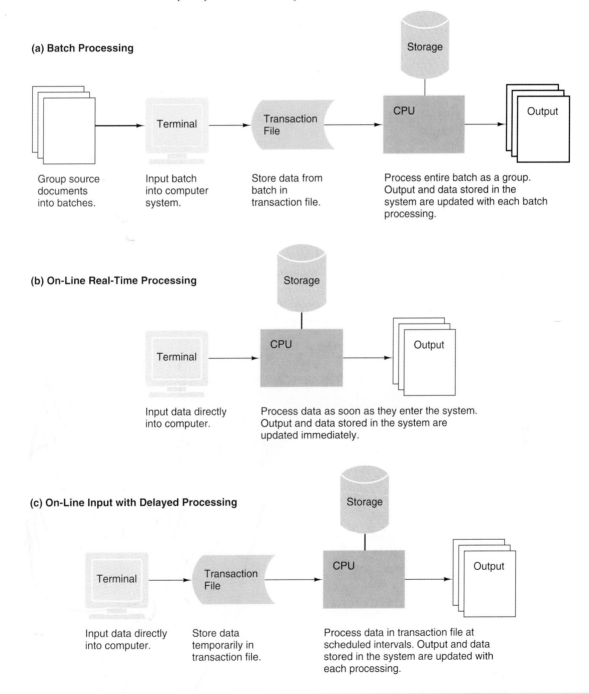

(a) Batch Processing

Storage — Terminal — Transaction File — CPU — Output

Group source documents into batches.

Input batch into computer system.

Store data from batch in transaction file.

Process entire batch as a group. Output and data stored in the system are updated with each batch processing.

(b) On-Line Real-Time Processing

Storage — Terminal — CPU — Output

Input data directly into computer.

Process data as soon as they enter the system. Output and data stored in the system are updated immediately.

(c) On-Line Input with Delayed Processing

Storage — Terminal — Transaction File — CPU — Output

Input data directly into computer.

Store data temporarily in transaction file.

Process data in transaction file at scheduled intervals. Output and data stored in the system are updated with each processing.

THE COMPUTER MOUSE

Computer mouse

A hand-held device that can be moved on a desk top to control the position of the cursor on a video display screen.

The **computer mouse** is a hand-held device connected to the computer by a cable; the mouse can be moved around on a desk top to control the position of the cursor on a video display screen. Once the cursor is in the desired location, the operator can push a button on the mouse to make a selection. The mouse can also be used to "draw" images on the graphics display screen. The "point and click" capability of the electric mouse is an alternative to keyboard and text-based commands.

A computer track ball is an inverted mouse that performs the same function as a mouse. A track ball unit has a small ball in a housing over which the user's palm can move. As the ball rotates in any direction, the screen cursor follows. The user selects elements on the screen by pushing a button or, on some units, depressing the track ball slightly.

PEN-BASED INPUT

Pen-based input

Input devices that accept handwritten input by allowing users to print directly on a sensitized screen using a pen-like stylus.

Handwriting recognition devices such as pen-based "tablets" or "notebooks" are emerging input technologies with many promising applications. These devices usually consist of a flat-screen display tablet and a penlike stylus. With **pen-based input,** users print directly on the tablet-sized screen. The screen, a liquid-crystal display similar to those on conventional laptop microcomputers, is fitted with an additional transparent layer composed of a grid of fine wires. The screen detects the presence of the special stylus, which emits a faint signal from its tip. The screen grows darker wherever the stylus touches. The screen can also interpret gestures made with the stylus such as tapping and flicking. Styluses come in both wireless and tethered versions. Letters and numbers written by users on the tablet can be recognized and changed into digital form, where they can be stored or processed and analyzed. The opening vignette about United Parcel Service described some of the benefits of this technology, but drawbacks remain, as the Focus on Technology explains.

Weighing less than 1 pound, the Apple Newton personal digital assistant uses pen-based input to transform handwritten notes into appointments and typeset documents. This handheld electronic organizer can schedule meetings and send documents to printers, fax machines, or microcomputers.

SOURCE: Courtesy of Apple Computer, Inc.

FOCUS ON TECHNOLOGY

IS THE PEN MIGHTIER THAN THE KEYBOARD?

Pen-based input to computers has a strong appeal—familiarity and ease of use. We have written by hand for many centuries; in contrast, keyboard writing is relatively new. Many people still do not have this skill or are uncomfortable with it.

Equally important, computers could be used more widely if the user were not burdened with a keyboard. Some occupations (e.g., insurance adjusting, financial consulting, sales, and maintenance) require forms that make use of a keyboard extremely difficult. Such occupations frequently require employee mobility, so that carrying a keyboard is simply too clumsy to be useful. People in other mobile lines of work, such as waiters, truck drivers, and journalists, also rely on ordinary notepads or appointment calendars because a keyboard is too ungainly to replace the pen. Pen-based computers could prove useful for people who don't like to use a keyboard or who need to fill out forms on the go.

Instead of a keyboard or mouse, pen-based computers use a stylus that looks and feels like a pen. People use the stylus to print directly on a tablet-sized screen. The writing is instantly captured and translated into digital form as if you had entered it with a keyboard. The stylus combines the best attributes of a mouse and a keyboard. You can use it not only to choose the software or document you want but also to edit or enter text or numbers. Tapping with the stylus on the name of a

document brings it up on the screen. Flicking the stylus at the bottom edge of the screen instructs the computer to scroll through long documents. Some pen-based models allow the user to draw pictures as easily as on paper. The computer straightens out wobbly lines and makes circles perfectly round.

Yet pen-based input is having trouble catching on. The basic problem with pen-based technology is the need to "recognize" cursive script in order to translate it into the binary code (such as ASCII or EBCDIC) that computers use to store each letter or number. We face a similar problem when we try to figure out the meaning of someone else's "scrawl" (or even our own at times). To accomplish this difficult task, the computer has some fundamental barriers to overcome. First, no two people write exactly alike. In fact, no individual writes exactly alike every time. This lack of human precision has proven to be a major stumbling block for a technology that is based on simple on/off (digital) distinctions. Second, while human beings can use the context of a word or letter to help them decipher it, computers have no such context knowledge to draw upon. Think of the creative newspaper headlines that we are able to decipher only because we know about current events and because we are used to the stylistic conventions of headline writing. Computers have no such knowledge. Another problem, the tremendous amounts of computing power required by handwriting applications, is being alleviated as newer, more powerful chips continue to appear.

Today's pen-based computers rely on recognition of hand-printed letters. Even this technology remains problematic, however, because hand-printed letters vary enough that block-print recognition is only 90–95 percent accurate. As a result, the user must correct

one of every 10 or 20 letters, a nuisance so great that many users abandon the technology altogether. Cursive recognition presents far greater problems.

Ronjon Nag, co-founder of Lexicus, a Palo Alto, California, company dedicated to developing software to solve computer handwriting problems, demonstrates his company's developing technology by writing the word *longhand* on a digitized tablet. Immediately the handwritten word appears on the screen; almost instantly, the word appears above it in standard computer print. Clearly Lexicus has made progress. However, if he then writes the word *Longhand,* the only difference being the capitalization of the *L*, the computer is stumped.

In August, 1993 Apple Computer released its palm-sized personal digital assistant, the Newton, which was supposed to be able to read handwriting. However, the Newton quickly gained a reputation for being rather mistake-prone and only sold at the rate of 12,500 per month during its first few months.

Apple and Lexicus are optimistic about solving the problems of pen-based computing and clearly have made progress, as have other companies. Many computer tasks, such as filling out a form or requesting a piece of data, require only a few numbers or words. With some additional refinements, pen-based computers will probably be widespread in industries that require mobility in their employees.

FOCUS Questions:
Name other occupations in which pen-based technology would be useful. What uses, not related to your occupation, could you personally find for such technology? What people, organization, and technology factors would you consider in deciding whether to use pen-based computers?

SOURCES: John Markoff, "Computers Advance Rapidly Back to the Pen," *The New York Times,* January 6, 1993, and "Marketer's Dream, Engineer's Nightmare," *The New York Times,* December 12, 1993.

VOICE INPUT

Voice input

Input devices that convert the spoken word into digital form.

Voice input devices convert spoken words into digital form. Special voice recognition software (see Chapter 6) compares the electrical patterns produced by the speaker's voice to a set of prerecorded patterns. If the patterns match, the input is accepted. This technology is still in its infancy. Most voice systems have limited "vocabularies" of several hundred to a thousand words and can accept only very simple commands. Even with limitations, however, this technology is already useful for simple applications or for assisting people with handicaps. For instance, the U.S. Postal Service uses a voice recognition system to expedite mail sorting. Users can speak ZIP codes instead of keying them in, leaving their hands free to sort packages. The Focus on Problem Solving describes how voice input and some other advanced input technologies have helped disabled people to contribute and communicate.

SOURCE DATA AUTOMATION

Traditional data input methods involve multiple steps, human intervention, and the handling of data as they are converted from one form to another. Not only can transcription errors occur at several points, but all the extra handling and duplicate effort add to costs. The most advanced data input technology focuses on **source data automation**, in which machine-readable data are generated at their point of origin.

Source data automation

Advanced forms of data input technology that generate machine-readable data at their point of origin; includes optical character recognition, magnetic ink character recognition, digitizers, and voice input.

The leading source data automation technologies—magnetic ink character recognition, optical character recognition, digitizers, and sensors—are more rapid and accurate than traditional input methods because they collect machine-readable data at the time the data are created. Such technologies eliminate the need for special data entry staff and are more accurate than keying in data. The error rate for bar code scanners, for example, is less than 1 in 10,000 transactions (keypunchers make up to 1 error per 1,000 keystrokes).

Magnetic ink character recognition (MICR)

A form of source data automation in which a MICR reader identifies characters written in magnetic ink; used primarily for check processing.

Magnetic ink character recognition (MICR) technology is used primarily by the banking industry for processing massive numbers of checks. The characters in the lower left portion of the check in Figure 5.7 are preprinted in special magnetic ink to indicate the bank identification number, the checking account number, and the check number. After the check has been cashed and sent to the bank for processing, a MICR reader senses the MICR characters on the check and feeds them into the computer. The amount of the check, which is written in ordinary ink, must be keyed in by hand.

Optical character recognition (OCR)

A form of source data automation in which optical scanning devices read specially designed data off source documents and translate the data into digital form for the computer; bar codes are an example of OCR technology.

Optical character recognition (OCR) devices read marks, characters, and codes and translate them into digital form for the computer. Optical character reading devices reflect light off characters on source documents and convert them into digital patterns that the computer can recognize. Only characters printed using special fonts can be read. For example, the optical reader will read only the optical characters on a charge account bill, not the characters in regular type. As the reader optically scans the data on the bill, it passes them immediately to the computer. The number of fonts that can be optically scanned has increased as OCR technology has grown more sophisticated.

Bar code

Specially designed bar characters that can be read by OCR scanning devices; used primarily on price tags and supermarket items.

Universal Product Code

A coding scheme in which bars and the width of space between them represent data that can be read by OCR scanning devices; frequently used in bar codes.

The most widely used optical code is the **bar code**, which can be found on supermarket items, clothing price tags, and other items. Scanning devices built into countertops or hand-held wands are employed to read the bar codes. Bar codes frequently utilize a **Universal Product Code** that records data based on the width of the bars and the space between them. The codes include manufacturer and product identification numbers (see Figure 5.8). Some point-of-sale systems, such as those found at Shoprite supermarket checkout counters, capture bar-coded data and use them to obtain the item's price from the firm's computer system. These data can also immediately update the firm's sales and inventory records.

FOCUS ON PROBLEM SOLVING

ENABLING THE DISABLED

How can someone who is totally paralyzed hold a job in a major corporation—and be productive? Mike Ward is an editor at Intel Corp., the giant maker of computer chips. He edits articles written by engineers about failure analyses of components used in various high-technology projects for *Failure Analysis Summit,* an Intel newsletter. Ward could not hold his job without a mix of technologies that allow him to communicate not only with his colleagues at Intel but with his computer.

Ward was diagnosed seven years ago with Lou Gehrig's disease, or amyotrophic lateral sclerosis, which progressively destroys the motor neurons that control all a person's muscles. He has been confined to a wheelchair for five years and can move only his eyeballs. He requires a ventilator to breathe and must be fed artificially. But his mind is fully productive. The key technologies that allow him to work are input and output devices that enable him to communicate with the computer which, in turn, communicates with others for him.

Because he can communicate only with eye movement, that became the key to input. LC Technologies, Inc., of Fairfax, Virginia, sells the Eyegaze computer system, which reads eye movement with great precision. The system

uses a low-power infrared system mounted below the computer monitor. The system illuminates the eye lens and takes a picture 30 times per second. It can detect where the person is looking to within one-fourth of an inch, allowing the user to activate keys as small as five-eighths of an inch. A key is "pressed" by the user looking at a key for one-quarter of a second or longer. The screen Ward uses contains a keyboard and other symbols as well to allow him to accomplish other tasks—typing, turning on lights or television, even "speaking" on the telephone. The keyboard emulator is Words+ Software Keyboard Emulator from Word+, Inc., in Palmdale, California. "I can't do anything myself," says Ward (via his computer). But, he adds, "This allows me as much control as I want." He claims the system works so well and fast that he can now write using full sentences and punctuation without a loss of time. To do his writing and editing, he uses an ordinary Compaq PC microcomputer running standard software.

In order to "talk," Ward uses a special text-to-speech output system called MultiVoice TM from the Institute of Applied Technology of the Children's Hospital in Boston. This system runs on a Toshiba 1200 HP laptop microcomputer that is mounted to his wheelchair. His MultiVoice speaks with a deep voice, although the quality and intonation of the voice can be adjusted.

Finally, to communicate with the rest of Intel's employees and to send and receive documents, he needs to use the same communication system they use, Intel's E-mail system. His Compaq PC

is connected to a corporate Digital Equipment Corp. VAX minicomputer, which is his gateway to the corporate E-mail system.

The three basic input/output systems he uses have very different origins. E-mail, of course, developed in response to a general need for intraorganizational communication. Eyegaze had a very different origin—the U.S. Air Force. It was developed to track a pilot's eye movements while the pilot sights a target. The text-to-speech system was developed within a medical environment to deal with the loss of the ability to speak.

Other disabled people are using new input/output technologies to start their own businesses. Don Dalton, who is paralyzed from the chest down and confined to a wheelchair, started Micro Overflow Corp. in his garage. He relied heavily on a microcomputer, initially operating the keyboard with a stick held in his mouth. Now he uses a microphone in a headset connected to the microcomputer and can activate all the computer's functions by voice, type 100 words per minute, and manage the company's finances and scheduling. Micro Overflow is a distributorship that adapts computer technology for the disabled. Dalton is helping other disabled entrepreneurs to profit from computer technology, just as he did.

FOCUS Question:
Suggest other computer systems that have been or could be developed to aid people with various disabilities, such as blindness, deafness, or the inability to walk.

SOURCES: Thomas Hoffman, "Knocking Down Barriers," *Computerworld,* August 30, 1993, and Timothy L. O'Brien, "Aided by Computers, Many of the Disabled Form Own Business," *The Wall Street Journal,* October 8, 1993.

Bar codes are used not only in supermarkets and warehouses but also in hospitals, libraries, military operations, transportation facilities, and every kind of manufacturing operation. For example, bar codes are used for the 2,500 items stocked by the pharmacy at Detroit's Henry Ford Hospital. Because bar codes can contain other useful pieces of

FIGURE 5.7

Checks: A Common Application for Magnetic Ink Character Recognition (MICR)

MICR is a common method of source data automation; it creates machine-readable data directly on the document. Banks, for instance, use checks with characters preprinted in magnetic ink that identify the bank and checking account number. A MICR reader "reads" the characters by identifying their shapes. This and other methods of source data automation eliminate the error-prone step of keying data into a computer.

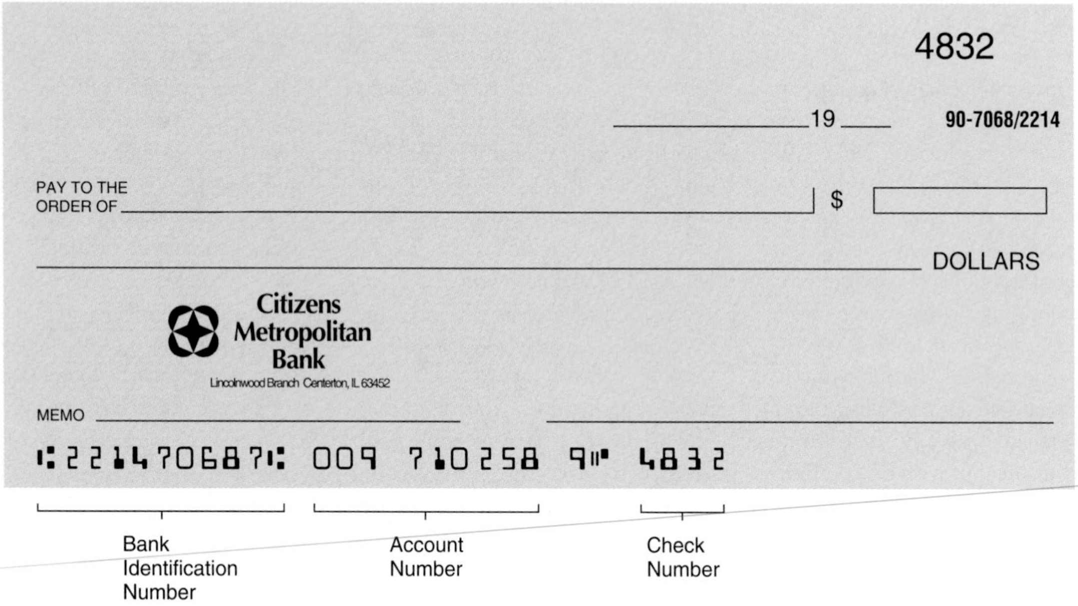

information, such as time, date, and location data in addition to identification data, they can be used to track an item, analyze its movement, and calculate what has happened to it during production or other processes.

To implement OCR technology successfully, input data must be carefully designed and organized. This subject is explored in the Focus on Organizations.

Image Processing and Digitized Images   Image processing is the use of computers and related equipment like digital scanners and high-resolution printers to enter, store, process, and distribute images such as pictures or documents. Image processing requires that an image be digitized or transformed into a series of digital bits so it can be processed by a computer. A scanner is a device that digitizes an image. Imaging technology is starting to be used extensively for solving business problems in which images as well as text must be captured in digital form. Chapter 14 describes imaging's new role in the business world.

Sensors

Devices that collect data directly from the environment for input into the computer.

Sensors   Sensors collect data directly from the environment for input into a computer system. For instance, sensors are used in General Motors cars with on-board computers and screens that display the map of the surrounding area and the driver's route. Sensors in each wheel and a magnetic compass supply information to the computer for determining the car's location. The South Coast Air Quality Management District's system uses sensors in smokestacks to supply data for monitoring pollution emissions. The

FIGURE 5.8

Bar Codes: The Most Commonly Used Optical Code

You are no doubt familiar with the bar code, which is used to identify merchandise ranging from designer clothing to dog food. Optical codes consist of special fonts, or shapes, that are converted into digital form by optical character recognition (OCR) devices. Here we see a common type of bar code, the Universal Product Code, which identifies each product with a unique code based on the width of the bars and the spaces between them. The codes include manufacturer and product identification numbers.

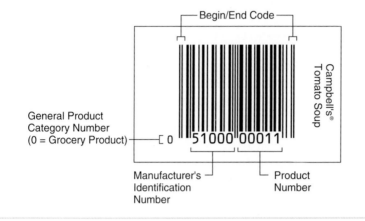

sensors continuously measure emissions; they are linked to microcomputers at the site of each smokestack that send the data collected by the sensors to the district's central computer for analysis.

5.4 OUTPUT TECHNOLOGY

When computers were in their infancy and performed only batch processing, printers were the primary output medium. Today, there are many more options for displaying

Speech scientist Vladimir Sejnoha carefully analyzes Kurzweil applied intelligence voice recognition software for mistakes. The screen displays the pattern made when the word *baby* is spoken. Voice input technology is useful for applications where the input consists of simple spoken commands.

SOURCE: © Hank Morgan, Rainbow.

FOCUS ON ORGANIZATIONS

DESIGNING FORMS TO AUTOMATE DATA ENTRY

Automating data entry often results in greatly increased productivity for organizations. Witness Florida's Department of Emergency Medical Services (EMS), which decided to automate its handwritten emergency reports. These reports are written by more than 8,000 emergency medical personnel and paramedics responding to accidents and other medical emergencies. Until recently, EMS could examine only a fraction of the paper reports they received. EMS could only review 200,000 trauma reports per year and were forced to ignore all other emergency reports. They now use Paper Keyboard ICR from Datacap, Inc. of Tarrytown, New York, a computer-aided data entry system that uses OCR to read in data from hand print on one side of a form and checked boxes on the other side.

Although the new forms contain more than three times as much data as the old manual forms, the agency can now examine more than1.5 million records per year (their total load in 1993 was approximately 1.2 million). However, like many companies, EMS found it had to redesign its input forms to take advantage of the benefits of automation. They had to determine what new data to include and how to set up the form. One important design change was to put all handwriting on one side of the form and all spaces for check marks on the other. At the end of the redesign process they found they were unable to move to a totally automated approach and that a combination of technologies was required.

When companies redesign forms for OCR, they are wise to seek recommendations from the people who will actually fill in the forms. The Illinois Department of Public Aid, which began using OCR in 1978, today handles more than 12 million medical forms annually. Over the years they have recognized the need for regularly modifying their forms in response to changing demands for the inclusion of new data items. Rather than strictly controlling their forms' content and appearance, the Department works with medical providers from across the state in the redesign process. Because the Department has learned that the number of required items increases over time, extra spaces are included on the form to give it room to expand.

Kristy Holch, director of scanning market strategies at BIS Strategic Decisions in Norwell, Massachusetts, says that organizations must be willing to redesign forms if they choose OCR data entry. "OCR is a very simple thing," she says, "when it is in a controlled environment." And Mark Blau, president of Datacap, warns that "As soon as you get into forms redesign, it sort of opens a Pandora's Box. Document forms are an organizational identity, and when you tinker with them, feathers get ruffled." Blau believes that the key to Datacap's success lies in customers' recognition that what they get when they buy Datacap's product is not necessarily character recognition but data entry productivity.

FOCUS Question:
Why do forms need to be redesigned for OCR data entry? Why is form redesign an organizational problem?

SOURCE: Ellis Booker, "Medical Agency Prescribes Record Cure," *Computerworld*, September 13, 1993.

The Canon BJ 600 color printer produces high-resolution color text and graphics output.
SOURCE: Courtesy of Canon USA.

computer output, such as video display terminals, color graphics, and voice output. The sophisticated array of output media allows us to further customize information technology to meet specific problem-solving requirements.

PRINTERS

Printers are still the medium of choice when permanent, hard-copy output is required. For example, bank statements and bills are still printed out. Printer output consists of characters, symbols, and occasionally graphics. A wide range of printer options is available, based on their speed and the way they print. The speed, cost, and quality of printer output are important considerations in selecting the right printer. Choosing the appropriate printer can be a crucial decision for a firm.

Character printers, which print one character at a time, are quite slow, outputting 40 to 200 characters per second. **Line printers** print an entire line at a time, reaching speeds of 3,000 lines per minute. **Page printers** print an entire page at a time, with speeds surpassing 120 pages per minute. High-speed line and page printers are typically found in large corporate computer centers that use mainframes and minicomputers.

Impact printers, such as a daisy-wheel printer or a dot-matrix printer, form characters by pressing a typeface device such as a print wheel or cylinder against paper and inked ribbon. **Letter-quality printers**, such as the daisy-wheel printer, produce a high-quality print image by pressing the image of a fully formed character against the ribbon. **Dot-matrix printers** use a print head composed of a series of tiny print hammers that look like pins. The print hammers strike the ribbon as the print mechanism moves across the print line from right to left and from left to right. Depending on the character to be printed, different pins are activated.

Dot-matrix printers tend to be faster than letter-quality printers and produce lower-quality output. Many dot-matrix printers can also produce graphical or color output. Letter-quality printers are most appropriate for important business letters or reports, whereas dot-matrix printers are used for drafts of documents, large-volume output, or graphics.

Character printer
A printer that prints one character at a time; such printers are very slow, outputting 40 to 200 characters per second.

Line printer
A printer that prints an entire line at a time; it can reach speeds of 3,000 lines per minute.

Page printer
A printer that can print an entire page at a time; it can reach speeds of over 120 pages per minute.

Impact printer
A printer that forms characters by pressing a typeface device, such as a print wheel or cylinder, against paper and inked ribbon.

Letter-quality printer
An impact printer that produces a high-quality image by pressing the image of a fully formed character against inked ribbon.

Dot-matrix printer
An impact printer that uses a print head composed of many small hammers or pins that strike an inked ribbon as the print mechanism moves from side to side; such printers are usually faster than letter-quality printers but produce lower-quality output.

Nonimpact printer

A printer (laser, ink-jet, or thermal-transfer) that does not form characters by pressing a typeface device against ribbon and paper.

Laser printer

A printer that produces an image by scanning a laser beam across a light-sensitive drum; the toner that adheres to the charged portions of the drum is then pulled off onto the paper.

Ink-jet printer

A printer that produces an image by spraying electrically charged ink particles against paper through holes in the printhead.

Thermal-transfer printer

A printer that produces high-quality images by transferring ink from a wax-based ribbon onto chemically treated paper.

Nonimpact printers do not strike characters between ribbon and paper and are usually less noisy than impact printers. The main categories of nonimpact printers are laser printers, ink-jet printers, and thermal-transfer printers.

Laser printers, perhaps the most familiar of these three, scan a laser beam across a light-sensitive drum, turning the beam on and off to produce dots that form an image. As the drum turns, it picks up toner. Toner particles adhere to the charged parts of the drum and are pulled off by paper as it passes by. Laser printers can generate from six pages per minute for personal computer models to over a hundred thirty pages per minute for high-volume work in large commercial and corporate data centers. These printers have become increasingly popular because they are relatively fast and can produce relatively high-quality graphic images and text, although the quality of their output is inferior to many letter-quality printers.

Ink-jet printers spray tiny electrically charged ink particles against paper through tiny nozzles, forming high-quality characters at speeds of over 200 characters per second. Since many models hold multiple color cartridges, they can be used for color output. **Thermal-transfer printers** transfer ink from a wax-based ribbon onto chemically treated paper, producing very high-quality character and graphic output.

Some processing and storage capacities are being built into printers and other input and output devices to reduce the load on the main computer. Almost all microcomputer printers, for instance, have at least 2K (2,000 bytes) of memory, called a buffer, that can store several sentences, and some printers have additional memory to store fonts and characters. The Xerox Corp.'s intelligent printing systems can be programmed to produce complex documents on their own so that CPU resources will not be tied up in the printing process. The printers can store forms, page-formatting instructions, logos, and signatures, thus eliminating the need for preprinted stocks. Using various professional-quality type fonts and halftones, they can merge text with graphics and forms. Microcomputer

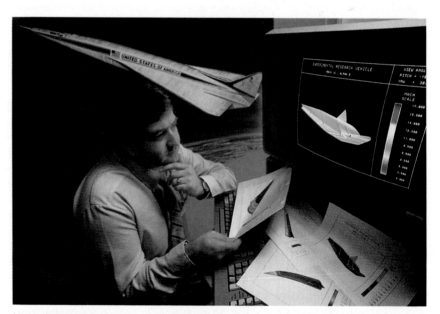

An engineer works on the preliminary design of the national aerospace plane's airframe at Rockwell International. Workstations with multiple output technologies—high-resolution color monitors, printers, and plotters—allow designers flexibility for displaying their work.

SOURCE: Courtesy of Rockwell International.

Apple Computer's ergonomically designed keyboard and mouse can be adjusted to meet the needs of any user. Carefully chosen input and output devices can reduce or eliminate many computer-related work disorders.

SOURCE: Courtesy of Apple Computer, Inc.

printers such as the Hewlett Packard Laserjet or the Apple LaserWriter are programmed to store graphic elements and various type fonts that can be used selectively by different pieces of software.

PLOTTERS

Plotters are special devices for outputting high-quality graphics, such as maps, charts, drawings, and graphs. They are commonly used by engineers and architects. A pen plotter is programmed to move in various directions to produce a series of straight lines; it draws curves as a series of very short lines. Electrostatic plotters produce images from tiny dots on treated paper using electrostatic charges.

VIDEO DISPLAY TERMINALS

Displaying output on a **video display terminal** (VDT) is appropriate when there is no need for a permanent paper record or when an immediate response is required. VDTs can be classified in terms of whether they are monochrome or color and whether they can display text only or text and graphics. The traditional technology for displaying output on a terminal screen is the cathode ray tube, or **CRT**. CRTs work much like television picture tubes, in that an electronic "gun" shoots a beam of electrons that illuminate tiny dots, called pixels, on the screen. The more pixels (a contraction of the phrase *picture element*) per screen, the higher the resolution, or sharpness, of the screen image.

Display devices for graphics often use **bit mapping**, which allows each pixel on the screen to be addressed and manipulated by the computer (as opposed to blocks of pixels in character addressable displays). This requires more computer memory, but it permits finer detail and the ability to produce any kind of image on the display screen. A high-resolution color monitor using the VGA (Video Graphics Array) standard for

Plotter

A device used for outputting high-quality graphics; pen plotters move in various directions to produce straight lines, whereas electrostatic plotters use electrostatic charges to produce images from tiny dots on treated paper.

Video display terminal

A screen on which output can be displayed; varieties include monochrome or color and text or text/graphics.

CRT

An electronic tube that shoots a beam of electrons that illuminates pixels, or tiny dots, on a video display screen; stands for cathode ray tube.

Bit mapping

A technology often used for displaying graphics on a video display terminal; it allows each pixel on the screen to be addressed and manipulated by the computer.

FOCUS ON PEOPLE

ARE VDTs SAFE?

Are VDTs safe for people? The question is being asked more and more frequently by employees, employers, public interest groups, and legislators.

Reports of workers who have developed irreversible eye strain or damage or repetitive strain injury—keyboard-related wrist and hand injuries—are becoming more common. The people most seriously affected are those who work at terminals for more than half the workday, such as data entry personnel, programmers, telephone operators, and journalists. A Department of Labor study noted that repetitive motion disorders accounted for 48 percent of all workplace illness in 1988, up 10 percent from the previous year.

VDTs emit electric and magnetic fields in very-low-frequency and extra-low-frequency ranges. These fields contain nonionizing radiation (gamma rays and Xrays emit ionizing radiation). Does the radiation from VDTs affect cell membranes or chromosomes? Does it cause high stress, depression, or disorientation? Can it be linked to cancer? Is it hazardous to pregnancy? Several studies have examined the effects of the low levels of nonionizing radiation emitted from VDTs, but none have been conclusive.

Another VDT-related disorder, computer vision syndrome (CVS), is characterized by dry, irritated eyes, blurry vision, headaches, and other symptoms associated with eye strain. CVS is caused by improper lighting, screen glare, and screens with poor resolution. A study by James E. Sheedy, chief of the VDT Eye Lab at the University of California at Berkeley, found that nearly 10 million people in the United States may suffer from this disorder.

All computer monitor manufacturers have reduced VDT emissions since the early 1980s, and European countries such as Sweden have adopted stringent radiation emission standards. State and local legislators are considering restrictions on VDTs, but such legislation has been difficult to enact. In December 1991 the city of San Francisco passed legislation to require that all companies with 15 or more employees spending at least four hours daily working with VDTs grant paid breaks of 15 minutes every two hours. Additionally, the employers were required to provide workers with adjustable terminals, keyboards, and chairs; proper lighting; and antiglare screens, wrist rests, foot rests, and document holders if requested. But the law was struck down two months later when San Francisco Superior Court Judge Lucy Kelly McCabe ruled that only the state, not individual cities, could regulate workplace safety. In the United Kingdom, court rulings have been divided about the harmful effects of computer input and output devices. One U.K. court awarded £11,371 ($16,858) to Sarah Munson, an editor who sued her employer, the *Portsmouth News*, claiming she was unjustly fired in 1991 for taking six months sick leave to recover from hand injuries incurred while working on the newspaper's electronic publishing system. The court decided the *News* was liable for Munson's injuries. But this verdict followed a ruling issued a week earlier by U.K.'s High Court, which cleared Reuters Agency of any responsibility for the RSI experienced by one of its employees. The court ruled that the term *repetitive strain injury*, as used to describe pain and swelling in the hands, arms, and shoulders suffered by people working long hours at a computer, had no medical meaning.

Many companies that either make or use computers have opposed local VDT regulations because it is burdensome to have each locality set its own rules. These firms believe they should be allowed to devise their own plans for protecting workers' health. Beyond educating workers about VDT risks, employers can pay more attention to ergonomics. The optimal computer work environment includes lower levels of light that reduce glare on the VDT screen, proper positioning of monitors, use of wrist rests, easily adjustable furniture and lighting, and brief, frequent rest breaks. Employers can also reduce the number of VDT work hours for pregnant employees or give pregnant employees the option to transfer.

FOCUS Question: Why do VDTs pose people problems?

SOURCES: Mitch Betts, "VDT Vision Problems May Affect 10 Million," *Computerworld*, February 8, 1993, and Andrew Pollack, "San Francisco Law on VDTs is Struck Down," *The New York Times*, February 14, 1992.

display devices supports graphics with 640 × 480 (307,200 pixels) resolution. A very-high-resolution color monitor using the Extended VGA standard to support CAD/CAM or sophisticated graphics work displays much clearer, sharper images because it has a 1,024 × 768 resolution (786,432 pixels).

Flat panel display devices use charged chemicals or gases sandwiched between panes of glass. Because they are compact, lightweight, and consume minimal power, they are used with portable laptop, notebook, and palmtop computers. The two leading flat panel technologies are plasma and liquid crystal. Flat panel screens with an active matrix display are brighter and sharper but more costly than screens with a passive matrix display.

As the Focus on People explains, controversy continues over the safety of VDTs. Since the late 1970s, suspicions have arisen that working long hours in front of these terminals creates health hazards.

MICROFILM AND MICROFICHE

Microfilm and **microfiche** have been used to record output as microscopic filmed images that can be stored compactly for future use. These media are cumbersome to search through, however, and are gradually being replaced by optical disk technology.

AUDIO OUTPUT DEVICES

Audio output includes voice, music, and other sounds. **Voice output** devices convert digital data into speechlike form. When you call for information on the telephone, for example, a computer "voice" may respond with the telephone number you requested. Sounds needed to process inquiries are prerecorded, coded, and stored on disk to be translated back as spoken words. Voice output is gaining popularity in toys, automobiles, and games as well as in situations in which visual output is not appropriate. We discuss other types of audio output in the following section.

5.5 LEADING-EDGE TECHNOLOGY: MULTIMEDIA

A sales representative presses a touch-screen function and a colorful video demonstration of the software she's learning fills a corner of her computer screen. An engineer runs through mathematical formulas with graphic animations that help to illustrate the principles involved. Both are examples of multimedia computing, a leading-edge technology for the 1990s and the twenty-first century.

Multimedia can be defined as the technologies that facilitate the integration of two or more types of media, such as text, graphics, sound, voice, full-motion video, still video, and/or animation into a computer-based application. By pressing a button a user can access a screen of text; another button might bring up video images. Still another might access related talk or music. Products and services that already use multimedia include imaging, graphics design tools, electronic books and newspapers, electronic classroom presentations, interactive entertainment, and multimedia video conferencing and electronic mail.

Digitizing graphics, full-motion video, and sound produces enormous quantities of data, requiring high-capacity microprocessor, storage, and communications technology to meld text, graphics, sound, and video data into a single application. For instance, storing a 4-minute song takes 2.4 megabytes of storage. A single-color picture or video frame requires 1 megabyte of storage, and full-motion video running at 30 frames per second requires 30 megabytes per second to store.

Flat panel display
A technology that uses charged chemicals or gases sandwiched between panes of glass to display output on a screen; used in lightweight, portable computers.

Microfilm and microfiche
Media that record output as microscopic filmed images that can be stored compactly.

Voice output
Output that emerges as spoken words rather than as a visual display.

Multimedia
The integration of two or more types of media such as text, graphics, sound, full-motion video, or animation into a computer-based application.

The Macintosh Quadra 660AV can be used as the foundation of a multimedia system. Desktop microcomputers require special hardware and software to blend text, sound, pictures, and full-motion video into a single digital experience.

SOURCE: Courtesy of Apple Computer, Inc.

A simple multimedia system that can run multimedia applications can be constructed from a microcomputer with a 32-bit microprocessor and a CD-ROM drive. The discussion of optical disks earlier in this chapter pointed out the enormous storage capacity of optical technology. A 5-inch optical disk holding more than 600 megabytes of information can store an hour of music, several thousand full-color pictures, several minutes of video or animation, and millions of words. A single optical disk can store all 26 volumes of *Compton's MultiMedia Encyclopedia*, which includes 15,000 drawings, charts, photographs, and paintings, many in full color; 45 animated sequences; an hour of audio clips of famous speeches and music; and *Webster's Intermediate Dictionary* plus about 9 million words.

Figure 5.9 shows the input, output, and storage devices for a multimedia system that can be used to create and run multimedia applications:

- A microcomputer with a 32-bit (or larger) microprocessor and 4 megabytes or more of RAM

- Special adapter cards (sound, video, and video compression cards) to digitize sound and video, integrate them into the computer, and digitally compress full-motion video

- A keyboard, mouse, or digitizer to input text and still images

- Microphones, CD players, music keyboards, and cassette players for audio input

- Camcorders, VCRs, and laser video disk players for video input

- CD-ROM disk

- A high-capacity hard disk (300 megabytes or more of storage)

- A very-high-resolution Super VGA or Extended VGA color monitor with a large screen

- Stereo speakers

FIGURE 5.9

Components of Multimedia Systems

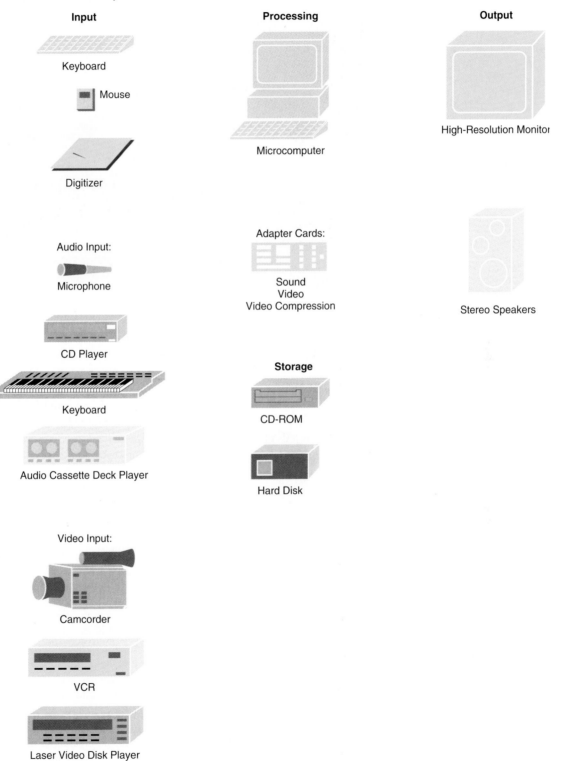

Apple computers come equipped with software called QuickTime™, which allows users to add multimedia features such as video clips, stereo sound, and animated sequences to existing applications without the addition of special internal hardware.

SOURCE: Courtesy of Apple Computer, Inc.

The most difficult element to incorporate into multimedia information systems has been full-motion video, because so much data must be brought under the digital control of the computer. While laser video disks and VCRs can deliver video images to microcomputers, this technology is limited to displaying images. The process of actually integrating video with other kinds of data requires special software or compression boards with dedicated video processing chips. The massive amounts of data in each video image must be digitally encoded, stored, and manipulated electronically using techniques that "compress" the digital data. Digital Video Interactive (DVI), the standard for Intel microprocessors, compresses video at a 150:1 ratio using special chips on a DVI board. The video compression process enables 1 hour of video to be stored on approximately 720 megabytes. Without compression, 110 gigabytes would be required. A new version of Intel's 486 microprocessor will incorporate DVI technology, eliminating the need for additional chips and boards for processing full-motion video.

Today, to run multimedia applications using the IBM personal computer standard, one must either purchase a specialized multimedia personal computer or use an upgrade kit to run information systems stored on CD-ROM. The original features of the Macintosh computer, such as its powerful graphics orientation, make it more easily adaptable to multimedia. In 1992 Apple Computer Corp. began delivering its computers with QuickTime™ software and the necessary hardware to enable the user to play multimedia disks containing text, video, and sound. Microsoft Corp. has developed multimedia standards that allow IBM microcomputers and IBM clone computers to author and play back multimedia presentations. By the end of the century all new computers will have built-in multimedia capabilities including text, graphics, music, full-motion and still-frame video, animation, voice messages, telephone, and fax.

At present, the most popular multimedia applications are for training and presentations. For training, multimedia is appealing because it is interactive and permits people to undertake training at any time of the day and at their own pace. Instructors can easily integrate words, sounds, pictures, and both live and animated video to produce lessons that capture students' imaginations. Andersen Consulting, for example, requires a microcomputer-based multimedia business practices course for all new consultants. Consultants work their way through a simulated company, solving a series of problems in various departments of this make-believe business. Andersen employees typically complete the course in as few as 35 hours, compared with 100 hours using traditional instructional methods. This dramatic cut in training time will enable Andersen to save $2 million annually in payroll and $8.5 million in delivery costs.

Using multimedia to train service agents solved a major problem for The New England, an insurance company based in Boston, Massachusetts. Agents retained little from the original course, which was full of difficult-to-recall mathematical figures and formulas. The multimedia training course, which features two actors going through the material with abundant audio and graphics, has proven much more memorable and takes half the time to complete.

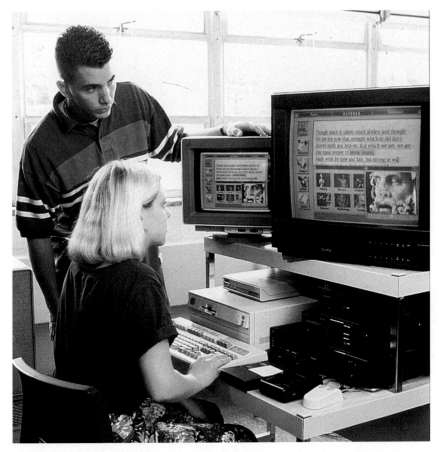

Corporations are taking advantage of new multimedia software and hardware to train employees and to upgrade their work skills. Multimedia applications are interactive, permitting people to respond to questions posed by the computer and to learn at their own pace.

SOURCE: Courtesy of International Business Machines Corporation Multimedia Training.

When multimedia is joined with telecommunications technologies (see Chapter 8), such as desk-to-desk videoconferencing, it will become a major tool for accessing corporate information, and it will change the way business is conducted. People will be able to exchange more than written documents. Members of work teams will share and manipulate text, graphics and image documents, including photographs and even full-motion video, without ever leaving their desks.

Even without networks, companies can use multimedia to improve the distribution and use of information. Minnesota Mining and Manufacturing Co. (3M) replaced its huge catalog of 2,400 office supply products with a multimedia application on a single CD-ROM. The application helps customers learn about products they need and even provides video demonstrations of some of 3M's more unusual products. The information is much easier to access than when it was in 5-inch-thick binders, so sales staff spend less time answering questions about products.

Another promising avenue for multimedia is interactive entertainment. Multimedia technology is creating exciting new video games and will be used to create interactive applications that combine text, graphics, video, audio, and animation into a single media experience delivered to the home using a television or computer monitor linked to telephone and cable television lines. For instance, while watching a nature show, a viewer could bring up a map of an animal's habitat or select more data from a list of facts. Viewers will be able to access vast libraries of movies, games, educational software, and other information, order a pizza, or read an on-line newspaper.[2] We will look more closely at this multimedia-rich information superhighway and at other aspects of multimedia in subsequent chapters.

SUMMARY

- The principal secondary storage devices are magnetic tape, magnetic disk, and optical disk.

- Magnetic tape is most useful for storing large volumes of data at a relatively low price. The disadvantages of magnetic tape are its slow access speed and the fact that it can only store data sequentially.

- Magnetic disk technology permits direct access to data, but it is more expensive than magnetic tape, is vulnerable to environmental disturbances, and needs to be backed up.

- There are two kinds of magnetic disks: hard disks and floppy disks. Removable-pack and fixed hard disk systems are used with larger computers, and Winchester hard disk systems are used primarily with small computers. Floppy disks are used in microcomputers; the most popular sizes are $3\frac{1}{2}$ inches and $5\frac{1}{4}$ inches.

- The cylinder method and the sector method are two ways of storing data on magnetic disks.

- Optical disks use laser technology to store vast amounts of data in a compact space. CD-ROM disk systems can only be read from. WORM optical disk systems can write data supplied by the user only once, but can be read many times. Rewritable optical disks are starting to be used.

- There are several approaches to input and processing: a batch approach, an on-line real-time approach, and on-line input with delayed processing.

- The principal input devices are keyboards, touch screens, computer mice, digitizing tablets, pen-based input, magnetic and optical character recognition, and voice input.

- The most advanced data input technology is source data automation, in which computer-readable data are generated at the point of origin.
- The principal output devices are printers, plotters, video display terminals, microfilm and microfiche, and voice output devices.
- Printers can be classified in terms of speed, as character printers, line printers, or page printers; and in terms of the way they print, as impact or nonimpact printers.
- Impact printers can be classified as letter-quality printers with a solid font mechanism or as dot-matrix printers with a dot-matrix mechanism.
- The main types of nonimpact printers are laser printers, ink-jet printers, and thermal-transfer printers.
- Video display terminals can be classified according to whether they are monochrome or color and whether they can display text only or text and graphics.
- Multimedia technology can integrate text, graphics, sound, and video into a single computer-based application.

KEY TERMS

Secondary storage	Key-to-tape
Magnetic tape	Key-to-disk
Magnetic disk	Touch screen
Direct-access storage device (DASD)	Digitizing tablet
Hard disk	Computer mouse
Read/write head	Pen-based input
Track	Voice input
Removable-pack disk system	Source data automation
Cylinder	Magnetic ink character recognition (MICR)
Winchester disk system	
RAID (Redundant Array of Inexpensive Disks)	Optical character recognition (OCR)
	Bar code
Disk access time	Universal Product Code
Floppy disks	Sensors
Sector method for storing data	Character printer
Single-sided disk	Line printer
Double-sided disk	Page printer
Recording density	Impact printer
Optical disk	Letter-quality printer
CD-ROM	Dot-matrix printer
WORM	Nonimpact printer
Batch input and processing	Laser printer
On-line input	Ink-jet printer
On-line real-time processing	Thermal-transfer printer
Keypunch	Plotter

Video display terminal   Microfilm and microfiche
CRT   Voice output
Bit mapping   Multimedia
Flat panel display

REVIEW QUESTIONS

1. What is the difference between primary and secondary storage?
2. What are the advantages and disadvantages of magnetic tape storage?
3. What are the two kinds of magnetic disks? In what situations is each useful?
4. What are the various ways of physically storing data on magnetic disk?
5. What is an optical disk? In what situations are optical disks useful?
6. What is the difference between CD-ROM and WORM?
7. Distinguish among the following: batch input and processing; on-line input and real-time processing; on-line input with delayed processing.
8. What are the traditional data input devices?
9. What are the new interactive data input devices?
10. Name and describe each of the leading source data automation technologies.
11. List and describe the major output devices.
12. Describe the various classifications of printers.
13. How can video display terminals be classified?
14. What is multimedia? What technologies does it involve?

DISCUSSION QUESTIONS

1. Why is source data automation becoming more widespread?
2. How do input, output, and storage technologies affect the design and performance of an information system?

PROBLEM-SOLVING EXERCISES

1. *Group exercise:* Divide the class into groups and have each group use magazine articles and research materials available in your library to prepare a report and oral presentation on VDT safety. Each group's report and presentation should include conclusions about VDT hazards. If possible, have each group take a position for or against VDT legislation, and have opposing groups debate whether government should regulate how VDTs are used in the marketplace.

2. The Bancroft Chemical Corporation is required by law to store information on its employees' medical histories for 25 years. Currently, employee medical claim forms are stored in document retention centers, where they are very difficult to access. Write

an analysis of how you could use information technologies to help Bancroft fulfill its legal requirements.

3.   *Hands-on exercise:* Many organizations need to compile and analyze the information collected on handwritten paper forms. Use appropriate software to design and create an application that analyzes medical emergency report forms similar to those described in the Focus on Organizations. The forms contain the following information:

Date	Patient Name	Age	Type of Accident	Trauma?	Medical Insurance?	Procedure Administered?
01/28/95	John Kelly	17	Auto	Y	N	Y
01/29/95	Audrey Stern	6	House	N	Y	N
02/03/95	Scott Schram	67	House	Y	Y	Y
02/05/95	Kara Wauters	33	Auto	N	Y	N
02/07/95	Pat Bohlen	18	Auto	Y	N	Y
02/12/95	Ben Thomas	51	House	Y	N	Y

Use your software to create a report or series of reports with the following information:

The total number of emergency report forms.

The number of reports in January 1995.

The total number of trauma cases.

The total number of emergency cases in which patients had no medical insurance coverage.

A list of all emergency patients under the age of 18 who had auto accidents.

NOTES

1. Laurie Flynn, "CD-ROM's: They're Not Just for Entertainment," *The New York Times*, April 24, 1994, and Clinton Wilder, "Data on a Silver Platter," *InformationWEEK*, March 21, 1994.

2. Jon C. Pepper, "Here Comes Multimedia," *InformationWEEK*, February 21, 1994; Eric Brown, "Will Multimedia Make College Obsolete?," *Newmedia*, July 1993; Terry Schwartz, "Corporate Paperwork Gets Sound and Action," *The New York Times*, July 7, 1993; and J. William Semich, "Multimedia Tools for Development Pros," *Datamation*, August 15, 1992.

PROBLEM-SOLVING CASE

THE RISE OF MULTIMEDIA KIOSKS

Many factors have combined to initiate a rapidly growing interest in kiosks as a way to sell products and serve customers. Kiosks are free-standing displays that use multimedia to allow customers to tailor products and services to their individual needs. The price of computer technology continues to fall, making kiosks more affordable, and fierce economic competition has fueled a continual drive to find new ways to market goods and services.

Kiosks that use a range of input/output technologies are appearing in music stores. These kiosks are a modern version of the old-fashioned music store listening booths that nearly disappeared with the advent of 33-rpm records, tape cassettes, and

CDs. The customer uses the kiosk to sample music from any of the 30,000 or more albums that many music stores carry.

Kiosks address the problem of the buyers' inability to know whether they really like some or all of a particular album, making an album purchase risky. In a bookstore the potential buyer can examine a book, but until now that has not been possible in most music stores. "Any information we can give [the customer] helps reduce [the] risk," according to Deborah English, a vice-president at Warehouse Records. "That's the key. Make it easier for them to buy." Intouch, produced by Muze Inc. of Brooklyn, New York, is a kiosk that allows customers to listen to 30-second samples of songs before deciding whether to buy.

To use the kiosk, the customer first completes a survey and then is issued a permanent bar-coded identity card that provides access to the kiosk. The Intouch I-station scans the card and logs the customer onto the computer system. The customer uses the scanner to scan the CD (or tape, record, or music video) bar code, and a menu of songs from the CD appears on the computer touch screen. The customer touches a specific song title to hear a 30-second sample of the song. Other ways to select specific songs are available; for example, customers can access a list of the top 50 sellers from *Billboard* magazine and select any of them. Or, using an on-screen keyboard, they can type in song names to locate specific albums. Having listened to one song, the customer can access lists of other songs by the same musicians by touching the screen. The station is also a marketing tool, displaying advertising specials and discount coupons.

The system produces a great deal of data for the sellers and producers of the albums as well. The system records all customer selections, and customers are asked to rate each album listened to. The data are collected each night by Muze (via a network) and are sold to stores and record producers.

The I-station runs on an Apple IIci that controls the screen and sound as well as the collection of data about customer tastes. The album and song titles are carried in a database along with performer names. The song samples are stored on digital audio tape.

Federal Express has developed a kiosk that makes it easy to send packages for overnight delivery. Their kiosks also contain touch screens and simulated keyboards. The customer must type in the shipping name and address and indicate one- or two-day delivery. Shippers who have an account can pay for the shipment by entering a customer number. Others can pay for it by running a credit card through a magnetic card reader. The computer checks all entered data, and if they are complete the computer prints out a bar-coded shipping label. The customer then attaches the label to the package and deposits it for pickup. Customers can also track their shipments at the kiosks and even print out a tracking report that includes the name of the person who signed for the package.

An unusual kiosk being installed by Hallmark Cards allows the customer to produce an individualized greeting card for any occasion. Using a touch screen, the customer answers a number of questions, such as the occasion and the recipient's name and sex. Customers can select from about 800 card designs and enter their own message at various places on the card. When the customer is finished, an Apple Macintosh prints the card using a Tektronix, Inc. ink-jet color printer. The 800 card designs are stored on compact disk and are changed monthly. Hallmark has networked all the kiosks, allowing company headquarters to collect and store sales data.

Although kiosks may be convenient, they do not always make money. Most shoppers still prefer to shop in stores, where they can talk to a live person before making a purchase. MicroMall, Inc., a unit of Microwave Systems Corp. in Des Moines, Iowa, installed 25 kiosks in office buildings and hotels in Chicago and in Wilmington, Delaware. The kiosks used interactive multimedia to entice shoppers with electronic pictures of wine accessories, gourmet foods, and clothing. Sales were disappointing, so MicroMall abandoned plans for installing additional kiosks to focus on home shopping. Kiosks appear to have a better track record as providers of information. When sales staff lack in-depth knowledge about their products, interactive kiosks can play a beneficial role.

SOURCES: Jeffrey A. Trachtenberg, "Interactive Kiosks May Be High-Tech, But they Underwhelm U.S. Consumers," *The Wall Street Journal*, March 14, 1994; James Daly, "Hallmark Offers Do-It-Yourself Cards," *Computerworld*, June 14, 1993; Matt Rothman, "A New Music Retailing Technology Says, 'Listen Here'," *The New York Times*, July 4, 1993; Linda Wilson, "Pressing All the Right Buttons," *InformationWEEK*, January 18, 1993; and "Multimedia Express," IBM Multimedia Innovations, October 25, 1993.

CASE STUDY QUESTIONS

1.   List and describe the function of all the many input, output, and storage technologies that are used in these kiosk examples. Name input and output technologies that are not used, and explain why you think they were not selected.

2.   Why do you think all three of these systems relied primarily on touch screens for input from the customers?

3.   What manual techniques are used as part of these applications? Could any of them be computerized? Why do you think they weren't?

4.   What problems are solved by using kiosks for sales and service? What problems can't be solved by using kiosks?

5.   Develop other ideas for kiosk applications and list the input, output, and storage technologies they would need and your reasons for those technology choices.

Chapter

→ S I X ←

INFORMATION SYSTEMS SOFTWARE

LEARNING OBJECTIVES

After reading and studying this chapter, you will:
1. Understand the roles systems software and applications software play in information systems.
2. Be familiar with the generations of computer software.
3. Know how the operating system functions.
4. Understand the strengths and limitations of the major programming languages.
5. Be able to select appropriate software for business applications.

FROM GARBAGE TO INFORMATION: SOFTWARE FOR WASTE MANAGEMENT

*D*o you know where your garbage goes after it is picked up? The answer is obviously important to your waste management firm, and it affects you as well: lack of accurate information to track trash can add to the cost of garbage disposal for consumers and to inefficient operation of landfills.

John Sexton Contractors Co., a waste management company in Hillside, Illinois, wanted accurate data to track the trash it handled. This 62-year-old company has 18 sites in four states and has acquired other landfill companies as it expanded. As a result, it could not effectively combine information from the different systems used by these companies. So Sexton Contractors turned to a fourth-generation software product called Progress, from Progress Software Inc., to create a new waste management system that could efficiently organize data from geographically widespread systems. This is flexible software and can run on various models of computer hardware.

The waste management software allows the firm to coordinate data from many regional offices while allowing the regional offices to access data collected from local offices. For instance, data are registered at a local landfill when a garbage truck arrives at a weigh station. The weigh station operator identifies the owner of the truck, the type of waste, and the party being charged for the bill. The truck is weighed and the operator registers where the waste will be dumped in the landfill. The entire process of recording this information into the computer requires four keystrokes for standard waste deliveries.

Credit agreements may limit designated customers to certain types and volumes of waste. The system may then issue a warning to the operator. Each *site can customize these parameters. The flexibility of the system helps Sexton cope with changing environmental regulations as well. The waste management software tells landfill operators where certain wastes are dumped in a landfill. If those wastes are later categorized as hazardous and require treatment, they can be easily located. Managers can use data such as how much space is consumed by a specific type of waste, how rapidly it decomposes, and how much the firm is paid for a particular commodity, such as aluminum, to charge more effectively for services and to maximize the benefits of recycling programs. For instance, a medical waste facility run by John Sexton recycles 89% of the plastic and paper wastes it collects.*

Sexton refines the methane gas produced by the waste decomposition process at its landfills and resells it to utility companies. The waste management software enables the company to calculate how much gas is pumped off. While other landfills merely burn off their methane, Sexton can use the information to generate revenue.

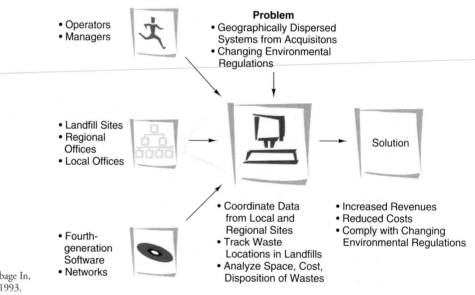

SOURCE: Melinda-Carol Ballou, "Garbage In, Info Out," *Computerworld,* June 21, 1993.

John Sexton Contractors' waste management system illustrates how a well-designed information system can bring both public and private benefit. While Sexton took advantage of the advances in computer hardware technology described in earlier chapters, it required software to make the computer a valuable problem-solving tool. Sexton had to write special software to tell its computer how to collect, process, and analyze data for waste management.

This chapter shows how computer software combines with computer hardware into useful information systems. We describe the features and capabilities of the two major types of software, systems and applications software, and show how to select appropriate software for problem solving.

6.1 INTRODUCTION

Software refers to the detailed instructions that control the operation of computer hardware. Without the instructions provided by software, computer hardware is unable to perform any of the tasks we associate with computers. Software has three principal functions: (1) it develops the tools for applying computer hardware to problem solving; (2) it enables the organization to manage its computer resources; and (3) it serves as an intermediary between the organization and its stored information.

SOFTWARE PROGRAMS

A software **program** is a series of statements or instructions to the computer. The process of writing or coding the program is called programming, and the individual who performs this task is called a programmer.

In order to execute, or have its instructions performed by the computer, a program must be stored in the computer's primary storage along with the required data. This is called the **stored-program concept**. Once a program has finished executing, the computer hardware can be used for another task by loading a new program into primary storage.

Program
A series of statements or instructions to the computer.

Stored-program concept
The concept that a program cannot be executed unless it is stored in the computer's primary storage along with the required data.

MAJOR TYPES OF SOFTWARE

There are two major types of software: systems software and applications software. Each handles a different set of problems.

Systems software consists of generalized programs that manage computer resources such as the central processing unit (CPU), printers, terminals, communications links, and peripheral equipment. In other words, systems software serves as the intermediary between the software used by end users and the computer itself.

Applications software consists of programs designed for applying the computer to solve a specific problem. Payroll processing programs or sales order entry programs are examples of applications software. Systems software provides the platform on which applications software runs. The relationships among people, the two different kinds of software, and computer hardware are illustrated in Figure 6.1. As the figure shows, people send instructions to the applications software, which "translates" the instructions for the systems software, which in turn forwards them to the hardware. Information flows in two directions: from the person using the computer to the hardware and back again.

Systems software
Generalized software that manages computer resources such as the CPU, printers, terminals, communications links, and peripheral equipment.

Applications software
Programs designed to handle the processing for a particular computer application.

GENERATIONS OF SOFTWARE

The sophistication and range of problems that can be addressed by programming languages can be attributed to the increased capacity of computer hardware. Just as computer hardware evolved over time, software has developed over several generations.

The first generation of computer software was **machine language**. Machine language, consisting of strings of the binary digits 0 and 1, was the only way to communicate with the primitive computers of the 1940s. It took highly trained, specialized programmers to understand, think, and work directly with the machine language of a particular computer. Machine language instructions must specify the storage location for every instruction and data item used. Consequently, writing software in this language

Machine language
The programming language used in the first generation of computer software; consists of strings of binary digits (0 and 1).

FIGURE 6.1

The Relationships between Hardware, Systems Software, Applications Software, and the User

Software serves as the intermediary between people and computer hardware. Most of the software that business professionals use directly is applications software: computer programs that "apply" the computer to perform a specific business function, such as calculating payroll checks or amount of sales. Systems software coordinates the various parts of the computer system and transforms instructions from applications software into instructions that will operate the hardware. Information flows both ways; the results of the hardware's operations travel through the systems software, and the applications programs transform them into results that people can use.

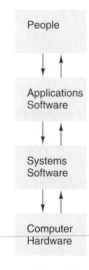

was excruciatingly slow and labor-intensive; very few problems could be addressed this way.

Machine language is no longer used to develop software, having been replaced by symbolic and high-level languages. Symbolic languages, or assembly languages, use symbols and alphabetic abbreviations in place of the 0's and 1's of machine language for representing operation codes, storage locations, and data elements. **High-level languages** consist of statements that, to varying degrees, resemble natural languages (e.g., English). Both symbolic and high-level languages must be translated into machine language for execution by the computer, however (Section 6.2 discusses language translators).

The second generation of software, which began in the early 1950s, consisted of **assembly language**. Assembly language is considered a symbolic language because it consists of language-like acronyms and words such as add, sub (subtract), and load. The programs that translate assembly language into machine code are called **assemblers**. Today assembly language has limited use for problems that require maximum execution efficiency or highly intricate manipulations.

Third-generation computer software, which prevailed from the late 1950s to the 1970s, featured high-level languages that were more sophisticated, easier to use, and directed toward specialized classes of problems. High-level languages also are less machine dependent and often can be used on more than one type of computer. Popular third-generation languages include FORTRAN (FORmula TRANslator) for scientific and mathematical problems, COBOL (COmmon Business-Oriented Language) for business problems requiring extensive file manipulation and large lists, and BASIC (Beginner's All-purpose Symbolic Instruction Code), a generalized programming

High-level language

A programming language that consists of statements that, to some degree, resemble a natural language such as English.

Assembly language

A programming language used for second-generation software; it consists of natural language–like acronyms and words such as add, sub(tract), and load and is considered a symbolic language.

Assembler

A program that translates assembly language into machine code so it can be used by the computer.

language popular for microcomputers. Third-generation software is still in wide use today.

Fourth-generation software was developed in the late 1970s and is used widely for application development today. Fourth-generation software consists of query software, report generators, graphics software, application generators, and other tools (discussed later in this chapter) that dramatically reduce programming time and make some software development tasks easy enough to be performed by nontechnical specialists.

The first three generations of software languages were procedural. Program instructions had to detail a sequence of steps, or procedures, telling the computer what to do and how to do it. In contrast, fourth-generation software has nonprocedural features. Program instructions need only specify *what* has to be accomplished rather than provide details about how to carry out the task. Consequently, the same process can be accomplished with fewer program steps and lines of program code than with third-generation languages.

Some fourth-generation software has natural-language features, meaning that commands are expressed in English-language form. Offices and factories are starting to take advantage of voice recognition software, in which users communicate with computers through spoken commands. For example, Burlington Industries in Greensboro, North Carolina, has equipped its quality control inspectors with Texas Instruments Voice Boards. As lengths of cloth pass, the inspectors describe the defects into microphones connected to their computers, while a yardage meter automatically reports the defect's location to the computer. Defects dropped 20 percent since the voice recognition system was adopted. Previously, inspectors wasted much time switching back and forth between their notepads and repair tools. The next wave of software will feature more prominent use of such natural-language tools, as well as graphical interfaces, touch screens, and other features that will make it easier for nontechnical specialists to use.

This programmer is working on voice recognition software used with a voice-activated word processor. The capabilities of each generation of software have come progressively closer to the way we speak and work.

SOURCE: © Hank Morgan, Rainbow.

6.2 SYSTEMS SOFTWARE

Systems software consists of programs that coordinate the various parts of a computer system and mediate between application software and computer hardware. The **operating system** is the systems software that manages and controls the activities of the computer. It supervises the operation of the CPU; controls input, output, and storage activities; and provides various support services. Other vital services, such as computer language translation facilities and utility programs for common processing tasks, are provided by language translators and utility programs (discussed later in this chapter).

Operating system

The systems software that manages and controls the activities of the computer.

THE OPERATING SYSTEM

The operating system can be visualized as the chief manager of the computer system. Like a human manager in a firm, the operating system determines which computer resources will be used for solving which problems and the order in which they will be used. As shown in Figure 6.2, it has three principal functions:

- Allocating and assigning system resources
- Scheduling the use of resources and computer jobs
- Monitoring computer system activities

Allocation and Assignment   A master control program called a supervisor, executive, or monitor oversees computer operations and coordinates all of the computer's work. The supervisor, which remains in primary storage, brings other programs from

---

FIGURE 6.2

The Tasks of the Operating System

The operating system is the systems software that manages the computer's operations. It has three major roles: it allocates hardware resources as needed; it schedules the various functions, such as input and output; and it monitors the functioning of the system.

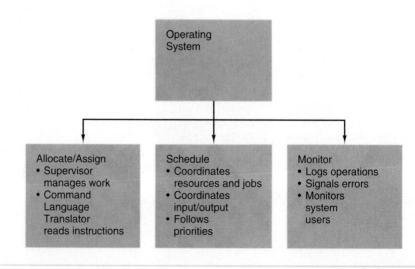

secondary storage to primary storage when they are needed. As each program is activated, the supervisor transfers control to that program. Once that program ends, control returns to the supervisor.

A command language translator controls the assignment of system resources. The command language translator reads special instructions to the operating system, which contain specifications for retrieving, saving, deleting, copying, or moving files; selecting input/output devices; selecting programming languages and application programs; and performing other processing requirements for a particular application. These instructions are called command language. The commands you use with your personal computer to format a disk or copy a file are examples of command language for microcomputer operating systems.

Scheduling   Thousands of pieces of work can be going on in a computer at the same time. The operating system decides when to schedule them, since computer jobs are not necessarily performed in the order they are submitted. For example, payroll or on-line order processing may have a higher priority than other kinds of work. Other processing jobs, such as software program testing, would have to wait until these jobs were finished or left enough computer resources free to accommodate them.

The operating system coordinates scheduling in various areas of the computer so that different parts of different jobs can be worked on simultaneously. For example, while some programs are executing, the operating system is also scheduling the use of input and output devices.

Monitoring   The operating system is also responsible for keeping track of the activities in the computer system. It maintains logs of job operations, notifying end-users or computer operators of any abnormal terminations or error conditions. It terminates programs that run longer than the maximum time allowed.

Operating system software may also contain security monitoring features, such as recording who has logged on and off the system, what programs they have run, and any unauthorized attempts to access the system. Security issues are explored in greater detail in Chapter 12.

If a computer can execute only one instruction from one program at a time, how can thousands of American Airlines reservation clerks use the computer simultaneously to book flights? How can American Airlines run its on-line reservation software 24 hours a day and still use its computers for accounting and other activities? Operating system software has special capabilities for these purposes.

Multiprogramming   Multiprogramming allows multiple programs to use the computer's resources at the same time through concurrent use of the CPU. Only one program actually uses the CPU at any given moment, but at this same instant the other programs can use the computer for other needs, such as input and output. Thus a number of programs can be active in the computer at the same time, but they do not use the same computer resources simultaneously.

Figure 6.3 shows three programs (1, 2, and 3) stored in primary storage. The first program (1) uses the CPU to execute until it comes to an input/output event (in this case, output). The CPU then moves to the second incoming program and directs a communications channel (a small processor limited to input/output processing functions) to read the input and move the output to a printer or other output device. The CPU executes the second program until an input/output statement occurs. It then switches to program 3, moving back and forth between all three programs until they have finished executing.

Multiprogramming

The concurrent use of a computer by several programs; one program uses the CPU while the others use other components such as input and output devices.

FIGURE 6.3

Multiprogramming Uses the CPU More Efficiently

Early computers could execute only one software program at a time. This meant that the CPU had to stop all processing until the program it had just processed finished outputting. This wasted a great deal of valuable CPU time that could have been more profitably spent in processing other programs. Multiprogramming means that the systems software allows the CPU to work on several programs simultaneously (see panel b). Even though the computer can still *process* only one program at a time, it can simultaneously perform input and output functions on other programs. This dramatically cuts down on the amount of idle time between CPU tasks.

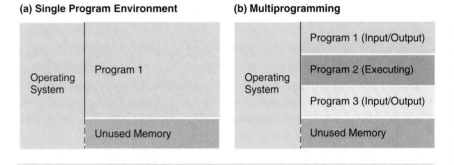

(a) Single Program Environment

| Operating System | Program 1 |
| | Unused Memory |

(b) Multiprogramming

Operating System	Program 1 (Input/Output)
	Program 2 (Executing)
	Program 3 (Input/Output)
	Unused Memory

The advantage of multiprogramming is that it enables computers to be used much more efficiently. Before multiprogramming, computers were a single-program environment; only one program could be executed at a time. The CPU had to stop and wait whenever a program had to read input or write output. With multiprogramming, more problems can be solved at the same time using a single computer.

Multitasking

The multiprogramming capability of single-user operating systems such as those for microcomputers; it enables the user to run two or more programs at once on a single computer.

Multitasking   Multitasking refers to multiprogramming capability on single-user operating systems such as those for microcomputers. It enables one person to run two or more programs concurrently on a single computer. For example, a stockbroker could write a letter to clients with a word processing program while simultaneously using another program to record and update client account information. Multitasking allows the broker to display both programs on the computer screen and work with them at the same time, instead of having to terminate the session with the word processing program, return to the operating system, and then initiate a session with the program handling client account information.

Multiprocessing

The simultaneous use of two or more CPUs under common control to execute different instructions for the same program or multiple programs.

Multiprocessing   The use of two or more CPUs linked together to work in parallel is **multiprocessing**. Two CPUs may be assigned to execute different instructions from the same program simultaneously so that they can be accomplished more rapidly than on a single machine, or instructions from more than one program can be processed simultaneously. The operating system is responsible for scheduling and coordinating the tasks of the various processors. The two CPUs can "communicate," or exchange information, in order to execute programs more efficiently.

Time-sharing

A technique in which many users share computer resources simultaneously (e.g., one CPU with many terminals); the computer spends a fixed amount of time on each user's program before proceeding to the next.

Time-Sharing   A technique that enables many users to share computer resources simultaneously is **time-sharing**. It differs from multiprogramming in that the computer spends a fixed amount of time on one program before proceeding to another. Each user is allocated a tiny slice of time (say, two milliseconds). The computer performs whatever operations it can for that user in the allocated time and then releases two milliseconds to the next user. (In multiprogramming, the computer works on one program until it reaches a logical stopping point, such as an input/output event. Then the computer starts processing another program.)

In a typical time-sharing environment, a CPU is connected to thousands of users at terminals. Many people can be connected to the same CPU simultaneously, with each receiving a tiny amount of CPU time. Since computers now operate at the nanosecond level, the CPU can actually do a great deal of processing in two milliseconds.

Virtual Storage   **Virtual storage** is a way of splitting up programs so that they can be managed more efficiently by the operating system. Before virtual storage was developed in the early 1970s, only a few programs could be loaded into primary storage. A certain portion of primary storage usually remained underutilized because the programs did not take up the total amount of space available. In addition, very large programs could not be loaded as whole programs in primary storage. Programmers had to split up such programs to find portions that would fit into limited memory space.

Virtual storage is based on the realization that only a few program statements can actually be used in the computer at any one time. Virtual storage divides programs into fixed-length portions called pages (each page is approximately 2-4 kilobytes) or into variable-length portions called segments.

A page is read into the CPU when needed and sent back to secondary storage, or disk, when it is no longer required. The CPU executes the instructions from each page, then moves on, either to the next page of the program or to a page from a different program (see Figure 6.4). Many portions of programs, broken down into pages, can reside

Virtual storage

A way of dividing programs into small fixed- or variable-length portions with only a small portion stored in primary memory at one time so that programs can be used more efficiently by the computer.

FIGURE 6.4

Virtual Storage Expands the Computer's Memory
Virtual storage is a feature of operating systems that expands the potential memory of the computer. Software programs are split into portions called pages (fixed-length, as shown here) or segments (variable-length). The pages are stored in secondary storage and shuttled into and out of main memory as needed for processing. Thus the CPU can process pieces of many programs almost simultaneously.

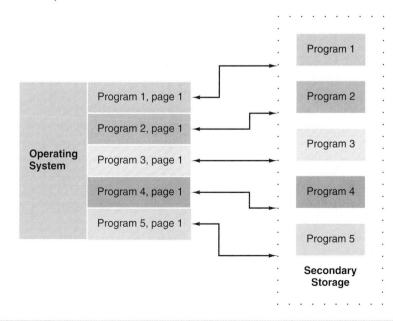

in primary storage at once. All other program pages are stored in a secondary storage peripheral disk unit until they are required for execution.

Virtual storage has several advantages. Not only does it promote fuller utilization of the CPU, but programmers no longer have to worry about program size because any program can be broken down into pages or segments. In addition, large programs do not need large machines to run; they can be executed on smaller computers.

LANGUAGE TRANSLATORS AND UTILITY PROGRAMS

Another important function of systems software is to translate high-level language programs into machine language so that they can be executed by the computer. The program statements in the high-level language are called **source code**, and the machine-language version is called **object code**. Before actually being executed by the computer, object code modules normally are joined together with other object code modules in a process called linkage editing. The result, called the load module, is what is executed by the computer.

There are three kinds of language translator programs: compilers, interpreters, and assemblers. A **compiler** translates an entire high-level language program into machine language. An **interpreter** translates each source code statement one at a time into machine code and executes it. Consequently, interpreted programs run more slowly than compiled programs. Many versions of BASIC use interpreters. An assembler is similar to a compiler but is used only for assembly languages. (See Section 6.3.) Figure 6.5 illustrates the language translation process for a compiler, the most common type.

Utility Programs   Systems software typically includes utility programs for important but common, routine, repetitive tasks, such as sorting records or copying programs from tape to disk. Utility programs are stored in libraries where they can be shared by all users of a computer system.

GRAPHICAL USER INTERFACES

When people work with a computer, the interaction is controlled by an operating system. Users interact with the operating system through the user interface of that operating system. Users communicated with earlier operating systems using text-based commands. For instance, to delete a file named FILED using the older DOS operating system for microcomputers, the user would have to type in the command DELETE FILED. In contrast, a **graphical user interface** (often called a **GUI**), uses icons, buttons, bars, and boxes instead of text-based commands to represent common operations. Icons are symbolic pictures that are used in GUIs to represent programs and files. Commands are activated by rolling a mouse to move the cursor to the appropriate icon and clicking a button on the mouse to make a selection. Many GUIs use a system of pulldown menus to help users select commands and pop-up boxes to help users select among various command options. Windowing features allow users to create, stack, size, and move various boxes of information.

How do GUIs affect problem solving? Proponents claim that they are easier for computing novices to master without prior training. For example, using the Macintosh microcomputer operating system GUI, a file can be deleted simply by dragging the file icon to the "trash" icon. A complex series of commands can be issued by linking icons. Commands are standardized from one program to the next, so new programs can often be used without additional training or studying reference manuals. For example, the steps involved in printing a letter created by a word processing program or a financial state-

Source code
Program statements in a high-level language that are translated by systems software into machine language so that the high-level programs can be executed by the computer.

Object code
The machine-language version of source code after it has been translated into a form usable by the computer.

Compiler
A language translator program that translates an entire high-level language program into machine language.

Interpreter
A language translator program that translates a high-level language program into machine code by translating one statement at a time and executing it.

Graphical user interface (GUI)
The feature of an operating system that uses graphical symbols, or icons; rather than typing in commands, the user moves the cursor to the appropriate icon by rolling a mouse on a desktop.

FIGURE 6.5

Language Translation

A compiler is a type of systems software that serves as a language translator: it "translates" software that people use into instructions that the computer can use. As shown here, the compiler transforms high-level language instructions (called source code) into their machine language equivalent (object code). A linkage editor combines modules of object code with those from other incoming programs into a load module, the group of instructions that the computer follows.

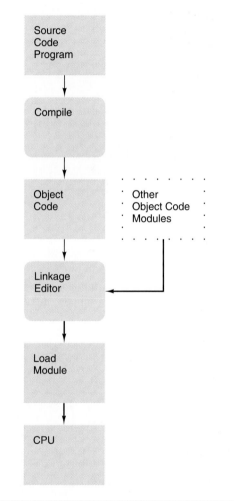

ment generated by a spreadsheet program should be the same. GUIs also encourage solutions communicated through graphics.

However, GUIs have not fully achieved these possibilities. The Focus on People shows that graphical symbols are not always easy to use or understand. Poorly designed GUIs may be confusing and inconsistent across different applications.

MICROCOMPUTER OPERATING SYSTEMS

Microcomputer software is based on specific operating systems and machines. Operating system software defines the "personality" of the microcomputer by specifying the way

Graphical user interfaces can make a computer easier to use by presenting system features through colorful menus, windows, and icons.
SOURCE: Courtesy of Microsoft Corporation.

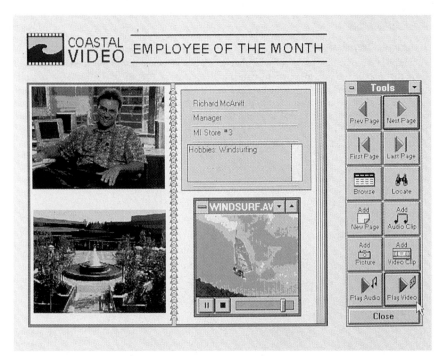

in which programs are controlled, files are stored and retrieved, and the hardware components of the system are held together. A software package written for one microcomputer operating system cannot run on another. Operating systems themselves have distinctive features, such as whether they support multitasking or graphics work,

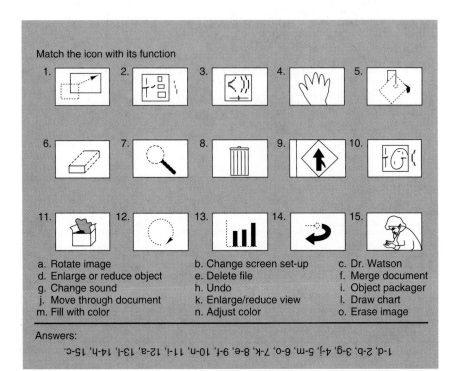

Some of the icons used in graphical user interfaces can be confusing.
SOURCE: Dave Kansas, "The Icon Crisis: Tiny Pictures Cause Confusion," *The Wall Street Journal*, November 17, 1993. Reprinted with permission of *The Wall Street Journal*. Copyright © 1993 Dow Jones & Company, Inc.

FOCUS ON PEOPLE

ARE ICONS THE ULTIMATE SOLUTION TO USER INTERFACES?

The graphical user interface (GUI) was one of the great computer developments of the 1980s because it made it easy for ordinary people (those who are not computer experts) to issue computer commands. No fancy terminology to be learned, no errors because of a misspelled word, just point the mouse at an easy-to-understand icon and click. Simple, efficient, error-proof. Suddenly the computer became a machine for all of us, not just for the hacker, the nerd, and the professional programmer. But GUI has so far depended on the use of icons, and icon technology, like all technology, has its limits.

In the early days of the microcomputer, people communicated with the computer via the keyboard. Commands were frequently confusing and all but required the user to be a programmer. The leap to icons was made in 1981 by Xerox and became popular after 1984, when Apple Computer released its easy-to-use Macintosh microcomputer. It was a gigantic leap —the icon culture became enmeshed with pride in not having to use any words at all.

At first icons were easy to understand. A picture of a manila file folder being opened represented the command to open a file. A blank sheet of paper represented the set-up for creating a new document. A trash can represented delete. But problems arose as computer users developed wider applications—spreadsheets, graphics, telecommunications. As each application became more sophisticated, more functions were added, each requiring a new icon. Small pictures can be only so subtle, and GUI developers discovered that many actions (verbs) are difficult to depict as icons. How, for example, does one draw one small picture to delete a document, another to delete a paragraph, a third to delete a line, and yet a fourth to delete a word? Some of these problems were solved creatively. For example, Lotus Development Corp., looking for a symbol for merging documents, used a highway "traffic merge" sign, a symbol with which most adults are familiar. But there are only so many commonly recognized symbols, and such solutions are becoming more difficult to find.

Other issues further complicate the problem. Some software companies desire to copyright their symbols. For software to be easy to use, all applications should use the same symbols so that users need only learn one set; in that way, users can learn new software with little effort. If companies succeed in copyrighting icons, users will have to learn different symbols for the same function if they use more than one software package. However, if they fail to copyright, a company may come along that likes a specific icon but wants to use it for a different function; then the user will have to learn more than one meaning for a given icon, depending on which application he or she is running. Clearly, this could get confusing. Yet another problem, given the internationalization of the computer field, is the cultural differences in response to certain pictures. For example, a particular hand position or pointed finger may be acceptable and easily understood in one culture but be thoroughly offensive in another.

Occasionally attempts at solutions aid individual users but cause confusion within groups. For example, some applications (e.g., Microsoft Windows) include software to allow users to make their own icons or to modify existing icons. Others give the user the facility to use the icons supplied but to change the meanings (functions) assigned to them. These solutions may work well for an isolated computer user, but can cause serious problems when people share computers.

To solve the problem, industry taboos against using any words are beginning to crumble. Some icons now include an action word with a picture above it. Other applications allow the user to choose between picture only, word only, or the two in combination. Many applications now offer the choice of using icons or pulldown menus that are word-based and accessed by an extra click or two but require no words to be typed and no knowledge of arcane computer terminology. More changes will be required as the need to use additional commands continues to grow.

Focus Questions:
Other than icons, what approaches to user interfaces do you think might be successful? What are their strengths and problems?

SOURCE: Dave Kansas, "The Icon Crisis: Tiny Pictures Cause Confusion," *Wall Street Journal*, November 17, 1993.

that make them conducive to work on specific classes of problems. To use microcomputers effectively, one must understand the capabilities of their operating system software.

DOS

An operating system for 16-bit microcomputers based on the IBM microcomputer standard.

Windows

A GUI shell that runs in conjunction with the DOS operating system.

OS/2

A powerful operating system used with 32-bit IBM microcomputers that supports multitasking and multiple users in networks.

Table 6.1 compares the leading microcomputer operating systems—DOS, OS/2, Windows NT, UNIX, and System 7. The most popular operating system for 16-bit microcomputers is **DOS** (which stands for Disk Operating System). There are two versions of DOS: PC-DOS, which is used exclusively with IBM microcomputers, and MS-DOS, which is used with other microcomputers with 16-bit microprocessors that function like the IBM PC. DOS has several limitations: it has a text-based command-driven user interface; it cannot take advantage of the power of 32-bit microprocessors because it can only address data in 16-bit chunks; and it limits the size of a program in memory to 640K. DOS on its own cannot support multitasking; it can run only one application at a time.

DOS can be given a graphical user interface by using Microsoft **Windows**, a GUI shell that runs in conjunction with the underlying operating system. Windows supports some limited forms of multitasking and networking, but like DOS, it can only run programs that use less than 640 K of memory. Early versions of Windows had problems with application crashes when multiple programs contended for the same memory space. Windows requires a minimum 386 or 486 microprocessor, 4–8 megabytes of RAM, and 80 megabytes of hard disk storage.

OS/2 (Operating System/2) is a robust operating system that can support multitasking and is used with the powerful 32-bit IBM Personal System/2 line of microcomputers or PS/2 clones. OS/2 runs faster than DOS because it can address data in 32-bit chunks and is used for applications that require massive amounts of memory (e.g., networking or multitasking). It can run large complex programs that require more than 640 K of memory. It provides a powerful desktop computer with many of the capabilities of mainframe operating systems, such as the ability to run multiple applications simultaneously and support for multiple users in networks. OS/2 is a more protected operating system than Windows running under DOS; an application that crashes is less likely to disrupt other applications or the entire operating system. OS/2 can run DOS and Windows applications at the same time in its own resizable windows, and it has its own GUI called the Workplace Shell. Later versions of OS/2 have multimedia capabilities and can support pen-based computing. However,

---

TABLE 6.1

Microcomputer Operating Systems: A Comparison

Operating System	Features
DOS	Operating system for IBM (PC-DOS) and IBM-compatible (MS-DOS) microcomputers. Uses text-based commands and limits use of memory to programs with less than 640 K.
OS/2	Operating system for IBM Personal System/2 microcomputers and PS/2 clones. Can take advantage of the 32-bit microprocessor. Supports multitasking and networking and can run large programs requiring more than 640 K of memory.
Windows NT	32-bit operating system for powerful microcomputers and workstations that is not limited to Intel microprocessors. Supports multitasking, networking, and multiprocessing and can run programs requiring more than 640 K of memory.
UNIX	Operating system for powerful microcomputers, workstations, and minicomputers which is portable to different models of hardware. Supports multitasking, multiuser processing, and networking.
System 7	Operating system for the Macintosh computer. Supports multitasking and has powerful graphics and multimedia capabilities.

OS/2 requires powerful computer hardware—a 386 or 486 microprocessor, a minimum of 4 megabytes of RAM, and at least 80 megabytes of hard disk storage.

Windows NT, developed by Microsoft Corporation, is a powerful yet flexible operating system designed for large applications in networked environments with massive memory and data requirements. It uses the same GUI as Windows but has considerably more powerful multitasking and memory management capabilities. Windows NT can run software written for DOS and Windows but it can take advantage of 32-bit microprocessors if required and can support multiprocessing with multiple CPUs. Windows NT can be used with Intel microprocessors as well as workstations and microcomputers based on other microprocessors, such as DEC's Alpha chip or RISC microprocessors from Mips Computer Systems. This operating system might be useful for companies that need to run a variety of applications with a common user interface using different types of computer hardware.[1]

UNIX, which was developed at Bell Laboratories in 1969 to link different types of computers together, is an interactive, multiuser, multitasking operating system that is highly supportive of communications and networking. Many people can use UNIX simultaneously, or one user can run many tasks on UNIX concurrently. UNIX was initially designed for minicomputers, but now there are versions for microcomputers and mainframes. At present, UNIX is primarily used for workstations, minicomputers, and inexpensive multiuser environments in small businesses, but its use in large businesses is growing because of its machine independence. Applications software that runs under UNIX can be transported from one computer to another with little modification. GUIs such as Sun Microsystems' Open Look and Open Systems Foundation's Motif have been created for UNIX.

UNIX does have limitations. It uses a complicated set of commands. It cannot respond well to problems caused by overuse of computer resources. It has weak security features because it allows multiple users and multiple computer jobs to access the same file simultaneously. It requires huge amounts of RAM and disk storage capacity.

System 7, the latest version of Macintosh system software, supports multitasking and has powerful graphics capabilities, with a built-in mouse-driven GUI. It can take advantage of the power of 32-bit microprocessors. An extension of this operating system, QuickTime™, allows Macintosh users to integrate video clips, stereo sound, and animated sequences with conventional text and graphics software. (See Chapter 5 for a discussion of multimedia.)

Windows NT

A powerful operating system for use with 32-bit microprocessors in networked environments; supports multitasking and multiprocessing and can be used with Intel and some other types of microprocessors.

UNIX

A machine-independent operating system for microcomputers, minicomputers, and mainframes; it is interactive and supports multiuser processing, multitasking, and networking.

System 7

Operating System for the Macintosh microcomputer, with multitasking, graphics, and multimedia capabilities.

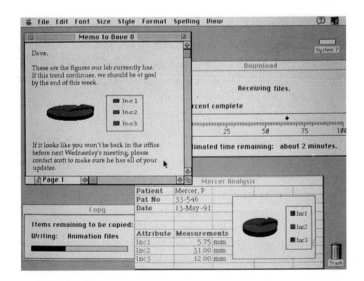

System 7, the operating system for the Macintosh computer, has a built-in graphical user interface and multitasking and multimedia capabilities. Users can view multiple windows and make selections by clicking on icons using pulldown menus.
SOURCE: Courtesy of Apple Computer, Inc.

As this brief survey suggests, the various microcomputer operating systems offer a variety of features as well as advantages and disadvantages. Therefore, when selecting a microcomputer operating system, one should ask several key questions:

What kind of computer hardware is required? How much processing power and storage capacity are required to run the operating system?
What kinds of applications software does it support?
How easy is it to learn and use?
How quickly does it run?
Are many problems anticipated that would best be solved in a multitasking environment?
Is the operating system primarily designed for single users or for networking?
How much technical and support assistance is available?

6.3 PROGRAMMING LANGUAGES

Each of the major kinds of software consists of programs written in specific programming languages. Each programming language was designed to solve a particular class of problems. It is important to understand the strengths and limitations of each of these languages in order to select appropriate software.

MAJOR PROGRAMMING LANGUAGES

Assembly Language   As we explained in Section 6.1, assembly language was developed to overcome some of the difficulties of machine language. Mnemonic (easy to remember) codes and symbols are used to represent operations (such as adding or moving) and storage locations. For example, A stands for "Add" and L stands for "Load." Assembly language is very machine oriented, because assembly-language instructions correspond closely to the machine-language instructions for a specific computer and spe-

---

FIGURE 6.6

Examples of Machine Language Code and Assembly Language Code to Add the Value of B to A

Assembly language is primarily used today for writing software for operating systems. As you can see, it is very different from English and much closer to machine language in its commands. Although this can make it inefficient for humans to learn, it is very efficient for computers to execute.

```
Machine Code

1111101001010010100100000000000001001000000001100

Assembly Code

AP TOTALA,    VALUEB
```

SOURCE: Figure 4–15, "Examples of Machine Language Code and Assembly Language Code to Add the Value of B to A (A = A + B)," from *Computer Information Systems* by Jerome S. Burstein and Edward G. Martin, p. 113, copyright © 1989 by The Dryden Press. Reprinted by permission of the authors.

cific microprocessor. Each assembly-language instruction corresponds to a single machine-language instruction (see Figure 6.6).

Assembly language emphasizes efficient use of computer resources. Minimal memory and CPU activity are required for processing with assembly language. Therefore, execution of assembly-language programs is extremely rapid and efficient.

Although assembly language is easier to use than pure machine language, it is still extremely difficult to learn and requires highly skilled programmers. Assembly language is used primarily for writing operating systems software, when highly detailed programs that are sensitive to a specific computer's machine language must be designed.

FORTRAN   FORTRAN (which stands for FORmula TRANslator) was developed in 1954 to facilitate the writing of scientific, mathematical, and engineering software. Although business applications can be written in FORTRAN, the language is most appropriate for scientific, engineering, and mathematical problems that use complicated formulas. A FORTRAN program is shown in Figure 6.7. It reads a list of students and their grade-point averages (GPAs) on a scale of 0 to 4. From the list shown below, the program selects those students with a GPA of 3.5 or more and prints their names and GPAs for the honor roll.

Student	GPA
Mary Smith	3.75
Robert Lopez	2.95
Christine Jones	2.85
Tom Toshiba	3.95
Janis Roberts	3.49
Ralph Brown	3.20
Ronald Chang	3.00
Susan O'Malley	3.50
Cathy Schwartz	3.00
Michael Ramirez	3.65

FORTRAN's great strength lies in its facilities for mathematical computations. It does not have strong facilities for input/output activities or for working with lists. Thus it would not be appropriate for business problems that involve reading massive amounts of records and producing reports. On the other hand, for business problems requiring sophisticated computations, such as forecasting and modeling, FORTRAN has been used successfully.

COBOL   COBOL (which comes from COmmon Business-Oriented Language) was introduced in the early 1960s and remains the predominant language for business problems. It was designed to process large data files with alphanumeric characters (mixed alphabetic and numeric data), which are characteristic of business problems. COBOL can read, write, and manipulate records very effectively. Business specialists also find it easier to learn than most other programming languages. It uses relatively English-like statements, is easily readable, and supports well-structured programs. COBOL does not handle complex mathematical calculations well, however, and its programs tend to be wordy and lengthy. Figure 6.8 shows the honor-roll program in COBOL.

PL/1   IBM created **PL/1** (which stands for Programming Language 1) in 1964 as a general-purpose programming language to support both business and scientific problem solving. PL/1 is very powerful but not widely used. Companies that had already invested heavily in COBOL and FORTRAN software and programmers did not want

FORTRAN

A programming language developed in 1954 for scientific, mathematical, and engineering applications; stands for FORmula TRANslator.

COBOL

A programming language with English-like statements designed for processing large data files with alphanumeric characters; the predominant programming language for business applications; stands for COmmon Business-Oriented Language.

PL/1

A programming language developed in 1964 by IBM for business and scientific applications; not as widely used as COBOL or FORTRAN.

FIGURE 6.7

The Honor-Roll Program in FORTRAN

FORTRAN is a relatively old computer language (created in 1954), but it is still in common use today. It is generally used for scientific, mathematical, and engineering calculations rather than for business.

```
      PROGRAM HONORF(INPUT,OUTPUT,SCOREF,TAPE60=INPUT,TAPE61=SCOREF)
C   THIS PROGRAM EXTRACTS THE NAMES OF THOSE STUDENTS WHO
C   HAVE A GRADE-POINT AVERAGE (GPA) GREATER THAN OR EQUAL
C   TO 3.50.   THE NAME AND GPA OF EACH QUALIFYING STUDENT, AND
C   THE TOTAL NUMBER OF THE QUALIFYING STUDENTS IS PRINTED OUT.
      CHARACTER * 20 NAME(10)
      REAL GPA(10)
      INTEGER COUNT
      COUNT = 0
        PRINT *,'     OAKRIVER UNIVERSITY HONOR ROLL REPORT'
        PRINT *,' '
        PRINT *,'          THE HONOR ROLL STUDENTS'
        PRINT *,' '
        PRINT *,'     STUDENT NAME                    GPA'
        PRINT *,' '
      DO 70 I = 1, 10
        READ(61,40) NAME(I), GPA(I)
40      FORMAT(A20,F4.2)
        IF (GPA(I) .GE. 3.5) THEN
           PRINT 50, NAME(I), GPA(I)
50         FORMAT(5X,A20,10X,F4.2)      IF THEN ELSE
           COUNT = COUNT + 1
        END IF
70    CONTINUE
      PRINT 80, COUNT
80    FORMAT(//,5X,'THE NUMBER OF HONOR ROLL STUDENTS IS:', I3)
      END
```

```
RUN

      OAKRIVER UNIVERSITY HONOR ROLL REPORT

          THE HONOR ROLL STUDENTS

      STUDENT NAME                    GPA

      MARY SMITH                      3.75
      TOM TOSHIBA                     3.95
      SUSAN O'MALLEY                  3.50
      MICHAEL RAMIREZ                 3.65


      THE NUMBER OF HONOR STUDENTS IS:  4
```

SOURCE: Figure 15–8, "The Honor Roll Problem in FORTRAN," from *Computer Information Systems* by Jerome S. Burstein and Edward G. Martin, p. 516, copyright © 1989 by The Dryden Press. Reprinted by permission of the authors.

to convert to another language. They were reluctant to spend millions of dollars rewriting software when software written in COBOL and FORTRAN was already solving problems well. It has also been difficult to teach PL/1 to programmers versed in COBOL.

BASIC

A programming language frequently used for teaching programming and for microcomputers; although it is easy to learn, it does not easily support sound programming practices.

BASIC   BASIC (which stands for Beginner's All-purpose Symbolic Instruction Code) was developed in 1964 to teach Dartmouth College students how to use computers. It has become an extremely popular programming language for microcomputers and for teaching programming in colleges and high schools. BASIC is easy to learn and has minimal memory requirements for conversion into machine code. Beginners with only a

FIGURE 6.8

The Honor-Roll Program in COBOL

As you can see, COBOL commands are much closer to English sentences than either FORTRAN or assembly language. Created to process large data files such as those used in business (e.g., payroll and accounting), COBOL is still the most common computer language in business programming.

```
IDENTIFICATION DIVISION.

PROGRAM-ID.             PROGRAM-SCORE.
AUTHOR.                 TOM LEE.
INSTALLATION.           ORISC.
DATE-WRITTEN.           JANUARY-12, 1990.

ENVIRONMENT DIVISION.

CONFIGURATION SECTION.
SOURCE-COMPUTER.   CYBER-174.
OBJECT-COMPUTER.   CYBER-174.
INPUT-OUTPUT SECTION.
FILE-CONTROL.
    SELECT RECORDS-IN ASSIGN TO SCORES, USE "RT=Z".
    SELECT PRINT-OUT ASSIGN TO OUTPUT.

DATA DIVISION.

FILE SECTION.
FD   RECORDS-IN
     LABEL RECORDS ARE OMITTED.
01   IN-RECORD              PIC X(72).
FD   PRINT-OUT
     LABEL RECORDS ARE OMITTED.
01   PRINT-LINE             PIC X(72).
WORKING-STORAGE SECTION.
77   STUDENT-COUNT          PIC 9(3)       VALUE ZEROES.
01   FLAG.
     05 END-OF-FILE-FLAG    PIC X          VALUE "N".
     05 NO-MORE-DATA        PIC X          VALUE "Y".
01   STUDENT-RECORD.
     05 NAME-RD             PIC X(20).
     05 GRADE-PT            PIC 9V99.
     05 FILLER              PIC X(49).
01   HDG.
     05 FILLER              PIC X(5)       VALUE SPACES.
     05 FILLER              PIC X(9)       VALUE "OAKRIVER ".
     05 FILLER              PIC X(11)      VALUE "UNIVERSITY ".
     05 FILLER              PIC X(17)      VALUE "HONOR ROLL REPORT".
     05 FILLER              PIC X(30)      VALUE SPACES.
01   HDG-1.
     05 FILLER              PIC X(10)      VALUE SPACES.
     05 FILLER              PIC X(15)      VALUE "THE HONOR ROLL ".
     05 FILLER              PIC X(8)       VALUE "STUDENTS".
     05 FILLER              PIC X(39)      VALUE SPACES.
01   HDG-2.
     05 FILLER              PIC X(5)       VALUE SPACES.
     05 FILLER              PIC X(12)      VALUE "STUDENT NAME".
     05 FILLER              PIC X(18)      VALUE SPACES.
     05 FILLER              PIC X(3)       VALUE "GPA".
     05 FILLER              PIC X(34)      VALUE SPACES.
01   HDG-3.
     05 FILLER              PIC X(72)      VALUE SPACES.
01   STUDENT-LINE.
     05 FILLER              PIC X(5)       VALUE SPACES.
     05 NAME-IN             PIC X(20).
     05 FILLER              PIC X(10)      VALUE SPACES.
     05 GRADE               PIC 9.99.
     05 FILLER              PIC X(33)      VALUE SPACES.
```

continued on page 198

continued from page 197

```
01    TOTAL-LINE.
      05  FILLER              PIC X(5)      VALUE SPACES.
      05  FILLER              PIC X(14)     VALUE "THE NUMBER OF ".
      05  FILLER              PIC X(11)     VALUE "HONOR ROLL ".
      05  FILLER              PIC X(12)     VALUE "STUDENTS IS:".
      05  STUDENT-NUMBER      PIC ZZ9.
      05  FILLER              PIC X(27)     VALUE SPACES.

PROCEDURE DIVISION.

MAIN-PROGRAM.
      PERFORM START-PROCESS.
      PEFORM DECISION-FOR-HONOR-ROLL
        UNTIL END-OF-FILE-FLAG = "Y".
      PERFORM WRAPITUP.
      STOP RUN.
START-PROCESS.
      OPEN INPUT RECORDS-IN OUTPUT PRINT-OUT.
      MOVE SPACES TO STUDENT-LINE.
      WRITE PRINT-LINE FROM HDG AFTER ADVANCING 2 LINES.
      WRITE PRINT-LINE FROM HDG-1 AFTER ADVANCING 2 LINES.
      WRITE PRINT-LINE FROM HDG-2 AFTER ADVANCING 2 LINES.
      WRITE PRINT-LINE FROM HDG-3 AFTER ADVANCING 1 LINE.
DECISION-FOR-HONOR-ROLL.
      READ RECORDS-IN INTO STUDENT-RECORD
        AT END MOVE NO-MORE-DATA TO END-OF-FILE-FLAG.
      MOVE NAME-RD TO NAME-LN.
      MOVE GRADE-PT TO GRADE.
```

```
      IF (GRADE-PT > 3.49)
        WRITE PRINT-LINE FROM STUDENT-LINE                    IF THEN ELSE
        AFTER ADVANCING 1 LINE ADD 1 TO STUDENT-COUNT.
```

```
      MOVE STUDENT-COUNT TO STUDENT-NUMBER.
WRAPITUP.
      WRITE PRINT-LINE FROM TOTAL-LINE AFTER ADVANCING 3 LINES.
      CLOSE RECORDS-IN, PRINT-OUT.

RUN

        OAKRIVER UNIVERSITY HONOR ROLL REPORT

           THE HONOR ROLL STUDENTS

        STUDENT NAME             GPA

        MARY SMITH               3.75
        TOM TOSHIBA              3.95
        SUSAN O'MALLEY           3.50
        MICHAEL RAMIREZ          3.65


THE NUMBER OF HONOR ROLL STUDENTS IS:  4
```

SOURCE: Figure 15–7, "The Honor Roll Problem in COBOL," from *Computer Information Systems* by Jerome S. Burstein and Edward G. Martin, p. 514–515, copyright © 1989 by The Dryden Press. Reprinted by permission of the authors.

few hours of instruction can use the software to solve small problems. Figure 6.9 illustrates the honor-roll program in BASIC.

BASIC can handle many kinds of problems, although experts point out that it performs few tasks very well. BASIC also lacks strong structures for enforcing a clear flow of logic and well-organized programs, so it is not conducive to teaching good programming practices.

Pascal

A programming language that consists of smaller subprograms, each of which is a structured program in itself; it is used on microcomputers and for teaching programming but has relatively few business applications.

Pascal   Named after Blaise Pascal, the seventeenth-century mathematician and philosopher, **Pascal** was developed by the Swiss computer science professor Niklaus Wirth

FIGURE 6.9

The Honor-Roll Program in BASIC

Here we see the BASIC instructions for performing the same task. BASIC is a popular language for microcomputers; it is similar to English and thus is easy to learn. However, it is not very good at performing sophisticated calculations or complex manipulations of data.

```
100  REM  HONOR PROGRAM
110  REM  This program prints NAMES and GPA for students
120  REM  whose GPA is 3.5 or higher. It also prints the
130  REM  total number of honor roll students printed on report.
140  REM  VARIABLES: N$ = Student Name  G = Grade Point Average
150  REM            S  = Total          I = Array counter
160  REM  * * * * * MAIN PROGRAM * * * * *
170  LET  S=0
180  OPEN  "i",1,"SCORES"
190  PRINT  "        Oakriver University Honor Roll Report"
200  PRINT
210  PRINT  "           The Honor Roll Students"
220  PRINT
230  PRINT  "        Student Name           GPA"
240  PRINT
250  FOR  I = 1 TO 10
260  IF  EOF(1)  THEN 320
270  INPUT  #1,N$,G
280  IF G>3.49 THEN 290 ELSE 310
290  PRINT USING "     \                \          #.##";N$,G
300  LET S=S+1
310  NEXT  I
320  CLOSE #1
330  PRINT
340  PRINT
350  PRINT  "    The number of honor roll students is: ";S
360  END

RUN

        Oakriver University Honor Roll Report

           The Honor Roll Students

        Student Name           GPA

        Mary Smith             3.75
        Tom Toshiba            3.95
        Susan O'Malley         3.50
        Michael Ramirez        3.65


    The number of honor roll students is:  4
```

SOURCE: Figure 15–5, "The Honor Roll Problem in BASIC," from *Computer Information Systems* by Jerome S. Burstein and Edward G. Martin, p. 511, copyright © 1989 by The Dryden Press. Reprinted by permission of the authors.

of Zurich in the late 1960s. Wirth wanted to create a language that would teach students structured programming techniques. Pascal programs consist of smaller subprograms, each of which is a structured program in itself. Figure 6.10 illustrates the honor-roll program in Pascal.

Pascal programs can be used on microcomputers, but Pascal itself is used primarily in computer science courses to teach sound programming practices. Pascal has limited features for input and output, so it is not well suited for most business problems.

Ada   Ada was developed in 1980 to provide the U.S. Defense Department with a structured programming language to be the standard for all its applications. In addition to

Ada
A programming language developed for the Department of Defense to be portable across diverse brands of hardware; it also has nonmilitary applications and can be used for business problems.

FIGURE 6.10

Pascal: Programs within Programs

The Pascal language was developed to teach students the techniques of designing logical, easy-to-read programs. Each Pascal program contains subprograms written to follow consistent patterns of instructions. Today Pascal is rarely used in business because its input and output features are limited.

```
PROGRAM HONOR(INPUT/,OUTPUT,SCOREP);

(* This program extracts the names of those students who *)
(* have a grade-point average (GPA) greater than or equal *)
(* to 3.50.  The name and GPA of each qualifying student, and *)
(* the total number of the qualifying students is printed out. *)

TYPE
     STRING = ARRAY[1..20] OF CHAR;

VAR
     COUNT, I, J: INTEGER;
     GRADEPT: REAL;
     NAME: STRING;
     SCOREP: TEXT;
BEGIN (* START OF PROGRAM *)
     RESET(SCOREP);
     COUNT := 0;
     WRITELN('      Oakriver University Honor Roll Report');
     WRITELN;
     WRITELN('           The Honor Roll Students');
     WRITELN;
     WRITELN('      Student Name           GPA');
     WRITELN;
     WHILE NOT EOF (SCOREP) DO
        BEGIN
           FOR J := 1 TO 20 DO
              READ(SCOREP, NAME[J]);
           READLN(SCOREP, GRADEPT);
           IF GRADEPT > 3.49 THEN
              BEGIN
                 COUNT := COUNT + 1;
                 WRITE(' ':5);                      IF THEN ELSE
                 FOR I := 1 TO 20 DO
                    WRITE(NAME[I]);
                 WRITELN(' ':10, GRADEPT :3:2);
              END;
           END;
     WRITELN;
     WRITELN;
     WRITELN('      The number of honor roll students is:', COUNT :3);
END.

RUN

          Oakriver University Honor Roll Report

             The Honor Roll Students

          Student Name              GPA

          Mary Smith                3.75
          Tom Toshiba               3.95
          Susan O'Malley            3.50
          Michael Ramirez           3.65


          The number of honor roll students is:  4
```

SOURCE: Figure 15–6, "The Honor Roll Problem in Pascal," from *Computer Information Systems* by Jerome S. Burstein and Edward G. Martin, p. 512, copyright © 1989 by The Dryden Press. Reprinted by permission of the authors.

military command and control systems, Ada is used in some nonmilitary government applications. The language is also useful for business problems: it can operate on microcomputers, is portable across different brands of computer hardware, and promotes structured program design. Ada also supports concurrent tasks and real-time programming.

Ada was named for Ada, Countess of Lovelace, the daughter of the English poet Lord Byron. The Countess was an able nineteenth-century mathematician who developed the mathematical tables for an early calculating machine. For this reason she is sometimes called the first programmer.

Ada has many attractive features. The language was initially conceived for weapons systems for which software is developed on a processor and then embedded in the weapon. It was explicitly designed so that it could be uniformly executed in diverse hardware environments. The language also promotes structured software design and reusable software components. (See the Focus on Problem Solving.)

Nevertheless, the question remains as to whether Ada will ever be widely applied to business problem solving. Many firms are not convinced that it is worth the investment and risk to abandon COBOL as the business standard. A large firm would have to retrain hundreds, even thousands, of COBOL programmers and scrap millions of dollars worth of COBOL software.

C   Developed under the auspices of AT&T's Bell Laboratories in the early 1970s, C is the language in which most of the UNIX operating system is written. C has much of the tight control and efficiency of execution of assembly language, yet it is easier to learn and portable across different microprocessors. Figure 6.11 illustrates a sample C program that determines the smaller of two numbers supplied by the user.

Much commercial microcomputer software has been written in C, and C is starting to be used for business, scientific, and technical applications on larger computers.

C
A programming language with tight control and efficiency of execution like assembly language; it is portable across different microprocessors and easier to learn than assembly language.

FOURTH-GENERATION LANGUAGES

Fourth-generation languages offer two major advantages: they allow end users to develop software on their own with little or no technical assistance, and they offer dramatic productivity gains in software development.

Fourth-generation languages tend to be less procedural than conventional languages, making them more suitable for end users. Thus, these languages have created the technical platform for nonspecialists to play a larger role in problem solving with information systems. In addition, fourth-generation languages can be employed by less skilled programmers, a quality that helps improve productivity. Studies have shown that fourth-generation languages can produce productivity gains of 300 to 500 percent over conventional languages.[2]

There are several major types of fourth-generation software tools:

1. Query languages

2. Graphics languages

3. Report generators

4. Application generators

5. Very-high-level programming languages

Fourth-generation language
Programming languages that are less procedural than conventional languages (i.e., they need only specify what is to be done rather than provide the details of how to do it) and contain more English language–like commands; they are easier for nonspecialists to learn and use than conventional languages.

FOCUS ON PROBLEM SOLVING

WHY NOT REUSE PROGRAMMING CODE?

Advocates of reusing software see a big payoff in the practice. The Pentagon estimates that it could save $300 million annually if it increased its software reuse by only one percent. GTE Data Services, Inc., in Tampa, Florida, estimates it has gained a 20 to 30 percent productivity increase by using reusable code. The Canadian National Railway built a new freight-car optimization system by writing only 10,600 lines of new code while using 137,600 lines from existing code libraries, allowing it to develop a 148,000-line application in just eight person-months of work. Raytheon Co., of Lexington, Massachusetts, has reused program code since 1976 and now gets 80 to 90 percent of its new application code from reuse libraries. Carma L. McClure, research vice-president at Extended Intelligence, Inc. in Chicago, Illinois, and an expert on reuse, believes that 40 to 60 percent of all new code could come from libraries of reusable components. With all this productivity promise, why is code reusability not more popular?

In fact, it is becoming more popular. McClure reports a sharp rise in interest in code reusability since 1992. However, the real problem may be that the concept of software reusability is deceptively simple, resulting in too many implementation failures. The U.S. General Accounting Office reports that code reusers work in an ad hoc way, foraging for code through old libraries until they find something that might help. Such a disorganized approach is bound to fail frequently, partly because it takes entirely too long to find useful code and partly because the selected code may be flawed or at least will not be tested to meet the needs of the new application. Code reuse requires careful planning; time and money must be spent before it will work well. Raytheon's success, for example, has taken a long time.

To build reusable code libraries, organizations must prepare the software to go into those libraries. The code must be generalized so that it can be used in a number of different applications, and it must be more thoroughly tested than if it is to be used in only one program. Finally, it must be well-documented and certified for reuse. Tight development schedules often prevent this type of initial extra effort in exchange for benefits that may not be achieved for a long time. In addition, a company must be selective about what it adds to the reuse library, adding only code that analysis shows has genuine potential for reuse.

Another significant issue is the categorization of the code in the reuse libraries. Horizontal code functions are generic and can be used across applications, such as sorting algorithms or graphical user interface code. Vertical code functions are designed for specific groups of applications, such as a routine to calculate total cost that might be used in a number of accounting applications. A good programmer will have to understand how to locate the code she or he needs.

The concept of reusability is spreading beyond program code. Some organizations are beginning to store designs, algorithms, test plans, test data, and documentation for reuse. Philip Kiviat, a vice-president at Knowledge Ware, Inc., in McLean, Virginia, goes further to claim that it is only at the design level that real gains can be made. "You should reuse designs," he says, "not code. Code is perishable. Reuse components that are further upstream."

Companies are also beginning to purchase code from other companies for reuse. When Canadian Airlines International Ltd. decided to build a frequent-flier application, they bought a "template" from Trans World Airlines, Inc. and saved 50 percent of the expected coding time. As an additional benefit, they learned a great deal about the new application they were building. Some companies market code specifically for reuse. For example, Andersen Consulting sells code for functions related to life insurance and insurance policy administration. Oracle Corp. now sells industry-specific templates that use business models to help generate applications for the pharmaceutical, oil and gas, and other industries.

A recent development that will affect the issue of code reusability is the growing popularity of object-oriented programming. Objects are software building blocks that can potentially be reused by other applications. Software developers are hoping that libraries of reusable objects will speed up future software work.

FOCUS Questions:

What are some of the dangers in reusing program code? What people, organization, and technology factors should be considered when deciding whether to reuse software?

SOURCE: Gary H. Anthes, "Software Reuse Plans Bring Paybacks," *Computerworld,* December 6, 1993.

FIGURE 6.11

C: An Efficient, Flexible Language
C is the programming language of the UNIX operating system. It executes very efficiently, but it is easier to learn than assembly language. It also has the advantage of operating with different microprocessors.

```
/*
 * MINIMUM
 *
 * This program determines the lesser of two
 * numbers supplied by the user.
 */

main()
{
        int lesser;              /* the result */
        int number1, number2;    /* the input values */

        /*
         * Prompt the user for two numbers and read them.
         */
        printf("Type the first number and press Enter: ");
        scanf("%d" &number1);
        printf("Type the second number and press Enter: ");
        scanf("%d", &number2);

        /*
         * Find the lesser value and report it.
         */
        if (number1 < number2)
                lesser = number1;
        else
                lesser = number2;
        printf("The lesser of %d and %d is %d.\n".
                number1, number2, lesser);

        return (0);
}
```

SOURCE: From *Learn C Now*, p. 96, reprinted by permission of Microsoft Press. Copyright © 1988 by Augie Hansen. All rights reserved.

Query languages are high-level, easy-to-use languages for accessing data stored in information systems. They are valuable for supporting ad hoc requests for information that are not predefined (as opposed to routine, predefined requests). These are one-time requests for information that cannot be produced by existing applications or reporting software.

Query languages tend to be very end-user oriented, although some may have sophisticated capabilities for updating data as well. Some query languages have strong natural-language features, such as statements that use English-like words and syntax. An example of an ad hoc query might be, "List all products with a unit price over $12.00." (Compare this with a similar request in COBOL.)

Figure 6.12 compares queries in two different kinds of query languages, Nomad2 and Intellect. Nomad2 is an application generator with a query language. An application generator is a software package that uses a high-level or fourth-generation language and/or graphical screen painting tools to quickly generate a software application. Intellect is a natural-language system that accepts English-like queries. Most query languages are highly interactive, allowing users to satisfy requests for information immediately on-line.

Query language
A high-level, easy-to-use, fourth-generation language for accessing stored data.

FIGURE 6.12

Nomad2 and Intellect: Two Different Query Languages
Query languages are fourth-generation languages that make it easier than ever before to access stored data. They allow nonprogrammers to "ask" computers questions pertaining to stored information. The query in panel a uses Intellect and prints total sales in 1989 for four cities. The Nomad2 query in panel b lists total salary for each department in a firm.

(a) Natural-Language Query Using Intellect

RANK TOTAL COPIER SALES BY MARKET
PRINT THE RANKED TOTAL 1989 ACT YTD $
IN EACH MARKET OF ALL SALES DATA WITH PRODUCT
LINE = COPIER & PRODUCT = TOTAL & MARKET NOT
TOTAL & CHANNEL = TOTAL

MARKET	1989 ACTUAL YTD SALES
CHICAGO	$33,340,528
LOS ANGELES	$30,211,200
WASHINGTON	$20,295,200
NEW YORK	$18,848,800

(b) Query Using Nomad2

>LIST BY DEPT SUM (SALARY)
PAGE 1

DEPARTMENT	SUM CURRENT SALARY
MARKETING	66,700
PERSONNEL	54,900
SALES	77,300

SOURCE: David H. Freedman, "Programming without Tears," *High Technology,* April 1986.

Graphics language

A fourth-generation language for displaying computerized data in graphical form.

Report generator

A software tool that extracts stored data to create customized reports that are not routinely produced by existing applications.

Graphics languages are specialized software for displaying computerized data in graphical form. Most numeric data can be understood more easily when presented as graphs. This is particularly true when making comparisons or spotting trends. Graphics software can retrieve stored data and display them in the graphic format requested by users. Some graphics languages can manipulate data and perform calculations as well. Harvard Graphics, Lotus Freelance Graphics, and Aldus Persuasion are leading graphics packages for microcomputers.

A popular mainframe graphics language, Statistical Analysis Software (SAS), is primarily a statistical analysis tool, but it also has easy-to-use graphics capabilities. It features English-like commands and menus that enable end-users to perform statistical operations, such as regression analysis and variance analysis, and to create reports. SAS has easy-to-use yet powerful color graphics features for charts, plots, maps, and three-dimensional displays. The graphs can be customized, and multiple displays can be presented on a single page.

Report generators are software tools that extract stored data to create customized reports that are not routinely produced by existing applications. In contrast to query languages, report generators give users more control over the way data are formatted, organized, and displayed. For example, report generators such as RPG III have facilities for specifying report headings, subheadings, page headings, column positioning, page numbering, and totaling of numbers. Report generators may have on-line capabilities, but they typically run in a batch processing environment.

Application generators are related pieces of software that can generate entire information system applications without customized programming. The end-user need only specify *what* needs to be done, and the application generator will create the appropriate program code. The most versatile and powerful application generators integrate tools such as a query language, screen painter, graphics and report generators, modeling software, and a special programming language. Application generators typically are too complex for end-users to work with alone, but they require less technical assistance than conventional programming and can create entire applications more rapidly. Some features of application generators, such as the query language or graphics languages, can be employed directly by end-users.

Very-high-level programming languages are primarily tools for professional programmers, but they have some capabilities that can be employed by end users. These languages are distinguished by their productivity-promoting features, which produce program code with far fewer instructions than conventional languages such as COBOL or PL/1. APL and Nomad2 are examples of such very-high-level programming languages.

> **Application generator**
> Software that can generate entire information system applications without customized programming; the end-user specifies what needs to be done, and the generator creates the appropriate program code.

> **Very-high-level programming language**
> A programming language that produces program code with far fewer instructions than conventional languages; used primarily by professional programmers.

SELECTING A PROGRAMMING LANGUAGE

To select the right software tool for problem solving, you must know the capabilities and limitations of the major programming languages (see Table 6.2 for a comparison of the various languages). The following are the most important considerations for selecting a programming language:

1. **The nature of the problem to be solved:** Is it a scientific problem, a business problem that requires mathematical modeling, or a problem that entails extensive file manipulation and input/output work?

2. **Computer hardware requirements:** Is the language compatible with your computer hardware resources? Is it essential that it be able to run on more than one kind of machine? Will it work on the operating system for your computer hardware (see Section 6.2)? Are there any limitations on memory size or computer resources? Do you need to use a microcomputer?

3. **Ease of use:** Is the language one that you can use, one that your technical staff is already familiar with, or one that can easily be learned?

4. **Maintainability:** Is it important that the language be highly structured? Can the language-support programs be modified and maintained by others over a long period of time?

6.4 APPLICATIONS SOFTWARE

A computer application is the use of a computer to solve a specific problem or to perform a specific task for an end user. Applications software is a major category of software that handles the processing for a particular computer application. There are numerous computer applications for which applications software has been written: business functions, such as accounts receivable or sales forecasting; scientific and engineering functions, such as molecular modeling or microprocessor design; law enforcement functions, such as computerized criminal-history record keeping; educational functions, such as computer-based mathematics instruction; artistic functions, such as the production

TABLE 6.2

Comparison of the Major Programming Languages

Programming Language	Key Features	Appropriate Tasks
Assembly language	Machine dependent; highly efficient; symbolic; difficult to learn.	Systems software.
FORTRAN	Strong facilities for mathematical computations and formulas; poor input/output facilities.	Scientific and mathematical problems and business problems requiring complex formulas; modeling.
COBOL	Strong input/output and file manipulation facilities; weak facilities for mathematical computations.	Business problems requiring extensive reading and printing of records and file manipulation.
PL/1	Powerful, multipurpose language developed by IBM; complex and somewhat difficult to learn.	Both scientific and business problems.
BASIC	General-purpose language; easy to learn; runs on microcomputers; does not promote good program structure.	Problems that can be solved primarily with microcomputers; teaching programming.
Pascal	Used to teach structured programming; limited input/output capabilities.	Education; scientific problems that can be solved with microcomputers.
Ada	Developed by Defense Department for weapons systems and business applications; powerful; portable across different machine environments.	Weapons systems; business problems.
C	Highly efficient and portable across different computer machine environments; somewhat difficult to learn.	General-purpose problems, especially those that can be solved with microcomputers; development of systems software.
Fourth-generation languages	Query languages, report generators, application generators, graphics languages, very-high-level programming languages; largely nonprocedural with many "user-friendly" features.	Simple problems that can be solved primarily by nontechnical specialists.

of computer-generated music and art; and the transmission of data via telecommunications. The Focus on Technology describes one kind of state-of-the-art applications software that can represent data geographically.

SOFTWARE PACKAGES

Software packages are prewritten, precoded, commercially available programs that eliminate the need for writing software programs. Software packages are available for systems software, but the vast majority of software packages are **applications software packages**. The spreadsheet, database, and word processing software for your personal computer are all software packages. A mainframe-based payroll system that issues checks each week for 30,000 employees and the checking and savings account processing system of a bank also typically use software packages.

The following is a list of areas for which commercial applications software packages are available. Some of these applications are solely mainframe or microcomputer

Applications software package
A prewritten, precoded, commercially available program that handles the processing for a particular computer application (e.g., spreadsheet or data management software for a personal computer).

FOCUS ON TECHNOLOGY

SOFTWARE THAT READS MAPS

If you were a vice-president for sales, your fourth-quarter sales report might look something like this:

Region	Sales	Change from Last Year
North	52,231	−4.1%
South	90,809	−2.6
East	132,553	+3.3
West	87,441	−6.0
TOTAL	363,034	−2.3

You can tell that sales in the East are doing better. But is one state outperforming the others in that region? Are there any "hot spots"—cities or counties where sales are taking off? How can you discover such details without wading through a 60-page report? The answer was known to ancient mariners: If data are linked to geography, use a map. Special software that displays geographically linked data can answer your questions.

Like all maps, mapping software presents data in a form that users can absorb more easily than by reviewing and analyzing written reports. For example, Quaker Oats Co. uses geographic software from MapInfo Corp. of Troy, New York, to target stores and regions in geographic areas with specific products. The software displays and analyzes customer data, store locations, and sales volume geographically on electronic charts, maps, and graphs. Quaker uses this information to develop cost-effective advertising programs.

Another advantage of mapping software is that data can be manipulated as well as mapped. Sales managers can use the software for territory design, site selection, and target marketing. Johanna Dairies of Union, New Jersey, used such software to create digital maps of streets and delivery locations to determine the best routes for delivery. By redesigning its delivery routes, Johanna Dairies was able to eliminate 13 percent of its routes for an annual savings of $100,000 per route. Businesses can analyze the effect of competitors on the geographic distribution of customers by physically viewing the concentration of customers in areas closer to and further away from competitor locations.

Banks use geographic information systems (GISs) to make sure their lending practices are equitable. The Community Reinvestment Act requires that banks lend money back to the same neighborhoods from which they receive deposits and that they report deposit and loan activity at a census-tract level within their market areas. The legislation is designed to prevent a practice called redlining, in which banks circled low-income areas on a map in red. Even if they had respectable incomes and credit ratings, inhabitants of those areas were either denied mortgage loans or were subject to more stringent loan application standards than the residents of more affluent areas. Banks use GIS to perform the analysis needed to create the required loan/deposit reports and to present the data in map form. When banks find areas where the loan/deposit ratio is out of balance, they can use the GIS to target markets to bring them into compliance.

GIS may even ease the health care crisis. One solution proposed for affordable health care is managed care, in which employees have a limited choice of physicians and hospitals. Managed-care networks use GIS to prove that their network of health care providers is geographically well-suited to a group of employees by generating maps that show employees' homes in relation to provider locations.

FOCUS Questions: What people, organization, and technology factors should a business examine when considering whether to use mapping software? Can you suggest other applications for mapping software?

Leads for hot tubs are primarily coming from upper-income ZIP codes. The map is used to create direct-marketing programs for the most promising areas. SOURCE: Courtesy of MapInfo Corp.

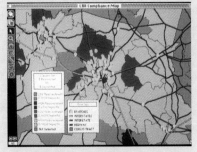

Banking and demographic census data are combined to analyze Community Reinvestment Act compliance. Census tracts are color-coded by level of reinvestment in comparison to level of deposits. SOURCE: Courtesy of Tactics International Ltd.

SOURCES: Nora Sherwood Bryan, "A Look at GIS," *Computerworld*, July 26, 1993; David Forrest, "Seeing Data in New Ways," *Computerworld*, June 29, 1992; and John C. Freed, "Mapping Software for Every Business," *The New York Times*, February 16, 1992.

based, but many have packages available in mainframe, minicomputer, and micro-computer versions.

- Accounts payable
- Animated computer graphics
- Arithmetic drill
- Automobile rentals
- Computer-aided design (CAD)
- Check processing
- Client management
- Desktop publishing
- Econometric modeling
- Equal Employment Opportunity reporting and compliance
- General ledger
- Hotel reservations
- Human resources
- Life insurance
- Mailing labels
- Management of personal finances
- Manufacturing resources planning
- Molecular modeling
- Mortgage account calculation
- Payroll
- Pension calculations
- Presentation graphics
- Process control
- Property management
- Purchasing
- Statistical analysis
- Tax preparation
- Videotape rental tracking
- Word processing

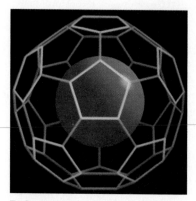

To facilitate design of new chemical compounds, scientists develop molecular models. The processing of commands and data that create these models is handled by applications software.

SOURCE: © Richard E. Smalley, Rice University

POPULAR MICROCOMPUTER APPLICATIONS PACKAGES

Some of the most popular pieces of applications software are the general-purpose applications packages that have been developed for microcomputers. Word processing, spreadsheet, data management, graphics, and desktop-publishing software have been widely adopted for business and other kinds of problem solving. Some of this software also has been widely copied and distributed, raising questions about violations of software copyrights and improper use. (See Chapter 3.)

Word Processing Software   Word processing software has dramatically enhanced the productivity of clerical workers, managers, and knowledge workers by automating the creation, editing, and printing of documents. Text data are stored electronically rather than typed on paper. The word processing software allows changes to be made in the document electronically in memory so that it does not have to be typed again. Changes in line spacing, margins, character size, and column widths can be made with formatting options in the software. WordPerfect, Microsoft Word, WordStar, and Ami Pro are examples of popular word processing packages.

Most word processing software has advanced features that automate other aspects of the writing process. Spelling checkers use built-in dictionaries to locate and correct spelling errors. Style checkers analyze grammar and punctuation errors and may even suggest ways to improve writing style. The thesaurus program provides on-line lists of synonyms and antonyms. Mail merge programs link letters or other text documents with names and addresses in a mailing list.

Word processing software
Software that handles such applications as electronic editing, formatting, and printing of documents.

Spreadsheets   Electronic **spreadsheet software** provides computerized versions of traditional financial modeling tools—the accountant's columnar pad, pencil, and calculator. A spreadsheet is organized into a grid of columns and rows. The intersection of a column and row, which is called a cell, can store a number, formula, word, or phrase.

Spreadsheets are valuable for solving problems in which numerous calculations with pieces of data must be related to each other. After a set of mathematical relationships has been constructed, the spreadsheet can be recalculated immediately using a different set of assumptions.

Spreadsheet software readily lends itself to modeling and "what if" analysis. A number of alternatives can easily be evaluated by changing one or two pieces of data without having to rekey in the rest of the worksheet. Figure 6.13 illustrates how spreadsheet software could be used to answer the question "what if sales revenue increased 10 percent each year over a five-year period?" Many spreadsheet packages include graphics functions that can present data in the form of line graphs, bar graphs, or pie charts. The most popular spreadsheet packages are Lotus® 1-2-3®, Quattro Pro, and Excel.

Spreadsheet software
Software that provides the user with financial modeling tools; data are displayed on a grid and numerical data can easily be recalculated to permit the evaluation of several alternatives.

Data Management Software   Although spreadsheet programs are good at manipulating quantitative data, they are poor at storing and manipulating lists or at extracting parts of files from larger sets of data. **Data management software**, on the other hand, is weak at manipulating quantitative data but is very good at creating and manipulating lists and at combining information from different files for problem solving. It has programming features and easy-to-learn menus that enable nonspecialists to build small information systems.

Data management software typically has facilities for creating files and databases (discussed in Chapter 7), storing data, modifying data, and manipulating data for reports and queries. Data management software and database management systems are treated in detail in Chapter 7. Popular database management software for microcomputers includes dBASE IV, Paradox, RBase, and Access.

Data management software
Software that is used for such applications as creating and manipulating lists, creating files and databases to store data, and combining information for reports.

Integrated Packages   Problem solving often requires a combination of software skills—some writing, some quantitative analysis, and some record management. To produce a polished sales forecast report using unintegrated word processing and spreadsheet programs, one would have to develop a sales forecasting spreadsheet and then reformat

FIGURE 6.13

Spreadsheet Software—An Important Business Tool

Spreadsheets have become very popular in business because they can perform "what if?" analysis. The top worksheet displays the results of asking the software to determine sales revenues over a five-year period if sales increased 10 percent each year. The bottom worksheet shows the formulas and data relationships that were entered to ask this question.

Breakdown of Sales by Region

SALES REGION	1993	1994	1995	1996	1997
Northeast	$2,304,000	$2,534,400	$2,787,840	$3,066,624	$3,373,286
South	$1,509,300	$1,660,230	$1,826,253	$2,008,878	$2,209,766
Midwest	$3,309,800	$3,640,780	$4,004,858	$4,405,344	$4,845,878
West	$2,667,000	$2,933,700	$3,227,070	$3,549,777	$3,904,755

% Annual Growth 10%

Breakdown of Sales by Region

SALES REGION	1993	1994	1995	1996	1997
Northeast	$2,304,000	+C23*(1+$C$11)	+D23*(1+$C$11)	+E23*(1+$C$11)	+F23*(1+$C$11)
South	$1,509,300	+C24*(1+$C$11)	+D24*(1+$C$11)	+E24*(1+$C$11)	+F24*(1+$C$11)
Midwest	$3,309,800	+C25*(1+$C$11)	+D25*(1+$C$11)	+E25*(1+$C$11)	+F25*(1+$C$11)
West	$2,667,000	+C26*(1+$C$11)	+D26*(1+$C$11)	+E26*(1+$C$11)	+F26*(1+$C$11)

% Annual Growth 10%

Integrated software package

A software package that provides two or more applications, such as spreadsheets and word processing, allowing for easy transfer of data between them.

that spreadsheet as a report by separately keying the data into both programs. **Integrated software packages** eliminate the redundant work by performing such tasks without having to switch from one program to the other. The spreadsheet data could be reworked in word processing mode by merely pressing a few keys on the keyboard.

Integrated packages typically combine the most common kinds of personal computer applications software—spreadsheet, database, and word processing. Some have recently added data communications, graphics, and project management functions. Popular integrated packages include Lotus Works, Microsoft Works, and ClarisWorks.

Integrated software packages should be distinguished from applications software suites, which are collections of applications such as a spreadsheet, database, and presentation graphics that are sold as a unit. An example would be Microsoft Office, which consists of Excel spreadsheet software, Word word processing software, Access database software, PowerPoint presentation graphics software, and Microsoft Mail electronic mail software. The software suites have some features of integrated packages, such as the ability to exchange data among different applications in the suite, but they consist of the full-featured versions of each type of software. Integrated packages generally offer fewer features and less versatility than the stand-alone versions.

6.5 LEADING-EDGE TECHNOLOGY: OBJECT-ORIENTED PROGRAMMING

What if all cars had nonstandard engines that were built by hand and each make of car required its own special blend of fuel? Automobiles could not play a large role in everyday life because they would be prohibitively expensive to run and hard to repair. Yet this is the situation that has prevailed for software. Most software is still constructed piece by piece by highly trained craftsmen, somewhat like medieval blacksmiths or woodcarvers.

Object-oriented technology promises to create an "industrial revolution" for software by allowing the use of interchangeable parts similar to those in modern manufacturing. These interchangeable software parts are called *objects* and consist of chunks of computer code that describe entities ranging from the concrete, such as an automobile part, to the more abstract, such as an airline reservation. Each object is an encapsulated collection of data and operations performed on that data.

Traditional software development methods treat data and procedures as independent components, similar to the ingredients and instructions in a cookbook recipe. A separate programming operation must be performed every time someone wants to take an action on a particular piece of data. For instance, a credit card company would have to store data on its customers' purchases and have the instructions for using that data to calculate a customer's balance in a separate billing program.

Object-oriented programming, on the other hand, combines data and the specific instructions acting on that data into one "object." In the credit card application, a customer object would contain both the data on the customer's purchases and the techniques for calculating the customer's balance. Because data and operations are combined, each object is an independent software building block that can be used in many different systems without changing the program code. Objects can be assembled by combining various objects; the objects themselves don't need to be altered. If modifications are required, the programmer can design new objects that "inherit" attributes from existing objects. Some proponents believe object-oriented technology will eventually enable unskilled computer users to create their own software programs out of premade software objects.

The main benefit of object-oriented programming is the reusability of the code. The various objects can be reused in different combinations. After programmers build

Object-oriented programming
Approach to software development that combines data and the instructions acting on that data into one "object."

NeXTSTEP software for the NeXT computer offers users an object-oriented development environment that makes creating a customized application relatively quick and simple. It is an example of an innovative programming solution for corporations with constantly changing information needs. This screen shows various programming options available by choosing the appropriate icons. A sample database is open in the center window.

SOURCE: Courtesy of NeXT Computers, Inc.

processing routines and data sources into objects, they can retrieve and insert them into other software applications without having to reinvent the wheel each time. Figure 6.14 illustrates how these features of object-oriented programming could be used in a bank program.

Future software work can draw upon a library of reusable objects. For example, Texas Instruments Corp. uses object-oriented software to provide customers with constantly updated electronic dossiers of semiconductor designs. It is working on a library of objects with current data on specific semiconductor designs that computer manufacturers and other customers can access electronically on a subscription basis.

One of the challenges of creating object-oriented programming is analyzing business functions so they can be portrayed as objects. Companies must analyze and dissect the way they operate. Dunkin' Donuts uses object-oriented software in a system to help franchisees manage inventory, production, and finances. Each object represents business functions along with information related to that function. The sales object, for

FIGURE 6.14

A Banking Application of Object-Oriented Programming

Object-oriented programming divides the program into objects that contain both data and instructions and can be reused in different combinations. One object can be defined as a subcategory of another so that the savings and checking account objects are subcategories of the customer account object. The bank can create a new interest-bearing checking account object by merely specifying the difference between the interest-bearing checking account and the checking and savings accounts. The new object can easily be linked to the objects in the existing program.

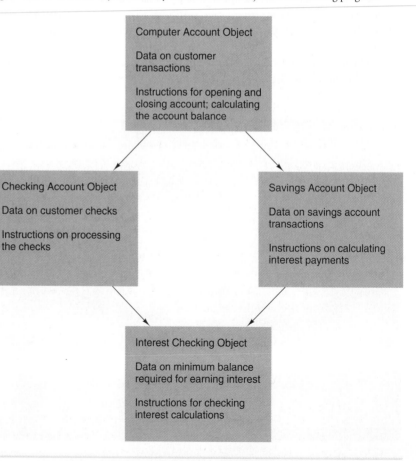

instance, allows a franchisee to scan rows of sales figures and display a growth chart based on those figures. Another challenge is that programmers trained in traditional software development techniques must be completely retrained, because object-oriented software represents a fundamental shift in thinking.[3]

FOCUS ON ORGANIZATIONS

CONTROL OF COMPUTER PROGRAMS: IS SOCIAL EQUITY AT STAKE?

When your car breaks down, how do you get it repaired? Unless you want to fix it yourself, you have two basic choices: you can take it to a dealer or an independent mechanic. The availability of alternative repair services offers automobile owners the advantage of convenience as well as increased competition in price and quality. Computer technology could change all this within the United States by eliminating independent mechanics as a choice for all but routine maintenance, a change that would put most independents out of business.

Many cars today are manufactured with computer chips that control certain basic functions, such as engine timing, and identify problems related to them. The 1990 Clean Air Act requires that from 1996 on, all automobiles sold in the United States must contain such on-board computers. In addition, the law mandates that their functions include the ability to detect failures in pollution-control equipment. Today, if a car has a problem with the on-board chip, or the chip program needs to be changed to adjust functions controlled by that chip (such as fuel mix),

the chip itself must be replaced. In the near future, however, that will change—these chips will be reprogrammable. If an automobile's catalytic converter requires an adjustment or the fuel mixture program needs to be changed, a quick check of the on-board computer will alert the mechanic to the problem. The mechanic will then be able quickly, easily, and inexpensively to reprogram the chip from programs stored on CD-ROMs.

If only authorized dealers have access to these programs, automobile owners will be forced to use only dealer mechanics for anything more serious than routine oil changes and lube jobs. Independent mechanics will not survive the loss of most of their business. This raises several key questions: who should have access to those programs? and who should have the ability to reprogram those chips? These questions are deeply intertwined with fundamental issues of social equity. The use of this technology, after all, is mandated to meet a social need, in this case, environmental protection. The first social equity question, then, is whether control of mandated technology should be allowed to take away the ability of a whole industry (here, the independents) to earn a living. Another closely related social equity question concerns the formation of a monopoly. Should control of mandated technology be allowed to create a monopoly, thereby likely raising the price to the general public while also reducing quality?

Automobile industry proponents argue strenuously for their maintaining exclusive control over the computer programs that they have developed.

While many observers believe greed may be the main issue, industry representatives articulate other arguments. They are concerned over liability, fearing that while independents might be doing repairs, the automobile companies themselves would be responsible for any recalls. They also argue that independent mechanics have inferior tools, which will result in consumers paying more and receiving less quality if these programs are given to independents. Frank Krich, a Chrysler Corp. regulatory planning specialist, even argues that if the programs are distributed to private mechanics, the dealers will suffer a discriminatory disadvantage because their automobile manufacturers require them to use high-quality, expensive repair equipment, resulting in higher costs. Independents have no such requirement.

The issue is to be decided by the U.S. Environmental Protection Agency (EPA), an organization whose interest in this matter is focused on clean air, not on rights of property, economics, or social equity. Lobbyists representing both sides are hard at work. Members of Congress have also become active on both sides of the issue and could make their weight felt at some point if they are dissatisfied with the decision of the EPA.

FOCUS Questions: As a member of the Environmental Protection Agency, how would you vote on this issue? Explain your reasoning. Should the EPA alone decide who should repair automobiles with on-board computers?

SOURCE: Julie Edelson Halpert, "Who Will Fix Tomorrow's Cars?" *The New York Times*, November 7, 1993.

Contemporary information technology has made software a valuable and powerful instrument in everyday life, opening up new ways of working and living. But as the Focus on Organizations shows, the use of software can give some groups in society more power than others, raising concerns about the impact of digital technology on social equity. Should everyone have an equal opportunity to use software and hardware in the digital age?

SUMMARY

- There are two major types of software: systems software and applications software. Systems software consists of generalized programs to manage computer resources and mediate between applications software and computer hardware. Applications software consists of programs designed for applying the computer to solve a specific problem such as a business problem.

- There have been four generations of software development: (1) machine language; (2) symbolic languages such as assembly language; (3) high-level languages such as FORTRAN and COBOL; and (4) fourth-generation languages, which are less procedural and closer to natural language than earlier generations of software.

- The operating system acts as the chief manager of the computer system, allocating, scheduling, and assigning system resources and monitoring the use of the computer.

- Multiprogramming, multitasking, multiprocessing, virtual storage, and time-sharing enable computer system resources to be used more efficiently so that the computer can attack many problems at the same time.

- Multiprogramming (multitasking in microcomputer environments) allows multiple programs to use the computer's resources concurrently.

- Multiprocessing is the use of two or more CPUs linked together, working in tandem to perform a task.

- Time-sharing enables many users to share computer resources simultaneously by allocating each user a tiny slice of computing time.

- Virtual storage splits up programs into pages or segments so that primary storage can be used more efficiently.

- To be executed by the computer, a software program must be translated into machine language via special language translation software—a compiler, an assembler, or an interpreter.

- A graphical user interface (GUI) allows users to interact with the operating system by using a mouse to select icons representing commands. Windows is a popular graphical user interface shell for the DOS operating system.

- The leading microcomputer operating systems are DOS, OS/2, Windows NT, UNIX, and System 7. These operating systems can be classified according to whether they support multitasking and multiple users and whether they are command driven or use a graphical user interface.

- The most popular programming languages are assembly language, FORTRAN, COBOL, BASIC, PL/1, Pascal, C, and Ada. Each has been designed to solve a special class of problems.

- Fourth-generation languages are more nonprocedural than earlier programming languages and include query software, report generators, graphics software, application generators, and other tools that dramatically reduce programming time and make some software tasks easy enough to be performed by nontechnical specialists.

• Software packages are prewritten, precoded, commercially available programs that eliminate the need for writing software programs. The most popular software packages for microcomputers are productivity aids such as word processing software, spreadsheet software, data management software, and integrated software packages.

• Object-oriented programming combines data and procedures into an independent software building block called an object. Each object is reusable in many different systems without changing the program code.

KEY TERMS

Program	Windows NT
Stored-program concept	UNIX
Systems software	System 7
Applications software	FORTRAN
Machine language	COBOL
High-level language	PL/1
Assembly language	BASIC
Assembler	Pascal
Operating system	Ada
Multiprogramming	C
Multitasking	Fourth-generation language
Multiprocessing	Query language
Time-sharing	Graphics language
Virtual storage	Report generator
Source code	Application generator
Object code	Very-high-level programming language
Compiler	Applications software package
Interpreter	Word processing software
Graphical user interface	Spreadsheet software
DOS	Data management software
Windows	Integrated software package
OS/2	Object-oriented programming

REVIEW QUESTIONS

1. Why do we need software to use computers?

2. What are the major types of software? How can they be distinguished?

3. What are the major software generations? When were they developed? Describe the characteristics of each generation.

4. Define an operating system. What functions does it perform?

5. How do a compiler, an assembler, and an interpreter differ?

6. Define multiprogramming, multitasking, time-sharing, multiprocessing, and virtual storage.

7. What is a graphical user interface? Describe some of the features that make graphical user interfaces easy to use.

8. Name the leading microcomputer operating systems. How can they be distinguished?

9. Name and describe four popular high-level programming languages.

10. What is a fourth-generation language? Give examples of fourth-generation software tools.

11. What is an applications software package? Name and describe the four major kinds of software packages used with microcomputers.

12. What is object-oriented programming? How does it differ from the traditional method of developing software?

DISCUSSION QUESTIONS

1. Why is the operating system considered the chief manager of a computer system?

2. Software will continue to become more user-friendly. Discuss.

PROBLEM-SOLVING EXERCISES

1. *Group exercise:* Divide the class into groups and have each group research the features of a major microcomputer operating system using computing magazine articles and vendor literature. For instance, one group could describe the features and advantages of DOS; another could discuss OS/2, Windows NT, or the Macintosh operating system. Alternatively, the class could be divided into groups assigned to describe the features of each of the major graphical user interfaces for operating systems—System 7; Microsoft Windows; Workplace Shell; and Open Look. Have each group present its findings to the class.

2. David Ashton is the superintendent of schools for the Herron Lake School District. His staff consists of a business manager, who performs all of the accounting for the district and manages the budget; a manager of pupil and personnel services, who maintains enrollment and test score data; and two secretaries. The secretaries are in charge of the superintendent's appointments and correspondence with district staff and parents. The District Office has one terminal connected to a countywide computer system that maintains student enrollment data and prints mailing labels. Otherwise, all work is performed with calculators, electric typewriters, or pen and pencil. Write a memo describing how the leading microcomputer software packages could help the superintendent and his staff. Identify applications that should be computerized and the type of software most suitable for each. What software selection criteria should be considered?

3. *Hands-on exercise:* The following list displays some of the information that needs to be maintained by waste management companies such as John Sexton Contractors Co., described in the chapter-opening vignette. The amount of waste represents tons of waste.

Landfill	Truck Owner	Type of Waste	Amount	Party Charged
Buford	Sherman	Garbage	10	Conti
Ulster	Higgins	Construction	14	O'Callahan
Buford	DeWitt	Garbage	14	Johnson
Buford	Sherman	Yard	22	Conti
Stony Ridge	DiNardo	Floor cleaner	15	McPherson
Ulster	Oliva	Garbage	17	Conti

Use appropriate software to develop an application that can store this data and create reports that would be of interest to companies such as Sexton Contractors. Some of these reports would be:

A list of all types of waste dumped at the Ulster site.

The total amount of garbage dumped at the Buford site.

All waste paid for by Conti classified by type of waste and landfill site.

NOTES

1. Robert D. Holmes, "OS/2 vs. Windows NT," *Computerworld,* January 21, 1994.

2. Jesse Green, "Productivity in the Fourth Generation," *Journal of Management Information Systems* 1 (Winter 1984–85).

3. Alan Radding, "Not Quite Ready for Prime Time," *Computerworld,* June 14, 1993; and Robert Haavind, "Software's New Object Lesson," *Technology Review,* February/March 1992.

PROBLEM-SOLVING CASE

CHOOSING AN OPERATING SYSTEM: A BIG BUSINESS DECISION

Most business managers don't understand what an operating system (OS) is or what it does. Happily, the choice of operating systems is something only the technical specialists will decide—it is not an issue of concern for the business manager. Or is it? To better understand the business implications of choosing an operating system, we will look at the reasons a few companies have given for their selection of an operating system.

The most popular systems software adoption in recent years has been Microsoft Windows, which sold 10 million copies in 1992 alone. In comparison, the other new PC operating system, IBM's OS/2, sold only 2 million copies that year. Why such a difference? Jerry Witowski, a manager of systems development at W.R. Grace & Co., says his organization selected Windows for an application using SAS Institute Inc.'s statistical and graphics software because of its easy-to-use graphical user interface. "People use Windows products at home, so they feel comfortable with them at work, too," he claims. George Weston Ltd., a Toronto-based food processing and distribution company, selected Windows for use in an employee health-compensation claim system for the same reason. As Weston consultant Bill Hamilton says, "We were able to create an electronic form that was easy to work with and allowed the users to interact with the system more naturally."

In addition, comfort and ease-of-use translate into development and training dollars saved. Galileo International markets the Windows-based Personal Galileo system, which is the front end to United Airlines' Apollo reservation system used by travel agents worldwide. Galileo finds that without the Windows user interface, six weeks are needed to train secretaries and clerks to use the Apollo system, whereas with Windows, very little training is required. Bill Hamilton calls Windows development costs "very cheap"; their compensation claim system application cost just $25,000 to create.

Ken Forster, a systems engineer at Lockheed, the aerospace company, chose Windows as the front end to a system of high-end computers that control a multimillion dollar automated metal-finishing facility for two reasons. First, it is off-the-shelf (he didn't have to write a front-end operating system). Second, it has open standards, enabling him easily to connect into the high-end systems the Windows application would control. He also mentions cost; the $28,000 in hardware and software and the nine person-months of work was half the cost of any other alternative.

The ability to easily display data in graphical format is Shane Ankeney's main reason for adopting Windows. Ankeney, a senior media research analyst at J. Walter Thompson, the giant advertising agency, was responsible for developing TV Reach to aid media planners in developing media plans using demographic statistics. A key aspect of such a system is the need to show statistical results to the company's clients. Ankeney believes that clients can grasp the data much more easily in graphical format.

With so much quality in Windows, why does anyone turn to any other operating system? Response time caused The Royal Bank of Canada to turn to the OS/2 operating system when developing a system to give account managers quick access to customer data stored on the mainframe. OS/2 is a full 32-bit operating system, whereas Windows is a 16-bit system. Rob Brodie, the bank's manager of technology planning, believes that the 32-bit OS/2 will give account managers a response time of just a few seconds, as opposed to up to two minutes with other operating systems.

The Royal Bank has also turned to OS/2 as the operating system to control their several thousand local networks. As the second largest bank in North America, they are one of the world's largest information processing firms. Again, the key feature causing the selection of OS/2 is its 32-bit technology, which allows more enhanced functionality than 16-bit systems do. They expect that OS/2 will result not only in faster performance for their existing hardware but will also reduce new hardware purchases by supporting the connection of 60 devices to each network rather than the 40 to which 16-bit systems are limited. In addition, OS/2 is packaged with added facilities they expect to be of value. For example, OS/2 includes software for remote network management and problem diagnosis, which greatly eases the burden of supporting so many local networks. With this facility, the networks can be supported centrally by a few people rather than having to have more than 2,000 trained programmers (one for each network).

Microsoft's new Windows NT operating system was the choice of Nordstrom, Inc., the Seattle-based national clothing store chain, because it combines many of the strengths of both Windows and OS/2. Nordstrom has about 60 stores, each of which was connected to the company's two centralized IBM 3090 mainframes. End-users at the stores and company headquarters used to access mainframe data through terminals. But Nordstrom wanted to bring all the mainframe data together so that departmental and central managers could obtain detailed product-by-product inventory information using an easy-to-use Windows interface. Store buyers can now determine what merchandise is popular at their particular stores and make immediate purchase decisions—daily if necessary—to keep inventory current with sales. Larry Shaw, Nordstrom's PC coordinator, is very concerned about network management, as the operating system controls a 1,300-plus user network that will connect all the chain's stores. Nordstrom selected Windows NT because it could support graphical user interface–based applications that were easy for users to learn while providing a single platform to support all the various types of machines in the network, from central computers to individual workstations. Price was an additional consideration.

Arthur Tisi, director of information systems at the nonprofit National League for Healthcare in New York City (an organization for health care professionals), also gives price as one of his reasons for selecting Windows NT for his networked application. He believes that with Windows NT he can build an application that will approach midrange computing capabilities for one-third or less the cost of alternatives. Performance is another reason. Tisi believes that he will eventually be able to move corporate accounting and other mainframe applications to Windows NT platforms.

As these examples suggest, the choice of operating systems can affect application ease-of-use as well as development and training costs. The right OS choice can make communication with other computer systems feasible. It can even affect the ability of business personnel to communicate their ideas effectively to clients. Thus, the choice of an operating system should not be left solely to technical specialists because it requires the knowledgeable involvement of business management.

SOURCES: Sally Cusak, "If You Build Them, Will Users Come?" *InformationWEEK*, September 6, 1993; John Pepper, "Admiring the View From Windows," *InformationWEEK*, June 28, 1993; J. William Semich, "NT: Is It Ready For Critical Apps?" *Datamation*, May 15, 1993; International Data Corporation, "The Royal Bank of Canada: 32 Bits at the Branches," *IDC White Paper*; and John McMullen, "OS/2 Gets the Royal Treatment," *InformationWEEK*, February 24, 1992.

CASE STUDY QUESTIONS

1.   Why is selecting an operating system an important business decision?

2.   What people and organizational issues should be considered when selecting an operating system?

3.   Given that operating systems tend to be considered very technical pieces of software, how might you as a nontechnician educate yourself about them so that you can participate in the selection of an operating system?

4.   What problems do you see with individual business groups within larger organizations making their own selection of operating systems based on their own business needs?

Chapter

SEVEN

ORGANIZING INFORMATION: FILES AND DATABASES

LEARNING OBJECTIVES

After reading and studying this chapter, you will:

1. Understand how the usefulness of information is affected by file organization.
2. Be familiar with traditional file organization methods.
3. Be able to describe how a database management system overcomes the limitations of a traditional file environment.
4. Be familiar with the three database models.
5. Know how to design a simple database.
6. Be able to describe new database trends.

Earthquake and brush fire loss in California can easily surpass hundreds of millions of dollars in a single year, which explains why insurance is so critical to Californians. Not surprisingly, the California Department of Insurance collects an immense amount of data on its insurance companies. What is surprising is that until 1991 the data were so scattered and isolated that they were not usable to adequately regulate the state's approximately 1,500 insurance companies. Some information was recorded only on paper and file cards; much of the information was stored on computer, but the computers were in department offices all over the state. As a result, too frequently the insurance department was unable to detect insurance company fraud or financial shakiness.

This precarious situation finally changed when, in 1991, the state discovered that two multibillion dollar insurance companies were failing—a condition discovered much too late to rectify. To protect California residents from the consequences of insurance company bankruptcy, the state insurance department was forced to take over the two companies. It was also forced to consolidate all its insurance company data so that employees could finally monitor the insurance companies for financial soundness and patterns of fraud.

A year later the California Department of Insurance had the basics of an integrated relational database management system in place; a full set of accompanying programs was completed in 1994. Data are collected from many locations and stored in a manner that allows department employees to access and relate the data in whatever format, order, and relationship they need. The system gives the California Department of Insurance early warnings of developing financial problems and patterns of fraud. It also allows the department staff to better serve the 50,000 Californians who call each month with insurance complaints.

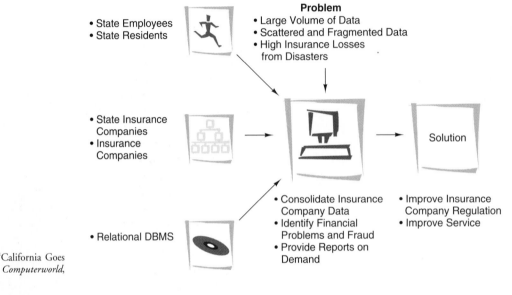

SOURCE: Jean S. Bozman, "California Goes After Insurance Cheaters," *Computerworld,* May 10, 1993.

The usefulness of information depends a great deal on how it is stored, organized, and accessed. Solving problems is difficult—sometimes impossible—unless the requisite information is easily available in the right form. Consequently, an understanding of files and databases is crucial for using information systems effectively. This chapter describes traditional file management technologies and database management systems, showing how a database approach can overcome problems in accessing data such as those faced by the California Department of Insurance.

7.1 INTRODUCTION

Information systems cannot provide solutions unless their data are accurate, timely, and easily accessible. Various file organization and management techniques have been developed to achieve these objectives. Each of these techniques works best with a different class of problems.

WHY ARE FILE ORGANIZATION AND MANAGEMENT IMPORTANT TO PROBLEM SOLVING?

In all information systems, data must be organized and structured so that they can be used effectively. But unless information can be easily processed and accessed, the system cannot achieve its purpose. Due to disorganized methods of storing and retrieving information, many firms with excellent hardware and software cannot deliver timely and

FIGURE 7.1

The Data Hierarchy

In an information system, pieces of data are organized into a hierarchy. The smallest piece of data that computers can handle is the bit (the 1s and 0s of binary representation). Next is the byte, a group of bits that forms a character such as a letter, number, or punctuation mark. A field is a group of characters that forms a word, a group of words, or a number. A record is a collection of related fields; a file is a collection of related records. The largest element in the hierarchy, a database, consists of related files.

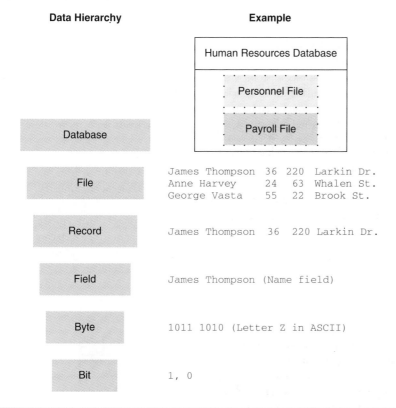

Data Hierarchy	Example
	Human Resources Database
	Personnel File
Database	Payroll File
File	James Thompson 36 220 Larkin Dr. Anne Harvey 24 63 Whalen St. George Vasta 55 22 Brook St.
Record	James Thompson 36 220 Larkin Dr.
Field	James Thompson (Name field)
Byte	1011 1010 (Letter Z in ASCII)
Bit	1, 0

precise information. Poor file organization prevents some firms from accessing much of the information they maintain.

Imagine how difficult it would be to write a term paper with your notes on 3-by-5-inch index cards if the cards were in random order. No matter how neatly they were stacked and stored, you would have no way of organizing the term paper. Of course, with enough time, you might be able to arrange the cards in some order. But often imposing an organization scheme after the fact, or modifying it to accommodate a change of viewpoint in your paper, will cause you to miss your deadline. Thus the role of file organization and management cannot be underestimated.

DATA ORGANIZATION TERMS AND CONCEPTS

Data are structured in information systems in a manner that keeps track of discrete data elements and related groupings of information. The data are organized in a hierarchy that starts with bits and bytes and progresses to fields, records, files, and databases (see Figure 7.1).

Field

A grouping of characters into a word, a group of words, or a complete number.

Record

A grouping of related data fields, such as a person's name, age, and address.

File

A group of related records.

Database

A group of related files; more specifically, a collection of data organized to appear to be in one location so they can be accessed and used in many different applications.

Entity

A person, place, or thing on which information is maintained.

Attribute

A characteristic or quality of a particular entity.

Key field

A field in a record that uniquely identifies that record so that it can be retrieved, updated, or sorted.

A bit, as we have seen, represents the smallest piece of data the computer can handle. A byte is a group of bits that represents a single character, which can be a letter, number, or other symbol. A grouping of characters into a word, group of words, or complete number, such as a person's name or age, is called a **field**. A collection of related data fields, such as a person's name, age, and address, is called a **record**. A group of related records is called a **file.** For example, we could collect all of the records described in Figure 7.1 into a personnel file. Related files, in turn, can be grouped into a **database.** For example, our personnel file could be grouped with a payroll information file into a human resources database.

Entities and Attributes   An **entity** is a person, place, or thing on which information is maintained. For example, *employee* is a typical entity in a personnel file, which maintains information on people employed by the firm. Each characteristic or quality describing a particular entity is called an **attribute**. For example, name, address, or number of dependents would each be an attribute of the entity employee. The specific values that these attributes have can be found in the fields on a record describing a particular entity.

Key Fields   Every record in a file or database must contain at least one field that uniquely identifies that record so that it can be retrieved (accessed), updated, or sorted. This identifier field is called a **key field**. An example of a key field would be an employee number or Social Security number for a personnel file or a product number for an inventory file. In the sample personnel record in Figure 7.2, which contains information about the entity employee, the Social Security number is the key field for the record, since each employee has a unique Social Security number.

Computers are used in hospitals to help diagnose patients, design treatments, prescribe drugs, and teach medicine. Records for patients typically include the patient's name and address, medical problems, allergies, and prescribed medications.

SOURCE: Courtesy of International Business Machines Corporation.

FIGURE 7.2

A Sample Record Containing Data about the Entity "Employee"

A personnel record with information about employees contains separate fields for attributes such as last name, first name, and so on. Social Security number is the key field because each employee has a unique Social Security number that can be used to identify that employee.

Entity = "Employee"

SSN Field	Last Name Field	First Name Field	Birth Date Field	Address Field
444367890	Johnson	Maureen	01/02/60	12 Valley Road, Croton, NY 10520
113467098	Kanter	Steven	11/04/44	33 Hillsdale Dr., Peekskill, NY 10566
224569801	Minton	Helen	08/04/57	46 Wood Road, Bedford, NY 10593
576018935	Thomas	George	04/04/59	11 Avery Drive, Croton, NY 10520

Key
Field

7.2 THE TRADITIONAL FILE ENVIRONMENT

The way data are organized on storage media determines how easily they can be accessed and used. In Chapter 5 we discussed the difference between sequential-access storage devices, such as magnetic tape, and direct-access storage devices (DASDs), such as magnetic disk. In a **traditional file environment**, data records are physically organized on storage devices using either sequential file organization or random (or direct) file organization.

SEQUENTIAL FILE ORGANIZATION

In **sequential file organization**, data records must be retrieved in the same physical sequence in which they are stored. In **random** (or direct) **file organization**, data records can be accessed in any sequence, independent of their physical order. Sequential file organization is the only file organization method that can be used with magnetic tape. Random file organization is used with magnetic disk technology.

Sequential files are becoming outmoded, but they are still used for older batch-processing applications, which access and process each record in sequential order. The classic example is a payroll system; the system must process all of the employees in a firm one by one and issue each a check. Most applications today, however, including those based on microcomputers, rely on some form of random file organization method.

Figure 7.3 compares sequential file access with the **indexed sequential-access method (ISAM)**, which stores records sequentially on a DASD but also allows individual records to be accessed in any desired order by using an **index** of key fields. Like the index for a book, the index for a file consists of a listing of record keys and their associated storage location. The index shows the actual physical location on disk of each record that

Traditional file environment
The storage of data so that each application has its own separate data file or files and software programs.

Sequential file organization
A way of storing data records so that they must be retrieved in the physical order in which they are stored; the only file organization method that can be used with magnetic tape.

Random file organization
A way of storing data records so that they can be accessed in any sequence, regardless of their physical order; used with magnetic disk technology.

Indexed sequential-access method (ISAM)
A way of storing records sequentially on a direct-access storage device that allows individual records to be accessed in any desired order using an index of key fields.

Index
A list, for a file or database, of the key field of each record and its associated storage location.

FIGURE 7.3

Two Methods of Organizing Data
The sequential file access method (panel a) retrieves records in the same sequence in which they are physically stored. It is useful for batch processing, in which records on a file are processed one after the other in sequential order, and it is the only access method for magnetic tape storage. In the indexed sequential-access method (ISAM) (panel b), records are also stored sequentially but can be accessed directly by using an index. The index lists every record by its unique key field and gives its storage location. With ISAM, records are stored on a direct access storage device (DASD) such as a disk.

(a) Sequential File Access Method

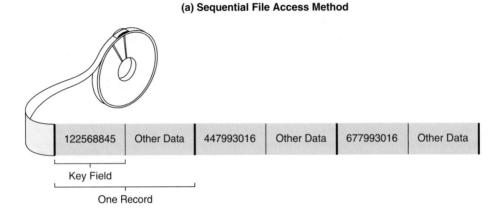

(b) Indexed Sequential Access Method (ISAM)

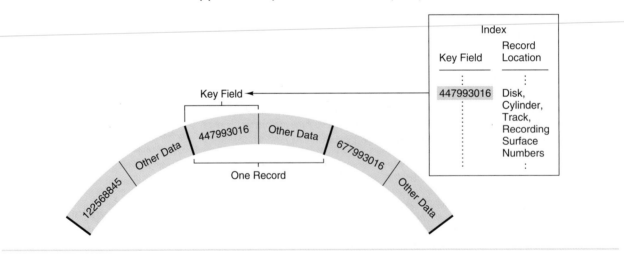

can be referenced with its key field. Any specific record can be located directly by checking the index for its storage address. ISAM is most useful for applications requiring sequential processing of large numbers of records in batch mode but with occasional direct access of individual records.

RANDOM FILE ORGANIZATION

Random, or direct, file organization also uses a key field to locate the physical address of a record but accomplishes this without an index. This access method uses a mathematical formula called a randomizing algorithm (also called a transform or hashing algorithm) to translate the key field directly into the record's physical storage location on disk.

FIGURE 7.4

Direct File Access Methods

Direct file access methods let users access individual records more quickly than either the sequential or indexed sequential methods. Direct file access involves a mathematical operation called a randomizing algorithm. In this example the algorithm involves dividing the record's key field (4467) by the prime number closest to the total number of records in the file (997). The remainder (479) is the storage address on disk of the record. Thus we can go directly to this record rather than sifting through all the records that may be stored ahead of it.

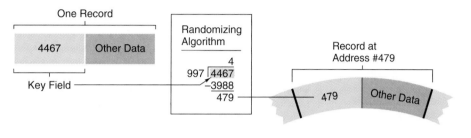

The algorithm performs some mathematical computation on the record key, and the result of that calculation is the record's physical address. For example, in Figure 7.4 the randomizing algorithm divides the record's key field number (4467) by the prime number closest to the total number of records in the file (997). The remainder designates the address on disk for that particular record.

This access method is most appropriate for applications requiring individual records to be located directly and rapidly for immediate on-line processing. Only a few records in the file need to be retrieved, and the records are selected randomly, in no particular sequence. An example might be an on-line order processing application.

FILE ORGANIZATION AND TRANSACTION PROCESSING

File organization not only determines how quickly data can be accessed from an information system, it determines how quickly data can be entered and processed as well. At their most elementary level, information systems keep track of the day-to-day transactions of a business, such as processing orders, airline reservations, or payroll checks. A transaction is an event to which a business must respond by collecting data relevant to the transaction and storing that data in either a manual or computerized information system. Transactions are used to update the firm's records and to produce documents required for business operations. The personnel record illustrated in Figure 7.2, for instance, could be created by entering a transaction to add an employee to the firm's personnel file. Other types of personnel transactions might involve changing the employee's address, or deleting the employee from the firm's personnel file if employment was terminated.

Chapter 5 introduced the concepts of batch and on-line input and processing. Transactions can be processed in either batch or on-line mode. Figure 7.5 illustrates a traditional batch transaction processing application—a payroll system. It has two files—a transaction file and a payroll master file. The master file contains relatively permanent data, such as records of each employer's name, address, Social Security number, gross pay, deductions, and net pay. The transaction file consists of data used to change the master file, such as data collected from time cards showing the number of hours an employee worked that will be used to calculate the employee's weekly pay. If the master file is organized sequentially, transactions can update the file only in sequential order. The key field of each record in the file must be examined to determine whether there

FIGURE 7.5

Batch Transaction Processing
The processing of payroll is a typical batch transaction processing application. The payroll master file contains employee records, and the transaction file contains data on the number of hours each employee works per payroll period. Only the key field for each record (employee identification number) is illustrated here. Processing both files together produces an updated master file, paychecks, and various payroll reports.

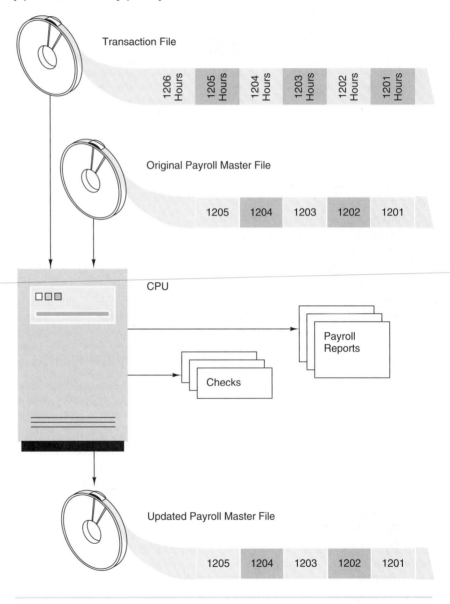

is a corresponding transaction to update it. Time-card transactions would be collected in a batch, sorted in the same order as the records in the master file, and then processed against the master file. A new updated master file would be created.

On-line transaction processing requires a direct-access storage device and some form of direct file organization. Making an airline reservation, illustrated in Figure 7.6,

FIGURE 7.6

On-Line Transaction Processing

On-line transaction processing is used for airline reservations and other applications in which information must be processed immediately. Direct file organization is required so that the reservation transaction can directly locate the appropriate reservation record and update it.

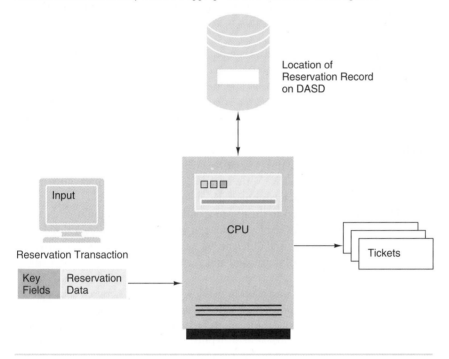

is a classic on-line transaction processing application. Airline reservation or travel agents key in airline reservations at desktop terminals. The key fields in the airline reservation transaction (date, destination, and flight number) are used to locate the address of the appropriate reservation record and update the reservation record. Passengers are immediately booked on the flight of their choice. If requested by passengers, agents with desktop printers can print out their tickets at the same time they are making the reservations.

The processing of transactions necessary to conduct the day-to-day activities of the business is the distinctive feature of a special category of information systems called transaction processing systems. Chapter 13 provides a detailed description of the role of transaction processing systems in business.

PROBLEMS WITH THE TRADITIONAL FILE ENVIRONMENT

All of these methods of file organization are associated with individual files and individual software programs. But what if the information required to solve a particular problem is located in more than one file? Often extra programming and data manipulation will be required to obtain that information.

For example, suppose you want to know all of the orders outstanding for a particular customer. Some of the information is maintained in an order file for an order entry application. The rest of the information is contained in a customer master file. Thus the required information is stored in several disparate files, each of which is organized in a different way. To extract the required information, you will need to sort both files repeatedly until the records are arranged in the same order. Records from the two files will have to be matched, and the data items from the merging of both files will have to be extracted and output. Obtaining this information entails additional programming and the creation of more files. Sometimes the effort to extract this information is so enormous that the problem remains unsolved.

Even with the most up-to-date computer hardware and software, the traditional file environment presents many obstacles to efficient and effective problem solving—high costs, poor performance, inflexible response to information requests, and information processing chaos. Most organizations have developed information systems one at a time, as the need arose, each with its own set of software programs, files, and users (the people in the organization who use that system). Over time, these independent applications and files can proliferate to the point that the firm's information resources may be out of control. Some symptoms of this crisis are data redundancy, program/data dependence, data inconsistency, and excessive software costs. This predicament is illustrated in Figure 7.7 for a bank in which customers maintain several accounts.

Data redundancy refers to the presence of duplicate data in multiple data files. The same piece of data, such as employee name and address, will be maintained and stored in several different files by several different systems. Separate software programs must be developed to update this information and keep it current in each file in which it appears.

Program/data dependence refers to the close relationship between data stored in files and the specific software programs required to update and maintain those files. Every computer program must describe the location of the data it uses. In a traditional file environment, any change to the format or structure of data in a file necessitates a change in all of the software programs that use these data. The program maintenance effort required, for example, to change from a five-digit to a nine-digit zip code may be exorbitant.

Data inconsistency refers to inconsistencies among various representations of the same piece of data in different information systems and files. Over time, as different groups in a firm update their applications according to their own business rules, data in one system become inconsistent with the same data in another system. For example, the student names and addresses maintained in a school student enrollment system and in a separate system to generate mailing labels may not correspond exactly if each system is updated with different software programs, procedures, and time frames.

Excessive software costs result from creating, documenting, and keeping track of so many files and different applications, many of which contain redundant data. Organizations must devote a large part of their information systems resources merely to maintaining data in hundreds and thousands of files. New requests for information can only be satisfied if professional programmers write new software to strip data from existing files and recombine them into new files.

Data redundancy
The presence of duplicate data in multiple data files.

Program/data dependence
The close relationship between data stored in files and the specific software programs required to update and maintain those files, whereby any change in data format or structure requires a change in all the programs that access the data.

7.3 THE DATABASE VISION

Many of the problems of the traditional file environment can be solved by taking a database approach to data management and storage. Here is a stricter definition of a database: a collection of data organized so that they can be accessed and used by many different

FIGURE 7.7

The Traditional Approach to Organizing Data

Most organizations have developed information systems one at a time, as they needed them, each with its own set of software programs and files. All too often this involves storing duplicate information in each system. The same piece of data might be updated in one system but not in others. Another problem is that the format in which the same piece of data is stored in different files could be inconsistent. Such a situation also drives up costs because there are so many files and applications to maintain, each serving a separate group of users in an organization. Can you identify any other potential problems?

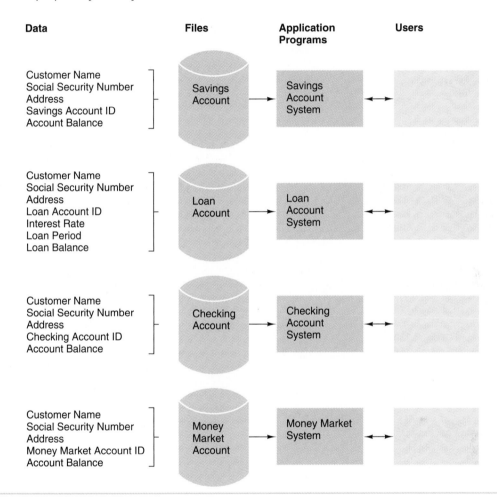

applications. Instead of storing data in separate files for each application, data are stored physically so that they appear to users as being stored in one location. A single common database services multiple applications. For example, instead of a bank storing customer data in separate information systems and separate files for savings accounts, money market funds, loans, and checking accounts, the bank could create a single common client database, as in Figure 7.8.

LOGICAL VERSUS PHYSICAL VIEWS OF DATA

The database concept distinguishes between logical and physical views of data. In the **logical view**, data are presented as they would be perceived by end-users or business

Logical view
The presentation of data as they would be perceived by end-users or business specialists.

FIGURE 7.8

How a Database Management System Helps a Business Organize Data

Here we see how a database management system could help the bank solve the data problems shown in Figure 7.7. The bank can combine all its data into a single customer database, and the database management system can make the data available to multiple applications and users. Combining all data into one database avoids duplicating data. It also means that a particular data element needs to be updated only once; all systems will be using the same updated piece of information.

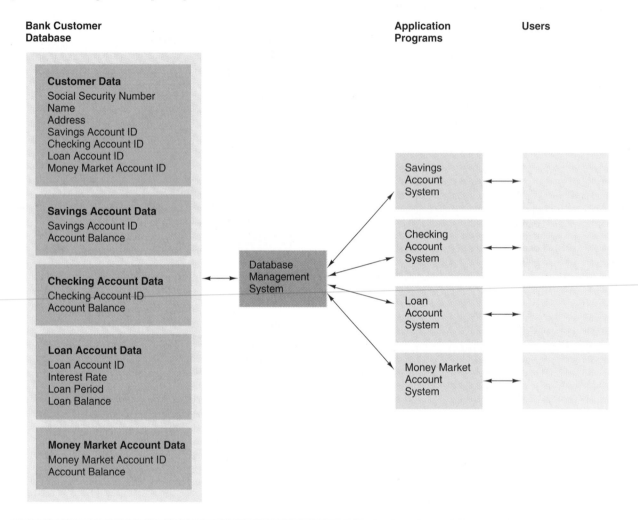

Physical view

The presentation of data as they are actually organized and structured on physical storage media.

Schema

The logical description of an entire database; it lists all the data items and the relationships among them.

specialists. The **physical view** shows how data are actually organized and structured on physical storage media. One physical view can support many logical views. A database management system uses special database management software to make the physical database available for different logical views presented by various application programs.

The **schema** is the logical description of the entire database; it lists all of the data items and the relationships among them. The specific set of data from the database that is required by each application program is called the **subschema**. The subschema could be considered the portion of the database that is used to solve a particular problem presented by a business specialist. For example, for the bank customer database in Figure

7.8, the savings account application would have a subschema consisting of client name, address, Social Security number, and specific savings account data such as savings account number and account balance.

COMPONENTS OF A DATABASE MANAGEMENT SYSTEM

Special software called a **database management system (DBMS)** permits these data to be stored in one place while making them available to different applications. Database management software serves as an interface between the common database and various application programs. When an application program calls for a data element like hourly pay rate, the database management software locates it in the database and presents it to the application program. There is no need for the application programmer to specify in detail how and where the data are found. A database management system has three components: a data definition language, a data manipulation language, and a data dictionary.

The **data definition language** defines each data element as it appears in the database before it is translated into the form required by various application programs. Database programming specialists use this language when they are developing the database.

The **data manipulation language** is a special tool for manipulating data in the database. It is used along with some conventional third- or fourth-generation programming languages. It has features that can be used by both end users and technical specialists to extract data from the database, to satisfy information requests, and to develop applications.

Subschema
The specific set of data from a database that each application program requires.

Database management system (DBMS)
Software that serves as an interface between a common database and various application programs; it permits data to be stored in one place yet be made available to different applications.

Data definition language
The part of a database management system that defines each data element as it appears in the database before it is translated into the form required by various application programs.

Data manipulation language
A special tool in a database management system that manipulates the data in the database.

To improve the detection of severe weather, data on storms, such as wind speed and direction, are collected and analyzed by the NEXRAD system created by Unisys Corporation. The information is stored in a database and sent to U.S. government weather bureaus and air traffic controllers.

SOURCE: Courtesy of Unisys Corporation.

FIGURE 7.9

An Example of a Data Dictionary Entry

Here is a sample report from a data dictionary for a human resources database. The data element is AMT-YTD-EARNINGS; its "alias" or alternative name is YTD-EARNINGS. The entry gives such helpful information as the size of the data element, what programs and reports use it, and which department "owns" it (i.e., is responsible for updating it).

```
NAME: AMT-YTD-EARNINGS
ALIAS: YTD-EARNINGS

DESCRIPTION: EMPLOYEE'S YEAR-TO-DATE EARNINGS

SIZE: 9 BYTES

TYPE: NUMERIC

OWNERSHIP:            PAYROLL

UPDATE SECURITY:      PAYROLL DATA ENTRY CLERK

ACCESS SECURITY:      PAYROLL DATA ENTRY CLERK
                      PAYROLL MANAGER,
                      ACCOUNTS PAYABLE MANAGER
                      PERSONNEL COMPENSATION ANALYST
                      BENEFITS ADMINISTRATOR

BUSINESS FUNCTIONS USED IN:    PAYROLL
                               PERSONNEL
                               BENEFITS

PROGRAMS USED IN:    PLP1000
                     PLP2020
                     PLP4000
                     PLP6000

REPORTS USED IN:    PAYROLL REGISTER
                    PAYROLL CHECK STUB
                    W-2 FORMS
                    941A REPORT
                    PENSION BENEFITS REPORT
```

Structured Query Language (SQL)

A data manipulation language for relational database management systems that is an emerging business standard.

Data dictionary

The component in a database management system that stores definitions and other characteristics of data elements; it identifies what data reside in the database, their structure and format, and their business usage.

The most prominent data manipulation language today is **SQL**, or **Structured Query Language**, which is the data manipulation language for mainframe database management systems such as IBM's DB2, with versions for microcomputer database management software.

A **data dictionary** is an automated file that stores definitions of data elements and other characteristics such as usage patterns, ownership (who in the organization is responsible for maintaining the data), relationships among data elements, and security. If properly documented, the data dictionary is an important problem-solving tool. It identifies for end users and business specialists what data reside in the database, their structure and format, and their business usage.

Figure 7.9 shows a sample data dictionary entry for a human resources database. This report describes the size, format, meaning, alternate name (alias), and usage of the data element AMT-YTD-EARNINGS, which is an employee's accumulated year-to-date earnings. The dictionary also shows which individuals, programs, reports, and business functions use this data element and what business function "owns" or has the responsibility for maintaining this piece of data. The "security" entries identify the people who have the right to access this information.

ADVANTAGES OF DATABASE MANAGEMENT SYSTEMS

Database management systems and a database approach to organizing information overcome many of the limitations of the traditional file environment:

- Data are independent of application programs. The DBMS distinguishes between logical and physical views of data so that many different application programs can use data from a common, shared database.

- Data redundancy and inconsistency are reduced. Because data are independent of application programs, there is no need to build isolated files in which the same data elements are repeated each time a new application is called for. Data are maintained in only one place.

- Complexity is reduced by consolidated management of data, access, and use via the DBMS.

- Information is easier to access and use. The database establishes relationships among different pieces of information. Data from different records and applications can be more easily accessed and combined.

Many of the advantages of a database approach are illustrated in the Focus on Problem Solving.

THE THREE DATABASE MODELS

The way data are organized in a database depends on the nature of the problems they are required to solve. There are three principal logical database models: the hierarchical model, the network model, and the relational model. Each model is best suited to solving a particular class of problems.

The Hierarchical Model   The **hierarchical database model** organizes data in a top-down, treelike manner. Each record is broken down into pieces of records called segments. The database looks like an organization chart with one root segment and any number of subordinate segments. The segments, in turn, are arranged into multilevel structures, with an upper segment linked to a subordinate segment in a parent-child relationship. A "parent" segment can have more than one "child," but a subordinate "child" segment can have only one "parent."

The hierarchical model thus works best for one-to-many relationships among pieces of data. Figure 7.10 shows a hierarchical database for personnel in a work department. The root segment, *Department*, is the point of entry into the hierarchy. Data are accessed by starting at the root and moving progressively downward in the hierarchy. Thus, to find information about employees, jobs, and performance ratings, one must start at Department, then access related data about the employees and jobs in a particular department. IBM's IMS (Information Management System) is the most widely used hierarchical DBMS.

Hierarchical DBMSs thus have well-defined, prespecified access paths. Any piece of data in the database must be accessed from the top downward, starting with the root segment and proceeding through successive layers of subordinate segments. Hierarchical DBMSs are best suited for problems that require a limited number of structured answers that can be specified in advance. Once data relationships have been specified, they cannot easily be changed without a major programming effort. Thus the hierarchical model cannot respond flexibly to changing requests for information.

Hierarchical DBMSs are also noted for their processing efficiency, making them ideal for systems in which massive numbers of records and changes to the database must

Hierarchical database model
The organization of data in a database in a top-down, treelike manner; each record is broken down into multilevel segments, with one root segment linked to several subordinate segments in a one-to-many, parent-child relationship.

FOCUS ON PROBLEM SOLVING

TRACKING SALMON WITH A DATABASE

The Northwest Power Planning Council (NPPC) was created in the early 1980s to develop a program to minimize damage to the salmon and steelhead rainbow trout in the Columbia River drainage system. The fish were endangered as a result of severe environmental damage caused partly, but not exclusively, by the construction of hydroelectric dams. The NPPC staff faced an immense challenge. The Columbia River basin, located in Oregon, Washington, Idaho, and Montana, contains about one-third of all free-flowing rivers in the entire United States; consequently, it produces an immense amount of data relevant to the struggle to save the fish. The database management system (DBMS) selected had to meet specific and extensive requirements.

To fulfill their charge, the NPPC needed to collect data that would yield information on current fish migration patterns, the quality of the fish habitat, dams, irrigation, and logging in the pertinent areas, even area geological

and archeological information. They needed to coordinate and centralize the data on fish counts, gathering information every half-mile on all affected rivers, a total of 300,000 collection spots. In addition, the Endangered Species Act required the agency to trace specific species of endangered salmon, which meant gathering data on hatchery releases. In total, the system had to contain hundreds of thousands of records of varying types and content. NPPC faced a major technical problem as well. Much of the data would come from many different state, local, and private agencies that collected data in a wide variety of incompatible formats. Equally important, users who were not computer professionals had to be able to access the data in meaningful ways, so that, for instance, they could predict the potential effects of building another dam.

The NPPC had used a hodge-podge of solutions that were inadequate to handle its huge volume of data. After several years of looking, the group finally selected the 1032 database from CompuServe Data Technologies. According to Peter Paquet, senior biological associate at the NPPC, they selected the software for a series of reasons based on NPPC needs:

● 1032 can coordinate data recorded in different formats. 1032 does this

well; it even includes a facility to transform data calculated in incompatible ways. For example, 1032 can convert data collected in feet per acre to the NPPC standard of feet per mile.

● It supports cross-referencing of coding schemes used in the four states, so that, for example, NPPC could combine data on the same stream identified four different ways.

● 1032 is able to handle the very large records and multiple data sets required by the NPPC system.

● The DBMS data manipulation language is easy to use, enabling end-users to develop their own applications.

● The data can be used by SAS System, a sophisticated statistical analysis package that NPPC uses to analyze the mountains of data they collect.

To make the data even more accessible to users, the NPPC staff recently developed an easy-to-use menu system.

FOCUS Questions: Describe the problem that the 1032 database was designed to solve. How effective was it? What other uses might there be for the same data?

SOURCE: Melinda-Carol Ball, "CompuServe Database Simplifies Fish-Tracking Task," *Computerworld*, January 4, 1993.

be processed. Hierarchical DBMSs would be ideal for solving problems such as the daily processing of millions of airline reservations or automated teller banking transactions.

Network database model

The organization of data in a database to depict a many-to-many relationship.

The Network Model   The **network database model** is best at representing many-to-many relationships between data. In other words, a "child" can have more than one "parent." For example, in the network structure for personnel in work departments in Figure 7.11, an employee can be associated with more than one department. Computer Associates' IDMS is a popular network DBMS for computer mainframes.

Network DBMSs are more flexible than hierarchical DBMSs, but access paths must still be specified in advance. There are practical limitations to the number of links, or relationships, that can be established among records. If they are too numerous, the software will not work efficiently. Neither network nor hierarchical database management

FIGURE 7.10

A Hierarchical Database: A Child Has Only One Parent

The design of a hierarchical database resembles a tree: it has a single "root" segment (in this case, "department") connected to several lower-level segments ("employee"). Each employee segment, in turn, connects to other subordinate segments ("performance ratings" and "job assignments"), each subordinate segment being the "child" of the "parent" segment immediately above it in the design. In a hierarchical database, each child segment can have only one parent; in order to access that child, we must "go through" the parent.

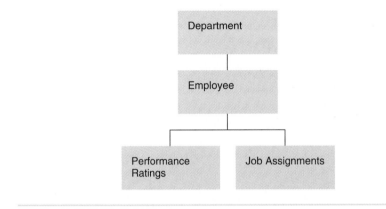

models can easily create new relationships among data elements or new patterns of access without major programming efforts.

The Relational Model   The most recent database structure, the **relational database model**, was developed to overcome the limitations of the other two models in representing data relationships. The relational model represents all data in the database in simple two-dimensional tables called relations. The tables appear similar to flat files, but the information in more than one file can be easily extracted and combined.

     The strength of the relational model is that a data element in any one file or table can be related to any piece of data in another file or table as long as both tables share a common data element. IBM's DB2 and Oracle from the Oracle Corporation are examples of mainframe relational database management systems. dBASE IV and

Relational database model
The organization of data in a database in two-dimensional tables called relations; a data element in any one table can be related to any piece of data in another table as long as both tables share a common data element.

FIGURE 7.11

A Network Database: A Child Can Have More Than One Parent

A network database permits many-to-many relationships. If we wanted to retrieve information on Employee 3, for example, we could access that information by going through either Department A or Department B. This means that network databases are somewhat more flexible than their hierarchical counterparts, although there are practical limits to the number of links that can be designed into them.

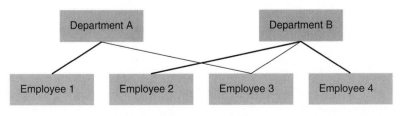

FIGURE 7.12

A Relational Database: The Most Flexible Approach to Data Retrieval

A relational database arranges data into tables or relations. What makes this approach so flexible is that a data element in one table can be related to any data element in any other table, as long as the two tables share a common data element. Thus, in the example here, the employee table can be combined with the job assignment table, because each of these tables has a field containing a job code. Similarly, the employee table can be combined with the performance rating table, because each one holds an employee ID field.

Table (Relation)

Columns

Department

Dept Code	Dept Name	Dept Location	Cost Center
398	Shipping	Warehouse 2	B1209
447	Accounting	Office Building 1	C4428
112	Purchasing	Office Building 2	C1133

→ Rows

Employee

Employee ID	Employee Name	Address	Age	Hire Date	Term Date	Salary	Job Code
113223394	David Sniffen	11 Scenic Dr, Rye, NY 11233	33	02/04/90		22,000	S88
432669764	Paula Hayes	22 Brook St, Croton, NY 10520	67	05/03/49	04/30/90	27,000	C42
135770964	Mark Hastings	6 Nordica, Elmsford, NY 11677	44	11/01/85		66,000	M55
445890264	Robert Flynn	3 Oak Pl, Harrison, NY 10767	55	11/01/77		46,000	M77

Job Assignment

Job Code	Job Description	Date Created	Salary Range	Dept Code
C42	Clerk	01/01/45	13,000-29,000	447
S88	Shipping Clerk	05/01/49	15,000-25,000	398
M55	Manager	01/01/45	40,000-150,000	112

Performance Rating

Employee ID	Performance Rating	Evaluation Date
113223394	2	12/14/95
432669764	3	11/23/95
135770964	1	12/07/95
445890264	2	12/14/95

Paradox from Borland International, Inc., and Microsoft Access are examples of microcomputer relational database management systems. (Oracle also has a microcomputer version.)

Figure 7.12 illustrates how personnel in work departments would be treated by a relational database. The relational database consists of four tables or files: a department file (Department), an employee file (Employee), a performance rating file (Performance), and a job assignment file (Job). Each file or table consists of columns and rows. Each column represents a different field, and each row represents a different record in the file. The database was arranged this way because most of the time these files or tables are updated and accessed independently. When information is needed from more than one table, however, it can be combined by using DBMS commands. Therefore, a request to show which department is associated with a particular job assignment and the department's name and location could easily be satisfied by a relational database model.

The standard data manipulation language for relational database management systems is SQL (Structured Query Language). SQL was developed by IBM in the mid-1970s for mainframe and minicomputer environments and was commercially introduced in 1979. It has recently been incorporated into some microcomputer environments. Using SQL, we can combine information from several tables or files, using the operations SELECT, FROM, and WHERE.

The basic structure of a SQL query for retrieving data is as follows:

```
SELECT <columns>
FROM <tables>
[WHERE <condition>]
```

The SELECT command identifies the columns or data fields to retrieve. The FROM clause specifies the tables or files from which to retrieve this information. The WHERE clause restricts the information output to only those records or rows matching a specified condition.

Figure 7.13 illustrates a typical SQL query to extract data from the Department and Job tables illustrated in Figure 7.12. The two tables share a common field, Dept_Code, which identifies each department. In the SQL query, the department code field in the Job table, called Job.Dept_Code, is given a prefix of Job to distinguish it from the department code field (Department.Dept_Code) in the Department table. The query described in Figure 7.13 joins the Department and Job tables to form a new table with the required information.

Database technology has provided many benefits, but it also allows organizations to maintain data that could threaten individual privacy. This issue is explored in the Focus on People.

FIGURE 7.13

A Sample Query Using SQL

SQL (Structured Query Language) is a popular data manipulation language for retrieving information from relational databases. Here we see an SQL query to obtain information by joining two different tables.

```
SELECT  Job.Job_Code,Job_Description,Job.Dept_Code,Dept_Name,
Dept_Location
FROM  Job, Department
WHERE  Job.Dept_Code = Department.Dept_Code
```

FOCUS ON PEOPLE

WHO'S LOOKING OVER YOUR SHOULDER?

Modern database technology allows organizations to combine the myriad information about you stored on computers. Organizations that do that know more about you than you would probably like. Think of all the ways you generate computer information about yourself: charge card purchases, telephone calls, video rentals, magazine subscriptions and book purchases, mail order purchases, banking records, credit application forms (including mortgages), local, state, and federal government records (including court and police records), travel tickets, entertainment tickets, and on and on. Put together and mined properly, this information could reveal not only your credit information, but also your driving habits, your tastes, your associations, and your political interests.

Currently the largest collectors of "private" data about individuals are the three giant credit bureaus—Equifax, TRW, and TransUnion Corp., which together have records on nearly 200 million people in the United States. These bureaus collect monthly information from retailers and banks. Besides your name and address (current and past), they know your income, job title, debts, credit limits, payment records, the value of your home and your car, and even who has requested credit information about you. Your credit card company knows your buying patterns—what you buy, where, and in what price range. They also know your travel patterns. The telephone company knows whom you call, when, and how long you talk. Much of this and other stored data is useful to others and is sold to anyone who pays the price. Too frequently, the data are inaccurate, and those errors can be damaging, as many people have discovered when they were denied credit and examined their own credit records to find out why.

Who wants to buy this information? Many organizations do. People with products to sell purchase relevant information. If you buy "upscale" merchandise from one catalog, you can be certain catalogs from other companies will soon arrive. If you buy gold stocks through your broker, you should not be surprised if within a month or two you receive sales literature about precious metal newsletters not published by your broker. You may get a phone call from a long-distance telephone carrier salesperson (not from your current carrier company) telling you how much you could save by switching, and citing your own long-distance calling patterns. Credit card holders who always paid their bills on time have had their nonbank credit card canceled because their bank account balance had fallen too low. Companies of all types mine their data and sell it to marketing companies. Governments can also be interested. In an effort to locate 18-year-old men who have not registered for the draft, the Selective Service Administration has been known to purchase birthday party lists from ice cream chains.

Concern over loss of privacy through this so-called database marketing has become so great in recent years that the federal government has

7.4 APPLYING DATABASE CONCEPTS TO PROBLEM SOLVING

In applying database concepts to problem solving, several points must be kept in mind: (1) how the database should be designed; (2) whether a traditional file access method or a database approach should be chosen; and (3) if a database approach is appropriate, which database model should be selected.

DESIGNING DATABASE SOLUTIONS

Since file or database organization has a profound effect on how information can be delivered, the design of a database must be very carefully considered. An information system solution must include the logical design and physical design of the database.

When people apply for a bank loan or a credit card, they must supply confidential information such as their Social Security number and annual income. Privacy experts worry that such sensitive personal information can be sold to other companies for use in marketing campaigns. While database technology has provided many benefits, it can also be used by organizations to infringe on individual privacy.

Source: Courtesy of International Business Machines Corporation.

become involved. The Federal Trade Commission (FTC) recently charged TransUnion Corp. with violating consumer privacy by selling lists of consumer information to telemarketing and mailing companies. Equifax stopped the practice in 1991 when it became clear that regulations were coming. TRW recently completed negotiations with the FTC and agreed to stop the practice. These companies will still be able to sell lists, but the data they can include will be severely limited (unless TransUnion Corp. wins the lawsuit). But federal intervention will not solve the problem. Data will still be purchasable from many other sources, including state and local governments, which sell information from birth records, driver's licenses, and even court records.

FOCUS Questions:

How do people benefit from these computerized databases? How can they be harmed? What steps could be taken to prevent this personal data from being misused?

SOURCES: Mitch Betts, "FTC Targets Credit Bureau Mailing Lists," *Computerworld*, January 18, 1993; Gary Levin, "Databases Loom Large for '90s," *Ad Age*, October 21, 1993; and Ruth Simon, "Stop Them from Selling Your Financial Secrets," *Money*, March 1992.

The logical design of the database shows how data are arranged and organized from a business, as opposed to a technical, perspective. There are three steps in logical database design:

- Identifying the functions the solution must perform.

- Identifying the pieces of data required by each function.

- Grouping the data elements in a manner that most easily and efficiently delivers the solution.

We will illustrate the data modeling for a simple purchasing system. (Real-world systems of this sort are more complex; we have simplified here for instructional purposes.) The problem consists of finding a way to track the orders for all the parts a ventilator manufacturer purchases from outside vendors. There may be more than one order for each part. The solution consists of a purchasing system with three basic functions:

Wetterau Incorporated's Maintenance Control Management System tracks nearly 15,000 warehouse and transportation equipment parts, identifying minimum and maximum inventory levels, determining lead times for automatic reordering, tracking repairs, and analyzing operating costs. In order to work efficiently and effectively, databases such as those used in the Wetterau system must be carefully designed.

SOURCE: Courtesy of Wetterau Corporaiton.

1. Issuing and tracking purchase orders.

2. Keeping track of parts on order.

3. Tracking parts suppliers.

The system will need to maintain the following data for each function:

1. Issue purchase orders:

- Order number

- Part number

- Part description

- Unit cost

- Number of units

- Total cost of order

- Vendor identification code

- Vendor name

- Vendor address

- Order date

- Delivery date

2. Track parts:

- Part number

- Part description

- Unit cost

- Vendor identification code

- Vendor name

- Vendor address

3. Trace suppliers:

- Vendor identification code

- Vendor name

- Vendor address

- Vendor payment terms

This laundry list of data must then be analyzed to identify redundant items and to find the most useful way to group data elements. From our list and description of functions, we can identify three basic data groupings or entities: orders, parts, and suppliers. Each of these groupings represents a single subject, or entity, and defines an individual file or record. The data elements are the details that are appropriate for describing each entity. We also need to add key fields so that we can identify unique records. Thus part number is the key field for the parts file, vendor identification code is the key field for the supplier file, and order number is the key field for the order file.

The final logical design describes all of the data elements to be stored in the database, the records and files into which they will be grouped, the relationships among these

FIGURE 7.14

The Logical Design for Building a Relational Database for a Purchasing System
The logical design for a database organizes the data according to an end-user perspective rather than a technical perspective. The final design groups the data elements into records and files that will best serve the information needs of the organization. It must also identify the key field of each file. In this illustration, we have marked the key field with an asterisk. It is essential to develop a useful and workable logical design before creating the physical database.

Order File	*Parts File*	*Suppliers File*
Order number*	Part number*	Vendor identification code*
Part number	Part description	Vendor name
Number of units	Unit cost	Vendor address
Total cost of order	Vendor identification code	Vendor payment terms
Order date		
Delivery date		

data elements, and the structure of the database (hierarchical, network, or relational). Figure 7.14 shows that the logical design for solving this problem uses a relational model with three separate tables, or files: a suppliers file, a parts file, and an order file. The key field in each table is marked with an asterisk.

Note that vendor name, vendor address, part description, and unit cost appear in only one file, although they are required for more than one function. Ideally, redundant data elements should be represented only once—in the group in which they are most appropriate. The data elements in each file pertain to the subject of that file, but they can be combined with each other if required. This is accomplished by using certain fields to establish links or relationships between files, a task facilitated by the relational database model. The vendor identification code in the parts file, for example, allows us to access further details about the vendor of a particular part from the suppliers file.

Once the logical database design has been finalized, it is translated into a physical database, the form in which the data are actually arranged and stored on computer storage media. The goal of physical database design is to arrange data in a manner that makes updating and retrieval as rapid and efficient as possible. Business specialists' data access patterns and frequency of data usage are important considerations for the physical design. The physical database design for our purchasing system using dBASE III+ or dBASE IV software appears in Figure 7.15.

The Focus on Technology describes the special considerations that must be addressed when designing very large databases.

CHOOSING A TRADITIONAL FILE ACCESS METHOD OR A DATABASE APPROACH

Problem solving must consider alternative file organization and access methods. The nature of the problem at hand largely determines whether one of the traditional approaches to file management or a database approach should be built into the solution design.

Very few application solutions today will be based on magnetic tape sequential files. But files using indexed sequential or random-access methods may be appropriate if the solution best stands alone as an independent application, or if the firm does not have the economic or organizational resources to commit to a database approach.

FIGURE 7.15

Building a Physical Database from a Logical Design

Here we see the physical database design developed from the logical plan in Figure 7.14. In this case we have used dBASE IV software to create the physical version. A well-designed database must take into account users' access patterns and how often they need to retrieve specific data elements.

```
Structure for database : C: \DBASE4\INSUPPL.DBF
Number of data records :           0
Date of last update    : 01/18/94
Field   Field Name   Type          Width   Dec   Index
    1    VEND_ID      Character         4           N
    2    VEND_NAME    Character        40           N
    3    VEND_ADDR    Character        50           N
    4    PAY_TERMS    Numeric           2           N
** Total **                          97

Structure for database : C: \DBASE4\INPARTS.DBF
Number of data records :           0
Date of last update    : 01/18/94
Field   Field Name   Type          Width   Dec   Index
    1    PART_NO      Character         4           N
    2    PART_DESC    Character        30           N
    3    UNIT_COST    Numeric           4           N
    4    VENDOR_ID    Character         4           N
** Total **                          43

Structure for database : C: \DBASE4\INORDER.DBF
Number of data records :           0
Date of last update    : 01/18/94
Field   Field Name   Type          Width   Dec   Index
    1    ORD_NUM      Character         5           N
    2    PART_NUM     Character         4           N
    3    NUM_UNITS    Numeric           5           N
    4    ORDER_COST   Numeric           6    2      N
    5    ORDER_DATE   Date              8           N
    6    DELIV_DATE   Date              8           N
** Total **                          37
```

Stand-alone microcomputer databases for personal or small business applications are easy to implement compared with large company-wide databases residing on mainframes or minicomputers. The data requirements of personal or small business databases tend to be quite simple; microcomputer database management software is much less complex and easier to master than mainframe DBMSs. However, a true database approach for a large corporation is a large-scale, long-term effort requiring deep-rooted organi-

TABLE 7.1

A Problem-Solving Matrix for Database Models

Problem Dimension	Hierarchical DBMS	Network DBMS	Relational DBMS
Data relationships	One to many	Many to many	Flexible
Transaction volume	High	Medium	Medium but improving
Flexibility of information retrieval	Low	Low	High
Ease of use for end users	Low	Low	High

FOCUS ON TECHNOLOGY

LEARNING TO LIVE WITH GIANT DATABASES

As computer technology has advanced, our ability to collect and store data has exploded and our ingenuity has developed ways to make use of much of that data. Some companies, such as Nynex Corp., use giant databases to improve their future business. Nynex's MITAS (Market Intelligence Tracking and Analysis System) is more than 400 gigabytes in size and contains telephone-customer use pattern data. Nynex product developers use it to simulate test marketing of new products. Other companies use huge databases because they can no longer perform their core business without them. United Parcel Service's 1.5-terabyte DIALS (Delivery Information Automated Lookup System) is needed to track the 12 million packages they deliver every day.

For other corporations, the huge database *is* the business. Information Resources, Inc.'s (IRI) 1.7-terabyte system comprises data collected from checkout scanners at 3,000 supermarkets. They sell that data to manufacturers and marketers who use it to analyze local and regional buying patterns.

Gigantic databases pose special problems. Access to so much data is difficult. IRI groups the data into 10–20 gigabyte "slices" based on product categories to make it more manageable for customers. They provide artificial intelligence programs to aid customers in navigating their way through the mass of data. So much data is also difficult to store. IBM's flagship mainframe relational database, DB2, has a physical limit of 2 gigabytes, forcing giant database users to divide the data into hundreds of datasets. Maintaining all this data in such a complex environment can require a staff of hundreds, a major cost that must be justified.

Data that are critical to the survival or success of a business must be backed up, no matter how large the quantity.

Backing up a 7-gigabyte Oracle database can take several hours. Yet these giant databases are many times larger than that. Scheduling backups while keeping the data on-line during business hours can be a critical issue.

These giant databases, created by the continual collection of massive numbers of transactions (such as supermarket purchases, telephone calls, or package deliveries), ultimately become larger than needed or can be handled. Some organizations archive or purge the oldest transactions on a regular, sometimes monthly, schedule. John Tedesco, Nynex's director of marketing IS, posed the dilemma all companies with huge databases must face: "The issues are what information do we want, how long should we hold it, and what should we index." Does maintaining so much data make sense?

FOCUS Questions:
What special challenges are posed by large databases? What criteria might you want to use to justify maintaining so much data?

SOURCE: Jean S. Bozman, "Grappling with Huge Databases," *Computerworld*, May 31, 1993.

zational and conceptual change. In order to fashion an application-independent database, organizational discipline must be applied to enforce common standards for defining and using data among diverse groups and functional areas. Defining and building files and programs that take into account the entire organization's interest in data is a long-term effort.

If a database approach is selected, the nature of the problem likewise dictates the most appropriate database model. Table 7.1 shows the kinds of problems each database model is best able to solve.

7.5 DISTRIBUTING INFORMATION: DISTRIBUTED AND ON-LINE DATABASES

Two recent trends in information distribution are distributed databases and on-line databases.

FIGURE 7.16

The Two Types of Distributed Databases: Replicated and Partitioned

As its name implies, a distributed database distributes data among several locations. There are two ways of doing this. A replicated database (panel a) places copies of the central database in each location. Every database is a duplicate of the central one. A partitioned database (panel b) "partitions" its data according to the needs of each location. Thus each local database contains a different portion of the organization's data, and none of the local databases contains all the data.

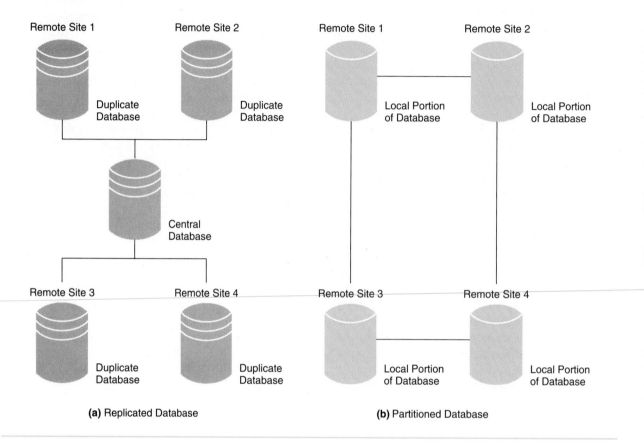

(a) Replicated Database   (b) Partitioned Database

DISTRIBUTED DATABASES

Distributed database

A complete database or portions of a database that are maintained in more than one location.

Replicated database

A central database that is duplicated at all other locations.

Partitioned database

A database that is subdivided so that each location has only the portion of the database that serves its local needs.

Databases can be centralized in one location or distributed among multiple locations. The movement away from centralization toward distribution of computing resources and the growth of computer networks has also spawned a trend toward **distributed databases**. With a distributed database, a complete database or portions of a database are maintained in more than one location. As Figure 7.16 shows, there are essentially two kinds of distributed databases: replicated and partitioned.

With a **replicated database**, a central database is duplicated at all other locations. This is most appropriate for problems in which every location needs to access the same data. A **partitioned database** is subdivided so that each location has only the portion of the database that serves its local needs.

Distributed databases provide faster response time and service at each business location. Firms can fill orders or service customer requests faster if their data are locally available. Distributed databases also reduce the vulnerability of consolidating all the firm's essential data at only one site. They can also increase security problems, however,

FOCUS ON ORGANIZATIONS

DISTRIBUTING DATA FOR WORLDWIDE BANKING

To meet challenges created by bank deregulation in the United States and the emergence of the global information economy, large U.S. banks have begun to operate nationally and internationally. To serve customers across wide geographic areas, these banks must rethink the way they organize their customer data. The challenge for $96 billion Chase Manhattan Bank NA was how best to accomplish this transformation as it expanded globally.

Chase has multiple business units, each of which has its own customer files. Many customers appear many times and in multiple locations in these customer files. When a large client with international holdings asks Chase for a quick picture of its current investments, that customer does not want to wait while Chase collects data from various customer files around the globe. Nor does it want only part of the data. Yet geographically dispersed banking units need to maintain their own data to better serve local clients, even if those clients are branches of larger, international customers. The new competitive environment also required Chase to have rapid and flexible access to its data.

Chase turned to database technology for part of the solution. In 1988, an international network was implemented that was well ahead of most of Chase's competitors. By 1993, 12,000 of Chase's 22,000 PCs worldwide were connected to the network. Chase installed relational databases as part of the technology infrastructure. The goals are to enable flexible access to data on the network and to present a unified view of large corporate accounts across Chase's far-flung global operations. The next step is to import data from Chase's mainframes onto local networks. Chief Information Officer Craig Goldman says Chase will use Sybase Inc.'s Sybase System 10 Replication Servers, which will copy data across multiple computers in offices worldwide. These Replication Servers will be able to replicate some data in some locations once every 24 hours. However, they will also update designated data continuously in true distributed database fashion. Banks dealing with customer inquiries about their accounts need to know the customer's last transaction.

According to Gene Friedman, Chase's vice-president of applied technology, these technology changes are being accompanied by a cultural change in the way people view their work. "It's a change in the paradigm that the doers and the maintainers of this technology are used to working in," he said.

FOCUS Questions: Was a replicated database appropriate for an organization such as Chase? Why or why not? What people, organization, and technology factors had to be addressed to implement this replicated database?

SOURCE: Jean S. Bozman, "Chase Unifies Database View," *Computerworld*, May 24, 1993.

because of their dependence on telecommunications links and widened access to sensitive data.

Distributing databases increases data redundancy, especially if a replicated database is chosen. Inconsistencies can easily arise among the data in central and local systems, especially if changes to the data in one system are not immediately captured by the other. These problems can be compounded if data from a central database are informally "distributed" by downloading portions of them to microcomputers.

The Focus on Organizations illustrates some of the advantages of distributed databases when organizations have worldwide operations.

ON-LINE DATABASES AND INFORMATION SERVICES

In addition to information maintained internally, many firms are taking advantage of **on-line databases** and information services. Such services supply information external to the firm, such as stock market quotations, general news and information, or specific

On-line database
A service that supplies information external to the firm, such as stock market quotations, general news and information, or specific legal and business information.

TABLE 7.2

Leading On-Line Database Services

Company	Service Provided
Prodigy	Business and general interest information
CompuServe	Business and general interest information
America Online	Business and general interest information
Dow Jones News Retrieval	Business and financial information
Dialog	Scientific, technical, medical, and business information
Lexis	Legal research
Nexis	News and business information

legal and business information. A valuable feature of these services is the ability to search the databases for specific information, such as key words and phrases, and to extract reports. If you were researching CAD workstations, for example, you could request references on the key words *workstation, CAD,* and *computer-aided design* and receive a list of articles containing those key words in the title. In addition to supplying information, these services may provide a network that lets two different users communicate with each other.

Table 7.2 lists the leading on-line database services. For example, a "general interest" supplier, CompuServe, provides not only on-line information but also electronic bulletin boards and airline reservation and shopping services.

7.6 LEADING-EDGE TECHNOLOGY: OBJECT-ORIENTED AND HYPERMEDIA DATABASES

As information needs change, methods of data storage and retrieval must also change. Two recent developments, object-oriented and hypermedia databases, are once again transforming the way we manage data. DBMSs were initially designed to store only homogeneous, structured numeric and character data that were predefined into fields and records. Today many applications need to store such traditional data together with drawings, images, photographs, voice, and even video within one database. CAD (computer-aided design) is a typical application. An engineer's design usually includes design specifications (numeric data), written descriptions (characters), and images (graphic data), that are often complex three-dimensional representations that can be viewed from all angles. A medical database might need to include doctor notes, laboratory reports, test results, chronological charts, X-rays, and magnetic-resonance image videos. A traditional DBMS could not automatically manipulate and link these different types of data in a single application.

Object-oriented databases

Databases that store data and processing instructions as objects that can be automatically retrieved and stored.

Object-oriented databases store data as objects that can be automatically retrieved and shared. Included in the object are processing instructions to complete each database transaction (see Chapter 6 for a discussion of object-oriented programming). These objects can contain various types of data, including sound, graphics, and video as well as traditional data and processing procedures. Object-oriented databases thus can handle all kinds of data, and the objects can be shared and reused. These features of object-

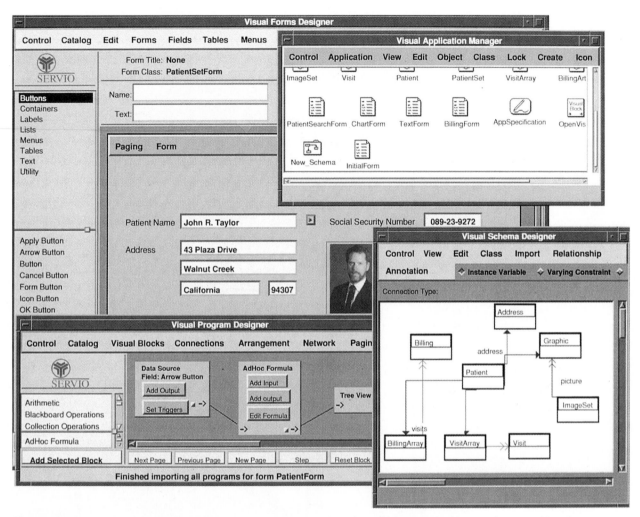

Object-oriented databases can store and organize data consisting of graphics, sound, video, and text, making them especially suitable for multimedia applications.

SOURCE: Courtesy of Servio Corporation.

oriented databases promise to facilitate software development through reuse and the ability to build new multimedia applications that combine multiple types of data. For example, Cold Spring Harbor Laboratory, a biology research center in Cold Spring Harbor, New York, uses the GemStone object-oriented database management system (ODBMS) to store images of DNA molecules. The GemStone ODBMS lets the laboratory model the DNA molecule in three dimensions, as it actually appears in the real world.

Hypermedia databases manage data differently than object-oriented DBMSs but also can contain diverse data. They store data as "chunks" of information, with each chunk in a separate node. Each node can contain traditional numeric or alphanumeric data, or whole documents, software programs, graphics, sound, or even full-motion video. Each node is totally independent—the nodes are not related by a predetermined organization scheme as they are in traditional databases. Instead, users establish their own links between nodes (see Figure 7.17). The relationship between records is less structured than

Hypermedia databases

Databases organized to store text, graphics, audio, or video data as nodes that can be linked in any pattern established by the user.

FIGURE 7.17

Hypermedia

In a hypermedia database, the user can choose his or her own path to move from node to node. Each node may contain text, graphics, sound, full-motion video, or executable programs.

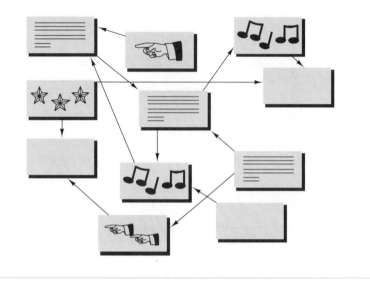

Apple Computer Corporation's HyperCard is an example of a hypermedia database, which can contain text, graphics, sound, full-motion video, or executable software programs. The card displayed on the screen can be linked to one or more other cards in any manner the user chooses.

SOURCE: Courtesy of Apple Computer Corporation.

in a traditional DBMS. Searching for information does not have to follow a predetermined organization scheme. Users can branch directly from one node to another in any relationship established by the author. For instance, one could relate an X-ray with a doctor's notes on that X-ray.

Hypermedia is best known for the technology behind Apple Corp.'s HyperCard, although the approach is becoming popular with other software vendors as well. An auto sales system using the HyperCard approach might link basic product information (e.g., auto name, model number, color, body type, suggested dealer price) with descriptive sales brochures, technical data, perhaps a three-dimensional image of the vehicle, a video showing it in action, and the location of authorized dealers in the area. Facts can be linked across traditional subject boundaries. For example, if you were studying chemistry, you could link a chemical compound to the biographical information about the compound's creator that is located in an entirely different reference work. Or you could connect the compound to grocery products containing it or to long-term health studies of the compound.

SUMMARY

- Data are organized in computerized information systems in a hierarchy that starts with bits and bytes and proceeds to fields, records, files, and databases.

- In the traditional file environment, data records are organized by using either a sequential file organization or a random file organization.

- Transactions can be processed in either batch or on-line mode. On-line transaction processing requires a direct-access storage device and some form of direct file organization.

- Problems associated with the traditional file environment include data redundancy, program/data dependence, data confusion, and excessive software costs.

- A true database approach to organizing information stores data physically in only one location and uses special database management software so that this common pool of data can be shared by many different applications.

- The three components of a database management system are a data definition language, a data manipulation language, and a data dictionary.

- Advantages of using a database approach to organizing information include independence of data from application programs, reduction of data redundancy and inconsistency, elimination of data confusion, consolidation of data management, and ease of information access and use.

- The three principal database models are the hierarchical model, the network model, and the relational model. The suitability of each model depends on the nature of the problem to be solved—specifically, the nature of the data relationships (one-to-many or many-to-many), the need for flexibility, and the volume of requests or changes to the database to be processed.

- The standard data manipulation language for relational database management systems is Structured Query Language (SQL).

- With a distributed database, a complete database or portions of a database are maintained in more than one location. There are two major types of distributed databases: replicated databases and partitioned databases.

• Commercial on-line databases such as CompuServe, Lexis, and Dow Jones News Retrieval can provide essential external information to firms easily and inexpensively.

• Object-oriented and hypermedia databases can store graphics and other types of data as well as numeric data and text, making them suitable for multimedia applications. Data in hypermedia databases can be linked together in any pattern established by the user.

KEY TERMS

Field	Schema
Record	Subschema
File	Database management system (DBMS)
Database	Data definition language
Entity	Data manipulation language
Attribute	Structured Query Language (SQL)
Key field	Data dictionary
Traditional file environment	Hierarchical database model
Sequential file organization	Network database model
Random file organization	Relational database model
Indexed sequential-access method (ISAM)	Distributed database
Index	Replicated database
Data redundancy	Partitioned database
Program/data dependence	On-line database
Logical view	Object-oriented database
Physical view	Hypermedia database

REVIEW QUESTIONS

1. Why should businesses be concerned about file organization and management?
2. List and define each of the components of the data hierarchy.
3. Why are indexes and key fields important tools for file management?
4. What is the difference between the indexed sequential-access method and the sequential-access method? Distinguish between the indexed sequential-access method and the random-access method.
5. What is the relationship between file organization and batch and on-line transaction processing?
6. Define a database and a database management system.
7. What problems associated with a traditional file environment can be overcome by a DBMS?

8. What is the difference between a logical view and a physical view of data?

9. List and describe the components of a DBMS.

10. Why are data dictionaries important tools for businesses?

11. Describe the three principal database models and indicate the strengths and limitations of each.

12. What are the three steps in logical database design?

13. What is a distributed database? List and define the two major types of distributed databases.

14. List two major commercial on-line databases and the services they provide.

15. How do hypermedia and object-oriented databases differ from a traditional database? What kinds of problems are they most useful in solving?

DISCUSSION QUESTIONS

1. Compare the database approach to the traditional approach to file management. What are the advantages and disadvantages of each?

2. It has been said that you do not need database management software to have a database environment. Discuss.

3. Which of the components of a DBMS (data definition language, data manipulation language, data dictionary) would you use for each of the following?

   a. The field for annual salary must be expanded from six to seven digits.

   b. A report listing all employees who work in the purchasing department must be produced.

   c. A new data element, taxable life insurance, must be added to the database. Personnel and payroll programs must be modified to keep track of the amount of company-funded life insurance that is taxable.

PROBLEM-SOLVING EXERCISES

1. *Group exercise:* A university typically maintains information about students and courses. Some of the pieces of data that must be maintained are student names and addresses, student identification numbers, course names, course descriptions, course numbers, grades, majors, course enrollments, number of credits per course, faculty member teaching each course, term offered, and department giving the course. Using the guidelines presented in Section 7.4, divide the class into groups, and have each group design a database for this application.

2. Develop a data dictionary for the purchasing system described in this chapter. List all of the data elements in the system and show their format, size, definition, and business usage.

3. *Hands-on exercise.* Use appropriate application software to create the relational database illustrated in Figure 7.12. Then develop an application to create the following reports:

- All employees with salaries over 30,000, listing the employee's name, identification number, job code, and salary.

- All employees with performance ratings of 2 or 3, listing the employee's name, identification number, and performance rating code.

- Jobs in the Shipping Department, listing the department name, department code, job description, and job code.

PROBLEM-SOLVING CASE

BETTING ON HORSE RACING DATA

"Data is our business," according to Nicholas D'Altilio, The Jockey Club MIS director. "We have no other products but data." He added, "We have to be able to get at it." With that realization, The Jockey Club recently launched a seven-figure project to overhaul its approach to data storage and access.

The nearly 100-year-old Jockey Club supplies data to the thoroughbred horse breeding and racing industries worldwide. The nucleus of their business is nonprofit—supplying thoroughbred pedigree and registry data on more than two million horses, including data on births, blood types, and markings. Breeders, horse owners, horse buyers, and racing specialists subscribe to this service. From their nonprofit beginnings, The Jockey Club has now branched out into the for-profit business of selling horse racing data. Together with the Thoroughbred Racing Association, they recently established Equibase Co., which has amassed data on 200,000 races after only 2½ years. Customers include not only their nonprofit subscribers but also paying publications.

D'Altilio and his staff recently concluded that they had two fundamental problems with their hierarchical mainframe database management system. First, rigid data structures made customer access to data difficult and frustrating. In addition, many of the data were closely linked to the specific applications separately designed for various business subsidiaries, which forced customers to go from one system to another, a slow and frustrating way to gather full information on a given horse. For example, subscribers were unable to correlate breeding information on a horse with its later racing record. Nor could a subscriber send in a check for service payment unless it had the horse's name on it. Otherwise, there was no way to apply it to an account. In other words, the data could not be related; customers had no point at which they could enter a keyword (such as a horse's name) and access all relevant data.

There were other problems. Because so much of the data were closely coupled with outmoded batch applications, they were not immediately available. The Jockey Club had to process the batch breeding data overnight, which required seven to 15 hours, to make it available the next day. Worse, the company was unable to implement plans to offer new, potentially profitable services because of their inability to relate the data. The company even had trouble linking services rendered to their financial systems, resulting in lost income. To add insult to injury, maintaining all this inaccessible data proved very costly. Clearly they had to make a change.

In 1993 The Jockey Club's high-level business managers set a goal to develop an enterprise business model that would become the basis for designing the new data storage and distribution system. They chose network technology, distributed processing (see Chapter 4), minicomputers and desktop computers, and relational databases. The Jockey Club selected Sybase Inc.'s relational database and HP 9000 UNIX computers and workstations. They plan to retire their IBM 3081K mainframe in 1995, replacing it with a single, networked, logical database that is totally separate from individual applications. It will be completely accessible across different businesses. The network technology and distributed processing will prevent overload from requests to access the data. They also expect to offer their customers dial-up or direct access to all the data. The icing on the cake? Robert Burch, The Jockey Club's computer operations manager, believes the new system will reduce operating costs by 25 percent.

SOURCE: Joanie M. Wexler, "Horse Club Races for Payoff from Database Overhaul," *Computerworld*, August 30, 1993.

CASE STUDY QUESTIONS

1. Why do you think The Jockey Club chose to go to a relational database model for data storage?

2. If you were Nicholas D'Altilio, how would you cost justify a project costing over $1 million?

3. Although the case mentions distributed processing as part of the solution, no mention is made of distributed databases. As the designer or this system, would you include distributed databases as part of the solution? Explain your reasons.

4. Review the business problems that caused The Jockey Club to launch this project. Which of those problems seem to be well addressed by the solution? Are any problems not adequately addressed? What changes or additions would you make to the design? Explain your answers.

Chapter

⟶ E I G H T ⟵

TELECOMMUNICATIONS
AND NETWORKS

LEARNING OBJECTIVES

After reading and studying this chapter, you will:

1. Understand the basic components of a telecommunications network.
2. Know how to measure telecommunications transmission rates.
3. Be familiar with the three basic network topologies.
4. Know the major types of telecommunications networks.
5. Be able to address telecommunications issues when designing a solution.
6. Be aware of important business applications using telecommunications.

According to aboriginal tribal ritual, when a person dies, his or her goods are distributed among kin so that the person's spirit can live on. For aborigines living in places like Yuendumu, a remote outreach of the Australian outback, this critical ceremony would have taken weeks or months to complete. Long, dry, dangerous treks across the Tanami Desert would have to be made to reach relatives in other pockets of this vast, nearly unpopulated region. Now, the spirit of the deceased can be rekindled within hours, using a satellite telecommunications network.

Fifty years ago the Australian government relocated the Tanami aborigines to reservations in the Tanami Desert. This move virtually stranded the tribes. Then Terence Nickolls, chief executive officer of AAP Communications Services, a supplier of video-based teleconferencing systems in New South Wales, found a way to help. Since the company operated its own network, why not use the technology to bring communication to the Tanami people?

The result was ConferNet, a flexible, multisite network that combines satellite telecommunications, low data-rate digital videoconferencing, and a customized Microsoft Windows graphical user interface. ConferNet delivers interactive childhood and adult education, emergency health diagnoses, and government support systems over distances of many hundreds of miles. The Tanami people developed their own plan for managing and using the network to link their far-flung community. Users at each site control scheduling and call reservations with commands based on the Windows graphical user interface icons.

Plans are under way to expand ConferNet to provide access to Australian media and information activities. ConferNet can be used for the international display and sale of Tanami paintings and crafts. The network will be extended from six to 30 sites. The Chinese government has expressed interest in ConferNet's technology as a solution to its long-distance communication problems.

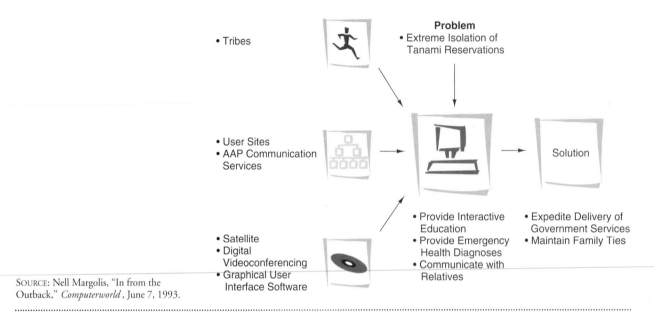

SOURCE: Nell Margolis, "In from the Outback," *Computerworld*, June 7, 1993.

The use of ConferNet to help the Tanami people cope with their relocation illustrates one of the many ways in which communications technology can be used to overcome barriers of distance for the benefit of communities and businesses alike. Today telecommunications networks are a critical ingredient for linking people, factories, stores, and offices in different locations, for improving organizational efficiency, and for creating new products and services. Many of the advanced features of information systems, such as on-line processing and access to information, are the products of telecommunications technology.

This chapter describes the elements of telecommunications technology and shows how they can be arranged to form various types of networks. We show the major kinds of network-based applications that can help organizations solve problems and the factors that must be considered when designing a network-based solution.

8.1 INTRODUCTION

Telecommunications can be defined as communication by electronic means, usually over some distance. A telecommunications system transmits information, establishes an interface or path between sender and receiver, directs messages along the most efficient paths and makes sure they reach the right receiver, edits data by performing error checking and reformatting, converts messages so they flow from one device to another, and controls the overall flow of information. Telecommunications systems can transmit text, graphic images, voice, or video information.

It is impossible to talk about contemporary information systems without addressing telecommunications issues. Today, most information systems for nonpersonal use feature on-line processing and remote access to information. Without communications technology, it would be impossible to solve problems requiring immediate, on-line access to information, sharing of information among different geographic locations, or transmission of information from one location or one information system to another. Table 8.1 lists some typical applications based on telecommunications and the problems they solve.

Recent changes in communications technology and in the ownership and control of telecommunications services have blurred the distinction between telecommunications and computing. Before 1984, telecommunications in the United States was virtually a monopoly of American Telephone and Telegraph Company (AT&T). But, in that year, legal action by the Department of Justice forced AT&T to give up its monopoly and allowed competing firms to sell telecommunications equipment and services. Other companies promptly began to offer telecommunications services, presenting firms with a bewildering array of alternative vendors and technologies from which to choose. AT&T, for example, now markets its own line of computers and computing services, while IBM has ventured into the telephone equipment market.

Telephone companies are starting to provide information services as well, as the Focus on Organizations points out.

TABLE 8.1

Common Uses of Telecommunications

Application	Purpose
Finance	Reducing the time and cost of funds transfer
Automated teller machines	
Electronic funds transfer	
Electronic clearinghouses	
Securities trading	
On-line account inquiry	
Sales and Marketing	Making it easy for customers to purchase
Point-of-sale terminals	
Telemarketing	
Airline and hotel reservation systems	
On-line order processing	
Credit cards and credit authorization	
Manufacturing and Production	Reducing production costs
Process control	
On-line inventory control	
Computer-integrated manufacturing	
Human Resources	Managing human resources
On-line personnel inquiry	
On-line applicant tracking	
Communication and Knowledge Work	Reducing the cost of knowledge and information transfer
Electronic mail	
Groupware	
On-line information services	
Shared design databases and specifications	
Videoconferencing	

**FOCUS ON
ORGANIZATIONS**

THE RACE FOR THE INFORMATION SUPERHIGHWAY

The race for the information super-highway could be the greatest business race of the century. Communications giants are locked in a struggle to build and control a vast web of electronic networks delivering information, education, and entertainment services to offices and homes. These networks will be information highways that could affect life as profoundly in the twenty-first century as railroads and interstate highways did in the past.

A series of court decisions, culminating in Federal appeals court rulings in 1993, allowed the seven regional "Baby Bell" telephone companies created by the breakup of AT&T to provide information services, such as news reports, electronic white and yellow pages, and the electronic retrieval of books and periodicals. The telephone companies were also permitted to become providers of entertainment, with the capability of transmitting tele-

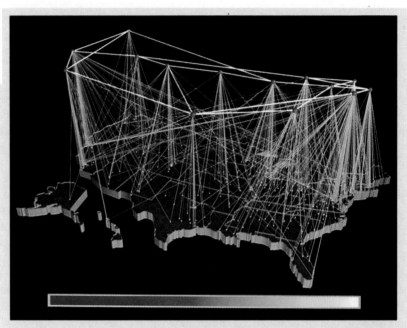

The information superhighway will connect businesses and homes in a vast web of electronic networks that will change the way people work and play.
SOURCE: Courtesy of the National Science Foundation.

vision and video programming.

Telephone lines can now be linked to television sets or computer monitors in the home. Telephone customers will be able to dial a special number to obtain a "video dial tone" that would offer a menu of programs. The programs could include movies, compact-disk quality music, home shopping, or two-way interactive educational services. Work force training, medical ser-

vices, shopping, the ability to see real estate before traveling, videoconferencing, telecommuting, exchanging purchase orders and product designs—all could take place on the network. According to Arthur Bushkin, president of Bell Atlantic Information Services, the range of potential services is endless.

To provide the full range of information services, including video, the

Analog signal
A continuous sine wave form over a certain frequency range, with a positive voltage representing a 1 and a negative charge representing a 0; used for voice transmissions.

Digital signal
A discrete flow in which data are coded as 0-bits and 1-bits and transmitted as a series of on-and-off electrical pulses; used for communication between computers and by some telephone systems.

Consequently, since many more communications choices are available than in the past, you will need some background knowledge on telecommunications systems in order to choose wisely among them. To understand how telecommunications systems work, you must become familiar with certain characteristics of data transmission, the capabilities of various transmission media, the manner in which the components of a telecommunications network work, and alternative ways of arranging these components into networks.

TYPES OF SIGNALS

Two types of signals are used in telecommunications systems: analog and digital (see Figure 8.1). An **analog signal** takes the form of a continuous sine wave over a certain frequency range. A positive voltage charge represents a +1 and a negative charge represents a 0. Analog signals are used to handle voice traffic and to reflect variations in pitch.

telephone companies need more transmission capacity than can be provided by traditional twisted-pair telephone wire. To meet this need they are laying millions of miles of high-capacity fiber optic cable and are purchasing cable companies or forming joint ventures with them. The coaxial cable used by the cable companies already has the capacity to transmit the graphics and video most of these new information services require. For example, Time Warner, the largest cable company in the United States, entered into a joint venture with U.S. West, a regional Bell telephone company, to build a cable system offering entertainment and information services, including video on demand.

Ultrafast switches will route video images as easily as ordinary telephone calls. Special dedicated computers called video servers will store movies and television programs in digital form for delivery over the network. The network will be two-way and interactive. Users will be able to send information—voice, video, data, and graphics—as well as to receive it. Subscribers will be able to select movies or programs from one of 500 channels. Suppose you are trying to furnish a room. You will be able to electronically "snip" images from various online catalogs—sofa, carpet, drapes—and arrange them on your TV screen, even programming the color of your choice. You will order by pushing a button. The network will have your address and credit card data on file.

The telephone companies are expected to help with the construction of another electronic superhighway that is being promoted by the federal government. This information superhighway will be a national network connecting universities, hospitals, research centers, and other institutions that need to exchange vast amounts of data. The Clinton administration wants to extend this national data highway into homes and schools to give students and families immediate on-line access to libraries and other rich sources of information. Although this national data highway will be public-oriented, the government expects it to be constructed by private enterprise.

The information superhighway race is heating up in Europe as well. Britain has allowed both television and telephone on the same network since 1991. Nynex, Southwestern Bell, U.S. West, Singapore Telecom, and Bell Canada are working with cable companies such as Videotron Corp. (a unit of La Group Videotron of Montreal, Canada, which owns cable companies throughout London), long-distance carriers, and media companies to install networks carrying video, voice, and data to British homes and businesses. Telecommunications is still tightly regulated on continental Europe, but experiments with information services are being encouraged. The city of Berlin and Deutsch Bundespost Telekom are testing a service for personalized electronic newspapers and one that will allow physicians to videoconference over patient X-rays and medical histories. In France, which pioneered the Minitel videotext system for home banking and shopping, Plaisance Television has launched two interactive cable TV channels; users can press the telephone touch pad to shop at home or play video games.

FOCUS Questions:
What problems are solved by having the telephone companies deliver information services? How could businesses benefit? How could individuals benefit? Are there any drawbacks to using the information superhighway?

SOURCES: "Yield Signs on the Info Interstate," *Business Week*, January 24, 1994; Paula Dwyer, "Britain Races Down the Information Superhighway," *Business Week*, September 27, 1993; and Andrew Kupfer, "The Race to Rewire," *Fortune*, April 19, 1993.

A **digital signal** is a discrete burst rather than a continuous wave; it represents data coded into two discrete states: 0-bits and 1-bits, which are transmitted as a series of on-and-off electrical pulses. Most computers communicate with digital signals, as do many local telephone companies and some larger networks. (Although telephone lines used to be analog only, digital lines, which can transmit data faster and more accurately than analog lines, are beginning to be used.) If computers communicate through analog lines, all digital signals must be converted into analog form and then reconverted into digital form for the receiving computer.

The process of converting digital signals into analog form is called **modulation**, and the process of converting analog signals back into digital form is called **demodulation**. A device called a **modem** (MOdulation and DEModulation) is used for this translation process. As Figure 8.2 shows, when computers communicate through analog

Modulation
The process of converting digital signals into analog form.

Demodulation
The process of converting analog signals into digital form.

Modem
A device used to translate digital signals into analog signals and vice versa, a necessity when computers communicate through analog lines; stands for MOdulation and DEModulation.

A Panhandle Eastern Corporation technician makes a routine check of a gas pipeline measurement station near Indianapolis. A telecommunications system at this station electronically sends volume data to the Houston operating headquarters.

SOURCE: Courtesy Panhandle Eastern Corporation.

FIGURE 8.1

Analog and Digital Signals

An analog signal is a continuous wave over a particular range of frequencies. A positive voltage charge represents a "1," and a negative voltage charge represents a "0." A digital signal contains discrete bursts representing "on" and "off" electrical pulses. Digital lines tend to be faster and more accurate than analog. Telecommunications systems are moving toward using digital signals exclusively, but some telephone lines still carry information in analog form.

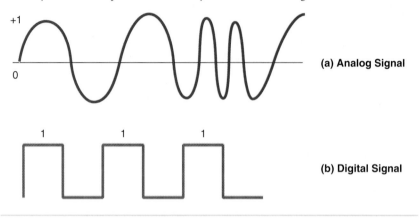

(a) Analog Signal

(b) Digital Signal

telephone lines, two modems will be needed—one to convert the first computer's digital signals to analog, the other to convert the analog signals back to digital for the second computer.

DIGITAL TRANSMISSION MODES

Once the signal type has been determined, the user must be aware of the alternative ways of arranging bits of data for transmission and must also consider the direction of data flow supported by the telecommunications medium.

Asynchronous and Synchronous Transmission   Data are transmitted from one computer to another as a stream of bits. How then does a receiving computer know where

FIGURE 8.2

The Function of Modems in Telecommunications

A modem (short for MOdulation/DEModulation) is a device that translates digital signals into analog, and vice versa. It is a vital piece of equipment in telecommunications systems that employ both types of signals.

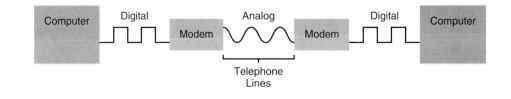

one character ends and another begins? Several conventions have been devised for communicating when a character begins or ends. In **asynchronous transmission**, characters or bytes are transmitted one at a time. Each string of bits composing a character is "framed" by control bits—a start bit, a parity bit, and one or two stop bits. The parity bit is set on or off, depending on whether the parity scheme is odd or even (see Chapter 4).

In **synchronous transmission**, several characters at a time are transmitted in blocks, framed by header and trailer bytes called flags. Synchronous transmission is faster than asynchronous transmission because the characters are transmitted as blocks with no start and stop bits between them. Consequently, it is used for transmitting large volumes of data at high speeds. Figure 8.3 compares synchronous and asynchronous transmission.

Simplex, Half-Duplex, and Full-Duplex Transmission   Transmission must also consider the direction of data flow over a communications line. In **simplex transmission**, data can travel only in one direction at all times; thus, data can flow from a computer processing unit to a printer but cannot flow from the printer to the computer. **Half-duplex transmission** supports two-way flow of data, but the data can travel in only one direction at a time. In **full-duplex transmission**, data can move in both directions simultaneously. Figure 8.4 compares the simplex, half-duplex, and full-duplex transmission modes.

FIGURE 8.3

Asynchronous and Synchronous Transmission

Asynchronous and synchronous transmission represent two ways of sending bits of data along telecommunications lines. Asynchronous transmission sends one byte (one character) at a time; each byte is preceded by a start bit and followed by a parity bit (for error checking) and a stop bit (to signal the end of that particular byte). Synchronous transmission sends several bytes at one time, preceded and followed by bytes called flags. Not surprisingly, synchronous transmission is much faster than asynchronous because there are fewer intervening bits slowing down transmission of data. Both of these examples use an ASCII representation of data.

Asynchronous transmission
A method of transmitting one character or byte at a time when data are communicated between computers, with each string of bits comprising a character framed by control bits.

Synchronous transmission
The transmission of characters in blocks framed by header and trailer bytes called flags; allows large volumes of data to be transmitted at high speeds between computers, because groups of characters can be transmitted as blocks, with no start and stop bits between characters as in asynchronous transmission.

Simplex transmission
A form of transmission over communications lines in which data can travel in only one direction at all times.

Half-duplex transmission
A form of transmission over communications lines in which data can move in both directions, but not simultaneously.

Full-duplex transmission
A form of transmission over communications lines in which data can be sent in both directions simultaneously.

(a) Asynchronous Transmission

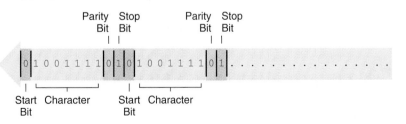

(b) Synchronous Transmission

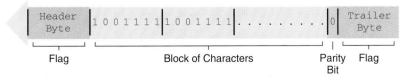

FIGURE 8.4

How Data Flow: Simplex, Half-Duplex, and Full-Duplex Transmission

There are differences in how telecommunications lines transmit data. Simplex transmission (panel a) allows data to flow in only one direction—in this case, from a computer to a receiving device. Half-duplex transmission (panel b) allows two-way flow, but data can travel in only one direction at a time. Full-duplex transmission (panel c) can transmit data in both directions at the same time.

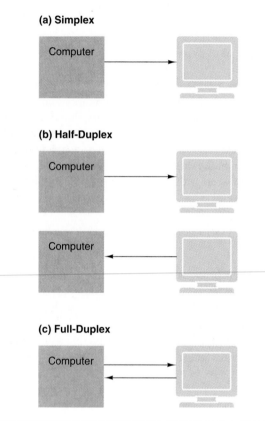

(a) Simplex

Computer

(b) Half-Duplex

Computer

Computer

(c) Full-Duplex

Computer

8.2 TELECOMMUNICATIONS TECHNOLOGY

A telecommunications system is a collection of both hardware devices and the software needed to control these devices. We will examine the major components of telecommunications systems in this section and then describe how these components are used to build networks in the following section.

TELECOMMUNICATIONS SYSTEM COMPONENTS

A telecommunications system is a network of interconnected hardware and software components that perform the telecommunications functions described above. Its essential components are as follows:

1. Computers to process information.

2. Terminals or any input/output devices that send or receive data.

3. Communications **channels**, the links by which data or voice communications are transmitted between sending and receiving devices in a network. Communications channels use various transmission media, such as twisted wire, fiber optic cables, co-axial cables, microwave, satellite, and other forms of wireless transmission.

4. Communications processors, such as modems, front-end processors, multi-plexers, controllers, and concentrators, which provide support functions for data transmission.

5. Telecommunications software, which controls input and output activities and other functions of the communications network.

Communications Processors   A telecommunications system contains a number of computer-like "intelligent" devices, each of which plays a special role in a network.

The **front-end processor** is a computer (often a programmable minicomputer) that is dedicated to communications management and attached to the **host computer** (main computer). It takes some of the load off the host computer by performing error control, formatting, editing, controlling, routing, and speed and signal conversion. The front-end processor is largely responsible for collecting and processing input and output data to and from terminals, and it also groups characters into complete messages for submission to the central processing unit (CPU).

A **multiplexer** is a device that enables a single communications channel to carry data transmissions from multiple sources simultaneously. The multiplexer divides the communications channel so that it can be shared by several transmission devices. The multiplexer may divide a high-speed channel into multiple channels of slower speed or may assign each transmission device a very small slice of time in which it can use the high-speed channel. Figure 8.5 illustrates components of a telecommunications system that includes two multiplexers.

Channel

A link by which voices or data are transmitted in a communications network.

Front-end processor

A computer that manages communications for a host computer to which it is attached; the front-end processor is largely responsible for collecting and processing input and output data to and from terminals and performing such tasks as formatting, editing, and routing for the host computer.

Host computer

The main computer in a network.

Multiplexer

A device that enables a single communications channel to carry data transmission from multiple sources simultaneously.

FIGURE 8.5

The Components of a Telecommunications System

The five major components of a telecommunications system are a computer, communications processors, communications channels, terminals (or other input/output devices), and telecommunications software. Here we see a telecommunications system that uses two multiplexers as communications processors. The multiplexers divide the communications channel to allow several devices to share it. The separate streams of data entering from terminals are routed through the channel into the computer. Multiplexers operate by splitting a high-speed channel into several channels of a slower speed, or by giving each terminal only a very small piece of time for using the high-speed channel.

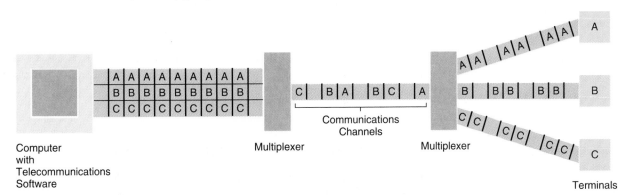

Concentrator

A device that collects and temporarily stores messages from terminals in a buffer or temporary storage area and sends bursts of signals to the host computer.

Controller

A device that supervises communications traffic between the CPU and peripheral devices such as terminals and printers.

A **concentrator** is a type of "store and forward" device (often a specialized minicomputer) that collects and temporarily stores messages from terminals in a buffer, or temporary storage area. When the messages are ready to be sent economically, the concentrator "bursts" signals to the host computer.

A specialized minicomputer called a **controller** supervises communications traffic between the CPU and peripheral devices such as terminals and printers. The controller manages the flow of messages from these devices and communicates them to the CPU, and it also routes output from the CPU to the appropriate peripheral device.

Telecommunications Software   Special software is required to control and support the activities of a network. This software resides in the host computer, front-end processor, and other processors in the network. The main functions of telecommunications software are network control, access control, transmission control, error detection/correction, and security.

Network control software routes messages, polls network terminals, determines transmission priorities, maintains a log of network activity, and checks for errors. Access control software establishes connections between terminals and computers in the network and controls transmission speed, mode, and direction. Transmission control software enables computers and terminals to send and receive data, programs, commands, and messages. Error control software detects and corrects errors, then retransmits the corrected data. Security control software uses log-ons, passwords, and various authorization procedures (see Chapter 12) to prevent unauthorized access to a network.

Protocols   Telecommunications networks typically consist of a wide variety of hardware and software technologies. In order for different components in a network to communicate, they must adhere to a common set of rules, called a **protocol**, that enables them to "talk to" each other. Each device in a network must be able to interpret the other devices' protocols. Protocols perform the following functions in a telecommunications network:

Protocol

The set of rules governing transmission between two components in a telecommunications network.

1. Identify each device in the communication path.

2. Secure the attention of the other device.

3. Verify the correct receipt of a transmitted message.

4. Verify that a message requires retransmission because it cannot be correctly interpreted.

5. Perform recovery when errors occur.

Although the need for standard protocols is widely recognized, different vendors have developed their own systems. Section 8.3 describes some of these systems of protocols and efforts to create universal standards that can be accepted and used by all manufacturers.

TYPES OF TRANSMISSION MEDIA

There are five principal telecommunications transmission media: twisted wire, coaxial cable, fiber optics, microwave (and other forms of radio transmission), and satellite. Each has certain advantages and limitations.

Twisted wire

The oldest transmission medium, consisting of strands of wire twisted in pairs; it forms the basis for the analog phone system.

The oldest transmission medium is **twisted wire**, which consists of strands of wire twisted in pairs. Most of the telephone system in a building relies on twisted wires installed to operate the analog phone system. Most buildings have extra cables installed for future expansion, so every office usually has a number of unused twisted wire cables that can be used for digital communications. Although it is low in cost and is already in place, twisted wire is relatively slow for transmitting data, and high-speed transmission causes interference called crosstalk. On the other hand, new software and hardware have raised the capacity of existing twisted wire cables up to 10 megabits per second, which is often adequate for connecting microcomputers and other office devices.

Coaxial cable, like that used for cable television, consists of thickly insulated copper wire that can transmit a larger volume of data than twisted wire. It is often used in place of twisted wire for important links in a telecommunications network because it is a faster, more interference-free transmission medium. Speeds of up to 200 megabits per second are possible. However, coaxial cable is thick and hard to install in many buildings; it also has to be moved when the computer and other devices are moved, and it does not support analog phone conversations.

Fiber optics technology consists of thousands of strands of clear glass fiber, the thickness of a human hair, that are bound into cables. Data are transformed into pulses of light that are sent through the fiber-optic cable by a laser device at a rate of 500 kilobits to 1.7 gigabits per second. Fiber-optic cable is considerably faster, lighter, and more durable than wire media and is well suited to solutions requiring transfers of large

Coaxial cable

A transmission medium consisting of thickly insulated copper wire; it can transmit a larger volume of data than twisted wire and is faster and more interference-free; cannot be used for analog phone conversations.

Fiber optics

A transmission medium consisting of strands of clear glass fiber bound into cable through which data are transformed into pulses of light and transmitted by a laser device; it is faster, lighter, and more durable than wire media but also more expensive and harder to install.

Fiber optic cable can transmit data that have been transformed into pulses of light at speeds of up to 1.7 gigabits per second.

SOURCE: © Matthew Borkoski, Stock, Boston.

Twisted wire used in analog telephone lines can be used for low-speed data transmission of up to 10 megabits per second, while coaxial cable supports high-speed data transmission reaching 200 megabits per second.

SOURCE: © Dan Bryant.

FOCUS ON
PROBLEM
SOLVING

THE CHRYSLER
TECHNOLOGY
CENTER

In the late 1980s, the Chrysler Corp. was sliding into another financial crisis. Its market share was slipping away to the Japanese. How could it sell more cars? Chrysler slashed its operating costs and decided to emphasize designs that would make its cars as striking as possible.

To support its new approach to product design and development, Chrysler built a 3.5 million–square foot Chrysler Technology Center (CTC) 30 miles north of Detroit at a cost of $1.3 billion. Seven thousand people are employed in "platform development teams" that can have as many as 700 members. In the past, Chrysler and the other U.S. automobile makers used a rigid "stovepipe" method of cre-

The Chrysler Technology Center's massive fiber optic network has enhanced productivity by allowing platform development teams to share and simultaneously work on automobile designs.
Source: Courtesy of Chrysler Corporation.

ating new cars in which functionally separate departments such as the engine department or the design department each performed one aspect of development in sequence. In contrast, the platform teams combine experts from diverse areas such as design, manufacturing, marketing, and purchasing to share ideas and expertise.

The CTC represents the heart of Chrysler's effort to re-engineer the automobile design process by coordinating the talents of its staff and information systems to speed quality products to market. At the new design center, engineers, manufacturing specialists, and even accountants review designs from the earliest days. As a result, they have

---

volumes of data. (See the Focus on Problem Solving.) On the other hand, fiber-optic cable is more difficult to work with, more expensive, and harder to install. It is best used as the "backbone" of a network rather than for connecting isolated devices to a backbone. In most networks, fiber-optic cable is used as the high-speed trunk line, while twisted wire and coaxial cable are used to connect the trunk line to individual devices.

Microwave systems transmit high-frequency radio signals through the atmosphere and are widely used for high-volume, long-distance, point-to-point communication. No cabling is required. Because microwave signals follow a straight line and do not bend with the curvature of the earth, terrestrial transmission stations must be positioned 25 to 30 miles apart, which adds to the expense of microwave. This problem can be solved by using microwave systems with other communications methods, such as satellites.

Communications satellites are preferred for transmitting large quantities of data over long distances because they do not have the distance limitations of terrestrial microwave transmission stations. Communications satellites orbiting more than 22,000 miles above the earth can receive, amplify, and retransmit microwave signals; thus the satellites act as relay stations for earth stations (microwave stations on the ground).

Satellite is not optimal for problems requiring extremely rapid exchanges of data because delays occur when data are sent thousands of miles into space and back down again. However, satellite is very appropriate for transmission of large quantities of

Microwave

A transmission medium in which high-frequency radio signals are sent through the atmosphere; used for high-volume, long-distance, point-to-point communication.

Communications satellite

Satellite orbiting above the earth that acts as a relay station for transmitting microwave signals.

more time to anticipate and work out problems. Designers are more sensitive to the manufacturability of their creations. Will a door permit enough side-impact protection? Will too much steel be wasted if the manufacturer tries to stamp this shape? Manufacturing and engineering, in turn, try to make the innovative designs work. For instance, when the Dodge Stratus and Chrysler Cirrus cars were on the drawing boards, designer Michael Santoro wanted to emphasize curves in the car sides. The curves would make the sedan feel roomier and artfully reflect light. But from an engineering standpoint, the curve was a nightmare. No hinge existed that would make car doors swing properly when a car's sides curved so sharply. A few years ago, the curve would have been straightened. But the curve survived because the team concept allowed designers and engineers to work out their mutual problems.

The CTC houses ten mainframe computers, two supercomputers, and control systems for all the center's computer networks. Every room in the CTC has 8-inch raised floors covering

10,000 fiber-optic cables. These cables can transmit massive volumes of data, such as design specifications and graphics, at very high speed. The cables also link CTC's buildings to its main computer center.

The CTC provides the technology—state-of-the art workstations and CAD/CAM software—to enable the platform teams to test designs by computer. Designs can be easily passed among team members and modified in the computer. Instead of building a series of expensive physical models of a car for crash tests (hand-built prototypes cost $250,000 to $400,000), designers can use their computers to compare crash data from a test with theoretical predictions, moving closer to a solution with succeeding prediction cycles. Only when they need to test a final solution would they actually have to crash a real model. Using this approach, engineers refined the design of the LH car so that it passed its first crash test.

The first new product from the CTC was the LH, a "cab-forward" line of midsized cars that directly competes with Japanese automobiles on price

and quality. The design of these cars expands passenger space and increases the driver's feeling of control by pushing the cabin out over the front wheels and moving the wheels out to the corners of the car to give the sense that it clings to the road. The LH line—the Chrysler Concorde, Eagle Vision, and Dodge Intrepid—have sold as fast as Chrysler can make them. Chrysler's redesigned Grand Cherokee and Dodge Ram pickup trucks and its Chrysler Cirrus and Dodge Stratus cars have also been well received.

Using the team concept and the CTC's advanced technology, Chrysler has greatly increased its productivity. New products such as the LH can be developed with half the design and production staff in 30 percent less time than before.

FOCUS Questions: Why was fiber optic cabling so important in the CTC? What kinds of problems are solved by using telecommunications technology in the CTC?

SOURCES: James Bennet, "The Designers Who Saved Chrysler," *The New York Times*, January 30, 1994; and Edward Cone, "Chrysler," *InformationWEEK*, September 7, 1992.

Satellite dishes facilitate telecommunications transmission to geographically remote areas.
SOURCE: © Stacy Pick, Stock, Boston.

information in one direction at a time. Figure 8.6 shows a typical VSAT (very small aperture terminal) private satellite communications system. Satellite networks are typically used for communications in large, far-flung organizations with many locations that would be difficult to tie together through cabling media. For example, the Chrysler Corp. uses a private VSAT network to connect its corporate headquarters in Detroit, Michigan, with nearly 5,000 dealerships and offices throughout the United States. Section 8.5 describes other forms of wireless communication.

MEASURING TRANSMISSION RATES

Baud

A change in voltage from positive to negative and vice versa. The baud rate at lower speeds corresponds to a telecommunications transmission rate of bits per second. At higher speeds the baud rate is less than the bit rate because more than one bit at a time can be transmitted by a single signal change.

The total amount of information that can be transmitted via any telecommunications channel is measured in bits per second (BPS). Sometimes this is referred to as the **baud** rate; a baud represents a voltage switch (signal change) from positive to negative or vice versa. The baud rate is not always identical to the bit rate, however. At higher speeds, more than one bit at a time can be transmitted in a single signal change, so the bit rate will generally surpass the baud rate. Since one signal change, or cycle, is required to transmit one or several bits per second, the transmission capacity of each type of telecommunications medium is a function of its frequency—that is, the number of cycles per second that can be sent through that medium measured in hertz (see Chapter 3). The

FIGURE 8.6

A VSAT Satellite Communications System

Satellite-based telecommunications are useful for systems that transmit large amounts of information over great distances. A VSAT (very small aperture terminal) satellite system uses a satellite that orbits over the earth. At the central site, a hub earth station and a host computer with a front-end processor manage the earth. At the remote sites—there can be hundreds of these—an outdoor VSAT or antenna links the remote site with the central location by picking up transmissions from the satellite. A control center at the remote site handles data from telephones, facsimile machines, and broadcasts.

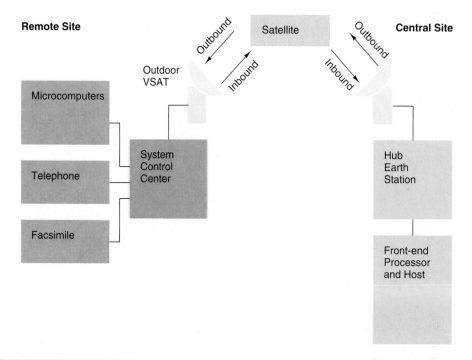

TABLE 8.2

Transmission Capacity of Telecommunications Media

In general, the high-speed transmission media are more expensive, but they can handle higher volumes (which reduces the cost per bit). A wide range of speeds is possible for any given medium, depending on the software and hardware configuration. Most microwave and satellite commercial systems support a standard of 6.2 MBPS for high-speed communication but theoretically have much higher transmission rates.

Medium	Speed		
Twisted wire	500 BPS	to	10 MBPS
Microwave	256 KBPS	to	100 MBPS
Satellite	256 KBPS	to	100 MBPS
Coaxial cable	56 KBPS	to	200 MBPS
Fiber-optic cable	500 KPBS	to	10 GBPS

NOTE: BPS = bits per second; KBPS = kilobits per second; MBPS = megabits per second; GBPS = gigabits per second.

range of frequencies that can be accommodated on a particular telecommunications medium is called its **bandwidth**. The bandwidth is the difference between the highest and lowest frequencies that can be accommodated on a single channel. The larger the range of frequencies, the greater the bandwidth and the greater the medium's telecommunications transmission capacity.

Deciding which telecommunications medium to employ depends not only on cost but also on how often the channel is used. For example, the monthly charges for satellite links are much higher than for twisted wire, but if a firm uses the link 100 percent of the time, the cost per bit of data could be much lower than leasing a line from the telephone company. Table 8.2 compares the speed and cost of the various transmission media.

Bandwidth
The range of frequencies that can be accommodated on a particular telecommunications medium.

8.3   TELECOMMUNICATIONS NETWORKS

There are several ways of organizing telecommunications components to form a network and hence several ways of classifying networks. They can be classified by their shape or **network topology**; they can also be classified by their geographic scope and the type of services they provide. Wide area networks, for example, encompass a relatively wide geographic area, from several miles to thousands of miles, whereas local area networks link local resources such as computers and terminals in the same department or office of a firm. This section will examine both the topological and the geographical classification of networks.

Network topology
The shape or configuration of a network; the most common topologies are the star, bus, and ring.

NETWORK TOPOLOGIES

The three most common network topologies are the star, the bus, and the ring, which are compared in Figure 8.7. Each configuration is appropriate for a particular class of problems.

In the **star network** (panel a), a central host computer is connected to a number of smaller computers, terminals, and other devices such as printers. This topology is popular for organizations in which some aspects of information processing must be centralized

Star network
A network in which a central host computer is connected to several smaller computers and/or terminals; all communications between the smaller computers or terminals must pass through the host computer.

FIGURE 8.7

Three Common Types of Networks: Star, Bus, and Ring

The star network (panel a) is managed by a central or host computer that is connected to all the other devices in the network. All communications must pass through the host computer; another computer cannot send output to a printer, for example, without first channeling it through the host. The bus network (panel b) connects equipment via a single circuit. There is no host computer to control the network, and all data are transmitted to the entire network in both directions. Bus networks are more reliable than star networks because they do not depend on one computer to run the network. A third topology or shape is the ring network (panel c), in which the connecting channel (wire, cable, or optical fiber) forms a closed loop. This allows each member of the network to communicate directly with any of the others, with data always flowing in one direction.

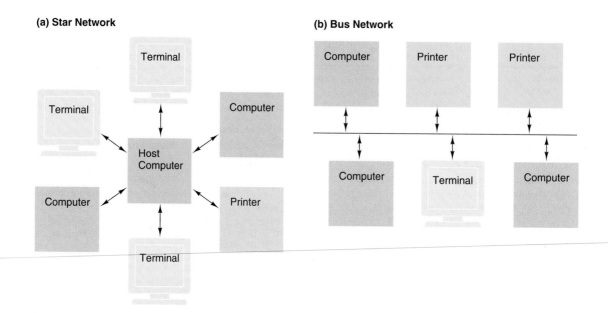

(a) Star Network

(b) Bus Network

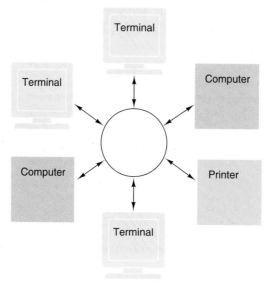

(c) Ring Network

and others can be performed locally. For instance, company-wide files like the master customer list are best stored on a central file. A star network allows data from the master list to be downloaded, or transferred to local computers for processing, and then uploaded back to the central file when the work is complete.

One problem with the star network is its vulnerability. All communication between points in the network must pass through the host computer. Because the host computer is the traffic controller for the other computers and terminals in the system, communication in the network will come to a standstill if the host computer stops functioning.

The **bus network** (panel b in Figure 8.7) links a number of computers and other equipment by a single circuit made of twisted wire, coaxial cable, or optical fiber. All the messages are transmitted to the entire network, with special software to identify which components receive each message; messages can flow in both directions along the cable. No central host computer controls the network, although a host computer can be one of the devices on the network. If one of the computers in the network fails, none of the other components in the network is affected; hence the network is far less vulnerable than a star network to a machine failure. The bus and ring topologies are commonly used for local area networks (LANs); these are discussed in the following section.

One difficulty of bus networks is that with many users, the system slows down because messages start colliding with one another and have to be re-sent. This network topology is also not appropriate for storing large data files that must be shared, such as a list of customers in a mail-order firm. Too many inquiries to the central file will collide and have to be retransmitted. For these reasons, bus networks perform best for applications such as electronic mail, sharing of resources like printers, and file transfers from one machine to another.

Like the bus network, the **ring network** (panel c in Figure 8.7) does not rely on a central host computer and will not break down if one of the component computers malfunctions. The connecting wire, coaxial cable, or optical fiber forms a closed loop that allows each computer in the network to communicate directly with any other computer. Data are passed along the ring from one computer to another, always flowing in one direction, but each computer processes its own applications independently. The most common ring network for microcomputers is IBM's Token Ring Network. Ring networks offer similar advantages and disadvantages as bus networks.

PRIVATE BRANCH EXCHANGES AND LOCAL AREA NETWORKS

The most common kinds of local networks are local area networks and private branch exchanges.

Private Branch Exchanges   A private branch exchange (PBX) is a private telephone exchange that handles a firm's internal voice and digital communications needs. A branch exchange is simply the equipment—found in many buildings—that switches incoming and outgoing telephone calls from the telephone company trunk line to individual offices. In the past, most premise exchanges were owned by the telephone company and manually operated by human operators. Today, many are fully automated and owned by the building or business firm.

Like the switching equipment in central offices, today's PBX is a special computer originally designed for handling and switching voice telephone calls. PBXs not only store,

Bus network
A network in which a number of computers are linked by a single loop circuit made of twisted wire, coaxial cable, or optical fiber; all messages are transmitted to the entire network and can flow in either direction, with special software identifying which component receives each message.

Ring network
A network in which a number of computers are linked by a closed loop of wire, coaxial cable, or optical fiber in a manner that allows data to be passed along the loop in a single direction from computer to computer.

Private branch exchange (PBX)
A central private switchboard that handles a firm's voice and digital communications needs.

forward, transfer, hold, and redial telephone calls, but they also can carry both voice and data to create local networks, switching digital information among computers and office devices. For example, a person can write a letter on a microcomputer, connect to the PBX using his or her own modem and telephone, and distribute a copy of the document to other people in the office or have it printed on the office copying machine. The PBX serves as the connection among all these various devices.

PBXs offer several advantages. First, they handle both data and voice communications and, in the future, may even handle video signals. For voice communications, PBXs allow a firm to exercise more control over its internal telephone system than systems provided by the telephone company. For data communications, they create networks without the expense of installing new cable or wire because they rely on the existing phone wires. Devices can be linked wherever there is a phone jack. Therefore, microcomputers can be networked together or linked to mainframes or minicomputers using existing telephone lines.

The primary disadvantage of PBXs is that they are limited to telephone lines and therefore cannot easily handle large volumes of data. Although they are good at connecting low-volume digital devices, they are less well developed than local area networks for accessing massive central databases like customer files.

Local area network (LAN)

A transmission network encompassing a limited area, such as a single building or several buildings in close proximity; widely used to link microcomputers so that they can share information and peripheral devices.

Local Area Networks   A local area network (LAN) encompasses a limited area, usually one building or several buildings in close proximity. Most LANs connect devices located within a 2,000-foot radius and are widely used to link microcomputers. In contrast to PBXs, which use existing telephone lines, LANs require their own communications channels.

LANs have higher transmission capacities than PBXs. LANs generally have bus or ring topologies and a high bandwidth. A very fast PBX may have a transmission capacity of over 2 megabits per second, whereas LANs typically transmit at a rate ranging from 256 kilobits per second to over 100 megabits per second, depending on the model and transmission medium. They are recommended for solutions requiring high volumes of data and high transmission speeds. For example, a problem requiring a solution expressed with graphics would need a LAN because graphic output is data-intensive.

LANs have become popular for network-based solutions for several reasons: Networks can be built independently of central computer systems. Instead of relying on a central main computer for processing (which can fail), LANs can be installed wherever the business need is the greatest. A LAN solution can be economical, since hardware and software can be shared by many locations. For instance, several offices or departments in a firm may share an expensive laser or color printer. Finally, LANs may be the only viable alternative for electronic mail, video conferencing, graphics, and on-line applications requiring a high-capacity network solution.

LANs are most commonly used to link microcomputers within a building or office so that they can share information and expensive peripheral devices such as laser printers. Another popular application of LANs is in factories, where they link computers and computer-controlled machines. Figure 8.8 shows a typical LAN for an office environment. It consists of several microcomputer workstations, a file server, a network gateway, and a laser printer. We have shown a LAN that uses the ring topology.

File server

A computer with a large hard disk whose function is to allow other devices to share files and programs.

Network gateway

The communications processor that links a local area network to another dissimilar network, such as the public telephone system or another corporate network.

A **file server** is a computer—often a high-capacity microcomputer—with a large hard disk. Its function is to allow other devices to share files and programs, The file server typically contains the LAN's network management software, which manages the file server and routes and manages communications on the network. The **network gateway** connects the LAN to public networks, such as the telephone network, or to other corporate networks so that the LAN can exchange information with dissimilar networks external to it.

FIGURE 8.8

A Local Area Network (LAN)

LANs are networks that link a limited area, such as one office building or several buildings located close to each other. They are often used for electronic mail, graphics, and shared on-line applications. Here we show a LAN with the ring topology. LANs with the bus topology are also common.

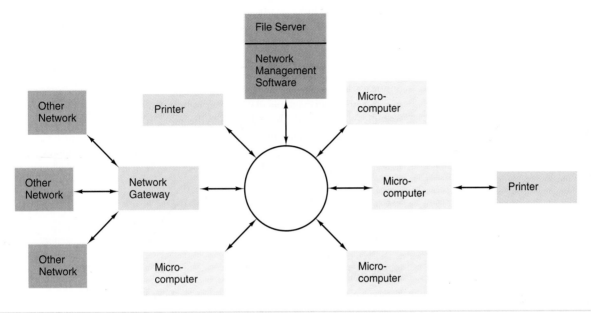

LAN technology components consist of metallic or fiber-optic cable or wireless transmission media linking individual computer devices, special adapters that serve as interfaces to the cable, and software that controls LAN activities. There are four principal LAN technologies for physically connecting devices: Ethernet, developed by Xerox, Digital Equipment Corp., and Intel; Appletalk from Apple Computer Corp.; Token Ring, developed by IBM and Texas Instruments; and Arcnet, developed by Datapoint. LANs employ either a baseband or a broadband technology. Baseband products, such as thin Ethernet, provide a single path or channel for transmitting text, graphics, voice, or video data. Broadband networks provide several paths or channels so that different types of data, or different messages, can be transmitted simultaneously.

LAN capabilities are also defined by the network operating system employed. The network operating system works with application software, such as word processing or electronic mail, to keep data traffic flowing smoothly. The network operating system can reside on every microcomputer in the network (as is the case with the Appletalk network for the Macintosh), or it can reside on a single designated microcomputer, which acts as the server for all the applications on the network. Leading network operating systems include Microsoft's LAN Manager, Novell's NetWare, and IBM's PC LAN.

The primary disadvantages of LANs are that they are more expensive to install than PBXs and are more inflexible, requiring new wiring each time the LAN is moved (unless the LAN uses wireless transmission). LANs also require specially trained staff to manage and run them.

WIDE AREA NETWORKS

Wide area networks (WANs) span a broad geographical distance, ranging from several miles to entire continents. WANs are provided by common carriers, which are companies

Wide area network (WAN)
A telecommunications network covering a large geographical distance; provided by common carriers but managed by the customer.

(such as AT&T or MCI) that are licensed by the government to provide communications services to the public. The common carrier typically determines transmission rates or interconnections between lines, but the customer is responsible for the content and management of telecommunications. In other words, individual firms are responsible for establishing the most efficient routing of messages, error checking, editing, protocols, and telecommunications management.

WANs may consist of a combination of switched and dedicated lines and microwave and satellite communications. Switched lines are telephone lines that a person can access from his or her terminal to transmit data to another computer; the call is routed or switched through paths to the designated destination. Dedicated lines, or nonswitched lines, can be leased or purchased from common carriers or private communications media vendors and are continuously available for transmission. The lessee typically pays a flat rate for total access to the line. Dedicated lines are often conditioned to transmit data at higher speeds than switched lines and are more appropriate for transmitting high volumes of data. Switched lines, on the other hand, are less expensive and more appropriate for low-volume applications requiring only occasional transmission.

Figure 8.9 illustrates a wide area network used by the Texas Instruments Corp. that spans the entire globe. It links 100,000 devices, many of which are arranged in LANs, using a combination of dedicated lines and satellite transmission.[1]

FIGURE 8.9

Texas Instruments' Worldwide Communications Network

Texas Instruments' global communications network illustrates just how complex worldwide networking can get. The LAN internetwork spans several different transmission methods, from dedicated modem lines to satellite links.

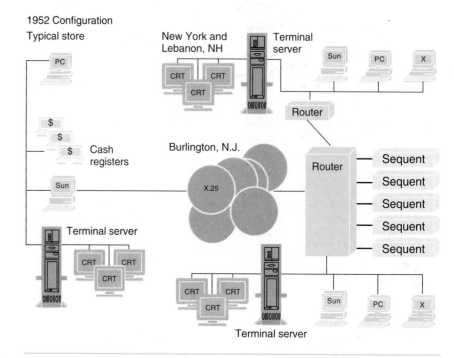

SOURCE: *Byte*, December 1993, p. 68.

The largest wide-area network in use today is the Internet, which connects thousands of smaller networks and millions of users around the world. The Internet was originally set up for research scientists and academics, but it is now accessible to anyone with a computer and a modem. The Internet allows millions of people to access vast stores of information in computer systems throughout the world and to exchange information anywhere in the world at any time. The Part 2 illustrated case study following this chapter describes the wonders of this vast network of networks.

Value-Added Networks   Value-added networks (VANs) are an alternative to firms' designing and managing their own networks. VANs are private, multipath networks for data only. They are managed by third parties that can provide economies of service and management to participating businesses. A private firm establishes and manages the VAN and sells subscriptions to other firms willing to use it. The network may use ordinary telephone or voice-grade lines, satellite links, and other communications channels leased by the value-added carrier. Subscribers pay only for the amount of data they transmit plus a subscription fee. Note that VANs are not common carriers in the sense that they are not regulated monopolies; instead, they are private firms offering a service for a fee. They cannot provide long-distance voice service, however, which is reserved for common carriers.

The term *value-added* refers to the extra "value" added to communications by the telecommunications and computing services these networks provide to clients. Customers do not have to invest in network equipment and software or perform their own error checking, editing, routing, and protocol conversion. They may also save on-line charges and transmission costs because the costs of using the network are shared among many users. Thus the resulting rates may be lower than if the clients had leased their own lines or satellite services. VANs are also attractive because they provide special services, such as electronic mail and access to public databases and bulletin boards. Compuserve, BT Global Network Services, Advantis, Tymnet, and GE Information Services Co. (GEIS) are popular VAN suppliers.

Another way VANs achieve economies is through **packet switching**. This entails breaking up a lengthy block of text into packets, or small bundles of data approximately 128 bytes long. The VAN gathers information from many users, divides it into small packets, and continuously searches for available communications channels that it leases from common carriers and others on which to send the packets. In contrast, an individual firm might use a single leased line for 1 hour and then not use it for 2 or 3 hours. Packets of data originating at one source can be routed through different paths in the network and reassembled into the original message when they reach their destination. Packet switching enables communications facilities to be used more fully and shared by more users.

Frame relay is a faster and less expensive type of packet switching. Since so many of today's digital lines are cleaner than in the past and networks have features for correcting transmission problems, frame relay transmits data in packets without performing error correction. Frame relay works successfully over reliable lines that do not require frequent retransmission because of error.

CLIENT/SERVER COMPUTING

Networks with powerful file servers have created a new model of computing called **client/server computing** in which diverse pieces of hardware work on the same processing problem. In addition to managing the activities of the network, the file server can store

Value-added network (VAN)
A multipath data-only network managed by a private firm that sets up the network and charges other firms a fee to use it.

Packet switching
The breaking up of a block of text into packets of data approximately 128 bytes long; a value-added network gathers data from its subscribers, divides the data into packets, and sends the packets on any available communications channel.

Frame relay
Network technology that organizes data into packets without error correction routines to transmit data over networks faster and cheaper than packet switching.

Client/server computing
Model of computing that divides processing tasks between "clients" and "servers" on a network, with each machine assigned the functions it performs best.

application programs and data files and can distribute programs or data files to other computers on the network as they request them. Servers can be mainframes or mini-computers, but often they are large workstations or powerful microcomputers. In the client/server model, some processing tasks are handled by the file server and others by the subordinate machines, called "clients," with each function being assigned to the machine best suited to perform it. In large, complex applications, more than one server can supply services to clients. The client portion of the application usually handles user interfaces, data input, querying a database, and obtaining reports, whereas the server part usually retrieves or processes data. The exact division of tasks varies with each application. The client/server model requires that application programs be written as two separate software components that run on different machines but that appear to operate as a single application.

Because of the immense power and range of capabilities of desktop computers, client/server computing has emerged as a serious alternative to traditional computing based on centralized mainframes. Many companies are trying to downsize by replacing the work performed by mainframes with some type of client/server network. For example, the Burlington Coat Factory in Burlington, New Jersey, replaced a system collecting transactions from its retail stores based on a Honeywell mainframe computer to one based on six smaller Sequent 2000/750 computers and Sun workstations (see Figure 8.10). Cash registers in each Burlington store are connected by LANs to the Sun workstation, which serves as the main store processor. The Sun machines act as file servers for the registers and as communications gateways to the company's host computers. They send each store's transactions via satellite to several Sequent computers at company headquarters. Users no longer have to request reports in advance, as they did with the mainframe system. They can access company databases from their desktops and use the data in their own spreadsheets and word processing applications. The network can run even if individual parts are not working properly.[2]

Client/server computing has become attractive because it appears to be less expensive yet more flexible than using a centralized mainframe. The hardware for a client/server network costs much less than mainframes, significantly reducing computer processing expenses. However, client/server computing has some "hidden" costs. Companies need to write new software that can divide the processing among clients and servers. Client/server networks are still not as reliable as centralized mainframes, with the potential for crippling the organization if they malfunction. Information systems specialists and end-users require extensive training to use client/server technology properly. Some of these issues were explored in the case concluding Chapter 4 and will be considered again in Chapter 12.

THE DRIVE TOWARD STANDARDS

Telecommunications networks are most effective when digital information can move seamlessly from one type of computer system to another, without regard for the hardware or software technology being used. This goal has been difficult to achieve because of the many disparate types of communications equipment and software. Government, industry, and professional groups are working to create telecommunications standards that can be accepted by all computer manufacturers. Some of the most important standards used today are Open Systems Interconnect (OSI), Transmission Control Protocol/Internet Protocol (TCP/IP), and Integrated Services Digital Network (ISDN).

Open Systems Interconnect (OSI)   In 1978, the International Standards Organization issued a model of network protocols called **Open Systems Interconnect**

Open Systems Interconnect (OSI)

Model of network protocols enabling any computer connected to a network to communicate with any other computer on the same network or a different network, regardless of the manufacturer.

FIGURE 8.10

Burlington's Client/Server System

Burlington's client/server system links all its stores and distribution centers to headquarters. Store transactions enter network-ready cash registers linked to Sun workstations, which also serve as communications gateways. Transactions are routed to a series of Sequent computers for processing. Terminal servers enable data entry and queries from workstations.

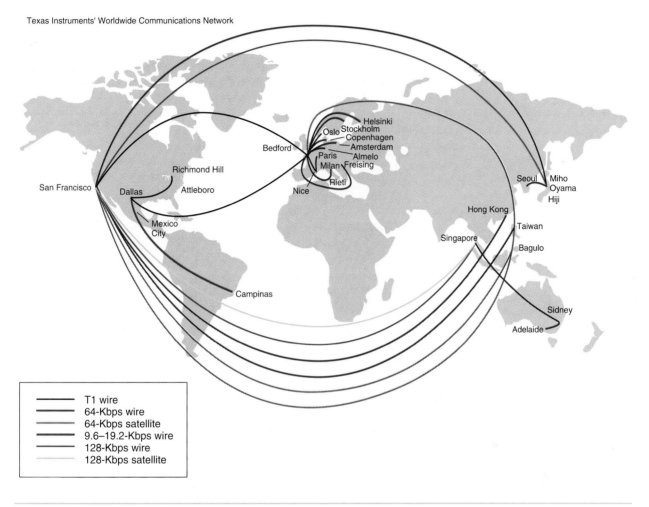

Texas Instruments' Worldwide Communications Network

SOURCE: *Byte*, June 1993, p. 98.

(OSI) that would enable any computer connected to a network to communicate with any other computer on the same network or a different network, regardless of the manufacturer.

OSI was designed to support global networks with large volumes of transaction processing. Figure 8.11 shows that the OSI model divides the telecommunications process into seven layers. Two different computers using OSI standards would each have software and hardware that correspond to each layer of the OSI model. A message sent from one computer to the other would pass downward through all seven layers. It would start with the application layer of the sending computer and pass through to the sending computer's physical layer. It would then travel over the communication channel and enter the receiving computer, rising upward through the seven layers in that machine. The process is reversed when the receiving computer responds.

FIGURE 8.11

The Open Systems Interconnect (OSI) Network Model

The OSI network model divides the communications process into seven layers to enable two networked computers to communicate with each other.

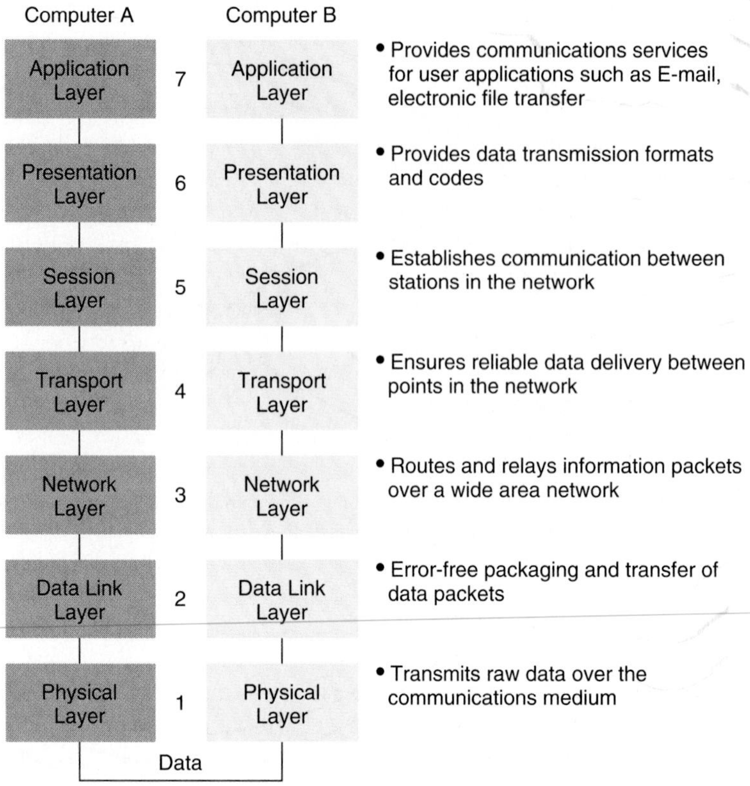

The top three OSI layers are responsible for turning formatted data into a "plain vanilla" version that can travel on a generic network defined in the bottom four layers. Each layer in the OSI model has one or several associated protocols. Each layer is independent of the others so that it can be changed without affecting the other layers.

For example, if a customer service representative wanted information about a particular client's order that was stored in the firm's central host computer, he or she would enter the instructions to retrieve the client's order record into his or her terminal under control of layer 7, the application layer. The presentation layer (layer 6) would change this input data into a format for transmission. Layer 5 (the session layer) initiates the session. Layer 4 (the transport layer) checks the quality of the information traveling from user to host node. Layers 3 and 2 (the network and data link layers) transmit the data through layer 1 (the physical layer). When the message reaches the host computer, control moves up the layers, reversing the sequence.

Transmission Control Protocol/Internet Protocol (TCP/IP)

Network reference model created by the U.S. Department of Defense and widely used in the United States.

Transmission Control Protocol/Internet Protocol (TCP/IP)   Another important network reference model is called **Transmission Control Protocol/Internet Protocol (TCP/IP)**, which was launched in 1972 by the U.S. Department of Defense. TCP/IP is the most widely used communications reference model in the United States (Europeans tend to favor OSI) and is associated with UNIX environments. The

Internet, described in the Part 2 illustrated case, is based on TCP/IP. TCP/IP divides the telecommunications process into five layers and contains special error-checking features for unreliable networks.

Integrated Services Digital Network (ISDN)   Integrated Services Digital Network (ISDN) is an emerging international standard for extending common-carrier digital service to homes and offices from central telephone company facilities. Imagine sitting in your office or dormitory room looking at your computer screen; in one window is a spreadsheet, and in the other is the moving picture of a friend or colleague located across the country with whom you are working. You can both share voice messages, digital information, and video pictures. All of this information comes over a single twisted-wire telephone line that is totally managed by the local phone company. That means you have integrated voice, digital, and video service and great flexibility with no expensive rewiring with coaxial cable; you just plug your computer/telephone into the wall socket. Briefly, ISDN is the everything network. The goal and promise of ISDN is to provide a more functional network to transport all kinds of digital information, regardless of its source or destination. It is a vision of the public switched-phone network turning into a vast digital superexpressway.

Two levels of ISDN service are available. Basic Rate ISDN delivers two 64-kilobit-per-second channels for voice, data, and video and one 16-kilobit-per-second channel for control information (such as the phone number of the calling party) to the desktop or room through ordinary phone wire. Primary Rate ISDN offers 1.5 MBPS of bandwidth divided into 23 channels for voice, video, and data and one channel for control information. This service can connect PBXs, central office switches, or computer systems with a need for high-speed data transmission. Plans are under way to increase the transmission capacity of both Basic Rate and Primary Rate ISDN. National ISDN service is emerging as local Bell companies upgrade their equipment. Currently, implementation of ISDN is restricted by its cost, regional limitations, and the difficulties organizations have experienced in learning how to use the technology. Once the technology is fully developed, however, and prices fall, ISDN will become a leading network alternative.

Asynchronous Transfer Mode (ATM)   Most corporations today use separate networks for voice, private-line services, and data, each of which is based on a different technology. **Asynchronous transfer mode (ATM)** may overcome some of these problems because it can seamlessly and dynamically switch voice, data, images, and video between users. ATM also promises to tie local and wide area networks together more easily (LANs are generally based on lower-speed protocols, whereas WANs operate at higher speeds.) ATM is a protocol that parcels information into uniform "cells," each with 53 groups of eight bits, thus eliminating the need for protocol conversion. It can pass data between computers from different vendors and permits data to be transmitted at any speed the network handles. ATM currently requires fiber-optic cable, but it can attain transmission speeds of hundreds of megabits per second.[3]

Integrated Services Digital Network (ISDN)
Standard for transmitting voice, data, and video over public switched telephone lines.

Asynchronous transfer mode (ATM)
Protocol for transmitting voice, data, and images over LANs and wide-area networks using computers from different vendors by parceling information into uniform cells of 53 groups of 8 bits.

8.4 TELECOMMUNICATIONS APPLICATIONS

Many of the information system applications discussed throughout this text employ telecommunications technology to help people make decisions faster and to accelerate the production of goods and services. Telecommunications has become essential to organizations with multiple geographic locations that must be closely coordinated. Here we discuss some of the leading telecommunications applications for communicating, coordinating, and speeding the flow of information: electronic mail, voice mail, fax, teleconferencing and videoconferencing, and electronic data interchange.

ELECTRONIC MAIL, VOICE MAIL, AND FAX

Electronic mail

The computer-to-computer exchange of messages.

Electronic mail, or E-mail, is the computer-to-computer exchange of messages that has become a way of eliminating telephone tag and costly long-distance telephone charges. It is possible for a person with a microcomputer attached to a modem or a terminal to send notes and even lengthier documents just by typing in the name of the message's recipient. Many organizations have created their own internal E-mail systems, but people can also send and receive E-mail by subscribing to a commercial (public) E-mail service, such as EasyLink, MCI Mail, and AT&T Mail. Value-added networks and on-line information services such as Compuserve and Prodigy also offer E-mail facilities.

By providing faster and more efficient communication between different functional areas of a firm, E-mail can speed up the production process. For example, Liz Claiborne, a leading U.S. clothing manufacturer, uses electronic mail to coordinate activities between its corporate headquarters in New York and New Jersey and its offices in Hong Kong, Korea, Taiwan, Singapore, the Philippines, and Shanghai. Marketing and administrative decisions are made in the United States, but Claiborne's production is handled in hundreds of factories in the Far East. Manufacturing activities and design and production decisions must be carefully coordinated. In a given fashion season, separate items must be color-coordinated, with matching dyes and consistent sizing. Since matching pieces may be produced in different factories, this is a complex process. Claiborne tried telex communication overseas but found it too cumbersome: telex messages could not be sorted by recipient, and critical messages that needed immediate attention could not be singled out. Claiborne now uses E-mail, which can automatically sort

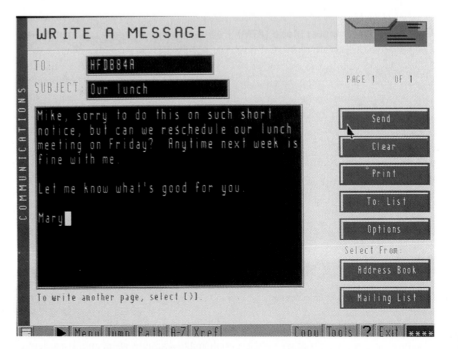

With electronic mail (E-mail), people can easily send notes, messages, or letters directly from their computer to another computer. Information services such as Prodigy provide E-mail facilities for their subscribers, or companies can develop their own internal E-mail systems.

SOURCE: Courtesy of Prodigy Services Co.

FOCUS ON PEOPLE

RUSSIANS EXPLORE CYBERSPACE

Is anyone looking for a few hundred Mercedes sedans? Does anyone want to barter for a 200-mile oil pipeline or a planeload of chicken parts? Is anyone in the market for a spouse? Viktor in Murmansk has potatoes for sale at 4 cents per pound, and will be happy to deliver them by flatbed truck, but only if you are willing to buy 20 tons or more. Using E-mail, Russians have created a giant electronic billboard to ask and respond to these questions.

Privatization speculators freely advertise their wares. Lonely men in ice-bound Siberia search for company. Russia's advanced theoretical physicists exchange theories, formulas, and small talk electronically with colleagues in Cambridge, Massachusetts, and Hong Kong. The food bulletin board Relkom, the largest Russian computer network, posts an average of more than 250 messages per day. Relkom has 200,000 users with connections in virtually every major city in the former Soviet Union; more join every day.

According to Anatoly A. Voronov, director of Glasnet, a Russian com-

puter network, *elektronnaya pochta*, or E-mail, is flourishing in Russia because almost all other methods of communication work so badly. In the United States postal, telephone, and overnight delivery services are abundant, fast, and reliable. In Russia one can send E-mail to Vladivostok or Boston in 5 seconds. One can search the archives of the Library of Congress and have results in a minute. Or one can wait 3 months to get a magazine by mail. Increasingly, Russian business cards list not only three or four telephone numbers, where callers have a slim chance of getting through, but also E-mail addresses.

During seven decades of Communist rule, this free exchange of information was forbidden. Yevgeny G. Vilovich, a young specialist in solid-state physics at Moscow State University, can't imagine life without E-mail. When he comes to work in the morning he can learn what new research was generated yesterday among his colleagues at Princeton. This world did not exist for Russian intellectuals like his father, a mathematician. In one day Vilovich can access research that his father would not have been able to read until 5 years after its publication. E-mail has opened up a new world to people for whom even Xerox machines used to be forbidden fruit: They can create and distribute as much information as they wish every day.

Although it is new to Russians,

most Westerners would find Russian cyberspace technology seriously outdated. Most Russian users rely on first-generation IBM microcomputer clones, technology that was abandoned by Americans years ago, and slow Russian modems with speeds of 2400 baud or less. Russian telephone lines are overtaxed and noisy—the crackle and hiss can garble signals on computer screens. On the other hand, Russian commercial services cost only a few dollars a month, and universities and institutes can connect to the Internet for free. A few high-capacity telephone lines have been made available in Moscow. Network services like Glasnet feature the latest workstations from Sun Microsystems and connect to the Internet through a satellite telephone line donated by the Soros Foundation. Some software offers users the choice of either Roman or Cyrillic letters. Sovam Teleport, a joint Russian, British, and American communications venture, provides packet switching services to 15 Russian cities and can transfer currency on-line in a network of several hundred Russian and international banks.

FOCUS Questions:
What problems does E-mail solve for people in Russia? What new opportunities does it create?

Source: Michael Specter, "Russians' Newest Space Adventure: Cyberspace," *The New York Times*, March 9, 1994.

messages by department and route them to the appropriate recipient. Using Infonet's value-added network, Claiborne sends 4,500 E-mail messages a day.

Because E-mail is generally more efficient than sending letters or using the telephone, it has become the preferred method of communication for many organizations. The Focus on People shows that it has also created new intellectual, social, and business opportunities in countries where communication has been traditionally difficult.

Voice Mail   In a **voice mail** system, the spoken message of the sender is digitized, transmitted over a telecommunications network, and stored on disk for later retrieval. When the recipient is ready to listen, the messages are reconverted to audio form. Various

Voice mail

A telecommunications system in which the spoken message of the sender is digitized, transmitted over a telecommunications network, and stored on disk until the recipient is ready to listen; at this time the message is reconverted to audio form.

FIGURE 8.12

A Voice Mail System

A voice mail system routes incoming telephone calls. If there is no answer at the requested telephone extension, the caller can leave a voice message that the system digitizes, transmits over a telecommunications channel, and stores on disk for later retrieval. When the recipient retrieves the message, it is converted back into audio form. This voice mail system uses an "auto attendant," which automatically routes calls and either rings the extension, screens calls, or holds calls.

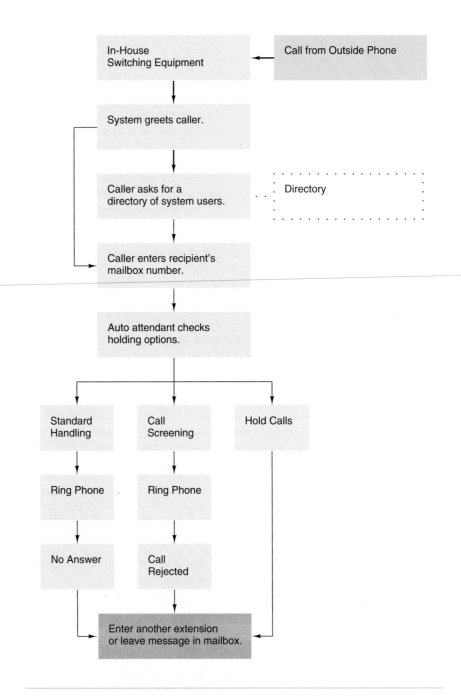

"store and forward" capabilities notify recipients that messages are waiting. Recipients can save these messages for future use, delete them, or route them to other parties. Sophisticated mainframe- or minicomputer-based voice mail systems can store hundreds of hours of messages and handle over 100 incoming phone lines; microcomputer-based systems are much smaller in scope.

The voice mail system in Figure 8.12 has an "auto-attendant" feature for automatically routing incoming calls. Calls can be transferred automatically to any phone extension; the system can also screen or hold calls. If the specified extension does not answer, the system will leave the message in the mailbox set up for that extension. The message can then be retrieved at a later time.

Facsimile   Facsimile (fax) machines can transmit documents containing both text and graphics over ordinary telephone lines. The image is scanned, digitized, and transmitted by a sending fax machine and reproduced in hard-copy form by a receiving fax machine. The process results in a duplicate, or facsimile, of the original.

TELECONFERENCING AND VIDEOCONFERENCING

Telecommunications technology provides **teleconferencing** capabilities that allow people to meet electronically. In electronic meetings, several people "confer" via telephone or E-mail group communications software (see Chapter 14). With video teleconferencing or **videoconferencing**, participants can see each other on video screens.

Videoconferencing requires complex video conference facilities, technology to integrate images with data and voice transmission, and appropriate technology and transmission media for relaying the massive volume of data required to transmit images. In the past, most firms could not afford this technology, but advances in transmission technology have now made video conferencing more affordable and easier to implement.

Teleconferencing helps bring ideas and people together from remote locations, reducing the need for costly business travel and saving travel time. For example, the British

Facsimile (fax)
A machine that can transmit documents containing both text and graphics over telephone lines; the sending machine digitizes and transmits the image, which is reproduced as a facsimile (fax) by the receiving machine.

Teleconferencing
The use of telecommunications technology to enable people to meet electronically; can be accomplished via telephone or electronic mail.

Videoconferencing
Teleconferencing in which participants can see each other on video screens.

The Union Pacific Railroad uses a network of 450 Pitney Bowes facsimile machines to link rail yards across the United States to a customer service center in St. Louis. This network allows Union Pacific to tell customers about how, when, and where their shipments are moving as they are moving.

SOURCE: Courtesy of Pitney Bowes Facsimile Systems.

By using videoconferencing technology, people can meet and work together from many different locations.

SOURCE: © Frank Siteman, Stock, Boston.

firm ICL Ltd. adopted video teleconferencing as a means of reducing executive travel and facilitating global sharing of information.

ELECTRONIC DATA INTERCHANGE

Electronic data interchange (EDI)

The direct computer-to-computer exchange of standard business documents, such as invoices, bills of lading, and purchase orders, between two separate organizations.

Electronic data interchange, or **EDI**, is the direct computer-to-computer exchange of standard business transaction documents, such as invoices, bills of lading, and purchase orders, between two separate organizations. EDI saves money and time because transactions can be electronically transmitted, eliminating the printing and handling of paper at one end and the inputting of data at the other. Figure 8.13 illustrates how EDI streamlines information processing.

EDI differs from electronic mail in that it transmits an actual transaction, as opposed to a primarily text message, and features standardized transaction formats, content-related error checking, and actual processing of the information.

Various transaction documents, such as purchase orders and invoices, can be generated electronically and passed from one organization's information system to another using a telecommunications network. Routine processing costs are lower because there is less need to transfer data from hard-copy forms into computer-ready transactions. EDI also reduces transcription errors and associated costs that occur when data are entered and printed out many times.

EDI can produce strategic benefits as well; it helps firms increase market share by "locking in" customers—making it easier for customers or distributors to order from them rather than from competitors. EDI also reduces transaction processing costs and can cut inventory costs by reducing the amount of time components are in inventory. For example, by handling 80 percent of its general merchandise orders through EDI, the Kmart Corp. in Troy, Michigan, reduced lead time for ordering most stock by 3 or 4 days, resulting in substantial interest savings.

For EDI to work properly, three key components are required:

1. *Transaction standardization:* Participating companies must agree on the form of the message to be exchanged. Transaction formats and data must be standardized.

FIGURE 8.13

Electronic Data Interchange (EDI)

EDI is the computer-to-computer exchange of standard business documents, such as purchase orders, invoices, and bills of lading, between two separate organizations. Transmitting these documents electronically, or on-line, saves time and money by cutting down on paperwork and data entry. This diagram illustrates an EDI system that transmits a purchase order (P.O.) from the buyer to the seller.

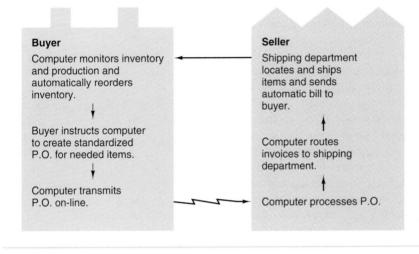

2. *Translation software:* Special software must be developed to convert incoming and outgoing messages into a form comprehensible to other companies.

3. *Appropriate mailbox facilities:* Companies must select a third-party value-added network with mailbox facilities that allow messages to be sent, sorted, and held until needed by the receiving computer.

The Focus on Technology describes another emerging telecommunications application, the use of intelligent software "agents" that can perform a diverse array of time-saving tasks on networks for their users.

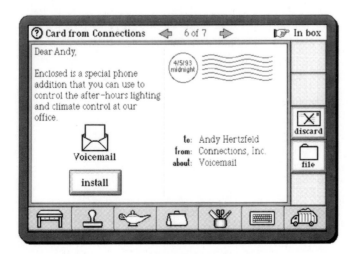

Telescript intelligent agent software can move through computer networks to perform many useful tasks, such as booking airline reservations, making purchases, or filtering messages.

SOURCE: Courtesy of General Magic Corp.

FOCUS ON TECHNOLOGY

SOFTWARE VALETS MAKE NETWORKS SMARTER

Overworked? Short on time? Too busy to make vacation plans to Florida or to keep up with the newspapers and magazines that have been piling up? Now you can relax and have an "intelligent agent" do many of these things for you. The agent is a set of software programs that works in the background on computer networks to schedule meetings and respond automatically to electronic mail by searching files and exchanging messages with other people's agents. Think of the agent as a digital valet.

The agent can find its way through computer networks to carry out useful tasks such as booking a flight on an airline's computer system or sifting through electronic retail catalogs to purchase a camera at the best price without any intervention by the consumer. Businesses based on electronic networks, such as America Online, the Official Airline Guides, Mead Data Central, and Rupert Murdoch's News Electronic Data are making their products and services accessible to these agents.

A leading intelligent agent technology is a new computer language called Telescript, which was developed by the software consortium General Magic, Inc. Telescript allows computer users to dispatch electronic agents onto computer networks to find and filter information. These agents can perform chores such as shopping or retrieving news. Telescript can also filter messages, select the most appropriate form of wired or wireless transmission, and link disparate types of hardware devices. General Magic's backers anticipate that over the next decade, intelligent networks will gradually form local and national electronic marketplaces where millions of buyers and sellers of products and services can meet.

Here's how Telescript works. A device such as a microcomputer or personal digital assistant has built-in software that interprets instructions from the user. With a click of a mouse or the tap of a stylus, the user can select instructions that send an agent directly to service providers such as airlines, news services, travel agencies, or banks or to a host network that provides a centralized electronic meeting place for buyers and sellers. (AT&T is launching an intelligent network called PersonaLink for this purpose.) You may want to buy a used Jeep. The network can match your agent with the agent sent by someone who wishes to sell a 1985 Jeep. The seller's computer is equipped with Telescript so that it can talk to your agent. The seller's agent automatically responds to a bid that is placed in your network mailbox.

To purchase an airline ticket, a person would enter her preferred travel date and time, airline, and credit card information into a wireless hand-held computer. The computer creates a software agent (we can call it Agent 1) and sends it via radio waves to the computer network connected to the airline's reservation and ticketing system. Another software agent on the airline's computer greets Agent 1, takes the travel specifications, verifies the credit card information, and books a flight. Agent 1 receives a ticket confirmation number and a flight itinerary. It creates a new software agent (Agent 2) to stay on the airline's computer. Agent 1 gives the confirmation number and itinerary to the user. On the day of the flight, Agent 2 checks the status of the flight each hour. Agent 2 notifies the traveler that the takeoff will be delayed 90 minutes because of a snowstorm in Chicago.

Critics voice concern about the complexity of building the first intelligent networks and the high costs of using them. Will people pay the costs of using electronic marketplaces? Moreover, the use of intelligent agents raises thorny technical, legal, and ethical problems, Millions of these autonomous agents would course through the world's data networks. What if they ran amok, creating the equivalent of an epidemic on digital networks? What if the agents were used maliciously to invade corporate and government computer systems? Could the interaction of countless agents cause network software to become unpredictable? Backers of Telescript argue that it is designed so that agents cannot sabotage the computer they enter. Telescript software in receiving computers can greet arriving agents, interpret their content, and bar access to programs that control how the machine processes and stores data. Proponents see Telescript as a breakthrough because it will find products, services, and information that are difficult to obtain and will save consumers time.

FOCUS Questions: What problems can agents solve for individuals and organizations? What people, organization, and technology factors would you use to decide whether to use an intelligent agent?

SOURCES: G. Christian Hill, "New Software Helps Networks Get Smarter," *The Wall Street Journal*, January 6, 1994; and John Markoff, "Hopes and Fears on New Computer Organisms," *The New York Times*, January 6, 1994.

PROBLEM SOLVING WITH NETWORKS: CAUTIONS AND CONCERNS

Several factors must be considered when a solution involves the use of a network:

1. *Response time:* This refers to the amount of time an on-line system takes to send a transaction or query over a network and receive a response. An example might be an inquiry about the balance in a client's checking account in an on-line banking system. Many factors affect response time, including the processing speed of application software and the ease of extracting information or records from databases. Many of these factors are network related, however, such as the transmission capacity of a telecommunications channel and related equipment, the distance data must be communicated, and the amount of traffic on the network. High error rates, which are primarily caused by line noise or power surges, also degrade response time because messages must be retransmitted.

2. *Reliability:* A network may be unable to deliver the required solution if it is crippled by excessive "downtime" (the period of time a network is nonoperational). Businesses such as MasterCard would come to a standstill if their network operations were interrupted for more than a few minutes. Network reliability is a function of the quality of telecommunications channels and equipment, error rates, and the quality of the personnel managing the network.

3. *Cost:* There are extra costs for using a network solution, such as the cost of installing or renting the channels, purchasing telecommunications equipment, and employing and training personnel to manage the network. Alternative network solutions may have different cost structures that should be considered—for example, a PBX is less costly to install than a LAN but has a lower transmission capacity. Savings may also be realized by increasing response time or by reducing transmission errors. The cost and performance trade-offs of alternative network structures must be figured into the solution design.

RUNNING CASE PART 2

AUTOMATING THE SALES FLOOR

What specific information system technologies would be most useful to large retail stores such as Macy's? Discounters such as Kmart and department stores such as JCPenney, Sears, and Saks Fifth Avenue have benefited from technology that helped them automate their sales floors. They are using point-of-sale-terminals, store-based local area networks, hand-held radio frequency scanners, and sophisticated customer databases to expedite purchases and to supply information to improve marketing and inventory management.

Point-of-sale devices: Point-of-sale devices such as hand-held scanning wands or guns or scanners built into countertops near the cash register record sales data at the point where the sales transaction is taking place. The captured data, which usually include the item sold, the number of units of the item sold, and perhaps the flavor, color, or size of the item, are transmitted to a computer. These data are used in information systems that track items in inventory, reorder items that are running out of stock, and analyze customer buying patterns. Some point-of-sale terminals are also connected to merchandise locator systems. For instance, sales associates at New York-based Saks Fifth Avenue can press a hot key on the store's point-of-sale terminals to order merchandise located at another Saks store and have the order shipped to the customer's home. Saks calls its merchandise locater system its "electronic store" and credits the system with $50 million in annual sales. Saks also uses point-of-sale data to feed an automatic inventory replenishment program similar to that described for Wal-Mart in Chapter 3.

Store-based local area networks (LANs): Stores can link their point-of-sale terminals via local area networks to in-store microcomputers to maintain their own sales data. Data specific to each store can also be transmitted to a central database for company-wide analysis. For example, branches of Neiman Marcus, the Dallas-based luxury department store, maintain their own data on purchases made locally using an in-store IBM RS/6000 workstation. The data are captured as purchases and are entered in point-of-sale devices. Neiman Marcus sales associates use this data to call or write their customers. The in-store data are also transmitted to corporate headquarters, where Neiman Marcus maintains a large company-wide database of all customer purchases made in all stores and all customer purchases made by mail order.

Hand-held radio frequency scanners: Handheld wireless radio-frequency-based scanners can be easily used by store employees as they roam the aisles to capture data about items on store shelves for automatic transmission to sales and inventory management systems. For example, Saks uses hand-held radio frequency scanners supplied by Telxon Corporation to transmit data on style, size, and color directly to a 486-based microcomputer running under OS/2. The scanners are in constant radio communication with the microcomputer, which acts as the store server. The microcomputer then transmits the data to Saks's corporate mainframe. By automating the tedium of counting inventory, the scanner gives sales staff more time to spend with customers.

Customer databases: The information maintained by department stores on customers and their credit card purchases is a veritable gold mine for direct marketing and sales promotions. By analyzing customer purchases and sales data captured by point-of-sale devices, department stores can target ads or direct marketing campaigns at customers most likely to respond to a specific type of promotion. Individual stores can tailor their particular product assortments to the brands, styles, sizes, and colors of merchandise that their customers are most likely to buy. In combination with sales data, customer databases can help stores fine-tune their inventory to ensure that the merchandise their customers want to buy is on the shelves when they want to buy it.

SOURCE: Linda Wilson, "The Big Stores Fight Back," *InformationWEEK*, April 26, 1993.

RUNNING CASE Questions:

1. How could sales floor automation technology help Macy's merchandise buyers?
2. How could sales data be used to give a firm a competitive advantage?
3. What kinds of problems can sales floor automation solve? What kinds of problems can't be solved by using this technology?

4. *Security:* Networks are vulnerable to disruption and penetration by outsiders at many points. A network solution must consider the critical nature of the data flowing through the network and the extent to which they need to be safeguarded by special security measures. This issue is discussed in detail in Chapter 12.

5. *Standards:* The vast array of existing hardware, software, and network standards makes it difficult for different devices and different networks to communicate with each other and exchange information. Designing a network-based solution requires consideration of compatibility and standards.

6. *Ethics:* Widespread use of networks raises new ethical issues for businesses when they need to determine whether to monitor the way their employees use their networks and set standards of professional conduct for managers and employees. We explore this topic in the case study at the end of the chapter.

8.5 LEADING-EDGE TECHNOLOGY: WIRELESS COMMUNICATION

Suppose you are sitting outside waiting for a tennis match to start. Several minutes remain before the game, so you check your hand-held portable computer. The screen shows a fax from a customer in Germany. You take a pen, mark the fax with comments, and instruct the personal communications assistant to send the fax back to Germany, all at the price of making a telephone call. Rapidly developing capabilities in wireless communications technology are beginning to make this scenario a reality.

When equipped with a special insert card and external modem, the Apple Newton personal digital assistant can serve as a pager, transmit E-mail, or send documents to printers, fax machines, or microcomputers. Portable communication devices using wireless technology will help people in mobile occupations stay in touch without being tethered to their desktops.

SOURCE: Courtesy of Apple Computer Corporation.

Until the past few years, telephones, computers, faxes, and other communications devices have been tethered to wires. But advances in microprocessors and software are changing that, and powerful wireless networks are starting to emerge. Wireless networks will allow people to communicate cheaply and easily without being tied to their desktop telephones or computers. They could change the way many people do their jobs; more employees could work at home or in the field, with central offices run by fewer people. As the work force becomes more mobile, the ability to move information without wires is essential. Today, the more than 50 million people who work in nontraditional environments as office nomads, business travelers, and telecommuters need portable network support.

The first users of wireless networks will be businesses who need to transmit information to and from employees in the field. As costs decrease, consumers will use the networks to make reservations for dinner or upcoming airline trips.

There are a range of wireless technologies. We have already described microwave and satellite transmission media. Other wireless technologies include the use of radio-based mobile data networks, paging systems, enhanced cellular telephones, personal communication services, and new satellite networks.

Mobile data networks are radio-based wireless networks for two-way transmission of digital data. These systems employ a network of radio towers to send text data to and from hand-held computers. They can send long data files efficiently and cheaply by transmitting them in packets (see the discussion of packet switching in section 8.3).

Ram Mobile Data Ltd. (a joint venture of Ram Broadcasting and BellSouth) and ARDIS (owned by IBM and Motorola) are two data-only national digital networks. These networks are used primarily by workers such as field technicians or sales representatives. For instance, from a single office in Connecticut, Otis Elevators uses the ARDIS network to dispatch repair technicians all over the United States and to receive their reports. Pitney Bowes, Inc., based in Stamford, Connecticut, trimmed its field service staff for mail and copy machines from 3,000 to 2,700 by using ARDIS for sending and receiving information. Before the wireless system was installed, dispatchers in 18 service support centers took calls from customers and either paged field service representatives or waited for them to call in. The new system routes customer calls directly to the field service reps. Switching to wireless data communications allowed Pitney Bowes to reduce the number of service support centers to six and to increase customer service representatives' productivity by 8 percent. These radio-based data networks could be expanded to provide electronic mail and other network services.

The most common use of portable **paging systems** has been to beep when the user receives a telephone call. Since the mid 1980s, paging devices have also been used to transmit short alphanumeric messages that can be read on the pagers' screens. These paging systems can now send (but not receive) data to mobile computers. Paging services operate at very low speeds, making them useful primarily for sending very short messages. Some organizations find one-way paging more economical and efficient than faxing. For example, Ethos Corp., a software maker in Boulder, Colorado, developed commercial mortgage-processing software that uses a paging system to electronically deliver mortgage rates from financial firms to nearly 2,000 brokers daily. These firms used to spend $30,000 per month to fax the same information from a service bureau, whereas paging costs $10,000 or less per month. Even more important, data transmitted through the paging network can be downloaded and manipulated, saving brokers perhaps 1½ hours of work each day. Two-way paging systems are in development.

Cellular telephones work by using radio waves to communicate with radio antennas placed within adjacent geographic areas called cells. When you place a call from a cellular phone, the call moves through a radio highway of these transmission towers,

Mobile data networks
Radio-based wireless networks for two-way transmission of digital data.

Paging systems
Wireless system for notifying users of telephone calls that can also be used to transmit short alphanumeric messages.

Cellular telephones
Telephones working in a system that uses radio waves to transmit voice and data to radio antennas placed in adjacent geographic areas.

In addition to providing wireless voice communication, cellular telephone networks are starting to be used for wireless data transmission.

SOURCE: Courtesy of McCaw Cellular Communications, Inc.

directed by advanced digital switches and computers. As a cellular call moves from one cell to another, a computer that monitors signals from the cells switches the signal to a radio channel assigned to the next cell. Although cellular phones are primarily used for voice transmission, cellular companies are developing capabilities to use the existing analog cellular phone network to transmit data in digital form. A standard called Cellular Digital Packet Data (CDPD) takes advantage of pauses in voice conversations during idle air time to send packets of data. McCaw Cellular Communications Inc. and seven regional Bell holding companies are putting a CDPD system of computers and digital signal processors atop the existing cellular analog system to allow users across the United States to send both their voice and data from a single wireless device.

Portable computers can be linked to cellular telephone services using internal and external wireless cellular modems or devices that interface between ordinary modems and cellular telephones. Small, low-power radio modems are being developed to fit into card slots for the transmission devices used in wireless data and cellular networks.

Companies are starting to build new kinds of microcellular digital networks called **personal communications services (PCSs)**. PCS technology is similar to cellular technology, but uses low-power, high-frequency radio waves. Compared with conventional cellular networks, PCSs use smaller, closely spaced microcells that require lower-powered radio transmitters and phones. Where a city might have a dozen cellular stations, a PCS system might have hundreds. PCS phones are much smaller (pocket-sized) and less expensive than cellular phones because they don't need to be as powerful. And they can be used in many more locations than cellular telephones—from inside office buildings, elevators, tunnels, trains, and subway platforms. Lower power requirements also allow this type of system to use the entire assigned radio frequency repeatedly in each microcell transmission area. In contrast, current cellular operators can't use parts of their allotted frequency to prevent radio interference with calls in adjacent cells.

Personal communications services (PCSs)

Systems for wireless transmission of voice and data sending low-power, high-frequency radio waves to closely spaced microcells.

FIGURE 8.14

Sky Phones

Several companies plan to use satellites to help calls travel over vast regions such as mountains, deserts, and oceans that are not served by cellular systems. Satellite phones will also help international travelers stay in contact where local cellular technology is not compatible with their phones from home.

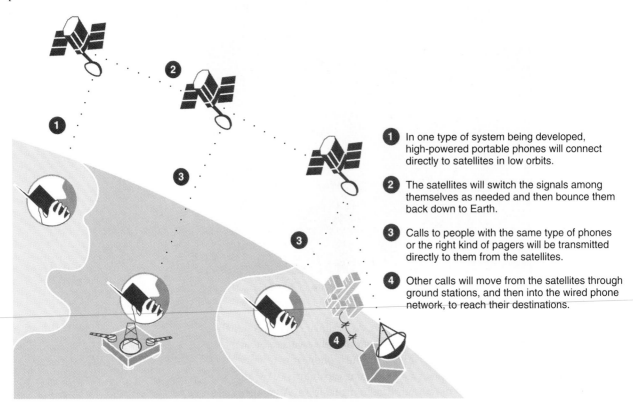

1 In one type of system being developed, high-powered portable phones will connect directly to satellites in low orbits.

2 The satellites will switch the signals among themselves as needed and then bounce them back down to Earth.

3 Calls to people with the same type of phones or the right kind of pagers will be transmitted directly to them from the satellites.

4 Other calls will move from the satellites through ground stations, and then into the wired phone network, to reach their destinations.

Personal digital assistant (PDA)

Pen-based, hand-held computer with built-in communication and organizational capabilities.

Some people believe PCS networks will be as much as 20 times more efficient than existing analog cellular systems, with vastly better service and quality.

PCS transmission is entirely digital, designed for sending data as well as voice. It can work with a **personal digital assistant** (PDA), a pen-based, hand-held computer with built-in communication and organizational capabilities. For instance, Apple's 1-pound Newton MessagePad can serve as an electronic scheduler, calendar, and notepad. Equipped with a special insert card, it can also function as a pager; when plugged into an external modem the size of a cigarette pack, it can transmit E-mail or send documents to printers, fax machines, or microcomputers. The Newton recognizes notes penned on its glass screen with a special stylus using intelligent software that not only executes but can also anticipate some common commands.

The Federal Communications Commission (FCC) has allocated a huge spectrum of network air space for these wireless personal communications services, which could eventually challenge local telephone systems. The slice of frequencies is wider than for cellular communications. Since PCSs operate at higher frequencies than cellular systems, where the spectrum isn't so crowded, PCSs will be able to offer a wider range of services, including video and multimedia communication.

A hierarchy of wireless networks is emerging. The most deluxe wireless networks will be the satellite networks (as shown in Figure 8.14), which can provide global wireless phone, data, and fax service by bouncing signals off low-orbit satellites. Low-orbit satellites are close enough to the earth to pick up signals from weak transmitters and consume less power and are less expensive to launch than conventional communications satellites. For example, Iridium, a $3.4 billion project sponsored by Motorola, Sony, and Sprint, will beam calls from a small hand-held set from any one point in the world to any other using a system of 66 low-orbit satellites encircling the globe. The Teledesic Corp., a joint venture of McCaw Cellular Communications and Microsoft Corp., is working on a $9 billion system using 840 small satellites to create a high-capacity wireless network capable of transmitting telephone calls, high-resolution computer images, and two-way video conferences to virtually any spot on the planet. Wireless satellite networks will be most useful for organizations wishing to bypass inadequate communications in underdeveloped or rural areas or for travelling business executives who cannot use cellular phones easily when they travel abroad.

While wireless networks hold great promise, they have several limitations. At present, transmission speeds of 2,400 to 8,000 BPS are only practical for short messages. Wireless transmission has a high incidence of errors because it is susceptible to many kinds of interference, especially when transmission occurs from moving vehicles. Elaborate error-correcting features, which reduce the actual throughput of wireless networks, are required. Data may have to be transmitted repeatedly until the entire message is received. Many wireless networks use different radio frequencies and disparate protocols, so that wireless modems that work with ARDIS can't work with RAM or cellular networks. To make wireless communication as easy to use as the wired telephone system will require complex software that lets incompatible networks and technologies work seamlessly together.[4]

SUMMARY

- Telecommunications can be defined as communication by electronic means, usually over some distance.

- Asynchronous transmission and synchronous transmission are two conventions for determining where a character begins or ends when data are transmitted from one computer to another.

- There are three different transmission modes governing direction of data flow over a telecommunications medium: simplex transmission, half-duplex transmission, and full-duplex transmission.

- Two types of signals are used in telecommunications systems: analog and digital. Analog signals are used primarily for voice transmission, whereas digital signals are used for data transmission and some voice transmission. A modem can be used to convert digital signals to analog form and vice versa.

- The essential components of a telecommunications network are computers, terminals or other input/output devices, communications channels, communications processors (such as modems, multiplexers, and front-end processors), and telecommunications software.

- Different components of a telecommunications network, which typically use a wide array of hardware and software technology, can communicate with each other using a common set of rules called protocols.

- The principal telecommunications transmission media are twisted wire, coaxial cable, fiber-optic cable, microwave, and satellite.

- Telecommunications transmission rate is measured in bits per second. The transmission capacity of a particular telecommunications medium is a function of its bandwidth, the range of frequencies that the medium can accommodate.

- The three common network topologies are the star network, the bus network, and the ring network.

- Local area networks (LANs) and private branch exchanges (PBXs) are used for local, short-range office and building systems. A PBX is a central, private switchboard that can be used for digital transmission among computers and office devices as well as for voice transmission. A LAN typically consists of a group of microcomputers linked together. LANs are useful for large-volume, high-speed communications among computers, whereas PBXs are most useful for mixed voice and data traffic involving low volumes and lower speeds.

- Client/server computing divides processing work between client computers on a network and servers, with each function assigned to the machine best suited to perform it. Client/server networks are starting to replace centralized mainframes.

- Wide area networks (WANs) cover large geographical areas and are provided by common carriers but managed by the customer.

- Value-added networks (VANs) are privately owned and managed networks that carry digital information over long distances. In addition to providing baseline communications, VANs also provide editing, storage, and redistribution of information for a firm.

- Standards are required to link different hardware, software, and network components together to transfer information from one computer to another. Open Systems Interconnect (OSI), Transmission Control Protocol/Internet Protocol (TCP/IP), and Integrated Services Digital Network (ISDN) are important standards.

- Electronic mail, voice mail, fax, teleconferencing, videoconferencing, and electronic data interchange (EDI) are widely used telecommunications applications.

- Six factors to consider when designing a communications network are response time, reliability, cost, security, standards, and ethics.

- New forms of wireless communication are being provided by mobile data networks, cellular telephones, paging systems, personal communications services, and satellite telephone services.

KEY TERMS

Analog signal
Digital signal
Modulation
Demodulation
Modem
Asynchronous transmission
Synchronous transmission
Simplex transmission

Half-duplex transmission
Full-duplex transmission
Channel
Front-end processor
Host computer
Multiplexer
Concentrator
Controller

Protocol

Twisted wire

Coaxial cable

Fiber optics

Microwave

Communications satellite

Baud

Bandwidth

Network topology

Star network

Bus network

Ring network

Private branch exchange (PBX)

Local area network (LAN)

File server

Network gateway

Wide area network (WAN)

Value-added network (VAN)

Packet switching

Frame relay

Client/server computing

Open Systems Interconnect (OSI)

Transmission Control Protocol/Internet Protocol (TCP/IP)

Integrated Services Digital Network (ISDN)

Asynchronous Transfer Mode (ATM)

Electronic mail

Voice mail

Facsimile (fax)

Teleconferencing

Videoconferencing

Electronic data interchange (EDI)

Mobile data networks

Paging systems

Cellular telephones

Personal communications services (PCSs)

Personal digital assistant (PDA)

REVIEW QUESTIONS

1. Name and briefly describe the principal functions of telecommunications systems.

2. What is the difference between an analog signal and a digital signal?

3. What is the difference between synchronous and asynchronous transmission? How do half-duplex, full-duplex, and simplex transmission differ?

4. Name and briefly describe the components of a telecommunications network.

5. How do a modem, a concentrator, and a controller differ?

6. What are the five principal telecommunications transmission media? Compare them in terms of speed and cost.

7. What are the measures of telecommunications transmission speed? What is the relationship between the bandwidth and the transmission capacity of a channel?

8. Name and briefly describe the three principal network topologies.

9. What is the difference between a local area network and a private branch exchange? Between a wide area network and a value-added network?

10. What is client/server computing?

11. Name and describe three important telecommunications standards.

12. What is the difference between electronic mail and electronic data interchange (EDI)?

13. Distinguish between teleconferencing and videoconferencing.

14. Name and describe the major wireless communication technologies.

DISCUSSION QUESTIONS

1.   What type of transmission medium is most suitable for the following situations? Why?

>   a. *USA Today* uses a network to relay each day's newspaper layout to 31 print locations across the world.

>   b. The law firm of Sidley & Austin wants to link 1,000 microcomputers used for legal document preparation and to send electronic mail between the firm's primary offices in Chicago and its branches in New York, Los Angeles, and Washington, D.C.

>   c. Lloyd's of London wants to link all of its 1,000 underwriters, located in the same building in corporate headquarters.

2.   Nathan Kaplan is a prominent obstetrician-gynecologist in Fairfield County, Connecticut, who is starting to use microcomputers in his busy office. His office staff includes one receptionist, one secretary, and one nurse. The office uses an IBM Personal System/2 for writing letters, simple office accounting (payroll, accounts payable, microcomputer billing), and maintaining patient files. Business has grown to the point where one PC is not enough. Kaplan wants to purchase another so that one PC can be used by the receptionist in the front office and one by the secretary in the back room. Both need access to the same data and files. What networking options should he consider? What factors should be taken into account in the final selection?

PROBLEM-SOLVING EXERCISES

1.   *Group exercise:* Newton's is a discount appliance and electronics retail chain with outlets in over 50 locations throughout the Northeast. Its inventory and other major application systems are processed by a minicomputer in corporate headquarters in Hartford, Connecticut. If an outlet runs out of a popular item, such as large air conditioners, it can obtain that item from another outlet or from the firm's central warehouse. Newton's currently has no way to maintain up-to-date data on inventory. Outlets collect purchase transactions at the checkout counter and mail them to corporate headquarters. Customer complaints have mounted, because customers are frequently told that an item is in inventory when it has been sold out for the season.

Newton's is afraid it will lose market share unless it develops an on-line, point-of-sale system with up-to-date inventory for each outlet and for its central warehouse. Divide the class into groups and have each group write a proposal for an on-line, real-time point-of-sale system using telecommunications technology. The group should include a diagram of the proposed network and an analysis of appropriate hardware, transmission, media, and network topology. The analysis should include reasons for the group's recommendations. Have each group present its findings to the class.

2.   Using Table 8.2 for reference, calculate approximately how long it would take to transmit this chapter over the following media: twisted wire, coaxial cable, fiber-optic cable, and satellite.

3.   *Hands-on exercise:* If your college or university computers are linked to the Internet and have an account that can be used by students, send a brief (one or two paragraphs) electronic mail message via the Internet to the President (president@whitehouse.gov) explaining your position on whether the federal government should pass additional legislation to protect E-mail privacy. If your school has no Internet connec-

tion, use an on-line service such as CompuServe, Prodigy, or America On-line to send the E-mail message via the Internet. Be sure to consult your instructor and your school's technical support staff before sending the message.

NOTES

1. Ben Smith and Jon Udell, "Linking LANs," *Byte,* December 1993.
2. Alok Sinha, "Client-Server Computing," *Communications of the ACM* 35, no. 6 (June 1992) and Ellen Ullman, "Client/Server Frees Data," *Byte,* June 1993.
3. Ellis Booker, "ATM Faces High Expectations," *Computerworld,* January 24, 1994.
4. G. Christian Hill, "Look! No Wires!," *The Wall Street Journal,* February 11, 1994 and Joanie M. Wexler, "Moving toward a Wireless Infrastructure," *Computerworld,* October 11, 1993.

PROBLEM-SOLVING CASE
CAN NETWORKS PROTECT PRIVACY?

The widespread use of networks has raised new ethical questions for information systems. Figures from the U.S. Office of Technology Assessment show that at least six million computer users are monitored, a larger number than ever before.

New software tools allow supervisors to electronically check on employees in a number of ways. A supervisor can use these tools to check an employee's performance by tracking the number of keystrokes per minute, the number of mistakes made, and the total time spent at the computer. Such electronic monitoring is routinely used in airline reservation sales, insurance companies, mail-order houses, and telephone companies to check on employees. The telephone system technology in most large business firms can record the time, length, and destination of employees' telephone calls or listen in on employees' telephone conversations with customers.

Some local area network remote control products let LAN managers remotely connect to other networked microcomputers. Managers can "jump" from system to system and even share screens and keyboards. A "no-notify" option in many of these LAN remote control products can hide this process from the computer users.

Lanstore, made by Secure Data, Inc., in Vernon, Connecticut, gives supervisors far-reaching surveillance capabilities. It is marketed as a tool to re-create commands that cause a system to "crash" to a halt, but it could also be used as a "Big Brother" aid to graph work activity minute-by-minute. Glenn Fund, principal research specialist at Lockheed Sanders, Inc., in Nashua, New Hampshire, asserts that Lanstore is used selectively and only for highly classified defense-related files at his firm. But he concedes that the device could be used to measure employee security.

Other products that can be used for monitoring employees using computers are available. Network Sniffer, for example, made by the Network General Corp., Menlo Park, California, can easily capture and display communications, including E-mail, that stream through networks.

While such devices can be used to monitor employee communications, employers note that there are legitimate reasons for using them. They believe that computer monitoring is a valuable quality control technique. Covert monitoring is accepted for many jobs classified by the government or the company. It is the responsibility of the information systems department to inform workers that they will be monitored and to make sure that the devices are not used maliciously.

The increasing use of E-mail has created new areas of conflict between employers and employees. Some companies have already been taken to court over E-mail privacy issues. In a widely-publicized case, E-mail administrator Alana Shoars filed a suit in March 1990 against her former employer, Epson America Inc., in Los Angeles Superior Court alleging wrongful termination, defamation, and invasion of privacy and seeking $1 million in damages. Four months later, Shoars followed with a class-action suit seeking $75 million for 700 Epson employees and approximately 1,800 outsiders whose E-mail may have been monitored. This suit alleged that Epson's interception of E-mail messages violated the privacy of employees. Ms. Shoars was responsible for installing an E-mail system and training 700 employees how to use it. She had assured her co-workers that their E-mail communications would be totally private. Later Shoars discovered that her supervisor was copying and reading employees' E-mail. When she complained, she was fired. Both cases were dismissed on grounds that E-mail does not fall within the state's wiretapping law, although they are under appeal.

Many companies contend that they have a right to monitor the electronic mail of their employees because they own the facilities and expect their use to be for business purposes only. In some instances—when there is evidence of safety violations, illegal activity, racial discrimination, or sexual improprieties—it may be appropriate for employers to monitor E-mail. Companies may also need to access business information, whether it is kept in an employee's file cabinet, desk, or E-mail system. Clear policies on E-mail use and administration must be established to prevent misunderstandings that can cause ill will and lead to litigation. The issues of privacy and property relating to E-mail are complex. Jerry Berman, director of the Information Technology Project for the American Civil Liberties Union, says they will be decided by the courts, Congress, and the institutions developing a culture around these technologies.

At present the only federal law to cover E-mail privacy is the Electronic Communications Privacy Act of 1986. This law prohibits interception or disclosure of E-mail messages by parties outside the company where the messages were sent, unless a warrant is obtained by law-enforcement agents. The act does not cover the interception of messages within a company.

Michael Godwin, legal adviser for the Electronic Frontier Foundation (EFF), an organization to protect the civil liberties of computer users, observes that some employers who would never think of monitoring your telephone calls might not hesitate to monitor your E-mail. When companies make large expenditures for office computer networks, bosses may feel they have the right to access what flows over the network. EFF recommends that at the very minimum, a company that expects to access its employees' E-mail should have a stated policy to that effect.

Some employers, such as Federal Express, Nordstrom, Eastman Kodak, and the Bank of Boston, have issued policy statements informing employees of the company's right to intercept and read their E-mail messages. These firms contend that the E-mail system is company property and its use should be for company business only. Other firms, such as General Motors and Hallmark Cards, have policies that give their employees greater privacy.

Regardless of their decision regarding E-mail privacy, employers can greatly reduce misunderstandings and legal actions by taking the time to develop internal policies that explicitly outline company rules and responsibilities regarding employee monitoring. Employees should be notified if a company decides to monitor electronic messages. Companies can add policy messages to screen menus, place stickers on equipment, or even require employees to sign affidavits indicating that they understand the rights and responsibilities of using corporate E-mail systems.

Some companies have already addressed this issue as part of sound company practice. Hallmark Cards Co. in Kansas City, Missouri, has an E-mail network of about 4,500 subscribers. User privacy is the top priority for Hallmark's E-mail system. At Hughes Aircraft Co. in Long Beach, California, technical, legal, and human resources staff are exploring E-mail issues to see if the company should develop a policy. Other companies hold the view that employees should assume that E-mail messages generated from company computers and stored on company hard disks are company property. Regardless of their views, companies should pay attention to E-mail issues. Existing policies should be enforced. If they don't exist, they should be developed.

Pending legislation may strengthen E-mail privacy. The federal Privacy for Consumers and Workers Act, introduced in late 1993 by Senator Paul Simon of Illinois, would prohibit secret monitoring of E-mail and require companies to notify employees of any monitoring policies. Several states, including Massachusetts, have introduced similar bills.

SOURCES: "Does E-Mail Mean Everyone's Mail?" *InformationWEEK*, January 3, 1994; David Bjerklie, "E-Mail: The Boss Is Watching," *Technology Review*, April 1993; and Jim Nash, "Technology Raises Many New Ethics Questions," *Computerworld*, October 14, 1991.

CASE STUDY QUESTIONS

1. Should businesses have the right to monitor employees using networks? Why or why not?

2. Should E-mail privacy be protected by law? Why or why not?

3. Develop a company privacy policy regarding E-mail and workplace monitoring.

›ILLUSTRATED CASE‹

WHAT IN THE WORLD IS THE INTERNET?

More and more people are becoming aware of the Internet and asking what it is, but no simple answer exists. To Shem Ochuodoho of Kenya, it is a lifeline, a connection to medical knowledge around the world that can be accessed when urgent needs arise. To Peter Ho, a network systems engineer at Unocal in Brea, California, it is a source of state-of-the-art seismic data-modeling software. To Jeff Dearth, president of the *New Republic* magazine, it is a way to garner new readers for his magazine. To Dr. Brendan McKay, a scientist at the Australian National University in Canberra, it is a tool making possible his transworld research collaboration with Dr. Stanislaw Radziszowsky of the Rochester Institute of Technology in Rochester, New York. To Michael Seidel, vice president of sales and marketing at San Diego's Mesa Ridge Technologies, it is a medium to avoid as a marketing tool. To

many it is the forerunner of the information superhighway envisioned by President Bill Clinton and Vice-President Al Gore. All may be correct on their views of the Internet. We can say only two things about it with certainty: It is changing rapidly, and that change is generating a great deal of controversy.

The Internet is without question the world's largest computer network. It is actually a network of other networks (individuals normally cannot connect to it). Estimates of its size vary widely because it is growing so rapidly and because its lack of organization makes estimates nearly impossible. In 1994 the Internet had approximately 21,000 connected networks and 2 million connected computers spanning 60 connected countries worldwide. It is commonly said that it has doubled in size every year since 1988. The *Internet Society News* estimates that in the United States alone between 30 and 45

By linking scientists, educators, and professionals all over the world, the Internet has accelerated the pace of scientific collaboration and the spread of knowledge.

SOURCE: Courtesy of International Business Machines Corporation.

million computers will be connected to local area networks by 1995, an immense pool for continuing expansion.

One reason the Internet (or simply the "net") is so difficult for many to understand is that it has no owner. Of course, the constituent networks are all owned by some organization—government at all levels, businesses, or not-for-profit organizations—but not the Internet itself. It also has no central management and no centrally offered services, an anarchic approach that goes against everything we believe about the requirements of successful computer telecommunications. It was created in the 1960s by the U.S. Defense Department's Advanced Research Projects Agency (ARPA) as an experimental network for sharing research data. In the 1980s, the National Science Foundation's NSFnet, a network for general researchers and academics, was linked to the ARPA network, and the phenomenal growth began. Scientific and educational networks were added as the net became a way for scientists and educators from around the world to converse daily, to share their work, to collaborate regardless of distance, and to gather information.

The technology that makes all of this not only possible but extremely popular is relatively simple. Users of the Internet need only agree to certain telecommunications standards to make such an open network possible. The net uses a popular network architecture known as TCP/IP (Transmission Control Protocol/Internet Protocol). Costs are also low because the net itself owns nothing and has no costs to offset; it only charges a connection fee for access to regional computer hubs. Organizations with networks must pay for their own networks, of course, as well as their connection to the Internet, but most costs are generated independently from their connection to the net. Once connected, the cost of E-mail communication is usually far lower than the equivalent postal, voice, or overnight delivery expense, and the communications are essentially instantaneous.

Before we can examine the problems within the Internet and the controversies that surround it, we must understand its value to so many people. Let us look first at typical uses and then at some of the available resources.

Recently a doctor in Kenya urgently needed information on how to administer a new medication to a critically ill patient. According to Shem Ochuodoho, "We could not get the hard copy of the article about this medication anywhere in Kenya, but we were able to download it from the Internet and put it on the doctor's desk" in time to save the patient's life. Similarly, Hasan Rizvi, a Pakistani physicist, tells about a 2.5-ton dump of toxic material inside the crowded city of Karachi. Scientists were able to identify the substance but did not know how to clean it up. They turned to the Association

Hundreds of library catalogues can be accessed on-line through the Internet.
SOURCE: Courtesy of International Business Machines Corporation.

for Progress of Conservation, an Internet grouping that includes Greenet, Econet, and the U.S. Environmental Protection Agency. The Pakistanis were flooded with electronic mail and fax responses that allowed them to solve their problem rapidly.

Many users look to the net for software. Numerous organizations make state-of-the-art packages they have developed available to others for the taking by using the Internet's File Transfer Protocol (FTP). For example, hundreds of research and development and medical staff at General Electric (GE) use GNU Emacs, a popular text editor and formatter available for free (they use hundreds of other programs downloaded from the net as well). In turn, GE has made available to medical R & D sites on the Internet a research medical imaging package they have developed. GE also supports the use of that package, for free, via the net.

Not only is the *New Republic* magazine available for free (in the hope of gaining new subscribers over the long run), but many other journals are also available, particularly scientific literature. With some 40,000 scientific journals being published around the world (some of them weeklies), mostly at a very high cost, libraries no longer have the space or funds to subscribe to them all. Making many of them available electronically solves these problems and brings them to eager readers far more rapidly than is possible using the traditional print-and-mail approach.

But the print field has found many more uses for the Internet. One boon to researchers all over the world are the several hundred library catalogs available on-line, including such giants as the Library of Congress and the library systems of the University of California and Harvard University. Hytelnet, available on the net, helps users determine which library catalogs to search. Addison-Wesley senior editor Tom Stone uses the net's E-mail facility to correspond with authors. He can sometimes receive and copyedit a manuscript without ever touching paper. Such major periodicals as *The New York Times, The Village Voice*, and *The Economist* use the net to collect information on readers' interests. Soon even whole books will be available on-line through the net, with royalties to be paid to authors where the copyright has not expired.

Along with E-mail, collaboration via the Internet is the most popular usage. The extent of network collaboration is breaking down the stereotype of the lone scientist making startling discoveries in an isolated lab. We are coming to understand that scientific discovery is a social process, a process significantly enhanced by the presence of the Internet. Dr. Brendan McKay in Australia is half a world away from Dr. Stanislaw Radziszowsky in New York. Yet the two have exchanged more than 1,000 messages in 3 years, allowing them

to work almost as if they were at the same site. Dr. McKay claims that thousands of researchers in Australia use the net this way, probably because of Australia's remoteness from the rest of the world. In another form of collaboration, scientists at Woods Hole Oceanographic Institution can share exciting new research data via the net. Using a robot to explore newly discovered forms of life more than a mile below the surface of the Gulf of California, they relay the data to a surface ship via a robot tether and then instantly radio them to a satellite, where they are disseminated via the Internet to waiting scientists all over the earth.

The commercial world has discovered the size and potential value of the net and is searching for ways to exploit it. Cygnus Support Inc., a Mountain View, California, software company, uses the Internet as an inexpensive way to link with their Cambridge, Massachusetts, office. SRI International, a research and consulting firm in Menlo Park, California, also links its London office via the net. General Motors uses it to gather research data when designing new automobiles. Microelectronics and Computer Technology Corp. uses the Internet for electronic data interchange (EDI), and software companies use the net to gather reports on software bugs and to distribute software fixes. Copytech Printing Inc., a

Hamilton / Diana
Jason Project 1990

Scientists at the Woods Hole Oceanographic Institution can send images directly from 20,000 feet below the ocean to labs worldwide over the Internet.

SOURCE: © The Jason Foundation and the Corporation of the City of Hamilton. Courtesy of Woods Hole Oceanographic Institution.

In the control room for the Woods Hole Oceanographic Institution network, powerful workstations help scientists relay oceanographic research data over the Internet to anxiously awaiting scientists.

SOURCE: Photo by Thonmas Kleindinst. © The Jason Foundation and the Corporation of the City of Hamilton. Courtesy of Woods Hole Oceanographic Institution.

printer of software manuals in Canton, Massachusetts, receives files for printing from clients via the Internet.

Organizations can make their specialty databases available via the Internet (some for free, others at a price). One can search hundreds of databases not only for information on administering medication, but also for information on agriculture, molecular biology, or zip codes. Advanced Network and Services claims that using the net for patent research is 40 percent faster than previous methods and also reduces the searching and legal costs related to patents. MSEN Inc. of Ann Arbor, Michigan, has made a career-counseling database available at no charge. Even the U.S. Central Intelligence Agency's world almanac is readily available.

Another source of information are the multitudes of mailing lists that allow an individual to send a single message to a large group of individuals using only one address. People who join these specialized lists can keep up with the field the list covers. Topics range from technology transfer to business studies. Some businesses receive daily oil price postings through a list; others receive hourly updates on the weather, including the latest satellite weather photographs.

The Internet's multimedia capabilities further increase its applications. For example, satellite weather photographs can be electronically distributed. The Internet uses Multipurpose Internet Mail Extensions (MIME) not only to send traditional alphanumeric messages but also messages that encompass graphics, sound, video, and foreign-language character sets. MIME technology supports all the functions described above as well as videoconferencing via desktop computers. The Internet Engineering Task Force (IETF) uses videoconferencing in its effort to establish Internet standards. Task force members can see each other via video cameras and can talk

during the meeting and exchange electronic messages. Internet users who are concerned about standards can "eavesdrop" to make sure the standards being developed match their own interests.

Educators also use the Internet's multimedia capabilities. In the spring of 1993, explorer and environmental author Will Steger "led" a group of elementary and high-school students from 100 schools in ten countries on an Internet-based hike through the Canadian Arctic. The students and Mr. Steger were linked via classroom desktop computers and the Internet. Mr. Steger reported on a trip of a scientific team he

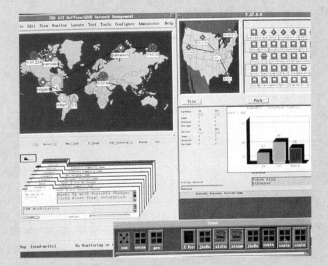

Text and graphic images can be transmitted over the Internet, making it suitable for some forms of on-line publishing.

SOURCE: Courtesy of International Business Machines Corporation.

had led through the area. The students not only saw the trip report and listened to Mr. Steger but were also able to interact with him.

Serious problems have emerged as the Internet has gained popularity. One obvious issue is security. When the net was only a data highway for the free exchange of ideas among scientists and educators, security was not an issue; most users wanted others to read what they wrote. However, with increased business usage, the transmission of proprietary or sensitive data in such areas as product development, manufacturing processes, marketing plans, and sales exchanges has mushroomed, and such proprietary data need to be protected from prying competitors. Companies offering products for sale and their customers are also concerned about the theft of credit-card information.

The greatest security problem on the net may be unauthorized access to connected computers. As large as it is, the Internet has proven vulnerable to hackers intent on creating trouble. Panix Public Access, a New York City on-line service, had to shut down for 3 days in October 1993, when they discovered that someone had inserted a rogue computer program in their network. The program watched network data communications and secretly recorded password information as Panix users connected to other computers over the net. With this data, hackers could gain access to many other computers connected to the Internet. Such hidden password detection programs are known as "Trojan horses" and are all too common.

Security experts are concluding that current password protection systems are no longer adequate. The biggest issue may be laxness on the part of those whose computers are linked to the net. According to Eugene Spafford, director of the Purdue University security center, "The vast majority of people have never really bothered to think carefully about what they may have to lose and what exposure they are taking for themselves by connecting to the network."

Another problem is information overload. The network is so large that an inquiry often leads to more responses than the recipient can handle. Susan Kubany, president of Omnet (a network for oceanographers), says she knows "people who have stopped using Internet because they get 500 messages a day." Mitch Kapor, founder of the Lotus Development Corp., equates the net to a library in which all books are dumped on the floor in no particular order. How can human beings possibly handle all this data? How can we locate what is there and make intelligent choices as to what we ought to access? (Similar questions are raised by predictions that the information superhighway will include 500-channel interactive cable television systems.)

For many people, the main problem with Internet is traffic jams. The net is a "data superhighway" that is often com-

pared to such superhighways as the Long Island Expressway and the Los Angeles freeways. Because the number of Internet users has exploded, many constituent networks can no longer handle the traffic. The National Center for Supercomputing Applications in Champaign, Illinois, reported that requests to access its electronic library rose from 100,000 per day in June 1993, to nearly 400,000 daily requests just 4 months later. Similar rises in usage are reported by many other Internet-connected services. MSEN Inc. was forced to limit access when daily queries rose to 12,000 (they plan a bigger computer when they can afford it).

One potential solution to the traffic jams is to begin to charge for access to services that are currently free. When Adam Curry, a host for the MTV music-video network, began posting an electronic gossip sheet on Madonna's private life on Panix, the crowds became so great that the Panix system was overwhelmed. After Panix asked Mr. Curry to change his method of distribution, he made his *Cyber Sleaze Report* available on his own computer and began asking $10 from subscribers. Other providers and users would like to expand the bandwidth, in essence widening the information highway. But this change would take time, and it would not solve the problems of a host computer that is too small to handle the traffic. As Allen Weiss, president of Advanced Networks and Services Inc., puts it, "After you get off the ramp from the data highway, you have to wait in line at the gas station."

The most obvious problem for new users of the Internet is the lack of a friendly user interface. Because there is no central management and no centrally offered services, there is no uniform interface. E-mail is less of a problem because an addressing standard does exist, and Internet's E-mail services can be easily accessed through popular on-line information services such as Compuserve, Prodigy, and America On-Line. Your address would be your local computer log-on identification followed by an @ symbol and then your local computer Internet network name. For example, to receive mail while logged on to Prodigy (assuming your Prodigy ID were ABCD00A), your E-mail address would be *ABCD00A@PRODIGY.COM.* However, there is no way to identify who is on the network at any one time, and there is no up-to-date "telephone book" listing all the users and giving their E-mail addresses. Even finding the specific computers that contain the data you want to retrieve can be a nightmare. And even when you find the correct computer, locating the data you need can be just as daunting a task.

It should be no surprise that a small industry has developed to help with this problem. For example, Hytelnet helps you find the right library catalog for the information you require. Wide-Area Information Servers (WAIS) make over 300 databases available and can search them for matches to key words entered by the user. The World-Wide Web can perform

College students can use Internet E-mail or research resources if their university computer system is linked to the Internet.

<small>SOURCE: Courtesy of International Business Machines Corporation.</small>

key word searches with hypertext capabilities. The new user either needs help from an experienced user or should turn to one of many books written to help beginners learn to use the network.

The problem dominating discussion of the Internet, however, is the specter of commercialization of the net. Michael Seidel of Mesa Ridge Technologies was "inundated with hate mail" when he tried to use the Internet for direct marketing. Seidel was quoted as saying "The vitriol was pouring off the screen." The problem? The original and still dominant body of users of the net, scientists and educators, view the network as an electronic vehicle for free speech. They have created a culture that abhors traditional advertising and the controls and inundation that can accompany it. Already overburdened, even overwhelmed, by the information they are seeking, users do not want to be deluged with unwanted advertising.

The battle between the traditional users and the business community runs far deeper than quarrels over direct advertising and "junk mail." The overall battle is so significant that *The Wall Street Journal* described it as a battle over the "Soul of Internet." Who will ultimately set the standards and policies for the network, and how will they develop it? What will it look and feel like? Who will be its dominant users? After all, it has always been primarily used by scientists and researchers at federal agencies and universities for the exchange of messages and research. Few seem to object to quiet commercial use such as employees communicating with each other via E-mail or to corporate scientists sharing data and programs with each other and with noncommercial users. Such

commercial usage is unobtrusive; it disrupts no one while it often contributes to the knowledge and work of others. Rather, the quarrel is over the larger commercialization of the net—will it evolve into a giant electronic shopping mall? Representatives of the education and scientific communities fear begin pushed aside.

A final Internet issue that we need to examine is its potential social and cultural effects (and those of future giant networks). It is obvious that the net breaks geographic barriers, that physical isolation no longer need imply intellectual isolation, as the McKay–Radziszowsky collaboration illustrates so well. With the Internet, the world is truly becoming smaller. But the net has other potential consequences.

Dr. Paul Ginsparg, a physicist at New Mexico's Los Alamos National Laboratory, sees a social revolution occurring. "The old means of distributing information were very unfair," he claims. Only a select few were able to access such key works as specific doctoral dissertations or published scientific articles. Now these important documents can be read worldwide by anyone with access to the Internet. Dr. Larry Smarr, director of the National Center for Supercomputing Applications at the University of Illinois, believes that such electronic networks are "the one unifying technology that can help us rise above the epidemic of tribal animosities we're seeing worldwide." He adds that the Internet "promotes a very egalitarian culture." However, others point out that while it is true that more people than ever have easier access to data worldwide, that access requires expensive technology that only a relatively small elite can afford. The knowledge elite may be becoming larger, more widespread, and more egalitarian than ever, but the gulf between that elite and the rest of the world continues to widen and becomes ever more difficult to bridge. The world is being permanently divided between a small, technologically based group of haves and a vast majority who are becoming a permanent underclass of have-nots.

Citing the millions of messages that are exchanged daily worldwide, some observers see the net as a productivity revolution comparable to Gutenberg's development of movable type in the medieval period. Dr. Ginsparg says that electronic reprints of his articles can now be instantly read in about 50 countries. He also points to the Los Alamos experience. In the 1980s the collection, printing, and distribution of genetic code data in the form of books required 13 months. Today, with two-way electronic network communication, the turnaround time has been reduced to 48 hours.

Dr. Robert Reich, Harvard University economics professor and Secretary of Labor in the Clinton administration, views networks such as the Internet as the foundation of an emerging economic and social revolution in which a unified international economy is replacing more traditional national economies. He states that corporations and individual entrepreneurs and consultants can now work anywhere in the world, and as a result they no longer feel an economic loyalty to the country of their origin. In this new economy, Americans (or residents of any national information economy) are no longer "in the same economic boat together." Instead, when a major national recession occurs, those who participate in the international economy through such international networks as the Internet will not suffer with the rest of their fellow citizens. As a result, we must begin to change the way we think about and act upon economic matters.

Perhaps the most far-reaching consequence of the net and other such networks, according to many, is the trivialization of information. The amount of overall information available is so great that cultural critic Neil Postman (referring to information networks in general) says that "information has now become a form of garbage." He claims we have lost a "sense of what things mean . . . as information pour[s] in from uncountable sources, directed at no one in particular, in unassimilable quantities."

For those who want to learn more about the Internet, many books are available, including Ed Krol's *The Whole Internet: User's Guide & Catalog* and *How to Use the Internet* by Mark Butler. In addition, the net has become a popular topic in periodicals. A check of your library or bookstore will guide you to alternative sources of information.

SOURCES: Gary H. Anthes, "Internet Tapped for Global Virtual Publishing Enterprise," *Computerworld*, March 23, 1993; William J. Broad, "Doing Science on the Network: A Long Way From Gutenberg," *The New York Times*, May 18, 1993; Robert E. Calem, "The Network of All Networks," *The New York Times*, December 6, 1992; George Johnson, "We Are Wired: Some Views on the Fiberoptic Ties that Bind," *The New York Times*, October 24, 1993; John Markoff, "A Web of Networks, an Abundance of Services," *The New York Times*, February 21, 1993, "Computer Insecurity on the Rise," *The New York Times*, November 1, 1993, and "Jams Already on Data Highway," *The New York Times*, November 3, 1993; John S. Quarterman, "To: ismanager@bigco.com, From: jsq@tic.com, Subject: What Can Businesses Get Out of the Internet," *Computerworld*, February 22, 1993; Robert B. Reich, *The Work of Nations* (New York: Knopf, 1991); Brian Robinson, "Internet's Business Degree," *InformationWeek*, August 30, 1993; Steve Stecklow, "Computer Users Battle High-Tech Marketers Over Soul of Internet," *The Wall Street Journal*, September 16, 1993; and Joanie M. Wexler, "Internet Commercial Uses Blossom," *Computerworld*, June 28, 1993, and "Internet Lends Global Helping Hand," *Computerworld*, September 16, 1993.

CASE QUESTIONS

1. As the vice-president of sales of an international corporation, what uses might you have your department make of the Internet? What problems do you see with using it, and how would you handle those problems?

2. Draw up a set of guidelines that you think might satisfy the traditional users of the Internet and yet allow the commercial world to increase its usage.

3. Develop ways to address the underlying problems that some fear will result in a small elite of worldwide computer and network users and a large, permanent underclass.

Part 3

PROBLEM
SOLVING WITH
INFORMATION
SYSTEMS

Chapter
✧ N I N E ✧

PROBLEM ANALYSIS: CRITICAL THINKING SKILLS

LEARNING OBJECTIVES

After reading and studying this chapter, you will:

1. Know how to solve problems using a simple five-step model.
2. Know how to develop your critical thinking skills.
3. Understand the three major factors to consider when approaching a business problem.
4. Be able to design logical and physical system solutions for a business.
5. Be familiar with the three major factors to consider when implementing a system solution.

IS RYDER'S ENGINE SPUTTERING?

*R*yder Systems, Inc. grew from a relatively simple truck-rental company into a conglomerate comprising more than 100 companies with assets of over $6 billion. But by the end of the 1980s the Miami-based transportation firm seemed to stall out. Profits lapsed, revenue growth slowed to a crawl, and the price of the company's stock began to fall. Stockholders began to pressure Ryder's chairman, M. Anthony Burns, to sell some of the nontransportation businesses Ryder had acquired and to shed excess layers of management. In response to these pressures, Ryder became leaner and smaller as it refocused on its original business—truck leasing, truck renting, and auto hauling.

By 1992, Ryder again posted high earnings. Burns believes that Ryder can turn a consistent profit in the trucking business by concentrating on highway transportation without being distracted by aviation, insurance, and other lines of business. But investors have serious questions about Ryder's long-term prospects. Despite intensified marketing efforts, Ryder's revenue growth in some of its trucking businesses has been disappointing. The company's businesses are in mature industries, meaning that they have passed their time of rapid growth. Consequently, the company's prosperity is more directly tied to that of the economy. How will Ryder be able to survive during periods of economic downturn?

What is Ryder's problem? A large portion of Ryder's revenue comes from its consumer truck-rental business. But when economic growth slows, people tend not to move. Businesses that rent trucks from Ryder reduce their orders as well. Even when the economy rebounds, the consumer rental business returns only a tiny profit, beset by stubborn competition from U-Haul

International and other firms. Ryder's auto transport operation, which accounts for 16 percent of its sales, has been sluggish because of continuing troubles at General Motors Corp., Ryder's largest customer.

Ryder's management still believes that most of its revenue will continue to come from the trucking business and is searching for ways to acquire new customers. Ryder is eyeing the "private carriage" market, in which trucking firms such as Ryder provide equipment, maintenance, fuel, and drivers for other companies. But convincing other companies to hand over some of their shipping operations to an outside firm is not easy. Ryder tackled this issue by putting more emphasis on sales and marketing. Its sales force was increased by 38 percent, and sales representatives are now equipped with laptop computers with which they can cut the time required to order a truck from over a week to 3 days. Ryder also worked to tailor its services to individual customers. For instance, Ryder agreed to redesign many of the 275 trucks it leases to Home Depot Inc., the Atlanta home-improvement retailer. To accommodate the growing numbers of professional builders who use Home Depot, Ryder equipped each of their flatbed trucks with a forklift.

Ryder has also found ways to obtain more business from existing customers. One promising area of revenue growth is dedicated logistics, whereby Ryder leases trucks to customers on a regular basis, instead of just providing trucks on demand. Ryder provides not only the trucks and drivers but also designs entire delivery systems for these leasing customers. Ryder drivers and trucks even carry the colors and logos of the customers. Many analysts believe international growth is essential, and Ryder is planning to expand its 67-site leasing and logistics business in Great Britain and to introduce services in Germany, Mexico, and other countries. Will these strategies help Ryder grow even when the domestic economy lags? The solution is neither clear nor easy.

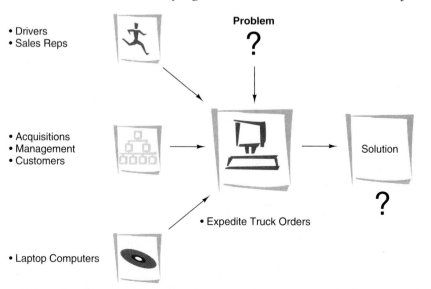

SOURCES: Emory Thomas, Jr., "Ryder Moves Back Home to Truck Leasing and Renting," *The Wall Street Journal*, December 14, 1993, and Jon Pepper, "On the Road to a Rebound," *InformationWEEK*, September 2, 1991.

The difficulties facing Ryder are typical of many companies that flourished and grew only to find themselves struggling with changes unleashed by a harsher, more competitive business environment. The problems these firms face are multifaceted and the potential solutions complex. Although technology offers a partial answer in many cases, experience shows that changes in organization and people are also required to save business firms like Ryder. Where would you start looking for solutions? Learning how to solve these and simpler problems is the subject of the next four chapters.

In this chapter you will learn some very important concepts about problem solving that can be applied in virtually all business settings. In Chapter 10 these conceptual skills will be applied to real-world cases. This conceptual framework is not tied to technology, although, as you will see, information technology can be useful in solving some business problems.

9.1 INTRODUCTION: CONCEPTS

At first glance problem solving in daily life seems to be perfectly straightforward: a machine breaks down, parts and oil spill all over the floor, and obviously somebody has to do something about it. So, of course, you find a tool around the shop and start repairing the machine. After a cleanup and proper inspection of other parts, you start the machine and production resumes.

No doubt some problems are this straightforward. But few problems are this simple, and, in general, when they are, they are not very interesting. Most real-world problems are considerably more complex. In real-world organizations, a number of major factors are simultaneously involved in problems. These major factors can be grouped into three categories: technology, organization, and people. When a problem occurs, it is usually not a simple technology or machine problem, but some mixture of organization, people, and technology problems. In other words, a whole set of problems is usually involved. Even establishing the existence of a problem, or declaring that a problem exists, can be controversial in a business or other organization. Why is this so?

DEFINING THE PROBLEM

Contrary to popular conception, problems are not like basketballs on a court just waiting to be picked up by some "objective" problem solver. There are an infinite number of solutions in the world, each with its own advocates. Choosing the right solutions in an organization depends on the ability of key organization actors to define the problem correctly.

Before problems can be solved, there must be agreement in an organization that a problem exists, about what the problem is, what its causes are, and what can be done about the problem given the limited resources of the organization. Problems have to be properly defined by people in an organization before they can be solved. Once you understand this critical fact, you can start to solve problems creatively.

Consider the following example. As you read the next paragraphs, try to answer these questions: Is technology the solution to Herman's Sporting Goods' problems? How have different people defined the problem in different ways?

Herman's Sporting Goods, founded in New York City over 75 years ago, fell victim to an ill-conceived expansion plan. It was acquired in 1989 by Isosceles Pl.c., a British holding company, which launched an ambitious plan to turn Herman's into a national sports retailing powerhouse. But the company spread its resources too thin and was easily outperformed by sports mega-retailers such as Sports Authority and Sportsmart Inc., companies that have prospered from offering a broad product selection and low prices in warehouse-style shopping outlets. These retailers are also leaders in the use of advanced information systems such as automatic inventory replenishment, which speeds the flow of merchandise to the retail floor.

In March 1993 Isosceles sold Herman's to a private investment group led by Whiteman, Heffernan, Rhein & Co. Inc. and Carl Marks Strategic Investments, two New York merchant banking firms. Herman's filed for bankruptcy protection and reorganized, downsizing from a national chain to a regional retailer in the Northeast, focusing on the Boston–Washington corridor. It closed 132 of its 256 stores. Hoping to capitalize on strong name recognition in this area, Herman's planned to open 50 new stores in the region over a 5-year period. It also instituted a plan to drastically reduce its debt and overhead expenses, which consumed more than 40 percent of its sales revenue.

Herman's outmoded logistics and merchandising systems contributed to the company's lack of success. By using an automated inventory replenishment system, Sports Authority can turn its inventory over an average of eight to 12 times a year. In contrast, Herman's can turn its inventory over only four times a year because it doesn't have the systems in place to automatically restock inventory when items are sold. Instead, the stores must carry additional items in inventory to make sure they are available when customers want them. Sports Authority can save on inventory and warehousing costs and pass these savings along to customers. Herman's also has antiquated point-of-sale systems that can provide point-of-sale data to its mainframe only on a batch schedule. The systems don't allow stores to poll the mainframe for inventory data or to exchange electronic mail with Herman's home office in Cartaret, New Jersey. Nor do these systems store the names and addresses of customers, which are valuable pieces of information for tracking purchases and designing direct-mail marketing campaigns.

Herman's can't afford to spend much money to overhaul its information systems because it is under such pressure to reduce operating costs. Yet it needs to be more aggressive in sales and to ensure that the right merchandise is available in its stores at all times. It needs to forecast sales, respond quickly to customers, and prevent product shortages. It needs to start using electronic data interchange (EDI) with its key suppliers and provide timely access to point-of-sale data and customer purchase records.

Herman's has been experimenting with an electronic purchase-order system with some of its vendors. It reduced the size of its distribution center by 40 percent and introduced electronic scanning of merchandise at the center. It also replaced its outdated point-of-sale terminals with more up-to-date point-of-sale technology in all its stores. All Herman's clerks now have scanners to take inventory, change prices, and perform other related tasks.

But industry skeptics and investors are not positive that Herman's has found the answer. The sporting goods market is sluggish, with an annual growth rate of only 5 percent during the 1990s. Critics not only believe that it will be difficult for any retailer to obtain new market share, but that the warehouse-style retailers have all the momentum.[1]

Obviously, people inside Herman's define the problems facing the company differently than outside critics and competitors do. Depending on how one defines Herman's problem, different courses of further research and action can be recommended. For instance, if Herman's problem is defined as one of competing with inadequate technologies, then the company was wise to start deploying these technologies with the ultimate goal of increasing sales and reducing operating costs. Alternatively,

FIGURE 9.1

The Five Stages in the Problem-Solving Process

We can think of problem solving as a five-step process. There are many possible solutions to a problem; the goal is to select the right solution through following these five steps. The first task is to define the problem. This may be more difficult than it sounds, since various people in an organization may have various ideas about what the exact problem is. The second step is to gather and analyze information, helping us to understand the problem better. Third is the decision-making stage, in which we look at possible solutions and select the best one. Next comes the process of designing the solution, and last is solution implementation, during which the solution is tested and refined. It is important to evaluate the results of each phase, including implementation, to make sure that the solution is indeed solving the problem.

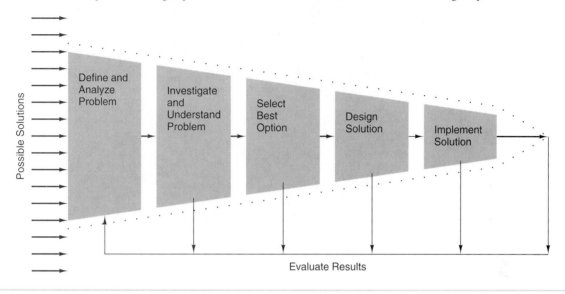

Herman's problem could be defined as a management failure to perceive changes in the competition and the overall business environment. Investors with this view would encourage a buy-out and breakup of the company. One could argue that Herman's management has defined its problem rather narrowly: it scaled down operations and implemented changes in software and hardware without asking a fundamental question: Can the business remain viable in the face of new merchandising strategies and formidable competitors?

Our point here is that "the problems" facing all companies are usually subject to complex and often controversial interpretation. These problems are not objective objects but, rather, subjective interpretations involving competing views of the world by powerful actors both inside and outside the company.

THE PROBLEM-SOLVING FUNNEL OF REAL-WORLD DECISION MAKING

The example of Herman's Sporting Goods can be used as a starting point to illustrate the typical stages problem solving goes through. Real-life problem solving can be seen as a kind of funnel (see Figure 9.1) with five stages.[2] The model begins by recognizing that there are a large number of solutions in the environment; our goal is to capture the correct solution from the many possibilities. A first step in problem solving typically involves the search for a consensus on what—in very general terms—the problem is and what general kinds of solutions might be appropriate. This is a critical period of

By investigating, analyzing, and defining problems, people can design and implement effective solutions. To solve a problem with the production of chemicals, Dow Corning manufacturing engineer Sue Jacob and her team studied procedures and analyzed production data. Their solution was an operating guideline that, when implemented, exposed a new problem: lack of communication between machine operators and their supervisors. Their solution to the second problem included clarifying the manufacturing process to both operators and supervisors to improve communications and training for operators.

SOURCE: Courtesy of Dow Corning Corporation.

Problem analysis

The consideration of the dimensions of a problem to determine what kind of problem it is and what general kinds of solutions may be appropriate; the first step in problem solving.

Problem understanding

The investigation—fact gathering and analysis—of a problem to gain better understanding; the second step of problem solving.

Decision making

The process of debating objectives and feasible solutions and choosing the best option; the third step of problem solving.

Solutions design

The development of a solution to a problem, including both logical and physical design; the fourth step of problem solving.

Implementation

The process of putting the solution of a problem into effect and evaluating the results and performance in order to make improvements; the fifth, and last, step of problem solving.

problem analysis and definition in which the definition of the problem is narrowed considerably. The second stage is **problem understanding**; this is a period of investigation—fact gathering and more analysis—hopefully leading to better understanding. Next comes a period of **decision making**, when objectives and feasible solutions are debated, and the best option is chosen. Fourth, once options are identified, the process of **solutions design** can begin. Note that each of the stages in the model has narrowed the possible solutions down to a smaller number. Finally, a period of **implementation** is entered, during which theoretical designs and concepts are tested in the real world and final changes are made in the design based on field experience. Evaluating the results and performance of this solution helps the firm to improve and refine it. As the business environment changes, feedback may signal that it is time to go through the decision-making process again.

We will use this real-world view of decision making later as the basis for a five-step model of how you can solve problems. First, however, we need to examine the early process of problem solving a little more closely.

CRITICAL THINKING

It is amazingly easy to accept someone else's definition of a problem or to adopt the opinions of some authoritative group that has "objectively" analyzed the problem and offers quick solutions. You should try to resist this tendency to accept existing definitions of any problem. Throughout the natural flow of decision making, it is essential that you try to maintain some distance from any specific given solution until you are sure you have properly identified the problem, developed understanding, and analyzed alternatives. Otherwise you may leap off in the wrong direction, solve the wrong problem, and waste resources. Wise decision makers wait until decisions are necessary and until they are as certain as they will ever be that the correct solution is at hand. Even then, wise decision makers carefully observe the early implementation period to see if they were right. To do this, you will have to engage in some critical thinking exercises.

Critical thinking can be briefly defined as the sustained suspension of judgment with an awareness of multiple perspectives and alternatives. It involves at least four elements:

- Maintaining doubt and suspending judgment.

- Being aware of different perspectives.

- Testing alternatives and letting experience guide.

- Being aware of organizational and personal limitations.

Simply following a rote pattern of decision making, or a model, will not guarantee a correct solution. The best protection against incorrect results is to engage in critical thinking throughout the problem-solving process.

First, maintain doubt and suspend judgment. Perhaps the most frequent error in problem solving is to arrive prematurely at a judgment about the nature of the problem. By doubting all solutions at first and refusing to rush to a judgment, you create the necessary mental conditions to take a fresh, creative look at problems, and you keep open the chance to make a creative contribution. Second, recognize that all interesting business problems have many dimensions and that the same problem can be viewed from different perspectives.

In this text we have emphasized the usefulness of three perspectives on business problems: technology, organizations, and people. Within each of these very broad perspectives there are many subperspectives or views. The **technology perspective**, for instance, includes a consideration of a firm's hardware, software, telecommunications, and database. The **organization perspective** includes a consideration of a firm's formal rules and procedures, culture, management, production process, and politics. The **people perspective** includes consideration of the firm's employees as individuals and their interrelationships in work groups.

You will have to decide for yourself which major perspectives are useful for viewing a given problem. The ultimate criterion here is usefulness: does adopting a certain perspective tell you something more about the problem that is useful for solving the problem? If not, reject that perspective as being not meaningful in this situation, and look for other perspectives.

The third element of critical thinking involves testing alternatives, or model solutions to problems, letting experience be the guide. Not all contingencies can be known in advance, and much can be learned by empirical experience. The experience of A. O. Smith's Automotive Products Co. is a good example of how a firm may have to test several alternatives before it arrives at a solution.

Smith, one of the world's largest producers of auto frames and parts, is a major supplier for the Detroit Big Three automakers. By 1981, despite concerted efforts to automate with new technology, Smith had reached a low point in productivity, growth, and quality. Up to 20 percent of the auto frames had to be reworked before being shipped. Bored workers toiled on assembly lines performing robotlike, repetitive actions; strong union work rules prevented any sharing of work; and union shop stewards spent much of the day arguing with shop foremen over speed and work rule enfringements.[3]

Critical thinking
The sustained suspension of judgment with an awareness of multiple perspectives and alternatives.

Technology perspective
A way of viewing a problem in which emphasis is placed on information technology hardware, software, telecommunications, and database as sources of business problems and the way in which they can contribute to a solution.

Organization perspective
A way of viewing a problem in which emphasis is placed on the firm's formal rules and procedures, production process, management, politics, bureaucracy, and culture as sources of its problems and the way in which they can contribute to a solution.

People perspective
A way of viewing a problem in which emphasis is placed on the firm's employees as individuals and their interrelationships as sources of its problems and the way in which they can contribute to a solution.

But in 1981, Smith began an 8-year odyssey of change. Its goal was not merely higher productivity but its very survival. Smith started with an employee involvement program that centered on creating quality circles. The union was not asked to participate. From 1981 to 1984, productivity improved somewhat, but without union involvement, there was little real change on the shop floor.

By 1984, as the Big Three automakers forced Smith to lower its prices, the union agreed to work with Smith to set up Problem-Solving Committees on the shop floor, Advisory Committees at the plant level, and a Top Planning Committee involving senior union and company management. With this move, the union gained a large say in both day-to-day decision making and long-term strategic planning.

Even with this change, however, workers still lifted, welded, and riveted in 20-second cycles, and absenteeism remained at around 20 percent on some days. The piecework pay system resulted in an enormous amount of poor-quality product.

By 1987, the Big Three had forced another round of price reductions on Smith. A decline in orders followed, and then 1,300 workers were laid off. In their 1987 negotiations, the union and Smith's management agreed to eliminate the old piecework pay system, set up production teams of workers, and freeze wages for 4 years so that no one lost money. In the production-team concept, small groups of workers perform integrated tasks in teams, switching off as needed to keep production rolling or just to change jobs. The teams elect a team leader and engage in most management activities, including setting work standards, ordering replacement parts, and stopping the line if problems arise. As one worked noted, "They just turned control of the shops over to us." The 1987 agreement eliminated the need for foremen, and many were let go. The ratio of foremen to workers went from 1 to 10 in 1987 to 1 to 37 in 1989.

With these changes, productivity finally improved. Workers were recently issued a $123 payment under a new profit-sharing plan. Although small difficulties still exist, Smith's management believes it has finally solved its basic production problems on the shop floor.

Careful examination of the A. O. Smith story makes it clear that the company ended up with quite a different solution than it originally anticipated. This is commonplace: solutions generally evolve over time rather than being "frozen" in time.

The fourth and final element of critical thinking involves an awareness of the limits on the human and organizational resources at your command. Remember, there is a difference between what an organization "should do" and what it "can do." And there is a difference between an "optimal" solution and a "satisfactory" solution. Generally, so-called optimal solutions may not be feasible, whereas satisfactory solutions are feasible, indeed even economical. Some solutions may be so expensive that the organization would go bankrupt if it adopted them (creating a whole new set of problems). An awareness of the feasibility of a solution—whether it is actually doable— will not only help you choose the right solution to problems, but will also help you save time and money by avoiding solutions that are beyond your organization's resources.

9.2 A FIVE-STEP MODEL OF PROBLEM SOLVING

As we noted in Figure 9.1, real-world decision making can be summarized in a simple five-stage model of problem solving that is applicable to personal problems as well as to business decisions. In the world of information systems, the first three stages are usually called systems analysis, and the last two stages are called systems design. Thus, "systems analysis and design" is another word for problem solving.

STEP 1: PROBLEM ANALYSIS

Problem analysis is somewhat analogous to "ball parking"—that is, estimating the dimensions of a problem. The most important question answered in this step is, "What kind of a problem is it?" The State Department of Motor Vehicles Office at White Plains, New York, discovered this when it set out to improve its quality of service.[4] As you read through the saga of the Motor Vehicles Office in the next paragraphs, pay particular attention to the way the office defined its problems.

In 1984, the office seemed to have nothing but problems. The average waiting time to register a car was 2½ hours. The building itself was a crumbling relic. Office hours were set for the convenience of employees (8:00 A.M. to 4:00 P.M.), making it difficult for working people to register.

Registrants had to wait in three separate lines: document examination, eye examination, and billing. New York State had instituted a 4-year license renewal program in which driver's licenses expired at the end of the month in which they were originally issued. Thousands of people would descend on the office at the end of each month, causing long lines. If any document was missing, or if applicants forgot to bring some documents, they had to leave the line and reenter at a later time.

There was no way for people to call in to ask questions and no information service on the premises. Therefore, people had to stand in line just to get information. Although cars could be registered by mail, few people were aware of this and came in to register their cars in person because that is how it had always been done. Computer capacity was stretched to the limit, with 4- and 5-minute delays in computer terminal response at peak hours.

What kind of problem did the Motor Vehicles Office have? Was it a people or labor problem related to poor attitudes of public workers or poor training? Was it a business problem related to outdated procedures and unnecessary bureaucratic red tape? Was the Motor Vehicles Department being starved for funds by the state legislature? Or was it a technology problem that more powerful computers could easily solve?

Let's look at how these problems actually were solved in the period 1984–1988.[5] First, the State Department of Motor Vehicles renovated and modernized the entire building and physical plant. Second, a new commissioner who was publicly committed to radical improvements in service was appointed in 1986. Third, in 1986, evening hours were added to serve working people. Fourth, computer capacity was expanded 20 percent to permit sales tax collection and registration in one operation, and a new cash accounting system was written to speed up service. Fifth, the end-of-the-month rush in license renewals was eliminated by making expirations effective at dates throughout the month. Sixth, a new employee training program was instituted involving 3 weeks of in-class training on subjects ranging from computer operations, dress codes, and courtesy to how to keep cool under pressure. Seventh, a centralized telephone information service was initiated in 1987; it now handles up to 6,000 inquiries a day. Eighth, mail-in registration was initiated for those who wanted to use it, reducing the load on local offices.

As a result of these improvements, a person has to wait in only one line at the Motor Vehicles Office and can check his or her documents at a central information booth before entering the line. The average time to register a car or obtain a license has been reduced to less than 30 minutes at peak times. In estimating the dimensions of the solution, planners at the New York State Department of Motor Vehicles identified a number of interrelated problems involving people, technology, and organization. The solution was multifaceted, took many years to implement, and was largely incremental—that is, it was implemented one step at a time.

STEP 2: PROBLEM UNDERSTANDING

What causes the problem? Why is it still around? Why wasn't it solved long ago? Those are some of the questions that must be asked in the second step of problem solving. Finding the answers involves some detailed detective work, some fact gathering, and some history writing. Facts may be gathered through personal interviews with people involved in the problem, analysis of quantitative and written documents, or attitude questionnaires. Generally, the more different kinds of data you have, the better understanding you will achieve.

In the case of the Motor Vehicles Office described above, managers used personal observation and interviews to understand the problems, along with agency documents, administrative data, and employee questionnaires.

At the end of this second step, you should be able to give a rather precise, brief account of what the problem is, how it was caused, and what major factors are sustaining it.

STEP 3: DECISION MAKING

Once a problem is analyzed and a sense of understanding is developed, it is possible to make some decisions about what should and can be done. We emphasize these two aspects of decision making because they are quite different.

Interviews and surveys can be used to gather facts about a problem or to verify satisfaction.

SOURCE: © Owen Franken, Stock, Boston.

What should be done has to do with objectives; these are the goals that the business hopes to attain. Is the firm's objective short-term profit maximization, intermediate-term growth, or long-term survival? Sometimes, to your surprise, you may find out that no one has ever asked that question. It is your job to understand precisely what the firm's objectives are.

Second, whatever the firm's objectives may be, it has resources to pursue only selected options. Your job is to understand what can be feasibly done within the resources of the business. Generally, a business cannot hire a whole new labor force, develop new products overnight, or enter entire new markets in the short term. All these may be things the firm should do but cannot do in the short term because of resource limits.

STEP 4: SOLUTIONS DESIGN

Most people think that once a decision is made to pursue a given option, the process is over. Actually, only the beginning is over. Solutions have to be designed and planned. In the process, the solutions will continue to be modified and changed. As we describe in Section 9.5, a design may be logical or physical. In a **logical design**, the general level of resources, the general operational process, and the nature of outputs that the solution should require are described. A **physical design** involves a more detailed description of equipment, buildings, personnel, and inventories than the logical design provides.

STEP 5: IMPLEMENTATION

Once a solution is designed, the last step in problem solving is implementation. The world's best solutions do not implement themselves. Virtually all real-world business solutions require a planned implementation strategy in order to work properly. You will have to consider when and how to introduce the solution, how to explain the solution to your employees, how to modify the planned solution to account for field experience, how to change existing business procedures so the solution can work, and how to evaluate the solution so you know it is working.

Figure 9.2 summarizes the five-step model of business problem solving described here. It is a very general model that can be used in a variety of business or personal settings. But we also need to be more specific in describing the problems businesses typically face. In the next section, we look at the first two steps and three major sources of business problems and their related solutions. In the next chapter, we describe logical and physical designs of solutions and illustrate some charting tools used to depict solutions graphically.

When this problem-solving methodology is applied specifically to information system–related problems, it is called systems analysis and design. **Systems analysis** is the study and analysis of problems of existing information systems; it involves both identifying the organization's objectives and determining what must be done to solve its problems. While systems analysis shows what the problems are and what has to be done about them, **systems design** shows how this should be realized. The systems design is the model or blueprint for an information system solution that shows in detail how the technical (hardware, software), organizational (procedures, data), and people (training, end-user interfaces) components will fit together. Sometimes a problem will not require an information system solution but an adjustment in management or existing procedures. Even so, systems analysis may be required to arrive at the proper solution.

Logical design

The part of a solutions design that provides a description of the general level of resources, the operational process, and the nature of outputs that the solution should require; it describes what the solution will do, not how it will work physically.

Physical design

The part of a solutions design that translates the abstract logical system model into specifications for equipment, hardware, software, and other physical resources.

Systems analysis

The study and analysis of problems of existing information systems; it includes the identification of both the organization's objectives and its requirements for the solution of the problems.

Systems design

A model or blueprint for an information system solution to a problem; it shows in detail how the technical, organizational, and people components of the system will fit together.

FIGURE 9.2

Systems Analysis and Design

In order to design effective solutions for business problems, we must first analyze and understand the problem. Systems analysis includes the first three stages in our five-step model, during which we identify the problem, gather information about it, and make a decision about the best solution. The best solution is not always the ideal solution, since the ideal may be too expensive or too difficult considering present resources. The final two steps encompass systems design: designing the logical and physical specifications of the solution and implementing this solution. Feedback from each step, and from the postimplementation evaluation, helps us judge the effectiveness of the solution: has it solved the problem it was intended to solve?

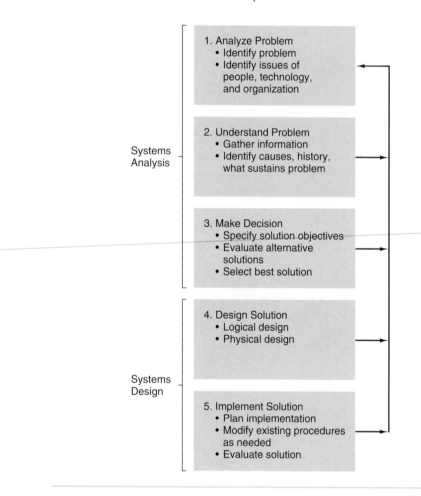

9.3 TYPICAL BUSINESS PROBLEMS: ANALYSIS AND UNDERSTANDING

We have suggested throughout this book that all problems (and solutions) can be seen as some combination of technology, organization, and people issues. These three perspectives can be applied throughout the problem-solving process. They are especially helpful in the first two steps of problem solving—problem analysis (what kind of problem

TABLE 9.1

Problem-Solving Perspectives and the Examples in This Chapter That Illustrate Them

Perspective	Example
Technology	
Hardware	CS First Boston
Software	
Telecommunications	
Database	
Organization	
Culture	Ryder Systems, Inc., A. O. Smith
Management	New York State Department of Motor Vehicles
Politics	
Bureaucracy	New York State Department of Motor Vehicles
Resources	Ryder Systems, Inc.
Turbulence	Ryder Systems, Inc.
Complexity	
People	
Ergonomics	A. O. Smith, TRW, Inc.
Evaluation and Monitoring	
Training	
Employee Attitudes and Involvement	A. O. Smith
Legal and Regulatory Compliance	

are we facing?) and problem understanding (where did the problem come from and why does it persist?)—but they can also be valuable in the decision-making and implementation steps.

Table 9.1 shows the matrix of perspectives we use throughout the book to guide the problem-solving process and lists the real-world examples in this chapter along with the particular perspective each illustrates.

TECHNOLOGY PERSPECTIVES

Problems—and solutions—are rarely technology problems per se. However, information technology is often one of the major sources of organizational problems. There are several kinds of technology problems, as shown in Figure 9.3. In general, when problem solving, you should ask yourself, "What changes in information technology hardware, software, telecommunications, and database are required to solve this problem?"

For all types of technology, the most common hardware problems are capacity, compatibility, and change. The expanding use of computers has quickly overwhelmed many central mainframe computers installed in the 1980s. You can usually tell when capacity is exceeded by looking at response time: When response times approach 30 seconds to a minute, you know a capacity problem exists. Expanding capacity is not as simple as it sounds. Often, a firm will want to change from one generation of computer to another to take advantage of new technology. But this may necessitate a change in software. What begins as a simple hardware upgrade may eventually require an expensive rewriting of all the organization's software. Compatibility issues must be considered as well: Will the new computer be compatible with all the older computers and related equipment, such as printers and communication networks?

FIGURE 9.3

Looking at Problems from a Technology Perspective

Information technology can often contribute to organizational problems. The most common technology issues are capacity (is the system overloaded?), compatibility (can the system's various components "talk" to each other?), and change (is the system still meeting organizational needs?). These issues affect hardware, software, databases, and telecommunications. It is wise to look at all of these aspects before ruling out technical problems.

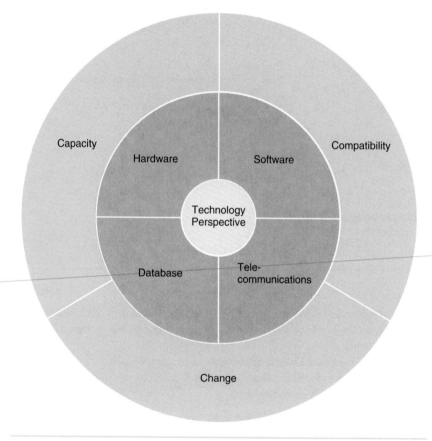

The experience of CS First Boston Corp. is typical. Its old mainframe computer could not handle the company's rapidly expanding computational needs. This multi-billion-dollar securities business required a system that could handle in 8 hours more than 1,000 transactions linking traders representing companies waiting to sell short-term securities with salespeople who sell them to investors. It took several minutes to over half an hour to assemble a list of offerings from a trader to investors. Only a few users could access the old system at one time, or the system would slow to a crawl. The slow computer performance was bad for business. Investors were frustrated because it took too long for them to buy what they wanted. Traders lost money because they could only complete a limited number of transactions and sales.

To alleviate these problems, CS First Boston replaced its worn-out mainframe system with a new client/server application called CPTrade that runs on a Sun file server networked to Sun workstations. The new system, which can generate a list of 50 offerings of interest to an investor in half a second,[6] will help First Boston increase its securities business, since sales staff can assist seven investors in the time it took them to help just one. Service for each customer has markedly improved.

Software often presents a problem when an organization wants to do something new or to accomplish traditional tasks in a new way. Existing software will have to be replaced with new software when the organization changes, develops new products, institutes new organizational structures, or initiates new procedures.

The most common software issues involve the creation of interfaces with existing software, management of cost and projects, and personnel. Organizations build large libraries of software applications over many years. New software typically will require inputs from the old software and may be required to output information to the old systems. Generally, software interfaces have to be built. This is a time-consuming, expensive, and difficult process. It is no secret that the typical software project is 50 to 100 percent over budget and behind schedule.[7] What looks like a 6-month project costing $100,000 can quickly turn into a year-long extravaganza costing $200,000 or more.

Part of the problem with the management of software projects involves personnel. Typically, organizations do not have in-house personnel trained in the techniques of building new software. Most of the existing staff is involved in maintaining the old software, not writing new software. Hence organizations must often hire outside consultants to write new software, and the outsiders may take many months to master the complexities of the organization.

Telecommunications has recently become a major source of problems for organizations because of the need to network large numbers of desktop computers and the desire to develop integrated systems that can link mainframes, minicomputers, and microcomputers into single networks. Typically, telecommunications issues involve standards (compatibility) and capacity planning.

Computers existed long before computer networks. This is quite different from the telephone system. Telephones were developed at the same time networks evolved, and there were well-established standards to assure that one phone could talk with all others on the network (this came about because the telephone companies in all countries have been regulated monopolies that both manufactured the equipment and owned, operated, and defined the networks).

Requiring only 35 percent of the "footprint" of a traditional SPARC-station, the SPARCstation Voyager is designed for environments where space is at a premium. With its quiet operation and energy-efficient design, professionals will find the system to be a powerful solution for work sites with a requirement for less noise and power consumption.

This is not the case with computers. Apple computers use a different language than IBM microcomputers, and both use a different language than mainframe computers, which in turn use a different language than minicomputers. Overcoming these differences and developing standards are major difficulties for organizations.

Fortunately, vendors are providing a growing number of communications solutions to the standards problem. Mainframes and microcomputers can effectively communicate in limited ways. Capacity planning, however, remains a guessing game. To put it simply, the problem is that it is extremely difficult to predict the demand on a communications network. Like improved highways that attract new traffic, when communications networks are made user friendly, the message traffic often skyrockets. The system can be overloaded the day it is installed.

A final technology area that causes problems for organizations is database. A firm often learns that it has a database problem when it discovers that needed information is located somewhere in the organization's computers, but it cannot be easily found or used. A second indicator of a database problem is an inability to write new software because the organization has no central repository or library showing what information is stored and where it is located.

Frequently, organizations inherit outmoded file structures that cannot adequately meet contemporary demands. Sometimes, organizations have thousands of application files but no real integrated database. Other organizations may have an integrated database, but it is an older hierarchical system that cannot easily be changed.

Solutions to these database problems are expensive. Typically, the database has to be completely redesigned. This requires a major and fundamental software effort.

Although technology problems are usually not the sole cause of an organization's difficulties, and they certainly are not the only solution, information technology is increasingly playing a larger role in problem solution. In large part, this is because what organizations want to do in terms of new products, new methods of manufacture, new organizational designs, and new methods of product delivery often directly involves information technology. But it should be remembered that information technology is only the servant of larger organizational purposes and issues.

The Focus on Technology describes a new option for firms facing technology problems—object-oriented software—and shows how visual programming techniques can address these technical issues.

ORGANIZATIONAL PERSPECTIVES

As Figure 9.4 shows, the organizational perspective on problem solving can be divided into internal institutional areas and external environmental areas (see Chapter 2). Let's look at some internal sources of problems first.

Internal Institutional Perspectives   At the most general level, organizational problems should be related to an organization's culture, management, politics, and bureaucracy. Organizational culture refers to the rarely questioned bedrock assumptions and publicly espoused values that most members of the organization freely accept. For example, at A. O. Smith it was simply assumed (until recently) that employees should be paid on a piecework basis. But times change, and old cultural assumptions often become outdated and even dangerous. When looking at an organization, you should ask, "Are the cultural assumptions of the organization still valid; that is, can the firm still survive by doing what it always did in the past?" Can the business survive with its traditional values, or are new public statements of its purpose needed?

FIGURE 9.4

Looking at Problems from an Organizational Perspective
The organizational perspective requires a multifaceted approach. Factors in the internal environment that can play a role include the organization's culture, management, company politics, and bureaucratic structure. Forces in the external environment must also be considered: resources that are available to the firm, the turbulence or rate of change in such important areas as technology and prices, and the complexity in inputs and products with which the firm must cope.

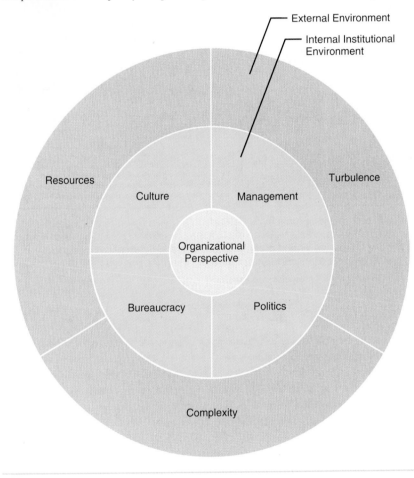

How can an organization change its culture? Think again of A. O. Smith's experiences over 8 years. The answer is that cultures change over long periods of time, with great difficulty, and largely through experimentation. Strong leadership from both management and employees is required. Many businesses cannot survive extensive cultural changes.

Management is expected to both control the existing organization and guide it into the future. Management problems become obvious when unexpected events happen and the business seems out of control. For instance, when profits fall due to cost overruns on major products, you will know there is a management problem. And although all managements have a strategic plan that purports to guide the future activities of the organization (this is a skill taught in business school and widely disseminated), not all plans work or are appropriate. Therefore, you should question strategic plans in

FOCUS ON TECHNOLOGY

VISUAL PROGRAMMING WITH OBJECTS

Object-oriented programming is the foundation for a new productivity-enhancing technology known as visual programming. Object-oriented programming is a method of programming in which data definitions and instructions for processing the data are combined into one object (see Section 6.5). Visual programming allows the programmer to create a program by working with groups of objects, clicking on a specific object and moving or copying it to another location or drawing a line to connect it to another object. Many desktop computer users already unknowingly use this technology when they customize the button bars that are now so familiar to users of Windows-based word processors and spreadsheets. Using their mouse, they point at the button they want to place on their button bar and then drag it to the desired location on the bar. This

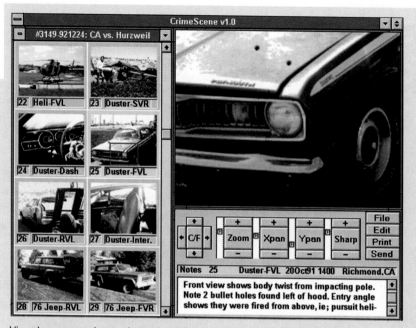

Visual programming tools such as Borland's ObjectVision enable non-programmers to create working applications by drawing, pointing, and clicking instead of writing program code. Visual programming is especially useful for building the user interface of an information system.

SOURCE: Courtesy of Borland International, Inc.

technology is now taking its place as a valuable productivity tool for both programmers and end-users.

Programmers find visual programming particularly useful in the building of user interfaces for client/server applications. The Dreyfus Corp., the giant mutual fund company, needed to bring together financial and client information stored in six different database management systems on two separate mainframes. Their

SOURCES: Barnaby J. Feder, "Sophisticated Software Set for Exotic Financial Trades," *The New York Times*, March 30, 1994, and Lawrence M. Fisher, "Helping Big Corporations Out of Computer Limbo," *The New York Times*, March 20, 1994.

terms of their ability to meet the challenges of a changing environment. When problem solving, ask yourself, "Can this management team control the business and, in addition, adequately plan for the future?"

Whatever organizations in fact do is often the result of a political struggle among major organizational players. One of the questions to ask when problem solving in an organization is, "Will the political struggles in this organization impede the adoption of suitable solutions?" If the answer is yes, you will have to devise ways to change the political landscape or tilt the balance in the political competition. You will have to choose sides and work for the side you believe in.

A last, very broad feature to consider when problem solving is business bureaucracy. Bureaucracy simply refers to the fact that all successful, large organizations develop specialized subunits (structure) over time that do most of the work; these specialized units, in turn, develop finely tuned procedures to get the work done in an accept-

goal was to create a "transparent" client/server application; users would be unaware of how the data were accessed or where they were stored. As with many client/server applications, the data were stored on mainframes, but processing was controlled by users on their desktops. Using the software package SQL Windows (Gupta Corp., Menlo Park, California), the programmers were able to create the interface much more easily and rapidly than had they used more traditional tools. The key to the productivity improvements is SQL Windows' "drag and drop" capability. The programmer selects a needed object (such as a button bar) from a list of existing objects, clicks on it, drags it to the position in the interface program where it is needed, and drops it there. The object brings with it all of its data and processing code. This software can have a major effect on building client/server systems because building the interface is often 80 percent of the in-house programming for such systems.

Drop and drag object programming is not being used only by programmers. The Ficad system (C.ATS Software Inc., Palo Alto, California), for instance, enables financial traders to create complex financial instruments. Ficad was designed for the specialized field of derivative trading instruments. Derivatives are highly sophisticated financial instruments, the values of which are linked to the price of an underlying asset, such as a stock, bond, or currency. They are primarily used to protect financial investments against major market reversals—in essence, a form of investment insurance. With $16 trillion in derivatives in the portfolios of financial institutions, this very large industry has a major effect on world economies. Because derivatives are so complex, creating them by using traditional programming methods has proven difficult and occasionally impossible when the needed derivative is too complex for existing methods. When the work must be performed manually, the procedures are extremely slow and expensive.

Ficad is a software system composed of objects that traders who are not programmers can manipulate to create their own programs. The objects can be stocks, stock dividends, bonds, options, or any number of financial instruments with which the traders are very familiar. They also can be actions, such as "pay quarterly" or "add these two accounts together." The software allows the users to link objects by drawing a line between them. In this way the traders join needed objects to create their own derivatives. Traders can even open some of these objects and change certain internal rules to meet the needs of the new derivatives they are creating. For example, the trader could change the time period for calculating the value of a stock option or even make changes to the underlying formula for calculating the value. Given the great flexibility and ease of use of this software's interface, traders are thus able to create derivatives more quickly and less expensively than in the past. They can even devise derivatives that are so complex they previously could not be created. And they often can do this without having to rely on professional programmers.

FOCUS Questions: What problems does visual programming solve? What other useful applications can you suggest for visual programming?

able manner. These standard operating procedures are difficult to change. In general, whatever a large organization does is an output of its bureaucratic subunits and their standard operating procedures.

When problem solving, you should ask yourself, "Are changes in bureaucratic structure or procedure required to solve the problem?" If the answer is yes, you will have to develop new, highly trained specialized groups to accomplish the solution and new bureaucratic procedures. The example above of the New York Motor Vehicles Office illustrates how simple changes in bureaucratic procedure can do wonders for customer service.

External Environment   Once you have examined these internal organizational issues, you should look further at the external constraints facing an organization. The most powerful environmental dimensions are resources, turbulence, and complexity.

All businesses need financial, political, cultural, and other resources from the environment. Some environments are rich with support for certain business firms but poor for other firms. For instance, for the last 25 years, computer manufacturers of all kinds have existed in an environment of growing market demand, growing legitimacy and acceptance by the broader culture (computers do not pollute like oil refineries), and large financial investments. Although these features do not guarantee survival, they are vital ingredients to longevity and prosperity and have been crucial to the success of many computer firms that may have been poorly managed but were fortunate enough to exist in a rich, forgiving environment. The same applies to home insulation manufacturers: during the last 25 years, the price of heating a home with oil or gas has tripled, leading to increased demand for insulation and keeping prices up as well.

When you examine an organization in trouble and are looking for solutions, you should ask, "Is this firm in a rich or poor environment? Is its market growing or declining?" Often firms fall into financial difficulty not simply because they are poorly managed, but because they are in declining markets and have failed to identify areas of growth to invest in. Obviously, if a firm is starved for funds, the solutions it ultimately chooses will have to be inexpensive and will have to show a return on investment in the very short term (1 year). In a cash-rich environment, a firm has many more options and can afford to take a longer-term view (3 to 5 years).

Turbulence refers to rates of environmental change in such areas as production technologies, sales, and prices. While computer manufacturers in general have benefited from expanding demand for their products (resource richness), they have been subject to incredible change in production technologies—that is, a turbulent environment. One result is a high level of failure among computer manufacturers. Having become competent in one set of production technologies, most firms find it difficult to adopt new techniques. Young, new firms built around the new technologies quickly rise to dominate older firms.

When you examine a problem at an organization, ask yourself, "Is this problem related in any way to broad environmental changes in production technology, sales, or prices?" If the answer is yes, you will have to consider ways in which the organization might respond.

Complexity refers to the number of inputs and products that a firm has as well as the geographical diversity of its production. Firms operating in a complex environment have many suppliers, a vast array of products, and widely distributed production facilities. The automobile industry and the petrochemical industry are typically identified as complex: they have a small number of suppliers but widely distributed production facilities and a vast array of products and niche markets. A chain of hamburger stands is marvelously uniform and not complex: a limited menu is served worldwide and each store is a carbon copy of the others.

In complex industries, administrative overhead is high, and decision making is difficult. Complex firms tend to have very large bureaucracies, with layer upon layer of middle management, whose job it is to control the complex organization. Profits and return on investment tend to be lower in complex industries than in "simpler" industries.

When you begin the analysis of an organization or seek better understanding, you should ask yourself, "To what extent are the problems visible here the result of a complex environment?" If environmental complexity is a problem, what solution might reduce that complexity?

Sometimes the solution to these organizational problems calls for fundamentally rethinking what the organization should be doing, defining new goals and ways of pursuing those goals, as described in the Focus on Organizations.

FOCUS ON ORGANIZATIONS

AETNA KEEPS REENGINEERING

Aetna Life & Casualty Co., the nation's largest publicly held financial services company, has been undergoing major changes in an attempt to cut losses. Faced with tighter government regulations, consumer revolts over prices, and mounting losses from costly pollution claims and bad real estate loans, Aetna has begun to rethink what, where, and how it sells.

Other large multiline insurers like Travelers Corp. and Cigna have also launched plans to cut middle management and reduce unprofitable lines of business. In the past, each of these companies tried to offer every type of insurance a customer could possibly want. They also worked through independent agents, which gave them higher expenses than companies such as Allstate Corp., which sells insurance directly to customers. The most successful insurance companies today are those that pay strict attention to costs.

Capital-rich companies such as Aetna tend to respond slowly to competitive pressures because they don't see an immediate monetary loss.

Robert E. Compton, Aetna's chairman, has launched a series of changes to make the paternalistic, old-line insurance company more competitive, lean, and mean. Aetna's greatest strength is in the individual life insurance business, including overseas and health care businesses. The company pulled out of automobile insurance in 28 states at significant short-term cost and is considering decreasing its property and casualty insurance business. The Aetna work force has lost nearly 8,000 jobs.

Some of the greatest changes Aetna has made affect customer relations. Aetna traditionally relied on independent agents who worked on commission and acted as intermediaries between the company and the consumer. Although agents still sell insurance, their intermediary role is now diminished. Customers are encouraged to bypass agents and to call the company directly when they have a claim. The company hopes that this kind of streamlining will reduce costs.

Aetna went into partnership with a Citicorp subsidiary in Florida to sell homeowners' insurance to people whose mortgages have just been approved. Only 15 policies were sold during the first 2 months, and protests by insurance agents initiated an investigation by the Florida Department of Insurance. Out-of-state banks are prohibited from selling insurance in Florida, and Aetna was asked to halt sales until questions are resolved.

The entire change process has taken its toll. Morale has eroded with employee layoffs, and burnout threatens those left. Although agents on reduced commission have become openly antagonistic, some officials and analysts view these developments positively. They believe that the entire delivery process has to be taken apart even though it will make people angry and uncomfortable.

While Aetna has increased its profits, its performance is still well below the expectations of investors. Aetna may need to continue downsizing, spinning off business, and reducing its work force to remain competitive.

FOCUS Questions:
What internal and external organizational perspectives would be useful in diagnosing Aetna's problems? Do you think the solution will be easy? Why? What kinds of changes are involved?

SOURCES: Greg Steinmetz, "Aetna Mulls Another Revamping Amid Sluggish Profits," *The Wall Street Journal*, January 14, 1994, and Kirk Johnson, "The New Marching Orders at Aetna," *The New York Times*, March 1, 1992.

PEOPLE PERSPECTIVES: STRATEGIC HUMAN RESOURCE ISSUES

One of the major findings of research on information systems in the last 10 years is that systems frequently do not achieve hoped-for productivity gains because insufficient attention has been paid to the "people" perspective, or human resource issues. Because business organizations are made up of people, just about any problem in a business is a "people" problem. Research has identified five strategic human resource issues (see Figure 9.5). By "strategic" we mean simply those issues that must be accounted for or dealt with to assure success in problem solving.[8]

Ergonomics is the science of designing machines, operations, systems, and work environments in general so that they best meet the needs of the human beings involved

FIGURE 9.5

Looking at Problems from a People Perspective:
Strategic Human Resource Issues

Research has identified five key areas that are especially important for identifying problems related to people in an organization. They are ergonomics, or the design of effective work environments to meet the needs of the human beings involved; evaluating and monitoring employees' work, which can backfire because it creates pressure and resentment; training employees, which is vital but all too often ignored; employee involvement, a controversial issue in many firms that can affect productivity; and legal and regulatory compliance, or making sure the organization protects its employees' legal rights. It is important to consider all these areas when analyzing a problem.

and optimize economic returns. This broad field encompasses the study of the physical design of hardware and furniture, the design of jobs, health issues, and the user/software interface design (e.g., the software logic and its presentation on the screen). Some typical ergonomic issues raised by information systems are VDT screen radiation (VDT means video display terminal or computer screen) and its potential to harm; the height of terminals above the floor, which can contribute to back strain and fatigue; the collection of too many (or too few) tasks into jobs, which can lead to fatigue and high absenteeism; and the way in which screens display information (software interface), which can also produce fatigue, monotony, and boredom. In addition, ergonomics has expanded its concerns to include the social psychology and physical results of screen design and software design. The "user interface" that the software creates has an important effect on the productivity of information technology (see the Focus on Problem Solving). Figure 9.6 illustrates many of the physical relationships that have to be taken into account when designing human-machine interfaces.

All jobs involve evaluation and monitoring by superiors to gauge the quality and quantity of work performed by employees. This evaluation can be fair and unobtrusive,

FIGURE 9.6

Some Physical Ergonomic Considerations in Designing a Computer System

There are many more issues to consider in designing a system than you might think. Such features as screen angle, viewing angle, and viewing distance can make the difference between comfortable viewing and eye strain. The correct knee angle, seat back angle, and back support can greatly reduce the possibility of back strain. The next time you sit down at a personal computer or terminal, notice how all these factors feel to you. Making computer systems more comfortable to use pays off in higher employee morale and productivity and lower absenteeism.

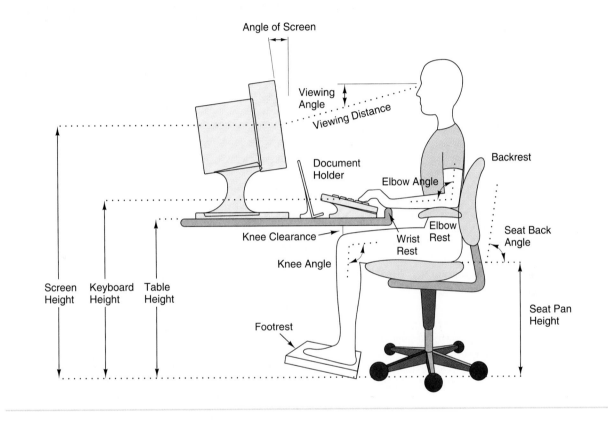

or it can be perceived by workers as unfair and intrusive. Computers permit much closer monitoring of the output of workers than the traditional means of monitoring and evaluating work, but they may be resented by workers. Computer monitoring may at first appear to be a "solution" to a productivity problem, but it can backfire into a human relations disaster.

It is obvious that training employees is a vital part of a successful human relations program. Training involves an investment of resources, however, and although many employers are willing to spend a great deal of money and time to ensure that employees are properly trained, many businesses and government agencies view formal training as an unnecessary expense. It is often the first budget to be cut when fortunes turn down. Inadequate training is a major source of information system failure, or at least disappointment.

Traditionally, American management has adopted a hostile attitude toward employee involvement, participation, and feedback. Since the turn of the century, a dominant attitude on the part of management has been that employees should follow orders, and if they disagree, they should resign. With very few exceptions, employment

F O C U S   O N PROBLEM SOLVING

MAKING THE INTERNET A CLICK AWAY

While the building of interfaces can be costly and time-consuming, they are not only necessary, but if done properly they can dramatically increase people's use of software. If analysis of a business problem indicates that a system is not being adequately used or that data are too difficult for nonprogrammers to access, it is likely that an easy-to-use interface will be a useful tool to address the problem. Seldom has the value of an easy-to-use interface been so clear as with Mosaic, a new way for novice computer users to access the Internet.

The Internet is a global network of networks, clearly the largest network in the world. As we explained in the Part 2 case, *What In the World Is the Internet?*, it is a worldwide window into immense quantities of information, including some of the world's largest libraries and most valuable databases. It is also a link to virtually millions of scientists, educators, and other professionals all over the world. But the Internet has a gigantic problem—it has no owner, no manager, no central organization; it is so disorganized that users have great difficulty finding anything. It has been likened to a library in which all the books are simply dumped in

FIGURE 9.7

A Click of the Mouse, a World of Information

❶ What the Computer User Sees First

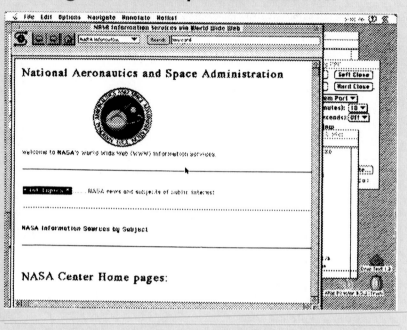

the middle of the floor. How can anyone find anything?

A whole industry has developed around this critical access problem. Various software programs have been developed to help people locate information or correspondents and then thread their way through the Internet maze to get to that information or person. However, early in 1993, with the introduction (and free distribution, in typical Internet fashion) of Mosaic, a revolution occurred in Internet usage. Mosaic is a graphical user interface (GUI) that was developed at the National Center for Supercomputing Applications in Champaign, Illinois

(see Figure 9.7). It integrates hypertext technology to greatly ease the difficulty of navigating through the Internet.

Hypertext is a relative of object oriented programming. On a screen built with hypertext, any highlighted word, phrase, or graphic can be clicked on to bring up another level of screens with more detailed information or information on a related topic. For example, if you are on the upper National Aeronautic and Space Administration (NASA) screen and want to get to NASA's "hot topics" listing, all you need do is click the highlighted phrase, and the hot topics screen will appear. The highlighted phrase "hot

SOURCE: John Markoff, "A Free and Simple Computer Link," *The New York Times*, December 8, 1993, page D-1+.

law allows employers great discretion in determining whom to hire, how the job will be done, and whom to terminate.

But these old attitudes are changing for many reasons. In a knowledge- and information-driven economy, skilled employees are in short supply and their views must be

② What the Computer User Sees Next

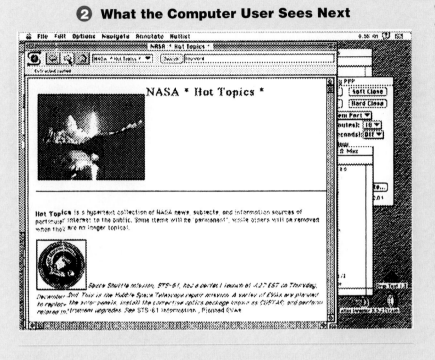

Although use had doubled every year since 1988, it grew dramatically when Mosaic was released. The National Center for Supercomputing Applications (the Mosaic developer) reported that requests from its electronic library rose from 100,000 per day in June to nearly 400,000 daily just 4 months later, and a similar usage rise has been reported by many other Internet-connected services.

In a number of cases organizations were forced to impose an access fee to distribute information they had formerly offered for free, not because they were trying to generate income but because they had to ration access to their traffic lanes so their computers would not be swamped. Commercial developers are starting to take advantage of Mosaic. O'Reilly & Associates, a technical book publisher, used Mosaic to create an on-line magazine that includes advertising.

Some barriers to using Mosaic remain. The user's computer must be directly linked to the Internet. While many businesses and universities have such connections, most personal computer users can only tie into the Internet using on-line information services such as AmericaOnline or Delphi. Companies are starting to work on software that will make connecting to the Internet as easy as dialing into these on-line services.

FOCUS Questions:
What problems might the installation of a flexible, easy-to-use interface cause an organization? What problems might it solve?

topics" is actually an object that has embedded within it the address of the network server where the document is stored, the document address on that server, and the network protocol needed by the server for the two computers to "talk" to each other. When the user clicks on the hypertext object, Mosaic finds the server (wherever in the world it is), locates the document, and displays it on the user's screen. The user has no long, exact, arcane address to type or even to locate. He or she does not need to enter a lengthy list of complicated instructions. Essentially, it is as easy as clicking an icon on a Windows GUI to run an application on your own computer—with a simple click you can connect to the University of California library, or read a copy of a speech by President Clinton that is stored at the University of Missouri, or see and hear a sample of musical recordings compiled by MTV. Mosaic users include librarians, magazine publishers, software developers, computer scientists, record companies, and catalog distributors, all of whom use Mosaic as a general-purpose navigational tool for the information highway.

Did making an easy-to-use navigation interface make a difference in the use of the Internet? It was almost as if the Internet had been hit by a tornado.

heeded. The overall productivity growth of the American economy is low relative to that of Japan, where a somewhat more participative style of management is encouraged. Hence many American managers have sought to imitate their Japanese counterparts by encouraging employee feedback, reducing the social distance between senior management and

Corporate chief executives learn how to use notebook computers in intensive training sessions at a technology "boot camp." Training is a key factor in successful information systems.

SOURCE: San Diego Union Tribune/ Charles Newman.

middle management, and promoting a family-like atmosphere. Still other managers have adopted Swedish and European-style employee participation schemes in which employees operate in teams with less direct supervision (see the example of A. O. Smith above). Finally, a number of federal and state laws have been enacted that have established a body of employee rights (described below).

When examining an organizational problem, you should ask yourself, "To what extent is this problem a result of poor employee attitudes related to lack of involvement, participation, and communication?" If this seems a problem, try to find solutions in this area.

The Focus on People explores how employers are beginning to seek employee feedback concerning the functionality and ease-of-use of software.

A last human resource issue to consider is legal and regulatory compliance. Because the American public is concerned about the welfare of all working people, since the 1930s both the federal government and most states have enacted legislation establishing a number of employee rights. The following are the most important:

- The right to join a union.

- The right to "no fault" worker compensation for injury on the job.

- The right to equal employment opportunity regardless of race, gender, or ethnicity.

- The right to a safe and healthy workplace.

- The right to have a pension and to have it protected.

- The right to freedom from reprisal for reporting violations of federal public-protection laws.

- The right of access to selected management information concerning toxic chemicals in the workplace.

Some states have also enacted laws that protect workers from arbitrary termination; under these laws, fired workers are entitled to a due process hearing.

These rights are often a source of organizational problems as well as part of the solution. The growth of information technology, the development of new systems, and their use by organizations have raised legal issues in health areas (as we explained above in the discussion of ergonomics), in matters related to employees' access to corporate information, and in the equal opportunity area. Briefly, the growth in management information made possible by computers has led employee groups and courts to subpoena information from the firm to support litigation against the firm. Women and minorities, for instance, who believe they have been discriminated against may demand that corporations release management and statistical information on employment practices. Likewise, workers who believe they have been illegally exposed to toxic chemicals can demand corporate management information on product composition, exposure levels, and internal reports. Employers cannot use the defense of claiming they did not or could not collect and analyze the information: statutes and court decisions make clear that, in this information age, it is the responsibility of employers to maintain complete employee data for periods of up to 60 years.

Usually, it will be obvious if legal and regulatory issues are a cause of the problems facing an organization. Generally, unions or groups of employees bring suits against the corporation for alleged violations of rights. Rather than waiting for suits to arise, however, wise managers periodically review their organization's compliance with existing regulations.

If employees were fearful of using VDTs, how could you resolve some of their fears? If employees believed they had been unfairly compensated for their work with information systems, how could you address this concern? If minorities and women claimed that they were unfairly relegated to low-level data entry jobs, or were not receiving promotions as rapidly as others, how could you address their complaints?

9.4 PROBLEM SOLVING: MAKING DECISIONS

If you have done a good job of analysis and understanding, the next step of the problem-solving process will be to choose among several alternative solutions. This should be a relatively simple process if you are properly prepared. What at first seemed like a hopelessly complex problem should at this point appear much clearer. The number of potential "solutions" or options should now be reduced to a manageable number—a few that stand some chance of working. In choosing among them, what criteria should be foremost? Figure 9.8 illustrates the three major steps involved in making a good decision.

ESTABLISH OBJECTIVES

The process of establishing objectives may be the most complicated part of decision making if only because many people in a firm have different perspectives. Nevertheless, in a firm, objectives must be carefully chosen and agreed on in a group process; otherwise, people will not be committed to a common course of action. One way to begin is to consider the overall corporate objectives as well as the major divisional or subunit objectives. The following might be a firm's overall corporate goals:

FOCUS ON PEOPLE

LEARNING FROM THE USERS

Business users have traditionally had major problems actually using application software developed or purchased for them. In fact, a high percentage of software developed or purchased by companies lies gathering dust or is only an added burden, a parallel system used alongside an older, manual business system. Some say that problems occur because the people who design systems are technicians who have trouble communicating with nontechnicians and getting useful feedback from them. Others point to the traditional American management hostility toward feedback from line employees. Whatever the cause, much business software is either poorly tested or never tested by the ultimate users.

Graphical user interfaces (GUIs) on desktop computers, such as the Macintosh or Windows on DOS machines, have certainly helped. But even desktop computers remain so difficult for some users that a book with the unlikely title of *DOS for Dummies*,

In "usability labs," technical specialists can observe end users trying out software to identify problems with the user interface. Feedback from end users is essential to a well-designed information system.
SOURCE: Usability Sciences, Dallas.

by Dan Gookin, became a runaway best-seller—1.3 million copies were sold in 18 months. This book spawned a series of books written for people who are willing to tag themselves as computer "dummies." Even *Mac For Dummies* has now appeared for the "easy-to-use" Macintosh. The problem is so serious that Apple Computer, Sony, Motorola, AT&T, Matsushita, and Philips have teamed up to establish General Magic Inc., a company whose goal is to find ways to make palm-sized

computers of the future easy and comfortable to use. Marc Porat, General Magic's chief executive, hinted at one of the real problems when he said "technology should never damage a person's self-esteem."

In a search for solutions, information systems (IS) professionals have begun seeking ways to successfully elicit feedback from end-users. Industry giants such as IBM and Microsoft Corp. operate research programs staffed by teams of psychol-

SOURCES: Steve Lohr, "Across the Computer Divide, The Nerds Face the Dummies," *The New York Times,* June 6, 1993; Elaine L. Appleton, "Put Usability to the Test," *Datamation,* July 15, 1993; and Christopher Lindquist, "User Software Takes to the Road," *Computerworld,* March 29, 1993.

- Long-term survival.

- Meeting a competitive challenge at any cost.

- Improving productivity.

- Increasing employee morale and loyalty.

Subunit goals might include the following:

- The introduction of new products.

- More effective marketing.

ogists, learning experts, and graphic designers. One approach they have copied from consumer product companies is to establish "usability labs" where users try out software while programmers observe them, often from behind one-way mirrors. Using this approach, programmers can identify and change interface terms that don't work, test the interface's ease of navigation through an application, learn how well the application flow matches the workflow of the users, and evaluate the clarity of the application's on-line and printed documentation. For example, in its usability lab, Microsoft Corp. programmers found that most users of Excel did not understand the term "preferences," whereas when they substituted the term "options," the difficulty virtually disappeared. In studying people working with Microsoft Publisher, they realized that users did not understand an icon with arrows pointing in all four directions that was meant to indicate that they could move boxes in any direction around the screen. Programmers modified the icon, embedding within the four arrows a moving truck with the word "move" on it, and the problem was solved.

However, many people believe that testing in an IS usability lab is unrealistic because it does not properly dupli-cate working conditions. Don Ballman, manager of usability laboratories at Mead Data Central, Inc., in Dayton, Ohio, claims "When I bring somebody into my lab, that in itself creates an unnatural environment." For example, in such labs users have the latest computer equipment to work on, not the old ones often found back on their own desks. Moreover, while in the lab, the users are able to concentrate on trying the new software with none of the everyday pressures from interruptions such as telephone calls, visits from co-workers, or trips to the copy machine. The solution? Portable labs—take the usability lab to the users' offices.

Portable labs actually cost very little. Ballman estimates that it takes only $5,000 to get started, including a hand-held video recorder, a portable television, videotapes, and software to index those tapes. One advantage of this approach (in addition to working in the users' own offices) is that users can view the videotapes at once and make comments while the experience is still fresh.

The ultimate management question is the cost-effectiveness of usability testing. Even if it does help, is it worthwhile, particularly given that hiring usability consultants can cost as much as $1,000 per day? In a 1990 study by Dr. Clare-Marie Karat, then of IBM's T. J. Watson Research Center, she found that usability testing of small application software programs resulted in changes that saved $2 in end-user time for every $1 spent. She further concluded that $100 was saved for every dollar spent in testing larger systems. Two brief examples:

American Airlines decided to test competing E-mail packages before purchasing one. The users heavily favored a package originally not considered seriously by management—it had less functionality but the users found it much easier to use. IS learned a great deal from the users and took their suggestions into consideration in finally purchasing and installing American's final system. At Mead Data Central, Ballman tested a commercial time-sheet application with users before installing it. He learned of a number of enhancements needed to make the system easier for the eventual 900 users to use effectively.

FOCUS Questions:
What problems can be solved by seeking end-user views on software when it is being developed? What kinds of problems can't be solved this way?

- Lower administrative costs.
- Lower manufacturing costs.
- Better financing terms.

Because a firm can pursue several objectives, you may want to list the goals in order of importance or establish the critical success factors that are absolutely essential for the firm to attain.

It is very important that problem solvers agree on a time frame over which a solution can and should be put in place. This entails deciding whether a short-term solution (starting this week) or a long-term solution (a program that lasts for several years)

FIGURE 9.8

What's Involved in Step Three: Making Decisions

In order to make an effective decision, first make sure that everyone agrees on the organization's objectives, both the broad corporate goals and the more focused subunit goals. Then determine the feasibility of each proposed solution, considering both internal and external constraints. Perform a cost-benefit analysis to determine the most appropriate solution for your firm. Remember to consider intangible benefits as well as tangible gains.

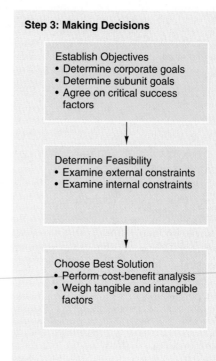

is appropriate. Some solutions can be staged: a short-term emergency action can head off imminent disaster while a long-term program is undertaken.

ESTABLISH FEASIBILITY

By now the number of possible solutions should have been pared down to a handful of options. At this point, you must decide which of the remaining solutions are doable given your firm's resources. Here you should consider both the external and internal constraints on your organization.

As we noted earlier, external constraints include the following:

- Financial resources.

- Legal/regulatory demands.

- The action of competitors.

- Suppliers.

- Customers.

Solutions to business problems must be practical and based on the company's resources and constraints. Milton Roy's Analytical Products division solved a production problem by creating ministockrooms throughout the manufacturing area to ensure that parts are located where they are needed.

SOURCE: Courtesy of Milton Roy Company.

You must consider how each of the proposed solutions is affected by these factors. For instance, it may be financially feasible to install a network of personal computers in your customers' order rooms (thus assuring customers they have easy access to your products), but you may fear the reprisals of competitors, which may lead to an unending technology war for customers.

Internal constraints are just as important. Can the subunits in the organization carry out the solution? Is the solution compatible with your company's culture? Are there major opposition groups that will try to scuttle your solution?

CHOOSE COST-EFFECTIVE SOLUTIONS

In the end, you will be left with a very small number of realistic solutions. Realistic solutions are those that meet your firm's objectives and are feasible. The last question is, "What solution is best in a financial sense?" In other words, you must try to determine the **cost-effectiveness** of a solution, or whether it is economical in terms of providing sufficient benefits for the cost.

The answer to this question can be estimated by conducting a cost-benefit analysis. Cost-benefit analysis involves adding up all the costs of a project and dividing by all its benefits. You will arrive at a ratio of costs to benefits. Ideally, you should chose the option or solution that is the least costly for a given amount of benefit.

For instance, if you had two options, one that delivered $2.00 in benefit for each $1.00 in cost and the other that delivered only $1.50 in benefit for each $1.00 in cost, you would choose the first option.

Cost-effectiveness

Being economical in terms of providing benefits that exceed costs; measured by cost-benefit analysis.

But adding up all the costs and benefits of feasible solutions is not easy, especially with large projects. Many factors, such as "speed of decision making," cannot be assigned a monetary value. These factors are called intangible, as opposed to tangible, factors. If a bank can process a loan in 1 hour instead of in 3 days, how much is that "worth" to the bank in terms of increased loan activity from enthusiastic customers and decreased clerical cost? Here, only "guesstimates" can be obtained. But good guesses are usually better than no estimate at all.

9.5 PROBLEM SOLVING: DESIGNING SOLUTIONS

Just because you have arrived at a solution that has broad support in your organization does not mean you have "solved" the problem. Once you have arrived at a feasible option, you will have to design the solution. At first, in the problem-solving process, solutions and options are only vaguely understood, even though many organizational actors pretend they understand precisely what is involved. When you get down to the nuts and bolts of specific solutions, however, you almost always discover new aspects of the solution—and the problem.

A design is a detailed description of a proposed solution in the form of a document. The document includes both textual description and graphs, charts, lists, and figures. As we mentioned earlier, there are two aspects to the design document: logical and physical design (see Figure 9.9).

FIGURE 9.9

The Two Stages in Step Four: Designing Solutions

There are two parts to the process of designing a solution: creating a logical design and translating it into a physical design. The logical design phase comes first; it involves developing a document that describes a conceptual model for the system. The emphasis is on what the system will do rather than on how it will work. The physical design translates the logical model into design specifications for hardware, software, manual procedures, and other physical considerations.

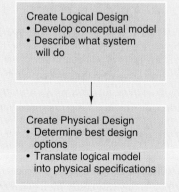

MAKING A LOGICAL DESIGN

The most critical steps in problem solving take place before the hardware or software for an application is considered. Unless the requirements for solving a problem are clearly understood beforehand, they can become obscured or even overshadowed by concerns with programming languages or hardware, and the result is an incorrect solution.

Therefore, in order to develop an information system application, a logical design, or model, of the proposed system is needed. This model must be built and understood in logical or conceptual terms before it can be translated into a specific, detailed system solution. The logical design presents the functional, or business, requirements of the proposed application solution as opposed to the technical requirements. It describes what the solution will do, not how it will work physically. The following are the basic components of a logical design (see Figure 9.10):

- **Outputs:** The information to be produced by the system. This includes reports, files, and on-line displays. The model must consider what pieces of output information are required and how they are to be organized and displayed.

- **Inputs:** The data required to be input into the system in order to create the desired output. The model must consider what pieces of data must be input and how they can best be arranged.

- **Processing:** The activities, both manual and automated, required to transform input data to output. The model must consider what kinds of decision rules, calculations, and modeling are required to perform the required manipulations on data.

- **Database:** The method of organizing and storing information in the system, through either computerized or manual means. The model must consider what pieces of data to store, when and how to update them, the relationships among them, and how they should be arranged.

- **Procedures:** The activities that must be performed by end-users and operations staff to run and use the system. The model must consider manual activities required to produce the desired information, business policies, and rules governing these activities, as well as the sequence of these activities.

- **Controls:** The manual and automated processes and procedures that ensure that the system is accurate, secure, and performing as required. The model must consider tests and measures for ensuring that the information produced is accurate and secure.

These components may be arranged in a number of ways. In problems in which one alternative is an information system application, the application itself can have alternative design solutions.

Although it may seem rather easy to determine what outputs a system should have (e.g., what reports should be produced, what screens of information are needed, and the like), in many cases the users themselves do not know or are not very good at describing what they want from their software. On the other hand, people are quite definite in their desires and tastes once they see a product. Many companies have developed software development systems that permit software engineers to build a mock-up or model of the software product before actual programs are written. Users can critique the prototype before large investments are made, and the end result is a more useful piece of software.

FIGURE 9.10

Scope of the Logical Design

The logical design is a document that specifies a system's functional business requirements. Here we show some of the issues and requirements that are crucial to building an effective information system. For instance, input procedures must take into account the content, format, and source of the input data, as well as the volume, frequency, and timing with which it enters the system. The design must also include controls to ensure the system's security, accuracy, and validity and must allow adequate supervision to maintain it on an ongoing basis. Note that these logical considerations are independent of specific types of hardware and software.

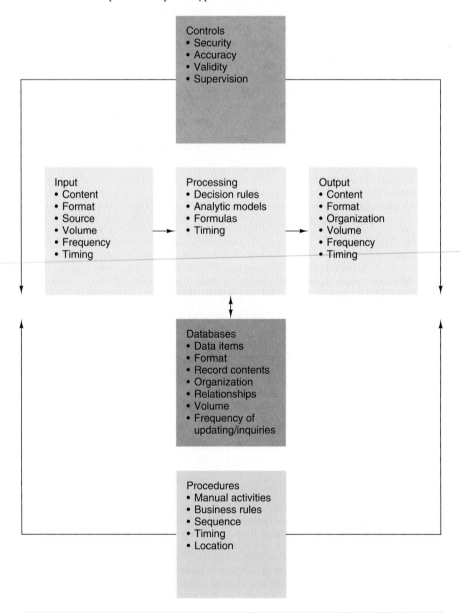

Most such prototyping systems do not take the human side of computing into account. But TRW, Inc., has developed a $5 million program that does just that. A central part of TRW's program involves using a psychologist and a sociologist on the staff.

The manager of TRW's office of system engineering technology says that "the sociologist is there to help us understand the interdynamics of the workplace—how users are organized and the protocol of the office. We need the psychologist to help us understand the individual because each user responds to a system differently based on his or her psyche."[9]

Some users think intuitively while others think systematically. The intuitive thinker wants the computer system to produce charts, graphs, and line drawings, while the systematic thinker wants quantitative information. It's possible to build a system that produces both kinds of reports, but first these needs must be identified.

TRW's prototyping systems work in four steps. First, the TRW staff and the user try to define what the system is supposed to do and for whom. Second, the staff observes prospective users in the workplace, asks them questions, and measures how they perform certain tasks. Next, an analysis of these data is used to produce the first prototype. In the last step, the prototype is tested, and corrections are made before a final version of the system is built.

In one project TRW was asked to automate the work of a cartographer who worked with satellite intelligence photographs of foreign countries. The cartographer found many faults with TRW's prototype. The position of the menu overlaid important intelligence details, so it was moved and highlighted in black; the resolution was poor and had to be enhanced; and, finally, the system did not project the photographs in a true north position, which was corrected by permitting the cartographer to rotate the map on the screen in any direction.

The process of logical design provides an opportunity to examine the way the organization itself works and to change management, jobs, and procedures to make it more efficient. Procedures may need to be streamlined, jobs rearranged, and functional areas combined to maximize the advantages of computerization. Sometimes the best solution will call for only minor changes to procedures, but in many cases, more extensive organizational change will be required. Chapter 3 introduced the concept of reengineering, whereby an entire business process is redesigned to reorganize the flow of work, eliminate repetitive steps, cut waste, and consolidate job responsibilities. The solution may call for such reengineering—rethinking and redesigning the way an entire organizational process works (review Section 3.4).

MAKING A PHYSICAL DESIGN

During the physical design process, the abstract, logical system model is translated into specifications for hardware, software, processing logic, input/output methods and media, manual procedures, and controls. The following are some of the detailed specifications that must be addressed by physical design (see Figure 9.11):

- **Databases:**
  What is the file and record layout?
  What are the relationships among data items?
  How much storage capacity is required?
  Through what path will data be accessed?
  How often will data be accessed or updated?

- **Software:**
  Is much complex logic required to transform input data to output?
  Do large files and lists need to be combined and manipulated?
  Does the application require modeling and mathematical formulas among interrelated pieces of data?

FIGURE 9.11

Physical Design Specifications

As you can see, there are many options for translating a logical design into a physical system. The physical design chooses among these possibilities to create the most effective design to meet business needs. Note that the physical design, like its logical counterpart, also includes specifications for procedures and controls.

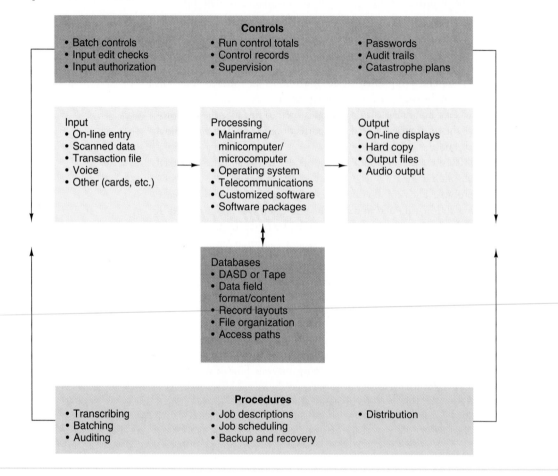

- **Hardware:**
  What hardware is already available?
  What processing power is required?
  Does the application require a special environment, such as a telecommunications network?

- **Input:**
  What medium should input data be collected on?
  How should data be collected for input?
  How often should data be input?

- **Output:**
  What medium should output information be displayed on?
  How should output be arranged and organized?
  How often should output be produced?

- **Controls:**
  What technology and procedures will make the system secure?
  How can the accuracy and integrity of data be ensured?
  How will the system be supervised?

- **Procedures:**
  What personnel are required to run the system?
  What activities must be performed for input, processing, and output?
  Where will these activities be performed?

As with logical design, there may be physical design alternatives. Some applications could be implemented on a personal computer or a mainframe; with software packages or custom programs; on a sequential file or a database; using on-line data entry or keypunched cards. The physical design options are myriad. But clearly the nature of the application plus the solution constraints will determine which design options are the most desirable.

9.6 PROBLEM SOLVING: IMPLEMENTING SOLUTIONS

In the last step of problem solving, the solution must be implemented. Often firms arrive at correct decisions, but their implementation is a failure. Effectively implementing solutions and decisions is a complex topic involving questions of psychology, organizational design, sociology, and finance. Here we present only a summary of the steps needed for effective implementation.[10] (See Figure 9.12.)

STEPS IN THE IMPLEMENTATION OF A SYSTEM SOLUTION

If the problem called for an application solution, the following activities would be performed:

- **Software development:** Software would be developed to perform any processing that had to be automated. Custom programs might be written, or the software might be based on an application package or on a personal computer spreadsheet or database management system.

- **Hardware selection and acquisition:** Appropriate hardware would be selected for the application and purchased if it was not immediately available.

- **Testing:** Each component of the system would be thoroughly tested to make sure that the system produced the right results. The testing process requires detailed testing of individual computer programs and of the entire system as a whole, including manual procedures. The process of testing each program in a system individually is called unit testing. System testing tests whether all the components of a system (program modules, hardware, and manual procedures) function together properly.

- **Training and documentation:** End-users and technical specialists would be trained in using the new application. Detailed documentation generated during

TRW, Inc., assigned a design integration manager to work with the U.S. Air Force to integrate and test new equipment for the underground command center of the Strategic Air Command. Testing components, training users, and providing documentation are integral parts of all systems' solutions.

SOURCE: Courtesy of TRW, Inc.

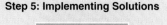

FIGURE 9.12

A Close-up of Step Five: Implementing Solutions

Four procedures make up the final step in the systems analysis and design process. First, we must develop software for the new system, whether it means writing totally new software or modifying existing programs. Second, we must select the right hardware to run the software we've written. In the testing phase, we run the programs and try out the hardware and manual procedures to ensure that everything is working properly. Finally, users must be trained to use the new system, and documentation must be written for it.

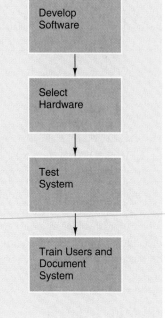

the development process for end-users and technical systems specialists would be finalized for use in training and everyday operations. Without proper documentation, it would be impossible to run or use an information system. The importance of technical and user documentation cannot be overemphasized.

CONVERSION STRATEGIES

Conversion strategies
Plans and methods for changing from an old system to a new system; include parallel conversion, direct cutover, pilot study, and phased approach.

Parallel conversion
A conversion strategy in which the old system and the new system run in tandem until it is clear that the new system is working correctly.

A final matter to consider is the strategy used to convert from the old system to the new system. In complicated systems, this will involve changes in personnel, procedures, databases, processing, inputs, and outputs. Such changes cannot be accomplished overnight and must be planned carefully beforehand.

The following are the most important **conversion strategies:**

- **Parallel conversion:** The old system and the new system are run in tandem until it is clear that the new system works correctly. The old system can serve as a backup if errors are found, but additional work is required to run the extra system.

- **Direct cutover:** The old system is replaced entirely with the new system on an appointed day. This carries the risk that no system is available to fall back on if errors are discovered.

- **Pilot study:** The new system is introduced to a limited part of the organization, such as a single department. Once the pilot is considered safe, the system is installed in the rest of the organization.

- **Phased approach:** The new system is introduced in steps. For example, a new payroll system could be phased in by introducing the modules for paying clerical employees first and managerial employees later.

In complicated projects, in which you expect that the solution will change as you gather field experience, the safest strategies are a pilot study or a phased approach. They will enable the solution to be deployed slowly over time. Direct cutover strategies are suitable for simple substitutions (when one kind of machine replaces another) and when human and social organizational changes are minimal. Perhaps the safest strategy is to run both the old system and the new system in parallel for a short period of time. In case the new system collapses, you will always have the old system to fall back upon. The disadvantage of this strategy is that it is expensive.

CHANGE MANAGEMENT

The introduction of a new business solution is an organizational change that affects the way various individuals and groups perform and interact in the firm. Different groups and individuals in organizations have varying objectives, goals, and levels of power. People typically resist new business procedures, job relationships, and technologies because they are uncertain of how they will be affected. A very well-designed solution may not work unless it is carefully planned and prepared for. The process of planning change in an organization so that it is designed and implemented in an orderly and controlled manner is called **change management**. The design of any business solution needs to take change management into account.

How can the change process be managed? In addition to determining people, organization, and technology factors that cause problems, one must determine the people, organization, and technology impacts of proposed solutions. Encouraging affected parties to participate in the development of a particular solution can make people more committed to realizing the solution and reduce their fears of change as well. People are more likely to accept a solution if they have had proper training and if the solution is supported by top management.

Direct cutover
A conversion strategy in which the old system is replaced entirely with the new system on an appointed day; no system is available if the new system fails.

Pilot study
A conversion strategy in which a new system is introduced to only a limited part of an organization; if the system is effective there, it is installed throughout the rest of the organization.

Phased approach
A conversion strategy in which a new system is introduced in steps.

Change management
The process of planning changes within an organization in order to ensure the changes are implemented in an orderly and controlled manner.

RUNNING CASE PART 3

WHAT HAPPENED AT MACY'S?

During the 1980s Macy's was bought by its management and once again became a privately held company. To buy the company back at a cost of $3.7 billion and to pay for new acquisitions, such as I. Magnin and the Bullock's retail chain, Macy's management borrowed heavily at very high interest rates. The debt was to be repaid from Macy's earnings.

The plan didn't work. By the late 1980s Macy's was losing money. In late 1991 Edward S. Finkelstein, Macy's chief executive officer, announced that he would increase television advertising by 25 percent, spending an unprecedented $150 million. The spending seemed outrageous, given Macy's deteriorating sales and staggering debt. Nevertheless, Finkelstein believed there was no reason to worry about Macy's financial obligations.

Macy's was known as a hierarchical, backbiting organization that was dominated by its imperious, if talented, chief executive. While management was preoccupied with financial affairs, Macy's could not keep pace with changes in the retail industry. It began losing younger customers to small, specialized stores, such as Benetton and The Gap. Customers interested in standard goods like pants, shirts, and shoes flocked to large discounters such as Kmart and Wal-Mart.

Macy's completed its fiscal year ending in August 1, 1992 with a $1.25 billion loss on sales of $6.4 billion and sales falling 3.7% at stores open a year or more. Suppliers refused to deliver goods, fearing they would not be paid. Macy's lenders demanded their money. By 1992, Macy's filed for bankruptcy and Finkelstein was out of a job.

That year, Macy's conducted its first customer survey in 25 years, surveying 8,000 shoppers. The survey indicated that Macy's customers often left the stores empty-handed because they couldn't find what they wanted in stock. They were also dissatisfied with Macy's service, complaining that there weren't enough sales associates to help them in departments such as high fashion, where they expected heavy attention. Customers also mentioned that it took too long to pay for Macy's purchases.

Kurt Salmon Associates, the consulting and research firm that conducted the survey, estimated that Macy's could increase sales by 17 percent simply by carrying the right stock. But Macy's had little or no idea of what merchandise was selling and what wasn't until weeks after the sales took place. Frequently store shelves would be empty of items that sold fast and filled with unpopular items that would have to be marked down.

SOURCES: Laura Zinn, "Prudence on 34th Street," *Business Week*, November 16, 1992, and Stephanie Strom, "A Key for Macy Comeback," *The New York Times*, November 1, 1992.

RUNNING CASE Questions

1. Use the three perspectives of people, organization, and technology to analyze and categorize Macy's problems. Rank the problems in order from most significant to least significant. How serious were these problems?
2. What steps would you take to better understand the problems you identified?

Individuals involved in developing solutions can act as change agents, working to win acceptance of their solutions among all parties involved. If an organization has successfully created an atmosphere that encourages creativity, innovation, and teamwork, new business solutions will be much easier to implement.[11]

SUMMARY

- Problem solving in business involves a number of conceptual steps and is rarely a simple process. An infinite number of solutions exists: The right solution depends on defining the problem correctly.

- Problems are not simply objective situations but depend greatly on how organizations and people define matters. Solutions depend on how problems are defined.

- Critical thinking is an important attribute of wise decision making. You should suspend judgment and sustain a skeptical attitude until you become convinced of the true nature of a problem.

- Problem solving involves five steps: analysis, understanding, decision making, solutions design, and implementation.

- Systems analysis is the study and analysis of problems of existing information systems and the identification of requirements for their solution. Systems design provides the blueprint for the information system solution.

- Most organizational problems involve a mix of technology, organizational, and people problems.

- Designing solutions requires both a logical and a physical design. A logical design describes the functional performance of a solution—what it is supposed to do—and a physical design describes how the solution actually works.

- Logical design presents the functional or business requirements of an application solution independent of technical considerations. It presents a model for solving a problem from an end-user or business standpoint. An information system will not be successful unless this business model is clearly visualized before technical factors (such as hardware and software) and considered.

- Physical design consists of detailed specifications for hardware, software, processing logic, input/output methods and media, manual procedures, and controls. Physical design will be shaped by the requirements of the logical business design and existing technical, economic, or operational constraints.

- Solution implementation involves four steps: software development, hardware selection, testing, and training. Four conversion strategies for implementing a solution are parallel conversion, direct cutover, pilot study, and phased approach.

- Change management facilitates the implementation of business solutions.

KEY TERMS

Problem analysis	Organization perspective
Problem understanding	People perspective
Decision making	Logical design
Solutions design	Physical design
Implementation	Systems analysis
Critical thinking	Systems design
Technology perspective	Cost-effectiveness

Conversion strategies   Pilot study

Parallel conversion   Phased approach

Direct cutover   Change management

REVIEW QUESTIONS

1. In what sense are problems "not like basketballs on a court"? Does this mean problems are not real?

2. What is the problem-solving funnel? Do all problems go through these stages?

3. What is meant by critical thinking?

4. What are the five steps involved in problem solving?

5. How are systems analysis and design related to the general model of problem solving presented in this chapter?

6. What is a technology perspective on problems? What makes technology problems easy (or difficult) to solve? Give some examples.

7. What is an organizational perspective on problems? What makes organizational problems difficult to solve? Give some examples.

8. What is a people perspective on problems? Give some examples.

9. What are the three facets of decision making that are required to arrive at a specific solution?

10. What is the difference between a logical design and a physical design?

11. What are the key features of the logical design of an information system?

12. What are the key features of the physical design of an information system?

13. Describe the steps involved in implementing a system solution. What factors should be taken into account when implementing a solution?

14. Name and describe the most important conversion strategies.

15. What is change management? Why is it important for business problem solving?

DISCUSSION QUESTIONS

1.   Review the Herman's Sporting Goods example. With a group of students, make a list of the company's possible problems. Then make a list of solutions for each problem you identify. If you were a Herman's senior executive, which solutions (and problems) would you prefer?

2.   With a group of students, identify a problem at your college or university that you all agree is indeed a problem. Next, identify the technology, organizational, and people features of this problem. Last, identify some feasible solutions.

3.   Calculate the costs and benefits of each of the solutions you identified in Question 2. What does this tell you about establishing the cost-effectiveness of solutions?

PROBLEM-SOLVING EXERCISES

1.   *Group exercise:* Divide the class into groups. In *Business Week, Fortune, The Wall Street Journal,* or some other business publication, have each group find a story about a business failure or mistake. Have the group write a short paper describing the situation and the errors made in the problem-solving process. Have each group tell the class how it might have improved on the problem-solving process.

2.   Locate a small business firm in your neighborhood and interview the owner. Make a list of the five most important problems identified by the owner and a list of the solutions (if any) the owner currently uses to "solve" or cope with the problems. Write a short paper analyzing how well the owner's solutions fit the problems. Can you suggest better solutions?

3.   *Hands-on exercise:* One of the principal activities of a financial planner is to recommend appropriate investment strategies to clients. Individuals can invest in stocks, bonds, and short-term instruments such as money market funds and bank certificates of deposit (CDs). Each has a different rate of return and a different risk. Stocks are considered to pay the highest rate of return in the long run, but have the greatest short-term risks. Bonds promise a fixed rate of return, but their value can fluctuate, depending on prevailing interest rates. Short-term instruments have a lower fixed rate of return than bonds, but their value is stable. The financial planner will recommend portfolios that represent a mix of each of these investments, depending on the client's tolerance for risk and time perspective. For instance, retirees who need to live off of their investments immediately and cannot afford to risk losing their original investment are recommended to have 50% of their investment in short-term instruments, 20% in stocks, and 30% in bonds. Individuals who do not need to draw on their investment for at least five years are recommended to have 40% in stocks, 40% in bonds, and 20% in short-term instruments. The adviser might use a worksheet like the following to analyze the client's assets.

	Market Value	**% of Total**
Stocks	_____	_____%
Bonds	_____	_____%
Short-term	_____	_____%

Doris Heinrich has enlisted the services of financial planner Marlene Jamison to help her allocate her investments. She is retiring in three months. Over the years she has accumulated $19,000 in stocks, $35,000 in bonds, and $17,000 in money market funds and bank deposits. Use appropriate software to develop an application that Marlene can use to help Doris revise her investment portfolio. Use the software to create a portfolio that would meet Doris's needs.

NOTES

1. Linda Wilson, "Two Outs, Bottom of the Ninth," *InformationWEEK*, October 4, 1993.

2. We do not argue that all real-world decision making follows this sequence in lockstep fashion, but rather that it is useful to conceive of problem solving with this sequence. Some real-world problem solving follows this sequence; other sequences are possible, even likely. See Michael D. Cohen, James G. March, and Johan P. Olsen, "A Garbage Can Model of Decisionmaking," *Administrative Science Quarterly* 17(1972). See also Karl E. Weick, "Educational Organizations as Loosely Coupled Systems," *Administrative Science Quarterly* 21(March 1976); and James G. March and Zur Shapira, "Managerial Perspectives on Risk and Risk Taking," *Management Science* 33(November 1987).

3. John Hoerr, "The Cultural Revolution at A. O. Smith," *Business Week*, May 29, 1989, 66–68.

4. Penny Singer, "Long Lines Gone at Motor Vehicle Office," *The New York Times,* November 6, 1988.

5. Ibid.

6. Mike Ricciuti, "The Best in Client/Server Computing," *Datamation*, March 1, 1994.

7. See Glenn L. Helms and Ira Weiss, "The Cost of Internally Developed Applications: Analysis of Problems and Cost Control Methods," *Journal of Management Information Systems* (Fall 1986); and Donald H. Bender, "Financial Impact of Information Processing," *Journal of Management Information Systems* (Fall 1986). For large-scale systems, see General Accounting Office, "Automated Information Systems: Schedule Delays and Cost Overruns Plague DOD Systems," GAO/IMTEC 89–36 (Washington, D.C.: U.S. Government Printing Office, May 1989).

8. An excellent description of "strategic human resource issues" can be found in Alan F. Westin, et al., *The Changing Workplace: A Guide to Managing the People, Organizational, and Regulatory Aspects of Office Technology* (White Plains, N.Y.: Knowledge Industry Publications, 1985).

9. Calvin Sims, "Personalizing Software," *The New York Times,* July 17, 1986.

10. The interested student can consult more advanced texts for a full treatment of the subject. See Kenneth C. Laudon and Jane P. Laudon, *Management Information Systems: Organization and Technology*, 3d ed. (New York: Macmillan, 1994).

11. John Seely Brown, "Research That Reinvents the Corporation," *Harvard Business Review*, January-February 1991; and Michael Beer, Russell A. Eisenstat, and Bert Spector, "Why Change Programs Don't Produce Change," *Harvard Business Review*, November-December 1990.

PROBLEM-SOLVING CASE

A STATE-OF-THE-ART AIRPORT CAN'T GET OFF THE GROUND

Denver's Stapleton Airport has been the sixth busiest airport in the United States, with 1,600 takeoffs and landings per day. But the airport, built in the 1920s, was clearly no longer capable of meeting Denver's needs. Mayor Federico Peña (later Secretary of Transportation in the Clinton administration) decided that the airport needed to be replaced, and the project to build the Denver International Airport began in the late 1980s.

As the first new major airport to be built since the Dallas–Fort Worth airport opened in 1974, Denver International was clearly designed for the future. Its 53 square miles makes it the largest airport in the United States. The voice and data networks for the airport campus are almost exclusively fiber optic and can operate at 100 megabits per second. An even higher-speed network—2.4 gigabytes per second—has been installed specifically for use by video security cameras, allowing the airlines to monitor such areas as gates and jetways. The airport traffic control tower is the tallest in the United States and contains the most modern electronic technology. It is supported by not just one but two surface detection systems (which locate plane positions while they are on the ground); three systems are planned for the future. The airport construction plans were approved at a budgeted cost of a little over $2 billion and with a completion date of October 1993.

Each functional unit of the airport, including facilities, security, heating and ventilation, and airline operations themselves, has its own computer systems operated by subcontractors. One of the airport's most advanced features is its automated luggage handling system, which is designed to carry 700 bags per minute (the modern United Airlines system at San Francisco airport handles only 100 per minute). The system is controlled by a network of desktop computers that processes millions of messages per second. All bags are tagged with a bar-coded route/destination label and then placed on a conveyor belt, much as they are in other airports. Every bag is automatically placed in a fiberglass baggage cart, and the bar-coded tag is read by a laser device. Each baggage cart has a small radio transmitter mounted on it. Every 150 to 200 feet the cart transmits to the computer system its location and the bar-code information on the luggage it is carrying. When a bag reaches the conveyor belt that will carry it to the appropriate airplane or baggage claim area, the cart flips the bag onto that conveyor belt. The belts and carts are propelled by over 10,000 motors and travel at 17 miles per hour. The designers claim that the system is so fast that in many cases the bag will reach the airplane before the passenger reaches the boarding gate (see Figure 9.13 for an overview of the system). Like the other distributed systems serving the airport, the baggage system operates outside the control of the airport's information systems department.

Denver's system is the first automated baggage system to serve an entire airport. It is also the first where baggage carts do not stop, but only slow down to drop off and pick up bags; the first to be run by networked desktop computers rather than a mainframe; the first to use radio links; and the first to handle oversize bags (in Denver, usually for skis). The system can quickly reroute bags for last-minute gate changes or send them to special inspection stations.

FIGURE 9.13

Denver International Airport's Baggage Handling System

Designed to handle 42,000 bags an hour, Denver International Airport's computerized baggage handling system can move up to 20 miles per hour. The system is controlled by a network of desktop computers and allows airport handlers to track and pinpoint the location of any checked bag in the airport. Electrical problems with the automated system, however, have caused long delays in the opening of the airport. This figure depicts the way the system was intended to work.

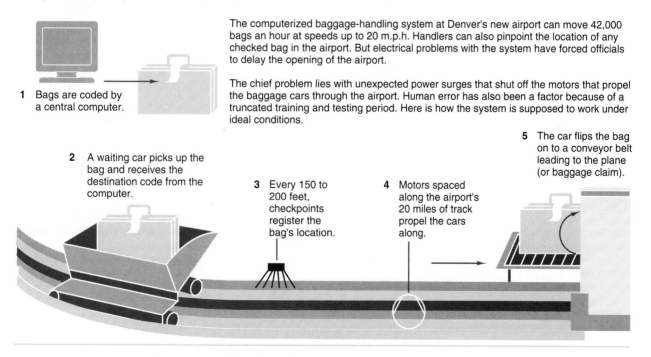

The computerized baggage-handling system at Denver's new airport can move 42,000 bags an hour at speeds up to 20 m.p.h. Handlers can also pinpoint the location of any checked bag in the airport. But electrical problems with the system have forced officials to delay the opening of the airport.

The chief problem lies with unexpected power surges that shut off the motors that propel the baggage cars through the airport. Human error has also been a factor because of a truncated training and testing period. Here is how the system is supposed to work under ideal conditions.

1 Bags are coded by a central computer.

2 A waiting car picks up the bag and receives the destination code from the computer.

3 Every 150 to 200 feet, checkpoints register the bag's location.

4 Motors spaced along the airport's 20 miles of track propel the cars along.

5 The car flips the bag on to a conveyor belt leading to the plane (or baggage claim).

SOURCE: "Spilled Luggage Grounds Denver's New Airport," *The New York Times*, March 2, 1994.

Troubles developed prior to the scheduled opening of the airport. Budget overruns exceeded $1 billion, so the final cost is now estimated to be about $3.2 billion. When problems with the baggage handling system appeared, the opening of the airport was delayed until March 1994. The system, which is owned by the city of Denver, was described as "the spine of the airport" by Michael Dino, an assistant to Denver Mayor Wellington Webb. Government officials insisted that the baggage handling system must be operable before the airport would be allowed to open. The system is being built by BAE Automated Systems of Carrollton, Texas. BAE president Gene Di Fonso wanted his company to be hired directly by the city to construct the system, but instead BAE became a subcontractor of a maintenance company which was hired by a consortium of airlines that will lease the system from the Denver city government. BAE also lost its bid to operate and maintain the system once it was built. BAE had built similar systems elsewhere, but they were all much smaller and operated at one-third the speed. When construction of the baggage system begin in mid-1992, airport construction work was already well under way, and Di Fonso was forced to accept an accelerated schedule. He agreed to the tight schedule but only with the provision that no changes be made to the plans. Di Fonso claims that in the following months city officials repeatedly made changes. City officials deny the charge.

The baggage system problems did not surface until the first test in September 1993, just a month before the airport was initially scheduled to open. Tested under realistic conditions, the system generated unexpected power surges that tripped the electric circuit breakers, automatically shutting down the motors. The city of Denver, United Airlines, and BAE all hired their own consultants. Special filters that could maintain an even power supply were needed to repair the problem, but the city delayed ordering them. As a result, the original airport opening was postponed until March 1994.

Although electrical glitches were the main reason for postponing the opening of the airport at that time, Di Fonso said that too little testing had been done to establish the reliability of the system. On March 9, 1994, with the surge problem corrected, a second full system test took place with hordes of reporters, photographers, and TV crews in attendance. When the system ran at full speed, bags flew everywhere, and many fell and broke open. About two-thirds of the bags were shunted to the hand-sorting area because the bar codes on the tags were too smudged to be read by the computer. The test was a dramatic failure, and the opening was again postponed, this time until May 15, 1994. The repairs to the system cost the airline consortium an additional $30 million. On May 1, 1994, mayor Wellington Webb postponed the airport opening indefinitely.

Other problems added to the complications caused by the snarled baggage system. Television monitors that flash flight information were not ready. A sign directing passengers to the baggage claim area led instead to a concrete wall. In the meantime, the old Stapleton Airport continues to serve the city, while the new airport costs Denver $500,000 for each day it remains closed.

Sources: Jean S. Bozman, "Denver Airport Hits Systems Layover," *Computerworld*, May 16, 1994; Allen R. Myerson, "Automation Off Course in Denver," *The New York Times*, March 18, 1994; Dirk Johnson, "Spilled Luggage Grounds Denver's New Airport," *The New York Times*, March 2, 1994; and Ellis Booker, "Airport Prepares for Takeoff," *Computerworld*, January 10, 1994.

Case Study Questions

1. Peter G. Neumann, the founder and manager of *Risks Digest*, an Internet forum on computer reliability and security, observed that an accidental glitch at an airport such as Denver's new airport could have a dramatic effect on air traffic around the country. Do you agree? Why?

2. Use the three perspectives outlined in the chapter—technology, organization, and people—to analyze and categorize the problems in the Denver International Airport construction project. Describe some of the possible interrelationships. Rank the problems in order from the most significant to the least significant.
3. What steps would you take to obtain a better understanding of the problems you identified in Question 2?
4. Take the project back in time to 1991, and in a short (three- to five-page) paper, design a plan that would avoid the problems encountered.

DESIGNING INFORMATION SYSTEM SOLUTIONS

LEARNING OBJECTIVES

After reading and studying this chapter, you will:

1. Be able to apply the five problem-solving steps to systems analysis and design.

2. Be able to devise and evaluate alternative systems solutions.

3. Be able to determine when a solution requires an information system application.

4. Understand the functional requirements of an information system application solution.

5. Be able to translate a logical or conceptual system design into a physical system design.

6. Understand how to use data flow diagrams, system flowcharts, and data dictionaries as tools for solution design.

Two straight years of business losses convinced management that Agway, the giant farm supply cooperative in the Northeast, was in serious trouble. Agway's 600 stores sold everything from cattle feed to garden trowels. The business, which operated like a retail chain, was supported by 18 warehouses and feed mills, a system that could no longer meet the needs of Agway's changing customer base. One of eight farms in the Northeast disappeared during the 1980s. Surviving farms were primarily large sophisticated agricultural businesses whose owners and managers wanted more expertise than store personnel could provide. Although Agway shipped many orders directly from its mills and warehouses, the farmers placed their orders at the stores. The stores then submitted them to the appropriate mill, plant, or warehouse. The net result was a costly tangle of bills and records. Agway's retail, manufacturing, and distribution facilities ordered from and billed each other—all to serve the same customer. Customers with billing problems had to talk to one, two, or three people to find an answer. A complaint might take several weeks to resolve.

Discount retailers like Wal-Mart started to take away general merchandise sales from Agway stores. Agway's ability to respond was hampered by its need to serve commercial farmers. Agway eventually solved its problem by splitting up its commercial and retail farming businesses and by deploying new information systems that made it more efficient and responsive to customers. It reengineered its entire ordering process so that farmers could place orders directly over the telephone to regional service centers. We show how Agway arrived at this solution later in the chapter.

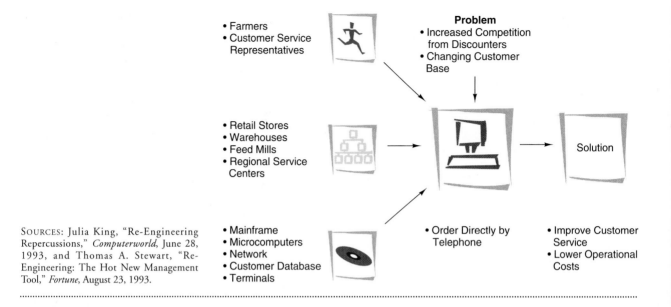

• Farmers
• Customer Service
  Representatives

Problem
• Increased Competition
  from Discounters
• Changing Customer
  Base

• Retail Stores
• Warehouses
• Feed Mills
• Regional Service
  Centers

Solution

SOURCES: Julia King, "Re-Engineering Repercussions," *Computerworld*, June 28, 1993, and Thomas A. Stewart, "Re-Engineering: The Hot New Management Tool," *Fortune*, August 23, 1993.

• Mainframe
• Microcomputers
• Network
• Customer Database
• Terminals

• Order Directly by
  Telephone

• Improve Customer
  Service
• Lower Operational
  Costs

The experience of Agway and other examples in this chapter illustrate how our problem-solving methodology can be applied more specifically to the analysis of information system-related problems and the development of information system solutions. The critical thinking skills you have learned in earlier chapters can be applied to a variety of situations. They can be used to analyze everyday business problems for which the answer lies in better procedures or better management. These skills can also be applied to the building of new information systems or the improvement of existing ones. As in Agway's case, they may even be used to help redesign organizations.

In many instances, the solution to a problem will be a "system solution." Indeed, this problem-solving framework lies at the heart of the analysis and design of information systems. No matter what hardware, software, and systems development methodology you use, you must first be able to understand a problem, describe it, and design a solution. Thus this process lays the groundwork for all subsequent systems development activities. Unless it is performed properly, it can result in major errors in a new system or even total failure.

Alternative systems-building approaches will be discussed in subsequent chapters. The purpose of this chapter is to illustrate the core problem-solving methodology that is the foundation for all of them.

10.1 PROBLEM SOLVING IN ACTION: DATABASE APPLICATION

Throughout this chapter, we use real-world cases to illustrate how problem solving and systems analysis and design actually work step by step. Our purpose is to focus on the process of analyzing a problem and visualizing the right business solution. Accordingly, we have simplified these cases for instructional purposes; their actual analysis and solution required many more details than can be presented here.

Database software such as dBASE for Windows can easily automate functions such as tracking clients and sales contacts. The database software not only maintains basic client and sales lead information, but can generate mailing labels and create customized input and output forms.

SOURCE: Courtesy of Borland International, Inc.

Let's start by looking at a fairly simple problem, one of a small start-up business grappling with a heavy load of record keeping and paperwork. For this case, as well as for all the other cases in this chapter, we need to answer the following questions:

1. What exactly was the problem?

2. What were its causes, and what was its scope?

3. What was the solution objective?

4. What alternative solutions were available?

5. What were the constraints on these solutions?

6. Why was a particular solution chosen?

THE PATIENT BILLING SYSTEM

Mark and Evelyn Springer are two up-and-coming child psychologists. After working in clinics for a decade, they decided to form their own private practice in Norwalk, Connecticut, an area with no therapists who could handle child disorders. Because of their excellent credentials and expertise with children, their practice is flourishing, and they have had to open a second office in nearby Bridgeport. But this leaves them with virtually no time for office record keeping.

Both psychologists must maintain detailed records of therapy sessions and periodic patient evaluations. They must also prepare a biweekly bill for each patient and keep records of payments. The Springers charge $95 per session, and most patients have sessions once or twice a week. Each patient's session is scheduled for the same day and time every week. The Springers find that they barely have time to maintain their patient evaluations, let alone send bills. Since they are still in a start-up situation, they do not have the resources to hire secretarial help.

In addition to patient charts, the Springers maintain patient records with the patient's name, address, date therapy started, time and day of the week for each session, and number of sessions per week. Do the Springers have a problem? If so, how can it be solved?

APPLYING THE METHODOLOGY

Step 1: Problem Analysis   The preceding case discussion serves as our fact-finding results.

Step 2: Problem Understanding   Once again, we apply our matrix and find that the Springers' problem involves mainly organizational factors.

Technology	**Organization**		**People**
Hardware	Culture		Ergonomics
Software	Management		Evaluation and Monitoring
Telecommunications	Politics		Training
Database	Bureaucracy	**X**	Employee Attitudes and Involvement
	Environmental Change	**X**	Legal and Regulatory Compliance

The Problem   The Springers do not have time to maintain adequate billing records or perform all the other record keeping required for a therapy practice.

Problem Dimensions   The Springers' problem has both external and internal dimensions:

- **External:** There is enormous demand for child therapist services in the Springers' area, so they are very busy.

- **Internal:** The Springers are in a start-up situation with very little capital or need for a permanent clerical employee. They have heavy record-keeping requirements. In addition to patient billings, very detailed patient charts and evaluations must be maintained. Higher priority is placed on patient charts and evaluations because they are critical to the treatment process. There is no systematic way to ensure that patient billing records are kept up to date.

Step 3: Decision Making   The solution objective would be to reduce the time and effort required to maintain patient records and send out bills. But we must also consider certain economic and operational constraints: The Springers cannot afford a full-time secretary or bookkeeper. In addition, they must maintain the patient evaluation records themselves and do not have any time left over for other kinds of record keeping.

Given these constraints, the Springers have three solution alternatives: (1) hire an office temporary to do the billing every 2 weeks; (2) develop an automated patient record-keeping and billing system; or (3) automate patient evaluations.

The most time-saving alternative would be an automated patient billing and record-keeping system. This would consist of a simple file with patient name, address, number of sessions per week, amount due, amount paid, and outstanding balance. Automating patient evaluations by using word processing would not save as much time as automating the billing process. Hiring a temporary to prepare bills would have little impact, because the Springers themselves would still have to keep track of payments on an ongoing basis.

Step 4: Solution Design The logical design for a patient billing and record-keeping system might look like this:

Inputs
  Basic patient data: Patient name, address, number of sessions per week.
  Payment transaction data: date paid and amount paid.
Processing
  Create and maintain patient records.
  Calculate amount owed by each patient every 2 weeks.
  Accumulate and total payment transactions for each patient every 2 weeks or on
      request.
  Adjust balance due every 2 weeks.
Outputs
  Semimonthly bill for each patient.
  Payment transaction listing that shows payment amounts and dates over each
      2-week period.
  Amount of bill and payment for each month.
  Listing of patients with overdue balances.
  Mailing labels.
Database
  A simple patient file with all of the fields for basic patient data.
  A payment transaction file showing patient name, payment amount, and payment
      date would also be required.
Procedures
  Input basic patient data when patient starts therapy.
  Update patient data for address changes or therapy session changes.
  Input payment data whenever a payment is received.
  Generate bills and mailing labels once every 2 weeks.
  Generate payment transaction listing on request.
Controls
  Reconcile checks with daily transaction listing report.

Several physical design options are possible. The Springers could use a time-sharing service. (A time-sharing service is a commercial firm that allows other firms to use its hardware and software for a fee for their information processing on a time-sharing basis.) A printer and terminal networked to the time-sharing company's mainframe or minicomputer could be installed in their office, but this would be too costly for such a small business with simple processing needs. The Springers require a very elementary application with small files that could be easily and inexpensively developed on a microcomputer using database software. Patient bills could be calculated with spreadsheet software, but the advantage of database software is that it could generate individual patient invoices and many different kinds of reports. This application requires flexibility and file management capabilities that are more readily available with database software. The microcomputer could also be used for word processing and other office tasks.

Figure 10.1 compares the physical design and sample contents of two files in the new system: the patient file and the payment transaction file. The designs were done on a microcomputer using dBASE IV or dBASE III Plus database software.

Step 5: Implementation The Springers would have to transfer required patient data from their manual records to the database. They would also have to develop and test the database software programs for printing the patient bills, mailing labels, lists of overdue payments, and payment transaction logs for calculating payments due. Finally, they

FIGURE 10.1

Physical Design and Sample Contents of Two Files from a Patient Billing System

This system, to be used on a microcomputer with dBASE III Plus or dBASE IV, is the result of applying our problem-solving approach to the needs of a small start-up business. The Springers must do a great deal of record keeping but cannot afford clerical help. The solution was to design a patient billing system that they could use themselves on a microcomputer. This figure compares the physical designs of the client and payment transaction files with the sample contents after information has been entered into the computer.

(a) Design of the Client File

```
Structure for database  :   A: CLIENT.dbf
Number of data records  :   5
Date of last update     :   01/01/95
Field Field Name      Type        Width      Dec
    1 LAST_NAME       Character       15
    2 FIRST_NAME      Character       15
    3 STREET          Character       25
    4 CITY_ZIP        Character       20
    5 TIMES_WEEK      Numeric          1
    6 AMT_DUE         Numeric          5
    7 AMT_PAID        Numeric          5
    8 BALANCE         Numeric          5
* *   Total    * *                    92
```

(b) Sample Contents of the Client File

Record #	LAST_NAME	FIRST_NAME	STREET	CITY_ZIP	TIMES_WEEK	AMT_DUE	AMT_PAID	BALANCE
1	Smith	Janet	33 Harmon Drive	Ossining, NY 10563	2	190	0	190
2	Harrison	Thomas	111 Cleveland Road	Danbury, CT 06601	1	95	0	95
3	Grover	Cynthia	88 Pleasant Ave.	Norwalk, CT 06888	1	95	0	95
4	Robertson	Hilary	99 Saw Mill Road	Danbury, CT 06502	2	190	0	190
5								

(c) Design of the Payment Transaction File

```
Structure for database  :   A: PAYMENT.dbf
Number of data records  :   3
Date of last update     :   01/01/95
Field Field Name      Type        Width      Dec
    1 PLAST_NAME      Character       15
    2 PFIRST_NAME     Character       15
    3 PAY_AMT         Numeric          5
    4 PAY_DATE        Date             8
* *   Total    * *                    44
```

(d) Sample Contents of the Payment Transaction File

PLAST_NAME-----	PFIRST_NAME-----	PAY_AMT	PAY_DATE
Smith	Janet	190	09/15/95
Harrison	Thomas	190	09/15/95
Smith	Janet	190	10/01/95

would have to change procedures for updating their patient files when they received payments or address changes and for generating patient bills.

In the Springers' case, a simple database was sufficient to solve their problem. An illustration of the Springers' patient billing and record-keeping system is shown later in the chapter.

While a well-designed database is an important element of an application solution, it may be useless if networking issues are not properly addressed. The Focus on Technology describes how one organization addressed these issues when it developed a network-based application.

FOCUS ON TECHNOLOGY

WORLD VISION CANADA LINKS UP

Attracting donors and maintaining their interest are major preoccupations for all charitable organizations, including World Vision Canada. The Toronto-based partnership within World Vision International, a global nonprofit relief organization, provides food, training, and care for needy children in under-developed countries. World Vision Canada relies on contributions from donors to pay for the relief, medicine, training, and other aid it dispenses. World Vision's 30-Hour Famine project, for instance, is a pledge-based "starvathon" in which participating students raise money for hungry children.

Because donors like to know where their money is going, what is happening to a child they are sponsoring, and what World Vision projects are in progress, it is essential that World Vision has ready access to its data. Donors are wary when charitable organizations cannot answer such inquiries. The reputation of the organization can be damaged, which subsequently causes donations to decrease. Fundraisers can also use such data to target donor prospects more accurately and efficiently and to speed the flow of food and training to those in need.

To improve its management of donor-related information, World Vision Canada developed a customized central database called Donor Centered Support System, which contains child and World Vision project histories and manages marketing, donation, and receipt information for tax purposes. The database is housed on an IBM AS/400 minicomputer that serves as a host computer for World Vision's wide area network (WAN). Once the database was built, however, the organization still had trouble accessing and manipulating its data in a timely fashion. Fundraisers in World Vision's 30 small offices throughout Canada could only connect to the database by using specially dedicated terminals. They wanted to be able to connect their microcomputers and local area networks to the central database yet use them for other purposes. They could not access services such as printing at remote locations that are available with the IBM PC Support software that comes bundled with the AS/400 operating system. Moreover, it cost thousands of dollars to link just one or two terminals in each remote location to the database at World Vision headquarters.

World Vision Canada solved the problem by purchasing a communications software package called PackagePC from Telepartner International in Farmington, Connecticut. PackagePC allows IBM PC Support software to be used with microcomputers over asynchronous dial-in packet-switched networks and eliminates the need for special terminals. If, for instance, the office for World Vision's Eastern Ontario territory in Kanata has a donor with a question, it can query the database remotely and receive the answer in less than a minute.

According to Tim Mills-Groninger, program director of the Information Technology Resource Center, a consultancy for nonprofit organizations in Chicago, most nonprofit organizations such as World Vision have trouble creating WANs. They can put together LANs quite easily, but linking up to WANs is more difficult.

FOCUS Questions: What kind of problem did World Vision Canada have? Was a technology solution appropriate?

SOURCE: Joanie M. Wexler, "WAN Gives Focus to World Vision," *Computerworld*, November 8, 1993.

10.2 PROBLEM SOLVING IN ACTION: SPREADSHEET APPLICATION

This case shows how a simple spreadsheet application can cut through a complex web of procedures and red tape in a firm with several hundred employees.

PARTNERSHIP ALLOCATION AT HASKELL, SIMPSON, AND PORTER

Haskell, Simpson, and Porter is a medium-sized New York City law firm specializing in trusts and corporate law. Its 35 partners and 150 associates generate annual revenues of over $25 million, with $5 million in total assets.

With user-friendly software and application development tools, microcomputers provide low-cost solutions to small businesses seeking to automate their recordkeeping.

SOURCE: Courtesy of International Business Machines Corporation.

Haskell, Simpson, and Porter's accounting department consists of a controller, assistant controller, and ten staff members. At the end of each fiscal year, one of the major public accounting firms audits Haskell, Simpson, and Porter's books, determines the accuracy of its financial statements, and approves the figure for net income.

In addition to a fixed salary, the 35 partners receive shares in the net income of the partnership. The percentage of each partner's share is determined by seniority and the amount of partnership revenue generated by the partner. Once the auditor approves the net income of the firm, the accounting department allocates partnership income. At year end, the law firm's accounting department also summarizes tax information for each partner, a task that requires numerous calculations of each partner's income and deductions.

The public accounting firm issues a first draft of financial statements during the first week in January, and then Haskell, Simpson, and Porter's accounting department finalizes the partnership income allocations. The auditing firm typically revises the bottom line of the drafted financial statements several times before the final version is approved.

Each time a change is made, the accounting department must prepare a new allocation of each partner's income. Each calculation is performed manually, including calculations for allocated partnership income, total income, unincorporated business tax, nondeductible insurance (which must be treated as additional income for tax purposes), retirement plan contributions, charitable contributions, and financial statement income.

Total income consists of each partner's fixed salary plus his or her allocated partnership income. (Total income is reported as ordinary income from the partnership on the federal income tax form 1040 Schedule E.) Each partner takes 6 percent of total salary for nontaxable retirement plan deductions, 0.3 percent of total salary for charitable contributions, 4.16 percent of total income for New York City unincorporated business tax (the law firm is a partnership), and 0.5 percent of total income for nondeductible insurance. Financial statement income consists of total income minus unincorporated business tax. It is reported as net earnings from self-employment on federal income tax form 1040 Schedule SE.

Mathematical errors are common, and the process of correcting them is tedious and even more time-consuming. For example, if the sum of the individual partners' allocations for an insurance deduction does not equal the partnership's total for that deduction, the assistant controller is forced to recalculate each number until the error is located.

In addition, the accounting department must prepare a tax letter for each partner listing his or her share of the firm's taxable income and deductions. This letter is required for individual record keeping and for preparation of the partners' federal, New York State, and New York City income tax returns.

Partners continually pressure the accounting department to complete their income allocation calculations and tax letters. During the past few years, several changes were made to the bottom line of the firm's income statement after the allocation calculations were completed. Since all the calculations are based on this figure, all of the partnership allocation calculations had to be performed again, which took an extra 3 days. Let's analyze this problem.

APPLYING THE METHODOLOGY

Step 1: Problem Analysis   Again, we can use the facts from the preceding discussion.

Step 2: Problem Understanding   Using our matrix, we find that this law firm's problem has both organizational and people dimensions.

Technology	Organization		People
Hardware	Culture		Ergonomics
Software	Management		Evaluation and Monitoring
Telecommunications	Politics	X	Training
Database	Bureaucracy	X	Employee Attitudes and Involvement
	Environmental Change	X	Legal and Regulatory Compliance

The Problem   Partnership allocations and tax calculations cannot be performed in a timely manner.

Problem Dimensions   The problem has both external and internal dimensions:

- **External:** The law firm is dependent on an external auditing firm for finalizing its bottom-line financial statement figures. It must base all of its partnership allocation calculations on input from an external source and work within a very narrow time frame to complete tax letters and income distribution for partners.

- **Internal:** Calculations for partnership allocations are complex and variable and require special approvals and bureaucratic procedures. The controller's office operates with primarily manual tools and technology and resists efforts to automate.

Step 3: Decision Making   The objectives here are to expedite and increase the accuracy of partnership allocations and tax calculations. At the same time, several constraints must be considered: The time frame for finalizing partnership allocations and tax calculations will remain very narrow because business rules require that the firm use an external auditor. The firm's internal accounting department is very resistant to extensive automation.

Given these constraints, the law firm appears to have two solution alternatives: (1) hire extra staff for the controller's office to perform the calculations manually once figures have been finalized. (2) Develop an automated model for partner income allocation that can be easily revised when bottom-line figures are changed.

The first alternative is not very desirable, since this process leads to mathematical errors and repetition of effort. The second alternative is feasible, provided that it can be done with minimum disruption to the accounting department.

Step 4: Solution Design   A system model for partnership income allocation would incorporate these requirements in a logical design.

Inputs
    Final bottom-line figure for net income.
    Each partner's percentage.
    Each partner's fixed salary.
    Unincorporated business tax percentage.
    Nondeductible insurance percentage.
    Retirement plan contribution percentage.
    Charitable contributions percentage.
Processing
    Compute each partner's gross partnership income allocation.
    Compute each partner's total income.
    Compute unincorporated business tax.
    Compute nondeductible insurance.
    Compute retirement plan contribution (deduction).
    Compute charitable contributions deduction.
    Compute financial statement income.
    Compute firm totals for each of the above.
Outputs
    Schedule of partner allocations.
    Individual tax letters.
Database
    A record must be kept for each partner with the following fields:
        Partner's name
        Partner's fixed salary amount
        Percentage of net income
        Amount of net income allocation
        Total income
        Unincorporated business tax amount
        Nondeductible insurance amount
        Retirement plan contribution amount
        Charitable contribution amount
        Financial statement reporting income amount
Procedures
    Input the net income figures after approval by the auditor and management.
    Mail tax letters and partnership income allocation statements to each partner.
Controls
    Require management's as well as the auditor's authorization of the final net
        income figure before it is input for partner income calculations.

Total all partners' shares of income and reconcile this total with the firm's net income figure used as input.

The physical design requires a very small file, with records on only 35 partners. Since the law firm does not need to have its own mainframe or minicomputer, the application could be farmed out to a time-sharing service. But the application is so small that it is most appropriate and cost-effective on a microcomputer, which could also be used for word processing and other office tasks. This application requires many calculations that are interrelated in a very small file. Spreadsheet software would be preferable to database software in this instance because it handles such problems more easily.

Figure 10.2 shows the physical design of the partnership allocation worksheet and a sample of the output. Panel a displays the organization of the worksheet, cell relationships, and calculation formulas. Panel b is a printout of the partnership allocation report. Data are extracted from the partnership allocation report for the tax letter sent to each partner, so the letters can be created much faster than before.

Step 5: Implementation   The firm would have to purchase a microcomputer and printer and compatible spreadsheet software. With the spreadsheet software, a template could be developed to produce the required partnership allocation calculations. Data formerly maintained manually (such as all of the partners' names and fixed income) would have to be entered into the template. The accuracy of the template would be tested by comparison with the same calculations performed manually. Procedures would have to be modified so that the calculations were performed on the template rather than by hand. The accounting department would have to be trained to use the microcomputer and spreadsheet software.

In addition to spreadsheet and database applications, multimedia systems are gaining use as application solutions. The Focus on People describes one such solution and the effect it is having on real estate agents' jobs and the entire real estate industry.

10.3 PROBLEM SOLVING IN ACTION: USER INTERFACE DESIGN

Sometimes a solution does not call for a completely new system but requires the redesign of its user interface. This problem focuses on improvements to the output part of an existing information system.

VARIABLE RATE MORTGAGES AT NORTH LAKE BANK

North Lake Bank is an old, well-established savings and loan institution headquartered in Montpelier, Vermont. One of North Lake's fastest-growing services has been supplying mortgages to purchasers of vacation homes and condominiums. The majority of these mortgages have been adjustable rate mortgages. North Lake will not issue fixed rate mortgages on condominiums, and many home owners have opted for the variable rate mortgages in the hope of later converting them to fixed rate mortgages when interest rates drop.

Under variable rate mortgages, the interest rate is adjusted annually. Effective September 1, the bank computes a new interest rate for the year, based on the Federal Savings and Loan Insurance Corporation (FSLIC) monthly median cost of funds index. This new interest rate is entered, via a control card transaction, into the bank's

FIGURE 10.2

Using Spreadsheets at Haskell, Simpson, and Porter: The Physical Design and Sample Output

This New York City law firm benefited greatly from a simple microcomputer-based spreadsheet (in this case, Lotus 1-2-3). Panel a is the worksheet that was developed for the partnership allocation system. The calculation factors are grouped at the lower left and are referenced by the formulas. The factor entitled "firm's net income" is the bottom-line figure, supplied by the auditor, that drives the rest of the calculations. Panel b shows a sample of the output, which displays the figures for each partner.

(a) Physical Design for Spreadsheet

PARTNER	PARTNERSHIP PERCENT	FIXED SALARY	ALLOCATED INCOME	TOTAL INCOME	UNINCORPORATED BUSINESS TAX
Donaldson, Paul	2.52%	48000	+$B5*$C$20	+$C5+$D5	+$E5*$C$21
Grover, Pauline	1.81%	48000	+$B6*$C$20	+$C6+$D6	+$E6*$C$21
Haskell, Thomas	3.83%	46000	+$B7*$C$20	+$C7+$D7	+$E7*$C$21
Porter, Arnold	4.42%	48000	+$B8*$C$20	+$C8+$D8	+$E8*$C$21
Simpson, Jeffry	2.76%	41000	+$B9*$C$20	+$C9+$D9	+$E9*$C$21
Thomas, Linda	3.12%	48000	+$B10*$C$20	+$C10+$D10	+$E10*$C$21
Westheimer, Charles	6.61%	55000	+$B11*$C$20	+$C11+$D11	+$E11*$C$21
TOTALS			@SUM($C5..$C11)	@SUM($D5..$D11)	@SUM($E5..$E11) @SUM($F5..$F11)

```
CALCULATION FACTORS

FIRM'S NET INCOME               $5,125,000
UNINCORPORATED BUSINESS TAX          4.16%
RETIREMENT PLAN CONTRIBUTION         6.00%
NON-DEDUCTIBLE INSURANCE             0.50%
CHARITABLE CONTRIBUTION              0.30%
```

(b) Sample Output

PARTNER	PARTNERSHIP PERCENT	FIXED SALARY	ALLOCATED INCOME	TOTAL INCOME	UNINCORPORATED BUSINESS TAX
Donaldson, Paul	2.52%	$48,000	$129,150	$177,150.00	$7,369.44
Grover, Pauline	1.81%	$48,000	$92,763	$140,762.50	$5,855.72
Haskell, Thomas	3.83%	$46,000	$196,288	$242,287.50	$10,079.16
Porter, Arnold	4.42%	$48,000	$226,525	$274,525.00	$11,420.24
Simpson, Jeffry	2.76%	$41,000	$141,450	$182,450.00	$7,589.92
Thomas, Linda	3.12%	$48,000	$159,900	$207,900.00	$8,648.64
Westheimer, Charles	6.61%	$55,000	$338,763	$393,762.50	$16,380.52
		$334,000.00	$1,284,837.50	$1,618,837.50	$67,343.64

automated mortgage account system. North Lake then sends out statements notifying each customer of the new interest rate and the change this will make in the customer's monthly mortgage payment. Customers are told to switch to the new monthly payment amount starting with the mortgage payment due October 1.

Most North Lake customers, especially the out-of-staters, pay their mortgages by mail. Until recently, each was issued a mortgage account passbook, which keeps track of his or her account (see Figure 10.3, panel a).

Amounts on the TOTAL line are entered by hand. They display changes in the amount of monthly mortgage payment, with the most recent payment amount listed on the right. The amounts in the other columns are entered via a passbook machine when

(a) Physical Design for Spreadsheet

RETIREMENT PLAN CONTRIB.	NON-DEDUCT. INSURANCE	CHARITABLE CONTRIBUTION	FINANCIAL STAT INCOME
+$E5*$C$22	+$E5*$C$23	+$E5*$C$24	+$E5-$F5
+$E6*$C$22	+$E6*$C$23	+$E6*$C$24	+$E6-$F6
+$E7*$C$22	+$E7*$C$23	+$E7*$C$24	+$E7-$F7
+$E8*$C$22	+$E8*$C$23	+$E8*$C$24	+$E8-$F8
+$E9*$C$22	+$E9*$C$23	+$E9*$C$24	+$E9-$F9
+$E10*$C$22	+$E10*$C$23	+$E10*$C$24	+$E10-$F10
+$E11*$C$22	+$E11*$C$23	+$E11*$C$24	+$E11-$F11
@SUM($G5..$G11)	@SUM($H5..$H11)	@SUM($I5..$I11)	@SUM($J5..$J11)

(b) Sample Output

RETIREMENT PLAN CONTRIB.	NONDEDUCT. INSURANCE	CHARITABLE CONTRIBUTION	FINANCIAL STAT INCOME
$10,629.00	$885.75	$531.45	$169,780.56
$8,445.75	$703.81	$422.29	$139,906.78
$14,537.25	$1,211.44	$726.86	$232,208.34
$16,471.50	$1,372.63	$823.58	$263,104.76
$10,947.00	$912.25	$547.35	$174,860.08
$12,474.00	$1,039.50	$623.70	$199,251.36
$23,625.75	$1,968.81	$1,181.29	$377,381.86
$97,130.25	$8,094.19	$4,856.51	$1,551,493.86

customers send in their monthly payments. The ESCROW PAYMENT and ESCROW BALANCE columns show how much of that monthly payment is held in an escrow account and the accumulated balance in that account. The LOAN PAYMENTS column lists the amount of the monthly payment actually applied to the loan after escrow payments have been deducted, and the INTEREST & CHARGES column lists the portion of the loan payment consisting of interest. The LOAN BALANCE column shows the outstanding balance of the loan.

North Lake has received many calls from customers complaining about their statements. They claim they are difficult to interpret and that the portion of the loan payment that consists of repayment of principal is not clearly spelled out. Sometimes the

FOCUS ON PEOPLE

WILL COMPUTERS REPLACE REAL ESTATE AGENTS?

Real estate has always been an information-driven business, based on informing customers about homes that fit their budgets and tastes. The function of providing this information to prospective home buyers was traditionally performed by the real estate agent, who was paid for providing information to customers so they could make a purchasing decision. Now, multimedia, on-line networks, and other information technology enable consumers to bypass agents and shop on their own.

Technology can furnish customers with much of the same information that was formerly provided by real estate agents. In some locations consumers can already order data to view houses from a CD-ROM disk or from an on-

line information service using their home computers. For instance, HomeView Realty Search Centers in Needham, Massachusetts, use multimedia imaging to showcase homes for prospective buyers. HomeView operates three automated viewing centers where home buyers can use touch screens to identify the house features or locations they want and scroll through digitized color photos of available homes that fit their requirements. The company charges no fee to buyers but shares the commission if it helps to make a sale. HomeView sends its own photographers to document the homes. HomeView's system consists of high-end microcomputer workstations and has mainframe-like storage capacity. Its database of listings is updated daily by the company's research and development staff. The quality of the imaging is so high that buyers can see cracks in the wall and vacuum marks on the rug. HomeView has almost 700 Boston-area real estate agents as subscribers and hopes to sell HomeView licenses and franchises nationwide.

Another information system application for real estate called ProSolutions,

created by Sector in Burlingame, California, downloads data on home listings, complete with digital color photos, to cellular telephones and fax machines. An agent can have access to the latest listings from Electronic Realty Associates' (ERA) comprehensive listings network en route to showing houses to clients. ProSolutions facilitates every aspect of home purchasing, from listing properties to applications for mortgage and insurance. The system includes software to help consumers apply for bank loans and software to track the performance of sales agents.

According to many industry analysts, such products will "fundamentally redefine" the role of the real estate broker. The National Association of Realtors (NAR) will probably lose its monopoly on the distribution and use of home listings. In time, customers will use CD-ROM technology or multimedia networks to locate home listings entirely on their own. Real estate agents will be needed only to show the homes and negotiate the deal. On the other hand, observes Harley E. Rouda, a Columbus, Ohio, real estate agent who served as NAR president in 1991, the current network of real estate agents is too well-established to be quickly supplanted by a more public, centralized source for real estate data. Systems like ProSolutions are helping real estate agencies to become a source of one-stop shopping for homes, where buyers can obtain listings, secure mortgages, initiate title searches, find insurance, buy homes, and even locate movers.

FOCUS Questions:
What problems are solved by using information system technology in the real estate industry? How much will information system technology change the role of real estate agents?

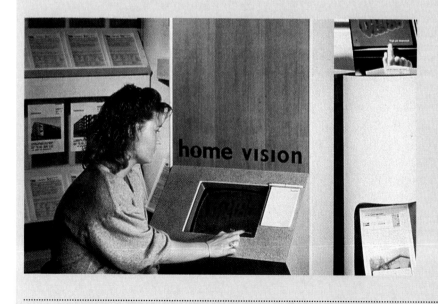

home vision

SOURCE: Chuck Appleby, "Real Estate Gets Real," *InformationWEEK*, March 2, 1994.

FIGURE 10.3

North Lake Bank's Mortgage Payment Reports: Old and New

Panel a is the old report. Amounts on the TOTAL line had to be filled in individually by hand, which sometimes caused trouble. If bank employees forgot to enter changes in monthly mortgage payments, customers would be unaware that the payments had changed—leading to some very angry telephone calls. Customers also complained that the old statements were difficult to interpret. Panel b shows the new report, on which the new software automatically updates mortgage payments and reports mortgage account information more precisely.

(a)

```
                          Acct. No 9999-99

   DATE     ESCROW      ESCROW      INTEREST    LOAN        LOAN
            PAYMENT     BALANCE     & CHARGES   PAYMENTS    BALANCE


   020193   12.00       24.00       492.29      530.86      58,268.08


   TOTAL    $623.41     $542.86     $
```

(b)

```
   ANNUAL RATE: 09.125    ACCOUNT NUMBER 9999-99
   DATE:    2/1/95


   BALANCES:
            PRINCIPAL               ESCROW
            $58,268.08              $24.00


   DATE     PRINCIPAL  INTEREST   ESCROW       LATE        TOTAL
   DUE                                         CHARGE      PAYMENT
   2/16/95  $38.57     $492.29    $12.00                   $542.86


   TOTAL PAYMENT DUE: $542.86
```

bank forgets to enter changes in monthly mortgage payments in the TOTAL fields. Some of the customers will forget to change their monthly mortgage payment on October 1. Those whose monthly mortgage payment has gone up will be billed a penalty for underpayment. Those whose mortgage payment has gone down will pay more than they owe. The difference will be applied to reducing the principal.

APPLYING THE METHODOLOGY

Let's apply our methodology to this problem.

Step 1: Problem Analysis   We can use the facts from the preceding discussion.

Step 2: Problem Understanding   As the matrix shows, this problem has both organizational and people dimensions.

Technology	Organization		People	
Hardware	Culture		Ergonomics	X
Software	Management	X	Evaluation and Monitoring	
Telecommunications	Politics		Training	X
Database	Bureaucracy	X	Employee Attitudes and Involvement	
	Environmental Change	X	Legal and Regulatory Compliance	

The Problem   Customers are making erroneous monthly payments toward mortgage accounts because of a poorly designed user interface. The Mortgage Department's time is not being used efficiently to resolve such complaints.

Problem Dimensions   North Lake's problem has both external and internal dimensions:

- **External:** North Lake's customer base is increasing, due to the Vermont vacation real estate boom. The bank's existing procedures are not sufficient to handle the influx of new customers.

- **Internal:** North Lake's procedures are very poor to begin with. There is no way to ensure that the new monthly mortgage payment amount will be entered manually on every passbook. Inconsistent information concerning changing monthly payments and interest rates is passed to clients. There is no management supervision to ensure that passbooks are consistently updated. Data in the mortgage payment passbook are broken out and displayed in a confusing manner.

Step 3: Decision Making   The objective here is to ensure that each customer's correct monthly payment amount appears on the monthly passbook when the payment amount changes. This must be done within the constraint that North Lake's mortgage payment system contains sensitive financial data that must always be accurate and timely. The bank cannot afford any errors or major disruptions.

Given these constraints, North Lake has two alternatives: (1) Tighten procedures to ensure that changes in the monthly payment amount will always be entered on the bottom of the passbook; or (2) Develop an application that produces an improved mortgage payment form, one that both notifies the customer of the correct monthly payment and tracks the same pieces of information in the customer's account. The application should also display the mortgage payment components in a clearer way.

Step 4: Solution Design   Alternative 2 was selected. North Lake maintained all the required data on its customer database internally and did not need any new inputs or changes to its databases. But the content and organization of its output document to customers needed improvement.

The logical design for this solution would mainly involve changes in outputs.

Inputs
Unchanged
Processing
Unchanged
Outputs
Design a new output document that can serve as both a mortgage payment coupon and a record of past payments and outstanding balances.

Field contents:
  Account number
  Annual mortgage rate
  Date
  Balance of mortgage principal
  Balance in escrow
  Date payment is due
  Amount of payment allocated to principal
  Amount of payment allocated to escrow
  Amount of payment allocated to interest
  Amount of late charge (from delay in previous month's payment)
  Total monthly payment amount
Database
  Same as before
Procedures
  Eliminate need to enter changes in monthly payment manually on mortgage payment passbooks.
Controls
  Same as before

North Lake did not need to make any physical design changes in existing hardware or files for its mortgage payment system. It did have to revise software programs to produce a different output report for customers. The new report, shown in panel b of Figure 10.3, serves as a turnaround document and payment form.

The bank also modified procedures so that mortgage interest changes were no longer entered manually on mortgage passbooks but were automatically updated on the payment report form.

Step 5: Implementation   In order to produce the new mortgage payment statement, the bank had to modify and test the output-reporting programs from its mortgage account system. No new hardware was required. The bank replaced its old mortgage payment passbooks with mortgage payment statement forms. No special training or documentation was required for this modification, since the mortgage payment statement is self-explanatory.

Another source of user interface problems is the design of data input or display screens. The Focus on Problem Solving describes how such problems can be created by inconsistent graphical user interfaces.

A BellSouth Corporation representative shows a customer the new design of a telephone bill. By improving the content and the organization of the output document, companies can make transactions simpler and less prone to error.

SOURCE: © 1989 Chipp Jamieson for BellSouth Corporation. Reprinted with permission.

FOCUS ON PROBLEM SOLVING

THE ROYAL BANK OF CANADA GRAPPLES WITH GUI STANDARDS

Graphical user interfaces (GUIs) are supposed to be easy to use. But if users have to learn seven different types of menus, if tapping the *D* key means *Delete* in one application and *Down* in another, many of the advantages of GUIs are lost. Users have to spend too much time learning how to make each new application work. If all applications with GUIs worked the same way, users would be more productive and less frustrated—standard GUIs would certainly decrease the number of calls from frazzled users to the company's help desk. Moreover, programmers would not have to start from scratch each time they developed a new application. The GUI standard would have a template for how the screen should look and operate, how users could browse a menu, and other GUI elements, supported by reusable program code.

But many companies do not know how to actually develop a GUI standard. Some believe that a consistent user interface design can be produced by creating a style guide for designers and developers. They buy a $2,000 electronic document of general design principles or rely on IBM's Common User access guidelines for the interface, but neither is sufficiently tailored to the specific needs of the company. Others mistake the Microsoft Windows environment for a GUI standard when Windows is actually a window manager that does not specify what should happen within the windows.

Companies can begin by creating a GUI standards committee to design the screens that fit the particular business needs of the company. The committee should gather data about users, the nature of the business, and the flow of work to identify the types of screens that will cover at least 85 percent of the company's needs. Such screens would include facilities for browsing, drilling down for more detail, and searching for data. The committee should select a real example of each type of screen and have technical specialists design the template for it.

The experience of the Royal Bank of Canada in Toronto illustrates that the hardest part of developing a GUI standard is not creating the standard but making sure that it will actually be enforced. The Royal Bank developed a GUI standard in 1993 but has experienced difficulty in keeping it updated, writing reusable code, and getting programmers to actually use it.

The bank wanted to reduce the amount of training and relearning necessary to use its applications. It developed successful working models of the standard screens but encountered resistance when it tried to get its software developers to use the standard rather than to create screens from scratch. According to Jamie Ingham, an internal usability consultant in the bank's information systems department, creating the standard was the easy part. The difficulty lay in getting it accepted. Ingham believes it will take years for the GUI standard to be widely adopted throughout the bank.

To surmount this hurdle, a firm can provide internal training classes and consulting advice to programmers. Proponents of standard GUIs can show top management that time and money would be wasted if the standard GUI templates were ignored. As a last resort, auditors can be assigned to shut down a systems development project that fails to use the standard. The critical factor is building consensus among the major interest groups affected by the standard and getting them willing to accept using it.

FOCUS Questions: What people, organization, and technology problems are solved by using GUI standards? What people, organization, and technology hurdles must be overcome to implement such standards?

SOURCE: Mitch Betts, "Standard GUIs Make Sense," *Computerworld*, March 14, 1994.

10.4 PROBLEM SOLVING IN ACTION: REENGINEERING

Sometimes the solution to a problem requires not merely changes in procedures or technology but a fundamental rethinking of the organization's goals and the best means to achieve them. The next case illustrates a problem that was solved by redesigning some of the core processes of the organization.

AGWAY

Agway's senior managers carefully reviewed its business strategy and decided to separate the retail and commercial farming businesses because the needs of these businesses were too different to be served in the same way. They decided to reengineer the ordering process used for sales to farmers to make Agway's farm business more efficient and responsive to customers. How and why did Agway choose reengineering as a solution? Let's put our problem-solving methodology to work again.

APPLYING THE METHODOLOGY

Step 1: Problem Analysis   The chapter-opening description of Agway provides sufficient facts for our investigation.

Step 2: Problem Understanding   Again we apply our matrix to find that Agway's problem was primarily organizational.

Technology	Organization		People
Hardware	Culture		Ergonomics
Software	Management		Evaluation and Monitoring
Telecommunications	Politics		Training
Database	Bureaucracy	X	Employee Attitudes and Involvement
	Environmental Change	X	Legal and Regulatory Compliance

The Problem   Agway was losing money because of a shrinking customer base, new competition, and an inability to service its traditional customers in an efficient and cost-effective manner.

Problem Dimensions   The problem had both external and internal dimensions.

- **External:** Agway's business environment is changing. There are fewer and fewer small farmers because changes in the farming industry favor large agribusinesses. These large agricultural businesses are willing to buy from Agway, but they require more service and efficiency. They do not want to take the trouble to visit stores to order.

- **Internal:** Agway had very inefficient ordering and customer service processes, with considerable duplication of paperwork and manual effort.

Step 3: Decision Making   The solution objective was to make Agway more attractive to customers and more profitable. Agway must be able to sell general merchandise at prices competitive with discounters such as Wal-Mart, yet many of its customers are commercial farmers with specialized product needs. Agway had three alternatives: (1) increase the number of store sales staff and customer service representatives helping farmers; (2) lower prices and focus on winning back customers from Wal-Mart; or (3) reorganize the business to differentiate more clearly between farm and nonfarm customers and to lower operational costs.

Agway selected the third alternative. It redesigned its organization so that farmers ordering farm supplies no longer had to go to the retail outlets. Instead, farmers could order all feed, crop, and seed supplies directly from regional service centers by calling (800) GO-AGWAY. It consolidated the number of ordering points to 15 regional customer service centers. Agway created an information system based on data collected from the point-of-sale system used in its retail stores. Customer service specialists can use microcomputers and terminals to access information on customer histories, credit information, and other data that are stored locally at the service centers and on Agway's Amdahl mainframe computer.

Step 4: Solution Design   To implement the third alternative, Agway simplified the ordering process. It eliminated the step requiring farmers to place their orders at retail stores. Instead, farmers can place orders directly over the telephone. The regional service centers receive the telephone calls and transmit the orders directly to Agway's mills and warehouses, which then ship the goods to the farmers. Figure 10.4 compares Agway's old and new ordering processes.

The solution also called for new information systems to support these changes. Agway did not build all the systems it needed at once. It installed an interim computer system for customer service that connects an older system that had been used by Agway's consumer group with two that had been used by its agricultural group. The result is an inefficient conglomeration of systems. For instance, Agway's customer service staff members can serve customers more knowledgeably by accessing background information on farmers' purchases, such as the kind of feed bought in the past. However, the system can only access the farmers' five previous orders. Some large farms put in five orders in only a week's time, so the system can't maintain enough order history data on them to be helpful. Although the customers are satisfied with the new ordering process, Agway realizes it needs new systems that will more fully support the use of regional service centers in the ordering process.

The logical design for this interim system would look like this:

Inputs
Orders (name or customer identification number, items ordered, order date).
Customer data (name, address, credit terms).
Payment data (name, order, amount of payment).
Processing
Verify customer credit.
Calculate order amount and outstanding account balance.
Transmit order to mill or warehouse.
Update customer database with order and payment data.
Outputs
Order invoice.
Order transaction listing.
Order status information.
Billing status information.
Database
Customer database with customer data and order history data.
Order file.
Procedures
Input orders on-line at regional service centers when farmers call them in.
Assign the same employee to respond to customer inquiries about the status of orders or problems with bills.
Input payment data whenever it is received.
Controls
Reconcile payment checks with order amounts.

The physical design uses Agway's central mainframe computer linked to microcomputers and terminals at its regional service centers. Agway's customer database is replicated at the regional service centers and at the company's central mainframe.

FIGURE 10.4

Agway's Reengineered Ordering Process

This figure illustrates Agway's ordering process before and after reengineering. The redesigned ordering process eliminated the need for farmers to visit retail outlets to place orders. Now farmers place their orders over the telephone.

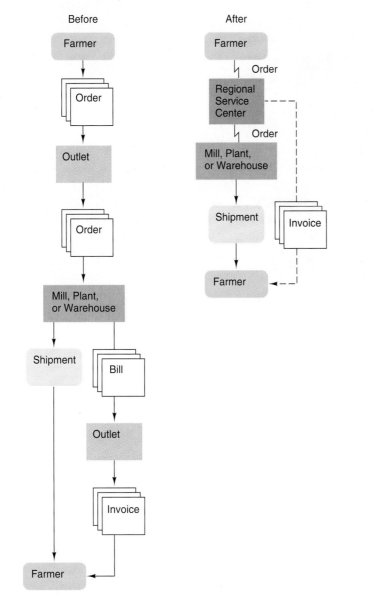

Step 5: Implementation After Agway reengineered, employees had to undergo extensive training. Agway eliminated the jobs of many clerks in its retail outlets and reassigned employees to the regional customer service centers. The firm retrained them as customer service representatives. These employees need continued training as new functions are added to their information system. Although the retraining process was largely successful, Agway had problems changing employee attitudes. Some employees could not understand the need for change.

Many companies conduct programs and workshops for employees that emphasize customer service. Employee training—whether in customer service or systems procedures—will often solve business problems and prevent new ones.

SOURCE: © Matthew Borkoski, Stock, Boston.

Although a reengineering solution may call for a new information system, the Focus on Organizations shows that the information system may represent a minor part of the solution compared with the larger changes occurring in the organization's structure, procedures, and culture.

Most problems you will encounter in the real world will be more complex than the preceding examples. Their solution will require in-depth research, analysis, and consideration of other factors, such as organizational culture or conflicting interest groups, that were not addressed here. In these cases, information system solutions were deliberately kept very simple so we could focus on the problem-solving process itself.

What stands out in all these cases is the importance of analyzing all the dimensions of a problem in order to derive the right solution. If an information systems application is called for, these cases demonstrate that the solution must be visualized first in business terms, as a business solution or logical systems model, before any details concerning computer hardware or software are addressed.

10.5 SYSTEMS-BUILDING TOOLS AND METHODOLOGIES

A number of tools and methodologies have been developed to document various aspects of the systems-building process. The most widely used are data flow diagrams,

FOCUS ON ORGANIZATIONS

FROM TAX DEADBEAT TO CUSTOMER

The Minnesota Department of Revenue collects an estimated $2 billion annually in sales tax from 151,000 businesses. Many of these businesses are delinquent accounts. Until recently, business owners who failed to pay were treated like criminals, and Minnesota's computer system immediately began sending them threatening letters. Out of $100 million in back taxes, all but $7 million was collected, but the process took 4 years. The average age of cases of late filers was more than 1 year.

The Minnesota Department of Revenue wanted to boost collections from delinquent accounts by $3.4 million annually. With a flat budget and a staff that was already stretched thin, the agency had to find ways of providing more service with the same resources. Several options were tried. A data analysis system was developed that can compare current filing results with typical filing patterns by industry or even by a particular company. The system looks for unexplainable patterns in return activity. For instance, if a music store files only $500 in sales tax, compared with an average of $2,000 for similar music stores, the revenue department would investigate. After employees pinpoint a potential compliance problem, they can use the system, which runs on an IBM RS/6000 file server networked to 600 microcomputers, to obtain more details about the taxpayer's filing history.

But Minnesota's major thrust was to change government's way of thinking about the tax collection process. When staff members went into the field to solicit comments and sugges-

tions, taxpayers voiced complaints that the revenue department had never heard because it was never asked. Many businesspeople found the tax payment process too complicated, confusing, and bureaucratic. For instance, if a business had a problem or question with its return, it had to wait up to 90 days for an answer. The customer's inquiry might be passed to two or three department employees before it could be resolved.

Instead of continuing to present citizens with an unresponsive bureaucracy, the revenue department believed that major results could be achieved by treating the citizen as a customer and improving customer service. Reasoning that if filing taxes were easier, people would be more likely to comply, the department tried to make filing sales tax a friendly, easy process. Tax forms were redesigned so that 80 percent of Minnesota businesses can file their sales tax with a simple four-line return instead of the two-page legal size form of the past. Businesses can file less frequently and can file their taxes electronically using electronic data interchange (EDI) and fax; businesses with small revenues can also file using touch-tone telephones. The revenue department eliminated the filing of estimated returns and improved service to answer businesses' questions about the status of their tax returns within the same day. The revenue department also created a databank of business profiles that could be used to help educate and train the state's businesses about how to file for taxes properly.

When a business is late paying sales tax, instead of sending another bill the revenue department assigns a staff member to call the taxpayer after the first billing is 10 days overdue. This new procedure has resolved 96 percent of late accounts within 90 days. Only 24 percent of delinquent accounts were collected within the same time by using the old impersonal billing procedure.

The new emphasis on customer service also helps the revenue department identify taxpayer problems earlier than before. It might discover that a taxpayer wants to comply but can't pay taxes because of business trouble. The revenue department can then direct taxpayers to resources to help them recover financial stability or put them on a payment plan. Revenue agents can make payment agreements with taxpayers over the telephone. The department also assists businesses that make mistakes filling out forms or that don't know how to file correctly.

Such assistance includes personal visits, phone calls, self-audit materials, complete audits, and classroom training. The revenue department sends tardy filers an industry-specific newsletter with filing tips. It dispatches representatives to work with businesses to prepare the next month's returns, and assists with self-audits. Complete audits are reserved for recalcitrant filers; the taxpayer is given every chance to pay voluntarily.

The change to a customer service orientation required the tax department to redefine its employees' jobs. The new civil service job, "revenue representative," emphasizes that providing information, education, and service to the taxpayer are just as important as auditing and collecting funds.

Response from the public has been overwhelmingly positive. According to Babak Armajani, CEO of the Public Strategies Group, a consulting group specializing in public sector reform in St. Paul, Minnesota, Minnesota's tax reforms demonstrate the effectiveness of putting the citizen first.

FOCUS Questions:
Was Minnesota's tax noncompliance problem a people, organization, or technology problem? Analyze the people, organization, and technology features of the solution.

Sources: Doug Bartholomew, "Not a Deadbeat, Just a Customer," *Information WEEK*, November 8, 1993.

data dictionaries, and system flowcharts. These can be used during analysis of a problem to document an existing system or during solution design to help visualize a new solution. They are most useful for describing large, complex information systems. Simple, microcomputer-based applications are often developed without these tools, especially if they involve only a limited number of data elements and one or two basic processes.

DATA FLOW DIAGRAMS

Data flow diagram

A graphic design that shows both how data flow to, from, and within an information system and the various processes that transform the data; used for documenting the logical design of an information system.

Data flow diagrams are useful for documenting the logical design of an information system. They show how data flow to, from, and within an information system and the various processes that transform those data. Data flow diagrams divide a system into manageable levels of detail so that it can be visualized first at a very general or abstract level and then gradually in greater and greater detail.

Basic data flow diagram symbols are shown in Figure 10.5. The arrow is used to depict the flow of data. The rounded box (sometimes a "bubble" or circle is used) is the process symbol; it signifies any process, computerized or manual, that transforms data. The open rectangle is the data store symbol; it indicates a file or repository in which data are stored. A rectangle or square is the external entity symbol; it is used to indicate an originator or receiver of data that is outside the boundaries of a system.

Data flow

The movement of data within an information system; a data flow can consist of a single data element or multiple data elements grouped together and can be manual or automated.

Data flows can consist of a single data element or of multiple data elements grouped together. The name or contents of each data flow are listed beside the arrow. Data flows can be manual or automated and can consist of documents, reports, or data from a computer file.

Data flow diagrams can break a complex process into successive layers of detail by depicting the system in various levels. For example, Figure 10.6 shows a general picture of the patient billing and record-keeping system described earlier in this chapter.

FIGURE 10.5

Data Flow Diagram Symbols

Data flow diagrams are a useful tool for depicting the flow of data and processes of a system. They can be constructed using only four basic symbols. Arrows represent the flow of data in a system. A box with rounded edges represents a process, whether manual or computerized, that changes input data into output. The open rectangle symbolizes a data store, a collection of data such as a file or database. Finally, a rectangle or square is an external entity that lies outside the system and serves as a source or destination of data.

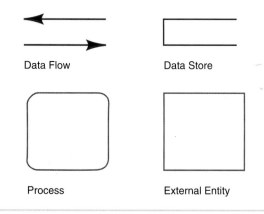

Data Flow   Data Store

Process   External Entity

FIGURE 10.6

A Context Diagram of a Patient Billing System

A context diagram is a data flow diagram that gives a broad picture of a system: a single process with its principal inputs and outputs. The process in this case is the patient billing and record-keeping system that we discussed earlier in the chapter. The patient and the therapist are the principal external entities, and the arrows depict the data flowing between the external entities and the system.

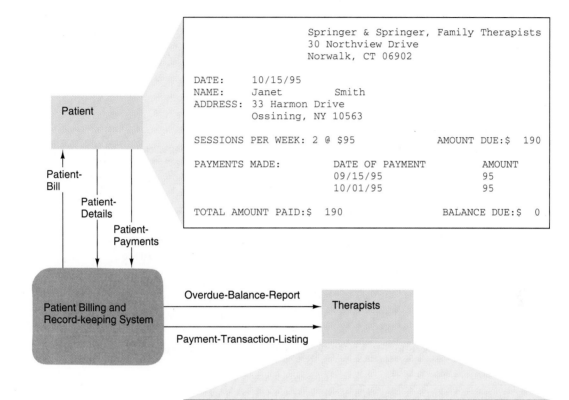

It is called a context diagram. The context diagram depicts an information system at the most general level as a single process with its major inputs and outputs. Subsequent diagrams then break the system down into greater levels of detail. Panel a of Figure 10.7, which is called a zero-level data flow diagram, shows the same system at the next level

FIGURE 10.7

Zero-Level and First-Level Data Flow Diagrams and Process Specifications

Data flow diagrams can be "exploded" into greater levels of detail. Panel a shows a zero-level data flow diagram, the next step in detail after the context diagram from Figure 10.6. Here the patient billing system includes three major processes: Capture Patient Details, Track Payments, and Prepare Bills and Reports. Panel b is a first-level data flow diagram that explodes process 3.0 into the next level of detail. We see that this process itself consists of three processes: Calculate Balance Due, Generate Bills and Reports, and Generate Mailing Labels. Panel c illustrates process specifications for process 3.3. Process specifications are a type of documentation that gives further information.

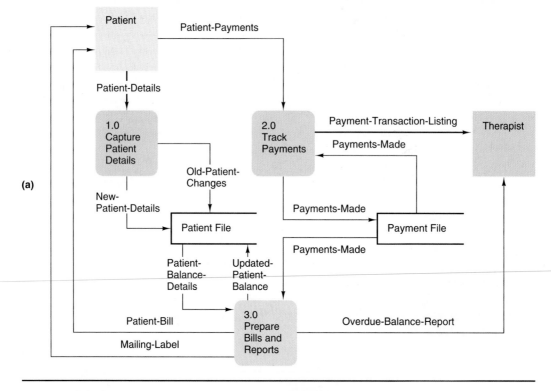

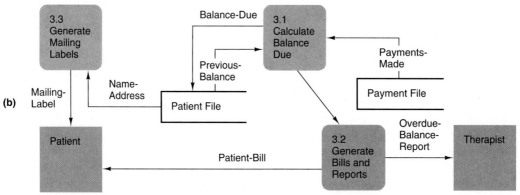

```
Generate Mailing Labels

For each patient in the patient file do the following:
     IF the amount due is greater than 0,
          Print client's first name, last name, street,
          city, state, and zip code on mailing label report.
```

of detail. It explodes the context diagram into multiple processes that are the major processes of the system: capturing patient details; tracking payments; and producing bills, mailing labels, patient listings, and other reports. Panel b is a first-level data flow diagram; it shows more specific detail about process 3.0, Prepare Bills and Reports. If necessary, lower-level data flow diagrams can be used to break this process and others into even greater detail.

Accompanying the data flow diagrams is additional documentation with more detail about the data in the data flows and the logical steps in each process. For example, panel c illustrates the **process specifications** (the logical sequence of steps for performing a process) for process 3.3., Generate Mailing Labels, in our first-level data flow diagram.

Process specifications
The logical steps for performing a process; they appear in documents accompanying lower-level data flow diagrams to show the various steps by which data are transformed.

THE DATA DICTIONARY

Details about each piece of data and the data groupings used in the data flows are maintained in a data dictionary. The data dictionary contains information about each data element, such as its name, meaning, size, format, and the processes in which it is used. Figure 10.8 shows sample data dictionary entries for our patient billing and record-keeping system. Panel a is a sample description of an individual data element from the

---

FIGURE 10.8

Two Data Dictionary Entries for the Patient Billing System
A data dictionary is a valuable tool for documentation. It "defines" each data element in a system by giving information such as its meaning, size, format, and the processes in which it is used. Panel a defines a data element called "Last-Name," which represents the patient's last name in the patient file. Panel b is an entry that defines a data flow, a group of elements that "travel" together through the system. This particular group is called Payments-Made. What information would you expect to find in that data flow?

(a)

	Data Elements
NAME:	Last-Name
DEFINITION:	Designates the patient's last name
TYPE:	Character
LENGTH:	15 positions
ALIASES:	LAST_NAME PLAST_NAME
FILE WHERE FOUND:	CLIENT.DBF PAYMENT.DBF
PROCESSES WHERE USED:	1.0: Capture Patient Details 2.0: Track Payments 3.0: Prepare Bills and Reports 3.1: Calculate Balance Due 3.2: Generate Bills and Reports 3.3: Generate Mailing Labels

(b)

	Data Flow
NAME:	Payments-Made
DESCRIPTION:	Patient's payment transaction
CONTENTS:	Last-Name First-Name Payment-Amount Payment-Date
PROCESSES WHERE USED:	2.0: Track Payments 3.0: Prepare Bills and Reports 3.1: Calculate Balance Due

patient file, the patient's last name. Panel b is a dictionary entry for a group of data elements traveling together as the data flow called Payments-Made.

The data dictionary can be in paper and pencil form, but it is often automated, since a large or medium-size information system application must keep track of many pieces of data, processes, and interrelationships. Data dictionaries are not used only when a new system is being developed. They can also be used to help an organization keep track of all of the data and groupings of data it maintains in existing systems. As discussed in Chapter 7, the data dictionary is a key component of a database management system. Data dictionaries thus provide a multipurpose data management tool for a business.

FIGURE 10.9

Basic System Flowchart Symbols

System flowcharts document the sequence of information flow and processing steps within a system. Notice that there are more symbols involved in building a system flowchart than in drawing a data flow diagram.

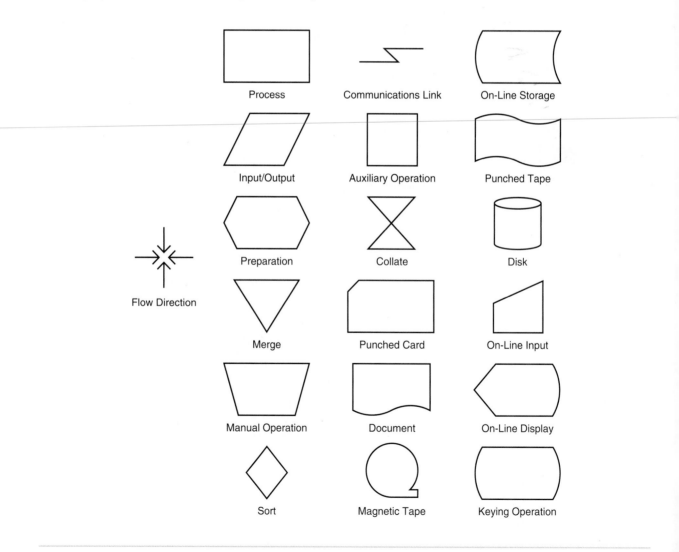

SYSTEM FLOWCHARTS

System flowcharts document the sequence of processing steps that take place in an entire system. They show the sequence of the flow of data and the files used by each processing step.

Figure 10.9 shows the basic symbols for system flowcharting. The most important are the plain rectangle, representing a computer processing function; the flow lines, which show the sequence of processing steps; and the arrows, which show the direction of information flow. Figure 10.10 illustrates how our patient billing and record-keeping system would be represented as a system flowchart.

System flowcharts differ from data flow diagrams in that more attention is paid to the sequence of processing events and the physical media used in processing. Data flow diagrams, in contrast, are a more logical and abstract way of representing a system.

System flowchart

A diagram that documents the sequence of processing steps that take place in an entire system; most useful for physical design, in which such diagrams show the sequence of processing events and the files used by each processing step.

FIGURE 10.10

A System Flowchart Depicting the Patient Billing System

This system flowchart illustrates the major steps involved in the patient billing system discussed earlier in this chapter. Note that this flowchart is more specific than a data flow diagram about the sequence and physical characteristics of processes, inputs, and outputs in this system. From the symbols, we learn that Payments and Patient Data both enter the system as documents and that they are then entered on-line. We can also see that the system contains two major files and produces three output documents and updated patient and payment files.

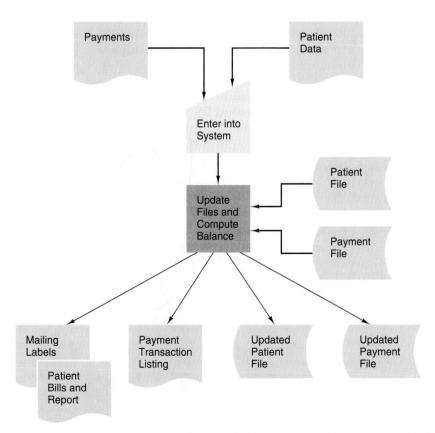

Data flow diagrams do not show the physical characteristics of the system or the exact timing of steps taken during processing.

STRUCTURED DESIGN AND PROGRAMMING

In order to develop good software, programs must be carefully thought out and designed. In the earliest days of computing, programmers wrote software according to their own whims, with the result that programs were often confusing and difficult to work with. Software today is expected to follow recognized design principles. The prevailing design standards are structured design and structured programming.

Structured Design   According to **structured design** principles, a program should be designed from the top down as a hierarchical series of modules. A **module** is a logical way of partitioning or subdividing a program so that each module performs one or a small number of related tasks. In **top-down design**, one should first consider the program's main functions, subdivide this function into component modules, and then subdivide each component module until the lowest level of detail has been reached.

The structured design is documented in a structure chart showing each level of the design and its relationship to other levels. Structure charts resemble corporate organization charts, but each box represents a program module. The chart shows how modules relate to each other but does not depict the details of the program instructions in each module.

Figure 10.11 shows a structure chart for a simple order processing program. There are three high-level program modules for the major functions of the program: inputting orders, updating inventory, and generating appropriate output documents. The structure chart shows that the modules for Input Orders and Output Order Reports can be

Structured design
A software design principle according to which a program is supposed to be designed from the top down as a hierarchical series of modules with each module performing a limited number of functions.

Module
A logical way of partitioning or subdividing a program so that each component (i.e., module) performs a limited number of related tasks.

Top-down design
A principle of software design according to which the design should first consider the program's main functions, subdivide these functions into component modules, and then subdivide each component module until the lowest level of detail has been reached.

FIGURE 10.11

A Structure Chart for an Order Processing Program
A structure chart is a tool for documenting levels and relationships within a computer program. Each box represents a module, a logical subdivision that performs one task or a few related tasks. We can see that the basic functions of this program are to input orders, update the inventory, and produce order reports as output.

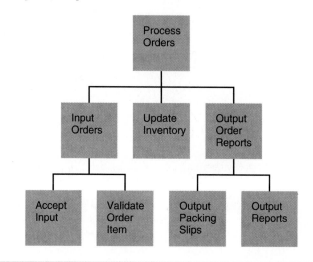

further broken down into another level of detail. The Input Orders module has subsidiary modules for accepting input and validating orders. The Output Order Reports module has subsidiary modules for generating packing slips and for generating various reports.

Structured Programming   **Structured programming** is a way of writing program code that simplifies control paths so that programs can be easily understood and modified by others. A structured program uses only three basic control constructs, or patterns, for executing instructions. These are the sequence construct, the selection construct, and the iteration construct (see Figure 10.12).

The **sequence construct** consists of a series of statements that are executed in the order in which they appear, with control passing unconditionally from one statement to the next. Panel a shows a sequence construct in which a program executes statement A, then statement B.

The **selection construct** tests a condition. Depending on whether the results of that test are true or false, one of two alternative instructions will be executed. In panel b of Figure 10.12, a selection construct tests condition D. If D is true, statement E is executed. If D is false, statement F is executed. Then control passes to the next program statement.

The **iteration construct** repeats an instruction as long as the results of a conditional test are true. In panel c of Figure 10.12, statement H will be executed as long as condition G is true. Once G is found false, H is skipped and control passes to the next program statement.

Proponents of structured programming claim that any program can be written using one or a combination of these control constructs. There is a single entry and exit point for each construct so that the path of the program logic remains clear.

Structured analysis and design embody a more traditional approach to developing software, which treats data and procedures as independent components. A separate

Structured programming

A way of writing program code that simplifies control paths so that programs can be easily understood and modified by others; it relies on three basic control constructs—the sequence construct, the selection construct, and the iteration construct.

Sequence construct

A series of statements that are executed in the order in which they appear, with control passing unconditionally from one statement to the next; one of three basic control constructs in structured programming.

Selection construct

A series of statements that tests a condition; depending on whether the results of the test are true or false, one of two alternative instructions will be executed; one of three basic control constructs in structured programming.

Iteration construct *(looping)*

A series of statements that repeats an instruction as long as the results of a conditional test are true; one of three basic control constructs in structured programming.

FIGURE 10.12

The Three Constructs of Structured Programming: Sequence, Selection, and Iteration
These three constructs, or patterns for executing instructions, are the building blocks of structured computer programs. Panel a shows the sequence construct, a series of statements that are executed in the order in which they occur. Panel b is the selection construct, which tests a given condition and then branches to one of two possible alternatives ("true" or "false"), depending on the outcome of the test. The iteration construct, panel c, repeats an instruction as long as the outcome of a test is "true."

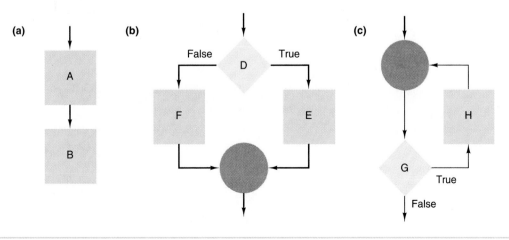

Structured program flowchart
A method of documenting the logic followed by program instructions; uses graphic symbols to depict the steps that processing must take in a specific program, using the three control structures of structured programming.

programming procedure must be written every time someone wants to take an action on a particular piece of data. Newer approaches to designing software, such as object-oriented programming, do not use such distinctions. (See Chapter 6.)

Documenting Program Logic   Two popular methods of documenting the logic followed by program instructions are structured program flowcharts and pseudocode. **Structured program flowcharts** use graphic symbols to depict the steps that processing must take in a specific program, using the three control structures of structured programming. Figure 10.13 explains the flowcharting symbols. The left portion of panel a of Figure 10.14 shows a structured program flowchart for a program that reads student records and prints out each record. The right portion of panel a is a second flowchart that details the steps involved in the predefined process "Process Records Routine."

FIGURE 10.13

Program Flowchart Symbols

Program flowcharts graphically document the steps that are followed in a specific computer program (as opposed to system flowcharts, which depict an entire information system). Structured program flowcharts are drawn using the three control structures of structured programming—sequence, selection, and iteration.

Process
Represents a group of instructions performing a processing function.

Predefined Process
Designates program instructions not detailed in the flowchart.

Input/Output
Designates movement of data into or out of a program's processing flow.

Connector
Links portions of a flowchart on the same page or separate pages.

Decision
Designates a point in a program where the decision construct is used and the program flow can take one of two alternative paths.

Terminal
Indicates the beginning or end of a program.

Flow Lines
Show the direction of the flow of program logic.

FIGURE 10.14

Program Flowcharts and Pseudocode for a Program that Reads and Prints Out Student Records

Somewhere in its information system, your school probably has a program that follows this logic. Panel a illustrates the program flowchart showing the sequence of instructions for a program that reads student records and then prints them out. Notice that there is a predefined process, Process Records Routine. To the right is another flowchart that represents the steps followed in Process Records Routine. Panel b shows the pseudocode statements that describe the logic in the first flowchart. Pseudocode is not a computer language itself, but it can easily be translated into a programming language.

(a) Flowcharts

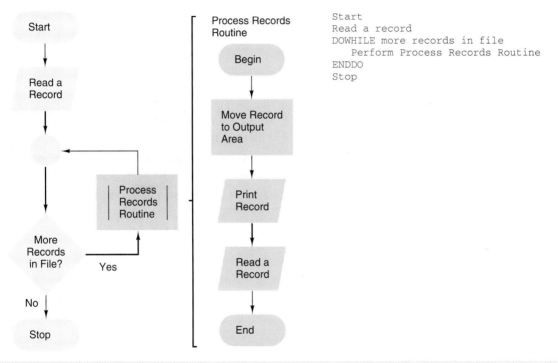

(b) Pseudocode

```
Start
Read a record
DOWHILE more records in file
    Perform Process Records Routine
ENDDO
Stop
```

Pseudocode uses plain English-like statements rather than graphic symbols or programming language to describe processing steps and logic. Once the outline for processing has been established, pseudocode can easily be translated into a programming language. Pseudocode uses the same control structures as structured programming. Panel b of Figure 10.14 shows the pseudocode for the first flowchart in panel a.

Pseudocode

A method of documenting the logic followed by program instructions in which English-like statements are used to describe processing steps and logic.

COMPUTER-AIDED SOFTWARE ENGINEERING

Special software has been developed to automate the generation of data flow diagrams, system flowcharts, data dictionaries, program code, and other tasks in the systems development process so that systems can be fashioned much more rapidly and efficiently. The automation of methodologies for software and systems development is called computer-aided software engineering, or CASE. Many different kinds of CASE tools are commercially available. The most sophisticated integrate multiple tasks, such as linking a description of a data element in a data dictionary to all data flow diagrams or process specifications that use this piece of data. The illustrated case concluding Part 3 describes the myriad capabilities of CASE tools.

SUMMARY

- You cannot successfully build an information system without first understanding a problem, describing it, and designing a solution using the five-step approach to problem solving introduced in the text.

- Even if a problem does not involve an information system application, the implementation of the solution will still require changes in the procedures, management, and personnel.

- Data flow diagrams are most useful for documenting the logical design of an information system. They show how data flow to, from, and within an information system and the various processes that transform those data.

- A data dictionary is used in solution design to define and describe each piece of data and the data groupings used in information systems.

- System flowcharts document the sequence of processing steps that take place in an entire system. They are most useful for physical design, in which they show the sequence of the flow of data and the files used by each processing step.

- Structured design and structured programming are software design principles that promote software with a simple, clear structure that is easy to follow and maintain.

- Structured design organizes a program into a hierarchy of modules from the top down, with each module performing a limited number of functions.

- Structured programming is a method of writing programs using only three basic control constructs: sequence, selection, and repetition.

KEY TERMS

Data flow diagram	Structured programming
Data flow	Sequence construct
Process specification	Selection construct
System flowchart	Iteration construct
Structured design	Structured program flowchart
Module	Pseudocode
Top-down design	

REVIEW QUESTIONS

1. Why should the solution to an application problem be worked out before hardware and software are considered?

2. How can you distinguish between a problem that requires an information system application solution and one that does not?

3. What is a data flow diagram? How is it used in systems analysis and design?

4. What is a data dictionary? How is it used in systems analysis and design?

5. What is a system flowchart? How is it used in systems analysis and design?

6. Define structured design and structured programming. How do they contribute to software design?

7. Name and describe the three basic control structures in structured programming.

8. Describe how each of the following is used in software development: structure charts, structured program flowcharts, and pseudocode.

DISCUSSION QUESTIONS

1. How would you decide whether an information system application should be processed on a microcomputer? How would you decide whether an application should be processed with spreadsheet or database software?

2. Why is programming such a small part of the development of an information system?

3. Why must procedures be considered in solution design as well as hardware and software?

PROBLEM-SOLVING EXERCISES

1. *Group exercise:* Divide the class into groups. Have each group use several levels of data flow diagrams, a data dictionary, and a system flowchart to document the solution design for partnership allocation at Haskell, Simpson, and Porter. The data dictionary need not contain all of the data elements in the solution, but it should contain a description of at least one individual data element and one data flow.

2. Develop a context data flow diagram and a high-level system flowchart to document the solution design for North Lake Bank.

3. *Hands-on exercise:* Use a structured program flowchart to document a program that reads a student file and outputs a report of names of students qualifying for the dean's list. To qualify, students must have a grade point average of at least 3.5. Then, document the same program using pseudocode. Use appropriate software to either write the program or develop an application that performs these functions. You can use the following list of students to test your solution:

ID	Name	Grade Average
323442373	Stephen Turkell	2.8
693920485	Carla Burton	3.6
405828451	Angela Myers	3.4
684092346	Timothy Shaw	3.5
583023988	Andrew Lund	1.9

PROBLEM-SOLVING CASES: SOLUTION DESIGN PROJECTS

RIVER EDGE SUPERMARKET

Profit margins in the supermarket business are only 1 to 2 percent of gross sales. The River Edge Supermarket in Peekskill, New York, is fighting against stiff competition from new Shoprite and Food Emporium markets several miles away. It has been able to survive on much lower sales volumes than its competitors by keeping operating costs to a bare minimum and specializing in fresh fruits, vegetables, baked goods, and natural beef for an upscale local village clientele.

Most products, with the exception of fresh produce, are marked with a price tag. The price of fruits and vegetables is calculated by weighing them and multiplying the weight by the cost of each item per pound. The cost of fresh produce changes daily and is posted above each cash register on a chart. However, some produce items, such as Idaho potatoes, are marked with a product code number, such as 547. The cashier at the checkout counter must consult the produce chart for the price of code 547. Sometimes the cashier rings up $5.47 instead. River Edge recently modernized its store facilities to attract more customers, and lines have been growing longer.

What is River Edge Supermarket's problem? How can it be solved?

THE OFF-CAMPUS HOUSING OFFICE

Finger Lakes University in upstate New York does not have sufficient dormitory space to house all its liberal arts, agricultural school, and graduate students. It uses a lottery system to determine which students can live in dorm rooms and which must find housing elsewhere. About half of Finger Lakes' students seek off-campus housing.

The ultimate responsibility for locating suitable housing rests with each student, but Finger Lakes offers assistance through its Off-Campus Housing Office (OCHO). OCHO maintains bulletin board listings of available housing and provides legal counseling services for students and landlords with questions about their leases.

Only 10 percent of OCHO's resources are devoted to legal services. Its most critical function is listing available housing in the surrounding area. Some landlords advertise in local newspapers, but virtually all openings flow through OCHO.

Landlords fill out an OCHO card describing the type of lodging they have available. This card is then placed on a bulletin board. Students review the bulletin board listings and copy down those of greatest interest. Then they call the landlords for appointments to view the rooms.

Cards are often put up haphazardly on the wrong bulletin board. Occasionally, a student will pull a card off to prevent other students from learning of the opening. Both students and landlords complain that listings remain posted several months after they have been filled. OCHO has no idea how many students actually use its services or the amount of student housing available. It does know, however, that around the time of the on-campus dormitory lottery, its office is jammed to capacity, to the point of being dangerously overcrowded, and students have difficulty seeing the bulletin board.

What is the problem at OCHO? How can it be solved? If an application solution is required, develop a logical model for the solution and determine whether it is a personal computer, database, or mainframe application. If the application can be developed on a personal computer, develop it using spreadsheet or database software, whichever is more appropriate. Justify your design and your decision. Document your solution design using data flow diagrams, the data dictionary, and a system flowchart.

VIDEO-SAVE MAIL-ORDER CASSETTES

James and Susan Branson found that they could make money in their own home by selling videocassette tapes through the mail at discount prices. They can sell a cassette that would normally retail for $29.95 at the video store for $10.00 less because they have almost no overhead expenses. Their inventory is stored in their garage and family room, and Susan Branson uses a home office with a WATS line to answer telephone orders. Many orders are also placed by mail as well.

The Bransons started out by advertising in several popular television and movie magazines. Now that they have a customer base of over 3,000, they would like to change their marketing strategy. Video-Save has an inventory of over 500 titles. Its full-color catalog with a description of each tape initially cost $15,000 to print and mail. The Bransons would like to find a more inexpensive way to contact customers, such as an occasional announcement of new releases or a special mailing directed to a special interest group—for example, purchasers of "self-help" tapes. They want to avoid expensive catalog mailings that do not bring in sales.

The Bransons recently purchased a microcomputer and printer with word processing, spreadsheet, and database software, but they are not sure what to do next. They do not need an elaborate accounts receivable system because all orders must be prepaid. Video-Save receives approximately 18 orders a day. Mrs. Branson uses preprinted invoice forms and types out the customer's name, address, charge card number, product number, quantity, title (product description), unit cost, shipping cost, and total cost of each order. The product numbers consist of five characters, with the first character designating the type of video: A designates adult-only videos; C, children's videos; S, sports videos; H, self-help videos; F, foreign films; and G, dramas or comedies of general interest. The Bransons maintain their customer list on index cards and have used a direct mail service to generate mailing labels for their catalogs and announcements.

Analyze the problem(s) at Video-Save. If an application solution is required, develop a logical model for the solution and determine whether it is a mcirocomputer spreadsheet, microcomputer database, or mainframe application. If the application can be developed on a personal computer, develop the application using spreadsheet or database software, whichever is more appropriate. Justify your design and your decision. Document your solution design using data flow diagrams, the data dictionary, and a system flowchart.

H. V. CONSTRUCTION COMPANY

Real estate development is a very high-risk method of investment, but one in which rewards can be substantial. In addition to a strong vision of a project, correct timing and accurate profit calculations are essential. Moreover, without adequate bank financing at supportable interest rates, a project will never be built.

The real estate boom of the past decade left the market very volatile. Costs of building materials and land spiraled upward, while an uncertain economy and high levels of consumer debt made the demand for housing much more uncertain.

Under such conditions, the H. V. Construction Company, a small general contracting firm, has been moving into development of residential townhouse complexes. H. V. hopes to combine its track record for quality construction with competitive pricing. To do this, the company tries to minimize overhead by subcontracting out most of the construction work and maintaining a small office with a skeleton staff. The permanent staff consists of only the owner, a secretary, a carpenter/superintendent, an additional carpenter, a general utility man, and a laborer.

H. V.'s owner, Harold Larson, feels this is the only way his company can compete with the development giants. But he finds himself overwhelmed, since he must find prospective properties, complete all financial calculations, prepare all proposal and correspondence documents, and shop around various banks for project financing. At present, he prepares all of his project estimates with a hand-held calculator. Any changes in relevant costs that alter the profitability of a project, such as interest rates, must be changed manually and retabulated.

Larson also knows that preparing a good bid is critical for survival. A sound estimate has double-edged objectives: it must be low and solid enough that the construction company will be awarded the job yet provide enough extra that the company can make a profit from the contract. If the bid fails on one or the other count, the company will soon be out of business. There is no margin for error. In bidding a job, there is no prize for second place. The company is either awarded the contract or it isn't.

The formula for a successful bid requires many ingredients: labor requirements, current labor rates, materials required and material costs, and total labor-hours anticipated. The cost of each component shifts constantly. When labor rates and prices from suppliers are volatile, the longer a company can wait before submitting its estimate, the better its chances are of being the low bidder.

The following cost components must be considered:

- Up-front fixed costs: Architect, developed lot, and legal and accounting fees.

- Sales and marketing.

- Total number of units.

- Cost of building materials per unit.

- Estimated labor cost per unit.

- Financing costs: Loan principal, interest rate, and financing period.

- Profit margin.

The company has a microcomputer with an 80-megabyte hard disk drive and printer. H. V. uses it primarily for word processing, and it has been a very cost-effective tool for generating correspondence and proposals.

Analyze the problem(s) at H. V. Construction Company. If an application solution is required, develop a logical model for the solution and determine whether it is a microcomputer spreadsheet, microcomputer database, or mainframe application. If the application can be developed on a microcomputer, develop the application using spreadsheet or database software, whichever is more appropriate. Justify your design and your decision. Document your solution design using data flow diagrams, a data dictionary, and a system flowchart.

Chapter

✦ E L E V E N ✦

ALTERNATIVE APPROACHES TO INFORMATION SYSTEM SOLUTIONS

CHAPTER OUTLINE

LEARNING OBJECTIVES

After reading and studying this chapter, you will:

1. Be able to apply the most important approaches for designing information system solutions: the traditional systems life cycle, prototyping, the use of software packages, fourth-generation development, and outsourcing.

2. Understand the relationship of each approach to the core problem-solving process.

3. Know the steps and processes of each design method.

4. Be aware of the kinds of problems for which each design method is most appropriate.

5. Know the roles assigned to end users and technical specialists in each system-building approach.

6. Understand the strengths and limitations of each system-building approach.

THE ARMY
ENLISTS AN
OUTSOURCER
TO DEVELOP ITS
NEW RESERVE
SYSTEM

U.S. Army Major General Gary A. Stemley said, "We had the Gulf War five years too soon." Stemley is a 1957 West Point graduate who was called back to active duty during the Persian Gulf War, as were many members of the Army National Guard and Army Reserve. Pentagon officials had difficulty during the Persian Gulf War obtaining such basic information as the number of fighting troops available from local National Guard and Reserve units. The thousands of Army Reserve units had unique computer-ized systems or had none at all. It could take several days to obtain the data from the reserve units' paper and electronic files for use by the U.S. military systems during the war.

The Pentagon recognized that it was time to replace this hodgepodge of manual and automated systems with a single nationwide Reserve Component Automation System (RCAS). The system provides the personnel management, equipment tracking and maintenance, supply, payroll, train-ing, and mobilization support functions that are required for the rapid mobilization of forces during wartime as well as for the daily activities of the Reserve units. It contains a database that holds unclassified, confidential, and secret data. The operating system allows individuals to access only the data that they are authorized to use. When RCAS is fully implemented, data needed for mobilization will be available in minutes.

RCAS is an ambitious systems project. It will link 60,000 users in 5,000 locations with 9,000 local area networks (LANs). There will be at least one RCAS LAN for every U.S. Congressional district. RCAS was cus-tom developed, with programs requiring 2,000,000 lines of Ada code. Its requirements specifications report was 35,000 pages long. The Pentagon *paid an outside contractor, the Boeing Company, $347 million to develop the system. Boeing won out over other bidders because its proposed solution had a more user-friendly graphical user interface and could flexibly accommodate future technology upgrades. Stemley, who became the RCAS program manager, noted that one reason the RCAS project was proceeding successfully was careful organization and homework. The requirements were very thoroughly detailed in the request for proposals, and solutions were left up to the bidders.*

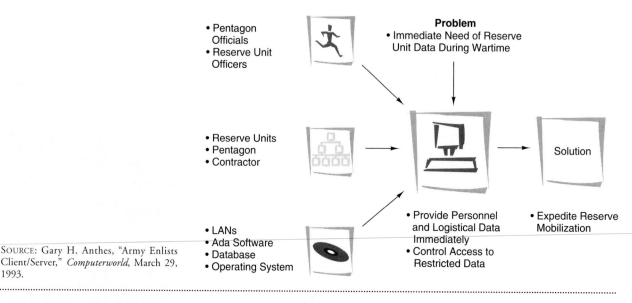

SOURCE: Gary H. Anthes, "Army Enlists Client/Server," *Computerworld*, March 29, 1993.

The Reserve Component Automation System was custom developed but its solution was designed and implemented by an external contractor. This approach, called outsourcing, is one of a series of alternative methods that can be used for creating information system solutions. Others include prototyping, the use of application software packages, end-user development, and in-house custom development using the traditional systems life cycle. Different problems call for different rules, procedures, and philosophies for building information systems. In this chapter we describe and compare these alternative approaches.

11.1 INTRODUCTION

The actual development of an information system solution can take many paths. The solution may require a large central mainframe connecting 20,000 people or a laptop personal computer, elaborate programming and testing or a simple word processing and graphics package. The problem to be solved may be fully structured or only semistructured. A structured problem is one for which the solution is repetitive, routine, and involves a definite procedure that can be used each time the same problem is encountered. For a semistructured problem, only parts of the problem have a clear-cut answer, provided by a definite procedure. Depending on the size, scope, complexity, and characteristics of the firm, different kinds of systems require different approaches to put them in place.

Some methods entail a more formal approach to solution design than others. Some call for clearly demarcated roles of end users and technical specialists; others blur this distinction. What is common to all of them is the core problem-solving methodology described in preceding chapters.

11.2 THE TRADITIONAL SYSTEMS LIFE CYCLE

The oldest methodology for building an information system is called the **traditional systems life cycle**. This method of developing systems originated with large operational systems in the 1950s and is still the predominant method for building large and medium mainframe-based systems today.

The "life cycle" metaphor partitions the development of a system into a formal set of stages, in much the same way as the life cycle of a human being or other organism can be divided into stages—a beginning, middle, and end. The systems life cycle has six stages:

1. Project definition

2. Systems study

3. Design

4. Programming

5. Installation

6. Postimplementation

Each stage is assigned activities that must be completed before the next stage can begin. Thus the system must be developed sequentially, stage by stage. Formal sign-offs, or agreements between technical staff and business specialists, are required to mark the completion of each stage.

Another characteristic of life cycle methodology is its clear-cut, formal division of labor between business specialists and technical specialists. Much of the solution design is relegated to technical staff such as professional systems analysts and programmers. Systems analysts are responsible for the analysis of problems in existing systems and for solution design specifications. Programmers are responsible for coding and testing the software components of a system. Both analysts and programmers use information and feedback provided by business specialists to guide their work, but the business specialists play a relatively passive role.

Traditional systems life cycle
The oldest methodology for building an information system; consists of six stages (project definition, systems study, design, programming, installation, and postimplementation) that must be completed sequentially.

THE RELATIONSHIP OF THE LIFE CYCLE TO PROBLEM SOLVING

The stages of the life cycle correspond to some degree to the steps in our problem-solving methodology. Figure 11.1 illustrates the stages of the life cycle, the corresponding steps in problem solving, and the appropriate division of labor between end

FIGURE 11.1

The Systems Development Life Cycle

The traditional approach to building an information system is the systems development life cycle, so called because it divides the process into a series of stages (similar to the life cycle of a human being). These stages correspond to the steps in the five-step problem solving process that we discussed in earlier chapters. As this diagram shows, the systems life cycle can be a very formal process. Each step of the cycle requires certain tasks from both end users and technical specialists, although with this approach, end users play a relatively passive role.

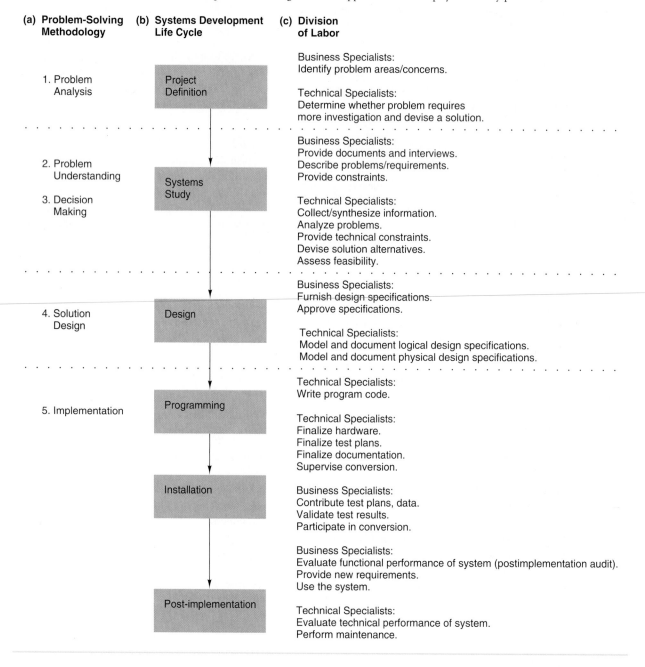

(a) Problem-Solving Methodology	(b) Systems Development Life Cycle	(c) Division of Labor
1. Problem Analysis	Project Definition	Business Specialists: Identify problem areas/concerns. Technical Specialists: Determine whether problem requires more investigation and devise a solution.
2. Problem Understanding 3. Decision Making	Systems Study	Business Specialists: Provide documents and interviews. Describe problems/requirements. Provide constraints. Technical Specialists: Collect/synthesize information. Analyze problems. Provide technical constraints. Devise solution alternatives. Assess feasibility.
4. Solution Design	Design	Business Specialists: Furnish design specifications. Approve specifications. Technical Specialists: Model and document logical design specifications. Model and document physical design specifications.
5. Implementation	Programming	Technical Specialists: Write program code. Technical Specialists: Finalize hardware. Finalize test plans. Finalize documentation. Supervise conversion.
	Installation	Business Specialists: Contribute test plans, data. Validate test results. Participate in conversion.
	Post-implementation	Business Specialists: Evaluate functional performance of system (postimplementation audit). Provide new requirements. Use the system. Technical Specialists: Evaluate technical performance of system. Perform maintenance.

users and technical specialists throughout the cycle. Notice that there is not always a one-to-one correlation between stages in problem solving and the systems life cycle, but they follow a similar process. The **project definition** stage of the life cycle investigates whether a problem actually exists and whether it requires further analysis and research. If so, a formal project to build a new information system or modify an existing system will be initiated. Thus this stage incorporates some aspects of our first step in problem solving.

The **systems study** stage incorporates some of the first step of problem analysis as well as the next two steps. Activities during this stage focus on describing and analyzing problems of existing systems, specifying solution objectives, describing potential solutions, and evaluating various solution alternatives. Constraints on solutions and the feasibility of each solution alternative are examined.

All of the information gathered from studying existing systems and interviewing business specialists will be used to specify information requirements. A systems solution must identify who needs what information, where, when, and how. The requirements must be specified in detail, down to the last piece of data, and must consider organizational procedures and constraints as well as hardware, software, and data.

It is important to emphasize that an information system solution will not work unless it is built around the correct set of requirements. If it is not, the system will have to be revised or discarded, often with a great waste of time and money. Perhaps the most difficult aspect of system building is capturing complex information needs when there are disagreements among users, poorly defined procedures, and data that are not clearly understood.

Once requirements have been captured, the design stage can proceed. At this point, logical design specifications are generated, usually with voluminous formal documentation and paperwork. Design and documentation tools such as the data flow diagram, data dictionary, and system flowchart introduced in Chapter 10 are likely to be employed because the life cycle puts so much emphasis on detailed specifications and paperwork. Business specialists and technical staff must review and approve these documents before physical design and programming can begin.

During the *programming* stage, detailed design specifications for files, processes, reports, and input transactions are translated into software for the proposed information system. Technical specialists will write customized program code using a conventional programming language, such as COBOL, FORTRAN, or a high-productivity fourth-generation language.

There is a widespread misconception that programming is the focal point of building an information system. In fact, the programming stage typically occupies only 10 percent of the system development effort. The bulk of time and resources are spent investigating and analyzing the problem, generating design specifications, and testing and installing the system.

During the *installation* stage, the software is tested to make sure it performs properly from both a technical and functional, or business, standpoint, and the old system is converted to the new one. Business and technical specialists are trained to use the new system. The activities surrounding programming, testing, conversion, and training correspond to the fifth and last step of our problem-solving methodology.

The systems life cycle also includes a stage for using and evaluating a system after it is installed. This is called the **postimplementation** stage. When a system is actually used on a day-to-day basis as the system of record, it is in production. At this point, it will be evaluated by both business and technical specialists to determine if the solution objectives specified earlier have been met. This formal evaluation is called the postimplementation audit.

The results of the audit may call for changes in hardware, software, procedures, or documentation to fine-tune the system. In addition, systems may have to be modified over the years to meet new information requirements or increase processing efficiency. Such changes to systems after they are in production are called maintenance.

Project definition
The process of investigating a perceived problem to determine whether a problem actually exists and, if so, whether it requires further analysis and research; the first stage of the traditional systems life cycle.

Systems study
The process of describing and analyzing problems of existing systems, specifying solution objectives, describing potential solutions, and evaluating various solution alternatives; the second stage of the traditional systems life cycle.

Postimplementation
The use and evaluation of a new system after it is installed; the last stage of the traditional systems life cycle.

The bulk of time and resources needed to build an information system is not spent programming. When William M. Mercer, Inc., was hired by Bechtel Group, Inc., one of the world's largest multinational engineering firms, to evaluate its employee benefits program, the team analyzed and evaluated existing benefits and alternatives; obtained management's opinion on cost and administrative concerns and employees' reaction to the existing plan; and designed several alternative plans, using a computer system to project costs and administration. After Bechtel selected its final plan, Mercer used its enrollment and administration computer system to implement it.
SOURCE: © Steve Chenn/Westlight.

As time goes on, an information system may require increasing amounts of maintenance to continue meeting solution objectives. When maintenance becomes overwhelming, the system is usually considered to have come to the end of its useful lifespan. The problem-solving process initiates a call for a completely new system.

PROBLEMS WITH THE LIFE CYCLE

Large mainframe- or minicomputer-based systems and systems with highly complex technical requirements will continue to use the traditional life cycle methodology. But 90 percent of today's applications will be based on workstations and microcomputers. Generating the paperwork and voluminous specifications and sign-off documents for life cycle methodology is very time-consuming and costly and may delay the installation of a system for several years.

Moreover, this approach may not be appropriate for simpler, less structured, and more individualized applications such as personal computer workstations or systems for which there are no well-defined models or procedures. The life cycle methodology is rather rigid and inflexible. Volumes of new documents must be generated and steps repeated if requirements and specifications have to be revised. Consequently, the methodology encourages freezing of specifications early in the development process. If a system solution cannot be visualized immediately—as is often the case with decision-oriented applications (see Chapter 16)—this methodology will not help.

Many firms have a two- to three-year backlog of application solutions requested by business specialists that cannot be implemented because of shortages of time, financial resources, and data processing personnel. Alternative system-building approaches focus on ways of reducing the time, cost, and inefficiencies of solution design.

ALTERNATIVES TO THE LIFE CYCLE

There are other ways of building information systems that can overcome some of the limitations of the life cycle. They too are founded on the problem-solving methodology we have outlined. However, the means of establishing requirements, developing software, and finalizing the system solution differ from the traditional life cycle, and business specialists play a much larger role in the solution design process. The usefulness of alternative solution design approaches depends on the nature of the information system solution and the level of uncertainty in establishing information requirements. The most important alternatives to the traditional life cycle are prototyping, the use of software packages, fourth-generation development, and outsourcing.

Prototyping entails building an experimental system or part of a system quickly and cheaply so that end users can evaluate it. As users interact with this prototype, they get a better idea of what their needs are, and the features of the final system can be adapted accordingly.

Application software packages are an alternative to writing software programs and developing a custom system internally. Instead, a firm can buy a software package in which all of the programs have already been written and tested and all of the input and output forms and screens have been designed. Software packages are most appropriate when the information system solution is one required by many organizations, and software packages to meet such needs are on the market.

Fourth-generation development promotes the development of information systems with little or no formal assistance from technical specialists. This approach is useful for smaller informal systems and for personal computer applications such as desktop

Prototyping
Building an experimental, or preliminary, system or part of a system for business specialists to try out and evaluate.

Fourth-generation development
The construction of information systems with little or no formal assistance from technical specialists; useful for smaller, informal systems and personal computer applications.

file management or graphics applications. Much of the solution design process can be performed by end users themselves. When users understand the requirements, they can design their own information system solutions with user-friendly fourth-generation software tools.

Outsourcing involves using an external vendor to develop (or operate) an organization's information systems. The organization develops an application solution using the resources of the vendor instead of its own internal information system staff. This approach is useful when the organization lacks the financial or technical resources to develop systems on its own.

Outsourcing
Using an external vendor of computer services to develop or operate an organization's information systems.

11.3 THE PROTOTYPING ALTERNATIVE

A prototype is a preliminary model of a system solution for end-users to interact with and analyze. The prototype is constructed quickly and cheaply, within days or weeks, using microcomputer software or fourth-generation software tools. End users try out this experimental model to see how well it meets their requirements. In the process, they may discover new requirements they overlooked, or they may suggest areas for improvement. The prototype is then modified, turned over to end users again, and enhanced over and over until it conforms exactly to what they want.

With prototyping, solution design is less formal than with the life cycle methodology. Instead of investigating and analyzing a problem in detail, prototyping quickly generates a solution design, assuming an application solution is called for. Requirements are determined dynamically as the prototype is constructed. Problem analysis, problem understanding, decision making, and solution design are rolled into one.

The prototyping approach is more explicitly iterative than traditional life cycle methodology. The steps to develop a solution can be repeated over and over again. Unlike the traditional life cycle, which must capture the correct version of a system the first time around, prototyping encourages experimentation and repeated design changes. Prototyping is also highly interactive, with end users working directly with solution designs at a much earlier stage of the development process.

Compared with the traditional life cycle, prototyping calls for more intensive involvement of business specialists in the problem-solving process. Business specialists must be in close contact with the technical specialists who fashion the prototype. With fourth-generation or microcomputer-based software tools, end users may actually design the prototype themselves. (This is discussed in more detail later in this chapter.) They will also have to make frequent decisions about further improvements each time the prototype is revised.

STEPS IN PROTOTYPING

As Figure 11.2 illustrates, prototyping involves four steps, which incorporate the steps of our problem-solving methodology:

1. **Identify preliminary requirements:** A technical specialist or analyst will work briefly with the business specialist to capture a basic solution model and information needs. The process is more rapid and less formal than life cycle methodology. Several steps of solution design are consolidated into one.

2. **Develop a working prototype:** A functioning prototype will be created rapidly. It may consist of only on-line screens or reports for a proposed system or an entire system with very small files of data.

At Du Pont European Technical Center near Geneva, Switzerland, a solid imaging system creates prototypes to assist customers in selecting the most appropriate engineering polymer for their projects. Prototypes allow users to handle experimental models, make improvements, and work out problems before final specifications are implemented.

SOURCE: Courtesy of Du Pont Company.

FIGURE 11.2

Prototyping: A Quicker Way to Develop a System

Prototyping can be faster and often cheaper than going through the more formal systems development life cycle. It involves constructing a prototype, or preliminary model, of a system aimed at solving users' needs. The end users then try out this model and suggest ways to refine it. The technical specialists enhance the prototype, and the users try it again. This process continues—as shown by the repetitive construct in this diagram—until the prototype is acceptable. Only then is the final version produced.

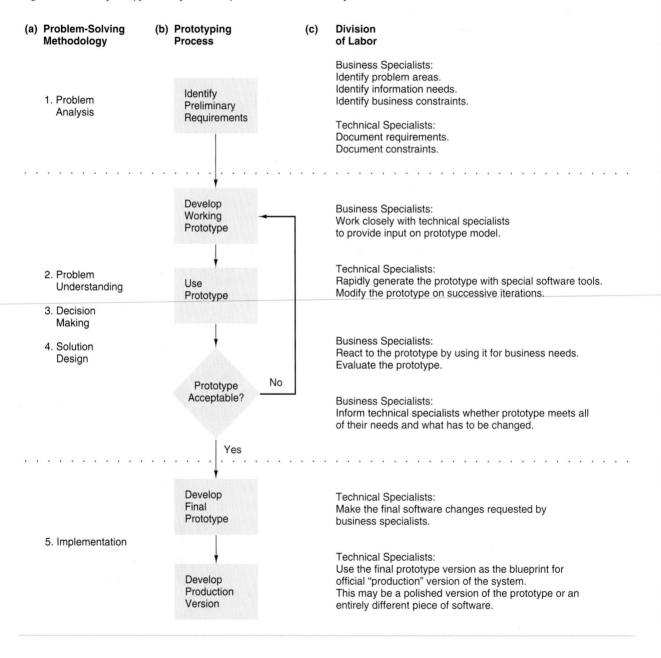

3. **Use the prototype:** The end-user works with the prototype to see how well it meets his or her needs. The user is encouraged to make recommendations for improving the prototype.

4. **Revise and enhance the prototype:** On the basis of end-user recommendations, the technical specialist or analyst revises the prototype. The cycle then returns to step 3. Steps 2, 3, and 4 are repeated over and over again until the user is completely satisfied. The approved prototype furnishes the final specifications for the information system solution. Sometimes the prototype itself becomes the final version of the system.

WHEN TO USE PROTOTYPING

Prototyping is most effective when user requirements are unclear. This is characteristic of many decision-oriented systems. Often the final system cannot be clearly visualized because the decision process itself has not been fully worked out. For example, TRW, Inc. has used prototyping to accommodate both users who think "intuitively" and those who think "systematically." The intuitive thinkers typically prefer graphs, charts, and trend lines, whereas the systematic thinkers generally want information displayed quantitatively as dates, numbers, and places. The advantage of working with a prototype is that business specialists can use a working system as a mechanism for clarifying the problem-solving process, which helps them arrive at a solution rapidly.

Prototyping is also useful for testing the **end-user interface** of an information system—those parts of the system that end users must interact with, such as on-line transaction screens or reports. The prototype enables users to react immediately to the parts of the system they will use. Figure 11.3 shows how a data entry screen for a human resources system was improved via prototyping. The old screen (panel a) was difficult to read and work with. Experienced human resources data entry clerks suggested ways of streamlining the arrangement of input data to create a clearer display (panel b).

End-user interface

The parts of an information system that end users must interact with—for example, on-line data entry screens or reports.

LIMITATIONS OF PROTOTYPING

Some studies have shown the prototypes that fully meet user requirements can be created in 10 to 20 percent of the time estimated for conventional development. To balance the impressive advantages of this approach, however, we should note that prototyping is not suitable for certain types of information systems.

Prototyping is most effective for smaller applications. It cannot be applied easily to massive, mainframe-based systems with complex processing instructions and calculations; in those cases, the traditional life cycle methodology is more appropriate. Prototyping a large system would require partitioning so that prototypes could be developed for one part at a time.[1] Another option would be to use prototyping for parts of the system, such as data entry screens and reports.

In addition, prototyping is not a substitute for all of the detailed research and analysis required to build an information system. Large systems will still necessitate thorough problem investigation, analysis, and requirements specification before prototyping can begin.

Some of the advantages of prototyping are also disadvantages. Often, critical activities such as testing and documentation are glossed over because it is so easy to create a prototype. The system can be changed so effortlessly that documentation may not be kept up-to-date. Sometimes a prototype system will be immediately converted into a production system. Yet, under real business circumstances, it may not be able to accommodate large numbers of users, process numerous transactions, and maintain large quantities of records.

FIGURE 11.3

The Benefits of Prototyping: A Data Entry Screen, Before and After

One advantage of prototyping is that it encourages participation and feedback from the people who will actually use the system to do their jobs. This can result in improvements that technical specialists, with no experience in doing those jobs, might not have considered. Here we see a data entry screen for a human resources system, both before (panel a) and after (panel b) prototyping. Human resources clerks tested the screen and suggested improvements, leading to a much more readable version.

(a) Old Screen

```
            1              2              3              4              5              6              7

                        CONSOLIDATED Corporation Personnel System
                                    Employee Profile

Search Value: | | | | | | | | | | | | | | | |   | | | | | | | | | | | | | | | | PEND DATE: xx/xx.
Name:     xxxxxxxxxxxxxxxxxxx   xxxxxxxxxxxxxxxxxxx   x
Employee #:     xxxxxx                        Position #:     xxxxxxx
HR Center:      xxxxx  xxxxx                   SNN #:          xxx-xx-xxxx
Budget Cntr:    xxxxxxxx                       Admin Center:   xxxxx
Ben Group:      xxx                            Ben Location:   xx
Co/Pay Level:   xx xxx                         Co of Origin:   xx
Work St Loc Code:   xxx                        Site Loc:   xx xxxxxxxxxxxxxxxxxx

Addr Line 1:    xxxxxxxxxxxxxxxxxxxxxxxxx      Telephone:      xxx/xxx-xxxx
Addr Line 2:    xxxxxxxxxxxxxxxxxxxxxxxxx      Birth Date:     xx/xx/xx
Addr Line 3:    xxxxxxxxxxxxxxxxxxxx           High ed Lvl:    xx      xx/xx
Zip:            xxxxx-xxxx                      Emp Status:     x
Sex Race Code:      x x                         AAP#:               xxxxx
Date of Empl:       xx/xx/xx                   Orig date of Hire:  xx/xx/xx
Termination:    xx/xx/xx      Reason:   xxxxxxxxxxxxxxxxxxxxxxxxxxxxxxxxxxxxxxx

| | | | | | | | | | | | | | | | | | | | | | | | | | error message area | | | | | | | | | | | | | | | | | | | | | | | | | |
PF1/EMP#       PF2/EMP NAME    PF3/HRCNTR      PF4/BUDCNTR       PF5/COMP    PF6/position
PF7/PREV       PF8/NEXT        PF9/PENDING     PF10/            PF11/       PF12/menu   CLE
```

(b) New Screen

```
        CONSOLIDATED    Corporation Personnel System
                        Employee Profile

Search Value: | | | | | | | | | | | | | | | | | | | | | |   | | | | | | | | | | | | | PEND DATE: xx/xx/xx

                Employee #: xxxxxx                    Position #: xx xx xxxxxxx
Name:    xxxxxxxxxxxxxxxxxxx   xxxxxxxxxxxxxxxxxxx x   SSNO:       xxx-xx-xxxx
    Addr Line 1: xxxxxxxxxxxxxxxxxxxxxxxx              Birth Date: xx/xx/xx
    Addr Line 2: xxxxxxxxxxxxxxxxxxxxxxxx              Sex/Race:   x x
    Addr Line 3: xxxxxxxxxxxxxxxxxxxx
    Zip:         xxxxx-xxxx                            Telephone:  xxx/xxx-xxxx

Emp Status:    x          Date of Empl:  xx/xx/xx    Orig Date of Hire: xx/xx/xx
Phys Work St:  xx         Site Loc:      xxx xxxxxxxxxxxxxxxxxxxxxxxx
Term Date:     xx/xx/xx   Reason:   xxxxxxxxxxxxxxxxxxxxxxxxxxxxxxxxxxxxxxxxx

    HR Ctr:      xxxxx xxxxx     AAP #:       xxxx      Ben Loc:     xx
    Admin Ctr:   xxxxx           Co/Pay Lvl:  xx xxx    Ben Group:   xxx
    Budget Ctr:  xxxxxxxxxxxx    High Ed Lvl: xx        Co of Orig:  xx

| | | | | | | | | | | | | | | | | | | | | | | | error message area | | | | | | | | | | | | | | | | | | | | | | | | | |
PF1  EMP#        PF3 HRCTR      PF7 NEXT       PF9 PENDING              PF11 POSITIONS
PF2  EMP NAME    PF4 BUDCTR     PF8 PREV       PF10 COMPENSATION        PF12 MENU
```

11.4 DEVELOPING SOLUTIONS WITH SOFTWARE PACKAGES

Chapter 6 introduced the topic of software packages—prewritten, precoded, commercially available programs that eliminate the need for writing software programs when an information system is developed. More and more systems today are being built with such packages for several reasons. For one thing, an increasing proportion of systems are based on desktop workstations and microcomputers that lend themselves readily to packaged software. In addition, some problems encountered by organizations require the same or very similar information system solutions. For example, payroll, accounts payable, accounts receivable, and order processing are standard needs for almost all businesses.

ADVANTAGES OF PACKAGES

Packages offer a number of advantages, especially for firms that do not have a large staff of technical systems personnel or whose staff lack the requisite technical skills for a particular application. Not only does buying packaged software take the burden of developing systems off in-house staff, but it can also be a source of technical expertise in the future. Leading package vendors maintain their own technical support staff to furnish customers with expert advice after the system has been installed. Thus a firm that buys packaged software has less need to maintain its own internal specialists.

A related advantage is the cost savings that organizations may achieve by purchasing packaged software rather than developing their own. A typical package vendor will claim that a system can be fashioned with a package in one-third to one-fourth the time required for custom development at a fraction of the cost. Packages also eliminate some of the need to work and rework the specifications for a system because users must accept the package as it is. Many features of the design solution have already been worked out, so the purchaser knows precisely what the capabilities of the system are.

PACKAGES AND THE SOLUTION DESIGN PROCESS

How do packages fit into our solution design methodology? As Figure 11.4 shows, even when considering a package, system builders still have to investigate and analyze the problem, specify solution objectives, consider constraints, and evaluate solution alternatives. During these processes, they can determine whether a package solution alternative will meet information requirements. Then, when they evaluate solution alternatives, they can weigh the feasibility of a package solution against other solution options.

The formality of the solution design process with a software package depends on the dimensions and complexity of the problem. For example, a problem requiring a simple mailing label or client database package on a personal computer can be easily addressed, whereas a mainframe-based manufacturing resources planning package to link four different production units may require all of the stages, activities, and formal procedures of traditional life cycle methodology. But whether formal or informal, the process still involves the basic steps of problem solving.

The package evaluation process is often based on the results of a **Request for Proposal (RFP)**. The RFP is a detailed list of questions that is submitted to vendors of packaged software. The questions are designed to measure the extent to which each package meets the requirements specified during the solution design process. An RFP is likely to include questions such as the following:

Request for Proposal (RFP)
A detailed list of questions for software vendors to answer as part of the process of evaluating a software package; the questions are designed to determine the extent to which the software package meets the requirements specified during the solution design process.

FIGURE 11.4

Prewritten Software Packages

Most organizations perform many of the same functions, such as payroll, accounting, and order processing, which has led to prewritten software that reduces the number of new programs that must be written for a new system. Even if a firm is considering basing a system on a software package, it should still follow the step-by-step solution design process. This diagram shows that system builders should still analyze the problem and evaluate alternative solutions.

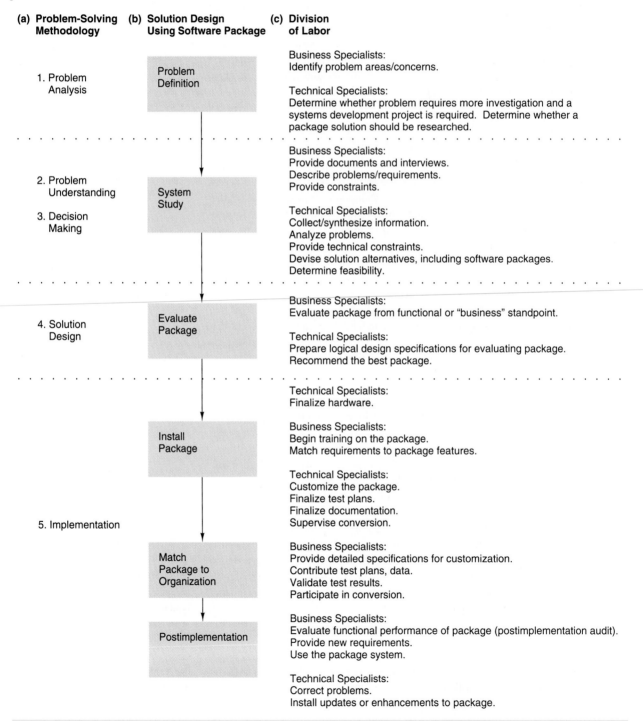

(a) Problem-Solving Methodology	(b) Solution Design Using Software Package	(c) Division of Labor
1. Problem Analysis	Problem Definition	**Business Specialists:** Identify problem areas/concerns. **Technical Specialists:** Determine whether problem requires more investigation and a systems development project is required. Determine whether a package solution should be researched.
2. Problem Understanding 3. Decision Making	System Study	**Business Specialists:** Provide documents and interviews. Describe problems/requirements. Provide constraints. **Technical Specialists:** Collect/synthesize information. Analyze problems. Provide technical constraints. Devise solution alternatives, including software packages. Determine feasibility.
4. Solution Design	Evaluate Package	**Business Specialists:** Evaluate package from functional or "business" standpoint. **Technical Specialists:** Prepare logical design specifications for evaluating package. Recommend the best package.
5. Implementation	Install Package	**Technical Specialists:** Finalize hardware. **Business Specialists:** Begin training on the package. Match requirements to package features. **Technical Specialists:** Customize the package. Finalize test plans. Finalize documentation. Supervise conversion.
	Match Package to Organization	**Business Specialists:** Provide detailed specifications for customization. Contribute test plans, data. Validate test results. Participate in conversion.
	Postimplementation	**Business Specialists:** Evaluate functional performance of package (postimplementation audit). Provide new requirements. Use the package system. **Technical Specialists:** Correct problems. Install updates or enhancements to package.

1. **Business requirements:** What business functions are supported by the package? (For example, does a payroll package generate W-2 forms automatically?)

2. **Ease of use:** Is the package easy for end-users to learn and use? How much training is required?

3. **Technical requirements:** What model(s) of computer hardware can the package run on? What operating system does it use? How much primary and secondary storage is required? Does the vendor supply source code?

4. **Vendor quality:** Does the vendor have an established reputation? Will the vendor provide updates to the package or technical support? Does the vendor supply training?

5. **Cost:** What is the cost of the package? Are vendor support and training extra? What would it cost to use the package for the proposed system solution?

6. **Flexibility:** Can the package be easily modified to incorporate other requirements or data that are not standard with the package?

The Focus on Problem Solving illustrates how these criteria can also be used to evaluate a foreign software package.

If a package solution is selected, the solution design step of problem solving will be carried out around the package. As a result, the work will proceed rather differently than in the other system-building approaches we have examined. In particular, logical and physical design will not proceed from scratch, tailored to the requirements and specifications generated first. Instead, the design work will focus on adjusting user requirements and specifications to meet the characteristics of the package. In other words, instead of end-users designing their own payroll register, the payroll register report provided by a payroll package will be used. In this sense, the organization and end-users have less control over the shape and design of solution outcome.

DISADVANTAGES OF PACKAGES

The main disadvantage of software packages is that they often are unable to meet all of an organization's requirements. As earlier chapters have pointed out, although organizations are alike in many ways, each has its own characteristics. Each organization treats even a standard function such as payroll a little differently. Consequently, there will be many instances in which a package will not be able to meet 100 percent of a firm's solution requirements. According to a study of corporations with payroll and personnel information systems, only 36.8 percent chose package software for personnel and only 40.3 percent for payroll in spite of the fact that these are standard business functions with a vast array of commercial packages available.[2] The difficulty in finding a package that will meet a firm's special needs may be one reason for these relatively low percentages.

Package vendors try to address this problem through **customization;** that is, the package includes features that allow it to be modified without destroying the integrity of the software. For example, the package may include areas on its files or databases where a firm can add and maintain its own pieces of data.

Some packages are modular in design; this allows clients to select only the modules that they need from an array of modules supporting different functions. Packages can also be customized through user exits, which enable clients to exit from the package programs to use programs they write themselves, then return to the package program. Figure 11.5 shows how a major payroll software package can be customized to accommodate different organizational reporting structures. This package allows firms

Customization

The modification of a software package to meet a firm's unique requirements.

**FOCUS ON
PROBLEM
SOLVING**

FINDING THE RIGHT PACKAGE FOR ROYAL MAIL

You may have assumed that when Royal Mail, the British government–owned postal system, needed a new human resources and payroll system, they would have built their own or purchased one from within the U.K. But they decided instead to buy from a U.S. company, Hyannis, Massachusetts–based Software 2000. This apparently surprising choice offers a lesson in software package purchasing.

The obvious factors argued strongly for the purchase of a British system. Royal Mail had been using software from Peterborough Software, in Peterborough, England, a company that was carefully considered during the selection process. Differing business practices between the U.K. and the U.S. create serious problems with the British use of an American financial system. The two countries use different monetary systems, have differing conventions for such key elements as sick-pay arrangements, and do not always share the same concerns in human resources. However, these issues were not the deciding factor. Underlying technology was.

John Harriman, Royal Mail's project controller, had two fundamental requirements. One was that the system would run on their current hardware, IBM AS/400 minicomputers, in order to protect their computer investment. That eliminated many contenders. Even Software 2000's software did not run on that particular piece of hardware, but it did run on the related IBM System/38 minicomputer, and it was easy for the software vendor to convert to the AS/400.

The other issue, even more paramount to Harriman, was that the system would be built on a single relational database. Each of Royal Mail's 64 districts used an independent system. Payroll and human resources were separate systems in which the data were stored in files related to specific programs. Managers found it almost impossible to obtain information about employees across the entire organization. Much of the data had to be entered multiple times, an expensive approach when maintaining data on 160,000 employees. Royal Mail also needed system flexibility so that processing modifications would be easy to make and custom applications would be easy to add on. A relational database addressed these problems.

Royal Mail's willingness to go against convention, combined with their careful needs analysis, paid off. They were able to make a 32 percent cut in payroll and personnel once the new system was installed, a reduction of 800 jobs. They estimate that the new system will save $14 million annually in administrative costs and will pay for itself in less than three years.

FOCUS Questions:
Royal Mail also considered the traditional build-it-yourself option. What factors might have caused them to reject that option and instead purchase a system that had so many drawbacks? What were the disadvantages of using a foreign software package?

SOURCE: George Black, "U.K.'s Royal Mail Boosts HR Efficiency," *Software Magazine*, April 1993.

FIGURE 11.5

A Customized Software Package

These diagrams show three possible organizational structures that can be created by the payroll/personnel system package from Management Sciences of America, Inc. The package allows each customer to organize employees into groups for reporting and control purposes. Data can be gathered and calculated for each organizational level defined. Each of these examples lists the highest level of the organization first.

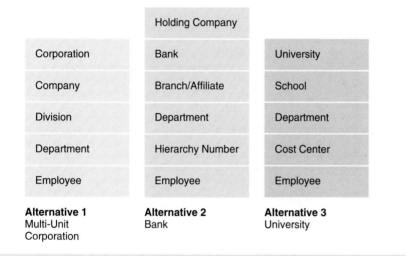

	Holding Company	
Corporation	Bank	University
Company	Branch/Affiliate	School
Division	Department	Department
Department	Hierarchy Number	Cost Center
Employee	Employee	Employee
Alternative 1	**Alternative 2**	**Alternative 3**
Multi-Unit Corporation	Bank	University

to define different types of organizational structures, such as a corporation, a bank, or a university.

Even with customization features, there are limits to how much packages can be changed. Firms experienced in using package software for major business applications have noted that a good package may only satisfy 70 percent of their application requirements. If the package cannot be modified to meet a firm's unique needs, the firm will have to change its procedures and ways of doing business to conform to the package. This may help streamline the firm's operations, or it may create additional confusion and complexity.

11.5 FOURTH-GENERATION DEVELOPMENT

Many information systems can be developed by end users with little or no formal assistance from technical specialists. This approach is called fourth-generation development. It incorporates some of the software tools introduced in Chapter 6, such as fourth-generation languages, personal computer tools, and graphics languages, which make it possible for end-users to perform tasks that previously required trained information systems specialists. (As you may recall, fourth-generation languages are programming languages that are not only less procedural than conventional languages but also contain more English-language commands; consequently, they are easier for nontechnical specialists to use.)

Computer Associates' CA Warehouse-BOSS is an application software package that provides a complete warehouse management system to control all operational aspects of a warehouse, including receiving, locating, putaway, order pool management, picking, replenishment, and shipping. Companies that purchase this package receive support services such as training courses, implementation support, documentation, and a 24-hour-a-day telephone helpline.

SOURCE: Courtesy of Computer Associates International, Inc.

Fourth-generation development has been used to build systems for mainframes, minicomputers, and microcomputers, although the majority of such systems are microcomputer based. Some examples of fourth-generation systems might include a mainframe-based application that provides on-line analysis of sales by sales region or sales representative or a microcomputer-based spreadsheet that projects five-year corporate earnings based on different levels of sales and operating costs.

FOURTH-GENERATION SOLUTION DESIGN

Fourth-generation development puts end users more in control of the problem-solving process. They can investigate and analyze a problem, specify solution alternatives, perform a limited amount of logical and physical design, and implement the solution themselves or with assistance from technical specialists. However, for end users to successfully develop applications using corporate data with little or no technical specialist involvement, the database (preferably a relational database) must have been designed by the specialists.

Figure 11.6 illustrates how fourth-generation development affects the solution design process. Note that solution design tends to be less formal than traditional systems development approaches, with technical specialists playing a relatively smaller role. Depending on the application solution, fourth-generation development may include prototyping, microcomputer packages, or more elaborate, custom-programmed software.

Generally, these fourth-generation systems tend to be quite simple and can be completed more rapidly than those using conventional life cycle methodology. This takes some of the pressure off the information systems department, so its staff can concentrate on more technically demanding projects. With less of their time allocated to applications development, more effort can be devoted to ensuring that users have appropriate tools to create their own system solutions. These tools include software development tools, a functioning relational database, and a telecommunications infrastructure.

FIGURE 11.6

Fourth-Generation Development

Fourth-generation development allows end users to do much of the development work themselves with easy-to-use software such as query languages and microcomputer packages. This takes a great deal of pressure off the information systems staff, since the users are responsible for identifying problems, designing and implementing solutions, and evaluating the results. Technical specialists take on a consulting role. Fourth-generation development works best with relatively simple applications and small files.

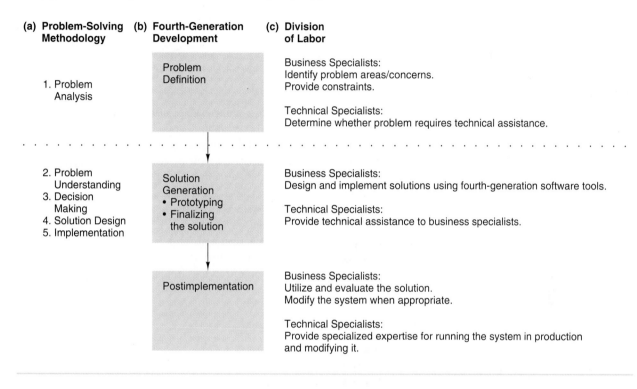

(a) Problem-Solving Methodology	(b) Fourth-Generation Development	(c) Division of Labor
1. Problem Analysis	Problem Definition	**Business Specialists:** Identify problem areas/concerns. Provide constraints. **Technical Specialists:** Determine whether problem requires technical assistance.
2. Problem Understanding 3. Decision Making 4. Solution Design 5. Implementation	Solution Generation • Prototyping • Finalizing the solution	**Business Specialists:** Design and implement solutions using fourth-generation software tools. **Technical Specialists:** Provide technical assistance to business specialists.
	Postimplementation	**Business Specialists:** Utilize and evaluate the solution. Modify the system when appropriate. **Technical Specialists:** Provide specialized expertise for running the system in production and modifying it.

The solution design process may actually be facilitated because end-users are in charge of problem analysis and requirements specification. Since end-users are in the best position to understand their own problems, there is less chance of issues being misunderstood, which often occurs when the problem-solving process is dominated by technical specialists. End-users are also more likely to choose systems they have built themselves as their preferred problem-solving tools.

FOURTH-GENERATION SOFTWARE TOOLS

As fourth-generation tools become more sophisticated and powerful, information system specialists themselves are also increasingly replacing third-generation languages with fourth-generation tools to develop many of the more complex applications. A key reason for this growing popularity is the spread of client/server technology, which removes processing from the mainframe and distributes it to desktops. When fourth-generation development tools were largely mainframe-based and competed with other applications for precious computer processing resources, they ran too slowly and required too much computer memory to be used to develop larger systems. Today, as more and more fourth-generation processing occurs on desktops, this problem is slowly disappearing.

Fourth-generation development requires easy-to-use software tools that can be employed by end-users alone or by technical specialists as productivity aids. The following are usually considered the major types of software tools for end-users:

1. Microcomputer tools

2. Query languages and report generators

3. Graphics languages

4. Application generators

5. Very-high-level programming languages

6. Application software packages

Figure 11.7 lists some representative, commercially available tools in each category and indicates the applications for which they are most appropriate.

Microcomputer tools consist of the microcomputer software described throughout this book: spreadsheet, database management, graphics, word processing, and communications software. Microcomputer software is especially well-suited to end-user development because it was designed for end-users rather than technical specialists and because microcomputer operating systems are relatively simple.

Query languages, graphics languages, report generators, application generators, and very-high-level programming languages were introduced in Section 6.3. Query languages are easy-to-use, fourth-generation languages that are used to access data stored in databases or files. Report generators extract data from files or databases to create cus-

FIGURE 11.7

Fourth-Generation Solution Design Tools

The term "fourth-generation tools" actually describes a broad range of products, as is evident here. It includes software for microcomputers such as Lotus 1-2-3 and query languages such as SQL, which are suitable for simpler problems. Other tools, such as very-high-level programming languages and application software packages, can address more technically sophisticated situations.

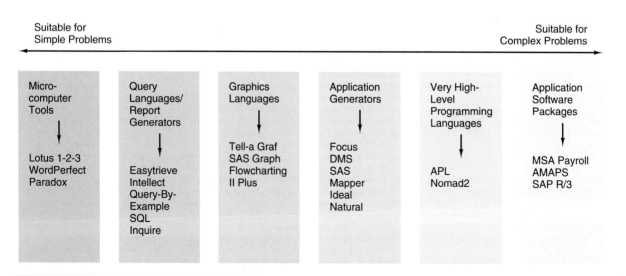

tomized reports. With an application generator, an entire information system application can be generated without customized programming; the end-user specifies what needs to be done, and the generator creates the appropriate program code. Very-high-level programming languages produce program code with far fewer instructions than are required by conventional languages.

Application software packages, described earlier in this chapter, can serve as fourth-generation computing tools if they are simple and can be installed by end-users. An example might be a mailing label or client database that can be installed by an end-user on a personal computer without any special programming or customization.

In recent years, fourth-generation development tool functionality has expanded so much that it will soon be difficult to categorize these tools in this traditional manner. Many database management systems (Chapter 7) now have end-user application generator tools, including query languages and report generators. Query languages and report generators are often capable of accessing other databases in addition to their own. Many application software packages now come with user-controlled report generators and graphics languages. Our Focus on Technology illustrates the complexity of selecting the appropriate fourth-generation tool for your work environment.

DISADVANTAGES OF FOURTH-GENERATION DEVELOPMENT

Although fourth-generation development offers many advantages, it can be used to solve problems only when the information system solution is relatively simple and easily understood by users. Fourth-generation languages and other end-user computing tools work best with small files and simple processing procedures. Unless they are developed on client/server technology, such tools typically require more computer resources to process information than conventional languages, so they are unable to handle large transaction-based applications efficiently. For example, the New Jersey Division of Motor Vehicles faced a backlog of 1.4 million vehicle registration and ownership records when it built its system using Ideal, a fourth-generation tool. The high transaction volume necessitated reprogramming part of the system in COBOL.

Because these languages are heavily nonprocedural, they cannot easily handle applications that require complex procedural logic. Information systems to support production scheduling or nuclear reactor design still require conventional languages.

Another disadvantage of fourth-generation development is the organization's potential loss of control over the solution design process and its information resources. Fourth-generation systems are developed much more informally and idiosyncratically than those using traditional methods. Consequently, no professional programmers or systems analysts may be involved to assist with problem analysis, evaluation of solution alternatives, and solution design. User-developed systems thus lack the independent review mechanism provided by the technical specialist when both groups participate in solution design.

In addition, standards for ensuring data quality, security, or conformity with the information requirements of the firm as a whole may never be applied. End-users may create many personal databases on desktop microcomputers containing data from corporate databases that, over time, are updated, defined, and transformed so that they no longer match the same data in other systems. This leads to confusion about where to turn for reliable data.

Given these advantages and drawbacks, how useful is end-user development? This question is explored in the Focus on People.

FOCUS ON TECHNOLOGY

FOURTH-GENERATION TOOLS TODAY: A WEALTH OF OPTIONS

Despite predictions of their early demise, fourth-generation development tools today are thriving because they evolved by integrating other advances in computer technology. Now, with so many capabilities, the choice of which fourth-generation tool to use is both complex and critical.

How have fourth-generation tools changed in recent years? The answer differs with different products, but in all cases they have added one or more of the recent popular technological advances, such as relational databases, graphical user interfaces, client/server technology, platform portability, prototyping, even object-oriented programming. Before the team responsible for selecting one of the fourth-generation language development environments investigates its choices, it must understand its own environment and needs. Then its members will have the complex task of comparing the functions, strengths, and weaknesses of the many choices to find the development tool that best fits their own requirements. We will look at a few available products to illustrate some of the factors that need to be examined and the many choices that are available.

One of the earliest, and still one of the most popular, of the fourth-generation languages is Focus from Information Builders, Inc. of New York

City. Many companies use Focus today because they have run Focus applications for a long time, and a new product would require expensive and time-consuming retraining. But Focus could not have survived if it had not modernized over time. Originally a mainframe system, Focus is now available on many hardware platforms and is easily ported between platforms. It is this portability that Steve Schneider, president of Fleet Lines of Avenel, New Jersey, values as one key reason his company stays with Focus. Focus has changed in other fundamental ways. Like many fourth-generation language products, Focus comes with its own database. Originally users could not access other databases using Focus, but today they can readily gain access to many databases such as Informix, Ingress, Teradata, and databases accessed using the SQL data manipulation language.

Progress, from Progress Software, Bedford, Massachusetts, is a multi-hardware platform fourth-generation language that runs on VAX/VMS, AS/400, MS-DOS, and about 50 other platforms. Client/server capabilities were incorporated into Progress in 1988, very early for such capability. Today, Progress users can access data across a large, heterogeneous network, and developers can use one development tool to develop both client/server and nonclient/server applications. Tony La Vecchio, programming manager of Interstate Batteries of Dallas, says his firm converted all its corporate systems to Progress both because of its good performance relative to COBOL and because of the ease with which system changes can be made.

The University of Texas uses Natural, a product of Software AG of Reston, Virginia, because it is so simple

to learn. With approximately 1,000 applications and 90,000 programs to run the university's police department, hospitals, libraries, and other facilities, ease of learning means increased productivity. According to Randy Ebeling, director of the university's data processing department, "Natural is easy enough so that anyone can learn it. We have 300 people writing Natural code, of whom 150 are not programmers."

Other products offer specific capabilities for particular markets. PowerHouse from Cognos, Inc., of Burlington, Massachusetts, is particularly appropriate for companies with networks on which only some of the users have converted to graphical user interfaces. With PowerHouse the user can develop a single system that will run with a character-based interface on one node of a network and a graphical user interface on another node. Cognos emphasizes that 35 to 40 percent of commercial applications that run in a UNIX environment still work in terminal (or character) mode. Empress from Empress Software, Greenbelt, Maryland, specializes in tools for developing multimedia systems that process graphics, image, and voice.

FOCUS Questions:
What people, organization, and technology criteria would you use to select a fourth-generation language? Should organizations with a wide range of requirements adopt two or more fourth-generation tools to meet their manifold needs? Why?

SOURCE: Lori Weitz, "4GLs Keeping Current with New Technology," *Software Magazine*, May 1993.

FOCUS ON PEOPLE

SHOULD USERS DEVELOP THEIR OWN APPLICATIONS?

While no one disputes the ability of end-users to develop their own isolated applications using desktop personal productivity tools such as databases and spreadsheets, agreement definitely ends there. When users employ such "easy" tools as Lotus Notes (groupware) or Focus (a fourth-generation language) to develop systems that connect two or more people or use corporate data, vociferous and sometimes adamant opposition emerges.

The arguments supporting end-user development are clear. First, end-users know their business and understand their needs and priorities far better than IS professionals ever can. Second, user-developed systems should result in fewer design flaws because users will design the system to operate according to the way they do their work, rather than operating the way technical specialists imagine the system should. Thus, user-developed systems should be more widely used once they are in production. Third, many IS departments have an application backlog of several years; user development would help to reduce that backlog.

Those who oppose user-developed systems do not dispute the first two of these arguments, making their own case more difficult to make. Why not let users develop their own systems? Opponents offer three fundamental reasons. The first involves technology. Tools such as Lotus Notes are deceptive in that they appear easy to use for application development but require extensive knowledge of programming and inter-system connections, knowledge only residing with IS professionals. For instance, to achieve productivity, most new systems require interaction with existing systems, primarily to retrieve data. Most business specialists don't know how to connect a Focus program to an Oracle database.

Second, opponents stress that even if the technology problems could be overcome, developing valuable organizational systems requires professional skills business staffs normally have not developed and often do not value. For example, users often are not skilled in and do not see the need for system design, project quality controls, data consistency and accuracy, rigorous testing, and system and data security. Yet experience has proven that all these skills are essential for successful system building.

Finally, many IS professionals claim that user development does not result in increased IS productivity and a reduction of IS backlog. On the contrary, IS must shift resources from development projects to deal with problems created by user-developed systems—for example, the need to create links to existing systems, to redesign the system to achieve data integrity, and to test to find bugs users could not isolate.

FOCUS Questions: How would you handle the issue of end-user development? Under what circumstances should users be allowed to develop their own systems? What people, organization, and technology factors would you consider?

SOURCES: Joe King, "If You Want Trouble, then Let Users Develop," *Computerworld*, November 15, 1993, and Jeff Papows, "User Developers Build Better Business Systems," *Computerworld*, November 15, 1993.

INFORMATION CENTERS

Information center

A facility that provides training, tools, standards, and expert support for solution design by end-users.

One way to manage fourth-generation development and maximize its benefits is through **information centers.** An information center is a facility that provides training and support for end-user computing. Its objective is to provide business specialists with tools to access computerized data and solve problems themselves. An information center furnishes computer hardware, software, and technical specialists, all of which are geared to fourth-generation systems development. The technical specialists serve as teachers and consultants; their primary goal is to train business specialists in the computing tools they will use, but they may also assist in the analysis, design, and programming of complex applications.

An information center may offer users access to mainframes and minicomputers as well as microcomputers, although some information centers contain only microcomputers. Information centers support end-user software tools such as spreadsheets, word processing, graphics, report generators, and query languages.

FIGURE 11.8

The Information Center Concept

An information center can help a firm provide fourth-generation development tools and benefits to all employees. It is a coordinating and consulting facility which, in addition to providing hardware and software, also provides services. This diagram illustrates the broad range of services that an information center typically performs, including training, documentation, and generating prototypes. A good information center can be a valuable resource for a company.

Information centers support the solution design process at many stages. Their staffs are prepared to work intensively to help end-users understand their problems and solve them as much as possible on their own. The services provided by an information center can be summarized as follows (see Figure 11.8):

- Referring business specialists to existing information system applications that may help solve their problems.

- Providing technical assistance by suggesting appropriate hardware, software, and methodologies for solving a particular problem.

- Training business specialists in the tools supported by the information center.

- Providing documentation and reference materials for information center resources.

- Generating prototypes for business specialists to evaluate.

- Evaluating new pieces of hardware and software.

- Giving staff access to terminals, microcomputers, associated software, and databases.

Information centers offer a number of benefits:[3]

1. Better use of information.

2. Increased job productivity.

3. Greater computer literacy.

4. Better relations between business specialists and technical specialists.

5. Reduced application backlog.

Another advantage of information centers is that they can establish standards for hardware and software so that end-users do not introduce too many incompatible pieces of equipment or data into a firm. Typically, an information center works with a firm's information systems department to establish standards and guidelines for hardware and software acquisitions by the firm; then the information center will provide assistance with only those brands of equipment and software.

For example, an information center may provide training only on WordPerfect, as opposed to other word processing packages, because that is the company standard. Otherwise, its staff would have to learn several different types of word processing software, each of which would be used by only a small number of people. Such a policy also contributes to the efficient use of information in an organization. Files created by one kind of word processing software cannot automatically be used by another. This restricts transportability of data across the organization.

11.6 OUTSOURCING

In recent years more organizations have concluded that they no longer want to maintain the internal resources needed for the development and operation of some or all of their information systems. They turn instead to outsourcing, the strategy of handing over to external vendors some or all of an organization's information systems functions.

Information centers provide computers, software tools, and training classes to help employees access data or create applications on their own.
SOURCE: Courtesy of International Business Machines Corporation.

Outsourcing firms provide a variety of services including:

- staffing and managing a company's computer center;

- operating some or all of a company's computer systems at the outsourcing firm's computer center;

- developing applications for an organization;

- operating an organization's telecommunications networks.

While outsourcing can be advantageous, companies must be careful not to view it as a way of relinquishing responsibility for the functions being outsourced. Outsourcing vendors must be managed as carefully as any internal system would be managed. Contracts must be carefully written to include measurable criteria for evaluating the vendor's performance. The organization must be certain, for example, that valuable data are being backed up and that the vendor actually provides systems maintenance as well as agreed-upon hours of systems operation. An outsourced development project must ultimately be supervised internally, and again detailed measurement criteria (e.g., deadlines) must be specified in advance.

FIGURE 11.9

Developing a System through Outsourcing

When a system is developed through outsourcing, the final design and implementation of the solution is assigned to an external vendor of information services. Outsourcing can be useful if an organization lacks the internal resources to develop a solution entirely on its own.

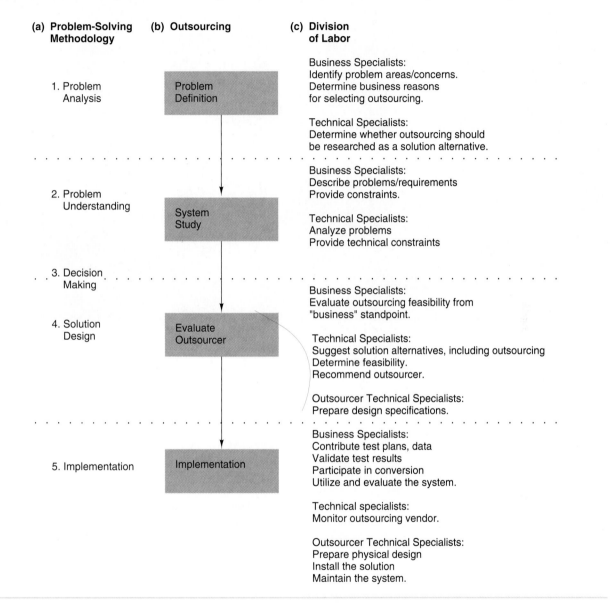

Selecting an outsourcing vendor takes skill. The vendor must have both technical and application skills. You would not want someone to run your payroll, for example, unless they clearly understood the tax and legal implications of a failure to maintain proper records. Similarly, if you plan to outsource the development of a chemical plant's process control system, you would want a vendor who is not only skilled in application development but also understands chemical processing controls. Figure 11.9 shows how the solution design process can be accomplished with outsourcing.

Electronic Data Systems (EDS), a leading vendor of information systems services, uses a specially equipped room to demonstrate its outsourcing capabilities to prospective clients. Firms can contract with EDS to develop applications and provide other information systems services for them.

SOURCE: Courtesy of Electronic Data Systems.

ADVANTAGES OF OUTSOURCING

Companies turn to outsourcing for a variety of reasons, the most common of which is economic. Outsourcing companies are specialists in the services they provide and therefore are able to provide those services at either a lower cost or with higher quality at the same cost. In addition, outsourcing vendors sell their services to multiple clients and thus can generate economies of scale that their clients cannot. Savings of 15 to 30 percent are not uncommon.[4]

Outsourcing can often reduce costs by turning fixed costs into variable costs. For many transaction-driven systems, such as payroll or accounts payable, the outsourcing vendor agrees to charge by the transaction (in these examples, an issued check) so that if the number of transactions (checks) go down, systems costs reduce also. The alternative, maintaining these systems internally, results in a fixed cost to support each system.

Outsourcing contracts offer still another economic advantage, that of predictability. The systems development process is notorious for cost overruns of 100 percent or more. Through outsourcing, the company can often negotiate a fixed price for the system. Care must be taken, of course, to specify system performance to be certain that the vendor does not cut costs by taking shortcuts.

Service quality is another common reason for outsourcing. Vendors specializing in a specific service, such as telecommunications, are often more skilled than is the more

FOCUS ON ORGANIZATIONS

CANADA POST OUTSOURCES FOR SERVICE

Canada Post's plan to outsource at first looks like a very ordinary, albeit rather large, outsourcing decision. Unlike many countries' postal services, Canada Post is expected to make a profit and to pursue new businesses as part of its strategy to be profitable. For this reason, this Canadian corporation decided to enter the electronic mail business—the very business that threatens to undermine the whole postal industry. To be successful, the company moved most of its processing from mainframes to a client/server environment with the help of SHL Systemhouse Inc.

The contract with SHL Systemhouse calls for them to manage the entire IS function at Canada Post—mainframe, distributed processing, networking, desktop systems and support, voice, imaging, and multimedia. Most of Canada Post's 235 IS professionals will become employees of SHL Systemhouse. The vendor will purchase much of Canada Post's computer and telecommunications infrastructure, financed with loans backed by Canada Post. Under the contract, E-mail, report

writing software, and application development tools will be moved from mainframes to the client/server environment during the first three years. Other functions will be moved in the following years.

The unusual aspect of this contract is the fee-for-service arrangement. Ron Keating, director of information technology at Canada Post, explains, "We're buying services, not hardware or people." Canada Post can add and subtract services, as needed, paying only for the services it requests. Its situation has been described as being similar to that of a telephone customer who can add or drop such services as call waiting and phone mail at will. If, for example, a department suddenly required a spreadsheet for year-end accounting, SHL Systemhouse would develop and deliver the application. Canada Post would be charged for that new service according to an agreed-upon pricing formula. Larger changes can be made in the same way. According to Keating, "If we decide we no longer need distributed processors in the Yukon, we can turn off those services."

FOCUS Questions: What do you think are the immediate and long-range organizational effects on Canada Post of such a large outsourcing contract? What people, organization, and technology factors would you consider in deciding whether to use outsourcing for a large company?

SOURCE: Mark Halper, "Canada Post Pays as it Goes," *Computerworld*, August 8, 1993.

general IS department of the firm buying the service. In addition, because the company can end the outsourcing contract if service is unsatisfactory, outsourcing vendors tend to place a heavy emphasis on quality.

Organizations with a limited number of IS professionals often use outsourcing as a way to free up talented IS staff for critical projects. Using staff to develop or maintain routine systems can be a waste of talent. Able analysts, for example, offer more benefit to their companies by developing new production-related systems than by maintaining a routine payroll system.

DISADVANTAGES OF OUTSOURCING

Outsourcing is not a solution for all companies or all situations. First, gains will not be realized unless the company effectively manages outsourcing. That means, above all, carefully selecting outsourcing functions and applications. Outsourcing can be costly and harmful if potential functions for outsourcing are not evaluated carefully. It is risky for a company to outsource applications on which its competitiveness depends. For example, because excellent performance of reservation systems is critical to the success of hotel chains and airlines, these systems probably should be managed internally. On the other hand, these same companies could probably outsource their medical claims systems because they will lose little if claims processing is occasionally interrupted. The same cannot be said of major health care insurance providers, for whom the medical claims system is pivotal. For them, occasional medical processing problems could be disastrous and could even threaten their survival. Thus, they would be wise to retain direct control of medical claims themselves.

Companies must guard against loss of control that can be the result of outsourcing. Firms sometimes find they have become overreliant on the vendor; in fact, the vendor may be the firm's only alternative for providing the outsourced service. In that unacceptable situation, the vendor is free to exploit the contract by raising fees and reducing the level of service. Overreliance also leaves a company vulnerable should the vendor develop financial difficulties or actually close down.

Finally, placing strategic applications in the hands of a poorly chosen third party can leave a company open to serious breaches of security. Proprietary or damaging information can leak out to competitors or the general public.

Ultimately, although outsourcing decisions can be complicated, outsourcing can benefit an organization if the functions to be outsourced and the vendors are carefully selected and managed. (See the Focus on Organizations.)

SUMMARY

- The traditional systems life cycle is the oldest methodology for building information systems solutions. It consists of a formal set of stages that must proceed sequentially, clearly demarcating the responsibilities of business and technical specialists.

- The six stages of the traditional systems life cycle are project definition, systems study, design, programming, installation, and postimplementation.

- The traditional life cycle is considered a very rigid and costly way to develop a systems solution. Moreover, it is not well suited for simpler, less structured applications for which requirements cannot easily be visualized.

- The most important alternatives to traditional life cycle methodology are prototyping, the use of software packages, fourth-generation development, and outsourcing.

- Prototyping entails building an experimental system or part of a system rapidly for business specialists to interact with and evaluate. The process is highly interactive and iterative.

- Prototyping involves four steps: identifying preliminary requirements; developing a working prototype; using the prototype; and refining and enhancing the prototype.

- Prototyping is most useful for simple, less structured applications for which solution requirements are vague. When the system solution is massive and complex, prototyping cannot substitute for comprehensive requirements analysis and careful programming, testing, and documentation.

- Software packages are commercially marketed, prewritten software that can considerably reduce system development costs if they meet solution requirements. Solution design using application software packages focuses on package evaluation and fitting the solution design to package characteristics.

- If a package does not meet an organization's unique requirements, it must be customized, or modified. However, extensive customization can elevate development costs to the point that a package solution is no longer feasible.

- Using fourth-generation development techniques, business specialists can construct information systems solutions with minimal assistance from technical specialists. This is possible because of the productivity and ease of use provided by fourth-generation development tools: microcomputer tools, query languages, graphics languages, report generators, application generators, very-high-level programming languages, and application software packages.

- Fourth-generation-developed solutions are most appropriate for applications with small files and relatively simple processing procedures. Potential problems from fourth-generation development include loss of organizational control and standards for solution design.

- Information centers can help control fourth-generation development by providing training, tools, standards, and expert support for solution design.

- Organizations can benefit by outsourcing applications development to an external vendor if such an arrangement reduces costs and allows the organization to control the solution design process.

KEY TERMS

Traditional systems life cycle	Outsourcing
Project definition	End-user interface
Systems study	Request for proposal (RFP)
Postimplementation	Customization
Prototyping	Information center
Fourth-generation development	

REVIEW QUESTIONS

1. Why is the oldest methodology for building an information system called the "systems life cycle"?

2. List and define each of the stages in the systems life cycle.

3. Why is it important to conduct a postimplementation audit of an information system?

4. What are the strengths and limitations of life cycle methodology?

5. What are the most important alternatives to conventional systems-building methodology?

6. Define information system prototyping.

7. What kinds of situations benefit most from prototyping the solution?

8. What are the four steps in prototyping?

9. What are the limitations of prototyping?

10. What kinds of situations benefit from using software packages to develop a solution?

11. Describe two advantages and two disadvantages of software packages.

12. What is customization? Why is it an important feature to consider in a software package?

13. What is fourth-generation development? Name the major kinds of software tools employed with this approach.

14. What problems are associated with fourth-generation development?

15. Define an information center. How can information centers solve some of the problems introduced by fourth-generation development?

16. What is outsourcing? What are its advantages and disadvantages as a solution design approach?

DISCUSSION QUESTIONS

1.   Discuss how the problem-solving methodology presented in this text is applied in the traditional systems life cycle, prototyping, software package–based development, fourth-generation development, and outsourcing.

2.   Describe the roles of business specialists and technical specialists in each of the approaches to information systems solutions presented in this chapter.

3.   Application software packages and fourth-generation computing tools eliminate the need for professional programmers. Discuss.

4.   It is impossible to develop a good solution design the first time around. Discuss the alternatives.

PROBLEM-SOLVING EXERCISES

1.   *Group exercise:* Divide the class into groups. Ask each group to obtain product information about a microcomputer application software package, such as Quicken, Kiplinger's CASimply Money, Microsoft Profit for Windows, or DacEasy Accounting. Have each group write an analysis of the package selected. What are its strengths and limitations? Under what circumstances could it be used for a system solution?

2.   What kind of approach (methodology) would you choose for the following application solutions? Justify your decision.

a. A system for tracking job applicants at six different branches of a nationwide retail chain.

b. A money market account system for a major regional bank.

c. A system to evaluate the financial and tax consequences of purchasing rental property.

d. A medical and dental claims administration and payment system for 14,000 employees of a major corporation.

3. *Hands-on exercise:* Use appropriate application software to create a prototype of a simple student recordkeeping system for a university. The system should maintain data on the student's name, address, age, sex, marital status, high school attended, citizenship, and grade point average. If possible, use your software tool to create an on-line data entry screen for inputting the data. Then modify the prototype to capture these additional data elements: student's social security number, parent's name, parent's address, and date of high school graduation. Present the first version of the prototype and the revision to your instructor.

NOTES

1. Maryam Alavi, "An Assessment of the Prototyping Approach to Information System Development," *Communications of the ACM 27* (June 1984).

2. John E. Spirig, "New HRMS Challenge: Section 89 in 1989," *Software Magazine*, January 1989.

3. Wayne L. Rhodes, Jr., "The Information Center: Harvesting the Potential," *Infosystems,* November 1985.

4. Lawrence Loh and N. Venkatraman, "Determinants of Information Technology Outsourcing," *Journal of Management Information Systems* 9, no. 1 (Summer 1992).

PROBLEM-SOLVING CASE

IMPLEMENTING "EXTENDED ENTERPRISE" FOR THE U.S. AIR FORCE

Writing software applications for the extended enterprise means writing applications that will run on different hardware platforms within more than one organization or company, often to connect an organization with its customers and suppliers. Launch Systems Co., a Martin Marietta Astronautics Group company located in Littleton, Colorado, has only one customer, the U.S. Air Force. They are the prime contractor for the Titan missile satellite launch system, which places satellites in orbit around the earth. They built the Titan Integrated Storage Information System (TISIS) to "extend their enterprise" to Air Force managers at various locations as well as to several of their five major subcontractors.

Each Titan missile launch is individual and requires a missile tailored to the specific needs of that launch. Therefore, each missile must be assembled-to-order from standardized parts. About 70% of these parts are supplied by subcontractors and stored at the suppliers' sites until the Titan is ready to be assembled. Ensuring that all the parts are available on time requires a great deal of coordination that had always been accomplished through numerous telephone calls to the many people involved. Bill Rierden, manager of data integration and analysis from the Mission Success group of Launch Systems, was concerned because the process was time-consuming and expensive. It was difficult to make precise predictions about when a particular component would be available for shipment to the launch site. He also knew that Launch Systems' contract with the Air Force tied compensation to operational efficiency and launch success. Errors and delays, therefore, directly affected Launch Systems' profits.

In response to these problems, TISIS was designed to link data at the various contractors' sites so that all involved could see what parts were available. When completed, TISIS gave everyone connected to the system the ability to check specific components, break components down to the lowest level of parts, or easily format reports on any component, part, or group of parts. The system could coordinate data from one subcontractor with data from all the other subcontractors. The number of phone calls was greatly reduced, and the information was available at all times. Moreover, says Rierden, TISIS lets the contractors "see how it all fits together," thereby giving them a more complete understanding of the overall launch effort.

The developers faced two key issues. First, the various contractors and Air Force managers worked on a variety of desktop platforms, including Macintoshes, PCs running under DOS using Microsoft Windows, and UNIX workstations running either Software Foundation's Motif or Sun Microsystems Inc.'s Open Look graphical user interfaces. TISIS had to be able to work equally well on all of these platforms. The other problem? How to develop this system economically.

Kurt Deshazer, leader of the project, decided to build the system in C, a very popular third-generation language. He would have preferred a fourth-generation language, but none could run with the speed of C. Moreover, Deshazer did not want to waste his staff's time learning a proprietary fourth-generation language, whereas C compilers are available on essentially all computer platforms. Code written for one platform can easily be ported to almost any other platform. Although C++, a newer, more advanced version of C, was available, it had not yet achieved the easy portability of C.

For the system to be accepted, users from the various organizations needed a graphical interface they found easy to use. More fundamental, however, the interface used on one platform in one organization would have to be able to access data on any other platform being used by any of the subcontractors. Skeptics did not think it possible to achieve that goal. Moreover, C presents a special problem because it is a bare-bones language that performs only fundamental (i.e., lower level) commands. More sophisticated functions must either be programmed or (the preferred solution) be performed by functions available in purchasable software program libraries. The appropriate C library would need to support all the various platforms and do so from a single coded C program. Separate development for each platform was risky and far too expensive to write and maintain.

After an extensive search, Deshazer found Open Interface, a library from Neuron Data Inc. of Palo Alto, California, which provided him the programming functionality and versatility he needed. Open Interface supports the graphical user interfaces for Microsoft Windows, the Macintosh operating system, UNIX Motif and Open Look, and IBM's OS/2. With this tool, any graphical user interface application can be developed and translated into any other graphical user interface by a simple recompilation of the programs.

Now that the system is in production, skepticism has been quieted. Bill Ball, Mission Success representative from subcontractor General Dynamics, described its ease of use, characterizing the new system as "nearly idiot-proof." He said he can easily select and build reports using whatever data he needs, whether he is in his own office or not, even if the data are in another subcontractor's system.

In 1992 Michael Goulde, senior consultant at Patricia Seybold Group, found that many IS managers in *Fortune* 500 companies agreed that as extended enterprise applications like TISIS become more extensive, the importance of such cross-platform tools as Open Interface will continue to grow.

SOURCE: Lee The, "The Extended Enterprise Blasts Off," *Datamation*, March 1, 1993.

CASE STUDY QUESTIONS

1.   What people, organization, and technology problems did Launch Systems face that caused it to build TISIS?

2.   Was the solution development approach appropriate for the problem? What other alternatives might the developers have employed?

3.   What were the technological and people problems Launch Systems encountered in implementing the new system? How did they overcome them?

4.   What were the benefits of the solution chosen? What were its drawbacks?

Chapter
❖ T W E L V E ❖

SAFEGUARDING INFORMATION SYSTEMS

LEARNING OBJECTIVES

After reading and studying this chapter, you will:

1. Be aware of the major threats to computer-based information systems, including computer crime, hackers, computer viruses, and information system quality problems.

2. Be able to describe the role of general and application controls in safeguarding information systems.

3. Be able to describe the most important techniques for promoting information system security.

4. Be able to assess software and data quality problems.

*I*n one of the most ambitious system-building projects in history, the Internal Revenue Service (IRS) is implementing a massive $23 billion Tax System Modernization (TSM) plan to give all its employees on-line access to taxpayer information. When the system is completed, what will happen if hundreds of IRS employees have already illegally "browsed" the tax records of friends, neighbors, relatives, and celebrities? Some employees have even altered files and created false tax returns.

A report prepared by the General Accounting Office (GAO) detailed this "computer voyeurism" and revealed inadequate measures to safeguard IRS data and lax enforcement by the IRS. The GAO report, drawing on internal IRS inspections, revealed that up to 350 employees in the IRS's Atlanta-based Southeast region alone had been caught snooping into tax records. At the time the report was prepared, 154 employees had been disciplined for improper browsing and at least four faced prosecution for preparing fraudulent returns. In one case, an IRS employee fabricated more than 200 fraudulent tax returns to obtain refund money. The bogus refunds have cost the IRS approximately $300,000. Up to 80 employees were under investigation for possible criminal prosecution. Senator John Glenn subsequently revealed that the IRS has investigated 1,300 employees for suspected security violations since 1989.

About half the IRS's 115,000 employees can use its Integrated Data Retrieval System (IDRS), an antiquated system about 20 years old that houses the largest database of taxpayer records at the agency. They can access the IDRS by using passwords and user identification numbers. All new *employees with access to the IDRS undergo security training that emphasizes the illegality of accessing tax records for other than official business. IRS Commissioner Margaret M. Richardson has insisted that the IDRS meets all security guidelines set forth by the National Institute of Standards and Technology for systems with sensitive data. The system does provide an audit trail documenting who used it and when, but IRS security managers have not consistently checked for abuses. Although they have been aware of the potential for security lapses for years, the managers did little to prevent them. According to an internal IRS audit, the IDRS security program had not been reviewed by local, regional, or national management for the past 2 years. Critics noted that IRS managers had not been held accountable for security breaches.*

Richardson insisted that the agency had not been trying to cover up these problems, pointing out that it was IRS inspectors who first alerted the GAO to the illegal browsing. She promised that the completed TSM would include internal controls to document all system activity and to flag usage transactions that indicated inappropriate access. Controls would also be instituted to prevent security breaches from outside hackers, since TSM computers can be accessed by dialing up from external networks. But security experts worry that such controls will be out-of-date and insufficient to solve the agency's problems. Technology alone can't prevent breaches of privacy and security. Robert Bales, executive director of the National Computer Security Association in Carlisle, Pennsylvania, notes that management must assume responsibility for the IRS employees' improper activities.

SOURCES: Gary H. Anthes, "IRS Cracks Down on Fraud," *Computerworld,* July 25, 1994 and Stephanie Stahl, "Internal Revenue Snoops," *InformationWEEK,* August 9, 1993.

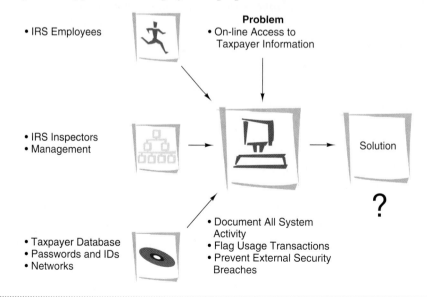

This story illustrates how vulnerable computerized systems are to theft, damage, disruption, or misuse. It also shows that the proper use and operation of information systems depends on the behavior of people as well as on technical, organizational, and design factors. The critical role played by automated information systems in business, government, and daily life requires special steps to protect them and to ensure that they are accurate and reliable. In this chapter we describe the considerations that must be taken into account when designing information system solutions to make sure that systems serve the purposes for which they were intended.

12.1 THE VULNERABILITY OF INFORMATION SYSTEMS

Although computer-based information systems can help solve a firm's problems, they are vulnerable to many more kinds of threats than manual systems. Events such as a fire or electrical power failure can cause massive damage because so much of a firm's information resources are concentrated in one place. Valuable data can be destroyed if computer hardware malfunctions or if individuals tamper with computerized files.

A nationwide study conducted by the Center for Research on Information Systems at the University of Texas at Arlington confirms that the longer computer services are disrupted, the more difficult it is to perform basic business functions. Almost

The California earthquake of January 1994 left thousands of buildings, homes, and offices in rubble, destroying valuable records and knocking out many computer systems. Computerized information systems are highly vulnerable to threats posed by natural disasters.
SOURCE: AP/Wide World Photos.

half the businesses surveyed predicted they would experience a total or critical loss of business functions if they suffered an outage lasting approximately 1 week. Such losses might occur in a matter of hours for banks or other financial institutions, where information systems themselves are the major sources of activity and revenue. Approximately 43 percent of companies that lose a major portion of their data through disruption or disaster will never reopen.[1]

THE MAJOR THREATS TO COMPUTERIZED INFORMATION SYSTEMS

The major threats to computerized information systems are disasters, such as fire or electrical failure, hardware malfunctions, software errors, user errors, and computer crime and abuse. These threats and their effects are summarized in Table 12.1.

On-line information systems and those based on telecommunications networks are especially vulnerable because they link information systems in many different locations. As a result, unauthorized access or abuse can occur at a multitude of access points. Figure 12.1 illustrates the vulnerabilities of a generic telecommunications network. New network technologies and computing patterns magnify these vulnerabilities. Wireless data networks are easily penetrated, since wireless data transfer uses devices that are essentially radio transmitters. Anyone with the right receiver can tune into a voice or data transmission. Client/server networks are especially difficult to safeguard because there are even more points at which the system can be accessed, which allows more opportunities to tamper with information. Local area networks (LANs) lack many of the backup and security features that are found in mainframe systems and are easily disrupted. Many things can go wrong, including file server crashes, faulty hard disks, problems with network operating systems, or application errors.

COMPUTER CRIME, HACKERS, AND COMPUTER VIRUSES

Of special concern to designers and users of information systems are the issues of security and computer crime. **Security** refers to all the policies, procedures, and technical tools used for safeguarding information systems from unauthorized access, alter-

Security

All the policies, procedures, and technical tools used to safeguard information systems from unauthorized access, alteration, theft, and physical damage.

TABLE 12.1

Major Threats to Computerized Information Systems

Threat	Effect
Fire	Computer hardware, files, and manual records may be destroyed.
Electrical power failure	All computer processing is halted; hardware may be damaged, and "disk crashes" or telecommunications disruptions may occur.
Hardware malfunction	Data are not processed accurately or completely.
Software errors	Computer programs do not process data accurately, completely, or according to user requirements.
User errors	Errors inadvertently introduced by users during transmission, input, validation, processing, distribution, and other points of the information processing cycle destroy data, disrupt processing, or produce flawed output.
Computer crime	Illegal use of computer hardware, software, or data results in monetary theft or destruction of valuable data or services.
Computer abuse	Computer systems are used for unethical purposes.

FIGURE 12.1

A Telecommunications Network Is Vulnerable at a Number of Points

Potential security problems—unauthorized access or abuse of the system—can occur at many points in a telecommunications network. Unauthorized access and illegal connections can occur at the input stage. It is also possible to "tap" communications lines and illegally intercept data. Within the CPU itself, either the hardware or software can fail, and stored files can be accessed illegally, copied, or stolen. Telecommunications systems linked by satellite are even more vulnerable because transmissions can be intercepted without using a physically attached device.

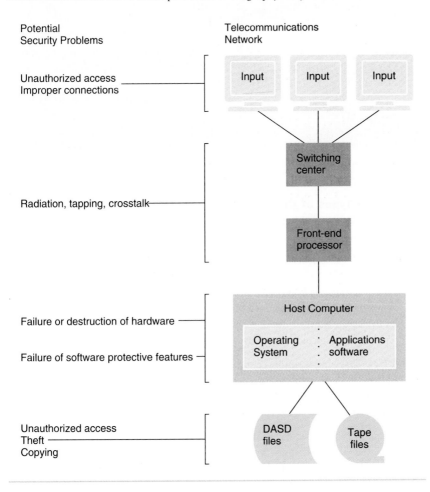

ation, theft, and physical damage. As organizations continue to store critical data on networks, the problems of unauthorized penetration are growing. USA Research Inc. in Portland, Oregon, estimated that the total volume of damage created by computer break-ins in the United States workplace reached $164 million in 1991, double the amount of damage 2 years earlier.[2]

Although the greatest threats to computer systems come from accidents and human error, a major objective of computer security is to prevent **computer crime** (which includes the deliberate theft or criminal destruction of computerized data or services, the use of computer hardware or software to illegally alter or destroy data, and the application of computer technology to perpetrate a crime) and to prevent legal but unauthorized access to computer systems.

Computer crime

The deliberate theft or criminal destruction of computerized data or services; the use of computer hardware, software, or data for illegal activities; or the illegal use of computers.

TRW's computer center houses one of the largest single databases in the nation. Security is multilayered to protect such important systems.

SOURCE: Courtesy of TRW, Inc.

Sources and Types of Computer Crime   Computer crime can range from a teenage prank to international espionage. Although monetary theft is the most common form of computer crime, it can also involve theft of services, information, or computer programs; alteration of data; damage to software; and trespassing. Here are some examples:

- Three technicians at AT&T's British headquarters in London set up their own company in 1992, assigned it a 900 number, and programmed AT&T computers to dial the number often. AT&T lost close to $500,000 before the fraud was accidentally detected.

- A New Jersey bank employee stole credit cards for her personal use by changing addresses on new accounts to her grandmother's home address. Bank officials eventually found the network the culprit was using and traced the transactions to her microcomputer by using special auditing software.

- In late 1991 a robber electronically snatched $25 million from one of the world's largest banks by using a microcomputer with network access to a Digital Equipment minicomputer in the bank's payroll department. Investigators suspect a bank employee but haven't been able to identify the culprit because hundreds of employees had access to the necessary data, and officials had no means of tracing the transactions to a particular workstation.

- John Draper discovered that the prize whistle offered in boxes of Cap'n Crunch cereal perfectly matched the frequency of an AT&T WATS line. He used the whistle to make free telephone calls. U.S. businesses may be losing up to $4 billion annually on unauthorized long-distance calls. A popular technique is to use an electronic monitoring device to intercept the electronic serial numbers and customer identification numbers of cellular telephones and then use them to make long-distance calls from other cellular telephones.[3]

Losses from computer crime are difficult to quantify because many computer crimes go undetected and corporations are reluctant to publicize such problems. Computer crime has been estimated to cost over $1 billion in the United States and billions more if cellular and corporate telephone theft are included. The concentration of assets in computer form makes computer crime a high-loss, high-risk proposition for a business firm. Even if the crime does not involve major theft, it can severely damage a business's operations or record keeping. For example, USPA, Inc., and IRA, Inc., two branches of an insurance and brokerage firm based in Fort Worth, Texas, could not pay 550 employees for several weeks when a former programmer wiped out 168,000 payroll records.

The vast majority of computer crimes are committed by authorized insiders. The National Center for Computer Crime Data in Los Angeles, California, estimated that 70 percent of reported computer crimes were perpetrated by people inside the organization. For example, employees from the magnetic peripherals arm of Control Data Corp. were arrested for diverting as much as $20 million in company goods and cash by using Control Data's automated purchasing and inventory records.

Hackers   Nevertheless, loss and damage from **hackers** attempting to penetrate information systems from the outside cannot be dismissed. The press has reported numerous incidents of inventive teenagers who invade computer networks for profit, criminal mischief, or personal thrills. Sophisticated personal computer users are becoming increasingly adept at connecting their personal computers to the nation's telephone network to eavesdrop, charge calls to another person's bill, destroy data, disrupt telephone switching services, or penetrate computer systems linked via telecommunications.

Hacker
A person who gains unauthorized access to a computer network for profit, criminal mischief, or personal reasons.

Between 5 and 10 percent of all bar code sales in supermarkets and merchandise chains are erroneous, resulting in many customers being overcharged for their purchases. Poor data quality is the single largest cause of information system problems.

SOURCE: Courtesy of International Business Machines Corporation.

Among the most notorious of these hackers were five young men under 22 years of age who belonged to a group called the Masters of Deception. The men broke into over twenty-five of the largest computer systems in the United States, including those of TRW Information Services (a leading credit reporting firm), Southwestern Bell Corp., New York Telephone, Pacific Bell, the Martin Marietta Corp., and universities. They stole and resold credit reports, credit card numbers, and other personal information. They were apprehended and charged in July 1992 with computer fraud, computer tampering, illegal wiretapping, wire fraud, and conspiracy.[4]

Computer virus

A rogue software program that spreads rampantly through computer systems, destroying data or causing the systems to become congested and malfunction.

Computer Viruses   Alarm has risen over hackers propagating **computer viruses**, rogue software programs that spread rampantly (like viruses) from system to system. Information systems become congested and malfunction as the viruses endlessly replicate themselves. Depending on the intent of the creator, the virus might flash a harmless message such as "Merry Christmas!" on computer terminals, or it might systematically destroy all the data in the computer's memory. A survey conducted by the National Computer Security Association and Dataquest Inc. found that viruses cost businesses $2 billion in 1994 alone. The average virus attack affected 142 microcomputers and took more than 2 days to eradicate. One-fourth of the attacks took more than 5 days to detect.[5]

The most notorious computer virus epidemic occurred in November 1988, when a brilliant computer science student introduced a program that spread uncontrollably throughout a nationwide Department of Defense data network. Created by Robert Tappan Morris, the son of one of the U.S. government's most respected computer security experts, the virus program rapidly reproduced itself throughout Arpanet (Advanced Research Projects Agency Network), which links research centers, universities, and military bases.

Morris introduced the program through a Cornell University terminal by signing on to a computer at the artificial intelligence laboratory at the Massachusetts Institute of Technology. The virus raged through computers that used a particular version of the UNIX operating system, moving from computer to computer as a piece of electronic mail through the Arpanet Sendmail program. Once inside Sendmail, however, the virus program used a "backdoor" feature to bypass Sendmail's electronic mailboxes, or files for storing personal messages, and entered the host computer's control programs. From there the virus moved to other computers and spread rapidly throughout the Arpanet network. Morris intended his program to reside quietly on Arpanet computers, but it was quickly detected as it echoed back and forth throughout the network in minutes, copying and recopying itself thousands of times.

Computer security experts concluded that this virus contained no harmful hidden features and left data files unharmed, but it did clog the Arpanet computers and eventually caused the network to shut down. More than 6,000 computers were infected. The Defense Department asserted that it was impossible for classified military networks that manage nuclear weapons systems and store vital secrets to be penetrated in this manner.[6]

Incidents such as this continue to occur on a smaller scale because personal computers are plentiful and their networking software and equipment are relatively easy to use. The following measures have been recommended for combating software viruses; these will decrease but never eliminate the problem:

1. Make backup copies as soon as you open a new software package and store the copies off-site.

2. Quarantine each new piece of software on an isolated computer and review it carefully before installing it on a network.

3. Restrict access to programs and data on a "need-to-use" basis.

4. Check all programs regularly for changes in size, which could be a sign of tampering or virus infiltration.

5. Be especially cautious with "shareware" and "freeware" programs, which have been a prime entry point for viruses.

6. Institute a plan for immediate removal of all copies of suspicious programs and backup of related data.

7. Make sure all purchased software is in its original shrink wrapping or sealed-disk containers.

Corporate Espionage   In addition to hacking and computer crime, the vulnerabilities of contemporary systems have opened new opportunities for committing commercial espionage. Corporations are storing more and more of their confidential information on computers, including strategic plans, sales data, production formulas, and even confidential memos and E-mail exchanges. This information is very valuable to competitors. Such valuable, confidential data are potentially more accessible because the growing use of telecommunications has dramatically expanded the number of points at which commercial spies are able to access a firm's system.

INFORMATION SYSTEM QUALITY PROBLEMS: SOFTWARE AND DATA QUALITY

While computer disasters such as fire, espionage, and viruses grab the headlines, software and data quality problems are a larger and more constant threat to computer operations. **Software bugs** (errors or defects in the code of a program), which can cost untold amounts of damage and losses in productivity, are everywhere. Developing high-quality software presents particularly difficult problems.

Software bug
Errors or defects in the code of a software program.

Software Quality Problems   Total quality management and zero defects are popular concepts in business today. They were pioneered by the Japanese, and the rest of the business world began to pay attention when the quality of Japanese products improved sharply and consumers began to demand Japanese goods. Zero defects is an appropriate target for most goods and absolutely essential for some products (think of the results of failed heart valves or airplane motors). Computer software, however, is different. Programs with zero defects cannot be achieved with current technology. Let's look at why.

In writing any but the simplest of computer programs, bugs cannot be avoided. The main technique in most computer programs is making decisions based on a given set of choices. For example, a simplified version of a part of an income tax program might contain lines like the following:

```
IF NET-INCOME IS LESS THAN 12,000
      THEN TAX-OWED EQUALS 0
      PERFORM PRINT-RETURN-ROUTINE
ELSE IF NET-INCOME IS EQUAL TO OR GREATER THAN 12,000 AND
      LESS THAN 24,000
      THEN TAX-OWED EQUALS (NET-INCOME MINUS 12,000)
      TIMES 0.14.
CALCULATE NET-TAX-OWED EQUALS TAX-OWED MINUS TAX-PAID.
IF NET-TAX-PAID IS GREATER THAN ZERO
```

THEN PERFORM OWES-TAX-ROUTINE
ELSE IF NET-TAX-PAID IS LESS THAN ZERO
THEN PERFORM REFUND-DUE-ROUTINE
ELSE PERFORM TAXES-EVEN-ROUTINE.

The code would continue with all the many tax possibilities and the accompanying mathematical formulas and actions. Most choices include a series of steps that contain further choices and steps, creating many complex paths. A program of several hundred lines will have many tens of such choices and paths. Important programs within an organization will have thousands or even millions of lines as well as hundreds or thousands of decision points. An ordinary payroll system for a large corporation, for example, may have hundreds of programs, each of which will require thousands or tens of thousands of lines of instructions.

With so many lines of code and so many decision points, a large number of errors will creep in. Errors occur for a number of reasons: typing errors, improper use of a complex programming technique to code a tricky passage, lack of clarity in program specifications, even misunderstandings by the end-users concerning what actions are needed under every possible combination of circumstances. The only way to make certain no errors exist within a program is to test every line of code, making certain that every possible path is executed through to its end, and that every kind of data error can be handled. However, studies indicate that testing every possible choice and line within a large system (such as a payroll, manufacturing control, or hotel reservation system) would require a minimum of thousands of years, even with the most powerful computers now available. Thus, complete testing of larger systems is a complete impossibility.

Worse yet, once testing has been "completed," no one can estimate with any accuracy how many bugs are left or what their effect might be. Hidden bugs will only surface when the lines of code that contain them are executed, triggered by an unusual combination of conditions. A hidden bug recently surfaced in a New York City–area bank that caused the bank to deduct $2 from each customer's account for every dollar the customer withdrew through the bank's ATM. The cost to the bank was enormous, not only in work to correct the bug and reinstate the funds in customers' accounts but also in negative public relations. The Focus on People provides a more detailed analysis of this event.

An AT&T long-distance failure in 1990 that forced all the New York financial markets to close for a day and shut down 800 lines for 9 hours was caused by a tiny, hidden program bug in a software upgrade to the firm's Signal System 7. Manufacturers have had to throw away whole batches of a product that were ruined during the computer-controlled manufacturing process when a new software bug surfaced. Imagine the havoc and death a hidden bug could cause in a railroad signal control system, an on-board airplane navigation system, or even an automobile brake control system.

Ultimately, the goal for most companies in relation to information systems bugs is not one of zero defects, but rather one of reducing the number and seriousness of bugs as much as possible within an acceptable time and cost framework, thus producing systems of as high a quality as is reasonably feasible.

One enormous issue faced by users of computer software is that of system maintenance. The maintenance phase of a system begins once a system goes into production, and it lasts for as many years as the system continues to be used. To many, maintenance refers to keeping the system running, particularly when hidden bugs do surface, and this is certainly a significant aspect of maintenance. When a critical system fails to act as required, it must be fixed immediately. However, maintenance also includes the need to keep the system up-to-date so that it supports the changing needs of the organization. If the business grows, a sales system might have to be modified to support added sales offices or additional products. It might also have to be enhanced so that it can be accessed

FOCUS ON PEOPLE

MIGHTY OAKS FROM LITTLE ACORNS GROW: THE RIPPLE EFFECTS OF A BUG

In the computer world mighty oaks can indeed grow from little acorns. On February 15, 1994, Chemical Bank of New York City installed some new software related to the operations of their ATMs. That night about 100,000 customers withdrew approximately $16 million from the cash machines and had their accounts charged twice: once for the ATM withdrawal, and a second time for a check for the same amount written against their accounts, checks they did not write. Chemical found the problem next day after receiving about 4,000 phone calls from customers complaining of two transactions against their accounts when there should have been only one.

The problem was a tiny bug in a single line of code. The ripple effects were enormous, affecting far more than the 100,000 accounts. For many customers, the double withdrawal brought their accounts below the minimum level for no-fee banking just as their statements were prepared for the next morning's mail, causing unwarranted fees to appear on their statements. Others had their accounts brought below the level needed to cover previously written checks that arrived at the bank that night or the next day. As a result, many checks bounced.

Although the software was installed in the morning, the problem did not surface until the following morning because the checking system is run only once a day, very late at night. Thus, the false transactions were not applied against the accounts until early morning. As a result, the damage was far more widespread than it would have been had the incorrect transactions immediately been deducted from customers' accounts. Once discovered, bank officials had several tasks to perform simultaneously. They had to assess the breadth of damage. Were only Chemical customers affected, or were customers of other banks who used the Chemical ATM machines also involved? Was the problem limited to New York state customers, or did it affect Chemical customers in New Jersey and other states? Were only withdrawals affected, or were deposits also doubled? Happily the problem was limited to withdrawals only by Chemical customers within New York. Officials then had to rapidly repair the software, a task that fortunately did not take long because the system was newly installed, and the programmers were familiar with the programs. Finally, the bank had to deal with all the problems that arose from the error.

Chemical immediately increased its customer relations staff by 30 percent. They called all 100,000 affected customers to inform them of the problem and what the bank was doing about it. They offered to write letters to the recipients of any bounced checks, taking full responsibility for the error. They also offered to pay all late fees and penalties that the customers might incur as a result of the problem, such as a charge for a delayed mortgage payment. To prevent further checks from bouncing until the erroneous transactions could be reversed, the bank had to ask for special permission from the Federal Reserve Bank of New York to delay their processing of checks a day beyond the normal legal limit. The special authorization was granted. The bank had to locate not only the transactions that were applied to accounts in error, but they also had to identify all transactions that were mistakenly generated as a result of the original error, such as monthly interest payments that were too low, charges for issuing the phantom checks, and bounced check charges. Statements mailed on February 16 contained the original error and other related errors. Those customers had to wait a whole month to obtain a corrected account statement. The bank also had to delay all statements the following day while all the problems were solved and correcting transactions were generated so that no other customers would receive statements that did not reflect the true condition of their accounts.

This affair was ironic in two ways. First, the reaction of the public was one of resignation. Although the magnitude of the effects of this error was unusually large, experts pointed out that nearly all banks have computer errors that affect their customers. Second, the new software had been installed as part of Chemical's year-long effort to *improve* the operations of its ATM system.

FOCUS Questions: What people, organization, and technology factors caused this problem? How serious a problem was this incident? Why?

SOURCES: Saul Hansel, "Bank Says Cash Machine Problems Are Fixed," *The New York Times*, February 19, 1994, and "The Greedy Cash Machines: 100,000 People Are Overbilled," *The New York Times*, February 18, 1994.

via a network in order to serve a more dispersed sales staff. A changing legal environment might require modifications to a payroll system or an environmental monitoring system. Increased cost pressures might cause a company to modify its manufacturing process, which in turn might require changes in production control systems. Maintenance is an ongoing need for most large systems and in many companies costs much more than does the development of new systems.

Data Quality Problems   The most common source of information systems failure, however, is not software quality but problems that result from data that are inaccurate, outdated, or incomplete. According to a recent study, 69 percent of corporate executives surveyed said that their corporate data had an unacceptable level of corruption. Corrupted data can wreak havoc. A tiny error in a percentage figure can cost a bank millions of dollars. But a single data error is not the most significant problem. Rather, the largest problem is the many bits of inaccurate data in massive numbers of records, from name and address errors in customer lists to mistakes made in individual accounts payable records. Credit histories of individuals, used to establish eligibility for all kinds of loans and credit cards, were so fraught with errors that the United States federal government forced the credit bureaus to give consumers access to their credit histories in order to improve credit record quality.

Here are some other examples of data quality problems:

- For months an airline had planes take off carrying only half the number of passengers listed for each flight because it had corrupted its database of passenger reservations while installing new software.

- J. P. Morgan, the New York investment bank, discovered that 40 percent of the data in its credit risk management database was incomplete and had to be double-checked by users.

- Several studies have documented that 5–12 percent of bar code sales at supermarkets and retail stores are erroneous and that the ratio of overcharges to undercharges runs 4:1. The problem stems mainly from human error in keeping shelf prices accurate.

- A comprehensive audit of FBI data published in 1988 found that 54.1 percent of the records in the FBI's National Crime Information Center system was inaccurate, ambiguous, or incomplete. Seventy-four percent of the records in the FBI's Identification Division system displayed similar problems.

When bad data go unnoticed, they can lead to product recalls, bad decisions, and financial losses. In the following sections we examine how organizations can address these problems and the other threats to their systems.

12.2 DEVELOPING CONTROLS FOR SYSTEMS

Controls
The specific technology, policies, and manual procedures used to protect assets, accuracy, and reliability of information systems.

General controls
Organization-wide controls, both manual and automated, that affect overall activities of computerized information systems.

As the preceding section shows, safeguarding computer information systems can no longer be treated as an afterthought but must be integral to the system design. Effective business problem analysis and solution design include considerations of how the information system can be protected and controlled.

The specific technology, policies, and manual procedures for protecting assets, accuracy, and reliability of information systems are called **controls**. There are two types of controls: **general controls**, which can be applied to the overall business and computing environment of an organization, and specific **application controls**, which govern individual information system applications.

GENERAL CONTROLS

General controls are all the organization-wide controls, both manual and automated, that affect the overall activities of computerized information systems. In other words, they provide an umbrella for all information systems in the firm. General controls ensure the following:

- The security and reliability of computer hardware.

- The security and reliability of software.

- The security of data files.

- Consistent and correct computer operations.

- Proper management of systems development.

They also include **management controls**, which provide appropriate management supervision and accountability for information systems. Table 12.2 presents examples of general controls in each area.

Documentation is a critical but often overlooked element of information system control. It is critical because information systems will not work properly unless clear-cut explanations of how they work from both end-user and technical standpoints are available. Each information system solution requires three levels of documentation: system documentation, user documentation, and operational documentation.

System documentation describes the design, structure, and software features of an information system solution. User documentation details manual procedures and how an information system solution is used from an end-user standpoint. Operational

Application controls
Manual and automated procedures to ensure that the data processed by a particular application remain accurate, complete, and valid throughout the processing cycle.

Management controls
A type of general control that provides appropriate management supervision and accountability for information systems (e.g., establishing formal written policies and procedures and segregating job functions in order to minimize error and fraud).

Documentation
A control that involves establishing and maintaining a clear-cut explanation of how an information system works from both an end user and a technical standpoint; includes system, user, and operational documentation.

A supervisor works with an on-line reservation agent at an airline reservation center. Ongoing management supervision and accountability are essential for ensuring that all the controls for an information system work properly.

SOURCE: © Jon Feingersh, Stock, Boston.

TABLE 12.2

General Controls for Information Systems

Control	Example
Hardware	Restricting access to machines/terminals; checking for equipment malfunction.
Software	Requiring logs of operating system activities; restricting unauthorized access to software programs.
Data security	Using passwords; restricting access to terminals to limit access to data files.
Operations	Establishing procedures for running computer jobs correctly; establishing backup and recovery procedures for abnormal or disrupted processing.
Systems development	Requiring management review and audit of each new information system project for conformity with budget, solution requirements, and quality standards; requiring appropriate technical and business documentation for each system.
Management	Establishing formal written policies and procedures; segregating job functions to minimize error and fraud; providing supervision and accountability.

documentation describes the steps for running and operating a system, or for backup and recovery, that would be used in a corporate data center. Table 12.3 provides examples of all three kinds of documentation.

APPLICATION CONTROLS

So far we have looked at general controls that monitor the firm's overall computing environment. In addition to these broad general controls, there are specific controls, called application controls, that govern individual information system applications. Application controls consist of both manual and automated procedures to ensure that the data processed by a particular application remain accurate, complete, and valid throughout the processing cycle. There are three types of application controls: input controls, processing controls, and output controls (see Figure 12.2).

Input controls ensure the accuracy and completeness of data when the data enter an information system. **Processing controls** ensure the accuracy and completeness of data during updating, and **output controls** ensure that the results of computer processing are accurate, complete, and properly distributed. Some of the most important application control techniques are procedures for authorizing and validating input and output, programmed edit checks, and control totals.

An organization can establish formal procedures that allow only selected individuals to authorize input of transactions into a system or to review system output to make sure that it is complete and accurate. These are known as authorization and validation procedures. For example, the signature of the head of the payroll department might be required to authorize corrections to employee time cards before such transactions are entered into the payroll system. The payroll department head might likewise be required to "sign off" on the results of each payroll processing run, indicating that he or she has reviewed the results and that they are complete and processed properly.

Programmed edit checks are a common technique for checking input data for errors before the data are processed. Transactions that fail to meet the criteria established in computerized edit routines will be rejected. For example, an order processing system

Input controls

Application controls that ensure the accuracy and completeness of data entering the information system.

Processing controls

Application controls that ensure that the accuracy and completeness of data during updating.

Output controls

Application controls that ensure that the results of computer processing are accurate, complete, and properly distributed.

Programmed edit check

An application control technique for checking input data for errors before the data are processed; it uses a computerized checking procedure.

TABLE 12.3

Examples of Information System Documentation

System Documentation
System flowcharts
Structure charts
File and record layouts
Program listings

User Documentation
Functional or business description of system
Data input instructions
Transaction authorizations
Sample data input forms or on-line input screens
Report distribution lists
Output report samples
Error correction procedures

Operational Documentation
Computer job setups
Run control procedures
Backup and recovery procedures
Hardware and operating system requirements
Disaster recovery plan

might check the product codes on the order transaction to make sure they are valid by matching them against the product codes on an inventory master file. If the product code does not conform to any existing product codes, the order transaction will be rejected. If the transaction passes this test, the program might then check the product price on the order to determine that it is accurate (if the item has a fixed price), appropriate (if the price may vary depending on quantity ordered), or reasonable (falling within present appropriate limits if the salesperson has discretion in setting the price). Sometimes

FIGURE 12.2

Application Controls and General Controls Work Together to Promote System Security and Accuracy
General controls govern the security and accuracy of the overall computing environment. They include such safeguards as data security measures, routine error checks in hardware, restriction of access to programs, and standards for system development. Application controls govern individual system applications. There are three types of application controls, corresponding to the three basic steps in computing: input, processing, and output. At each step there are specific types of application controls that check for errors, incomplete data, and inappropriate data. Note that the same control techniques, such as control totals and authorization checks, can be used at different points in the processing cycle.

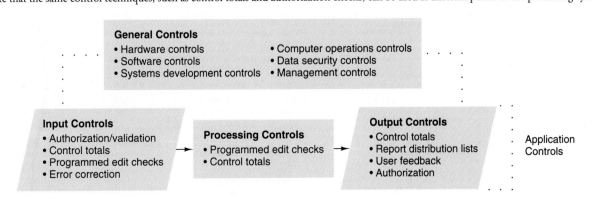

Control totals

A manual or automated count of the number of transactions processed during input, processing, or output, or of critical quantities, such as order amounts; this count is then compared manually or by computer to a second count; discrepancies in the counts signal errors.

preprogrammed edit checks are used as a processing control as well. Figure 12.3 describes some of the most important techniques for programmed edit checks.

Control totals are used at all points in the processing cycle to ensure completeness and some level of accuracy. An information system can make a manual or automated count of the number of transactions processed during input, processing, or output or of total critical quantities, such as order amounts. These totals can then be compared manually or by computer; any discrepancies will signal potential errors. Table 12.4 summarizes the major types of control totals—record counts, quantitative totals, hash totals, and run-to-run control totals.

PROBLEM SOLVING WITH CONTROLS

An integral part of solution design is making sure an information system has the proper controls. It is essential that vulnerabilities are identified during problem analysis and that solution alternatives consider different options for controls. We can apply our people, technology, and organizational framework to control issues.

Technology	**Organization**	**People**
Hardware malfunction	Management supervision	Insider crime
Software errors	Segregation of functions	Training
Program security	External pressure (privacy	Ease of use of controls
Telecommunications	laws, need to distribute	User errors
security	systems and data)	
Database security		

TABLE 12.4

Major Types of Control Totals

Control	Description	Example
Record counts	Counts the total source input documents and compares this total to the number of records at other stages of input preparation.	Number of order forms should match the total number of order input transactions for a batch order entry system.
Quantitative totals	Totals a quantitative field such as total sales or total orders for a batch of transactions and compares this number with a manual total established for this group of transactions.	Total order amount should match the order total for a batch of order transactions in a batch order entry system.
Hash totals	Totals nonquantitative data fields for control purposes and compares them with a total manually established for a group of transactions.	Total product code numbers should match a total established manually for a batch order entry system.
Run-to-run controls	Totals can be generated during processing to compare the number of input transactions with the number of transactions that have updated a file or with output totals. The totals can represent total transactions processed or totals for critical quantities.	Total number of time cards input should equal the total number of employees updated on the payroll master file during processing and the total number of employees with paychecks generated.

FIGURE 12.3

Programmed Edit Checks Are a Valuable Application Control Technique

Programmed edit checks can be used in both the input and processing phases to ensure data accuracy. Special edit check programs read input transactions and scan their data fields for accuracy. The most common types of edit techniques are the format check, the existence check, the reasonableness check, and the check digit. Transactions that do not meet the criteria of these checks are rejected and reported. The transactions must be corrected to pass the edit criteria before they can become part of the updated files.

Programmed Edit Checks

Technique	Description
1. Format check	The system checks the contents, size, and sign of individual data fields. Example: A telephone long distance code should be a 3-position numeric field.
2. Existence check	The system checks for valid codes by comparing input data fields to tables or master files. Example: State code should be one of the valid state codes on a state code table.
3. Reasonableness check	The system checks to see if selected fields fall within specified limits. Example: An employee's gross pay can't exceed six figures.
4. Check digit	The check digit is an extra reference number added to an identification code bearing a mathematical relationship to the other digits. The check digit is input with the other data, recomputed by the computer, and compared with the one input. Example: The check digit for vendor code 29743 is 9. The vendor code with appended check digit would be 297439.

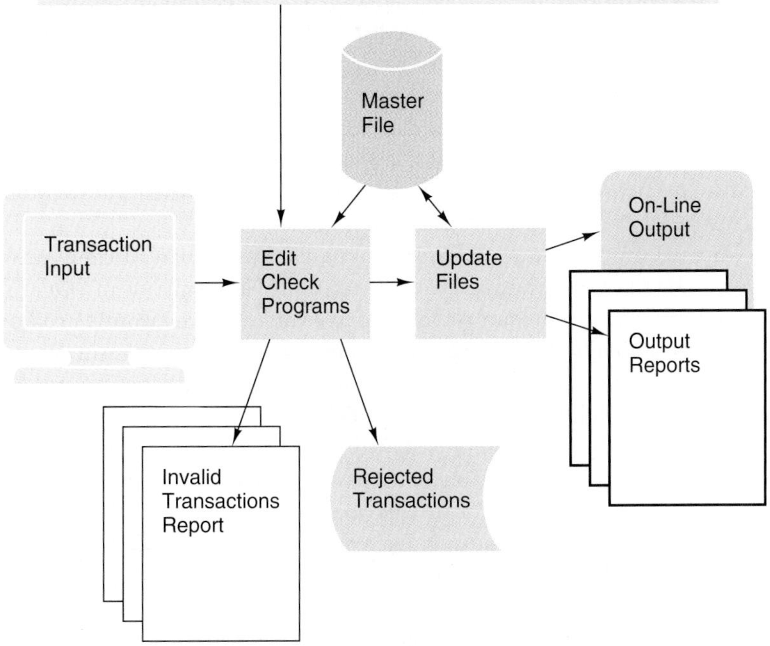

The logical and physical design of an information system solution should establish the criteria for ensuring completeness and accuracy of input, processing, and output. Figure 12.4 illustrates how analysis and design of controls fit into the problem-solving process. At each step in the problem-solving process, there are specific control issues that must be addressed.

Not all information systems use application controls to the same degree, nor do they all need to. Much depends on the nature of the application and how critical its data are. We can expect major banking and financial systems to use more controls than other systems because so much money and credibility is at stake.

Safeguarding information systems can be a costly and complicated process. Moreover, a system that has too many controls—one that is "overcontrolled"—can be so unwieldy and difficult to use that people may be discouraged from using it at all. The problem-solving process must weigh the benefits of each control or safeguard against financial costs and ease of use to determine the right mix for each application.

12.3 SECURING INFORMATION SYSTEMS

Securing information systems includes securing computers from disruption and unauthorized use and programs and data from unauthorized modification. Three important aspects of security are ensuring data security, safeguarding microcomputers and networks, and developing recovery plans for disasters affecting information systems. All of these areas require more attention now than ever before because of the growing reliance on networking and telecommunications.

DATA SECURITY

Data security
A control aimed at preventing the unauthorized use of data and ensuring that data are not accidentally altered or destroyed.

Data security entails both preventing unauthorized use of data and ensuring that data are not accidentally altered or destroyed. Data security must be provided for both data storage and data usage in both on-line and batch systems. The organization needs to determine what data are stored in its systems, how they are used, and who is allowed to access and update the data. A fundamental data security policy is to restrict access on a "need-to-know" basis—in other words, allowing individuals only the kind of data they need to do their jobs. Especially sensitive kinds of data, such as salaries or medical histories, may need a very strict definition of "need-to-know."

Data security must be especially tight for on-line information systems, since they can be accessed more easily by nontechnical specialists than batch systems. One of the principal data security techniques is the use of passwords, or secret words or codes giving individuals authority to access specific portions of an information system or systems. A password may be required to log on to a system, to access data and files, to change data in the system, and to view sensitive data fields.

Data security is often multilayered, with passwords for logging on tied to overall operating system software and additional passwords and security restrictions established by data security features of specific applications. Figure 12.5 illustrates the multilevel data security system for a mortgage loan system. User identification and authorization are checked at the system software level when staff first log on. A former employee whose password has been deleted would be unable to access the system at all. The banking specialist and loan officer must then provide a password to access customer mortgage account files; a clerk would be unable to access these files. At the individual

Control Issues Must Be Considered at Each Step of the Systems Development Process

Earlier in this book we examined the problem-solving steps involved in developing a new system. This diagram illustrates that at each step in the problem-solving process, there are crucial control issues to be considered. From the very beginning of the systems development process, criteria should be established for both general and application controls.

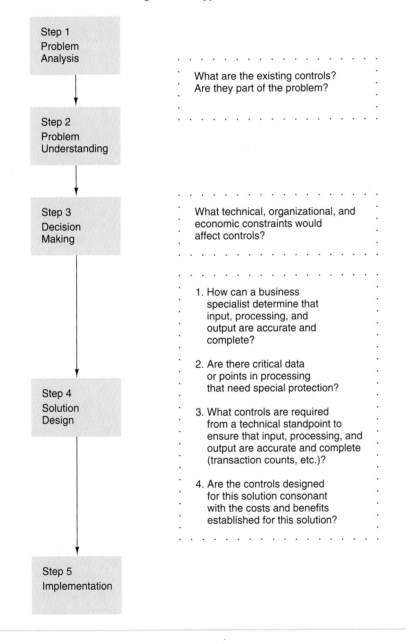

data field level, only the loan officer would be allowed access to annual income data. The banking specialist would not be allowed to view this sensitive information.

One problem with passwords is that they are not guarded carefully enough. Unauthorized individuals can easily discover another person's password if he or she writes

FIGURE 12.5

A Data Security System

Data security is a vital consideration for all firms. It involves protecting sensitive data by preventing unauthorized access and making sure that the data cannot be changed or erased. This figure illustrates a multilevel data security approach for a mortgage loan system that requires all employees to provide an authorized password when logging on. Staff must supply an additional password to access customer mortgage account files. A former employee whose password has been deleted would be unable to access the system at all; a clerk would be able to access the system but not the mortgage account files. A banking specialist could access mortgage account data but would be restricted from viewing the Annual Income field. A loan officer, however, would be able to view all the data.

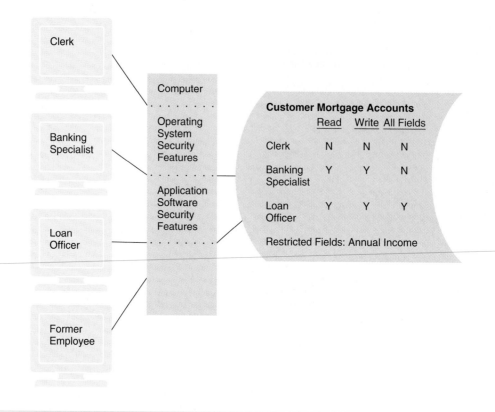

Customer Mortgage Accounts	Read	Write	All Fields
Clerk	N	N	N
Banking Specialist	Y	Y	N
Loan Officer	Y	Y	Y

Restricted Fields: Annual Income

it down on a piece of paper and carelessly leaves it by a desk or terminal. Yet individuals cannot be expected to memorize all their passwords, especially if they need a different password for each application, or if the passwords are periodically changed. They must be guarded when used on a network also. The Focus on Technology describes the way passwords are stolen on networks and some of the potential solutions to this problem.

As a result of the increased use of telecommunications, organizations have turned to an additional data security safeguard in the form of data encryption. Data are scrambled into a coded form before transmission on a telecommunications network and then decoded on arrival. An authorized user enters a unique, secret key that is not stored anywhere on the system to trigger the encoding process. The U.S. Bureau of Standards adopted the Data Encryption Standard (DES) in 1977 for encrypting commercial data such as that used by banks, government agencies, and other organizations. The Problem-Solving Case at the end of the chapter raises some issues related to data encryption.

FOCUS ON TECHNOLOGY

THE "TROJAN HORSE" OF THE INTERNET

The Internet, the world's largest network, is under siege from within. As with most other networks, the security of the Internet is vital. Those who break that security are called "crackers" because they "crack" the network's security system. Crackers steal all kinds of vital data and services, obtain and use credit card information, and carry out commercial espionage. According to James Settle, supervisory special agent of the FBI's National Computer Crimes Squad, today's cracker is not like the hacker of the past who was in it for fun. Today the typical motivation is profit. A whole underground network of crackers exists. Once crackers find a loophole in a network's operating system, they spread the news through underground publications, cracker conventions, and computer bulletin boards. They even use these channels to distribute programs to exploit network security defects. Settle claims that once a cracker breaks into the system, very few users are safe. Even if you are only connected to someone who is connected to the Internet, you are vulnerable also.

The magnitude of the problem became clear in October 1993, when Public Access Network Corp. (known as Panix), which sells access to the Internet, announced a major security breach. It announced that it was closing its connection to the Internet for 3 days while it dealt with a Trojan horse. A cracker (or group of them) had planted a rogue program in Panix's computers to track all passwords. When an individual signed on to a computer anywhere on the Internet through Panix, the crackers were able to steal the password and then gain access themselves. Once inside the second computer, the rogue software would be planted there also, thus making available more passwords and computer access in a never-ending chain.

The problem faced by Panix was not unique; in fact, it is all too common. The Trojan horse approach to breaking security has been used for years. The Panix incident differed because Panix decided to publicize the information to let other Internet users know the extent of the problem. Dain Gary, manager of the Computer Emergency Response Team that deals with Internet security problems, says his organization gets three to four reports of security breaches per day, and the number is growing. However, experts estimate that only about 15 percent of known break-ins are ever reported.

Part of the problem is that few people think about security issues related to the Internet. They focus only on the gain and the glitter, according to Eugene Spafford, the director of a Purdue University security center. The problem is multiplied in the case of the Internet by the fact that at least 2 million computers are connected to it, and the number is growing rapidly.

The ultimate issue, however, is not the Internet. It is security on all networks, and the lack of security consciousness in general. Other than in magnitude, the problems faced by the Internet do not differ from those faced by other networks.

If stealing passwords is so easy, what can be done about it? First, encryption is becoming more important—stealing an encrypted password or data that neither the thief nor another computer can read is of no value. Moreover, some networks require that you change your password each time you log on, an approach that erases the value of the stolen password, although it is a nuisance as a long-range solution. Another solution being used by some companies is a credit card–sized computer that creates a unique password each time it is used, but this is an expensive and clumsy method. The latest and perhaps most promising solution is a system called Kerberos that was developed at the Massachusetts Institute of Technology. Kerberos codes passwords in such a way that they cannot be viewed while they are traveling along the network. No solution is possible, however, until network managers and senior corporate management become alert to the risks and take steps to protect their systems as much as possible while the technology continues to improve.

FOCUS Questions:
What people, organization, and technology factors are responsible for Internet security problems? How would you recommend that your company deal with these problems?

SOURCES: John Markoff, "Staking a Claim on the Virtual Frontier," *The New York Times*, January 2, 1994, and "A Dose of Computer Insecurity," *The New York Times*, October 30, 1993; Jared Sandberg, "Computer 'Cracking' Is Seen on the Rise," *The Wall Street Journal*, November 1, 1993.

SAFEGUARDING MICROCOMPUTERS AND NETWORKS

Stand-alone microcomputer systems have tended to have less formal and stringent controls than those that are mainframe or minicomputer based. Control requirements change, however, when microcomputers are networked or linked to mainframes and other computers for cooperative processing. As applications formerly relegated to mainframes are downsized to microcomputers, they too will require serious controls if they entail critical data. Safeguarding microcomputers raises special problems and requires a special approach. Table 12.5 lists some considerations for microcomputer security.

Providing security is more difficult when microcomputers are networked into LANs or when the organization uses client/server computing. The wide distribution of and easy access to critical information in client/server networks open new channels through which users can alter or destroy data and intruders can gain access. Many of the tools that are available for mainframe and minicomputer security are not available for client/server environments.

Special steps must be taken to address network security as information system solutions are being designed. They include:

- **Backing up critical data.** Critical data should be copied to a variety of media so that data can be restored if there is a hardware failure or the data are corrupted or destroyed.

- **Providing redundant file servers or disk drives.** Redundant file servers and disk drives should be included in the design so that the system can keep working if one piece of hardware breaks. The organization should keep a supply of spare file servers, workstations, and disk drive components on hand for such emergencies.

- **Controlling access to workstations.** Physical access to networked workstations should be restricted and protected.

- **Classifying network users.** Network users should be carefully classified and assigned a level of security appropriate to their jobs. Users who need system data to perform their jobs should have fairly easy access, while users who do not need such data should have little or no access.

- **Documentation.** Procedures for restoring parts of the network and the telephone numbers of key technical specialists should be thoroughly documented for use during emergencies.

- **Antivirus software.** Special software for detecting and eradicating computer viruses can be installed to limit the risk of virus damage.

TABLE 12.5

A Microcomputer Security Checklist

1. Is microcomputer equipment stored in a locked room or attached firmly to work areas?
2. Are disks locked in drawers or filing cabinets? Are disks with critical data stored in a fireproof place?
3. Are data on hard disks backed up regularly?
4. Have individuals authorized to use each machine and application been formally identified?
5. Does each microcomputer application have input, processing, and output controls?
6. Have a procedure and individual been authorized for verifying the data in each application?
7. Are there standards, passwords, and other precautions for downloading and uploading data between microcomputers and mainframes or minicomputers?
8. Are individuals using microcomputers held accountable for security?
9. Have training and formal documentation for microcomputer security been instituted?

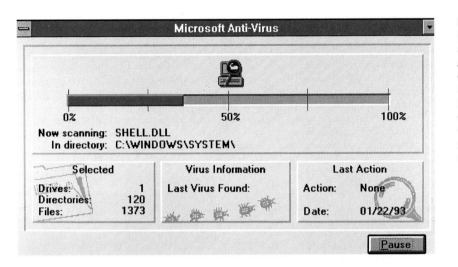

Microsoft Anti-Virus is one of the leading antivirus software packages for microcomputer systems. Antivirus software can detect and eradicate computer viruses and should be used along with other protective measures to prevent computer viruses from infecting an organization's information systems.

SOURCE: Courtesy of Microsoft Corporation.

DISASTER RECOVERY PLANNING

A wise step for firms that are highly dependent on computerized information systems is to develop a **disaster recovery plan.** Such a plan describes how firms can resume operations after disasters such as fires, floods, power disruptions, or sabotage have disrupted their computer processing. A disaster recovery plan typically provides for immediate access to alternative computer hardware and restoration of software programs, data, and telecommunications facilities. The following are key elements of a disaster recovery plan.

Disaster recovery plan
A plan detailing how an organization can resume operations after disasters have disrupted its computer processing.

- Identifying the most critical business functions and their vulnerabilities.

- Knowing what hardware, software, files, and human resources are required to resume processing of critical applications.

- Training personnel to follow the recovery plan correctly.

- A step-by-step course of action for implementing the plan.

A key component of disaster recovery is backing up and restoring data for critical applications. Disaster recovery plans must also be sensitive to how much of these data flow through microcomputers and telecommunications links and how much reside in mainframes. Firms use either internal or external disaster recovery facilities.

For example, the Beneficial Data Processing Corp., the data processing subsidiary of Beneficial Corp. in Peapack, New Jersey, relies on its own distributed processing facilities for disaster recovery. It has distributed processing to local branches so that the branches can operate for several days if the main computer center is lost. Figure 12.6 illustrates another option—the use of multiple computer centers. The Elkay Corp. split its applications between two mainframe computers, one in Oak Brook, Illinois, and the other in Broadview, Illinois. The mainframes are connected to each other and to remote sites via dedicated data lines. Each mainframe can back up the other. In fact, when operations at the Oak Brook site were disrupted by a fire at an Illinois Bell switching station in 1988, Elkay transferred data tapes and personnel to its Broadview data center and continued functioning.

FIGURE 12.6

Using Multiple Computer Centers to Protect a Firm against Disasters

The Elkay Corp. in Illinois protected itself against possible disasters by splitting its operations between two mainframe computers. Its Oak Brook mainframe handles corporate applications, while the Broadview site controls manufacturing applications and order entry. However, the two computer centers are connected using telecommunications lines, both to each other and to remote sites, and each can take over the other's functions in less than a day. The plan paid off when a fire at an Illinois Bell switching station disrupted phone service to the Oak Brook center. Elkay transferred data tapes and personnel to the Broadview center and continued operating from there.

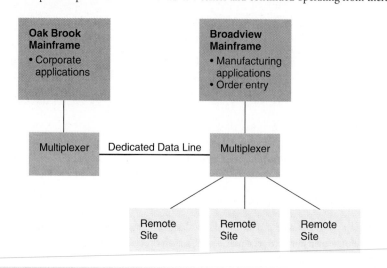

Sungard Disaster Recovery Services and Comdisco Disaster Recovery Services are specialized external disaster recovery services. They provide fully operational data processing and telecommunications backup facilities to subscribers on less than 24 hours notice. These include computer hardware and software for a firm to run its applications when needed, plus technical assistance in disaster planning testing and use of recovery centers.

The Focus on Organizations examines the resurgence of interest in disaster planning and some special problems that need to be addressed.

12.4 SOLVING SYSTEM QUALITY PROBLEMS

While zero-defect computer systems may not be possible, system and data quality can be improved dramatically if developers draw on the knowledge and skills in system-building gained over the past three decades.

ENHANCING SOFTWARE QUALITY

Software quality assurance is a major, ongoing issue for information systems professionals. Although progress is being made, no magic bullet exists that can improve the quality of software. Moreover, as we indicated above, problems cannot be totally solved with today's technology. However, software quality can be improved by considering the problem from a number of angles.

Development Methodologies   Any good quality program should begin with the adoption of a **development methodology**. The primary function of a development methodology is to provide discipline to the whole development process. A good methodology is based on proven methods of accomplishing all the standard tasks that are part of the development process. It establishes an organization-wide standard approach for gathering specifications, and designing, programming, and testing the new system. In addition, the methodology usually indicates the appropriate tools acceptable within the company to perform these tasks. By standardizing the building of systems in this way, a methodology makes systems easier to develop, test, audit, and maintain. Standardization offers two additional benefits: it reduces the cost of training, making it more feasible for a company to properly train its staff, and it results in more flexible staff members, who can be moved easily into priority projects. Most important, however, experience indicates that while not all system defects can be eliminated, a disciplined approach greatly reduces the number that remain.

A sound development methodology begins with methods to gather business specifications in an effective manner and to design a system to meet those specifications. It then provides programming standards that result in modularized computer programs that are understandable during development and maintainable after implementation. It also includes guidelines for establishing quality measurements for a system that are agreed on in advance by all parties involved. Testing guidelines and procedures are also central to a development methodology. We discuss quality measurements, programming standards, and testing separately below.

Finally, a development methodology includes methods and tools for controlling the development project itself. Lack of proper project control is one of the most important causes of project and system failure. Proper project control should include project milestones for schedule and budget review by both technical and business management. Planned testing tasks by business and technical staff, which help ensure that the system will be adequately tested, should also be included in the methodology. Such an approach results in projects that are more likely to stay within budget, be completed on time, and satisfy the users.

Development Resource Allocation   Traditional methods of building systems allocated the largest portion of resources to the programming phase of systems development. Experience and numerous studies show that a minor error in logic at the analysis and design phase that would take an hour to correct at the time will require at least 10 times as much work to correct in the programming phase and 90 times the effort once the system has been implemented. The clear lesson for development project leaders is that project resources, including time, should be shifted to earlier in the systems-building process and that greater emphasis must be placed on analysis and design. In addition, companies need to stress analysis and design skills in hiring and training staff. The result should be that fewer bugs are created in the first place.

Quality Measurements   People do not automatically recognize quality or agree on its definition, although what quality is and how it is defined are often assumed in application development projects. Measurement of quality requires careful planning, including agreements in advance as to what quality is and how it is to be measured. Those party

Development methodology
A proven method of accomplishing the tasks of systems development to provide standards for guiding the activities of a systems development project.

FOCUS ON ORGANIZATIONS

DISASTER HEADLINES ENCOURAGE DISASTER PLANNING

Major disasters have been front page news in recent years—the 1990 and 1993 California earthquakes, Hurricane Andrew in Florida, the Chicago and midwest floods, the World Trade Center bombing. Until recently, information system disaster recovery has not been taken seriously by many organizations. Although disasters have severely affected the information system facilities (and hence the operational abilities) of many companies, only about 40 percent of large organizations even have disaster recovery plans. Not surprisingly, concern over planning for possible disaster has grown as disaster headlines have multiplied.

Some disasters have affected many companies simultaneously. Figure 12.7 shows the ten worst U.S. information technology disasters, most of which drew a great deal of media attention. Together these ten disasters interrupted systems at almost 2,000 data centers, causing enormous financial and productivity losses. For example, the Chicago flood of April 1992 caused extensive power and telecommunications outages and water damage that crippled major banks, retail stores, and government centers. Billions of dollars were lost. Management of many organizations have been forced to recognize the obvious fact that disasters are unpredictable; it is too late to prepare for them after they occur.

Examples of successful disaster planning have also contributed to this changing attitude. Brody, White & Co., a commodities brokerage firm in the World Trade Center in New York City, had established a New Jersey hot site (an alternate site where operations can continue in case of a disaster at the main site) as a protection against an unexpected disaster. After the 1993 terrorist bombing they were able to shift to their hot site almost without interruption, continuing operations there for a month until their main site was again operational. News coverage contrasted this story about Brody, White with the many stories of other companies who lost a great deal of business while they scrambled for days or even weeks to find alternate computer facilities. Brody, White's insurance—disaster planning—clearly paid off.

Changing business perspectives have also increased disaster planning awareness. Computers are pivotal to an increasing number of companies as businesses become more reliant on the information stored in computers or on telecommunications systems. As a result, managements have begun to value the uninterrupted operation of their computers ever more highly. In addition, for many businesses the only long-range strategy for success is qual-

ity customer service. Many organizational leaders have concluded that the cost of a disaster can no longer be measured only in terms of the cost of repair and the immediate business lost. The larger, if more nebulous, cost is the customers who go elsewhere for more reliable service.

Today's disaster planners must think about a disaster's effect on their staff as well as their customers. When a widespread disaster occurs, an organization will naturally find many staff members more concerned with caring for their families than their computers. At the University of Miami, for example, officials had difficulty persuading staff to operate their systems after Hurricane Andrew hit. Plans must take this people factor into consideration. Methods of planning for disasters are also changing. Today a company can purchase a software package designed to aid the complex disaster planning process. For example, the American Automobile Association, based in Heathrow, Florida, uses the PC-based Total Recovery Planning System from Chi/Cor Information Management, Inc. of Chicago. New ways of dealing with disaster backup are also being developed. In Section 12.3, we explained how two companies, Beneficial Data Processing and Elkay,

SOURCES: Joseph C. Panettieri, with Chuck Appleby, "Survival of the Fittest," *InformationWeek*, January 10, 1994, and Bob Francis, "Recovery from Distributed Disasters," *Datamation*, December 1, 1993.

FIGURE 12.7

Days of Infamy
The 10 worst U.S. IT Disasters

Incident	Date	Data Centers Hit
1. Nationwide Internet virus	May 16, 1988	500+
2. Chicago flood	April 1992	400
3. New York power outage	August 13, 1990	320
4. Chicago/Hinsdale fire	May 8, 1988	175
5. Hurricane Andrew	September 1992	150
6. Nationwide Pakistani virus	May 11, 1988	90+
7. San Francisco earthquake	October 17, 1989	90
8. Seattle power outage	August 31, 1988	75
9. Chicage flood	August 13, 1987	64
*10. East coast blizzard	March 1993	50
Los Angeles riot	April/May 1992	50

*Tie

use geographically separated sites to internally back up their own data. The University of Miami has developed a partnership with a northern Florida company whereby each organization performs a weekly backup of the other's data. In this way an off-site (and out-of-area) backup occurs at no charge for both organizations.

The biggest change in disaster planning, however, is the result of the changing configuration of computers. Traditional disaster planning focused on the data center, an approach that was adequate for centralized mainframe systems but today leaves vital networks unprotected. Organizations that have been doing disaster planning for years may find themselves vulnerable as they decentralize their information systems. Because disasters tend to be localized, wide area networks actually have some disaster protection inherent in them. That is, a disaster in one location will leave the hardware at other locations untouched. Nonetheless, because software and data for all locations will usually be affected when even one key node is hit by disaster, the entire system will probably stop. Planning to operate a key, widespread network after a disaster hits one site is a complex matter and must be planned carefully, possibly using software designed to support network disaster planning. Traditional hot site services, such as those offered by Sungard and Comdisco (discussed in Section 12.3), emphasize mainframe use in case of disaster. But today, operating the mainframe without being able to operate the networks can cripple a company. Because organizations need hot sites for networks as well as mainframes, IBM, Hewlett Packard, and a number of other companies have begun to offer network hot site services; Comdisco is redesigning its sites to provide client/server recovery capabilities.

FOCUS Question:
How would you justify the expense of disaster planning to your company? What people, organization, and technology issues should be addressed by a disaster recovery plan?

to the agreements must include all who have a major stake in the project, including analysts, programmers, end-users, and auditors. Quality measurements must reflect the organizational goals established by the user and must also consider the limits of technology and cost of achieving certain goals (e.g., improving on-line response time may cost more than it is worth to the organization). Issues of quality, from a business perspective, will include interface ease of learning and use; computer response time; systems hours of availability; location and hours of service of telecommunication connections; number of bugs per 1,000 lines of programming code; and any other elements the user requires. Determining quality measurements can be complex; the development methodology will help. Interface ease-of-use might be measured by surveys and by training time required. Response time must include not only speed but also the number of users and the lowest percentage of response time that is acceptable. For example, a customer service unit may require a 5-second response time 90 percent of the time with 100 simultaneous users signed on to the system. Such measurements must be agreed on in advance of building the system so that they can be used during and after development.

Programming Standards   Traditional programming code was aptly nicknamed "spaghetti" code because it was so tangled that it was often impossible to follow its logic. Programs could not be reviewed by other programmers to ensure quality while they were being written. Once the system was implemented, finding and fixing bugs was a long, expensive, and frequently impossible task. Today, structured programming standards produce programs that are written in English-like language (e.g., a data name might be "gross-income" rather than the more mysterious name "GI1") and that are modularized (review the discussion of structured programming in Chapter 10). Other programmers, and often even end-users, can follow the code and review it for correctness. When bugs do appear, they are more easily isolated and corrected. If necessary, whole sections (modules) can be changed without affecting the basic logic of the program. Such code will contain fewer bugs and be more easily maintained. Moreover, standardized programs are more flexible, making them easier and less expensive to modify in response to changing business needs.

Testing   Testing standards are critical to improving system quality. Testing is often misunderstood. Most project team members, information systems professionals and end-users alike, will test to prove that the system works. While this is the obvious goal, a good development methodology will modify the project team's goal to emphasize testing as a means of discovering as many problems and bugs as possible. The bugs and operational problems are there; the more that are eliminated before implementation, the higher the quality of the system. Testing is also a skill with tried-and-true methodologies and useful tools. Test cases must be developed for each specification, and test banks developed so that the data for testing will be reliable. Testing must take place at all phases, including specification and design, and not just once programs are completed. Adequate time must be allocated for testing, and its importance must be stressed by project management. The Focus on Problem Solving describes the successful use of testing methodology at the discount broker Charles Schwab & Co., Inc.

Development Tools   Many automated tools are available to support the developer while improving the quality of the software. Some tools that can assist in improving the quality of application systems development were developed for use in general areas, such as project management and graphics software. Other tools were designed specifically for use in developing software, such as the CASE tools described in the Part Three

FOCUS ON PROBLEM SOLVING

SCHWAB TESTS ITS SOFTWARE

Effective testing requires planning and discipline. It is also a frame of mind. To test successfully, an organization must know why it is testing, have a methodology it actually follows, and be committed to devoting the time and resources to test effectively. Charles Schwab & Co., Inc., is one of the largest stock brokerage firms in the United States. An error in a Schwab application system could cost the company (or its client) millions of dollars, so new systems must be properly tested.

To Schwab, testing is important enough that they maintain a testing-services group that is skilled and experienced in testing. In one recent project (a testing program for the Windows interface of a new order entry system to handle trades for institutional investors), the testing group selected Auto-Tester for Windows as an automated testing tool because of its ability to support a structured testing methodology. They then developed a formal test plan that defined the scope of testing, responsi-

bilities for testing throughout the project, and deliverables from the testing process. The overall project then defined the functional business requirements by using a prototype. Business specialists representing the traders in the field reviewed the prototype and made recommendations for the system functions that would help them perform their jobs effectively, efficiently, and accurately. These business functions became the basis of the test requirements. From the requirements, the test team developed a test requirements matrix based on almost 300 individual business functions.

The next step was to develop test cases for each item in the matrix. According to Herb Isenberg, testing services technical lead, the goal was to cover the entire set of requirements "with the least possible number of cases." Part of the development of the test cases was to determine data requirements. In many companies, testing is done by simply taking recent live data and running them through the system being tested. But such an unsystematic "hit-or-miss" approach will fail to test many types of data. Schwab testers developed data requirements not only to make certain of proper coverage of data but also to assure test data independence. In other words, each test case should be executable independent

of the others. If a trader wants to sell stock, for instance, an account must hold sufficient shares to process the trade; the account balance must not depend on another test case.

Since the developers had no control over the 12 different production databases in which the live data are actually stored, they extracted test data that could be added to the databases instead of writing over them. The final preparatory step was the development of scripts to run each test case. Each script included the action to be taken, the state of the application, the data to be supplied or retrieved, and the actual results. Once the test cases were developed, the test-services group made them available to the programmers who were coding the software. In this way, programmers could use the test cases as they tested their own work before submitting the completed product to the test group.

FOCUS Questions:
In your opinion, why do so few companies test their software as Schwab does? Should they be doing more structured testing? Why? What people, organization, and technology issues should be addressed by a testing program?

SOURCES: Kevin J. Farley, "Final Exam," and Kevin Weeks, "School Yourself: Seven Steps to Better Testing," *Windows Tech Journal*, April 1994.

Illustrated Case. For example, code-generating tools can be used to generate a large portion of the program code of many systems. These generators produce structured, easy-to-follow code. Fewer bugs are produced by using a generator, and the tool can save a great deal of time. Experience shows that development tools cannot take over most development work, but their appropriate use will improve the quality of the final system.

ENSURING DATA QUALITY

Data quality can be improved in a number of ways. Data can be edited when they are first entered, so that obviously bad data are rejected. For example, a stock price can be automatically checked to make sure that it is all numeric and that it falls within a certain range. A stock that normally ranges in price from $20 to $50 might be rejected and brought to the attention of a monitor if it were entered at more than $100. The trained monitor would then check the price to see whether it had jumped that high. If so, the monitor would change the editing parameters; if not, the monitor would trace the source of the error and correct it. By using computer security procedures, data can also be protected so that only designated programs or persons are authorized to add, delete, or modify them. If others who have access to the data attempt (accidentally or purposefully) to alter them, such activity will be blocked.

Data quality is also being improved through the growing use of DBMSs, which we discussed in Chapter 7. A DBMS centralizes the data and stores them separately from the processing programs. One piece of data can be stored in only one place instead of in many files, thereby reducing data redundancy and eliminating most of the data integrity problems that accompany data redundancy. Moreover, a DBMS makes the editing of data input relatively easy so that more input errors can be caught before they corrupt the data. Most important, however, DBMSs make the data easily accessible for use in reporting and analysis while securing them from unauthorized updating. Set up properly, for example, a DBMS would be able to support the security pattern illustrated in Figure 12.5, which allows a bank's loan officer to view and update all mortgage data while restricting access by other bank employees.

Data quality audits are also important to improving the quality of data. By regularly scheduling such audits, business units can spot emerging data quality problems and take early corrective action. Such audits can be done in several ways: by interviewing end-users to determine their perceptions of problems with the data, or by actually checking data or data samples manually or with auditing software. The Social Security Administration has established a regular audit procedure that checks 20,000 sample beneficiary records each month.

Data quality audits
Surveys of data in information systems to ascertain their level of accuracy and completeness.

SUMMARY

- Computer information systems are more vulnerable to destruction, error, abuse, and crime than manual systems because data are concentrated in an electronic form in which they can be more easily accessed, altered, or destroyed. Networked systems are especially vulnerable.

- The major threats to computerized information systems are disasters, such as fire or electrical failure, user errors, hardware malfunction, software errors, and computer crime.

- Computer crime involves using software and hardware to alter or destroy data or applying computer technology to perpetrate a crime. The major types of computer crime are monetary theft; theft of services, information, or computer programs; alteration of data; damage to software; and trespassing. The vast majority of computer crimes are committed by insiders.

- Hackers and computer viruses are growing threats to information systems because of the upsurge in networked computing.

- Information system quality problems caused by software errors and data that are inaccurate, outdated, or incomplete are major causes of malfunctioning information systems.

- Controls refer to the specific technology, policies, and manual procedures for protecting the assets, accuracy, and reliability of information systems. General controls govern the overall business and computing environment of a firm, and specific application controls govern individual information system applications.

- General controls consist of hardware controls, software controls, data security controls, systems development controls, computer operations controls, and management controls. Complete user, system, and operational documentation are essential for maintaining a sound general control environment.

- Application controls consist of input, processing, and output controls. Principal application control techniques include control totals, programmed edit checks, and procedures for authorizing and validating input and output.

- Analysis and design of information system controls must be included at various stages of the problem-solving process. A solution design must consider the costs and benefits of each control as well as ease of use.

- Security encompasses all the policies, procedures, and technical tools for safeguarding information systems from unauthorized access, alteration, theft, and physical damage. Three important aspects of security are data security, safeguarding microcomputers and networks, and disaster recovery planning.

- Data security, which involves restricting access to data in computer information systems, is essential, especially in on-line information systems. Two important techniques for promoting data security are the use of passwords and encryption.

- A disaster recovery plan is a plan for restoring critical information system operations after physical disasters or sabotage have disrupted computer processing. It provides access to alternative computer hardware and tools and procedures for restoring software programs, data, and telecommunications capabilities.

- Software quality problems can be solved or minimized by using appropriate software development methodologies and standards, development tools, and careful testing. Data quality can be improved by carefully editing input data, using database management systems, and performing regular data quality audits.

KEY TERMS

Security	Documentation
Computer crime	Input controls
Hacker	Processing controls
Computer virus	Output controls
Software bugs	Programmed edit check
Data quality problems	Control totals
Controls	Data security
General controls	Disaster recovery plan
Application controls	Development methodology
Management controls	Data quality audits

REVIEW QUESTIONS

1. Why are computer information systems more vulnerable than manual systems? What kinds of computer information systems are the most vulnerable?

2. List the major threats to computer information systems.

3. What is computer crime? Name various types of computer crime.

4. What is security? What is its relationship to computer crime? To hackers?

5. What is a computer virus? How can computer virus attacks be prevented?

6. Describe the major quality problems that prevent information systems from functioning properly.

7. What are controls? Distinguish between general controls and application controls.

8. List and describe each of the general controls required for computer information systems.

9. Why is documentation so important for safeguarding and controlling information systems?

10. What are the three types of application controls? Describe the techniques that are used for each.

11. What kinds of techniques can be used for promoting data security?

12. Describe some steps that can be taken to safeguard microcomputers.

13. Describe some steps that can be taken to safeguard client/server systems.

14. What is a disaster recovery plan? What are some of the key elements of such a plan?

15. What steps can be taken to improve software quality?

16. How can data quality be improved?

DISCUSSION QUESTIONS

1.   There is no such thing as a totally secure system. Discuss.

2.   If you were designing an information system, how would you determine what controls to use?

PROBLEM-SOLVING EXERCISES

1.   *Group exercise:* The solution design for the North Lake Bank mortgage payment system in Section 10.3 notes that the controls for this application remain the same as before. With three or four classmates, use the information supplied in this text to write a description of what those controls might be. Present your findings to the class.

2.   Write an analysis of what might happen if each of the general controls for computer information systems were not in place.

3.   *Hands-on exercise:* Using appropriate software, develop an application to help security specialists analyze the data provided in Figure 12.7. Your application should be able to provide reports that can answer the following questions:

How many major IT disasters were caused by power outages?

Which major IT disasters caused by viruses took place in 1988?

How many IT disasters involving more than 100 data centers occurred after 1991?

NOTES

1. Steven R. Christensen and Lawrence L. Schkade, "Surveying the Aftermath," *Computerworld*, March 13, 1989.
2. James Daly, " 'Open' Security: Resolving the Paradox," *Computerworld Client/Server Journal*, August 11, 1993.
3. Bob Violino, "Are Your Networks Secure?" *InformationWEEK*, April 12, 1993.
4. Mary W. Tabor with Anthony Ramirez, "Computer Savvy, With an Attitude," *The New York Times,* July 23, 1992.
5. James Daly, "Virus Vagaries Foil Feds," *Computerworld*, July 12, 1993.
6. "Computer 'Virus' Injected in Military Computers," *The New York Times*, November 4, 1988.

PROBLEM-SOLVING CASE

THE CLIPPER CHIP: GOVERNMENT INTRUSION OR CITIZEN PROTECTION?

A hot debate is raging over the Clipper chip. Is it a tool for "Big Brother" to spy on United States citizens? Or is it a necessary weapon for the U.S. government to protect its citizens against criminals and terrorists?

As the industrialized economies have globalized and been transformed into knowledge and information economies, cross-country and around-the-world data movement have become essential: telephone calls, faxes, orders, shipping information, product research, product specifications, strategic plans, marketing plans, sales results, personal medical records, and electronic meetings are necessary to conduct business. Organizations and individuals must protect confidential data from commercial or military espionage, and encryption has long been the favored method of doing so— many will remember the key role the breaking of the Japanese code played in some World War II allied victories.

Encryption software today has become so sophisticated that codes are virtually unbreakable. At the same time, encryption has become easy to use. When using encryption, the sender and receiver must agree upon a "key" to encode and decipher the communication. Encryption software automatically and instantaneously encodes the voice and/or data communication at the sender's end and deciphers it at the receiver's end. Anyone trying to steal the communications finds that without the key, they will have only garbage. In recent years, widespread reports of hackers breaking into corporate and government computers, the stealing of passwords on the Internet, and increased commercial espionage have caused a dramatic growth of interest in encryption. At the same time, the growth of wireless (satellite and microwave) communications has made the theft of noncoded information easier.

Governments have long used wiretapping and other devices to "eavesdrop" on telephone conversations in order to break up criminal conspiracies and to gain evidence for criminal prosecutions. Court-approved wiretaps in the United States have played a key role in the conviction of many organized crime leaders, spies, and terrorists. For example, in the famous 1993–94 spy case of Aldrich Ames, who sold CIA secrets to the Soviet KGB, wiretapping played a key role in the ability of the FBI to break the case. As telephone communication is gradually digitized and the use of E-mail expands rapidly, the encryption of more and more communications is possible. U.S. government officials know that without the ability to break these unbreakable codes, they will lose the ability to wiretap, a valuable weapon in the fight against crime, spying, and terrorism. As the Clinton Administration's February 1994 statement said, "Unfortunately, the same encryption technology that can help Americans protect business secrets and personal privacy can also be used by terrorists, drug dealers, and other criminals." John Markoff, technology reporter for *The New York Times*, summed up the problem this way: "How to preserve the right of businesses and citizens to use codes to protect all sorts of digital communications without letting criminals and terrorists conspire."

The Clipper chip is the U.S. government's proposed answer to the conflict between the need to encrypt and the government's need to eavesdrop. It is a microprocessor chip that contains software for encrypting any telecommunications in unbreakable codes. Connected to a telephone or data terminal, it will scramble communications as any other contemporary encryption device does. When two people want to secure their communications, they activate their encryption devices to exchange secret numerical keys, using the Clipper chip to encode and decode their data. However, the Clipper chip has an added feature, a so-called "back door" that under certain circumstances would allow U.S. federal agents to unscramble communications. The federal government would have a key to the Clipper chip. To protect communications privacy, the plan is to split the key into two parts, storing one part at the Commerce Department's National Institute of Standards and Technology and the other part in the Treasury Department. Use of the keys would require both halves, so that no individual could act on his or her own. As with any wiretap today, use would require a court order. Anyone using the back door key without a court order would be subject to severe criminal penalties. Figure 12.8 shows a diagram of how the security will work.

While the government has not announced any plans to require the use of the Clipper chip for all encryption, it is debating establishing conditions that would likely bring about that effect. The long-term goal is that the National Security Agency (NSA) and the FBI will be able to continue to wiretap legally. First, the federal government is requiring the use of the Clipper chip in all the computers and data terminals it purchases. Given that the federal government is the largest single purchaser of such equipment in the world, this requirement could create the Clipper chip as a standard within the U.S. In addition, the government plans to require all encryption communications with its departments to be done with the Clipper chip. Just two departments, the Internal Revenue Service and the Department of Defense, could involve millions of ordinary citizens in this way. Finally, the administration has made it illegal to export any encryption device (hardware or software) other than the Clipper chip.

But this issue involves more than the Clipper chip. Proposed legislation—the Digital Telephony and Communications Privacy Improvement Act of 1994—would require telecommunications companies to use specified technology that would enable the interception of telecommunications. The law would also require phone companies to collect and make available "setup" information—who is phoning whom—for each call made. Louis J. Freeh, the Director of the FBI, defends this legislation as necessary for surveillance and urges its passage. The law-enforcement value of this technology came to public notice in early 1994 when it was used to solve the case of the attack against Olympic figure skater Nancy Kerrigan.

Organized, vocal opposition has arisen from many quarters. Opponents paint a picture of a spying Big Brother trampling on citizens' rights to privacy in a free society. The ultimate fear is the loss of privacy and freedom at the hands

FIGURE 12.8

Putting Privacy in Escrow

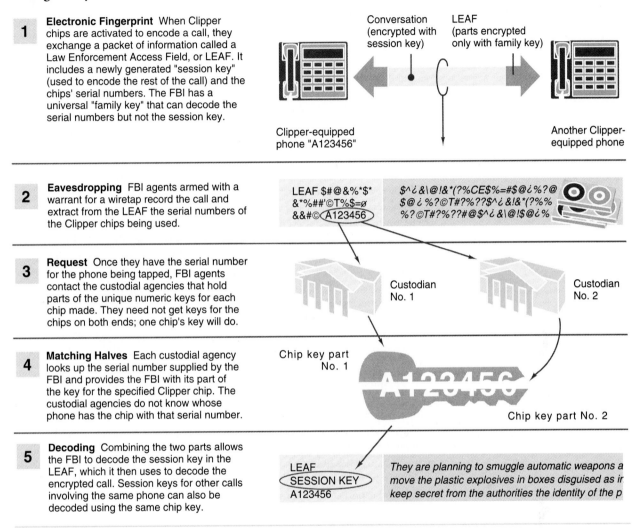

1 **Electronic Fingerprint** When Clipper chips are activated to encode a call, they exchange a packet of information called a Law Enforcement Access Field, or LEAF. It includes a newly generated "session key" (used to encode the rest of the call) and the chips' serial numbers. The FBI has a universal "family key" that can decode the serial numbers but not the session key.

Conversation (encrypted with session key)

LEAF (parts encrypted only with family key)

Clipper-equipped phone "A123456"

Another Clipper-equipped phone

2 **Eavesdropping** FBI agents armed with a warrant for a wiretap record the call and extract from the LEAF the serial numbers of the Clipper chips being used.

LEAF $#@&%*$* &*%##'©T%$=ø &&#© A123456

$^¿&\@!&*(?%CE$%=#$@¿%?@ $@¿%?©T#?%??$^¿&!&*(?%% %?©T#?%??#@$^¿&\@!$@¿%

3 **Request** Once they have the serial number for the phone being tapped, FBI agents contact the custodial agencies that hold parts of the unique numeric keys for each chip made. They need not get keys for the chips on both ends; one chip's key will do.

Custodian No. 1

Custodian No. 2

4 **Matching Halves** Each custodial agency looks up the serial number supplied by the FBI and provides the FBI with its part of the key for the specified Clipper chip. The custodial agencies do not know whose phone has the chip with that serial number.

Chip key part No. 1

A123456

Chip key part No. 2

5 **Decoding** Combining the two parts allows the FBI to decode the session key in the LEAF, which it then uses to decode the encrypted call. Session keys for other calls involving the same phone can also be decoded using the same chip key.

LEAF SESSION KEY A123456

They are planning to smuggle automatic weapons a move the plastic explosives in boxes disguised as ir keep secret from the authorities the identity of the p

of an overly powerful government. Critics contend that the technology will enable the government not only to listen to the contents of conversations, but also to monitor transactions and so learn a great deal of personal information about private citizens, including their spending habits (credit card transactions), their network of friends, their locations, even their sexual preferences. William Safire, the syndicated *New York Times* columnist, perhaps spoke best for this viewpoint when he wrote that federal snoopers can overhear "everything we say on a phone, everything we write on a computer, every order we give to a shopping network or bank or 800 or 900 number, every electronic note we leave our spouses or dictate to our personal-digital-assistant genies."

What about the protection afforded by the split key and the need for a court order? NSA expert James Bamford points out that one court that issues wiretap warrants, the Foreign Intelligence Surveillance Court, is a little-known court that publishes almost no public documents. In its entire 20-year history, Bamford claims, it has never turned down a wiretap request, so that it affords little protection. Supporters claim that the 8,000 wiretaps that were authorized in the decade prior to 1994 resulted in about 22,000 convictions. Freeh points to the World Trade Center bombing in 1993—and its $5 billion estimated damages—as an example of why the FBI needs this authority, but critics counter that telecommunications played no role in breaking that case.

In addition, many critics believe that officials with access to the electronic key could be bribed; enough money could jeopardize the system. Others fear that hackers could break into government computers and steal the codes. Still others believe the government's approach is unnecessary. A 1993 study by the Computer Professionals for Social Responsibility claims they could find no instances in recent years in which FBI agents were unable to wiretap due to technology problems. The FBI claims that hundreds of such cases exist.

Commercial opposition is high-powered and visible. In January 1994, 38 leading computer scientists from such major companies as Xerox and Sun Microsystems stated that they fear the Clipper chip because it "was developed in secret by Federal agencies primarily concerned about electronic surveillance, not privacy protection." Many indicate that large commercial organizations will not use an encryption device they cannot trust because its whole system is secret and is not susceptible to being tested. They are turning instead to other encryption standards. In the past the U.S. government's DES standard became widely used. Today, the leading commercial standard, produced by RSA Data Security, Inc., is being adopted by such computer giants as Hewlett Packard, Apple, IBM, Digital Equipment Corp., and Sun Microsystems as well as by Bankers Trust Co. Ultimately, most businesses are not too worried about spying by the government, but they do want full control over encryption because of their fear of commercial spying.

Major opposition to the Clipper chip centers around the argument that foreign companies and governments will not trust and thus will be unwilling to adopt an encryption device for which the United States government holds a key. A recent count showed that at least 215 competing encryption products are available around the world. If the U.S. standard is not adopted abroad, critics believe it will result in a great loss of business to U.S. firms. The CEOs of such software giants as Microsoft, Lotus, and Novell recently told Vice-President Gore that the tight encryption export controls already cost the U.S. software industry the loss of some $9 billion per year in encryption software sales and in sales of other software that integrates encryption capability. Michael Packer, managing director of financial services technology at Bankers Trust in New York (the seventh largest U.S. bank), expresses grave concern over the ability of the domestic financial services industry to compete in a global economy if U.S. companies cannot be part of an internationally accepted standard.

Critics of the Clipper chip point out that besides being a bad idea, it doesn't work as advertised. Matthew Blaze, a computer scientist at AT&T Bell Laboratories, discovered a basic flaw in the chip's design that would allow someone with sufficient computer skills to encode messages that could not be cracked by the government. Two people could then have secret conversations that law enforcement officials could not unscramble. The Clipper chip would be no more useful to the government than existing encryption technology on the market where law enforcement officials do not hold the mathematical keys.

Perhaps the ultimate argument against the Clipper chip was made in *The Wall Street Journal* by Bob Metcalfe, inventor of the Ethernet LAN technology and now publisher of *InfoWorld*, who says, "I am against Clipper simply because it will not

SOURCES: John Markoff, "Flaw Discovered in Federal Plan for Wiretapping," *The New York Times*, June 2, 1994; Peter H. Lewis, "Of Privacy and Security: The Clipper Chip Debate," *The New York Times*, April 24, 1994; John Carey, "Big Brother Could Hobble High Tech," *BusinessWeek*, March 21, 1994; James Daly, "Security Pros, Clinton Clash Over Encryption Standards," *Computerworld*, January 31, 1994; John Markoff, "A Push for Surveillance Software," *The New York Times*, February 28, 1994, and "U.S. Code Agency Is Jostling for Civilian Turf," *The New York Times*, January 24, 1994; Bob Metcalfe, "Clipper Chip Won't Stop Internet Pirates," *The Wall Street Journal*, March 22, 1994; Michael Meyer and Daniel Glick, "Keeping the Cybercops Out of Cyberspace," *Newsweek*, March 14, 1994; and Mary E. Thyfault with John P. McPartlin and Clint Wilder, "The Data Security Furor," *InformationWeek*, February 14, 1994.

work." Because of its secrecy, it will not be adopted, either within the U.S. or abroad. There are, he claims, better and cheaper alternatives. Moreover, he believes that smart criminals will use additional encryption to foil the Clipper chip while stupid criminals will continue to be caught for the same reasons they are caught now.

CASE STUDY QUESTIONS

1. Use the three perspectives of technology, organization, and people to categorize and analyze the problems the U.S. government is attempting to solve with the Clipper chip.

2. Given the strong opposition to the Clipper chip, why do you think the government persists in supporting it?

3. As a member of the U.S. Congress, would you support the Clipper chip and accompanying legislation and policy? Why?

4. Taking into consideration the needs of the FBI, the NSA, business organizations, and citizen privacy, suggest any compromises or other approaches that might meet most of the needs of all sides to the dispute.

❖ ILLUSTRATED CASE ❖

AUTOMATED SOLUTIONS WITH COMPUTER-AIDED SOFTWARE ENGINEERING (CASE)

As Chapters 9–12 have shown, designing information systems to solve an organization's problems can be a complex, multifaceted process. When a proposed solution entails a system with many inputs, outputs, and processing steps, developing it usually requires the joint efforts of information systems specialists and end users. The solution will need to be described using both narrative and graphics. Much time is required to generate, revise, and refine these descriptions and then translate them into software code.

Now, through computer-aided software engineering (CASE), some of the repetitive aspects of developing system solutions have been automated, freeing time for the more creative aspects of problem solving. For example, CASE can automatically produce charts and diagrams, draw prototypes of screens and reports, generate program code, analyze and check design specifications, and generate documents in standard formats.

While some CASE vendors are trying to create software that addresses all aspects of the problem-solving process, most CASE tools either focus on the early stages of problem understanding, decision making, and solution design, or else support implementation. Examples of the former are CASE tools that automatically produce data flow diagrams, structure charts, systems flowcharts, data dictionaries, and documentation. These are sometimes called front-end CASE tools.

In contrast, back-end CASE tools primarily support the implementation step of problem solving and some aspects of solution design. Thus, they address coding, testing, and maintenance activities. Examples of such tools include testing facilities, compilers, linkers, code generators (which generate modules of source code from higher-level specifications), and application generators. A number of CASE products allow system designers to model desired data entry screens and report layouts or menu paths through a system without complex formatting specifications or programming.

Many CASE tools contain a central information repository, which serves as an "encyclopedia" for storing all types of information related to a specific project: data descriptions, screen and report layouts, diagrams, project schedules, and other documentation. The people working on the project can easily look up the information, share it, and reuse it to solve other problems. Information is especially easy to share with CASE tools that are microcomputer-based and that can be put on local area networks. Thus, not only do CASE tools help system designers create clear documentation, they also help coordinate group problem-solving activities. CASE capabilities for supporting object-oriented and client/server applications are starting to be developed.

CASE products such as Andersen Consulting's FOUNDATION attempt to support the entire problem-solving process. They contain design and analysis tools that can be integrated with tools for generating program code and for managing systems development. For instance, the DESIGN/1 component of FOUNDATION allows users to do word processing, design data entry screens and report layouts, diagram the flow of data through a system, generate structure charts, design databases, and prototype the flow of on-line screens. Figure 1 shows how this tool is used during database design to model relationships among the entities for a bank customer services database.

DESIGN/1 tools are integrated through a shared repository. Problem solvers can define relationships among various design components, combine text and graphics within a single design component, and move or copy material from one component to another. For instance, one can establish relationships between a process in a data flow diagram and the data elements used in that process and use text to describe the process or to add personal notes. As information is changed in one diagram (for instance, the addition or deletion of a data flow), the CASE software ensures that it will be automatically

FIGURE 1

Use of FOUNDATION during Database Design
An entity-relationship diagram is a technique used to develop a model of a database that shows relationships among entities—one-to-one, one-to-many, many-to-one, or many-to-many. A user of FOUNDATION's Data Modeller can automatically define these relationships among entities by using a mouse, pull-down menus, symbols, and icons.
SOURCE: © 1990 Andersen Consulting. All rights reserved. Reprinted with permission.

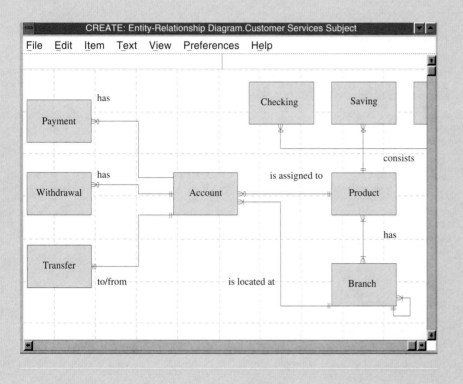

changed in related diagrams and other design components. DESIGN/1 also enables the user to review design data for completeness, accuracy, and consistency.

DESIGN/1 is integrated with INSTALL/1, the implementation and support component of FOUNDATION, which automates application generation. Design components stored in the DESIGN/1 repository are transferred to the INSTALL/1 repository, where they serve as specifications for generating the program code for applications.

Another useful component of FOUNDATION is METHOD/1, which provides a comprehensive methodology plus automated tools to support various approaches to systems development—a custom systems approach, a package system approach, and an iterative development (prototyping) approach. Figure 2 illustrates a Gantt chart, which is used for tracking tasks, budgets, and completion dates when managing a project. The Gantt chart can be automatically revised so that appropriate action can be taken if budgets are changed or

if various tasks are completed ahead of or behind schedule.

To use CASE tools effectively, members of a problem-solving team must adhere to common standards for diagramming; conventions for naming data flows, data elements, or program modules; and an agreed-upon solution design discipline. If each system builder were to cling to his or her own way of developing systems, the incompatibility between the old approaches and new tools could generate confusion. Educating users and technical specialists in how to use these tools effectively is an intricate process of change management.

Creating a new environment for using CASE tools can take a long time—in some cases, up to two years—so companies must be committed to adequate planning and training for CASE. When a firm introduces CASE tools, employees are often afraid they will lose their creativity. They need to be told that they'll be able to retain their creativity, but that instead of figuring out the best way to write program code, they'll be

FIGURE 2

Gantt Chart Used for Managing a Project

METHOD/1 contains automated project management tools with estimation, planning, and scheduling capabilities. The Gantt chart illustrated here details various tasks in a systems development project, their estimated duration, start and end dates, and which tasks overlap.

SOURCE: © 1993 Andersen Consulting. All rights reserved. Reprinted with permission.

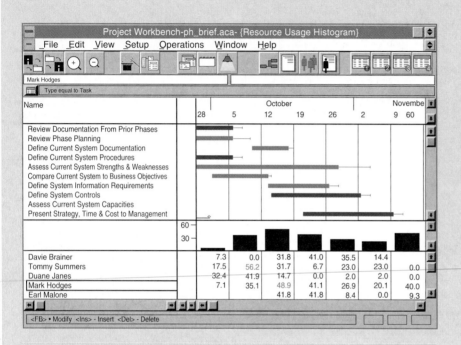

learning how to solve business problems. Training for using CASE tools should show employees how to retain their creativity.

Employees may also fear that CASE tools will eliminate their jobs. For instance, United Data Services in Overland Park, Kansas, had to figure out how to address rumors among its 400 programmers that their jobs would be made obsolete by the new tools. The firm responded by holding 30-minute presentations to reassure small groups of programmers about their jobs, explain how CASE could help them, and get them involved from the beginning.

CASE QUESTIONS

1. How useful are CASE tools for developing information system solutions? What aspects of problem solving cannot be addressed by CASE tools?

2. What human, organizational, and technological factors must be addressed when using CASE tools to design information system solutions?

3. It has been observed that firms that use CASE tools as a quick, low-cost path to creating new systems often lose money on their investment. Why?

OVERVIEW OF INFORMATION SYSTEM APPLICATIONS

Chapter

✦ THIRTEEN ✦

BASIC BUSINESS SYSTEMS

CHAPTER OUTLINE

LEARNING OBJECTIVES

After reading and studying this chapter, you will:

1. Know how information systems are used at the most elemental level in each of the major functional areas of the firm: manufacturing and production, sales and marketing, accounting and finance, and human resources.

2. Be aware of the kinds of problems that basic business systems help to solve.

3. Understand the purpose of fault-tolerant computers.

4. Understand the organizational, technical, and people challenges of building basic business systems.

*U*ntil recently, J.R. Simplot Co. in Boise, Idaho, used very simple systems to track inventory at its five main warehouses. Its warehouses used large wallboards with maps of the facilities and colored magnets to note the location of different frozen potato and vegetable products. Inventory records and order information for the $1 billion food business of this diversified company were kept on paper. In essence, the warehouses were technology-free zones.

Such simplicity had serious drawbacks. Simplot required extra clerical staff to maintain its paper records. It had problems shipping orders placed by high-volume customers such as McDonald's Corp., Burger King, and KFC Corp. Sometimes things went wrong. A warehouse visitor noticed some magnets stuck to the board at angles and straightened them, unaware that the sideways placement indicated special product information.

The warehouses were prime candidates for automation, especially since Simplot's food group accounts for half its total annual sales of approximately $2 billion. In 1992 the company began work on a new computerized client/server system using Unix workstations from Digital Equipment Corp. (DEC) and an SQL Server database from Sybase Inc. Each warehouse has two DEC R3000 workstations. One serves as a database server for the SQL Server database. The other acts as a client, running the warehouse applications. Hand-held radio frequency terminals used by warehouse crews to view and enter information about products and orders are connected to the client system, as are several terminals for office staff. All the warehouses are networked to the food group's order database at company headquarters in Boise.

Except for the bills of lading given to truckers, the new system eliminates paper from the inventory and order-filling process. Simplot installed the new system at its largest warehouse in Caldwell, Idaho in the fall of 1992; by February 1994 all five Simplot warehouses were automated.

Some of Simplot's workers found the new system challenging. People hired to drive a forklift had to be retrained to run a computer. Some had to overcome mental blocks to make the transition. But the system has produced many benefits. Labor costs were reduced. Simplot was able to eliminate 9 of the 138 jobs in the Caldwell warehouse and a few jobs in each of the other warehouses. And Simplot is profiting from improved inventory management. It can use its warehouses more efficiently, reducing costs by maintaining lower inventories. The Caldwell warehouse, which ships about 800 million pounds of food annually, can turn over its inventory 14 times a year. Before, it could change inventory only 12 times during the same time. This increased efficiency is especially important because Simplot's product line has grown as it has increased private-label sales and sales to club stores. The company's accuracy rate in filling orders has also improved. In September 1991 a survey found that only 78% of orders were shipped exactly as customers had specified. Now the accuracy rate is up to 97%.

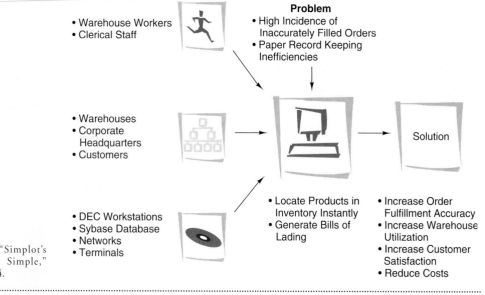

SOURCE: Craig Stedman, "Simplot's Modernization Far from Simple," *Computerworld,* January 31, 1994.

Simplot had to develop a more powerful information system to make the process of tracking products in inventory more accurate and efficient. Its inventory control system is an example of a basic business system that monitors, records, and performs the essential day-to-day activities of firms. This chapter describes how basic business systems work and the role that they play in organizations.

13.1 INTRODUCTION: BASIC BUSINESS SYSTEMS

At the most elementary level, information systems keep track of the day-to-day activities of a business, such as sales, receipts, cash deposits, credit decisions, and the flow of materials in a factory. These **basic business systems** perform and record the routine transactions necessary to conduct the business.

A **transaction** is a record of an event to which the business must respond. For example, data about an order that has just been recorded constitute a transaction. The company responds to this transaction by filling the order, adjusting its inventory to account for the items used to fill the order, generating a packing slip, packaging and shipping the order, and billing the customer. The transaction thus triggers a whole series of events that eventually update the firm's business records and produce appropriate documents. Another name for these basic business systems that use transactions to update company records is **transaction processing systems**.

Many organizations, especially those in banking or financial services, could not survive for more than a day if their basic business systems ceased to function. For example, MasterCard cannot even afford a few minutes' disruption to its system, which processes billions of credit card transactions each day from all over the world. MasterCard employs multiple backup power supply systems for its World Data Center in St. Louis, which is the clearing center for all credit transactions. The First Interstate Bank of California in Los Angeles, which handles from $3 billion to $5 billion of securities trading transactions daily, continually reviews and tests its disaster recovery plan.

Basic business system
A system that serves the most elementary day-to-day activities of an organization; it supports the operational level of the business and also supplies data for higher-level management decisions.

Transaction
A record of an event to which a business must respond.

Transaction processing system
A basic business system that keeps track of the transactions necessary to conduct a business and uses these transactions to update the firm's records. Another name for a basic business system.

13.2 FEATURES OF BASIC BUSINESS SYSTEMS

Basic business systems serve the most elementary level of an organization by processing data about the operations of that enterprise. Such systems keep records of routine business activities—bank deposits, long-distance calls and charges, tax returns, payrolls, and university grades and transcripts. They support the functions of recording, monitoring, and evaluating the basic activities of the business. These systems are important suppliers of data to the operational level of a business and to higher levels of the firm as well. Much of their output is critical to the day-to-day survival of the firm.

THE FUNCTIONS OF BASIC BUSINESS SYSTEMS

The principal purpose of basic business systems is to answer routine questions and to track the flow of transactions through the organization. How many parts are in inventory? What happened to Mrs. Talbert's payment? How many employees were paid this month? The kinds of problems solved by such systems involve very short-term issues. Information for their solution is structured and based on the firm's routine standard operating procedures.

Basic business systems support lower levels of the firm, where tasks and resources are predefined and highly structured. For example, the decision to pay an active

Agents and clients of The Travelers Corporation can call the customer hotline for instant access to insurance policy information such as cash value, coverage, and premium status. Basic business systems such as this one permit companies to efficiently perform their fundamental business activities.

SOURCE: © R. J. Muna.

employee is based on two predefined criteria: Is the employee on the company's payroll, and did the employee work that week? It does not require much management deliberation. All that must be determined is whether the employee meets those criteria. Consequently, these systems are used primarily by people with little or no management responsibility—payroll clerks, order entry clerks, or shop floor stewards. The systems require few, if any, decisions from the people who operate them.

Basic business systems enable organizations to perform their most essential activities more efficiently (see the Focus on Organizations). Business firms need them to function on a day-to-day basis, but often the systems have far-reaching strategic consequences that make them valuable for more than just operational efficiency alone. The SABRE and Apollo systems for processing airline reservations gave American and United Airlines a lead in the computerized airline reservation market and helped them promote their flights over those of competitors.

Although much of the information in basic business systems comes from inside the firm, these systems must also deal with customers, suppliers, and factors external to the firm. For example, an order processing system will contain customer data; a purchasing system will contain supplier data; a personnel system must incorporate government regulations concerning occupational safety, unemployment, and benefits accounting practices; a payroll system must incorporate changes in federal, state, and local tax laws. Thus basic business systems help solve problems concerning the firm's relationship with its external environment.

Most basic business systems are in constant use because they are the underpinnings of the day-to-day activities that drive the business. Many (although not all) of these systems take a high volume of input and produce a high volume of output. A large firm may process thousands or millions of transactions daily. Input data can come from several sources: data entry, punched cards, scanning devices, audio input, or computerized files. The outputs may consist of finished pieces of goods or documents such as paychecks, packing slips, or purchase orders (see Figure 13.1).

FOCUS ON ORGANIZATIONS

BENETTON BENEFITS FROM ELECTRONIC COMMERCE

Every morning, when Asuncion Henry arrives at her office at Fideta, in the heart of the garment-buying district on Paris's Right Bank, she first logs onto her network. The network is a value-added network operated by General Electric Information Services (GEIS) for Benetton Group SpA, the world-famous Italian clothing manufacturer and retailer. Henry is an office manager at Benetton's Fideta office, which manages more than 300 Benetton clothing stores throughout France. She uses the network to forward a new batch of orders to company headquarters in Ponzano, Italy, or to download information from Benetton.

From a small family clothing company in northern Italy, Benetton has grown into a global fashion merchandising and manufacturing giant. It operates more than 6,500 retail outlets in over 100 countries. The network is a vital link between Benetton and its offices and trading partners in 28 countries, handling more than 8 million transactions per year for the firm.

Whenever Benetton introduces a new fashion collection, it adds the new clothing items in the collection to its master file of product items and revises its price list. Benetton transmits its item master file and price lists over the network. Its country agents, such as Asuncion Henry, use the network to transmit orders back to Benetton. The agents can connect directly through the network to Benetton's IBM 3090 mainframe in Ponzano to obtain up-to-the-minute information on-line about the state of an order and its transport or about customer credit. Agents can also review Benetton's master file and price lists on-line.

The network connects the country agents to Benetton's factories in France, Brazil, Spain, Italy, and Argentina. Benetton maintains separate production agencies in Italy: Benetton for sweaters, Benetton Undercollar for underwear, Azimut for shirts, SAP for accessories, and Divarese for shoes. The country agents can use the network to contact the production agencies as well.

After a country agent places an order, an orders management program analyzes the order transactions before they are sent to Benetton. The software compares the agent's identification number and item numbers in the order to Benetton's database of product codes. When it encounters a discrepancy, it generates a "wait file" that lists the client number and the problem with the item. For instance, the item ordered might be the wrong color or size, or the agent might not have ordered the minimum number of items required. After the agent corrects the problem and re-enters the data, the system assigns an order number to the transaction. Each day, after order numbers have been generated for each agent's transactions, they are grouped together in batches and transmitted on the network to Benetton's main computer. Benetton's system groups the order transactions by country and sends them to the appropriate production agency. The production agencies extract orders from the system three times daily.

Benetton ships finished garments from its factories to customs agents in the appropriate country. It uses the network to send importation documents for these garments to one of 13 independent transport firms in 11 countries. The transport agency forwards the importation documents electronically on another network to customs agents. The import documents arrive before the boxes of garments, cutting the time for customs processing from 3 to 5 days.

FOCUS Questions:
How important is Benetton's network for its business? What transactions does it process? What problems does it solve? Draw a diagram of how Benetton processes order transactions.

SOURCE: Marsha Johnston, "Electronic Commerce Speeds Benetton Business Dealings," *Software Magazine*, January 1994.

Another form of output supplied by basic business systems is the data they provide for other systems used by managers. The basic business systems are the primary suppliers of data for information systems that support middle-level managers, who use summaries of transaction data for monitoring and controlling the firm's performance. For example, a typical report for a middle manager in a firm's Sales Department would be a summary of sales transactions by each sales region for a month or a year. In many instances, the basic transaction data and summarization of that data for management control will be produced by the same system. Systems specifically serving managers are discussed in Chapter 16.

FIGURE 13.1

The Concept of Transaction Processing in Basic Business Systems
A transaction processing system is the mainstay of a company because it performs the basic procedures that keep the firm in business. Exactly what kind of transaction is processed depends on the nature of the firm. However, the basic concept of transaction processing is the same, regardless of the company's line of business. The system accepts input related to a transaction event, processes it, and produces output that enables the firm to continue functioning. The primary users of transaction processing systems are staff at the operational or lowest level within a firm. However, these systems can supply data for other systems that serve different levels and functions.

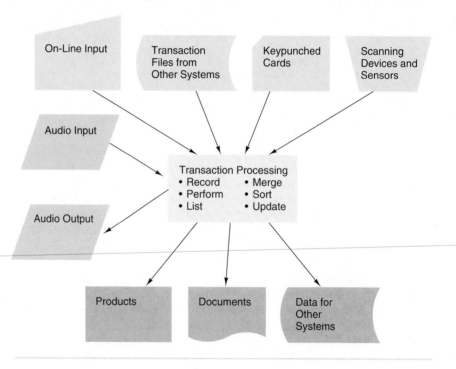

FAULT-TOLERANT SYSTEMS

Imagine the consequences to American Airlines if its reservation system were "down" for more than a few minutes or if a bank's customers were deprived of their automated teller machines. Such firms have heavy **on-line transaction processing** (OLTP) requirements, with multitudinous requests for information and changes to files occurring each instant. Their on-line transaction processing systems, in which massive numbers of transactions are processed instantly by the CPU, can create major business disruptions if they break down.

To forestall such calamities, many firms with heavy OLTP requirements rely on **fault-tolerant computer systems** with extra hardware, software, and power supply as backups against system failure. Fault-tolerant computers contain extra processors, memory chips, and disk storage. They can use software routines or self-checking logic built into their circuitry to detect hardware failures and automatically switch to a backup device. Parts can be removed or repaired without disrupting the computer system.

About half of the systems of the Securities Industry Automation Corp., the computing trading arm for both the New York and American Stock Exchanges, are fault

On-line transaction processing (OLTP)

A transaction processing mode in which transactions entered on-line are immediately processed by the CPU.

Fault-tolerant computer systems

Systems with extra hardware, software, and power as backups against system failure.

FOCUS ON TECHNOLOGY

SHUN TAK TRANSPORT HEDGES ITS BETS WITH OLTP

Shun Tak Ferries transports millions of people each year from Hong Kong to the nearby island of Macau, where the main attraction is its lively casinos. In 1989 Shun Tak took a gamble of its own and moved to client/server on-line transaction processing for JetTix, Shun Tak's critically important ticketing and reservation system. JetTix issues up to 13 million tickets annually. Its processing load was growing at a rate of 650,000 additional tickets each year.

The company's aging PDP/11 Digital Equipment Corp. minicomputer could not handle the increased transaction processing load. The firm could not afford a mainframe to deliver the processing capacity required for its large volume of transactions. Instead, it opted for a client/server computing platform that allowed the company to purchase the required computer processing power at much lower cost.

Was this a good idea? JetTix issues from 36,000 to 50,000 jetfoil, ferry, and helicopter tickets each day from locations such as subway stations, hotels, travel agencies, and the Macau terminal. The system accepts telephone reservations for tickets and last-minute purchases at ferry ticket windows. The system must be flexible, so that Shun Tak can increase the number of sales terminals. It must function 24 hours per day and be able to handle peak ticket purchase periods such as Sundays, the only full day that many Hong Kong residents have off from work.

Client/server systems have been considered somewhat risky for businesses that depend on mission critical transaction processing systems because they are more subject to network disruptions and failures than proven mainframe or minicomputer technology. Even though Shun Tak needed a system that could reliably process a huge number of transactions daily, the company took the risk with client/server computing by using fault-tolerant technology.

Shun Tak built a network of 100 IBM-compatible microcomputers that were linked to three redundant fault-tolerant processors from Stratus Computer Inc. of Marlborough, Massachusetts. The system contains duplicate hardware and software that reduce the chances of complete system failure. The microcomputers are located at Shun Tak's various ticket stations in Hong Kong and Macau and are connected to the main ferry terminal via a wide area network (WAN). There is also a LAN at company headquarters. The Stratus computers act as network servers for both the LAN and the microcomputers distributed in the WAN.

All data for the system are maintained in a central database that is accessible from all locations. This arrangement allows all ticket outlets to see what seats are still available but ensures that a ticket can be sold only once. The database uses a relational database management system from Sybase Inc. and runs on Stratus hardware.

Shun Tak began building this system in the fall of 1989 with the help of Information Systems Management, a Canadian systems integration firm. By January 1990 the jetfoil portion of the new system, which accounts for 80 percent of Shun Tak's business, was functional, but Shun Tak waited until the end of the peak travel season in September to switch over. By February 1991 the entire system was up and running. The total cost was approximately $2.5 million (U.S.) plus additional hardware acquisition costs in Hong Kong. Although David Hill, Shun Tak's executive director, is pleased with the system, he remains skeptical about pioneering in both client/server hardware and software for such a critical transaction processing system. He believes that Shun Tak's client/server fault-tolerant system is less reliable than systems built on more conventional minicomputers and mainframes.

FOCUS Questions:
Why did Shun Tak ferries use fault-tolerant technology for its transaction processing system? How useful was it?

SOURCE: Connie Winkler, "Hong Kong Transport Firm Risks C/S OLTP for Ticketing," *Software Magazine*, August 1993.

tolerant. Major airline and hotel reservation systems also depend on fault-tolerant technology. The Focus on Technology describes why firms that use client/server networks increasingly turn to fault-tolerant technology for their critical applications as well. Fault-tolerant systems are typically one and one-half to two times more expensive than traditional minicomputers or mainframes but their reliability makes the extra costs worthwhile for certain critical applications.

With computerized inventory control systems, businesses can automatically locate items in inventory, reorder items that are running low, and calculate the size of their inventory. These basic manufacturing systems can reduce inventory costs and improve performance in shipping orders to customer specifications.

SOURCE: Courtesy of International Business Machines Corporation.

13.3 EXAMPLES OF BASIC BUSINESS SYSTEMS

A typical firm will have basic business systems for all its major functional areas: manufacturing and production, sales and marketing, finance and accounting, and human resources. Depending on the nature of the firm's goods and services, these basic business systems will be more prominent in some functional areas than in others. For example, a bank or brokerage house may have only a small production system, since it primarily deals in financial services, but it will have extensive financial systems. Conversely, a firm that manufactures carburetors will put more weight on manufacturing systems; its financial systems will be less important.

BASIC MANUFACTURING AND PRODUCTION SYSTEMS

Information systems support basic manufacturing and production functions by supplying the data to operate, monitor, and control the production process. They collect data and produce reports concerning the status of production tasks, inventories, purchases, and the flow of goods and services. Such manufacturing and production systems are not limited to manufacturing firms. Other businesses such as wholesalers, retail stores, financial institutions, and service companies use manufacturing and production systems to monitor and control inventories, goods, and services. Table 13.1 lists typical basic manufacturing and production systems.

Purchasing systems maintain data on materials purchased for the manufacturing process, such as files on vendors, prices of purchased items, and items on order. Receiving systems maintain data on purchased goods that have been received and their delivery dates and supply this information to the production, inventory, and accounts payable functions. Shipping systems track the placement of finished products into inventory and shipments to customers; this information is then passed on to inventory and accounts receivable. Inventory systems track inventory levels, stockout conditions, and the location and distribution of stock in the organization.

TABLE 13.1

Standard Manufacturing Systems

Application	Purpose
Purchasing	Enter, process, and track purchases.
Receiving	Track the receipt of purchased items.
Shipping	Track shipments to inventory and to customers.
Materials	Catalog usage of materials in production processes.
Labor costing	Track the cost of labor as a production cost.
Equipment	Track the cost of equipment and facilities as production costs.
Quality control	Monitor production processes to identify variance from quality control standards.
Process control	Monitor ongoing physical production processes.
Numerical control (machine)	Control actions of machines.
Robotics	Use programmed intelligence to control actions of machines.
Inventory systems	Record the number, cost, and location of items in stock.

Materials systems track the usage of materials in the production process. The bill-of-materials system described in Chapter 2 inventories the raw materials and component parts needed to fashion a specific product. Labor-costing systems track the usage of personnel resources in the production process, and equipment systems track the costs of equipment and facilities for production.

Quality control systems collect data using shop floor data collection devices, such as counters, assembly-line data entry terminals, or process control sensors. The latter might be used to monitor the gauge of metal as it is fabricated into sheets, bars, or wire. If the system detects any variance, signifying that an item fails to meet established standards, it notifies supervisory personnel. **Process control systems** use computers to monitor an ongoing physical process, such as the production of paper, food products, or chemicals.

Numerical control systems, also called machine control systems, use computers to control the actions of machines, such as machine tools in factories or typesetting machines. Numerical control programs for machine tools convert design specifications and machining instructions into commands that control the action of the machinery.

Robotics is a more intelligent version of machine control. Robotic devices are machines with built-in intelligence and computer-controlled, humanlike capabilities (such as movement or vision) that can control their own activities. For example, a robot might be used in automobile manufacturing to pick up heavy parts or to paint doors.

In addition to performing these tasks, manufacturing and production systems are important sources of data for other systems. They interact with the firm's inventory, order processing, and accounting systems and supply data for systems serving middle- and higher-level management, such as capacity planning, production scheduling, and facilities planning.

Significant economies, efficiencies, and competitive advantages have resulted from integrating basic manufacturing and production systems. (See the Focus on Problem Solving.) Many firms have implemented manufacturing resource planning systems, which coordinate materials requirements planning, process control, inventory management, and capacity planning and exchange data automatically with the firm's financial accounting systems. Computer-integrated manufacturing (CIM) systems tie together all the computer systems used in manufacturing—computer-aided design, computer-aided manufacturing, computer-aided engineering, and manufacturing resources planning, replacing uncoordinated islands of automation with seamless integration and control.

Elco's statistical process control system, which is described in the next section, illustrates key features of basic manufacturing systems. As you read this case study, ask yourself, Where does a basic manufacturing system obtain its data? What does it actually do with the data? What business problems does a manufacturing system solve? What difference does this manufacturing system make for the firm?

A Typical Manufacturing and Production System: Elco's Statistical Process Control System   A major producer of fasteners and precision metal components for the automotive and electronic industries, Elco Industries in Rockford, Illinois, must guarantee products with accurate dimensions. Elco uses the cold-heading method of production, in which rod or wire is fed into dies, cut to length, positioned, and struck by a punch. The force of the punch blow causes the metal to flow into the shape of the punch and die, thus forming the part. The firm must maintain tight tolerances, often in ten-thousandths of an inch, over long production runs. Variations in production will occur if any of the Ms—machine, materials, measurement, and man (the machine operator)—are slightly off. The company's inspection and quality control departments rely on constant production sampling and control charts.

Quality control systems
Manufacturing and production systems that monitor the production process to identify variances from established standards so that defects can be corrected.

Process control systems
Manufacturing and production systems that use computers to monitor the ongoing physical production processes.

Robotics
The use of devices with built-in intelligence and computer-controlled, humanlike capabilities that can control their own activities.

FOCUS ON PROBLEM SOLVING

DELIVERING THE PRODUCT WHEN THE CUSTOMER WANTS IT

When Wheaton Industries takes an order, it can tell the customer within seconds when that order can be scheduled and delivered. Until last year, that process alone took from 3 to 10 days. Wheaton is a century-old plastic and glass packaging manufacturer located in Millville, New Jersey. Wheaton overhauled its production scheduling, order processing, manufacturing, and procurement so that it can deliver the product when the customer wants it instead of when the company thinks it can get it there.

Like many old-line manufacturers, Wheaton was burdened with a laborious and time-consuming customer service function. After taking orders over the telephone, customer service representatives researched the product and other information and usually had to call the customer back. Wheaton's order-taking was complicated because the company has extensive product lines. The firm makes glass and plastic packaging for the cosmetics, pharmaceutical, and liquor industries. Advil, Vick's Nyquil, and Anacin are among the scores of products that use Wheaton's plastic containers. Wheaton's containers group alone has 11 plants with 350 plastic blow-molding machines fashioning billions of containers for thousands of products each year.

Manually scheduling work for this army of machines was no easy matter. Wheaton had no materials resource planning system. Depending on the type of packaging the customer wanted, order takers had to call the firm's various plants in 35 locations throughout the United States, China, and South America. After determining the availability of materials and machines to make the specified product, the order taker called the customer with the anticipated delivery date. Finally, the sales staff relayed the production order to the manufacturing department.

Not surprisingly, this arrangement created considerable duplication and wasted effort. One plant could be producing a standard pharmaceutical bottle and another plant would not know it. Moreover, because the company's manufacturing facilities operated independently of one another, separate plants might make the different components of a container. Glass bottles would be made in one plant, labels in another, caps in another, and the plastic inserts for the caps in yet another plant.

Manual scheduling predictably resulted in occasional human error. A wrong delivery date could be a major problem because on-time delivery is crucial for Wheaton's customers. A customer trying to launch a new product could be seriously hurt if Wheaton missed even a day on promised delivery.

The new system solves these problems by combining order entry and customer service. Wheaton selected its best staff members to interact with customers and retrained them for their increased responsibilities. The staff members needed a broad understanding of Wheaton's manufacturing capacity, inventory, and scheduling requirements for their new roles.

Wheaton used a mainframe software package called R/2 from SAP America of Lester, Pennsylvania, as the foundation of its new system. R/2 software integrates sales, manufacturing, and financial functions so that data can be coordinated. Wheaton uses this software to coordinate order entry and production scheduling so that customer service representatives can immediately project a delivery date when a customer calls. Mainframe computer operations are outsourced to Sungard Data Systems in Wayne, Pennsylvania, which runs R/2 and other mainframe software for Wheaton. Terminals and microcomputer-based LANS in Wheaton's offices, plants, and warehouses are connected to Sungard's mainframe, which is located in Voorhees, New Jersey.

Wheaton hopes that this enterprise-wide approach linking ordering, production, scheduling, and manufacturing will eliminate duplication and wasted effort and enhance coordination across the entire order and production process. Some observers note, however, that R/2's production planning and control system may not be able to handle Wheaton's complex scheduling problems, which require plants to routinely make quick changeovers in the manufacture of a variety of products.

FOCUS Questions:
Why couldn't Wheaton tell customers when their orders could be scheduled? What people, organization, and technology issues had to be addressed to solve the problem? How successful was the solution?

SOURCE: Doug Bartholomew, "Schedule in a Bottle," *InformationWEEK*, March 28, 1994.

Statistical process control measures groups of sample parts to plot averages and ranges in a production run. During production, a number of measurements of groups of sample parts will be taken. A particular group of sample measurements, such as dimensional measurements, are averaged, as are those for other groups. These averages are plotted on a chart along with the ranges of each sample group. Machine operators and quality control staff use this information to determine how a production run is progressing and whether some remedial action is required to bring the dimensions within acceptable range.

Elco found that manual methods of statistical process control took roughly 2½ hours for a study of 20 groups of five samples each—much too long to be practical. Ninety-five percent of this time was consumed by calculations and constructing charts. By the time production runs were measured and calculations performed, many defective units had been produced.

One of Elco's quality control engineers developed a computer program to produce the required calculations and charts. Utilizing a tiny hand-held computer, the software calculates control limits, prints entered values, and draws charts, histograms, and bell curves. Figure 13.2 shows some sample output. The system allows for corrections, deletions, recalculations of control limits, and redrawing of charts.

FIGURE 13.2

Sample Output from the Elco Statistical Process Control System

Elco's statistical process control system is a good example of a transaction processing system that improved a firm's manufacturing function. This system automated Elco's quality control, which involves measuring sample products to gauge production performance. Output from the system includes charts, histograms, and bell curves. Also shown are measurements for the samples and acceptable limits.

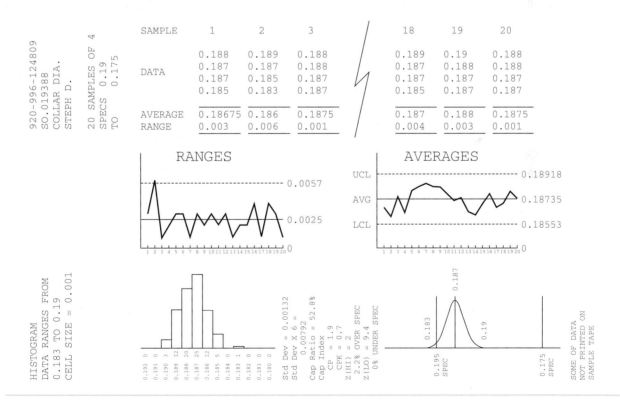

FIGURE 13.3

How the Elco Statistical Process Control System Works

Automating its statistical process control has allowed Elco Industries to reduce process control time by an impressive 95 percent, in addition to reducing defective output. Staff key the measurements of sample products into a hand-held computer, which compares the samples to the control limits. Output includes reports and charts, such as those in Figure 13.2.

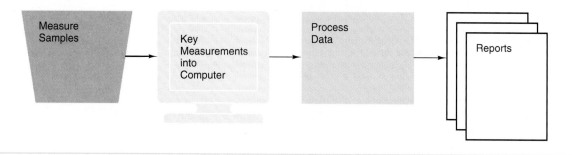

Elco's statistical process control system is so easy to use that anyone equipped with its brief *Operating Instructions* booklet can learn to run a statistical check in half an hour. Instructions carried on the display remain until answered. Data on a particular study are retained until new material is inserted.[1]

Let's return now to the questions that we raised at the beginning of the case study:

- **Where does a basic manufacturing system obtain its data?** Elco's statistical process control system, shown in Figure 13.3, obtains its information from dimensional measurements of sample products—in this case, wires and fasteners—in a given production run.

- **What does a manufacturing system actually do with the data?** The statistical process control system performs calculations based on measurements of samples from the production line. It plots averages of sample measurements for each group studied in the production run. The averages and ranges for each sample group are plotted on a chart to provide a statistical and visual concept of how a production run is progressing. Machine operators and quality control staff monitor these charts to determine whether the output of a production run is within the acceptable range, or tolerances.

- **What business problems does a manufacturing system solve?** This system helps guide and monitor the flow of production by identifying output that does not conform to specifications so that machine operators can take corrective action before the dimensions of the products exceed the acceptable range.

- **What difference does this manufacturing system make for the firm?** The system reduced production costs by automating a calculation process that formerly took close to 2½ hours. Man-hours consumed by calculations have been reduced by 95 percent. There is less wasted output from the production process because calculations are produced in time for machine operators to take corrective action against defects. The system promotes quality control by making it easier to measure whether production runs are falling within tight quality control limits. This enables the firm to back up its reputation for high-quality fasteners and wires, potentially increasing customer satisfaction and market share.

TABLE 13.2

Standard Sales and Marketing Systems

Application	Purpose
Sales support	Track customer contacts and prospective customers.
Telemarketing	Track the use of the telephone to make contacts, offer products, and follow up on sales.
Order processing	Enter, process, and track orders.
Point-of-sale systems	Record sales data.
Customer credit authorization	Inform sales staff about a customer's maximum allowable credit.

BASIC SALES AND MARKETING SYSTEMS

At the most elemental level, information systems support the sales and marketing function by facilitating the movement of goods and services from producers to consumers. These systems collect and process routine, repetitive data concerning locating customers, offering goods and services, processing sales and orders, and authorizing customer purchases. Table 13.2 lists typical sales and marketing information processing systems.

Many firms use telecommunications-based telemarketing systems to locate prospective customers, offer products for sale, and provide customer support.

SOURCE: © Bob Daemmrich, Stock, Boston.

Telemarketing systems

Sales and marketing systems that track the use of the telephone for contacting customers, offering products, and following up sales.

Order processing systems

Sales and marketing systems that record and process sales orders, track the status of orders, produce invoices, and often produce data for sales analysis and inventory control.

Point-of-sale systems

Sales and marketing systems that capture sales data at the actual point of sale through the cash register or hand-held scanners.

Sales support systems help sales staff identify potential customers, make customer contacts, and follow up on a sale. These systems record and keep track of prospective customers and customer contacts. They may include information such as the prospect or contact's name, address, and product preferences. **Telemarketing systems** track the use of the telephone for contacting customers, offering products, and following up on sales.

Order processing systems record and process sales orders by tracking the status of orders, producing invoices, and often producing data for sales analysis and inventory control. **Point-of-sale systems,** which were described more fully in Chapter 2, capture sales data at the actual point of sale through the cash register or hand-held scanners.

Customer credit information systems provide sales representatives or credit managers with information concerning the maximum credit to be granted to a customer; they may contain credit history information. These systems are often integrated with the firm's order processing and accounting systems.

Like other basic business systems, sales and marketing transaction systems supply data to other systems. Data from order processing and point-of-sale systems, for example, are used not only to track sales but also in sales management information systems to help sales managers evaluate sales performance or to shape sales targets. Sales systems are also linked with information systems from other business functional areas, such as purchasing systems and accounts receivable systems.

The one-stop sales and payment system used by Circuit City Stores, Inc., which is described in the next section, is an example of a leading-edge sales system. As you read this case study, ask yourself, Where does a basic sales and marketing system obtain its data? What does it actually do with the data? What business problems does this system solve? What difference does this system make for the firm?

A Typical Sales and Marketing System: No Lines at Circuit City   Circuit City Stores, Inc., a national electronics and home appliance retailer based in Richmond, Virginia, makes shopping easier through a system that allows customers in its 125 branch stores to pay for different items from different departments at a single register. The system uses special internally developed software and an in-store minicomputer that can handle up to 64 devices, including point-of-sale terminals and printers.[2]

When a customer selects a microwave oven, for example, the salesperson enters the sale on his register and prints out the customer's number. The customer can then move on to another department and purchase a television by simply giving her customer number to the salesperson in that department. When the customer's shopping expedition is over, she goes to the checkout stand. The checker enters the customer's number and the total appears. In the meantime, the system has transmitted the order to the printer on the receiving dock. By the time the customer arrives with her car for the merchandise, the purchases are already waiting there. This system is shown in Figure 13.4.

Before Circuit City installed this system it used a network of Hewlett Packard HP 3000 minicomputers based in company headquarters. The firm decentralized to in-store minicomputers to avert disruptions from telecommunications failures. A by-product of the new system is improved customer service, because each store maintains its own database of customer purchase records, which can be referenced by customer service representatives and equipment repair staff.

Let's return to our list of questions to examine more carefully what a sales and marketing system does:

- **Where does a basic sales and marketing system obtain its data?** The raw information comes from actual customer purchase transactions in each store. Each time a customer purchases an item, the purchase is recorded on the system. These sales

FIGURE 13.4

The Circuit City Sales System

Circuit City Stores, Inc., a large electronics and appliances retailer, has automated its sales/marketing system to allow customers to pay only once, regardless of how much they buy. With a customer's first purchase, a clerk enters the sale into the register and obtains a printout of the customer's number. This number is all that the customer needs to make further purchases. When the checker enters the number into the computer, the system tallies the total sale and forwards the data to the dock, where a printer outputs the customer's order and bill. The merchandise is ready for pickup when the customer drives up to the dock.

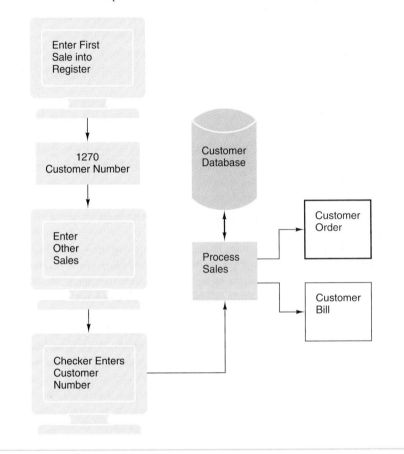

transactions are tracked, recorded, and totaled by customer number, which is an identification number assigned to each customer when he or she comes to the cash register with the first item purchased.

- **What does a basic sales and marketing system actually do with the data?** Like other basic business systems, this system primarily records transaction events—that is, the purchase of each item. The system then transmits the order to the receiving dock printer. The order is printed out, and warehouse clerks retrieve the items for the customer. In other words, this sales system tracks purchases, totals sales by customer, and transmits order information to inventory.

- **What business problems does this system solve?** The system solves the problem of how to record individual purchase transactions and how to supply customers with their purchases. These are very routine, repetitive, structured problems that require no decision to be made: if a customer purchases an item (and has the means to pay for it), he or she must receive that item from the warehouse unless it is out of stock.

In addition, customer purchase transactions from this system feed a database of customer purchase records. This provides information such as the brand and model of videocassette player a customer purchased and whether the customer purchased a service contract as well as the appliance. This information can be used by customer service representatives to assign appropriate repair staff and to stock the necessary repair parts.

- **What difference does this system make for the firm?** Circuit City's sales system primarily expedites the purchasing and delivery processes. Because purchase data are transmitted directly to the receiving dock, the customer can be supplied immediately from the warehouse. His or her order is immediate, direct, and not subject to discrepancies caused by time lags or transcription errors.

The system creates some strategic advantage by providing superior service to customers. It reduces lines in individual departments, at the cash register, and at the receiving dock. Customers can make payments and receive delivery in a much smoother and more timely manner.

BASIC ACCOUNTING AND FINANCIAL SYSTEMS

Some of the earliest computer systems automated accounting and financial functions. Accounting systems maintain records concerning the flow of funds in the firm and produce financial statements, such as balance sheets and income statements. Financial systems keep records concerning the firm's use and management of funds. Table 13.3 lists the basic accounting and financial systems.

Accounts receivable systems keep records of amounts owed by customers and credit information, based on customer invoice and payment data. **Accounts payable systems**, in contrast, keep track of amounts owed to the firm's creditors. They generate checks for outstanding invoices and report payment transactions.

Accounts receivable systems
Accounting systems that keep track of amounts owed to the firm.

Accounts payable systems
Accounting systems that keep track of amounts owed by a firm to its creditors.

TABLE 13.3

Standard Accounting and Financial Systems

Application	Purpose
Accounting	
Accounts receivable	Track money owed the firm; issue bills.
Accounts payable	Track money the firm owes.
General ledger	Summarize business accounts used to prepare balance sheets and income statements.
Payroll	Manage payroll records and produce paychecks.
Finance	
Cash management	Track the firm's receipts and disbursements.
Loan processing	Track transactions for consumer and commercial loans and credit card transactions; calculate interest and issue billing statements.
Check processing	Track checking account deposits and payments; issue statements of checking account activity and balances.
Securities trading	Track buying and selling of stocks, bonds, options, and other securities.

```
THE UNIVERSAL CORPORATION                              Nov 15 1995
Display Vendor Transactions - Current transactions
Vendor number [   200] Chloride Systems          On hold?: No

Comments:
Last activity on: Oct 06 95          Purchases this year:      16,246.08
┌─Transaction Detail─
  Type: PA Number:            5366   Reference:                    5366
  Description:
  Original amount:        2,529.25-  Last activity on:      Nov 06 95
  Transaction date:       Nov 06 95  Maximum payment:            0.00
  Active/Due date:                   Discount date:
  Current amount:             0.00   Base for discount:          0.00
  Posting sequence:              3   Total discounts:           47.95-
  ┌─Applied Transactions─
    Type     Number    Applied Amt.      Date      Disc. Taken

    IN         386         179.50    Nov 06 95        0.00
    IN        2993          95.75    Nov 06 95        1.95
    IN      W330001      2,254.00    Nov 06 95       46.00




ESC=Exit   CURSOR KEYS=Scroll                            F1=Help
```

ACCPAC Plus Accounting provides multi-user accounting software for medium-sized businesses and divisions of large corporations that have sophisticated accounting requirements and large transaction volumes. The system has fourteen different modules for functions such as accounts payable, accounts receivable, payroll, and general ledger. The various accounting modules can be operated independently or integrated to share data.

SOURCE: Courtesy of Computer Associates International, Inc.

General ledger systems use data from the accounts receivable, payroll, accounts payable, and other accounting systems to record the firm's income and expenses. They produce the income statements, balance sheets, general ledger trial balance, and other reports.

Payroll systems are sometimes treated as human resources systems, but they also perform important accounting functions. They calculate and produce employee paychecks, earning statements for the Internal Revenue Service and state and local taxing authorities, and payroll reports.

Cash management systems track receipts and disbursements of cash. Firms use this information to identify excess funds that can be deposited or invested to generate additional income. Cash management systems may also produce cash flow forecasts that managers can use for planning and development of alternative investment strategies.

Cash management systems

Financial systems that keep track of the receipt and disbursement of cash by a firm; they may also forecast the firm's cash flow.

The accounting and financial systems described above are found in virtually all firms, whereas loan processing, check processing, and securities trading systems are industry specific, serving primarily the banking and securities industries. Loan processing systems are used by banks to record transactions that initiate and pay for consumer and commercial loans and credit card transactions. Such systems keep track of principal and interest and issue customer billing statements. Banks use check processing systems to track deposits and payments in checking accounts and to produce customer statements of account activity. Securities trading systems are used by the New York and American Stock Exchanges to track the purchase and sale of stocks, bonds, options, and other securities.

The transaction processing system for credit card payments described in the next section is an example of a financial system that is shared by multiple companies. Visa's credit card payment system acts as an accounts receivable and billing system for the merchants and stores whose customers charge their purchases using the Visa credit card. The system is also an industry-specific system, a source of revenue for participating banks and the principal source of revenue for the Visa Corp. The description of Visa's system can help us understand the workings of basic financial systems if we keep in mind the following questions: Where does a basic financial system obtain its data? What does it

FIGURE 13.5

Visa's Plan to Reduce Errors and Fraud

In Visa's credit card payment system, a charge transaction goes through several steps involving the cardholder, the merchant, the merchant's bank, the bank issuing the credit card, and Visa itself.

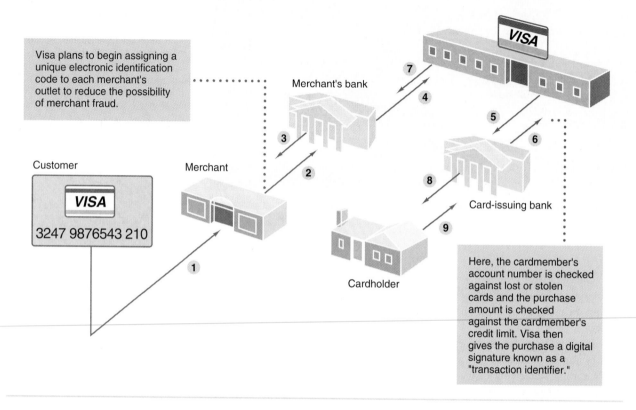

Visa plans to begin assigning a unique electronic identification code to each merchant's outlet to reduce the possibility of merchant fraud.

Merchant's bank

Customer

VISA

3247 9876543 210

Merchant

Cardholder

Card-issuing bank

Here, the cardmember's account number is checked against lost or stolen cards and the purchase amount is checked against the cardmember's credit limit. Visa then gives the purchase a digital signature known as a "transaction identifier."

actually do with the data? What business problems does the system solve? What difference does this system make for the firm?

A Basic Financial System: Visa's Credit Card Payment System   About 10 million merchants worldwide accept Visa and Mastercard credit cards. Visa and Mastercard's credit card networks represent two of the most massive transaction processing systems in the world. Let's examine Visa's credit card payment system, which processes 20 million transactions a day. Figure 13.5 shows how the system works.

When a customer makes a purchase of, say, $100 using a Visa card, the merchant or clerk swipes the card through a special electronic terminal connected by telephone lines to the computer network linking the merchant's bank, Visa, and the cardholder's bank. As shown in Figure 13.5, about 20,000 banks worldwide belong to this network. The credit card machine records the customer's credit card number, expiration date, and purchase amount and dials a number at the store's bank (1).

The merchant's bank is linked via Visa's network to the bank that issued the credit card. The card-issuing bank approves the charge. Then the merchant submits the charge to the store's bank (2). The bank subtracts an average fee of 1.9 percent and pays the rest to the merchant (3). For a purchase of $100, the merchant would usually receive $98.10.

The merchant's bank submits the charge to Visa (4), which charges the amount of the purchase to the bank that issued the Visa card (5). The cardmember's account number is checked against lost or stolen cards. The purchase amount is checked against the card member's credit limit. To reduce error and fraud, Visa assigns a special digital signature called a "transaction identifier" to the transaction. This identifier remains attached to the purchase transaction until everyone is paid. The card-issuing bank subtracts an interchange fee of approximately 1.3 percent (6) from the purchase amount and pays the rest ($98.70) to Visa, which then pays the merchant's bank (7). (The merchant's bank paid the merchant only $98.10 and gets to keep the 60-cent difference.) Both the issuing bank and the merchant's bank then pay small fees to Visa.

The card-issuing bank bills the customer for the original amount of $100 (8). When the customer pays the bill, the bank will either receive $100 immediately or $100 plus interest over time (9).[3]

Now let's return to the questions we posed earlier:

- **Where does a basic financial system obtain its information?** The Visa credit card payment system obtains its information initially from the merchant and the customer holding the credit card. The customer supplies his or her credit card number, name, and expiration date, which help identify the card-issuing bank. The merchant supplies the purchase amount and data identifying the merchant and the merchant's bank for the system.

- **What does a basic financial system actually do with the data?** The credit card payment system tracks purchase transactions, authorizes these transactions, and issues payments to the merchant, the bank issuing the credit card, the merchant's bank, and Visa. It also provides a bill for the purchase to the card holder.

- **What problems does this system solve?** The credit card payment system provides a relatively simple and instant way for merchants to receive payment for their sales. Merchants do not have to set up their own accounts receivable and billing systems or administer them. Visa does all the work. Additionally, the credit card payment system encourages consumers to buy more by providing nearly instant credit all over the world at little or no extra cost to them. The various banks involved profit from the transaction fees and interest. The system is Visa's core source of revenue, since it receives about 5 cents to process each credit card transaction.

- **What difference does this basic financial system make for the firm?** The Visa credit card payment system actually represents two types of financial systems. For the merchant, it represents a variant of an accounts receivable system, instantaneously granting credit to customers, tracking money owed, and issuing bills. For the merchant's bank, the card-issuing bank and the Visa Corp., the system is an industry-specific system that provides an essential service to subscribers and an important source of revenue.

BASIC HUMAN RESOURCES SYSTEMS

At the most elementary level, human resources information systems deal with the recruitment, placement, performance evaluation, compensation, and career development of the firm's employees. Basic human resources systems collect data concerning employees and support repetitive, routine tasks such as tracking new hires, promotions, transfers, and terminations and maintaining records of employee benefits and beneficiaries.

Table 13.4 lists the most important basic human resources systems. In addition to the systems listed, some firms treat payroll systems as human resource systems

TABLE 13.4

Standard Human Resources Systems

Application	Purpose
Personnel record keeping	Maintain employee records.
Applicant tracking	Maintain data about job applicants.
Positions	Track positions in the firm.
Training and skills	Maintain employee training and skills inventory records.
Benefits	Maintain records of employee benefits and perform benefits accounting.

because they maintain employee data that is used by the human resources function. Others consider payroll primarily an accounting function.

Personnel record-keeping systems maintain basic employee data such as name, address, marital status, dependents, age, Equal Employment Opportunity (EEO) category, and job performance appraisals, and they also record hiring, termination, transfer, promotion, and performance evaluation transactions. **Applicant tracking systems** maintain data about applicants for jobs and provide reports to satisfy federal, state, and local employment regulations.

Positions systems, by contrast, do not maintain information on employees but on the positions in the firm. A position can be defined as a slot in the firm's organization chart. Positions systems maintain data about filled and unfilled positions and track transactions concerning changes in positions and job assignments.

Training and skills systems maintain records of employees' training and work experiences, interests, and special skills and proficiencies. Such systems can identify employees with appropriate skills for special assignments or job requirements.

Benefits systems maintain data about employees' life insurance, health insurance, pensions, and other benefits and track transactions such as changes in beneficiaries and benefits coverage.

Basic human resources systems may also provide data for managers or supply data to other systems specifically serving management. For example, positions systems are used for management analysis of turnover problems and recruitment strategies as well as for succession planning.

Traditionally, the basic business systems in large firms have been based on mainframes and minicomputers. Today, with powerful microcomputers and workstations, many high-volume transaction processing tasks can be performed using these smaller machines or client/server networks. Compaq Computer's Employee Self-Service Personnel System is an example of how transaction processing can be accomplished with client/server technology. Again as you read the following account, keep our list of questions in mind: Where does a basic human resources system obtain its data? What does it actually do with the data? What business problems does this system solve? What difference does this system make for the firm?

A Basic Human Resources System: Compaq Computer's Employee Self-Service Personnel System The trend in human resources, as in all business functions, is to have fewer people handle benefits, pay raises, pension plans, vacations, and related administrative functions. Yet many human resources systems, even those that are on-line and networked, still rely on employees to send in paper forms for processing. The forms are keyed into the system by a central data entry staff. It might take as many as 31 steps involving multiple telephone calls and paper flows for a Compaq manager at a remote site to give an employee a pay raise.

Applicant tracking systems
Human resources systems that maintain data about applicants for jobs at a firm and provide reports to satisfy federal, state, and local employment regulations.

Positions systems
Human resources systems that maintain information about positions (slots in a firm's organization chart); they maintain data about filled and unfilled positions and track changes in positions and job assignments.

Training and skills systems
Human resources systems that maintain records of employees' training and work experience so that employees with appropriate skills for special assignments or job requirements can be identified.

Benefits systems
Human resources systems that maintain data about employees' life insurance, health insurance, pensions, and other benefits, including changes in beneficiaries and benefits coverage.

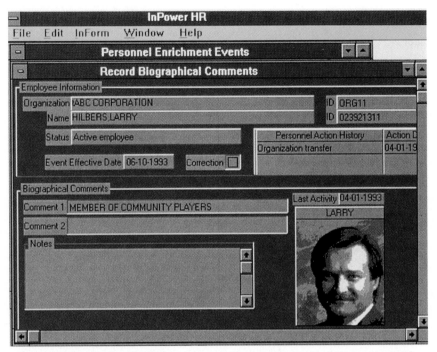

Integral Systems' InPower HR human resources management system operates in a client/server environment on a variety of database management systems and server operating systems. It can display employee records and related information using a graphical user interface.

SOURCE: Courtesy of Integral Systems, Inc.

To reduce some of the inefficiencies and expense associated with processing human resources transactions, Compaq Computer developed a new on-line human resources system that turns over nearly all of the data entry and validation work to its 6,000 employees and their supervisors on its 800-acre corporate campus in Houston, Texas. The new system is expected to reduce the human resources staff from 300 to 90 people within 2 years and to produce $313,000 in annual savings.

We can see how the "employee self-service" strategy features of this system work by looking at how it handles the process of enrolling employees in a cafeteria-style flexible benefits program. In an effort to cut costs and improve service to employees, Compaq, like many large corporations, implemented a flexible benefits plan that lets employees choose from a menu of benefit options. This cafeteria approach provides employees a fixed number of dollars that can be spent any way they wish on medical or life insurance coverage. For instance, employees might have the option of two different medical plans—a conventional plan that reimburses them for medical care provided by a physician of their choice, or a less expensive health maintenance organization plan in which they must use prespecified physicians and services. Employees can spend their dollars on either one of the medical plans and use the rest for additional life or disability insurance.

Good benefits packages such as flexible or cafeteria-style benefits plans are an important way for organizations to attract and retain good employees and to offset spiraling health insurance costs. Instead of paying more and more each year for one standard health care or life insurance plan, companies can stabilize these costs by giving each employee a fixed amount to spend on benefits. Employees gain by having the ability to choose among many benefits options.

Compaq Computer's On-Line Human Resources System

In Compaq Computer's on-line human resources system, employees and their supervisors can enter benefits data directly into the system using either a microcomputer or a telephone. Employee benefits plan selections update the employee database. The system then creates transactions for benefits plan contribution deductions to be taken from the employees' paychecks. These deduction transactions are passed to Compaq's payroll system. The system also displays the benefits plan options selected by each employee.

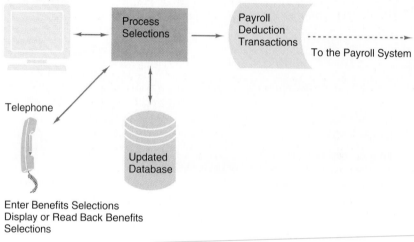

Compaq employees can interactively craft their own benefits plans using either a microcomputer or a telephone. The microcomputer prompts them for information about themselves and dependents and guides them through a menu of health and life insurance choices. As the employee selects these options, the bottom of the microcomputer display screen shows how many of their benefits dollars have been allocated to the options they have selected and how many dollars remain. The employee's selections update the employee database, which is maintained on a Compaq SystemPro 486/33 file server. (The application software for the human resources system is maintained on a separate SystemPro 486/33 file server.) When the benefits allowance is exhausted, the system notifies the user of deductions that can be taken from the person's paycheck to pay for the benefits.

Alternatively, the employee can enroll in a flexible benefits plan using a TouchTone telephone with an automated voice response capability. This interface captures the employee's voice input, validates it, and reads back enrollment information to the employee. Employees can enroll at home by telephone and later check their enrollment data on a microcomputer at work, or they can enter the data at work using the microcomputer and later listen to the enrollment choices at home. In either case, the system creates deduction transactions and passes them to the firm's payroll system, which runs on a Hewlett-Packard HP 3000 minicomputer.[4] Figure 13.6 illustrates this system.

Once again, we return to the questions we raised at the beginning of the chapter:

- **Where does a basic human resources system obtain its information?** The human resources system obtains its data directly from employees and from their supervisors. Both can input transactions directly into the system. Supervisors can input transactions for pay increases or for hiring and terminating employees. Employees can input transactions to select their benefit plans, providing data such as their name, department, health and life insurance choices, and coverage amounts.

- **What does a basic human resource system actually do with the data?** Employee selections of health care and life insurance benefits plans and coverage amounts are the transactions for the benefits portion of the human resources system. These transactions create or update the employee records on the human resources database (which is stored on the file server). Output consists of displays of benefits options; the number of dollars left in the employee's benefits allowance after the choices have been made; and payroll deduction transactions passed to the payroll system.

- **What problems does this system solve?** To comply with both internal record-keeping and external legal requirements, all organizations must keep accurate records of employee participation in benefits plans and their payments to these plans through payroll deductions. This system solves the operational problem of determining what benefits options were selected by each employee, the amount of each employee's benefits allowance that has been spent, and who must have benefits plan payments deducted from their paychecks. The system automates this record keeping and the transactions that feed related business systems such as payroll.

- **What difference does this basic human resources system make for the firm?** The new human resources system enabled the company to move to a more flexible yet more complex benefits program with no increase in administrative and support costs. In fact, the company was able to sharply reduce the number of people and the expense of administering the human resources function. The system also helped the company strategically by providing a way to attract and maintain desirable employees. Flexible benefits programs are believed to increase employee satisfaction and motivation by giving employees choices in constructing their benefits plans.

13.4 THE CHALLENGES OF BUILDING BASIC BUSINESS SYSTEMS

Because basic business systems are deeply ingrained in the day-to-day operations of the business, organizational, people, and technical challenges are posed when these systems have to be built afresh or revised.

ORGANIZATIONAL CHALLENGES

Basic business systems are the lifeblood of organizations, embodying the organization's fundamental procedures. Although some of these procedures may be automated, many procedures may still have to be performed manually between the initiation of a transaction and the time it is finally recorded in a system.

A major organizational challenge is to fully understand, capture, and, if possible, rationalize or streamline these procedures so that a basic business system can function

FOCUS ON PEOPLE

ELECTRONIC TAX FILING BACKFIRES

Each year the Internal Revenue Service (IRS) receives tax returns from 130 million individuals and 70 million businesses and other organizations. The IRS must also annually collect and process 170 million tax payments amounting to $1 trillion. Traditionally these returns have been filed on paper forms, such as the 1040 form, comprising 170 billion pieces of paper.

The enormity of the undertaking has created massive transaction processing problems. The IRS maintains a huge data entry staff to key in essential pieces of information from these paper forms into its automated information system. There, the information on each taxpayer is stored by the taxpayer's tax identification (Social Security) number in a computer database for further analysis and reporting. Errors must be corrected manually and re-entered. But because not all of the information on the paper forms is captured by the sys-

Electronic filing of tax returns has cut down on paperwork for the Internal Revenue Service and resulted in sending tax refunds more quickly. Unfortunately, the system has also created opportunities for people to obtain fraudulent tax refunds.

SOURCE: © Bob Daemmrich, Stock, Boston.

tem, the paper returns must be retained.

To reduce the mountain of paperwork, the IRS has encouraged the electronic filing of tax returns. It has offered to pay tax refunds due on electronic returns in 3 weeks instead of the normal 6 weeks for paper-based returns. Refund processing time can be cut to 2 weeks if the refund is deposited directly into the taxpayer's bank account. Electronic filers can even receive refund anticipation loans from their banks, which can typically obtain the taxpayer's refund money within 3 days.

SOURCE: Robert D. Hershey, Jr., "IRS Finds Fraud Grows as More File by Computer," *The New York Times*, February 21, 1994.

smoothly with as few steps as possible. Another challenge is to structure data so that they can flow smoothly into other systems and facilitate management decisions in higher levels of the firm.[5]

Perhaps the greatest challenge of this category of systems is the fear of rebuilding them. Basic business systems are so deeply embedded in a typical business's plans and day-to-day activities that they are exceedingly difficult to change and restructure. The sheer size and complexity of large basic business systems, such as the payroll system of the City of New York or the Internal Revenue Service Tax Administration system, make it impossible for them to be understood by one or a few individuals. Businesses typically resist changing their major business systems unless they are faced with a major crisis.

Electronic filing has been confined primarily to simple returns. It has great appeal among low-income groups, for whom quick refunds have special importance. In 1993 12 million returns (a little over 10 percent of all tax returns) were processed through electronic filing. The IRS hopes the number will rise to 80 million, or two-thirds of all returns, by 2001. The agency's goal is to computerize almost all aspects of the tax payment process that are currently paper based.

While the IRS would like electronic tax filing to gain widespread acceptance, electronic filing has experienced a high number of fraudulent returns. More than 25,000 fraudulent electronic returns were detected in the first 10 months of 1993, more than double the number in the corresponding period the year before. In 1993 electronic filing accounted for about 40 percent of all detected fraud. The IRS estimates that electronic filing produces losses of tens of millions of dollars a year, but outside specialists fear the amount is much higher.

People have taken advantage of the ability of electronic filing to send refunds very quickly—apparently much faster than the system can determine the validity of the claims. The infor-mation to verify a refund claim is still stored on paper documents like W-2 forms or depends on handwritten signatures that are mailed after the return is filed electronically. To verify a claim, IRS agents must examine each return individually and manually assemble all these pieces of information. Consequently, agents can't easily identify suspicious claims and delay those refunds until the claims are proven legitimate. The huge volume of returns means that the IRS is able to audit only 1 percent of all tax returns.

Not surprisingly, the IRS refuses to specify the techniques used to commit electronic fraud. Typically, however, people try to overstate the amount of income tax withheld from their paychecks or the amount of refundable tax credits. While some perpetrators use their own names and social security numbers, others use the names of unsuspecting honest taxpayers or create new fictitious identities. Frazier B. Todd, Jr., an electronic filer who was apprehended and convicted of tax fraud, had collected more than $500,000 by registering fictitious companies with the IRS over the telephone.

Congressional critics have charged that the IRS caused the problem by promoting the system before adequate steps had been taken to ensure that the system addressed the associated risks. The IRS has started numerous criminal investigations and no longer issues refunds to people filing tax returns for the first time, as first-time filers are especially likely to be fraudulent. It no longer makes refunds using direct deposit, since issuing paper checks allows more time for verification. The agency defers payment of earned income credit when a child's Social Security number is missing but pays the rest of the refund while verifying eligibility. Another part of the counter-offensive consists of using IRS supercomputers to detect anomalies in returns and identify suspicious patterns.

The IRS is in the midst of a $10 billion modernization program aiming for nearly total computerization of tax payments. Will it succeed in eliminating its labor-intensive handling of paper?

FOCUS Question: What people, organization, and technology factors were responsible for the high incidence of fraud in electronic tax filing?

PEOPLE CHALLENGES

Information for basic business systems is relatively fixed, structured, and routine. People have less difficulty specifying the inputs, processes, and outputs for this class of systems than for higher-level systems. The primary people challenge is one of consistency and completeness—ensuring that all of the firm's operating procedures have been adequately defined, captured, and automated when the procedures are multitudinous, complex, and poorly documented. Another people challenge is designing transaction processing systems that truly streamline basic business processes and make better use of people's time and skills. The Focus on People examines this challenge in more detail.

TECHNOLOGY CHALLENGES

Basic business systems have traditionally required hardware and software that can handle large numbers of discrete transaction events, collecting, updating, and listing up to millions of transactions each day. In the past, this required mainframe computing power and larger and larger machines as transaction volume soared. Client/server networks are now being used for this purpose. Fault-tolerant technology is essential for large-scale on-line transaction processing.

The primary technical question for basic business systems has become one of integration—how to link disparate islands of automation on the factory floor, in the warehouse, and in the accounting office so that their systems can exchange information with each other. Sometimes basic business systems do not efficiently supply the data required by management, and they need tighter integration with systems supporting higher levels of the firm.

SUMMARY

- Basic business systems keep track of the most elementary, day-to-day activities of the firm, dealing with routine, repetitive problems for which the solution is based on the firm's standard operating procedures. These systems support the operational level of the business but also supply data for management decisions at higher levels of the firm.

- A transaction is a record of an event to which a firm's system must respond. Basic business systems, which keep track of the elementary transactions necessary to conduct a business, are also called transaction processing systems.

- In on-line transaction processing (OLTP) systems, transactions are immediately processed by the CPU. Firms that have to process massive numbers of transactions on-line are turning to fault-tolerant computer systems with backup hardware, software, and power supply to forestall major business disruptions if their on-line transaction processing breaks down.

- Basic business systems are used primarily by people at lower levels of the firm who have little or no management responsibility.

- Basic business systems help solve internal operating problems and problems concerning transactions with the firm's external environment—customers, suppliers, and government regulations.

- Output from basic business systems may consist of finished goods, paychecks, other documents, or data supplied to other systems. Basic business systems supply data to higher-level systems in the same functional area (for example, an order entry system supplies data for a sales management system) or to systems in different business areas.

- The basic business systems support the manufacturing and production functions by supplying data to operate, monitor, and control the production process. Materials, purchasing, receiving, shipping, process control, numerical control, equipment, quality control, labor-costing, and robotic systems are examples of basic manufacturing and production systems.

- The basic business systems support the sales and marketing function by collecting and processing routine, repetitive data concerning locating customers, offering goods and services, processing sales and orders, and authorizing purchases. Sales support, telemarketing, order processing, point-of-sale, and customer credit authorization systems are examples of basic sales and marketing systems.

- The basic business systems support the accounting and finance function by recording the flow of funds in the firm, by tracking the firm's use of funds, and by producing financial statements. There are also industry-specific financial systems for the banking and securities industries. Accounts receivable, accounts payable, general ledger, payroll, cash management, loan processing, check processing, and securities trading are examples of basic accounting and financial systems.

- The basic business systems support the human resources function by tracking the recruitment, placement, performance evaluation, compensation, and career development of the firm's employees. Personnel record-keeping, applicant tracking, positions, training and skills, and benefits systems are examples of basic human resources systems.

- The primary organizational challenge for basic business systems is to fully understand, capture, and, if possible, rationalize or streamline myriad operating procedures so that these systems can function smoothly with as few steps as possible. The primary technical question for basic business systems is how to integrate separate systems when there are disparate islands of automation throughout the firm. The primary people challenge of basic business systems is to ensure that all of the firm's multitudinous operating procedures have been adequately defined, captured, and automated in a system.

KEY TERMS

Basic business system	Order processing systems
Transaction	Point-of-sale systems
Transaction processing system	Accounts receivable systems
On-line transaction processing (OLTP)	Accounts payable systems
Fault-tolerant computer systems	Cash management systems
Quality control systems	Applicant tracking systems
Process control systems	Positions systems
Robotics	Training and skills systems
Telemarketing systems	Benefits systems

REVIEW QUESTIONS

1. Define a basic business system. What functions do basic business systems serve?

2. What is a transaction? Give examples of three transactions used by businesses.

3. What kinds of problems do basic business systems solve? What kinds of positions in the firm use basic business systems?

4. What are the outputs of basic business systems?

5. What are fault-tolerant systems? Why are they necessary?

6. How do basic business systems support the manufacturing and production function? List and describe five kinds of manufacturing and production systems.

7. How do basic business systems support the sales and marketing function? List and describe four kinds of sales and marketing systems.

8. How do basic business systems support the accounting and financial functions? List and describe three accounting systems and four financial systems.

9. How do basic business systems support the human resources function? List and describe three human resources systems.

10. What are the principal organizational challenges of basic business systems? Technical challenges? People challenges?

DISCUSSION QUESTIONS

1. An important function of basic business systems is to produce information for other systems. Discuss.

2. Why can failure of basic business systems for a few hours or days lead to a business firm's failure?

3. To be most effective, sales and marketing systems should be closely coordinated with basic business systems from other functional areas, such as manufacturing and production, and accounts receivable systems. Discuss.

PROBLEM-SOLVING EXERCISES

1. *Group exercises:* As the director of Equal Economic Opportunity affairs for your firm, you are responsible for gathering the data concerning your firm's record in hiring and promoting women and minorities. How could you use human resources transaction processing systems for your work?

Divide the class into groups. Have each group develop two or three reports from the human resources systems described in this chapter that could assist the EEO director in this task. Each group should design a mockup of each report, showing column headings, data fields required, and any kind of totals that would be useful. Have each group present its reports to the class.

2. Herman's Hardware is a mom-and-pop business in a neighborhood that is becoming increasingly gentrified on New York City's Upper West Side. Store space is limited, and rents have doubled over the past 5 years. Consequently, Herman and Ida Stein, the owners, are under great pressure to use every square foot of space as profitably as possible.

The Steins have never kept detailed records of stock in inventory or of their sales. Stock items are just automatically placed on shelves to be sold. Invoices from wholesalers are kept only for tax purposes. When an item is sold, the item number and price are rung up at the cash register. The Steins use their own judgment and observation in identifying stock items that are moving fast and might need reordering. Many times, however, they are caught short and lose the sale.

How could the Steins use the information they already maintain to help their business? What data would these systems capture? What reports would these systems produce?

3. *Hands-on exercise:* Advanced Cartridges in Hayward, California, is a small manufacturer of cartridges for computer laser printers. Its Quality Control Department prepared the following report of the number of defective cartridges per 1000 cartridges produced between 1988 and 1994:

Defects per 1000 Cartridges Manufactured

Year	Defects per 1000
1988	1.89
1989	2.27
1990	2.72
1991	3.26
1992	3.17
1993	3.91
1994	4.23

The Department would like to display this information graphically for management to determine whether new quality control measures should be instituted. Use appropriate software to create a graph showing the number of defects per 1000 units produced each year. Print out your graph.

NOTES

1. "SPC Programmed Computer," *Manufacturing Systems*, March 1985, and Elco Industries Communications Department.

2. Kathy Chin Leong, "Store Systems Help Retailers Give Shoppers What They Want," *Computerworld*, November 28, 1988.

3. Roert E. Calem, "Taking the Worry Out of Paying with Plastic," *The New York Times*, November 14, 1993.

4. Gary H. Anthes, "Compaq Empowers Employees," *Computerworld*, August 2, 1993.

5. Mary J. Culnan, "Transaction Processing Applications as Organizational Message Systems: Implications for the Intelligent Organization," Working Paper 88-10, 22nd Hawaii International Conference on Systems Sciences, January 1989.

PROBLEM-SOLVING CASE

CAN COMPUTERS TAME THE HEALTH CARE MONSTER?

Walk into any U.S. hospital and you'll see patients surrounded by high-tech devices—glowing monitors, imaging machines, lasers. But most of the data being churned out by these machines is painstakingly written in a paper file. For the same patient there might be one paper file in the radiology department, one in the pharmacy, and one for surgery. About 30 percent of the patient information needed during a typical clinical visit is stuck in different files.

The $900 billion health care industry consumes 14 percent of the value of annual economic production in the United States and continues to grow by 10 percent each year, more than three times the rate of inflation. If unchecked, U.S. health care costs could double by the year 2000. There are many causes of this problem, but one is the staggering cost of health care record keeping. Administrative costs alone account for 24.8 percent of all hospital spending.

A study by Arthur D. Little, Inc. reported that the annual U.S. health care bill could be reduced by more than $30 billion merely by compiling and transmitting patient information electronically. There are many ways in which information systems could help. One is by simplifying the task of submitting patient bills for medical insurance.

The job of Madeleine Hunter, coding supervisor for Stamford Hospital, in Stamford, Connecticut, exemplifies the problem. Hunter completes medical claims for hospital procedures performed on patients and submits them to Medicare and other insurers. In addition to basic information, such as the patient's name, address, Social Security number, age, and sex, each claim form must list the medical procedure or procedures performed on the patient, the date of these procedures, the diagnostic code for each procedure, a description of the procedure, and the charge. Every procedure must be properly documented and related to the physician's diagnosis. Hunter's office shelves are filled with thick books detailing thousands of procedure codes, diagnosis codes, billing codes, and annual revisions to these codes.

Hunter can wade through only 18 patient records per day, each hundreds of pages long. If she misses a diagnosis code, Stamford Hospital loses revenue. If a procedure code or physician signature is missing, the insurer will ask for corrections or an audit. Both are costly and time-consuming tasks.

Hunter and her four clerks don't make many mistakes. Medicare amended only eight of over 700 cases in one quarter. But those eight exceptions represent an enormous undertaking. For each case audited, records must be photocopied and delivered to the auditing agency. Two Stamford hospital workers are assigned full time to gather evidence to refute the insurer's objections. Doctors and nurses spend hours each week appealing the insurer's evaluations. Two other full-time employees spend all of their time ensuring that a medical procedure has been approved before it is performed.

Hunter's job is not made easier by the fact that different insurers use different types of claims forms. Many private insurers reimburse claims based on a standard form that can be completed by a hospital's computer system and sent as an electronic data interchange (EDI) transaction to the insurer, but 40 percent do not. They require hospitals to use their own claims submission forms, which ask for the same data as the standard forms arranged in a different format. They may also demand copies of records or additional data on specialized forms.

The Workgroup for Electronic Data Interchange (WEDI) is a quasigovernmental group working to develop standards for electronic submission of health care claims. It prepared a study predicting that EDI alone could save $4 billion to $10 billion in health care claims processing costs annually in the United States. Joseph T. Brophy, WEDI's co-chairman, believes the savings could be as high as $40 billion each year.

Some regional groups have established EDI networks. The Chicago-based Blue Cross and Blue Shield Association teamed up with IBM and Medical Management Resources Inc. (MMR) to launch EDI-USA, which should save an estimated $1.5 billion each year in transaction costs. IBM provides networking support and MMR provides hardware, software, and operational support. Subscribers to the system can submit electronic claims to insurers for 40 to 50 cents per claim, compared with $2.50 per claim for processing paper forms. Robert Schult, managing director of interplan technology at the Blues association, sees the eventual adoption of a standard claims submission format for EDI. Today, the 72 Blues plans in the United States each use their own EDI format.

SOURCES: Catherine Arnst and Wendy Zellner, "Hospitals Attack a Crippler: Paper," *Business Week*, February 21, 1994; "The Administrator," *Business Week*, January 17, 1994; and Chuck Appleby, "Is Technology the Cure?" *InformationWEEK*, May 10, 1993.

CASE STUDY QUESTIONS

1. What are the people, organization, and technology factors that explain the high costs of submitting health care claims today?

2. How much are automation of claims forms and the use of EDI a solution to this problem? What people, organization, and technology factors would a hospital have to address when converting health care claims processing to EDI?

3. Design a standard transaction that could be used in an electronic health care claims submission system. What pieces of data would it contain? Draw a diagram of how an electronic claims system would work.

KNOWLEDGE WORK: SYSTEMS FOR OFFICES AND PROFESSIONALS

LEARNING OBJECTIVES

After reading and studying this chapter, you will:

1. Know what is meant by an "information and knowledge" economy, knowledge workers, and data workers.

2. Be able to describe the role of the office in contemporary organizations and how it can be supported by office automation technology.

3. Understand the role knowledge work and knowledge workers play in the modern firm.

4. Understand the generic information requirements of knowledge work and how they can be supported by special knowledge work systems.

5. Understand the people, organizational, and technological challenges of supporting professional knowledge workers.

Price Waterhouse is one of the world's premier accounting and consulting firms. Knowledge—experience and expertise—is the firm's principal product. But with over 45,000 employees in 400 offices located in 100 countries, Price Waterhouse had a problem. Management knew that clients would benefit significantly if experts best suited to work on their specific projects could be rapidly assigned to work on those projects, regardless of their location. By offering clients the combined knowledge and expertise of the entire firm, while competitors offer only the expertise of consultants located near the specific project, Price Waterhouse reasoned that it would gain a significant competitive advantage.

After an extensive study, Price Waterhouse built a proprietary, networked, global information system that could collect, analyze, and store data from its worldwide staff. Consultants now store their project documentation on the network, creating a permanent record of their work. The new network also gives its users (the Price Waterhouse consulting staff) direct access to much of the outside information consultants need to do their job.

Today, the system offers Price Waterhouse (and its clients) many advantages:

- *Through a search of a company-wide database, relevant consulting expertise anywhere in the world can be quickly identified and the appropriate staff can be assigned to work on specific projects.*
- *Consultants scattered around the world can collaborate without spending time and money on travel.*
- *Price Waterhouse staff can remain up-to-date on leading-edge research taking place within their company.*

- *The network maintains electronic bulletin boards on more than 1,000 different topics that can be accessed by 18,000 employees in 22 countries.*
- *The system gives Price Waterhouse an "institutional memory." Documentation on current and previous projects is now fully available to the whole organization, even long after the consultants involved have left the company. This institutional memory not only helps current consultants gain an understanding of clients' needs and characteristics, but it also is used to train consultants by making available to them others' experience in handling similar situations and technology.*
- *Price Waterhouse uses the network to convene emergency conferences of relevant experts anywhere in the world when new developments, such as tax law changes, occur. Their conclusions are distributed to the whole organization the next day via the network, allowing Price Waterhouse consultants to offer their clients expert advice on a new development within 24 hours.*

Interestingly, it was not easy for Price Waterhouse to make full use of this system. Management had to change the culture of the organization by convincing its staff of the value of open communications, a concept that was central to the new system. The effort seems to have been worthwhile. Price Waterhouse has found a way to leverage its main product, consultant knowledge, through the strategic use of cutting-edge information technology designed for knowledge worker use.

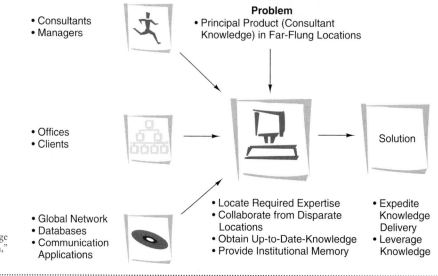

SOURCE: "Price Waterhouse—Knowledge Fully Shared Solidifies Leadership Position," *Computerworld*, September 27, 1993.

Price Waterhouse's global network illustrates the growing need for information systems that can help knowledge workers share and distribute knowledge. Information systems that help organizations create, coordinate, and distribute knowledge have become increasingly important as advanced industrial societies have shifted from industrial production to knowledge and information production as the primary basis of their wealth.

This chapter describes the role played by knowledge work and knowledge workers in contemporary organizations and shows how they can be supported by information systems applications for the creation and distribution of knowledge and information. We examine both office automation applications for clerical and managerial workers and knowledge work systems that support the work of highly trained professionals.

14.1 INFORMATION AND KNOWLEDGE WORK IN THE INFORMATION ECONOMY

What is information work and what is an information worker? The Bureau of Labor Statistics defines **information work** as work that primarily involves the creation or processing of information. Information workers are, therefore, people who primarily create or process information. Advanced industrial countries such as the United States, Canada, and most European nations employ more information workers than workers who work with their hands. This shift toward information work and workers has profound implications for the kind of information systems found in organizations and the ways they are used.

At a conservative estimate, over half of the U.S. labor force consists of information workers. Information workers produce about 75 percent of the value—$3 trillion—in our $4 trillion economy. The productivity of the entire economy depends greatly on their productivity. Because information work and workers play such a large role in the American economy, scholars refer to our society and other economically advanced societies as **information and knowledge economies**. These can be defined as economies in which the majority of new wealth (gross domestic product) is produced by creating or processing information.

Information work

Work that primarily involves the creation or processing of information.

Information and knowledge economy

An economy in which the majority of new wealth (gross national product) is produced by creating or processing information.

THE TRANSFORMATION OF THE AMERICAN ECONOMY

The transformation of the advanced industrial economies from economies centered on the production of manufactured goods toward economies based on the production of information and knowledge products and services is not new. Since 1900, the percentage of people who work in offices using information and knowledge to produce economic value (white-collar workers) has been rising, and the percentage of workers who work with their hands in factories or on farms (blue-collar workers) has been declining (see Figure 14.1). Among these so-called white-collar workers, the fastest growing occupations have been clerical, professional, technical, and managerial.[1] Recently the terms "knowledge" and "information" workers have been used to describe these employees. They are distinguished not by the color of their shirt collars, but rather by how they produce economic value through the use of knowledge and information.

These trends appear to have accelerated since 1960 in the United States and to have spurred worldwide changes in production and consumption. Since 1976, the value of goods produced in the information sector of the economy has been greater than the value of goods produced by manufacturing. Table 14.1 provides some examples of information, goods (manufacturing), and service industries.

FIGURE 14.1

The Growth of White-Collar Occupations Since 1900

At the turn of the century, blue-collar workers formed the majority of the American work force. Since then the trend has been a steady decline in the number of blue-collar workers, while the number of white-collar workers has risen. White-collar workers produce economic value through the use of knowledge and information. Since 1976 white-collar workers have outnumbered their blue-collar counterparts in the U.S. economy.

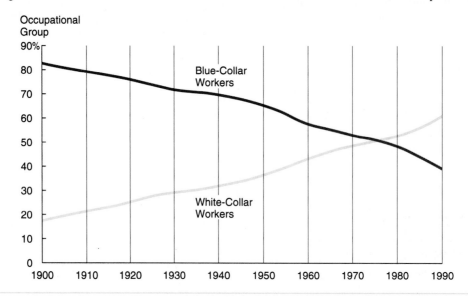

SOURCE: Vincent E. Giuliano, "The Mechanization of Office Work," *Scientific American,* September 1982, pp. 148–52.

Knowledge- and information-intense products

Products that require a great deal of learning and knowledge to create and often require information technologies to deliver in a timely fashion.

Information and service industries produce **knowledge- and information-intense products,**[2] which are defined as products that require a great deal of learning and knowledge to create; often information technologies are required to deliver these products in a timely fashion. Nintendo and other video games and all computer software are knowledge- and information-intense products because a great deal of knowledge and information is required to create them, and specialized information technology is needed to produce and use them. The airline industry, which provides a service—transportation—requires a vast computer network simply to book its seats and make a profit. Hence the airline reservation systems used in the United States are information-intense services. This is clearly less true of traditional industries such as mining and extrac-

TABLE 14.1

Some Representative Information, Goods, and Service Industries

Information	Goods	Service
Telephone	Agriculture	Hotels
Retail and wholesale trade	Logging	Business service
Finance	Chemicals	Auto repair
Insurance	Steel	Medical service
Education	Farm machinery	Amusements

SOURCE: Edward N. Wolff and William J. Baumol, "Sources of Postwar Growth of Information Activity in the U.S.," C.V. Starr Center for Applied Economics, New York University, June 1987; U.S. Census, 1980.

FIGURE 14.2

Shifting Demands for Labor in the United States since 1960

Since 1960 the increasing demand for information products and services has spurred the demand for—and the economic importance of—white-collar and service workers. This graph shows the sharp decline in manufacturing workers since 1960 and the corresponding increase in various types of white-collar and service occupations.

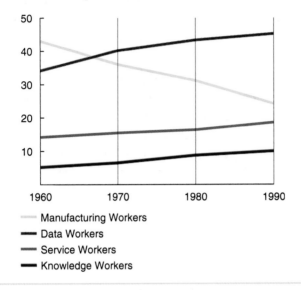

Manufacturing Workers
Data Workers
Service Workers
Knowledge Workers

SOURCE: Edward N. Wolff and William J. Baumol, "Sources of Postwar Growth of Information Activity in the U.S.," C.V. Starr Center for Applied Economics, New York University, June 1987. Reprinted with permission.

tion, although even in these industries, information and knowledge are playing new roles, as we describe later.

The increased demand for information products and services has touched off a very rapid shift in the demand for labor: More and more information and knowledge workers are required to produce the new goods and services. The airlines have had to hire many more computer specialists than pilots in the last 25 years. Even with traditional manufacturing businesses, more knowledge and information workers are being used to produce manufactured goods. The automobile industry, for example, has cut back on blue-collar production workers but has dramatically increased its hiring of designers, engineers, and computer specialists.

Figure 14.2 provides an overview of the changing composition of the U.S. labor force since 1960. Clearly, goods workers—those who work in factories or manipulate physical objects—have declined relative to data workers (those who work with information), service workers (those who provide a service), and knowledge workers (those who create new information).

Before describing how information technology serves these new types of workers, we should develop a more precise understanding of what we mean by information and knowledge workers and what kinds of jobs they perform. Only in this way can we understand the specific information requirements and technology solutions for information workers.

TABLE 14.2

Examples of Occupations of Various Types of Workers

Knowledge	Data	Service	Goods
Architect	Salesperson	Waiter	Teamster
Engineer	Accountant	Garbage collector	Welder
Judge	Data entry clerk	Cook	Machine operator
Scientist	Pharmacist	Nurse	Logger
Reporter	Railroad conductor	Hairdresser	Fisherman
Researcher	Foreman	Child care worker	Farmer
Writer	Draftsman	Gardener	Construction worker
Lawyer	Real estate broker	Cleaner	Miner
Programmer	Secretary	Barber	Glazier
Manager*	Manager	Clergy*	Mechanic

*Many occupations—like managers or clergy—cannot be easily classified. Managers, for instance, sometimes create new knowledge and information when they write reports; hence they often act like knowledge workers. At other times, they read and disseminate reports like data workers. Scholars handle this situation by classifying half of the managers as knowledge workers and half as data workers. A similar situation exists with clergy: they provide a service and disseminate information. Obviously, in the future we will need better data on specific occupations.

SOURCES: Edward N. Wolff and William J. Baumol, "Sources of Postwar Growth of Information Activity in the U.S.," C.V. Starr Center for Applied Economics, New York University, 1987; Marc Uri Porat, *The Information Economy: Definition and Measurement*, U.S. Office of Technology Special Publication 77–12 (1) (U.S. Department of Commerce, Office of Telecommunications, May 1977).

INFORMATION WORKERS: DATA VERSUS KNOWLEDGE WORKERS

The U.S. Department of Labor and the Bureau of the Census define information workers as all those people in the labor force who primarily create, work with, or disseminate information. The Department of Labor and the Bureau of the Census also distinguish two kinds of information workers: data workers and knowledge workers.

Knowledge workers are defined as those who create new information or knowledge; thus, **knowledge work** refers to work that primarily involves the creation of new information or knowledge. Data workers are defined as those who use, manipulate, or disseminate information; **data work**, then, is work that involves the use, manipulation, or dissemination of information. Service workers are those people who primarily deliver a service, while goods workers are those who work with physical objects or transform physical materials. Table 14.2 gives some examples of each kind of worker.

Notice in the table that knowledge workers are distinguished by the amount of formal schooling required to perform their jobs and by a large creative component in their work. Knowledge workers—for example, architects, engineers, judges, scientists, and writers—are required to exercise independent judgment and creativity based on mastery of large knowledge bases. In general, knowledge workers must obtain a Ph.D., master's degree, or certificate of competence before they are accepted into the labor force. In contrast, data workers typically have less formal training and no advanced educational degrees. They also tend to process information rather than create it and have less discretion in the exercise of judgment than knowledge workers do.

Given these differences, it is not surprising that these two types of workers have different requirements. Data workers are primarily served by office automation systems (described in the following section). Knowledge workers, although they certainly rely on and use office automation, also require much more powerful professional workstations (described in Section 14.3).

Knowledge work

Work whose primary emphasis is on the creation of new information or knowledge.

Data work

Work that primarily involves the process, use, or dissemination of information.

Although all persons in an organization depend on the office for support, information workers all work in offices. Or, to put it another way, all office workers are information workers of one kind or another. Sometimes the office is a "virtual office"—any place like a car, plane, train, or home where an information worker can get work done (see the Focus on People). These virtual offices are possible because of information technology like cellular telephones, fax machines, and a host of other office automation technologies described below.

THE PRODUCTIVITY CONNECTION: INFORMATION WORKERS AND OFFICES

With more than half of the labor force now composed of information workers who predominantly work in offices, and with most of our fastest growing industries being those that produce information- and knowledge-intense products that require high proportions of information workers, any overall advance in productivity for the advanced economies will almost certainly depend on increasing the productivity of information and knowledge workers. For this reason, there has been a massive increase in the capital investment in office workers.

Although total capital spending in the United States has slowed since the 1950s, there has been a dramatic shift toward capital investment in information technology of all kinds, with most of this going to the information sector of the economy. To put it another way, over 70 percent of all capital investment in the United States in 1989 was investment in information technology! Although some of this went to factories, most ended up in offices.

For this reason, office automation systems and professional work systems were the fastest growing applications of information technology in the 1980s and 1990s and will continue to grow in the future. Thus, it is not an exaggeration to say that office and professional systems have come to symbolize computerization in American work life and the hope for future gains in productivity. But the extent to which computers have enhanced the productivity of information workers is still open to debate, as described in the Focus on Problem Solving.

A British Petroleum engineer studies a computer-generated view of Prudhoe Bay. Her analysis of the data and skill in interpreting it can lead to profits—or losses—for the company.
SOURCE: Courtesy of BP America.

14.2 OFFICE AUTOMATION: AUTOMATING INFORMATION WORK

Office automation is any application of information technology that is intended to increase the productivity of office information workers. Office automation has been going on since the dawn of the Industrial Revolution or even earlier. In fact, you might trace the beginning of office automation to the year 1460, when Johannes Gutenberg and other German printers first used movable type to publish books and thereby semi-automated the printing process by permitting multiple strikeoffs of single pages and rapid page composition.

The automation of specific office tasks accelerated in the nineteenth century with the first desktop mechanical calculators (1840) and desktop typewriters (1860), which were designed to semi-automate hand calculations and handwritten notes, respectively. With the advent of electricity in 1900, filing cabinets, typewriters, and adding machines were converted to electro-mechanical devices based on small motors. Added

Office automation
The application of information technology to increase the productivity of office information workers.

FOCUS ON PEOPLE

THE BIRTH OF THE VIRTUAL OFFICE

Chiat/Day, a leading U.S. advertising agency with offices in New York and Los Angeles, is in the process of eliminating its offices. Its information workers are being issued laptop computers (IBM notebooks) with modems plus digital car phones and are being told to work for us, but not here. For some employees, this is the realization of a dream—flexibility and control over one's own time. For example, one recent morning, Peggy Roswell, Chiat's account executive for Home Savings of America, impulsively decided to see her daughter perform in her school choir. With a virtual office (VO), she has that flexibility.

Where do you work if your office disappears? Of course, you can work at home, or at the client's office, or in your mobile office, otherwise known as the car. VO workers often find themselves in hotel lobbies and airport terminals. Moreover, if the VO concept is to succeed, the employer must still supply some centralized work facilities. Chiat/Day has reconstructed its entire Los Angeles facility; by January 1994, no one had an office. The New York office is next. In their place will be a "campus" where employees will have lockers, a media center with video equipment and CD-ROM computers, and a "student union" where employees such as Roswell can register for a work space. Work spaces include traditional conference rooms, a "flop room" where people can work in easy chairs or lying

on the floor, and private work spaces that resemble amusement park rides.

Chiat's explanation for taking such a dramatic step is that they want their organizational structure to support the organizational need to be nimble in our fast-changing business environment. Skeptics believe Chiat's real motive is to divert attention away from the firm's troubles after they lost their lucrative Reebok account and lost the competition to get IBM's personal computer account. Ernst & Young, the accounting firm, moved their auditors from offices into a "hoteling" system because it reduced office space 15 to 18 percent and thereby reduced costs. Robert Cook, senior vice-president of Interior Architects Inc. in San Francisco, California, believes that one motivation for the VO is to force one's sales staff to spend more time with customers. Yet another possible explanation is the U.S. government's Clean Air Act, which requires companies with 200 or more employees in major metropolitan areas to reduce commuter automobile mileage 25 percent by 1996.

Whatever the reason, increasing numbers of people do not work in traditional offices. According to Link Resources, by 1993 some 25 million people were working at home, double the number 10 years earlier. Most of them were independent consultants, contractors, or entrepreneurs rather than employed VO workers. However, Link also claims that telecommuting—the practice of having corporate employees work at home—has increased 40 percent in the past 5 years. Because the VO may be appropriate for as much as 40 percent of our work force, we should expect to see it continue to grow.

Many employees are fearful of the VO. To some it sounds too much like

downsizing, part-time work, or a "virtual" work force of consultants. They are frightened for their jobs. Others respond poorly to the loss of daily social contact. A virtual office can be very lonely—there is no water cooler where employees can meet and chat. A Bell Telephone study done years ago on employees working from their homes found that their productivity and morale plunged precipitously unless they kept in close personal contact with the office. Some fear the breakdown of the separation between the refuge known as home and the pressure-cooker environment known as work. Paul Saffo of the Institute for the Future in California's Menlo Park sums up the conflict between having one's freedom in a VO and the loss of the work-home separation: "Heaven is the anywhere, anytime office. Hell is the everywhere, everytime office."

To be prepared to become a VO worker, you will need to be acquainted with some of the new vocabulary spawned by the VO movement. For example, an office used in turn by many employees is known as a *drop-in office; face time* is the time spent meeting face-to-face with clients; setting up temporary offices in places like hotels becomes *hoteling;* and the *virtual water cooler* is some technology device, such as a videophone, that keeps those not working in the office in touch with office gossip and relationships.

FOCUS Questions:
What do you think are the problems in managing people who work in VOs? If VO workers can be managed properly, does this hold any lessons for us on how to manage people who are in offices?

SOURCE: Phil Patton, "The Virtual Office Becomes Reality," *The New York Times,* October 28, 1993.

FOCUS ON PROBLEM SOLVING

CAN COMPUTERS MAKE OFFICE WORKERS MORE PRODUCTIVE?

Beset by recession and intense competition, companies are beginning to apply to office workers what they did to factories—attempts to make office workers more productive. Are computers the solution? Not necessarily. Computers can speed up high-volume, assembly-line activities such as bill paying, check clearing, or claims processing. But using computers to bolster the productivity of knowledge workers can backfire. Personal computers, electronic mail systems, and multifunction telephones can actually generate more drafts, more memos, more spreadsheets, and more messages. According to Paul Strassman, former chief information officer for Xerox and the Defense Department, the United States for three decades used computers to speed up the kind of work that accentuates bureaucracy. Unless offices and service companies have a detailed plan when they automate, computers may wind up being used for work that is trivial, peripheral, or downright counterproductive.

Stephen Roach, senior economist for Morgan Stanley, estimated that white-collar productivity increased an average of only 0.28 percent annually during the 1980s. Recently he has been more optimistic, however, because service sector productivity accelerated, growing over 3 percent annually by 1992. What made the difference? Roach and others believe that businesses started using computers to overhaul the way work is done in the office. Instead of blindly computerizing, firms such as Motorola, IBM, Security Pacific, and Corning Glass dramatically boosted white-collar productivity by re-engineering office work. They realized that automating something that shouldn't have been done manually in the first place won't make workers more efficient. Instead, the firms have focused on eliminating bottlenecks, improving customer service, and eliminating mistakes first before introducing new technology.

Sea-Land Service, the largest containerized ocean shipping company in the United States, increased productivity by streamlining its business procedures in conjunction with the use of information technology. Customers do not like to wait for accurate bills of lading. If shippers send paperwork with mistakes, clerks are now empowered to call the shipper and correct the problem instead of going through a maze of bureaucratic procedures. For instance, if a shipper misclassified bamboo umbrellas as bamboo goods (which are

shipped at a lower rate), the clerk calls the shipper and asks the shipper to reclassify them. In the past the clerk would have waited for the irritated consignee to call and ask for a revised bill of lading to be prepared at additional expense to Sea-Land. By getting the bills right the first time, Sea-Land has reduced the average cost of preparing the documents from around $22 to $14 each. The firm prepares 1.3 million bills of lading per year.

It used to take a corporate auditor at the Motorola Corp. an average of 7 weeks to draft a report and deliver a final version to top management. The auditor would visit a plant to examine its books, return to corporate headquarters in Schaumburg, Illinois, write the first draft of the report in longhand, give it to a typist, make revisions, send the report to his or her supervisor, revise again, have the report retyped, remit the report to an audit manager, revise the report again, send the report to the auditee for comment, incorporate changes, and type up a final version. Now each auditor uses a personal computer to write the report in the field, shows it to the auditee, and incorporates comments from the auditee and an auditing department manager in the field. The entire process now takes just 5 days, a tenfold improvement in cycle time.

FOCUS Question:
Why can't computers make office workers more productive?

SOURCE: Myron Magnet, "Good News for the Service Economy," *Fortune*, May 3, 1993.

to these devices were entirely new technologies: teletype, telephone, dictation and recording machines, automatic telephone switching, duplicating machines, copiers, and small offset presses. With the development of transistors and integrated circuits in the 1960s and the digital revolution, which saw the development of very-high-capacity digital storage devices like floppy disks and hard disks, much of this early electromechanical equipment was converted to digital machinery.

With the development of personal computers in the 1980s and the later emergence of powerful desktop machines such as the IBM XT, AT, 386, and 486 machines and the Apple Macintosh, the focus of automation shifted from mainframes to desktop computing and networks of desktop computers. Suddenly, office automation became something that small companies or even individuals could develop.

The meaning of "office automation" has changed with each generation of technology. In 1980 office automation largely referred to document management and processing, but as hardware and software have improved, virtually all office activities—from sophisticated color graphics to personal databases to communications—can now be assisted by information technology. Before we describe office automation today, however, we must first take a look at the role of the office in the organization.

THE THREE ROLES OF THE OFFICE IN ORGANIZATIONS

Office roles

The functions played by an office in an organization, consisting of (1) coordinating and managing people and work, (2) linking diverse organizational units and projects, and (3) coupling the organization to the external environment.

At least three primary **office roles** in organizational life can be discerned:

1. Coordinating the work of a diverse collection of business professionals who work together to achieve some common goal.

2. Geographically and functionally linking diverse parts and units of the business.

3. Spanning the boundary between the business and its external environment to connect the firm to its clients, suppliers, and other organizations.

Many features of offices and their roles in business are not immediately apparent to the casual observer. Most people think that offices predominantly involve secretaries and clerical work, but this is the most superficial aspect of office life. If you look closer, you will discover a diverse array of professional, managerial, sales, and clerical employees who work in the office or depend on the office to perform their daily jobs (see Figure 14.3).

If you look even more closely at the typical business office, you will discover a rich, informal social life involving intense interpersonal interactions across professional and status lines. A kind of equality exists in offices that is not found in the outside world. What unites diverse people in an office is a commonality of place, sometimes a sense of mission, and often their ultimate fate. When the organization no longer needs an office for a business purpose, everyone's life changes—the boss, the secretary, the accountant are all either placed elsewhere or terminated. Offices are work groups composed of people who work together as individuals toward shared goals. Office work is complex and cooperative, yet highly individualistic. It is not so much a factory of collaborating workers as an orchestra of highly trained individuals.[3] The office, in other words, is the closest thing to a "family" or "team" that information workers experience when they go to work.

The office is a major tool for the coordination of diverse information work and the allocation of resources to projects; it also serves as a clearinghouse for information and knowledge. In much the same way that a market establishes a relationship between sellers and buyers, the office creates a relationship between creators of information and knowledge and those who use, disseminate, or work with that information. The centrality of offices to organizational life and work is a key feature of modern life.

In addition, the office plays a critical role in linking diverse functional areas and physically distant units of the firm. The office is a significant node that gathers information and knowledge and distributes it to other work groups and offices in the organization. In this sense, the office is an information and knowledge conduit or channel.

FIGURE 14.3

Primary Role of the Office

An office is more than a room with people sitting in it; it is an organizational group consisting of employees who work together to achieve a common goal. Within an office are staff members from many organizational levels who perform a variety of information-intensive tasks. Office systems must therefore address various needs to help the office function more efficiently and coordinate the work of diverse groups of employees.

The office is the eyes and ears of the organization. The information and knowledge that the office decides to send up or down or across the hierarchy critically affect the fate of organizations.

Figure 14.4 illustrates the role of the office in linking a firm's functional areas as well as its third major role: The function of the office as the major link to the external environment. When you call an organization, you call an office. A specialized work group in that office handles your call in accordance with some well-established routine. The office is where the sales staff reports, where records are kept on customers, and where clients are tracked. Without the office, there would be no sales. Offices are also key purchasing units of the organization and are linked directly to vendors and suppliers of materials and to outside auditors. The human resources office must ensure that the firm follows government standards for employment practices.

Viewing offices in terms of these three major roles can help you understand how and why businesses need to use information technology in the form of the office automation systems described below. At the same time, you should remember that all offices do not face the same problems. Some offices are swamped by paperwork. Other offices have telephones ringing off the hook and going unanswered. Still others routinely lose engineering drawings. Each of these problems has a different information systems solution.

ROLES, ACTIVITIES, AND SYSTEMS IN THE OFFICE

As Table 14.3 illustrates, the roles played by offices and the activities performed in them present different information challenges that can be met by various types of information technology. Table 14.3 identifies five major **office activities** that occur to some degree in every office: managing documents, scheduling, communicating, managing data, and

Office activities

The activities performed by an office in an organization, consisting of (1) managing documents, (2) scheduling individuals and groups, (3) communicating with individuals and groups, (4) managing data on individuals and groups, and (5) managing projects.

FIGURE 14.4

Two Other Major Roles of the Office

Offices connect the different functional areas of a firm. Each office gathers and distributes information according to its particular role in the organization. In addition, offices have a third major role: They connect an organization to its external environment. Offices in the production area deal with the firm's suppliers of raw materials, while those in finance deal with outside auditors. Sales and marketing offices are the organization's link to its customers. The human resources office is responsible for ensuring that the firm meets government standards for fair employment practices. Offices in several of these functional areas may also be linked to databases, which provide businesses with pools of externally derived information.

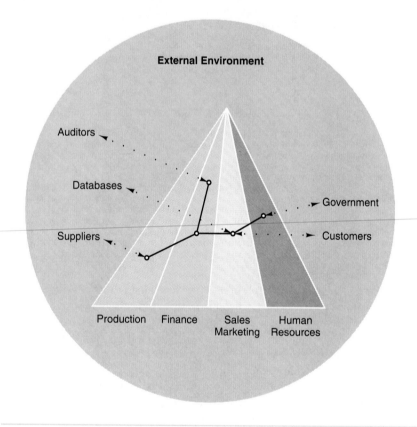

managing projects. We have also provided an estimate—based on our own experience as office systems implementors and software writers—of the average percentage of office effort involved in each activity. Effort can be defined either in terms of capital investment or time allocated to that type of activity. For instance, managing documents typically involves about 40 percent of the total hours worked in an average office. Communicating involves another 30 percent of office time.

At the far right of the table, five major groups of information technologies (both hardware and software) are listed that are designed to support these five office activities. Some of these technologies support more than one activity.

In the next sections, we examine each major group and explain what each of the technologies is and how it works. The hardware and software discussed here have

TABLE 14.3

Offices and Office Automation: Functions, Activities, and Systems in the Modern Office

General Functions of Offices	Activities in an Office	Percentage of Effort*	Information Technology Assistance
Coordinating and managing people and work. Linking organizational units and projects. Connecting the organization to outside groups and people.	Managing documents: Creating, storing/retrieving, and communicating image (analog) and digital documents.	40	Document management Word processing hardware and software. Desktop publishing. Optical and digital disk storage. Digital local area networks.
	Scheduling individuals and groups: Creating, managing, and communicating documents, plans, and calendars.	10	Digital calendars Electronic calendars and schedules. Electronic mail.
	Communicating with individuals and groups: Initiating, receiving, and managing voice and digital communications with diverse groups and individuals.	30	Communications Private branch exchanges and digital phone equipment. Voice mail. Group work support software.
	Managing data on individuals and groups: Entering and managing data to track external customers, clients, and vendors as well as internal individuals and groups.	10	Data management Desktop database for client/customer tracking, project tracking, and calendar information.
	Managing projects: Planning, initiating, evaluating, and monitoring projects; allocating resources; and making personnel decisions.	10	Project management Desktop project management tools. Critical Path Method (CPM) and Program Evaluation and Review Technique (PERT).

*Based on the authors' experience with office systems.

already been described in previous chapters (see Chapters 4–8), so you may wish to review these chapters briefly to refresh your memory of some of these terms.

Document Management Technologies Document management technologies are the information technologies used in the processing and management of documents; they include word processing, desktop publishing, and optical disk storage.

Word Processing **Word processing** refers to the software and hardware used to create, edit, format, store, and print documents. Word processing systems are the single most common application of information technology to office work, in part because producing documents is what offices are all about. A word processing system has four basic components: input, processing, output, and storage. A typical word processing system includes many possible devices and software elements (see Figure 14.5). Most of the terms in Figure 14.5 were introduced in previous chapters. The following provides a brief review:

- **Scanner:** An electronic device that reads text or graphics and inputs the information into a computer automatically without human typing.

Document management technology

Information technology that is used for producing and managing the flow of documents in an organization; includes word processing, desktop publishing, and optical disk storage.

Word processing

Software and hardware that are used to create, edit, format, store, and print documents.

FIGURE 14.5

A Typical Word Processing System

Word processing systems are the single most common application of information technology in today's offices. A word processing system consists of the hardware and software necessary for creating, editing, storing, and printing documents, and their importance reflects the importance of written documents in business transactions. As with other systems we have discussed, a word processing system includes devices for input, processing, storage, and output. This diagram shows possible devices that can perform or enhance the word processing function.

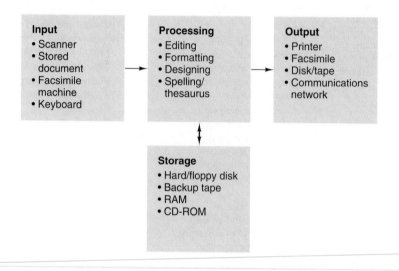

- **Disk-stored document:** A disk is a magnetic medium used to store digital information. Disks can be hard disks inside machines, which store a great deal of information, or floppy flexible disks, which can be removed from a machine but store less information.

- **Facsimile machine (fax):** An electronic device that reads a document and transmits it through the telephone system to another machine that prints a facsimile of the document.

- **Backup tape:** A device that makes a copy of files and disks on magnetic tape for safekeeping.

- **RAM:** Random-access memory is a computer's immediately available memory; it is used to store programs, data, and text.

- **CD-ROM:** Compact disk read-only memory is an optical disk similar to the 5-inch optical audio disks used for music. In the computer world, these disks are used to store very large amounts of data and text. The memory is "read only" because data can be placed on the disk only once but read many times. The data cannot be changed or updated, and the disk cannot be used to record new data.

- **Communications network:** A series of devices that work together to transmit information.

Many enhancements can be added to this bare-bones system. If we required access to large warehouses of information, we could add a CD-ROM storage unit with 500 megabytes of capacity as opposed to a mere 80-megabyte disk. Another option would be to add a magneto-optical disk, which would permit us to write on an optical disk as many times as we wanted. In addition, for a few hundred dollars, we could purchase desktop publishing software to produce higher-quality output.

Desktop Publishing   The term **desktop publishing** covers a variety of systems and capabilities. In general, it refers to applications for producing documents that combine high-quality type, graphics, and a variety of layout options. Working on the computer screen, the user arranges words and graphics on pages. The user can type in words or charts, and use an electronic scanner to scan photographs and drawings, converting them into data that instruct the printer to generate a duplicate of the image by printing tiny dots. An advanced system can even reproduce color graphics. The system enables the user to enter commands for how the various elements are to be printed on the page. The user then sends the document to a laser printer, which produces the final output quickly and in excellent quality.

If the user of such a system has good judgment in matters of design, he or she can use desktop publishing to single-handedly produce reports, advertisements, or other documents of a quality that closely approximates the work of professional typesetters and graphic designers. For example, the user can select various styles and sizes of type to fit a given design and layout for the document. Thus, desktop publishing enables users to do their own typesetting and page makeup at home or in the office. With a basic microcomputer–based system, even the smallest businesses can afford ads, brochures, reports, or other documents that might be too expensive if they were prepared by professionals.

But what good is all this equipment with its beautiful output if we cannot share the results with others? We need to add some communications to our typical office so we can connect workstations and communicate with our colleagues and the rest of the world.

Desktop publishing

Applications for producing documents that combine high-quality type and graphics with a variety of layout options, allowing users to produce professional-quality reports and documents.

Aldus PageMaker 5.0 for Windows desktop publishing software allows creative professionals to rotate text and graphics and to share text and graphics among different publications, expediting layout, design, and document production. Many companies use desktop publishing software on microcomputers to publish newsletters, sales brochures, and training documents.

SOURCE: Courtesy of Aldus Corporation.

Office Communications Technologies   For much of the early 1980s, the typical office relied on individual word processing workstations based on stand-alone personal computers. This did not present a problem for a person working alone in a tiny office or at home, but the purpose of documents is to communicate ideas, so stand-alone work-stations in a large office made no sense. What if you wanted to send a document to another computer for processing, editing, formatting, or review?

The most common office communications systems are local area networks (LANs), which are digital communications systems that connect digital devices such as computers, printers, fax machines, and storage devices (see also Chapter 8). A LAN usually operates in a small area of up to half a mile; after that, a more powerful network design is required. LANs are designed to integrate word processing and other microcomputer–based or workstation projects (like spreadsheets or database applications) into a single, coherent system that permits documents, pictures, and related graphics to be shared and communicated. With a LAN, for instance, only one laser printer is needed in an office because many microcomputer workstations have access to it via the network.

Office scheduling technology

Information technology used to coordinate individual and group calendars, such as electronic calendars.

Groupware

Software that attempts to expedite all the functions of a typical work group—for example, tracking the calendars of all or related individuals in an office, scheduling meetings, and sharing ideas and documents.

Office Scheduling Technology   Keeping track of appointments, activities, and meetings is an important job in the modern office. A variety of software tools, known collectively as **office scheduling technology**, is now available to coordinate individual and group calendars. A simple electronic calendar keeps track of personal appointments and activities.

More sophisticated software—sometimes referred to as **groupware**—tracks the calendars of related individuals, or all individuals, in an office and makes that calendar available to a central receptionist. In this way, for instance, if a customer calls and asks for an appointment with a specific salesperson who is out of the office, the receptionist can use an electronic group calendar to guide the customer to an available salesperson. Likewise, if a senior executive wants to meet with all his or her subordinates, a group calendar will show when all the subordinates are available. Other aspects of groupware will be discussed in the following pages.

Office data management technology

Information technology that centers around desktop databases for client or customer tracking, project tracking, calendar information, and other information required for office jobs.

Office Data Management Technology   Although business firms store basic transaction and client data in huge corporate databases on mainframes, the development of **office data management technology** has provided many office workers the opportunity to develop their own client tracking systems, customer lists, and supplier and vendor lists using desktop machines. With contemporary database packages like dBASE IV, Access, and Paradox, information workers can create their own databases on clients, customers, suppliers, and other data they need to do their jobs.

Most information workers do not create their own databases, however. In general, the microcomputer database languages are still too difficult to use without special training. Instead, they turn to personal information managers (PIMs), a new kind of software that is customized for specific positions such as salesperson, manager, real estate agent, stockbroker, and the like. Personal information managers are packaged database tools designed to support specific office tasks. They offer much greater flexibility than corporate databases and can easily be customized for individual preferences.

An example of a desktop database is The Financial Manager, which is designed to serve the desktop information needs of account executives and portfolio managers in the financial services industry. Financial managers typically have from 500 to 1,000 clients, each of whom has one or more portfolios of investments. In addition, financial managers usually have a full calendar of events, activities, and planned actions, as well as several routine projects such as contacting clients and prospects for business. The Financial Manager keeps track of all these various activities and functions—clients, portfolios, calendars, and projects (see Figure 14.6).

FIGURE 14.6

Personal Information Management Software

Personal information management packages are a relatively new type of software tool that is proving to be very useful in offices. More flexible than traditional corporate databases, they can be customized for a variety of office functions. This figure shows two screens from "Financial Manager" (© 1994 Azimuth Corp.), a desktop information management package for account executives and portfolio managers in the financial services industry. The opening screen (top) presents a schedule of each day's events. The client screen (bottom) records background information and investment objectives for each client. This first screen is for prospects—people who are not yet clients. Additional screens with more detailed information, including the names of spouse and children, follow this screen.

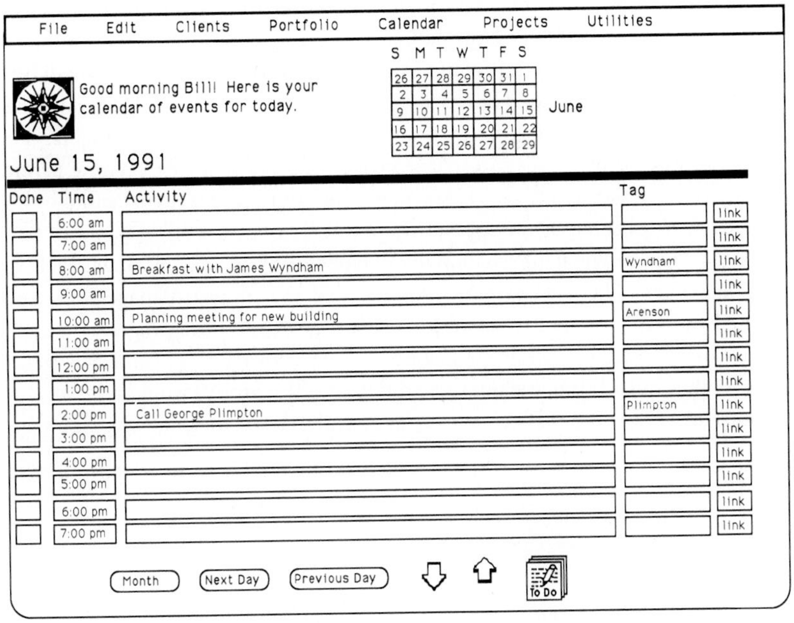

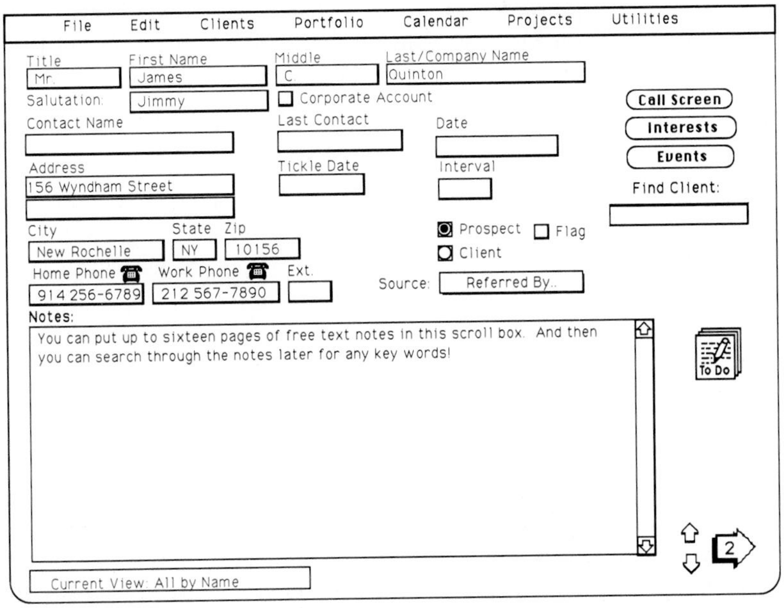

Project management technology

Software that helps managers track and plan projects.

Project Management Technology   Offices are hotbeds of individual projects. At the same time, they are central control points that coordinate the flow of resources to projects and evaluate the results. **Project management technology** is software that helps managers track and plan a multitude of projects.

Project management software breaks a complex project down into simpler sub-tasks, each with its own completion date and resource requirements. Once a user knows what is needed, how much, and when, delivery schedules and resources can be provided precisely when needed. Some software provides suggestions about how resources should be allocated to tasks. Two traditional techniques of project management that most project managers use are CPM (Critical Path Method) and PERT (Project Evaluation and Review Technique). These techniques can save thousands of dollars in inventory costs because a user does not have to stockpile resources.

Figure 14.7 shows how these information technologies might be used in a single office, such as a branch office of a large national stock brokerage firm. One would find clerical workers, office managers, account executives (the sales force), and a small professional support staff of analysts. The clerical group would primarily use document management software to keep track of sales and manage the flow of documents. The receptionist(s) would route calls through a private branch exchange (a central private switchboard that handles a firm's voice and digital communications needs) and use electronic calendars to schedule clients' appointments with account executives. Account executives would rely on personal information management software and customer databases to assist their sales. The management group would use project management, sales management, and group support software to set sales goals and track progress. The analysts would use statistical packages to measure office performance or track new trends in industry sales. In addition, each of these different office groups would use the communications network of the office to communicate with one another and with customers.

FIGURE 14.7

Information Technologies Used by Employees in a Branch Office

In a branch office of a large stock brokerage firm, we would find several functional groups of employees, with each group being served by certain information technologies. The clerical staff, including receptionists, for instance, would be likely to use document management software and electronic calendars to do their jobs and a PBX system to route telephone calls. Account executives located in the same office would be more likely to use such tools as customer databases and personal information management software like that shown in Figure 14.6. All the staff would use a network to communicate with each other and with customers.

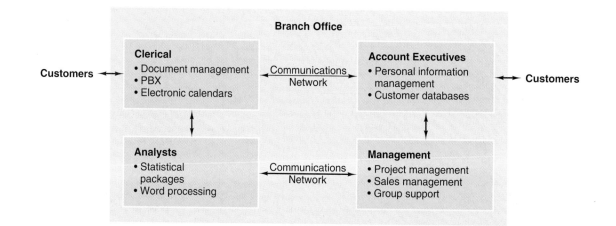

IMAGING: STEMMING THE TIDE OF PAPER

Businesses today deal with mountains of papers—letters, reports, forms, sales literature, and vital records. Offices throughout the United States store more than three trillion documents, 95 percent of them in paper form. Can information technology help to stem the rising tide of paper? One promising approach is the use of imaging systems. **Imaging** is an umbrella term that incorporates a variety of systems and software tools. With modern imaging technology a document can be digitized into a bit-mapped image that can be stored and made available within a database. The image can then be immediately retrieved and distributed if required.

 The benefits of imaging include increased productivity, efficient use of physical storage space, and improved information management. Most important, imaging helps businesses quickly access information, eliminating extensive, exhaustive searches for documents and files that are often buried in traditional storage facilities.

 The following components are typically found in complete imaging systems (see Figure 14.8):

- Scanners and optical character recognition software for digitizing hard-copy documents

- Workstations with high-resolution displays

- Software designed to manage document retrieval, work-flow automation, and communications functions

- High-capacity storage devices, especially optical disk

- Output devices such as printers

 Optical storage media significantly reduce the amount of storage space for archival (long-term) storage and thereby reduce operating costs. The information contained in 20 file cabinets can be stored on a single 5-inch optical disk.

 Documents are stored using optical or magnetic disks and can be retrieved on-line instantaneously, based on values in key fields. Compare this to waiting minutes or

Imaging

Systems and software that convert documents into digital form so that they can be stored, accessed, and manipulated by the computer.

Consolidated Freightways' image processing system makes digitized document images immediately available on-line. Imaging systems can save companies time and money by reducing the number of steps required to process a document and by making documents easier to locate.

SOURCE: Courtesy of Consolidated Freightways, Inc.

FIGURE 14.8

Components of a Typical Imaging System

Documents are scanned into the system. The scanner digitizes the document, creating an electronic image, which is compressed for storage and indexed for future retrieval. Compressed and indexed documents are stored either on magnetic or optical disks. The system controller moves images in and out of storage and routes them from one workstation to the next over a LAN, which can be limited to other departments or a host computer. Workstations allow users to access the document index, view the documents only, or both view and edit them.

System Controller
$30,000–$1,000,000

Storage
$25,000–$250,000

Scanner
$20,000–$150,000

Printer
$12,000–$60,000

Workstation
$8,000–$20,000

hours to retrieve a file from a file cabinet or even days to retrieve a file that has been archived in a warehouse. Files can also be accessed in different ways, such as by date, case number, or type, without creating multiple copies. Because the electronic document is like any other computer record, it can be accessed by more than one person at a time.

Files stored electronically are less likely to get lost or physically damaged. It is also easy to create backups of electronic documents and store them in another location for

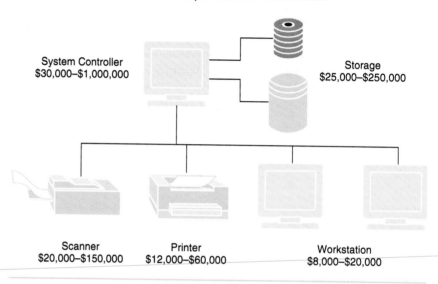

One form of output in image processing is digitized pictures of original documents accessed on video monitors.

SOURCE: Courtesy of Wang Laboratories, Inc.

FIGURE 14.9

How Imaging Streamlines the Paper Trail

Consolidated Freightways, Inc., a major player in the freight transportation industry, streamlined their paper trail by converting the equivalent of a 75-mile-high stack of paper documents into 2,500 12-inch optical disks. Bills of lading and delivery receipts and attachments are electronically scanned into an information system. The electronic images are then transmitted to the main data center where they are stored on optical disks. The day after a freight pickup or delivery, customers can access documents either through a telecommunications link or a phone call to their local image document service department. A hard copy of the requested document is sent to the customer's fax machine within minutes.

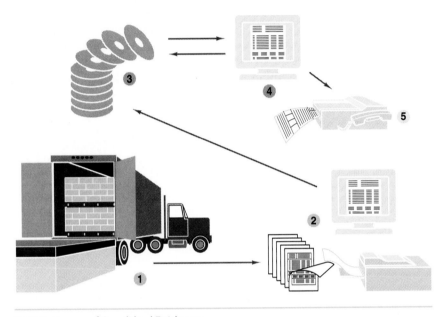

SOURCE: Courtesy of Consolidated Freightways.

added security. Fewer paper copies of documents are needed and the physical space for paper is greatly reduced (see Figure 14.9).

Imaging has several different functions. The first is document storage and filing and includes the ability to scan, store, and display documents on-line as digitized images. This is essentially an electronic replacement for the traditional filing cabinet, except that the electronic file cabinet can be accessed by more than one user at the same time. The second function is work-flow automation. Imaging technology allows digitized documents to be electronically routed throughout the firm from one workstation to another, streamlining the entire work procedure. Processes such as approval cycles, schedules, productivity measurement, and report generation are automated as well. A third function integrates digitized documents with existing information system applications. Tools can collect all the information required for a specific purpose and deliver it to a specific user.

While the basic application of imaging technology in business is to store and retrieve images of documents, the biggest payback comes from using imaging to manage work flow. Work-flow automation actively routes documents through a system based on rules that reflect the decision criteria for processing the documents. This results in a streamlined processing and distribution of documents, with fewer people required to process documents. To maximize the effect of imaging, organizations must change their work procedures. If a firm automates only its current work flow, it can't take full advantage of this tool.

The Focus on Organizations describes how Massachusetts Financial Services used imaging technology as an integral part of a solution for a major work-flow problem.

GROUPWARE: A NEW OFFICE TECHNOLOGY

A new kind of software aimed specifically at coordinating the efforts of work groups is now available. Called groupware as a generic category, this new technology requires a network to connect group member computers. Groupware attempts to expedite all the functions of a typical work group (we introduced one form of groupware in the discussion of scheduling technology above). Whereas early office automation software and hardware focused on using PCs to enhance the productivity of individual workers, there is a growing recognition that much of what gets done in a business depends on the effective functioning of small work groups.

But how can information technology help these small work groups? To answer this question, think of what happens in work groups: ideas develop, documents are shared for comment or modification, messages are sent, meetings are scheduled and held, and topics are discussed. Notice that these activities are similar to the five generic categories of office activities identified in Table 14.3. Groupware appropriate for each of these areas is available (see Table 14.4).

FOCUS ON ORGANIZATIONS

REDESIGNING THE ORGANIZATION WITH IMAGING TECHNOLOGY

Massachusetts Financial Services of Boston, which now manages $30 billion in mutual funds, experienced dramatic growth in the 1980s. Lacking the appropriate information systems to support its growth, the company "threw people at the problem," according to senior vice-president James F. Bailey. With 600 separate business steps involved in assisting customers, they required a staff of 1,000 people. Bailey

knew they had a problem. Working with DST Systems in Kansas City, Missouri, they developed a document management system that has paid off despite its initial cost of $5 million.

An internal business process review revealed to Massachusetts Financial that too many people were handling each business transaction. For example, they found that a customer's request to redeem mutual fund shares triggered activity involving 20 separate steps before the process was complete. The study concluded that the key to success for Massachusetts Financial was to redesign the work flow before automating it.

Once the work flow was redesigned, the system they developed was centered on imaging technology. Customer requests are scanned and stored on a network server. The customer service staff has easy, direct access

to all documents through desktop workstations connected to a client/server network.

The work-flow redesign has combined with the new imaging-based client/server document management system. A customer request to redeem fund shares now requires only six separate steps. Overall, customer service steps were reduced by 55 percent to a total of 270. Massachusetts Financial headcount decreased by 40 percent to about 600 employees—accomplished through attrition, not layoffs, so that the staff would support the changes. The $5 million investment has certainly proven cost effective.

FOCUS Questions:

How did Massachusetts Financial Services' imaging system contribute to work-flow redesign? What problems did it solve?

SOURCE: James M. Connolly, "Financial Firm Banks on Imaging," *Computerworld,* April 5, 1993.

TABLE 14.4

Examples of Groupware and the Five Major Office Activities

Managing Documents
Group writing and commenting
Electronic mail distribution
Screen sharing

Scheduling
Team and project calendars
Office calendars and appointment books

Communicating
Electronic mail
Electronic meetings
Conversation structuring
Computer conferencing
Screen sharing

Managing Data
Group decision support systems
Shared data files and databases

Managing Projects
Shared time lines and plans
Project management software on networks

Users of groupware define their own work groups, with separate groups being defined for separate functions. Employees frequently belong to a variety of groups. For example, the same employee may belong to his reporting work group, a special project development group, a group studying some new technology, a group of all employees dealing with a specific product line, a group consisting of all employees in his department, and a company-wide group. Only those who belong to a specific group will be able to access that group's applications.

A range of commercially available groupware products addresses specific group activities. For example, ForComment allows multiple users to comment on and edit a single document; Higgins permits access to group calendars and shared project information; Caucus accommodates up to 16 users in a single electronic meeting. We will describe the leading groupware software, Lotus Notes from Lotus Software (Cambridge, Massachusetts), to illustrate the worth of work group software.

Lotus Notes operates on IBM-compatible microcomputers and is accessed through an easy-to-use, Windows-like user interface. It allows sharing of information through collections of documents stored in databases. Text, graphics, spreadsheet data, sound, image, and video can all be contained within a single document. Each application belongs to a specific group and can be accessed only by members of that group. The application also has its own separate database.

Using Lotus Notes, group members can create documents using either predefined forms supplied by Lotus Notes or by creating their own forms. The form will automatically be stamped with the date and time of creation, the originator of the document, and any indexing keys the originator supplies. Group members can access the document, comment on it, or use the application to distribute other material to the rest of the team. The application logs and saves all application communications, thereby creating a history of project communications.

We can appreciate the value of this software by understanding how it is used on the global network of Price Waterhouse, the worldwide accounting and consulting firm described in the chapter-opening vignette. Rick Richardson, who is in charge of all the work that Price Waterhouse does with New York City banks, begins each day by clicking on Lotus Notes to see his E-mail messages (he receives 20–25 such messages daily). He then uses Notes to see news articles on topics he has given the computer standing orders to track and to call up a bulletin board specifically dedicated to the firm's financial services business. A Washington staffer has reported an account regulation charge.

Richardson adds a comment. A Miami manager needs Spanish-speaking consultants for an assignment in Buenos Aires. Richardson sends him a name via E-mail. Finally, Richardson checks another bulletin board called PW Alert, where employees post general information and queries. Richardson bypasses a message from Dublin asking for a consultant with experience auditing a cheese plant and other messages in which he is not interested, but he carefully scrutinizes a query from Chicago listing candidates for a chief financial officer position for a client firm.

In addition to managing the routine work flow and communications of small groups, groupware such as Lotus Notes can facilitate a firm's more urgent business. Price Waterhouse used Notes to assemble a proposal in just 4 days to win a multimillion dollar consulting contract. On Thursday, Price Waterhouse was invited to bid on work to develop a complex new trading operation for a major securities firm. The proposals were due the following Monday. The four executives required to write the proposal were in three different states, but with Notes they were able to conduct a four-way dialogue on screen. They also used Notes to extract from various databases key components of the proposal, such as passages from similar successful proposals and resumes of the Price Waterhouse experts from around the world who could be assigned to the job. Each contributor modified the draft as it evolved, with Notes keeping track of the changes. Other executives were able to tap into Notes to view the proposal over the weekend. The proposal was ready Monday. Price Waterhouse won not only the consulting contract but a subsequent contract to audit the new operation as well.[4]

Two scientists in the fermentation research group at the Bristol-Myers Squibb Research Institute in Tokyo collect soil samples that will be screened for substances that might eventually become new therapeutic agents. New products and businesses are frequently the result of knowledge work.

SOURCE: Courtesy of Bristol-Meyers Squibb Company.

14.3 KNOWLEDGE WORK: PROFESSIONAL WORK SYSTEMS

The information needs of highly skilled knowledge workers and professionals differ from those of data workers like secretaries or file clerks. To understand the different information problems and requirements of knowledge workers, we need to understand a little more about knowledge work and the role of such workers in the business world.

THE CHARACTERISTICS OF KNOWLEDGE WORK

What is the difference between technique, know-how, experience, and knowledge work? Doesn't all work involve the application of knowledge? Doesn't a lathe operator use knowledge and experience to cut a piece of metal in much the same way that a surgeon uses a knife to remove an appendix?

These are difficult questions. To some extent, the distinctions among knowledge workers, information workers, and just plain "workers" are arbitrary. But some important differences can be noted. Technique and know-how refer to rules of thumb gained from long experience in a line of work. Knowledge is quite different from know-how.

Sociologists and economists who study occupations believe that four characteristics define knowledge work and knowledge workers (see Figure 14.10). This definition is accepted by the Bureau of the Census, the Bureau of Labor Statistics, and professional demographers. First, knowledge work is work that is supported by a body of knowledge, a collection of books, articles, and findings that are widely accepted as

---

FIGURE 14.10

Four Characteristics of Knowledge Work

What exactly is knowledge work? Definitions vary, but the one presented here is accepted by the Bureau of the Census and the Bureau of Labor Statistics. Knowledge work has four characteristics: it is based on a codified body of information; it can be taught in a school as a collection of principles and procedures; proficiency in knowledge occupations is certified by the state or the school; and knowledge workers are regulated by independent professional associations that set standards for their work.

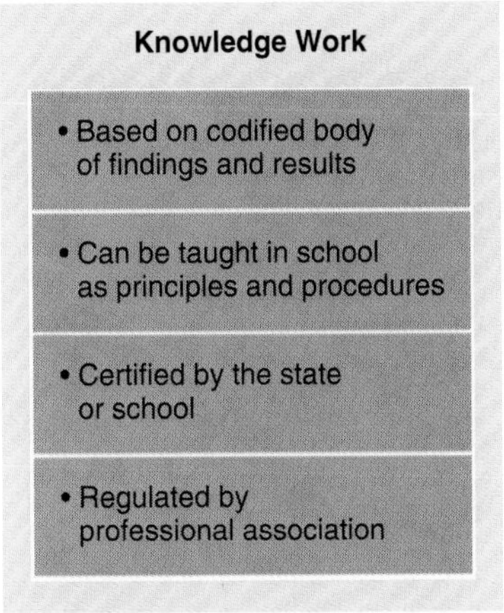

Knowledge Work

- Based on codified body of findings and results

- Can be taught in school as principles and procedures

- Certified by the state or school

- Regulated by professional association

valid, can be tested, and are stored somewhere (usually a library). In other words, knowledge is codified.

Second, this body of knowledge must be capable of being taught at major universities rather than merely being passed on as experience. Thus, principles, procedures, and methods must exist independent of pure experience for work to be labeled knowledge work.

Third, the people who learn the body of knowledge generally must be certified by the state (or university) to prove their mastery. Fourth, the field or profession must be regulated by independent professional bodies that maintain standards of admission and make independent judgments, based on their knowledge, of members' credentials as well as the social uses of their knowledge. At a minimum, these professional bodies maintain a published statement of ethics and educational or professional standards.

What kinds of work meet these qualifications? A list of knowledge workers would certainly include engineers, lawyers, doctors (to at least some extent), architects, biologists, scientists of all kinds, managers (to some extent), and even professors.

THE ROLE OF KNOWLEDGE WORK IN THE ORGANIZATION

As we described earlier in this chapter, there has been a fundamental shift in developed economies toward the production of information- and knowledge-intensive products

---

FIGURE 14.11

Three Unique Roles of Knowledge Workers in a Business
The roles of knowledge workers are unlike those of any other employees. Part of their mission is to interpret the always-growing external knowledge base for the organization so that the firm can remain competitive. A second role is to serve as internal consultants and advisers for management. Third, knowledge workers often serve as change agents who develop and facilitate projects that bring new knowledge into the firm. Managing knowledge workers can be difficult because their roles do not fit neatly into the traditional corporate hierarchy.

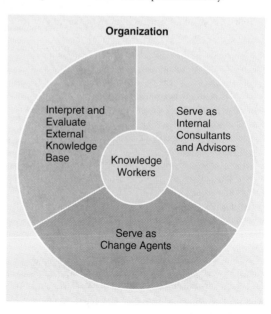

and services. More and more services, such as financial advising, ecological analysis and reporting, materials testing, and medical testing, require professional degrees. Some business firms are composed predominantly of knowledge workers. It is becoming apparent that knowledge workers' roles in business firms are both unique and becoming more important (see Figure 14.11).

Perhaps the most distinctive role of knowledge workers is to interpret the **external knowledge base** (which is always growing) for the organization. From the firm's point of view, a central purpose of hiring knowledge workers is to keep the business abreast of developments in science, technology, the arts, and social thought. Developments in these areas of knowledge often contain business opportunities. Consequently, knowledge workers are expected to refresh their skills and keep up-to-date so that the corporation may benefit from the latest developments in a field. This means knowledge workers must continually scan the environment and keep up with developments by participating in professional seminars and meetings.

Second, knowledge workers are uniquely qualified to play the role of advisers and internal business consultants. Rather than merely writing reports, they are expected to use their expertise to play an active corporate role in advising managers. Although most firms hire external consultants at some point, internal knowledge workers constitute a major source of advice and professional expertise on a continuing basis.

Third, knowledge workers are change agents. They are expected to initiate, promote, and evaluate change projects that incorporate developments in science, the arts, and other areas into the corporation. Knowledge workers are a little like evangelists: They are expected to believe strongly in their professional values and to share their views with other workers with the aim of improving the firm's behavior.

As this analysis of their roles suggests, knowledge workers are really quite different from other information workers like file clerks or secretaries and quite different from lathe operators. Because their position depends on understanding a formal knowledge base, knowledge workers really cannot be told what to do and cannot be subject to the same kind of authority relationships that exist elsewhere in the firm. Knowledge workers often know more than the boss. Consequently, they tend to be independent and autonomous.

Generally, knowledge workers are physically segregated from other line workers and staff in special research areas or centers. In part, this is because knowledge workers tend not to conform readily to a corporate image or mold. Major American firms like IBM and AT&T have developed specialized research centers far removed from daily corporate life where knowledge-intensive work is conducted.

External knowledge base
A knowledge base that is outside the organization, such as libraries of articles, collections of scientific or legal findings, and links to other professionals in universities or other organizations.

KNOWLEDGE WORK SYSTEMS

Due to their unique roles and setting in the firm, knowledge workers as a group have very different information requirements from data workers. As a result, a new class of systems has emerged—called knowledge work systems—that uses different hardware and software to serve knowledge workers. These systems must satisfy four requirements, as shown in Figure 14.12.

The first requirement is easy access to electronically stored knowledge bases external to the organization (see the Focus on Technology). These knowledge bases could be libraries of articles, collections of chemical or legal findings, or electronic mail links to other professionals working in universities or other businesses. Thus, one characteristic of knowledge work systems is that they are more directed toward external data and information than typical corporate systems.

FIGURE 14.12

Four General Requirements of a Knowledge Work System

Given that knowledge workers are unique, it follows that the information technologies they use must also be unique. Four characteristics distinguish knowledge work systems from the more usual corporate workstations. First, knowledge work systems must provide easy access to an external knowledge base. Second, they must provide software that differs from the usual business software by offering greater capabilities for analysis, graphics, document management, and communications. Third, they need to support "computing-intense" applications that may require unusually large numbers of calculations and data manipulations. Finally, they should have a friendly, easy-to-use interface.

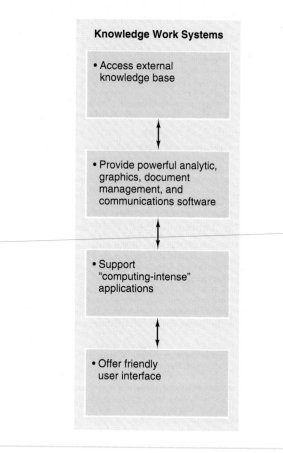

Second, knowledge work systems typically require different software than other corporate systems. They need much more powerful analytic, graphics, document management, and communications capabilities than a typical microcomputer can provide.

Knowledge work often requires much more computing power than typical information work. Some intensive simulations (called virtual reality) require very large and very fast supercomputers (see the Leading-Edge Technology description of virtual reality). Engineers may wish to run thousands of calculations before they are satisfied that a specific part is safe. Lawyers may want to scan thousands of legal findings before recommending a strategy. Designers using **computer-aided design (CAD)** systems to design a wide range of products from houses to automobiles to hand tools frequently need to use three-dimensional graphics software to fully visualize a model of a product. The computerized design can be easily modified, reducing both design time and expensive engineering changes once the production process begins.

Computer-aided design (CAD)

Automation of the creation and revision of designs using sophisticated graphics software.

FOCUS ON TECHNOLOGY

EXPERTS BY E-MAIL

A journalist with Radio Canada wanted to find an agricultural expert in the United States who could speak, in French, about the environmental problem posed by pig manure. A reporter for the *Poughkeepsie Journal* wanted to find people who keep crickets as pets. A few years ago, it would have taken hours on the telephone and a well-stocked Rolodex to complete these assignments, if they could be completed at all. Today, both reporters found what they wanted right away using Profnet, a computer network of university public information officers.

Reporters can relay queries by fax, E-mail, or toll-free telephone calls to Profnet headquarters at the State University of New York at Stony Brook. Within hours, or even minutes, the messages are transmitted free of charge by computer to nearly 600 colleges, universities, and research centers. Public information officers search for experts on their staff who can fulfill these requests. Profnet provides reporters with a wider range of sources, while helping lesser-known institutions draw attention to their faculty and researchers.

Dennis Kipp, the Poughkeepsie reporter, had twice tried and failed to write a column on pet crickets because of inadequate information. After learning about Profnet, he sent a query asking for information about the virtues of pet crickets. Within two days, he received four responses with the phone numbers of recognized cricket experts. One reply was a profile of Dr. David Shetlar, an Ohio State University entomologist who advocated cockroaches as children's Christmas presents. Kipp knew this man could tell him what to feed a pet cricket.

Stan Ernst, media coordinator for the College of Agriculture at Ohio State University, used Profnet to arrange for a faculty member to be interviewed on Iowa public television and to put a San Francisco newspaper in touch with an expert on coffee cartels. Other requests from reporters are less unusual. Chris Feola, an editor at *The Waterbury Republican-American* in Waterbury, Connecticut, received more than 100 responses to a query about the roots of urban poverty and decay. He likened Profnet to reading the *Encyclopaedia Britannica* because you can start reading something and "six hours later you're still reading."

Profnet was established in 1992 by Dan Forbush, an associate vice president for university affairs at Stony Brook. He had previously worked at Gehrung Associates in Keene, New Hampshire, a public relations firm rep-

resenting about 40 colleges, where he took calls from reporters and tried to link them to professors. Forbush created a directory of E-mail addresses for public relations officers in 16 countries.

Profnet differs from other research assistance services, such as the database of 30,000 experts maintained by the Scientists' Institute for Public Information (SIPI) in Manhattan, in that it relies primarily on the knowledge of public information officers to locate experts. (SIPI provides the names and telephone numbers of experts already listed in its database to reporters seeking assistance.) Forbush compared using Profnet to sending a telegram at no charge to more than 1,000 people around the world who would act as research assistants. Profnet receives about 14 to 20 queries each day.

Profnet costs about $2,500 a year to operate, not counting the time of university public information officers and volunteers. There is no charge to use the network. Forbush believes that if a fee were imposed, much of its attractiveness would be lost.

FOCUS Questions:
What other kinds of knowledge work would benefit from Profnet? What technology is required to use this network? Should such networks provide information for free? Why or why not?

SOURCE: Jonathan Rabinovitz, "Computer Network Helps Journalists Find Academic Experts," *The New York Times,* May 23, 1994.

Finally, knowledge work systems should have a user-friendly interface so that professionals can gain access to knowledge and information without spending a great deal of time learning how to use the computer. A user-friendly interface is somewhat more critical for knowledge workers than for ordinary information workers because knowledge workers are expensive. Wasting a knowledge worker's time is more costly than wasting a clerical worker's time. Unfortunately, many knowledge work systems need a great deal of work before they can be said to be user-friendly.

The term "workstation" is typically used to describe the hardware platform on which knowledge work systems operate. As we saw in Chapter 4, workstations differ from

A tool design screen from a computer-aided design/computer-aided manufacturing (CAD/CAM) system. Because such systems provide high levels of design, manufacturing, and testing precision and efficiency, many companies are investing in them.

SOURCE: Courtesy of International Business Machines Corporation.

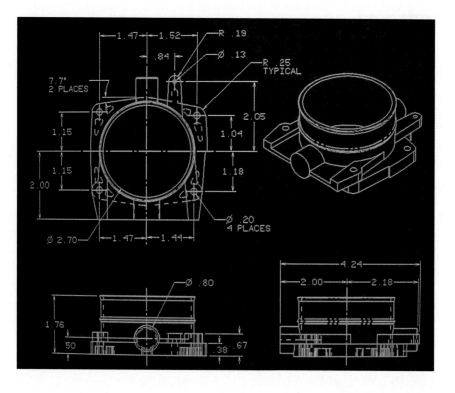

simple microcomputers in both power and applications. Microcomputers are designed to meet the very general requirements of diverse groups ranging from secretaries to financial analysts. In contrast, a professional workstation—whether built for a sales manager (managerial workstation) or a chemist—must generally be fine-tuned and optimized for a particular occupation. Table 14.5 provides some examples of knowledge work occupations that rely on professional workstations.

The specific technology features of knowledge work systems depend on the profession supported. Designers want machines with powerful graphics displays, whereas lawyers may be more interested in the huge database storage capabilities provided by optical disks. Financial analysts typically desire a 600-megabyte optical disk, refreshed each week, with a complete listing of the financial data for all 4,000 public corporations.

LEADING-EDGE TECHNOLOGY: VIRTUAL REALITY

Virtual reality

Technology that creates computerized simulations that allow users to feel they are participating in "real-world" activities.

Virtual reality is a rapidly developing knowledge work technology that has turned fantasy into reality. Imagine that you are an aircraft designer designing a new, large passenger aircraft. You would need to make certain that all parts of the aircraft would be accessible to the mechanic for maintenance. The mechanic may be 5 feet, 2 inches tall or may be 6 feet, 7 inches. In either case he or she must be able to get the wrench to the correct place and be able to turn it as needed. The only way you can test your design for proper maintenance access is to build a mock-up of the craft, a slow, expensive process that may have to be repeated a number of times. You have designed the aircraft using CAD software. Think of the time and expense that could be saved if you could only enter and test that aircraft while it is still digitized data stored on a computer disk! You would want to be able to change your own height to test access for both a small and a large mechanic. You could reach into a tight spot on your left and then test to see if both a

TABLE 14.5

Examples of Knowledge Workers and the Knowledge Workstations that Help Them Do Their Jobs

Specialized workstations involving unique hardware and software have been developed for many knowledge occupations. Architects can now use CAD (computer-aided design) software to design structures and test areas of stress to improve the structure's safety. Other knowledge workstations help scientists perform molecular modeling or help lawyers eliminate time-consuming legal research.

Architects	**CAD (computer-aided design):** Design building and floor plans.
Engineers	**CAD/CAM (computer-aided design/computer-aided manufacturing):** Manage manufacturing operations and control machinery.
Judges, Lawyers	**Legal research workstations:** Access legal databases, write legal briefs and opinions.
Scientists	**Visualization workstations:** Perform three-dimensional modeling.
Reporters	**Text publishing workstations:** Write news stories and translate into newspaper layout.
Programmers	**Programmer workbench systems:** Use CASE tools to produce software programs.
Managers (some)	**Management workstations:** Access large databases, provide graphic displays, electronic mail, and word processing.

By donning special goggles and headsets and using instruments attached to sensors, pilots-in-training can be presented with computerized images that make them feel they are actually flying an aircraft. Flight simulation, medical training, product design, and interactive entertainment are but some of many promising applications for virtual reality.

SOURCE: Courtesy of CAE Electronic Ltd., Quebec. C.A. Barbier, Photographe.

left- and a right-handed mechanic could turn a wrench. You could turn around to see if you could access an area behind you. All this design testing could occur in an aircraft that doesn't yet exist. This is the fantasy world of virtual reality, and it is the technology being used today by Boeing Corp. to design its new model 777 jet aircraft.

Virtual reality technology allows the user to feel immersed in a computer-created "world" as if that world actually existed. How is this possible? The world—in this case, the aircraft—is first created in the computer. To "enter" that world, the user of virtual reality dons special clothing that contains sensors to record the user's movements and transmit that information to the computer. The user also wears a pair of special goggles that are really two tiny video screens. Audio attachments and "feeling" gloves can be included if such feedback is important to the application. The user will see the "virtual aircraft" in front of him. If he walks forward, the image will move closer. As he reaches out with his arm, he will see the arm reach out into the virtual aircraft. If he turns his head, his view of the aircraft will shift just as it would in real life.

This technology is new and rather expensive because of the special clothing that is needed. Nonetheless, practical applications are in development. The most obvious application for this technology is related to architecture. The city of Berlin, Germany, is using virtual reality equipment to design a new subway station. Users can "walk" through the stations to critique the structures before they are ever built. Hewlett-Packard is designing its new European office building using this technology. Matsushita Electric has brought the fantasy world of virtual reality to the retail public through its department store chain. The department stores sell kitchen cabinets and appliances. To promote its products and make it easy for the customers to make a purchase decision, Matsushita has created an application called Virtual Kitchen. Shoppers give the trained staff their kitchen layout, which is entered into the computer. Shoppers also designate the cabinets and appliances to be purchased and their locations in the kitchen. Wearing the necessary special clothing, customers find themselves in their new kitchen. They can walk around (having already designated a location for their kitchen table) to feel the ambiance of their new kitchen. They can test the stove for location and height. They can open cabinet doors and drawers to test them for proper height, size, and functionality. They can check for the convenience of left- or right-handed door openings. If something is wrong, they can move or substitute the piece of equipment. When they are satisfied, they can buy with more than the normal confidence that all will work properly. The store, in turn, benefits from this technology by making many more on-the-spot sales.

The medical world, not surprisingly, is beginning to find practical applications for this imaginative new technology. Cine-Med, a small producer of medical training videos in Woodbury, Connecticut, has created a virtual clinic in which physicians can practice gall bladder removal using a virtual gall bladder from a virtual model patient. The software has been demonstrated at medical conventions. The technology can be used in medical schools to train students in surgery. A surgeon can program the software model with data from an actual patient so that she can practice a real operation in advance. The data for the live patient is obtained through computer-assisted tomography or magnetic resonance imaging scans. This medical technology has advanced far enough so that the National Library of Medicine of the National Institutes of Health is now creating industry-standard digital cadavers. Students will be able to study human anatomy with a detail and specialization previously impossible. Moreover, students will share standardized "cadavers" at different schools.

At General Electric's Research and Development Center in Schenectady, New York, GE scientists are working with a group of surgeons from Boston's Brigham and Women's Hospital to develop a virtual reality system that will allow a surgeon to have at her side a three-dimensional image of the relevant portion of a patient's body that she can consult during surgery. The ultimate goal of their project is to give the surgeon the ability to "walk" through a giant virtual image of the patient, approach the organ to be oper-ated on (such as the liver), and perform the operation on the virtual image rather than on the patient. With such a very large image, the surgeon will be able to be very pre-cise in her cuts, preventing any damage to surrounding tissue. The computer would con-trol the actual instruments performing the operation on the patient, duplicating the actions of the surgeon in a real-life, very precise, operation. While this goal is still a long way off, the project is already able to create three-dimensional images of a patient's brain and project them on the patient's head, allowing a brain surgeon to plan precise surgi-cal pathways through the brain to the location where surgery is needed. The current vir-tual reality system can also create an image of that brain, rotate it, and peel off layers to expose the parts below where the surgery is needed.[5]

Now let's review the questions we typically ask of information systems:

- **Where does a knowledge workstation obtain its information?** The systems described in this section obtained a great deal of information (and expertise) from external scientific, engineering, and legal databases. This information often must be internalized, or stored on local disks. Of course, much of the information is generated as a result of local knowledge workers' experiments and writing.

- **What does a knowledge workstation do to the information?** Knowledge work-stations process far more information and data than typical transaction or man-agement systems do. Generally, this occurs because knowledge work often requires the application of sophisticated mathematical routines and procedures in order to function. In the case of graphics systems, engineering CAD/CAM sys-tems, and virtual reality applications, the amount of processing speed and power exceeds that of microcomputers and usually requires specialized workstations. Yet as microcomputers become more powerful, they will be capable of performing more and more knowledge work.

- **What problems does a knowledge workstation solve?** How can business orga-nizations interested in making a profit make use of basic science? This is the over-all problem that knowledge work systems address. Obviously, businesses must first hire knowledge workers. But then business must support these knowledge work-ers for them to be effective. Since World War II, science and business have moved much closer together. Knowledge work systems can provide a critical link between science and business by speeding up the dissemination of scientific findings to business. This, in turn, can make the realization of business goals (like product development) more rapid. This is one of many ways in which knowledge work systems can have strategic impact.

CHALLENGES OF BUILDING KNOWLEDGE AND INFORMATION WORK SYSTEMS

Knowledge work systems are in many respects on the leading edge of information tech-nology and system development. Although the rewards are potentially great, the costs can be high and the challenges steep. Here we describe the challenges and leave the dis-covery of solutions for class discussion.

Technology Challenges   Many of the technologies involved in information and knowledge work are uncertain and change rapidly. Often before machinery can be paid for, new technologies are available, and sometimes they cost less than existing equipment. Although office automation equipment—like microcomputers and printers—appears at first glance to have been reasonably stable over the last 5 years, a closer look reveals a great difference between the first personal computers of the early 1980s and the models available today. Rapid change and rapid obsolescence make investment in knowledge work systems risky.

People Challenges   With technologies and techniques changing so rapidly, employees are under a great deal of pressure to continue learning and training once they are on the job. Moreover, because techniques can change within a few years, people need to accept the possibility that they will have to learn several new and different jobs in a short time. Since employers often do not provide training, cautious employees may have to obtain training in community colleges and elsewhere just to keep their skills current and valuable. On balance, as jobs require more skills and knowledge, individuals are under increased pressure to raise their levels of skills in order to remain employed.[6]

Organizational Challenges   Organizations face several challenges in building solid information and knowledge work environments. It is difficult to integrate information and knowledge workers into a traditional, hierarchical organization. Changes in the authority structure and work arrangements must be made to accommodate the goals and ambitions of contemporary workers. Second, organizations have to be much more careful about hiring: they must identify and recruit workers who have the capability and desire to learn. Third, organizations must devote more resources to training. When retraining does not work, organizations often must retire experienced older workers much earlier than in the past. This raises costs as well as significant social issues (discussed in Chapter 3).

SUMMARY

- Advanced economies such as those in the United States, Canada, and most European nations have been transformed from industrial economies, in which most wealth came from the production of goods and most employees worked in factories and assembled goods, to information economies, in which most wealth derives from information and knowledge production and the majority of workers process and create information. This new type of economy is known as an "information and knowledge economy."

- As the economy becomes more dependent on information and knowledge to produce economic value, our productivity and wealth as a nation depend on the effective use of knowledge work systems.

- Information workers are those whose primary job is to create or process information. There are two kinds of information workers: knowledge workers, whose primary job is to create new information, and data workers, whose primary job is to process, use, or disseminate information.

- Office automation is any application of information technology that is intended to increase the productivity of information workers in the office.

- Offices coordinate work, link diverse groups in the business, and connect the firm to its external environment. Offices and office work are therefore central to the success of any modern business.

- The major office activities are document management, scheduling, communications, data management, and project management. Information technology can support all of these activities.

- Word processing and desktop publishing systems support the document management activities of the office. Systems based on local area networks support the communications activities of the office. Electronic calendar and groupware systems support the scheduling activities of the office. Desktop data management systems and customized personal information managers support the data management activities of the office. Project management systems break down complex projects into simpler subtasks, producing delivery schedules, allocating resources, and supporting the project management activities of the office. Imaging systems can help streamline organizational work flow.

- Knowledge work systems are applications of information technology expressly designed to enhance the productivity of knowledge workers.

- Knowledge work is distinguished from other work by its reliance on a body of knowledge, its place in a university curriculum, its certification by the state, and the presence of professional societies with regulatory power. Knowledge worker roles include interpreting the body of knowledge to business managers and leaders, acting as internal consultants, and playing the role of change agents.

- Knowledge work systems require access to an external knowledge base, more powerful hardware and software platform than office systems, and a friendly user interface. Computer-aided design systems and virtual reality systems require powerful graphics and modeling capabilities.

- Building effective information and knowledge work systems is challenging because of the pace of technological change, the need for continual training and change on the part of employees, and the requirements for organizational learning.

KEY TERMS

Information work

Information and knowledge economy

Knowledge- and information-intense products

Knowledge work

Data work

Office automation

Office roles

Office activities

Document management technology

Word processing

Desktop publishing

Office scheduling technology

Groupware

Office data management technology

Project management technology

Imaging

External knowledge base

Computer-aided design (CAD)

Virtual reality

REVIEW QUESTIONS

1. What does the phrase "transformation of the economy toward an information economy" mean? When did this transformation begin?

2. Give some examples of information, goods, and service industries. Give some examples of knowledge, data, service, and goods occupations.

3. What are knowledge- and information-intense products? Give some examples.

4. What is the difference between data work and knowledge work? Give some examples.

5. How is information work related to the productivity of a business?

6. Define office automation. How has office automation technology changed over time?

7. What are the three roles of offices in modern organizations?

8. What are the five major activities that go on in all offices? Give an example of how information technology supports each activity.

9. Describe the importance of imaging systems in organizations today.

10. What is groupware and how does it differ from traditional office technology?

11. What are the four distinguishing features of knowledge work?

12. What role do knowledge workers play in the organization?

13. What are the generic elements of a knowledge work system?

14. Define and describe CAD and virtual reality.

15. What are the three kinds of challenges involved in building knowledge and information work systems? Give an example of each kind of problem or find an example in a business magazine.

DISCUSSION QUESTIONS

1. Some people argue that our country cannot survive as an information economy, that we need to produce manufactured goods as well, and that we should invest more money in factories and less money in offices. Divide into two groups to debate this issue.

2. Why are knowledge work systems playing an increasingly important role in organizations? Do you expect that this trend will continue or reach a plateau?

3. Other than a document imaging system, devise some knowledge work systems that Massachusetts Financial Services of Boston (described in the Focus on Organizations) would find useful to carry out their business.

PROBLEM-SOLVING EXERCISES

1. *Group exercise:* Divide the class into groups. Have each group locate a small business firm in your neighborhood and write a short report that analyzes how the firm currently deals with office correspondence and publications—letters to customers, suppliers, sales force (if any), and the general public. The group should identify where documents originate, how they are processed, and what communications technologies are used. Be sure to have the group identify the people, hardware, and software separately. The report should trace the flow of example documents (e.g., letters to suppliers). The last page of the report should be a list of recommended improvements. Have each group present its findings to the class.

2. University students are knowledge workers in training. As such, they have unique workstation requirements. Write a description of what you think would be an ideal "student workstation."

3. *Hands-on exercise:* Companies such as Price Waterhouse need information systems that will allow them to easily access knowledge about the skills, background, and experience of highly trained employees. Choose appropriate software and develop a simple application that could be used by a firm such as Price Waterhouse to maintain information about the experts on its staff. The information to be maintained by the system

might include the employee's name, area(s) of expertise, work location, age, telephone number, and research interests.

NOTES

1. Vincent E. Giuliano, "The Mechanization of Office Work," *Scientific American,* September 1982, pp. 148–52. See also Martin L. Ernst, "The Mechanization of Commerce," *Scientific American,* September 1982, pp. 132–45.

2. The phrases "knowledge-intensive organization" and "information-intensive organization" originated with Professor William Starbuck, Department of Management, Stern School of Business, New York University. The author is indebted to him for several stimulating conversations about the issue. Doubtless, over the next years, a great deal of attention will be paid to the various kinds of knowledge and information organizations, their peculiar work forces, and unique management problems.

3. Tora K. Bikson, J.D. Eveland, and Barbara A. Gutek, "Flexible Interactive Technologies for Multi-Person Tasks: Current Problems and Future Prospects," Rand Corporation, December 1988.

4. David Kirkpatrick, "Groupware Goes Boom," *Fortune,* December 27, 1993.

5. John Holusha, "Carving Out Real-Life Uses for Virtual Reality," *The New York Times,* October 31, 1993, and Harvey P. Newquist, "Virtual Reality's Commercial Reality," *Computerworld,* March 30, 1992.

6. For evidence on the overall aggregate rise in skill levels (despite earlier expert predictions that computers would "de-skill" the labor force), see David R. Howell and Edward N. Wolff, "Changes in the Skill Requirements of the U.S. Labor Force, 1960–1985," C.V. Starr Center for Applied Economics, New York University, August 1988.

PROBLEM-SOLVING CASE
THE DEBATE OVER GROUPWARE

Groupware encompasses an astonishing breadth of office functions: creating, storing, retrieving, and tracking documents, sending electronic mail, establishing conferences and calendars, organizing work flow, and holding computerized meetings. Their common thread is the activities of the individual within his or her work group.

This technology has greatly affected how people work in their offices, and it has also generated a great deal of controversy. Some users emphasize productivity gains. Fred Bonner, director of computer systems for The Discovery Channel, has documented a 40 percent increase in meeting-room vacancies since they began using groupware. According to Barry Barron, information systems (IS) manager for the Port of Oakland, California, "Every department stays informed about what everybody [else] is doing. . . . We hold fewer meetings now, and those that we do hold involve fewer people." Studies by the Massachusetts Institute of Technology (MIT) show that groupware can make design and sales teams more efficient and bring companies closer to customers and suppliers.

However, others express concern, citing such problems as perceived coercion and unwanted work-style standardization. Voucher routing is an obvious application of work-flow automation. An employee intending to distribute a memo creates a work-flow script that controls the routing of the memo, the timing of the routing, and the scheduling of the tasks associated with it. One groupware product, The Coordinator Workgroup Productivity System from Action Technologies, Inc. (ATI), has added a function it calls Conversation Management. Before a memo is electronically dispatched, the sender classifies the memo (an order, request, consultation, acceptance, rejection, and so on), establishes a goal, and provides action deadlines. Because the action deadlines automatically update group as well as individual schedules, the deadlines are accessible not only by those who receive the memo but also by management. As a result, critics believe these products create anxiety among employees. They might be afraid of a product that automatically schedules people, puts priorities on things, and possibly sends messages to management when they fail. Employees might feel Big Brother is watching.

The product has engendered surprising hostility. It has been called "fascist existentialism" and "a power tool for authoritarians." In a study at MIT's Sloan School of Management, Christine Bullen found that an unexpectedly large number of people purposely found ways to override many of the system's features. They particularly objected to the requirement that memos be classified in advance. The management of Aetna Life & Casualty Insurance Co. rejected the software, claiming that its inflexible work style did not fit well with their corporate culture.

Document creation has generated a different kind of controversy. The original author(s) of a document can place it on a network and make it available to a controlled list of people for comment and editing. Matthew Ghourdjian, IS director of the Los Angeles law firm Hennigan & Mercer, uses Instant Update (from On Technology, Inc., Cambridge, Massachusetts) when speed is critical. "When you have to move fast to get a temporary restraining order, we put all the tasks into an Instant Update file. Everyone writes to that file, with the secretary acting as a moderator."

Yet while such simultaneous access can significantly reduce writing time and improve the final product, it also creates complications that threaten the integrity of the document. Some people fear the loss of author control. They believe that no one but the original author of a document should be able to make revisions, a concept purposely not enforced by most groupware products. Others are concerned about the accidental corruption of documents in such an open editing atmosphere. One such problem not addressed by many groupware systems is the coordination and timing of updates. If two individuals happen to edit the same document simultaneously, the alterations in the first version to be saved will be overwritten (erased) when the second person saves her edited version.

One particularly innovative application of groupware is its use in meetings. KPMG Peat Marwick of Hartford, Connecticut, uses computerized meetings to develop strategic planning documents. Using Aspects from Group Technologies, Inc., within a meeting format, the attendees work simultaneously on the same document in the same room. Senior consultant Bob Piwko sees several benefits. "In a traditional meeting, only one person can talk at a time, so the spontaneity of brainstorming is lost." Furthermore, he adds, "Some people are intimidated by others." He believes that both these problems are eliminated by using groupware in this way. Such meetings can be expensive, however, because all participants need networked computers at their desks.

The E-mail function of groupware raises unique issues due to the multiplicity of corporate E-mail systems already in place. Most corporations have not standardized their E-mail function. US West Communications, Inc., of Denver, Colorado, estimates that it has 38,000 users employing 14 different systems in 15 states. They currently use IBM's Profs, Wang Laboratories' WangOffice, and Digital Equipment Corp.'s (DEC) All-In-1 as well as a variety of Unix-based and local area network-based systems. Does it make sense to install another E-mail system? Many proponents hope groupware could solve this problem. Corporations are interested in these systems for their breadth of functions, not just for E-mail. Installing groupware company-wide offers the corporation the opportunity to settle on a single E-mail system for all while taking advantage of groupware's other coordinated functions.

However, according to Steve Dickson, US West's message-network manager, the groupware packages now available are "very, very, very uni-platform." That is, individual systems run only on IBM mainframes or IBM PCs or Wang computers or DEC Vaxes, but not on all these platforms simultaneously. Their installation would only further complicate his already complex environment. Rather than purchase a commercially available system, Dickson's company has decided to build its own groupware system, a project that will take at least 5 years to complete.

Despite these controversies, groupware usage continues to show strong growth, fueling the traditional problems between user departments and IS units. The IS-user issues are significant. When networks were first introduced, users led the drive to use the new technology, and now they are repeating that effort with groupware. Traditional IS departments, on the other hand, tend to be more comfortable with older, more centralized technology. They often do not know desktop technology, and they don't understand users' desire for it. Systems professionals with traditional skills such as COBOL often find user-controlled desktop technology threatening. Animosity can develop, and users may simply bypass IS professionals and install the software themselves. For example, engineers have been attempting to link Lotus Notes with SQL databases to be able to store and retrieve notes and reports together with mathematical engineering data.

Serious problems can ensue when users and IS staff do not work together. Often user-installed systems are poorly used or not used at all. That is because users usually do not have the technical skills necessary to make groupware work, particularly when it is used in ways not originally intended, such as joining Notes with SQL databases. In addition, when IS departments are not fully involved, technology decisions are made that may be contrary to overall organizational strategic architecture. Thus, for example, a user group might install a new network for groupware software when the company has already decided to standardize by using a different network technology. Finally, major systems like groupware that are installed without IS support usually further weaken corporate control over its valuable data, leaving the company vulnerable to loss of that data.

SOURCES: Michael Vizard, "Power to the People," *Computerworld,* August 16, 1993; John J. Xenakis, "Documents by Committee," *InformationWEEK,* December 9, 1991 and "Shared Interests," *InformationWEEK,* December 30, 1991.

CASE STUDY QUESTIONS

1.   What are some of the implicit assumptions about how people work that are built in to groupware software? What problems do you find with those assumptions? How would you address them?

2.   If you were the president of a large corporation, would you install one of these products? Why? What benefits would you be looking for? What are the negatives?

3.   How does groupware increase productivity? At what cost? In what ways does this kind of software negatively affect productivity?

4.   Assume you are a secretary in a large corporation that is about to install a groupware system. What would your reaction be to the coming changes? Why? What might management do to prepare you and your fellow workers for the coming changes? Ask yourself these same questions as if you were a research scientist, an accounts receivable manager, and a divisional vice-president.

ARTIFICIAL INTELLIGENCE

LEARNING OBJECTIVES

After reading and studying this chapter, you will:
1. Know what artificial intelligence is and how it has evolved.
2. Be familiar with the many varieties of artificial intelligence.
3. Be able to define and describe expert systems.
4. Know what neural networks are and how they operate.
5. Understand what is meant by "intelligent" techniques and how they are used in the computer-based decision process.
6. Know how and why organizations use artificial intelligence techniques.

KEEPING ADS IN LINE WITH EXPERT SYSTEMS

*C*hannel 4, the largest commercial broadcaster in the United Kingdom, confronted scheduling decisions that were too complex for humans to solve regularly and on time. It needed to determine the best order in which to run ads during commercial breaks. This apparently routine business problem was unusually difficult because so many options were available to advertisers. One option involved placement in the break, such as first or last in order. Another was where to transmit the ads. While Channel 4's programming is broadcast nationwide, the advertisements shown during commercial breaks vary by region. Advertisers can choose to have their ads transmitted among six "macro regions" or to specific combinations of regions. One more complication: an advertisement sold to run in more than one region during a specific commercial break must be broadcast simultaneously in all the selected regions. In other words, each 4-minute commercial break can have up to 50 advertisements in various sequences.

In an effort to accommodate clients, the sales staff of Channel 4 wanted to determine the advertising sequence as late as possible. The transmission staff, on the other hand, wanted to finalize the sequence as early as it could. Channel 4's staff in charge of break sequencing would get a list of all the ads in each commercial break from the channel's mainframe transaction processing system. Schedulers would then arrange the advertising spots as fast as possible and feed the new list back into the computer. Doing the job manually was not impossible, but it was difficult and time consuming, requiring four highly skilled full-time staff members.

Channel 4 found it could schedule advertising spots more effectively by using artificial intelligence software based on Xpert-Rule from Attar Software Ltd. in Lancashire, England (marketed in the United States by Cincom Systems Inc.). The software uses the Windows graphical user interface and needs only a 486 microcomputer to run. The software determines the best solution to a problem by trying different combinations of rules and discarding those that do not make progress against the problem. It evaluates random solutions against the hard constraints (must haves) and soft constraints (desirables) of the problem. The solutions that score well are combined to create a new solution. This process is repeated until the best acceptable solution has been generated. The application takes 10 seconds to sequence a commercial break and has reduced staff time and errors. Channel 4 no longer needs to deploy four full-time schedulers and can use any one of a half-dozen people to do the job.

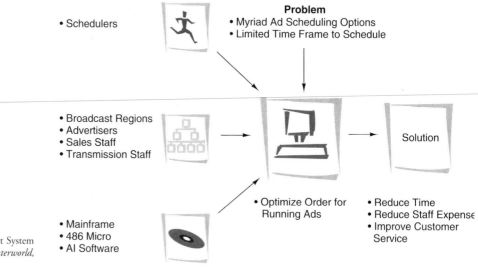

- Schedulers

Problem
- Myriad Ad Scheduling Options
- Limited Time Frame to Schedule

- Broadcast Regions
- Advertisers
- Sales Staff
- Transmission Staff

Solution

- Optimize Order for Running Ads

- Reduce Time
- Reduce Staff Expense
- Improve Customer Service

- Mainframe
- 486 Micro
- AI Software

SOURCE: Elizabeth Heichler, "Expert System Keeps UK TV Ads in Line," *Computerworld,* December 20, 1993.

The experience of Channel 4 illustrates how powerful information systems can be if they display some intelligence. In many areas of business, science, and everyday life, from banks and credit card companies to medical laboratories and machine manufacturers, new kinds of information systems based on artificial intelligence technology are used to guide human experts, diagnose problems, and help managers make decisions. This chapter explains how expert systems, neural networks, and other artificial intelligence systems work and the kinds of problems they are now capable of solving.

15.1 INTRODUCTION

Imagine that someday you could go to a desktop computer in your room and in simple English speak into a microphone attached to the computer: "Summarize the major points of all articles dealing with artificial intelligence in computer magazines published

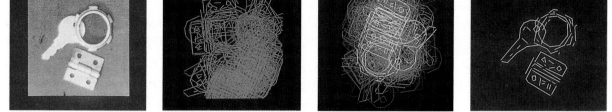

Scientists and engineers working in the field of artificial intelligence are creating machines that can "see." These machines break the task of "seeing" into several steps, matching the shape of the objects on view to objects they know, then eliminating the options before "recognizing" the objects.

Source: Courtesy of Thinking Machines Corporation.

since 1990! Then print the summaries on my printer and give me an oral report of no longer than 5 minutes!" What would your desktop computer need in terms of hardware and software to be able to handle your request? Here are some requirements:

- Your desktop machine would have to understand and speak English.

- Your desktop machine would have to be linked to a main library collection of magazines or have access to a very large optical disk on your desktop.

- Your machine would have to know something about how to conduct research in order to summarize articles; that is, your software would need some real expertise.

- Your software would have to read and "understand" natural English language statements found in articles and newspapers.

No machine or software yet in existence has these capabilities, but information scientists are working on building such machines and some with other capabilities as well. The promise of artificial intelligence is in part the promise of providing humans with some intelligent assistance so that people can do their work more efficiently and effectively and stay out of danger as well.

THE NATURE OF ARTIFICIAL INTELLIGENCE

Put simply, **artificial intelligence** (**AI**) is the study and creation of machines that exhibit humanlike qualities, including the ability to reason. Even the seventeenth-century scientists and engineers who built the first calculators and mechanical robots that could play musical instruments may have dreamed of this goal, but none of these early machines had quite so ambitious a program as contemporary efforts in artificial intelligence. Experts in artificial intelligence believe that one day, computers will be able to learn natural languages like English, perceive objects just as humans do, and exhibit all the qualities that we think of as human reason—the ability to think, make judgments, arrive at conclusions, and make comparisons. These systems will not look like robots, or R2-D2 in the film *Star Wars*. Instead these systems will reside inside desktop computers, similar to the ones we now call personal computers. Artificial intelligence is also the stuff of military dreams in which AI machines fight future wars largely independent of human intervention.

Artificial intelligence (AI)
The study and creation of machines that exhibit humanlike qualities, including the ability to reason.

FIGURE 15.1

Artificial Intelligence (AI) Involves Many Fields of Study

Artificial intelligence is not one discipline; it is many. Shown here are the major initiatives that AI currently includes: natural language, robotics, perceptive systems, expert systems, neural networks, and intelligent software. What do all these activities have in common? In brief, they are attempting to emulate human abilities.

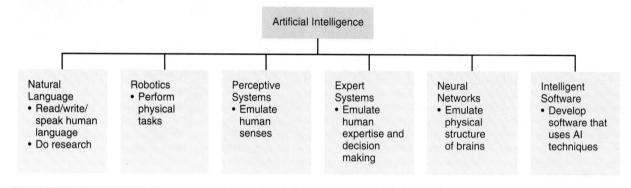

How would we know if a machine possessed these qualities of intelligence? How could we tell that we had built a war machine capable of conducting an autonomous war? One test was proposed by the British computer scientist Alan Turing in 1948. In the so-called **Turing test**, a human and a computer are placed in separate rooms connected by a communications link; if the person cannot tell whether he or she is talking to a machine or another human, then the machine is intelligent.

So far no machines have passed Turing's test, although the Focus on People describes how computers are coming closer. While computers are still a long way from behaving like humans, what has been accomplished is quite remarkable.

THE FAMILY OF ARTIFICIAL INTELLIGENCE TECHNIQUES

Artificial intelligence is not a single phenomenon but a family of sometimes related activities, each of which seeks to capture some aspect of human intelligence and being (see Figure 15.1). Computer scientists, electronic engineers, psychologists, linguists, physiologists, and biologists are all involved in that search, which leads them into research on natural language, robotics, perceptive systems, expert systems, neural networks, and intelligent software.

Natural Language   **Natural language** focuses on computer speech recognition and speech generation. The basic goal is to build computer hardware and software that can recognize human speech and "read" text and that can speak and write as well. A related goal is to build software that can do research requested by humans. The major impetus for this research began in the 1950s when the military attempted to develop computers that could automatically translate Soviet texts and speech for national security purposes. These early efforts largely failed: machines have a very difficult time understanding idiomatic expressions or translating sentences such as "Jane took a swing at the ball." A computer would not know whether "swing" refers to a movement or an object and might produce a translation in which Jane used something like a porch swing. Nor would the computer know that "bat" is implicit in the sentence even though just

Turing test

A test devised by Alan Turing to determine if a machine is intelligent. A computer and a human are placed in separate rooms connected by a communications link; if the human is not aware that he or she is communicating with a machine, then the machine is intelligent.

Natural language

Languages, including idioms, that are used by humans (e.g., English, Swahili, French).

FOCUS ON PEOPLE

STEAMY NOVELS FROM A COMPUTER?

Can a computer write a novel? That question so intrigued Scott French that he spent 8 years trying to answer it. In 1993 the 43-year-old electronic surveillance consultant and Hal, his Macintosh computer (aided by an expert system from Neural Data, Inc., of Palo Alto, California), published a steamy novel titled *Just This Once*. His effort tells us a great deal about the strengths and limitations of the attempt to teach computers to "think" like human beings.

French decided to "teach" his computer to write novels patterned after the works of Jacqueline Susann, the best-selling author of *Valley of the Dolls* and *Once Is Not Enough*. Since a computer had never written a novel, he first had to determine a methodology. After an extensive and detailed analysis of Susann's two top sellers, French devised thousands of rules to capture the tone, vocabulary, and plot of these works. Once he had coded both the rules and the data into the software, he began the process of having Hal write the novel.

According to French, the work is clearly a joint effort. He says he "wrote about a quarter of the prose, the computer cranked out about the same amount, and the remainder can only be described as a collaboration of man and machine." The writing process was actually a dialogue between French and Hal because the computer could not write more than two or three sentences at a time without human involvement.

The computer would begin by suggesting a typical Jacqueline Susann plot situation and would then offer possible characteristics of the situation. For example, Hal might propose a plot of two women after the same man, and then indicate that in this situation there is a "high probability" that one of the women would use both sex and drugs in her effort to seduce the male character. It would ask French some specific questions. For example, in the case of two competing women, the computer would ask French to rate (on a 1–10 scale) the "cattiness factor." If he entered a high number, the computer-generated sentences would include words like "screaming" and "shrieking." After the computer produced a few sentences, French would correct spelling, change a word here or there, and sometimes make more substantive changes.

The book received decent reviews for a "trashy" novel, although it apparently received reviewer attention primarily because of the role of the computer. The *Dead Jackie Susann Quarterly* (Susann died in 1974) speculated that "she would be proud," adding "lots of money, sleaze, disease, death, tragedy, and the good girl gone bad." Thomas Gifford for *USA Today* reviewed it together with another novel of the same genre and concluded: "If you do like this stuff, you'd be much, much better off with the one written by the computer."

FOCUS Questions: What do you think the computer *is* capable of doing in terms of writing like humans? What is it *not* capable of doing well? What human characteristics is the computer missing that would be needed for it to write more like humans?

SOURCE: Steve Lohr, "Potboiler Springs from Computer's Loins," *The New York Times*, July 21, 1993.

about every child knows that you swing at balls with a bat. The Focus on Problem Solving describes the difficulties of programming computers with these "common sense" capabilities.

Robotics

The study of physical systems that can perform work normally done by humans, especially in hazardous or lethal environments.

Robotics   The goal of **robotics** research is to develop physical systems that can perform work normally done by humans, especially in hazardous or lethal environments. The origins of robotics lie in seventeenth-century clockworks in which human forms mimicked human actions. Modern robotics is more concerned with the development of numerically controlled machine tools and industrial fabrication machines that are driven by CAM (computer-aided manufacturing) systems.

Perceptive systems

Sensing devices used in robots that can recognize patterns in streams of data.

Perceptive Systems   Like humans, robots need eyes and ears in order to orient their behavior. And humans who look for patterns in huge data streams need extensions of their own senses (see the visualization techniques described in Chapter 14). Since World War II, computer scientists and engineers have worked to develop **perceptive systems,** or sensing devices that can see and hear in the sense of recognizing patterns. This field, which is sometimes called "pattern recognition," has focused largely on military applications like photo reconnaissance, submarine echo sounding, radar scanning, and missile control and navigation. Progress has been uneven because of problems teaching computers the differences between decoys and the real thing.

Expert system

A software application that seeks to capture expertise in limited domains of knowledge and experience and to apply this expertise to solving problems.

Expert Systems   Expert systems are relatively recent software applications that seek to capture expertise in limited domains of knowledge and experience and apply this expertise to solving problems. Perhaps more media attention has focused on expert systems than on any other member of the AI family. In part, this is because such systems can assist the decision making of managers and professionals when expertise is expensive or in short supply. These systems are described at greater length in Section 15.2.

Neural network

Hardware or software that emulates the physiology of animal or human brains.

Neural Networks   People have always dreamed of building a computer that thinks, a "brain" modeled in some sense on the human brain. **Neural networks** are usually physical devices (although they can be simulated with software) that electronically emulate the physiology of animal or human brains. We describe in detail how these systems work in Section 15.3.

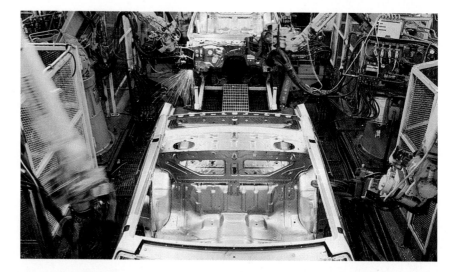

Automobile manufacturers such as the Ford Motor Company use industrial robots in their automobile assembly lines. The robots perform tasks that are difficult or hazardous for humans, such as lifting and positioning heavy parts.
SOURCE: Courtesy of Ford Motor Company.

FOCUS ON PROBLEM SOLVING

TEACHING COMPUTERS "COMMON SENSE"

The problem of supplying computers with "common sense" is deceptively simple. Even a 5-year-old child has a vast storehouse of the commonsense knowledge needed to understand her immediate world. A child knows, for example, that children are younger than their parents. But computers lack this kind of essential commonsense knowledge, and no one has yet developed a workable way to program such information. A Microsoft linguistics team, headed by computational linguist Karen Jensen, is beginning to make progress on the problem, although it will be years, if ever, before their approach will be commercially viable.

The six-person Microsoft team begins with a linguistic problem such as the sentence, "The spaceship photographed Seattle, flying to Mars." A computer cannot tell whether the spaceship or Seattle is flying to Mars. In contrast, most 5-year-olds would not only understand the sentence, but many would giggle at the image of Seattle flying to Mars. The research team's linguistic approach presently focuses on dictionary definitions to give the computer access to some of the commonsense information it needs to decipher this type of sentence.

The first computer step in deciphering the meaning of the sentence is to analyze its syntax. Grammar parsers now exist that can identify the part of speech of each word. "Spaceship" and "Seattle" will accurately be tagged as nouns, and "flying to Mars" will be identified as a participle that must be attached to one of the two nouns. The second step will use a computerized version of the *Longman Dictionary of Contemporary English* to examine the two nouns, and it will be able to conclude that a spaceship is more likely to fly than Seattle. In the third step, the computer might increase the clarity of the sentence by changing it to "Flying to Mars, the spaceship photographed Seattle."

The project will take years because the dictionary is only one of many sources of commonsense information. When the Microsoft team is satisfied with the dictionary portion of the project, they plan to turn to other sources, such as encyclopedias, newspapers, magazines, and novels. They hope eventually to cull enough information from these sources to create structured databases of word relationships that might permit machines to understand and use language the way humans do.

Success in "teaching" computers to understand and use language as we do has many implications. Such programming possibilities could be central to speech- and handwriting-recognition systems. Computer queries could be less structured and more natural. They could also have far-reaching social implications. For example, this technology could replace people in such jobs as telephone operator and airline reservation agent.

FOCUS Questions: Why is common sense a feature of intelligence? Why is it so difficult to program computers with common sense?

SOURCE: John Markoff, "Trying to Program Common Sense," *The New York Times,* September 1, 1993.

Intelligent Software   Many products now on the market claim to use AI techniques or to be "intelligent." Some of this is pure advertising hype, but software design is advancing beyond the contemporary Von Neumann computer model described in Chapter 4 in which a single processor executes one instruction at a time. Later sections of this chapter describe some of these developments, including parallel coordinated computing, in which many small computers work on a problem at once; "information refineries," in which thousands of parallel sensors summarize huge data streams; and intelligent databases, in which parallel processors search very large files for patterns.

THE DEVELOPMENT OF ARTIFICIAL INTELLIGENCE

Research into artificial intelligence has actually been conducted in two directions, each of which has its own story.[1] One involves the history of efforts to develop **intelligent machines** that mimic what people at the time think is the way an animal or human brain

Intelligent machine

A physical device or computer that mimics the way people think.

Bottom-up approach
An approach to intelligent machines that concentrates on trying to build a physical analog to the human brain.

Top-down approach
An approach to intelligent machines that concentrates on trying to develop a logical analog to the human brain.

Feedback
The return to a machine of part of the machine's output; the machine then uses the input information to improve its performance.

works. This is called the **bottom-up approach;** it is essentially the effort to build a physical analog to the human brain. The second story involves the **top-down approach,** the effort to develop a logical analog to how the brain works.

The effort to develop intelligent machines is hardly new. In fact, Charles Babbage, who invented a mechanical calculator in 1834, called his proposed calculating machine an "analytical engine," or thinking machine, and believed it could play chess at some point. This was perhaps the first top-down intelligent device. Figure 15.2 illustrates major developments in the top-down and bottom-up methods over the last 50 years.

Contemporary AI research can be traced to World War II and the concept of **feedback.** In feedback, part of a machine's output is returned to it as input, and the machine then uses the input information to improve its performance. Norbert Wiener, a scientist and mathematician at the Massachusetts Institute of Technology (MIT) in the 1940s, developed a method of radar control of antiaircraft guns for the U.S. Army in which the expected location of an aircraft was calculated based on new information—

FIGURE 15.2

A Brief History of the Top-Down and Bottom-Up Approaches to AI
Since World War II there have been two main thrusts in AI research. The top-down approach seeks to develop a logical model of human intelligence and the workings of the human brain. The bottom-up school tries to build a physical analog to the human brain and thus reproduce human thought patterns. Both techniques have played an important role in current AI research.

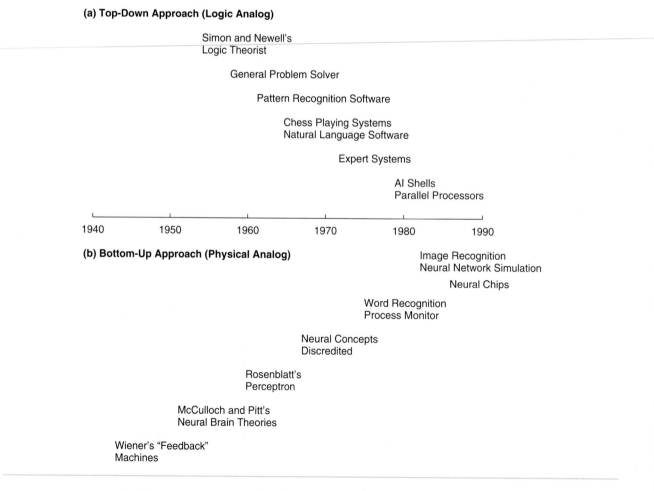

feedback—from radar. Wiener went on to propose in several books that feedback could explain how humans think and suggested that the principle could be applied to make machines think like humans.

Thus started the physiological or bottom-up approach to artificial intelligence. Warren McCulloch, a biologist interested in brain function, and Walter Pitts, a mathematician, used Wiener's idea of feedback to develop a theory of how the brain works. In this theory, a brain was composed of millions of neuron cells that both processed binary numbers (they were either "on" or "off") and were connected into a network that took in feedback or information from the environment. Learning was simply a matter of teaching the neurons in a brain how to respond to the environment.

These ideas were taken further by Frank Rosenblatt, a Cornell psychologist and scientist, who in 1960 demonstrated a machine he called a **Perceptron**. This machine was composed of 400 photoelectric cells that could perceive letters or shapes and 512 neuronlike relays that conveyed information from the photoelectric cells to response units. The machine could recognize letters (as long as they were all of the same size and type) and could be taught: operators would increase or decrease voltages in certain areas of the machine when mistakes were made.

In 1969 the top-down logical school led by Marvin Minsky and Seymour Papert, both at MIT, published a book called *Perceptrons,* which "proved" mathematically that such devices could never approach the intelligence of even lowly animals. This book ended serious research in the bottom-up, or cybernetics, school for many years. Since then, Minsky has withdrawn his critique and now supports neural network machine research. The resurgence of interest in neural networks is discussed in Section 15.3.

Although machines like the Perceptron received more media attention, the theorists of the logical, top-down school of AI were also hard at work. This school has developed through three stages. In its earliest stage, the goal was to develop a general model of human intelligence. This was followed by a period in which the extraordinary power of third-generation computers—the machines of the 1960s—was applied to more limited problems, like playing chess, or specialized areas, such as machine tool control. Finally, beginning in the 1970s, expert systems emerged in which the goals were scaled down to understanding knowledge in specific and highly limited areas.

In 1956 at the Dartmouth Summer Research Project on Artificial Intelligence, Herbert Simon (a Carnegie Mellon psychologist and scientist) and Alan Newall (a Rand Corp. scientist) announced they had developed a thinking machine, which they called a **Logic Theorist.** Its software could prove certain mathematical theorems found in the famous mathematical treatise *Principia Mathematica* by Alfred North Whitehead and Bertrand Russell. The software mimicked deductive logic: that is, it selected the correct rules and postulates to create a coherent logical chain from premises to conclusion.

Unfortunately, the Logic Theorist could not easily be adapted to other areas of life where deductive reasoning was used. The problem with following chains of "if a, then b" statements is that hundreds of thousands, or millions, of such rules are required for even simple real-world problems. In response to the difficulties of applying the Logic Theorist to real-world problems, Simon and Newell attempted in the late 1950s to discover the general principles of human problem solving. If a few principles could be found, then perhaps a few simple rules of thumb could be used to avoid a **combinatorial explosion.** This is the problem that arises when a computer must test more rules to solve a problem than it has the capacity to examine. Regrettably, no general or simple principles of human problem solving were discovered. The search for a General Problem Solver ended.

In the 1960s advances in hardware offered some hope of coping with the combinatorial explosion. The newly developed third-generation computers—the first computers to use integrated circuits—made it possible to consider thousands of computations

Perceptron

A machine devised by Frank Rosenblatt that could perceive letters or shapes and could be taught, or corrected, when it made mistakes; an example of the bottom-up approach to artificial intelligence.

Logic Theorist

Software developed by Herbert Simon and Alan Newell that mimicked deductive logic; that is, it selected correct rules and postulates to create a coherent logical chain from premises to conclusion.

Combinatorial explosion

The difficulty that arises when a problem requires a computer to test a very large number of rules to reach a solution; even a very fast computer cannot search through all the possibilities in a reasonable amount of time.

per second. Attention turned to pure "power" approaches: using the new machines to test out millions of rules, one at a time. But even a simple game like chess contains 10^{120} possible moves, so ways had to be found to pare down the search tree to avoid a combinatorial explosion. An exhaustive search through all possibilities on a chess board would have quickly swamped all the computers known to exist in the 1960s. On the other hand, in restricted domains—like chess—and with sufficient processing power, a number of problem-solving rules or strategies that are specific to the game of chess can be pursued and processed with some success.

One result of these developments was the first expert system—a system of rules limited to a very specific domain of human expertise (like chess). Unfortunately, the rules and strategies developed to play chess are not really applicable to any other area of life. Expert systems, which use heuristic, or rule-guided, searches, have helped to solve some of these difficulties.

Random or exhaustive searches through all the possible rules can be extremely time-consuming and can lead to a combinatorial explosion; in contrast, a heuristic search, based on certain rules of thumb that guide the search by indicating the most promising branch at a given point, can pare down the decision tree and make searching more efficient. In limited areas of expertise, such as diagnosing a car's ignition system or classifying biological specimens, expert systems have succeeded in codifying the rules of thumb used by real-world experts and placing them in a machine.

15.2 EXPERT SYSTEMS

Expert systems represent the latest evolution of top-down artificial intelligence thinking in which the computer is used to assist or even replace human decision makers. Unlike robotics or perceptive systems, expert systems have a very wide potential application to many areas of human endeavor in which expertise is important.

CLUES (Countrywide's Loan Underwriting Expert System) is a microcomputer-based expert system designed to make preliminary decisions about the credit-worthiness of loan applicants. The system contains about 400 rules that were provided by loan underwriters. The final decision for granting a loan is made by an underwriter, but CLUES can assist underwriters with their evaluations.
SOURCE: Courtesy of Countrywide Home Mortgage Loans.

THE NATURE OF EXPERT SYSTEMS

As we noted earlier, expert systems can be defined as systems that model human knowledge in limited areas or domains. Such systems are intended to solve problems as well or better than human decision makers, to apply human knowledge to well-understood problems, and to be able to account for how they arrive at decisions. At the same time, it is important to recognize the limitations of expert systems: they do not draw analogies, they cannot reason from first principles (i.e., they have no understanding of the larger world beyond their expertise), and they are hard to teach. Briefly, expert systems lack common sense and for this reason may not be useful in some areas of business, such as general management, that require an open-ended search for solutions.

THE COMPONENTS OF AN EXPERT SYSTEM

An expert system contains four major components: the knowledge domain, or base, in which one is building the system; the development team, which tries to capture relevant portions of the knowledge base; the shell, or programming environment in which the system is programmed; and the user, who must interact with the system to guide it. Figure 15.3 illustrates these components.

The Knowledge Base   What is human knowledge? Artificial intelligence developers sidestep this thorny issue by asking a slightly different question: how can human knowledge be modeled or represented so that a computer can deal with it? Three ways have been devised so far to represent human knowledge and expertise: rules, semantic nets, and frames. These constitute the **knowledge base** in an expert system.

A standard programming construct (see Chapter 10) is the IF-THEN construct in which a condition is evaluated and, if it is true, an action is taken. For instance:

IF
    INCOME > $50,000 (**condition**)
    PRINT NAME AND ADDRESS (**action**)

A series of these rules can be used to represent a knowledge base. Indeed, as you can easily see, virtually all traditional computer programs contain IF-THEN statements, and one can argue that these programs are intelligent. What, then, is the difference between an expert system and a traditional program?

The difference between a traditional program and a rule-based expert system program is one of degree and magnitude. AI programs can easily have 200 to 3,000 rules, far more than traditional programs, which may have 50 to 100 IF-THEN statements. Moreover, as Figure 15.4 indicates, in an AI program, the rules tend to be interconnected and nested to a far greater degree than in traditional programs.

The order in which rules are searched depends in part on the information the system is given. There are multiple paths to the same result. If the system is given "F" in Figure 15.4, then "H" will be performed, and if the system is given "A", "H" will also be performed. The system is also nonsequential: if "H" occurs when rule #5 fires, then #3 will be fired on a second pass through the rule base.

Could you represent the knowledge in the *Encyclopaedia Britannica* this way? Probably not, because the rule base would be too large, and not all the knowledge in the encyclopedia can be represented in the form of IF-THEN rules. In general, expert systems can be efficiently used only in situations in which the domain of knowledge is highly restricted (such as granting credit) and involves only a few thousand rules.

Knowledge base
A model of human knowledge used by artificial intelligence systems; consists of rules, semantic nets, or frames.

FIGURE 15.3

The Four Basic Elements in an Expert System

An expert system represents an effort to reproduce human expertise in a computer. There are four major components that combine to create an expert system. First, there is the knowledge base, the area of expertise for which the system is being built. Second, a development team composed of experts and knowledge engineers works to discover and develop the rules of thumb used by experts into a programmable and coherent whole. The third element consists of the development environment, which can either be a special-purpose AI language such as LISP or PROLOG or a more user friendly expert system shell (described more fully later). The final element is the user, who must guide the system with instructions, data input, and questions.

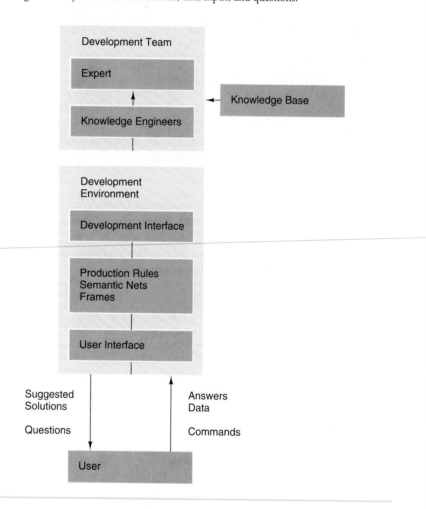

Semantic nets

A way of representing knowledge composed of objects with interrelated characteristics; objects are classified according to the principle of inheritance: objects in lower levels of the net "inherit" the general characteristics of the objects above them.

Semantic nets can be used to represent knowledge when the knowledge base is composed of easily identified chunks or objects of interrelated characteristics. Figure 15.5 shows a semantic net used to classify kinds of automobiles, based on size, high or low drag coefficient, and other traits. Semantic nets use the property of inheritance to organize and classify objects and also use a condition like "IS A" to tie objects together. "IS A" is a pointer to all objects of a specific class. For instance, all specific automobiles in the lower part of the diagram inherit characteristics of the general categories of automobiles above. Insurance companies, for instance, can use a semantic net to classify cars into rating classes. A clerical worker merely types the name and model of a car into a terminal, and the system can properly classify the car and decide on a rate.

FIGURE 15.4

Production Rules in an Expert System

A simple credit-granting expert system contains a number of rules to be followed when interviewing applicants on the telephone. The rules themselves are interconnected, the number of outcomes is known in advance and is limited, there are multiple paths to the same outcome, and the system can consider multiple rules at the same time.

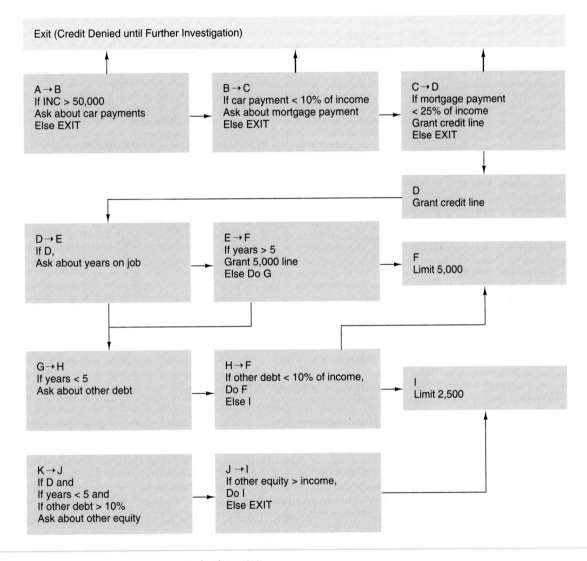

SOURCE: Copyright 1990 Azimuth Corporation. Used with permission.

Knowledge **frames** are similar to semantic nets in that knowledge is organized into chunks, but the relationships between chunks is less hierarchical and is based on shared characteristics rather than inherited characteristics. Figure 15.6 shows a part of a knowledge base organized by frames. A "CAR" is defined by characteristics or slots in the frame as a vehicle, with four wheels, a gas or diesel motor, and an action like rolling or moving. This frame could be related to just about any other object in the database that shares any of these characteristics. The manner in which the frames are connected can be determined by the user. Frame-based AI systems are somewhat similar to a

Frames

A way of organizing knowledge based on shared characteristics; an object is defined by its characteristics and can be related to any other object in the database that shares those characteristics.

FIGURE 15.5

Expert System Using Semantic Nets

Semantic nets employ the characteristic of inheritance to form associations between objects and traits. For instance, in this semantic network, which is used to classify cars, each item "inherits" characteristics from the item above it. Thus, all Dodge Caravans and Ford Escorts are family cars, and all family cars are automobiles.

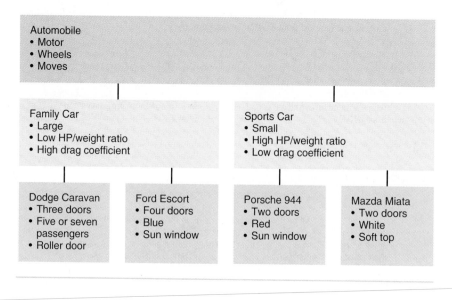

HyperCard database, which is organized into cards (see Chapter 7) with each object described on a card.

The Development Team   An expert system development team is composed of one or several "experts," who have a thorough command of the knowledge base, and one or more **knowledge engineers**, who can translate the knowledge (as described by the expert) into a set of production rules, frames, or semantic nets. A knowledge engineer is a specialist trained in eliciting information and expertise from other professionals. The knowledge engineer interviews the expert or experts and determines the decision rules and knowledge that must be embedded into the system. Thus, the knowledge engineer works with the expert to refine and improve the system until a useful system has been created. While AI software continues to improve, the process of eliciting knowledge from an expert remains a major challenge. Because knowledge engineering requires some background in diverse fields (such as software design, clinical psychology, and anthropology) plus finely tuned communications skills, knowledge engineers are rare.

Indeed, according to many experts, the hard part of writing an expert system is knowledge engineering. Knowledge engineer Helen Ojha of Coopers & Lybrand, a prominent accounting and consulting firm, described knowledge engineers as "visitors to another culture they have not grown up in." At work they're much like anthropologists, who are trained to observe things they do not fully understand.

The Artificial Intelligence Shell   The **artificial intelligence shell** is the programming environment of an expert system. Currently, expert systems can be developed in just about any programming language, including BASIC, C, or Pascal. In the early years of expert systems, computer scientists developed specialized programming languages, such as Lisp and PROLOG, that could process lists of rules efficiently. Although these

Knowledge engineer

Specialist trained in eliciting information and expertise from other professionals in order to translate the knowledge into a set of production rules, frames, or semantic nets.

Artificial intelligence shell

The programming environment of an artificial intelligence system.

FIGURE 15.6

Expert System Using Knowledge Frames

In a manner similar to semantic nets, knowledge and information can be organized by "frames" that capture the relevant and important characteristics of objects of interest. This approach is based on the belief that humans use "frames," or concepts, to narrow the range of possibilities when scanning incoming information, to make rapid sense out of perceptions. For instance, when a person is told to "look for a tank and shoot when you see one," experts believe humans invoke a concept or frame of what a tank should look like. Anything that does not fit this concept of a tank is ignored. In a similar fashion, AI researchers can organize a vast array of information into frames. The computer is then instructed to search the database of frames and list connections to other frames of interest. The user can then follow the various pathways pointed to by the system.

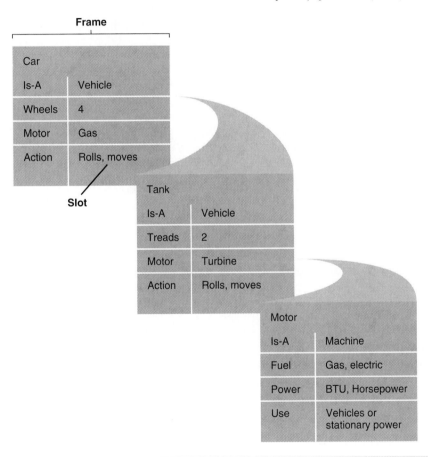

languages were efficient, they have proved difficult to standardize and even more difficult to integrate into a traditional business environment. Hence a growing number of expert systems today are developed using either C or, more commonly, AI shells, which are user-friendly development environments capable of quickly generating user interface screens, capturing the knowledge base quickly, and managing the strategies for searching the rule base. AI shells reduce the time and cost of expert system development and open up AI systems to nonexperts.

One of the most interesting aspects of the AI shell is the **inference engine**; this is simply the strategy used to search through the rule base. Two strategies are commonly used: forward reasoning and backward reasoning.

Inference engine
The strategy for searching through the rule base in an expert system; either a forward reasoning strategy or a backward reasoning strategy is used.

Forward reasoning

A strategy for searching the rules in a knowledge base in which the inference engine begins with information entered by the user and searches the rule base to arrive at a conclusion.

Backward reasoning

A strategy for searching the rules in a knowledge base in which the inference engine begins with a hypothesis and proceeds by asking the user questions about selected facts until the hypothesis is either confirmed or disproved.

In **forward reasoning,** the inference engine begins with information entered by the user and searches the rules in a knowledge base to arrive at a conclusion. The strategy is to "fire," or carry out the action of the rule, when a condition is true. Figure 15.7 shows two sets of rules that allow a user to search a rule base in order to decide whether a client is a good prospect for a visit from an insurance sales representative. If the user enters the information that the client has an income greater than $100,000, the inference engine will fire all rules in sequence from left to right. If the user then enters the information that the same client owns real estate (panel b), another rule base will be searched again, and more rules will fire. The rule base can be searched each time the user enters new information. Processing continues until no more rules can be fired.

In **backward reasoning,** an expert system acts more like a problem solver who begins with a hypothesis and seeks out information to evaluate the hypothesis by asking questions. Thus, in Figure 15.7, the user might ask the question "Should we add

FIGURE 15.7

How the Inference Engine Works

The inference engine is the strategy that has been programmed into an expert system to guide its search through the rule base. In forward reasoning, the inference engine takes its cue from the information entered by the user. In this example, if the user tells the machine that a certain client has an income greater than $100,000, the inference engine "fires," or carries out, a series of further rules based on additional information. If the user tells the machine that the same client owns real estate, this spurs a separate set of rules, some of which branch into the income rules. In backward reasoning, the engine would begin with the information at the right side of the diagram and reason "backward" through the same decision points.

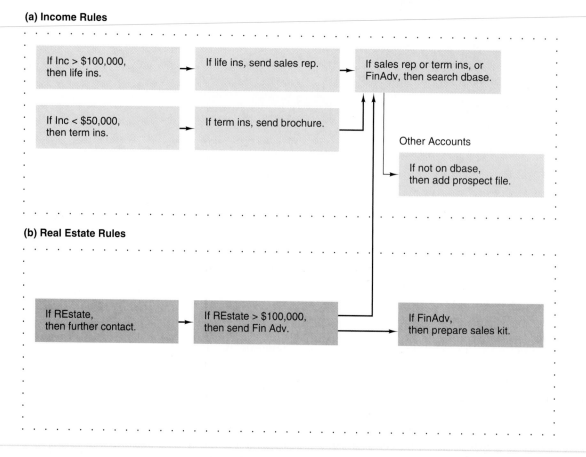

this person to the prospect data base?" The inference engine begins on the right of the diagram and works toward the left. Thus the person should be added to the database if a sales representative, term insurance brochure, or financial adviser will be sent to the client. But will these events take place? The answer is yes, if life insurance is recommended.

The User   The role of the user in an expert system is both to pose questions for the system and to enter relevant data to guide the system along. In most cases, the expert system will simply be an adviser to human experts and users, but on rare occasions, decision making may be turned over to the expert system entirely.

BUILDING EXPERT SYSTEMS

Building an expert system is basically similar to building any information system. A systems analyst (here a knowledge engineer) sits down with a user of the system (called an expert), and together they work out what the system should be able to do. They develop a preliminary version, which is tested and refined to produce the final expert system. Figure 15.8 depicts the process of expert system development.

Developing expert systems differs from building conventional systems in that expert systems rely much more heavily on experimental versions of the system and frequent, intense interactions with the user. Thus, as Figure 15.8 suggests, much time is spent on the preliminary version(s), testing, and improvement. One reason for this is that experts often discover that they cannot clearly articulate the rules they actually use when making decisions.

THE ROLE OF EXPERT SYSTEMS IN ORGANIZATIONS

Expert systems were at first developed as stand-alone applications, largely unrelated to the business systems that surrounded them. This has changed, however, as developers realized that expert systems often required data directly from mainstream corporate systems and often had to work cooperatively with knowledge workers' and managers' desktop computers. This has led to a significant reform in expert systems' development and a rethinking of their role.

In many respects, expert systems are not much different from traditional programming techniques, and the entire exercise might even be called "advanced programming" rather than artificial intelligence. After a decade's experience, some limitations in the technique are also becoming clear.

First, it takes a very long time and a large commitment of resources to build interesting expert systems. Many institutions have found it cheaper to hire an expert than to hire a team of knowledge engineers to build an expert system. Although simple expert systems of up to one hundred rules can be built quickly using one of several AI shells sold for personal computers, these applications tend not to be particularly important or powerful. Second, expert systems are brittle and cannot learn. They must be reprogrammed whenever knowledge changes in a field. Because knowledge does change often in an information society, expert systems maintenance costs are considerable. Third, expert systems require that knowledge be organized in an IF-THEN format. This is appropriate for some knowledge and expertise, but much expertise cannot be organized in this fashion without producing erroneous results. Fourth, for all these reasons, expert systems are limited in application to taxonomy problems (i.e., problems in which the goal is to

FIGURE 15.8

The Process of Developing an Expert System
The first step in developing an expert system is to capture the relevant information from the knowledge base. A knowledge engineer works with an expert in the knowledge base to determine what the system needs to know. Then they develop a preliminary version of the system, which is tested for accuracy and completeness. The final step involves implementing the finished system.

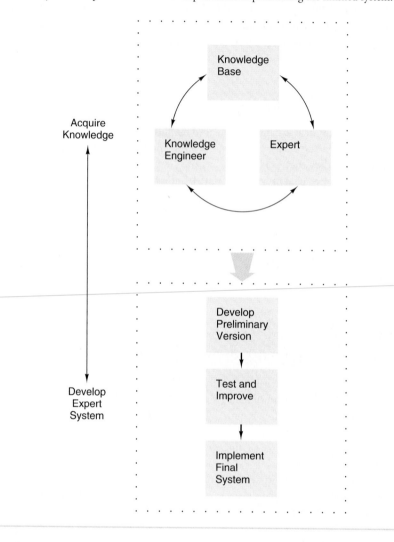

diagnose or assign objects to classes). Expert systems are not very good at typical management problems, which tend to be open ended, involve synthesis rather than deduction, require many different kinds of expertise, and rely on expertise that is widely distributed in an organization.

LEADING-EDGE TECHNOLOGY: CASE-BASED REASONING

Case-based reasoning
Artificial intelligence technology that represents knowledge as a series of cases stored in a database.

While the most widely used expert systems today are built on rules that experts follow in analyzing problems or making decisions, a newer type of expert system known as **case-based reasoning** (CBR) is fast gaining popularity. As we explained earlier, rule-based expert systems are actually a large number of IF-THEN-ELSE constructs used to evaluate specific conditions. The underlying technology of CBR is quite different. The fundamental unit of knowledge is not a rule but a case, a scenario, or an actual historical experience or occurrence. The cases are stored in a database for later retrieval when the user encounters a new case with similar characteristics. The system searches for similar cases, finds the closest fit, and applies the solutions of the old case to the new case. Successful solutions are tagged to the new case and stored together in the knowledge base applied to the new case. Unsuccessful solutions are also appended to the new case along with an explanation of why the solutions didn't work. In contrast to rule-based expert systems, the knowledge base for CBR systems is continuously expanded and refined by users.

The most popular use of CBR is as a help-desk tool to aid computer and technology company staffs in analyzing end-user problems (see the Focus on Organizations). For example, to build a CBR system to analyze printer problems, the cases would be actual printer problems the help desk (or technical support staff or customer service department) will have encountered—"the sheets came out blank," "the printing is smeared," "I press print but nothing happens," "the printing is all there but a black streak prints down the middle," "I didn't understand the error message," and so on. CBR systems are increasingly valued because their knowledge bases are continually updated as new data (cases) are received—the more experiences the knowledge base contains, the smarter the software. On the other hand, rule-based systems are changed only on occasion, when the business rules themselves are altered.

Case descriptions are entered in textual format into CBR systems by trained CBR staff. The person entering the description makes certain it contains key words necessary

Case-based reasoning technology is valuable for automated help desks, storing expert knowledge of problems with products and their solutions in a database of cases that can be instantly retrieved by customer support staff. Many customer queries can be resolved in a few minutes without calling on technical experts.

SOURCE: Courtesy of International Business Machines Corporation.

HELPING CUSTOMERS WITH COMPUTERIZED HELP DESKS

How strategic is customer service to Andy Gale, vice-president of finance at Landa Inc.? "If I'm not taking care of the customer, no matter how secure I am, no matter how mature my business, someone's going to come along and take care of 'em, and take 'em away from me." In other words, at Landa, a Portland, Oregon, manufacturer of washing and wastewater reclamation equipment, customer service means survival. Business survival helps explain the spread of help-desk and related software from the computer hardware and software industries to a wide range of other companies. Gale, for example, installed Point.Man customer-service software from Spectrum Associates, Inc. to link the customer database with accounting, product design, and other related data. Now, when a customer calls for help, Landa is "not jerking the customer from one department to another" to respond to questions.

A help desk is a staff of people who answer internal or external customer calls with problems that need to be solved. Traditionally, help-desk staff members went through lengthy on-the-job training. They were not technical experts and could answer only relatively routine questions. More complicated questions required calling a technical person or a specialist while the customer was kept waiting on hold. Today automated help-desk software systems are programmed with the information a nontechnical staff person needs to solve most customer problems.

Companies have found many ways their organizations benefit from automated help-desk software. In the past, when a customer called an equipment company like Landa with a problem, the company often had to send a maintenance staff person to the site to diagnose the problem and determine what to do. If the solution required new parts, the staff person had to return to the customer site for part installation. Today, with the support of help-desk software to analyze problems, the

SOURCES: Elaine L. Appleton, "Bonding with Customers through Better Service," *Datamation,* November 1, 1993; Bruce Arnold, "Expert System Tools Optimizing Help Desks," *Software Magazine,* January 1993; and William M. Bulkeley, "Your Pet Iguana Swallowed a Staple? Computerized Help Desk Will Try to Help," *The Wall Street Journal,* November 3, 1993.

to identify the problem ("smear," "blank," "streak"). The CBR expert also enters a series of questions to be asked that, if answered properly, will either help identify this case as the problem or, alternatively, may eliminate it. Finally, of course, the solution to the problem is entered. When the case is saved the software executes a complex routine to index key words so the case can be properly identified during a later search.

When the user (a help-desk staff member) is given a problem, he or she will answer a series of general questions posed by the CBR system that allows the software to use the key words to narrow the search to a specific set of cases, eliminating all others. Then the software will ask questions drawn from those selected cases. With each answer, every case within the set is assigned a weighting depending on the answer given. When one (or several) case(s) achieves a high enough rating, it is selected and solutions are displayed for the user. If no appropriate case can be found, a technician is assigned to analyze the problem, determine its cause and solution, and create a new case to be added to the CBR knowledge base, making it even "smarter" than before.

Compaq Computer used CBR to create its automated help-desk system. When Compaq management saw revenues and earnings declining in 1991, they increased their focus on customer service by establishing customer-support desks. A serious problem quickly surfaced: Studies showed that the technical staff assigned to support the help desk spent at least 50 percent of their time solving problems that had already been solved. Compaq's answer? Automate the help desk. Compaq turned to CBR Express from Inference Corp., El Segundo, California. The system they developed, known as Smart (Support Management Automated Reasoning Technology), benefited Compaq in a number of ways. First, the amount of time the technical staff devoted to solving customer

number of needed site visits is greatly reduced. Problems can be managed and required parts can be identified on the telephone. When a site visit is necessary the installer can carry the part, thus making only one visit.

Kathleen Frazer, consumer-service manager at Black & Decker in Towson, Maryland (the world's largest manufacturer and distributor of power tools for the home repair market), sees help-desk software as a way to reduce staff size and costs. Black & Decker supplies information on approximately 4,000 current and old power tools and accessories. In the past, product specialists only handled customer service calls during business hours. Now that Black & Decker uses automated help-desk software, customer-service representatives handle 100 calls per day, a 67 percent productivity improvement from

their previous average of 60 calls. The help-desk system contains solutions to problems with all products. Any customer-service representative can now handle most calls—the customer no longer has to be put on hold, for instance, while a circular-saw specialist is located.

Color Tile, Inc., a home improvement retailer based in Fort Worth, Texas, has used help-desk software to change the function of their help-desk group. The software has resulted in an average reduction in help-desk call time from 10 minutes to 2 minutes. As a result, the same staff is now also responsible for customer returns, refunds, and even appointment scheduling.

At Aircast Inc., a Summit, New Jersey, manufacturer of orthopedic braces, the help-desk software has become a strategic marketing tool. This

firm linked its help-desk software to its fax server. According to system manager Ralph Bagen, customer-service representatives can automatically fax appropriate diagrams and medical information to the patients of the physicians they deal with. Then the patient and physician can review the information together to determine the best course of treatment.

FOCUS Questions:
Why is help-desk software so important? What problems does it solve? Think of and describe other ways that help-desk software can be used internally (within the organization) to help a business.

problems was reduced. Second, help-desk staff training could be reduced while staff efficiency and effectiveness were increased. Third, help-desk staff turnover at Compaq was no longer a problem because expert knowledge remained embedded in Smart rather than in the customer-service staff. Compaq now resolves 95 percent of its customer queries in 10 minutes or less, a dramatic improvement for the customer and a major cost saving for Compaq. Figure 15.9 illustrates how Compaq's CBR system works.

Compaq and other companies view CBR as a valuable resource and are finding new ways to use it. To reduce their costs even further while giving customers even faster service, Compaq now supplies a CBR system, QuickSource, with its PageMarq laser printers. Customers can quickly diagnose most of their printer problems themselves by using their own computers. Compaq estimates that QuickSource saves the firm $10–$20 million annually through a reduction in technical support staff.[2]

CBR is spreading to other areas besides customer service when organizations want to make knowledge gained from past experiences available to employees. For example, the oil industry uses CBR technology to rapidly classify the age of exploration drilling samples by fossil content. CBR is also widely used in medical fields and quality assurance. General Dynamics' Electric Boat Division in Groton, Connecticut, which builds America's nuclear submarines, developed a database of cases concerning experiences with faulty parts and valves used to manage the flotation system of submarines. When an engineer finds a faulty valve, he or she consults the corporate case base to find valves and situations that are roughly similar. Once found, the engineers examine the solutions used in the past cases, adjust those solutions to the current case, and record their procedures for future reference by other engineers.

FIGURE 15.9

A Case-Based Reasoning System
Case-based reasoning uses accumulated memories of past problems and solutions as a guide for solving current problems. While humans use it instinctively, computers need artificial intelligence software, called expert systems, to show them how. This figure shows a simplified example of how a case-based system works.

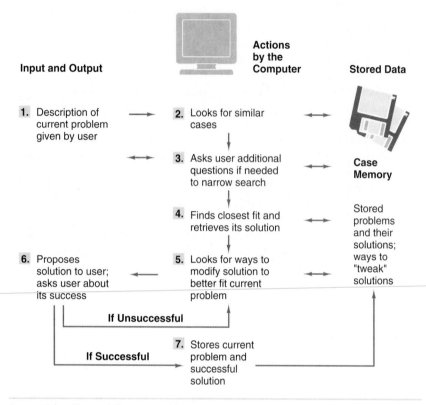

SOURCE: Sabra Chartrand, "Casing a Problem," *The New York Times,* August 4, 1993.

15.3 OTHER INTELLIGENT TECHNIQUES

It is clear that the pursuit of artificial intelligence will be a persistent theme of the 1990s. Although progress will continue to be made in expert systems, the development of parallel processing at the hardware level—the idea of breaking up a problem into many small components and then processing each component simultaneously using hundreds or even thousands of computers operating in parallel—is likely to unleash a host of new possibilities.[3] Here we review briefly the intelligent computing techniques that stand the best chance of developing into major fields for applications today and in the future.

NEURAL NETWORKS

There has been an exciting resurgence of interest in bottom-up approaches to artificial intelligence in which machines are designed to imitate the physical thought process of the biological brain. Figure 15.10 illustrates the natural version—in this case, two neurons from the brain of a leech—and its man-made counterpart. In the leech's

FIGURE 15.10

Two Neural Networks: A Computer and a Leech

Neural networks are an area of research in artificial intelligence in which programmers attempt to emulate the processing patterns of the biological brain. Panel a illustrates part of an animal brain, that of a leech. Each neuron contains a soma, or nerve cell. Axons and dendrites are the branches by which it connects to other neurons; each connection point is called a synapse. Panel b represents the man-made version, in which each neuron becomes a switch or processing element. Axons and dendrites are wires, and the synapses are variable resistors that carry currents representing data.

(a) Natural Neuron

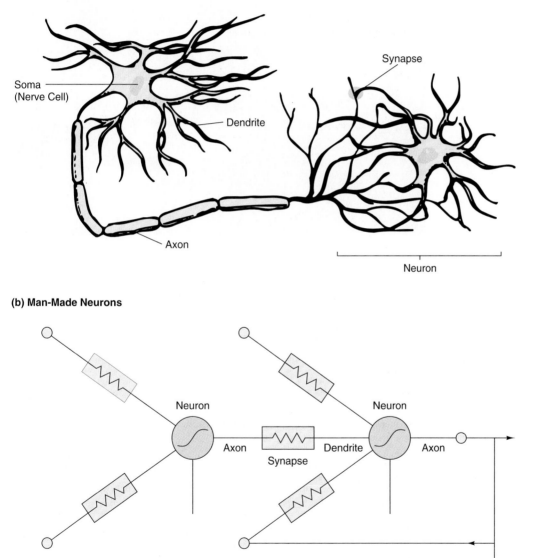

(b) Man-Made Neurons

SOURCE: Defense Advanced Research Projects Agency (DARPA), "DARPA Neural Network Study, October 1987–February 1988," DARPA 1988.

brain, the soma or nerve cell at the center acts like a switch, stimulating other neurons and being stimulated in turn. Emanating from the neuron is an axon, which is an electrically active link to the dendrites of other neurons. Axons and dendrites are the

Papnet by Neuromedical Systems, Inc. uses neural network technology to examine all the cells in a Pap smear and selects the 128 most abnormal cells for display on a monitor. The system was taught to distinguish between normal and abnormal cells. Using this system, a laboratory technician requires less than one-fifth the time to examine a smear while achieving ten times the accuracy of existing manual methods.

SOURCE: Courtesy of Neuromedical Systems, Inc.

"wires" that electrically connect neurons to one another. The junction of the two is called a synapse. The synapse converts the activity from the axon into further electrical effects that either excite or inhibit activity in the adjoining neurons. This simple biological model is the metaphor for the development of neural networks.

The human brain has about 100 billion (10^{11}) neurons, each of which has about 1,000 dendrites, which form 100 trillion (10^{14}) synapses. The brain operates at about 100 HZ (each neuron can fire off a pulse 100 times per second)—very slow by computer standards. For example, an Intel 80486 chip operates at up to 100 megahertz, or millions of cycles, per second, executing one instruction at a time. But the brain's neurons operate in parallel, enabling the human brain to accomplish about 10 quadrillion (10^{16}) interconnections per second. This far exceeds the capacity of any known machine—or any machine now planned or ever likely to be built with current technology. The human brain weighs 3 pounds and occupies about 0.15 square meters.

No technology now known can come close to these capabilities, but elementary neuron circuits can be built and studied, and far more complex networks of neurons—neural networks—have been simulated on computers. Figure 15.10 (b) shows an artificial electronic hardware equivalent of a biological neural cell. The transistors take the place of the nerve cells and act as switches. Wires replace the axons and connect one cell to another. Resistors take the place of synapses, the places where a decision is made as to whether the "firing" (the switching on) of one or more cells should cause the firing of other connected cells. Most neural networks are not built from hardware switches because hardware-based neural networks are very expensive to construct. Instead, the patterns of hardware switching are emulated by software programs. However, chip makers are starting to manufacture neural network chips because they foresee many uses for such chips, from sorting your E-mail the way you like it to balancing the laundry load in washing machines.

Neural networks are quite different from expert systems, in which human expertise has to be modeled with rules and frames. In neural networks, the physical machine emulates a human brain and can be taught from experience.

To explain how neural networks learn, let us examine one current application actually in use—spotting bad apples in a batch ("bad" here might mean spoiling or the wrong size or type of apple). First a color TV camera is connected to the neural network system. Then, as training examples, the net is shown apples one at a time and told whether each is good or bad. Soon the system will begin to categorize them without prompting, although it will make many mistakes. Each time it makes a mistake, the "trainer" corrects it. Gradually it will improve until ultimately it is accurate enough to be used. It can then be connected to a mechanical device that will automatically set aside bad apples based on instructions given it by the neural net.

Neural networks can be trained to recognize any number of patterns—letters, animal sizes and shapes, tanks, patterns in pictures, and patterns of credit charging by individual customers. They excel at pattern recognition. Generally, within a 24-hour period, a neural network can be taught to speak English when presented with text input or write text output when presented with speech input. Although today's neural networks can't begin to approximate the brain power of animals or humans, they can do some jobs better than humans, as described in the Focus on Technology.

Although there have been some impressive neural network applications, it is important to be aware of their limitations. Like expert systems, neural nets work best when the decision is simple—a binary "Yes" or "No"—and when the problem involves classifying cases into one of these predetermined categories. These machines do not achieve generalizable intelligence that could be applied to new situations. For instance, you could never ask an existing neural network to do anything it had never been trained to do, to synthesize the results of several research reports, or to write a term paper. A neural system trained to trade stocks would not have known how to respond to the outbreak of the Persian Gulf War unless it had been fed examples of how the stock market reacted to earlier wars. Since a neural network is not "programmed" as an expert system is, no one knows how it works or understands the problem any better after building the network. Human judgment is still required to keep the networks running properly. In most

Neural net technology mimics the brain's network of neurons to solve a problem. GTE's neural network tracks variations in heat, pressure, and the chemicals used by Sylvania to make fluorescent light bulbs. This neural net will help reveal the best manufacturing conditions.

SOURCE: © Hank Morgan, Rainbow.

FOCUS ON TECHNOLOGY

WHAT CAN NEURAL NETWORKS DO?

What is the hottest emerging computer technology today? When *Electronic Engineering Times* asked that question of engineers in the United States, Europe, and Japan, 85 percent replied neural networks. One reason for this consensus is that neural networks are finally moving from the lab into real-life applications.

The ability of this technology to discern patterns sooner than either human beings or other computer technology further explains its growing popularity. For example, IBM France has developed a diagnostic product called Neuroscope that monitors machinery and gives an early warning of machine failure. The system can be used on a range of industrial equipment, such as motors, cleaning tools, and pneumatic robots. It uses sound to detect changes in machine operation too subtle for humans to notice. A microphone is connected to the network, which is then trained in the correct sound of a piece of equipment. The neural net then quietly monitors equipment operations until it "hears" a problem. By identifying problems days earlier than any other system, Neuroscope allows users of expensive equipment to perform "predictive maintenance."

According to Jean Yves Leclere, who helped develop Neuroscope, "It's very difficult to write an expert system. The signs of normal and abnormal operation of machines are difficult to describe." Neural networks offer a way to solve this problem. IBM first used Neuroscope on its own production

lines and has started marketing it to other companies in Europe and the United States.

Neuromedical Systems, Inc. in Suffern, New York, has created a neural network system to increase the reliability of Pap smear tests, which are used to detect cervical cancer. A Pap smear slide can contain 500,000 cells, only a tiny percentage of which may be abnormal. When human technicians analyze Pap slides with a microscope, they miss the abnormal cells 30 to 50 percent of the time. The Papnet System selects 128 of the most abnormal-looking cells based on criteria that it has learned in the same way human lab technicians learn—by trial and error. The system is fed thousands of normal and abnormal cells in various positions of overlap and juxtaposition. Eventually, it learns the difference. Once it finds what it thinks is an abnormal-looking cell, the system displays it on a color monitor for a human technician to examine more closely. The error rate for Papnet in several independent tests was less than 3 percent.

Mellon Bank in Pittsburgh, Pennsylvania, uses a neural network system to detect credit card fraud. Mellon used to employ an expert system for this purpose, but it examined only a few factors, such as the size of the transaction. The expert system flagged too many legitimate cardholders who slightly altered their spending, angering the bank's customers and wasting the bank's resources. The bank then turned to a neural network Fraud Detection System (FDS) application developed by Nestor Corp. of Providence, Rhode Island. FDS was taught to recognize irregular charge card patterns and to rate the situation on a fraud-possibility scale. Here's how it works: Suppose Jane Doe routinely uses her MasterCard only twice a month, once at a restaurant and once at a local department store. Suddenly she—or someone who has

gained access to her card or card number—runs up four or five purchases in 1 week's time. The next time Doe's card is presented to a shopkeeper or used for a telephone order, FDS matches the current buying patterns against her charging history and returns either a flat denial or a prompt to ask for positive identification. The neural network can detect patterns of activity in massive pools of historical data that a busy human can't. To determine these patterns, FDS draws on 6 months of credit card transactions by Mellon Bank's 1 million active customers. The system is linked to Visa's and MasterCard's authorization centers. When a shopper presents his or her Visa card to a merchant, the merchant transmits pertinent data to Visa, which sends it to Mellon Bank, the card issuer. FDS then determines the chances the purchase is fraudulent and issues one of three instructions: accept, deny, or refer. A referral means the salesperson must ask the customer for proof of identity. The neural network system selects one-tenth the number of cases and with far greater accuracy than the old expert system. Investigators can usually follow up on suspicious transactions in less than 2 hours. Mellon Bank estimates that the nearly $1 million system will have paid for itself in 6 months.

Other neural net applications are currently being used in stock trading, real estate appraisal, optical character recognition, and even horse race betting.

FOCUS Questions: Neural networks are still a new technology. What people, organization, and technology factors would you consider in deciding whether to use this technology? Can you suggest other applications in which a neural network's ability to detect subtle changes would be useful?

SOURCES: Gene Bylinsky, "Computers that Learn by Doing," *Fortune,* September 6, 1993, and Kim S. Nash, "Bank Enlists Neural Net to Fight Fraud," *Computerworld,* December 23/January 2, 1992.

current applications, neural networks are best used as aids to human decision makers instead of substitutes for them.

PARALLEL SENSOR SYSTEMS

One of the problems of the Star Wars defense program (officially called the Strategic Defense Initiative) was that it proposed that the heavens be seeded with thousands upon thousands of sensors, all of which would be aimed at countries that might launch missiles against the United States. How could a computer, or collection of computers, keep track of all this information? Similar problems arise in hospitals: how can all patients be watched and monitored at once, or how can all the indicators on a single patient be closely monitored simultaneously to alert nurses in case something is wrong or to analyze the health status of the patient continually?

One possibility is a **parallel sensor system** called a Trellis machine by one of its inventors, David Gelernter, a computer scientist at Yale (see Figure 15.11). One might think of each node in the machine as a processor or computer that continually receives information from lower-level sensors, evaluates the information, requests more if needed, and reports to higher-level machines. Notice how each piece of information leads upward to possible diagnoses of the cause. The machine depicted in Figure 15.11 is only one portion of a Trellis machine showing how blood pressure is tracked. Other parts of the machine monitor other indicators of health.

Parallel sensor systems
A system in which each node continually receives information from lower-level sensors, evaluates the information, requests more if needed, and reports to higher-level machines.

AN INTELLIGENT DATABASE SEARCH MACHINE

Imagine you have to search the Library of Congress (90 million items including journals and technical reports) for all articles or book chapters having to do with computer security. One possibility, of course, is to have a massively large computer go through each volume, one by one, looking for articles that match the descriptions you have given. Another possibility is to use an **intelligent database search machine**. Instead of working alone, an intelligent database search machine, called the master, gives your descriptions to many machines, called workers, which search the database simultaneously. When a lower-level machine finds a possible match, it passes it back to the master for a final assessment. Figure 15.12 shows an intelligent database search machine used to match a particular DNA sequence against a massively large database of all known sequences.

Intelligent database search machine
A "master" machine that can direct a search of a very large database by giving the target pattern to many machines that search simultaneously; when a machine finds a possible match, it sends it to the controller machine, which makes the final assessment.

FUZZY LOGIC

Even expert system languages, which can capture very fine-grained logic for decision making, have limited ability to replicate human thought processes when a thought process can't be expressed in discrete IF-THEN rules. There are many instances in which a response depends on judgment and "shades of gray." For instance, what is a tall American male? If we use IF-THEN rules, we might define tall as being over 6 feet, 6 inches tall. But in real life, the range of heights considered tall is not well defined. Most people would recognize anyone over 7 feet as tall and anyone under 5 feet as short, but what about people who are 5 feet, 11 inches or 6 feet, 2 inches?

Until recently, computers had trouble handling situations that involved some imprecision and ambiguity. The traditional logic behind computers is based on things that can be categorized as true or false, yes or no, black or white.

Fuzzy logic, a relatively new, rule-based development in AI, is designed to overcome these limitations. Fuzzy logic consists of a variety of concepts and techniques for representing and inferring knowledge that is imprecise, uncertain, or unreliable.

Fuzzy logic
A variety of concepts and techniques in AI for using rules to represent knowledge that is imprecise, uncertain, or unreliable.

FIGURE 15.11

A Medical Application for Artificial Intelligence: A Trellis Machine

A Trellis machine is one attempt to apply AI principles to the problem of monitoring a large amount of data on an ongoing basis and drawing conclusions based on continual changes in the data. The Trellis machine monitors a hospital patient's condition through sensors that track such measures as blood pressure and heart rate and send this information (blue) upward through the "trellis" to computers that evaluate the data. As data rise, they travel through a hierarchy of processors that evaluate them and direct them to other processors as indicated by preliminary diagnoses. Higher-level units may send queries and comments (orange) downward to elicit additional information or change the behavior of a lower-level unit based on a high-level hypothesis.

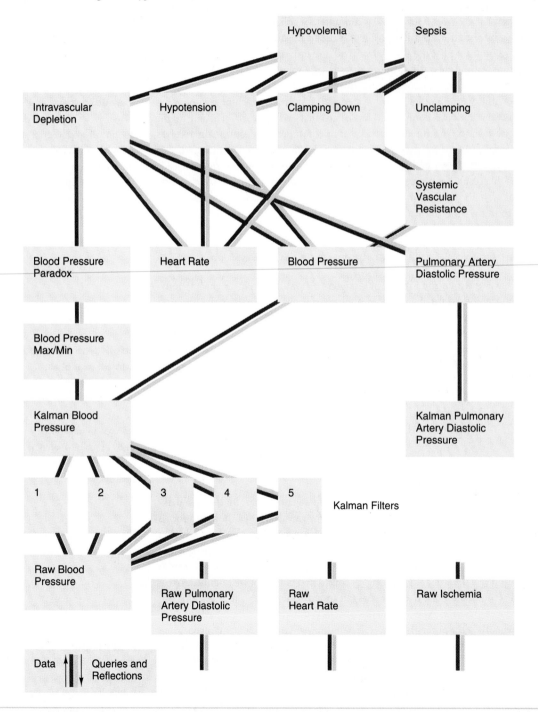

FIGURE 15.12

The Intelligent Database Search Machine
The intelligent database search machine applies principles of artificial intelligence to the problem of searching a large database. In this example the machine has been asked to match a certain DNA sequence against an enormous database of all known sequences. It accomplishes the task by delegating. A controlling computer, the master, copies the sequence and transmits it to many smaller computers called workers. The workers search the database simultaneously. When they locate a possible matching sequence, they send the information back up to the master for evaluation. The master selects the correct answer.

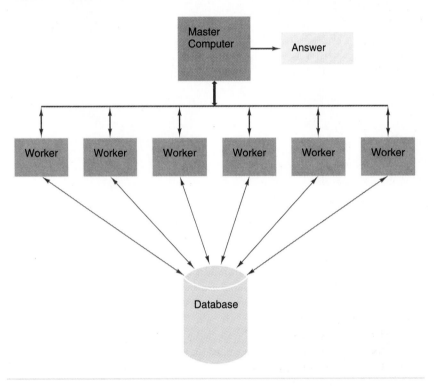

Fuzzy logic can create rules that use approximate or subjective values and incomplete or ambiguous data. By allowing expressions such as tall, very tall, and extremely tall, fuzzy logic enables the computer to emulate the way people actually make decisions, as opposed to defining problems and solutions using restrictive IF-THEN rules.

For instance, using traditional computer logic, a temperature controller on a room heater might react to 35°C as hot but 34.9°C as cold. Such a sharp boundary would cause abrupt changes in the heater's output. In contrast, fuzzy logic turns the hard-edged world of hot/cold, fast/slow into "soft" grades (warm/cool, moderately fast/somewhat slow). A temperature of 20°C can be both "warm" and "a little bit cool" at the same time. This is especially useful for heating systems or electric motors requiring smooth and continuous output.

Fuzzy logic is based on the concept of sets and the degree of membership in a set. In traditional computer logic, a set has rigid membership requirements—an object is either true or false, completely included or excluded. Fuzzy logic, on the other hand, allows "degrees" of truthfulness that measure the extent to which a given numerical value is included in a "fuzzy set." Terms (known as membership functions) are defined so that, for example, it might be 15 percent true that a 6-foot man belongs to the "very tall" fuzzy

Auto-focusing cameras use fuzzy logic to determine the spot that has the highest probability of being the main focal point in a picture.

SOURCE: © Oscar Palmquist, Lightwave.

set, 60% true that he belongs to the "tall" set, and 30% true that he belongs to the "medium height" set. (Since these "truth values" refer to different sets, they don't have to add up to 100%.) The computer would combine the membership function readings in a weighted manner and, using all the rules, describe a measured height in a qualitative way, as very tall, tall, or medium, using English words.

Fuzzy logic has enabled AI to be applied to problems we could not have solved before. One important use has been in embedded controllers that allow a piece of equipment to make constant operating adjustments by calculating its reaction to current conditions. In Japan, the Sendai Metro subway system uses a Hitachi fuzzy control system that stops with much greater accuracy than a manual control system and accelerates and brakes so smoothly that passengers don't need handrails. Fuzzy control systems are frequently used for speed, fuel injection, and transmission control in automobiles. Many Japanese consumer products, such as air conditioners, washing machines, televisions, camcorders, and auto-focusing cameras, also use the technology.

Fuzzy logic applications are beginning to appear in the U.S., and experts predict that within the next few years, they are likely to expand significantly beyond the field of controllers. For example, fuzzy logic can be used in building applications in which there is uncertainty about the exact characteristics of the data to be retrieved, which might be the case for insurance and financial risk assessment applications. Users can ask about good and bad insurance risks without having to specify a plethora of IF-THEN rules. Recently a system has been developed to detect possible fraud in medical claims submitted by health care providers anywhere in the United States. Fuzzy logic technology is rapidly becoming a major factor in the AI field.

ASSESSING MACHINE INTELLIGENCE

Assessing the intelligence of machines is no different from assessing the intelligence of people. This is an obvious corollary of the Turing test described at the beginning of the chapter. Intelligence is in the eye of the beholder and reflects the culture and zeitgeist (or spirit) of every age. Machines like the Trellis and intelligent database search machines exhibit such power in the sense of mastery over an environment that, in the eyes of many, they assume the quality of "intelligence," a quality normally reserved for humans.

But we must always remember that we are using the word "intelligence" metaphorically. These machines are not human. Instead they are programmed reflections of human intelligence, artifacts of humans that we hope are under our control. And it is well to remember their limitations.

SUMMARY

- Artificial intelligence refers to a number of different techniques and practices that have as their common goal the emulation of human intelligence and perception.
- The artificial intelligence family has six members: natural language, robotics, perceptive systems, expert systems, neural networks, and intelligent software.
- There are two approaches to artificial intelligence: top-down approaches seek to emulate the logic of human problem solving; bottom-up approaches seek to emulate the biological brain.
- Expert systems exemplify the top-down approach by modeling human reasoning in restricted domains.
- Expert systems are composed of four major components: the knowledge base, the development team, the AI shell, and the user.
- Case-based reasoning is a type of expert system technology in which knowledge is collected in a database of cases rather than rules.
- Neural networks exemplify the bottom-up approach to artificial intelligence because they are based on a biological metaphor of the brain.
- Neural networks can learn and excel at recognizing patterns that are not easily discerned by humans.
- Intelligent machines provide another approach to artificial intelligence. Because of their massive parallelism, these machines offer the prospect of greatly expanding computing power by performing "intelligent" functions we might expect of humans. The Trellis machine and the intelligent database search machine are two examples.
- Fuzzy logic technology expresses logic with carefully defined imprecision to solve problems that can't be handled with restrictive IF-THEN rules.

KEY TERMS

Artificial intelligence (AI)	Bottom-up approach
Turing test	Top-down approach
Natural language	Feedback
Robotics	Perceptron
Perceptive systems	Logic Theorist
Expert systems	Combinatorial explosion
Neural network	Knowledge base
Intelligent machines	Semantic nets

Frames

Knowledge engineer

Artificial intelligence shell

Inference engine

Forward reasoning

Backward reasoning

Case-based reasoning

Parallel sensor systems

Intelligent database search machine

Fuzzy logic

REVIEW QUESTIONS

1. How would you define artificial intelligence?

2. What are the members of the AI family?

3. What is meant by a domain of knowledge?

4. How would you characterize the history of AI? What were the major stages in its development, and when did they happen?

5. What is meant by a "combinatorial explosion"? How can intelligent systems solve this problem?

6. How would you define an expert system?

7. What are the major components of an expert system?

8. Name and describe the three ways in which a knowledge base can be modeled.

9. Define and describe forward and backward reasoning.

10. How does building an expert system differ from developing a traditional system?

11. How has the relationship between expert systems and other business systems changed?

12. What is case-based reasoning?

13. What is a neural network? How does it differ from an expert system?

14. What kinds of problems are appropriate for neural networks?

15. Define a parallel sensor system and explain how it differs from an ordinary information system in an organization.

16. Define and describe fuzzy logic.

DISCUSSION QUESTIONS

1.   Many people say that someday intelligent expert systems will replace high-level business managers. Do you think this will be possible?

2.   Examine an office in your college or in a local business, and describe how a small expert system might be used to make work more efficient and pleasant.

3.   What is the proper role of expert systems or neural networks in a business or a government agency? Should key decisions be left to AI devices? Describe a range of possible roles.

PROBLEM-SOLVING EXERCISES

1.   *Group exercise:* Divide the class into groups and have each group locate a small business in your neighborhood, and within that business locate a single occupation, such

as supervisor, clerk, or shelf stocker. Have the group interview the person who occupies this position, and try to discover at least ten "rules of thumb" that that person follows to accomplish his or her job. Each group should write a short paper and make an oral presentation about what it discovered.

2.   Look through several computer magazines, such as *Byte, PC Magazine, InformationWEEK,* or *Computerworld,* for a case study of an expert or neural network system. Review this article and write a two-page critical report. Was the system as successful as originally planned? How did the system fall short?

3.   *Hands-on exercise:* A popular expert system application is one that assists banks to decide whether to grant credit for consumer loans, such as automobile loans. North Side Bank in Erie, Pennsylvania, uses the following rules for granting a car loan. Applicants must be over 21 years of age and make over $20,000 per year. The total value of the loan cannot exceed 25 percent of the applicant's annual salary. The bank would like you to use appropriate software to develop a simple expert system application to evaluate the following information. Which candidates qualify for loans?

Name	Age (yrs)	Salary	Loan Amount
Joan Elliott	19	$22,000	$4,000
Robert Morrissey	35	$34,000	$5,000
Sheila Burke	57	$17,500	$2,000
Carl Zeigler	22	$24,700	$4,000
Miranda Kase	44	$55,000	$15,000

NOTES

1. Actually, the story of AI is much more complex and controversial than can be presented here in such a brief introduction. Involved in this larger debate are questions about the nature of human beings and knowledge, the proper relationship between responsible human beings and machines, and the difference between promise and reality. The interested student is directed to two diametrically opposed books. For a positive view of AI, see Edward A. Feigenbaum and Pamela McCorduck, *The Fifth Generation: Artificial Intelligence and Japan's Computer Challenge to the World* (Reading, Mass.: Addison-Wesley, 1985), and Paul M. Churchland and Patricia Smith Churchland, "Could a Machine Think?" *Scientific American,* January 1990. For a counterview of AI, see Hubert L. and Stuart E. Dreyfus, *Mind over Machine: The Power of Human Intuition and Expertise in the Era of the Computer* (New York: The Free Press, 1986), and John R. Searle, "Is the Brain's Mind a Computer Program?" *Scientific American,* January 1990.

2. See Bruce Arnold, "Expert System Tools Optimizing Help Desks," *Software Magazine,* January 1993, and Sabra Chartrand, "Compaq Printer Can Tell You What's Ailing It," *The New York Times,* August 4, 1993.

3. This section benefits from an article by David Gelernter, "The Metamorphosis of Information Management," *Scientific American,* August 1989. The article outlines a number of possibilities for extending computing through parallel processing.

PROBLEM-SOLVING CASE

RULE-BASED SYSTEM KEEPS REUTERS DATA ACCURATE

Inaccurate stock market data can be very costly to its users. Yet when markets are open, data flow by so swiftly that validating their accuracy is nearly impossible for human commercial data suppliers. Reuters, the London-based, internationally known news organization, is also a major supplier of real-time financial information. To gain a competitive edge, its managers needed to find a real-time way to reduce data errors.

Traditional methods of financial market quality control have been either minimally effective or too expensive to use. Data suppliers usually use rather simple, crude computer algorithms to attempt to catch corrupt data as they flash by. Assigning trading experts to the task of data validation might be effective, but it is far too costly and still prone to many errors. Reuters' response, the Intelligent Quality Toolkit (IQT) rule-based computer system, which went into production in London in March 1993, can validate British and Irish financial market numbers. It has fully met Reuters' objectives and is being installed in Reuters' offices around the world.

Experienced financial traders have a great deal of experience in rapidly evaluating data as they pass by them. They incorporate a variety of rules in their work, many of which are useful in detecting errors. For example, a simple rule is that the bid price at which someone buys a share must be less than the ask price at which it is to be sold. A more complex rule involves the method of incorporating night trades into the previous day's trading statistics. The IQT knowledge base includes many such practical trading rules and checks every piece of data that flows from the British and Irish exchanges.

The knowledge base contains a model of all commonly traded financial instruments, such as stocks, bonds, currencies, and commodities. The model contains information on the fields a particular type of data should contain, and how those fields relate to each other. The model also contains rules relating to that instrument type and specific rules for subtypes. Data are first checked against the model. If they agree with the model's specifications, then the system moves on to the next data item.

Should IQT spot problems at the model level, the data are flagged as "of interest" and passed to the next step, where they will be checked against a set of more complex "analysis rules." If a problem is found here, the system will flag a probable error and call it to the attention of the system user. The user will evaluate the data— they may be correct even though IQT flagged them. If necessary, the user will make appropriate adjustments to the data and notify subscribers of the error.

In one way important way the system resembles a case-based reasoning system more than a traditional rule-based expert system. If the user finds that the data have been flagged incorrectly, he or she can make corrections to the rules on-line and in real-time, so that the system continually "learns" from new solutions.

The development team chose not to write IQT using an expert system shell. Rather, with aid from consultants, they built the system themselves using object-oriented programming. Markets change swiftly, and object-oriented programs offer flexibility. In addition to changing rules in response to incorrectly flagged data, Reuters wants its market experts to be able to make rule changes on-line, without help from a software engineer, whenever trading regulations and practices change. Market experts can even add new data items themselves, associating them with existing data item models so the new items can inherit the rules of the existing items.

Six months after its initiation, the system found about 500 data items per day to be "of interest." About 25 percent of these were flagged for the attention of users, half of which were found to be genuine errors. According to Herbert Skeete, Reuters' United Kingdom exchange data manager, "As a result of this system we can now be sure of the accuracy of our data." IQT has also helped Reuters to improve the quality of the incoming data, for as Skeete adds, "We also now know the causes of any errors and we can put them right as they happen."

Reuters has found other uses for the system as well. They have linked it to their help desk so help-desk staff can answer queries on data accuracy. As with other help-desk software, customers no longer need to be put on hold while a specialist is found to deal with their question. IQT also shows commercial promise. Reuters' customers have asked to license the software for use in their own market operations. The system also has potential use by financial market regulatory agencies.

SOURCE: George Black, "Reuters Stays Accurate with Rules-Based System," *Software Magazine,* November 1993.

CASE STUDY QUESTIONS

1.   What people, organizational, and technology problems did Reuters face that caused them to develop the IQT system?

2.   What problems does the system solve? What problems can't it solve?

3.   What potential effects does this new system have on the organization, technology, and people of Reuters?

4.   Why do you think so many people want to acquire the system? Can you think of other uses for this (or a similar) system?

MANAGEMENT SUPPORT SYSTEMS

LEARNING OBJECTIVES

After reading and studying this chapter, you will:

1. Be aware of what managers do in a business and how they use information.
2. Understand the characteristics of management support systems.
3. Be familiar with management information systems and how they work.
4. Be able to describe individual and group decision support systems and how they work.
5. Know what executive support systems are and how they work.
6. Understand the significant challenges of building management support systems.

*Taco Bell Corp., the $3.3 billion fast-food chain, calls itself a
virtual taco stand. Although it cooks millions of tacos each year, it considers
itself more a service company that sells meals and snacks than a preparer of
fast food. Fast and efficient service is the key to success in the fast-food industry. By carefully monitoring what customers want and how the best service
can be delivered, the firm has all but removed kitchens from its restaurants.*

*Instead of preparing items when customers place their orders, Taco Bell
prepares most of its food in consolidated facilities with lower production and
labor costs. The menu items are then delivered to individual Taco Bell
restaurants. Taco Bell managers can order the items they expect to sell in
their restaurants with a high degree of accuracy because of their powerful
information systems.*

*A system called, appropriately enough, TACO (Total Automation of
Company Operations) provides detailed information for managers at 70
percent of the 3,000 company-owned restaurants and 1,000 franchises. The
system performs inventory control, labor scheduling, sales forecasting, product
ordering, management analysis, and sales recording. Each Taco Bell restaurant is equipped with a 486 microcomputer. Every night three IBM
RS/6000 workstations in the firm's corporate headquarters in Irvine,
California, poll data from the microcomputer in each store. They then
manipulate and organize the data so that regional managers can analyze
factors such as sales trends, staffing levels, portion control, or the success or
failure of promotional campaigns.*

*According to Jim Mizes, Taco Bell's Vice-President of operations and
services, "We know what goes on in 15-minute increments—how many*

customers came in, what they ordered, and how fast they were served." This detailed information lets each Taco Bell market manager oversee about 30 restaurants, a marked contrast to the fast-food industry average of eight units per manager.

Since store managers don't have to spend much time overseeing food preparation, they can spend more of their time dealing with customers, and the cost of managing each Taco Bell restaurant is lower. By reducing the costs of management, Taco Bell can lower prices to stay competitive. Taco Bell was the first fast-food chain to institute "value pricing," offering main meal items for less than a dollar. Value pricing can lead to profits because customers who pour in for 39-cent tacos will buy nachos and sodas at the regular price. Most costs, such as a restaurant's labor and physical plant, are fixed, so more customers equal more profits, even if the prices of a few food items are reduced. Taco Bell can compete effectively by offering good value, low prices, speed, and efficiency.

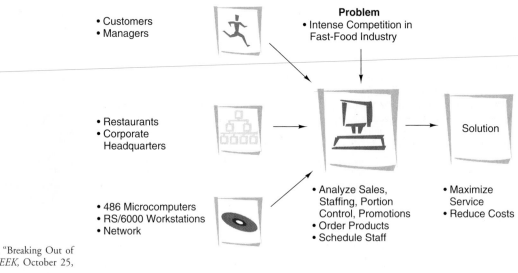

- Customers
- Managers

Problem
- Intense Competition in Fast-Food Industry

- Restaurants
- Corporate Headquarters

Solution

- 486 Microcomputers
- RS/6000 Workstations
- Network

- Analyze Sales, Staffing, Portion Control, Promotions
- Order Products
- Schedule Staff

- Maximize Service
- Reduce Costs

SOURCE: Clinton Wilder, "Breaking Out of Its Shell," *InformationWEEK,* October 25, 1993.

Keeping track of thousands of customers, controlling business finances, and planning for the future are just some of the tasks of modern managers. What should we do if profits fall below expectations? Why are so many employees leaving after 4 or 5 years? How can we increase the quality of our products without raising prices? How can we make our business more competitive? What changes should we make in our organization? These are typical of the questions that managers face every day.

Such questions rarely have simple answers, and they require managers to use a great deal of judgment. Managers require special kinds of information systems to help them find answers and develop solutions. Information systems can play a powerful role in helping managers meet the major challenges we present in this text. In this chapter we describe what managers do and explain how information systems can support them in their work.

16.1 INTRODUCTION: MANAGEMENT SUPPORT SYSTEMS

In Chapter 13, we described how information technology directly supports the transactions of a business—the functions in which the product is actually made and sold. In this chapter, we are concerned with how information technology supports the management of a business. We describe the three generic kinds of management support systems: management information systems, decision support systems, and executive support systems. Each type of system will be illustrated by a real-world example.

Figure 16.1 shows the characteristics of the various management support systems and where they fit into the hierarchy of the firm. **Management information systems (MIS)** provide routine summary reports about the firm's performance; such systems are used to monitor and control the business and predict future performance. **Decision support systems (DSS)** are interactive systems under user control that provide data and models for solving semistructured problems. A **semistructured problem** is one in which only parts of the problem have a clear-cut answer provided by a well-accepted methodology.

Both MIS and DSS are generally concerned with daily operations and with problems that are structured or semistructured. (**Structured problems,** such as those described in Chapter 13, are repetitive and routine and have a specified procedure for

Management information systems (MIS)

Management support systems that provide routine summary reports on the firm's performance; used to monitor and control the business and predict future performance.

Decision support systems (DSS)

Interactive systems under user control that are used in solving semistructured problems.

Semistructured problem

A problem in which only parts have a clear-cut answer provided by a well-accepted methodology.

Structured problem

A routine, repetitive problem for which there is an accepted methodology for arriving at an answer.

FIGURE 16.1

The Three Types of Management Support Systems

An executive support system (ESS) serves the senior or executive management level in an organization. It supports the strategic, long-term planning that is required of this level. Executives often must use data from outside the firm, such as information about legal regulations, market conditions, and competing firms' activities. Many of the decisions they must make are unstructured—that is, the questions are open-ended and the decisions involve unpredictable factors. Management information systems (MIS) and decision support systems (DSS) serve middle and low-level managers, who must deal with short-term, daily operational issues. Much of the information required for these systems is internal, and the systems help managers make structured or semistructured decisions.

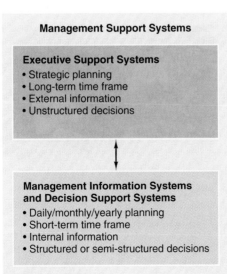

handling them; in contrast, unstructured problems are novel and nonroutine, with no agreed-upon procedure for solving them. Semistructured problems combine elements of both types.) Most of the information for these kinds of decisions comes from within the business, and the time frame is relatively short term (e.g., this week, this month, or this year).

Executive support systems (ESS) generally support the strategic planning function in a business, for which the time frame is relatively long term. Such activities involve largely unstructured, open-ended questions and decisions pertaining to unpredictable future events; they also tend to require a great deal of information from a business's external environment. Senior executives, for example, need information on government activities and regulations, new laws, the actions of competitors, market conditions, and so forth. ESS also tend to be more graphics oriented than other management support systems.

Although all these management systems are different, they often exchange information with one another and are related to one another through this information flow. These various systems can be seen as layers in a business organizational cake.

But before we examine each of these systems in detail, we must take a look at what managers do when they manage a business. That will give us a good idea of the kinds of problems managers face and why they build information systems to help solve those problems.

Executive support systems (ESS)

Graphic-oriented systems designed for senior management that provide generalized computing and telecommunications facilities and combine internal and external information; used for long-term planning.

16.2 WHAT MANAGERS DO

There are many descriptions of what managers do, including "getting things done through other people,"[1] "leading an orchestra,"[2] and using business resources to accomplish goals. Each of these descriptions has some validity. Since ancient times, management has been associated with great accomplishments and achievements, such as the irrigation works of the Sumerians (6500 B.C.), the pyramids of Egypt (4000 B.C.), the Great Wall of China

Honeywell, Inc. manager Kathryn Ybarra won a technical achievement award for leading a 30-person engineering team that contributed to the success of Honeywell's Traffic Alert and Collision Avoidance System. Managers must juggle planning, organizing, leading, and controlling functions to accomplish business goals.

SOURCE: Courtesy of Honeywell, Inc.

(third century B.C.), and the like. Managers have traditionally been concerned with criteria for measuring progress toward some goal. Management also involves the coordination of many (sometimes thousands) of workers.

Managers clearly are not the people who actually do "the work"; instead, they are responsible for determining what work will be done, where it will be done, and for what purpose. And because any business is composed of specialists, managers are in a sense like symphony orchestra conductors trying to get individuals to work together so that "music" results.

TRADITIONAL VIEWS

Classical writers on management, like the French industrialist Henri Fayol (1841–1925), who rose to become the director of a major French mining company, described management as involving five activities: planning, organizing, commanding, coordinating, and controlling, Contemporary writers on management have reduced these features to four management functions: planning, organizing, leading, and controlling (see Figure 16.2).[3] Thus, according to **traditional theories of management, managing** can be defined as the effort to accomplish business goals through planning, organizing, leading, and controlling.

Traditional theories of management
Views of management that see its primary functions as planning, organizing, leading, and controlling.

Managing
The process of using business resources to accomplish goals, coordinate the work of many workers, and establish criteria for measuring progress toward the established goals.[3]

FIGURE 16.2

The Four Major Functions of Management:
Planning, Organizing, Leading, and Controlling
The classical view defines management as the effort to meet business goals through these four activities. By planning, the manager establishes the goals of the firm and sets up tasks by which employees will work to achieve these goals. Organizing involves assigning staff and resources to accomplish these tasks. Effective managers lead their employees by motivating them to do their work well, and they control employees in the sense of monitoring business activities and making corrections as necessary.

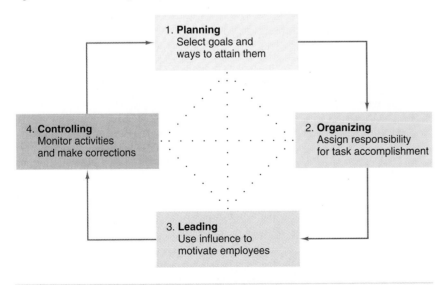

SOURCE: Exhibit 1.1, "The Four Functions of Management," from *Management* by Richard L. Daft, p. 8, copyright © 1994 by The Dryden Press. Reprinted by permission of the author.

Planning refers to defining the goals of the business and describing how it will fulfill these goals. Organizing involves assigning responsibility for accomplishing the necessary tasks and assigning appropriate resources. Leading means motivating employees to achieve organizational goals. Controlling involves monitoring the activities of the business and making corrections as necessary.

THE BEHAVIORAL VIEW: MULTIPLE ROLES

The traditional view is perfectly adequate for describing the basic functions of management, but it does not tell us how managers do what they do. How do managers actually go about planning, organizing, leading, and controlling? For this we must turn to contemporary behavioral scientists who have studied managers in daily action. The results are surprising. A typical manager's morning might look like this:[4]

- **7:35 A.M.:** Wendy Henshaw arrives at her office, unpacks her briefcase, gets some coffee, and looks over a "to do" list.

- **7:40:** Wendy and her immediate subordinate, Frank Williams, discuss their weekend activities. Wendy shows Frank some recent pictures.

- **8:00:** Wendy and Frank discuss a meeting for next week with production managers.

- **8:20:** Another subordinate, Janet Watson, drops in and joins the conversation about next week's meeting. Janet will start preparing slides for the presentation next week and wants some guidance on appropriate slide colors.

- **9:00:** Wendy attends a meeting of marketing specialists planning for a new product release. She is upset that her department has not been informed even though it is responsible for the marketing effort.

- **11:00:** Wendy's boss, Harrison White, drops by for a short unplanned meeting. He wants a report as soon as possible on last week's production shortfall. Wendy promises to get it out this afternoon.

- **11:20:** Wendy's secretary comes in with an office get-well card for another secretary who is hospitalized. Her secretary reminds her that tomorrow is the staff luncheon to celebrate the birth of a co-worker's child.

- **11:40:** A staff person stops by with the figures on last week's production shortfall. Wendy has to show the staffer how to reformat them for her boss.

- **11:45:** Wendy takes a call from a friend.

- **12:00:** Wendy goes to lunch with a human relations recruiter to discuss corporate recruitment policies.

Wendy spends the afternoon in one brief meeting after another, interrupted by several phone calls and appointment requests; she also devotes 1 hour to returning calls. This is what a typical manager does to fulfill the functions of planning, organizing, leading, and controlling.

This realistic world of the manager has six characteristics. (1) Managers perform high-volume, high-speed work, involving a large number of very different topics. (2) The pace is unrelenting, and the phone rarely stops ringing. (3) The work is characterized by variety, fragmentation, and brevity. There is very little time to "think about things."

(4) Managers tend to be issue oriented because they spend attention on the things that need attention immediately. If something is not an issue, it often is not attended to. (5) Managers also have a complex web of personal contacts and interactions, which range from working with clerical workers to sympathizing and working with other managers. (6) Managers have a strong preference for verbal communications.[5]

According to **behavioral theories of management,** the traditional notion of management as planning, organizing, leading, and controlling is a little simplistic. All these functions are performed, but not in any rational, sequential manner. Moreover, behavioral theorists perceive the manager's roles a bit differently than traditional theorists do.

When John T. Kotter observed real-world managers, he found that they engage in three basic activities:[6]

- **Establishing agendas:** Managers set long-term (3 to 5 years) goals.

- **Building a network:** Managers develop a network of business and community contacts at all levels.

- **Executive agendas:** Managers use their personal networks to accomplish their goals.

A contemporary researcher, Henry Mintzberg, studied the characteristics of management work and found that managers perform ten roles, which fall into three major categories (see Table 16.1). A role is a set of expectations for a person who occupies a specific status. In other words, occupants of the manager position are expected to perform three types of roles:

Behavioral theories of management

Views of management based on behavioral scientists' observations of what managers actually do in their jobs.

TABLE 16.1

Management Roles

Category	Role	Activity
Interpersonal	Figurehead	Perform ceremonial and symbolic duties such as greeting visitors or signing legal documents.
	Leader	Direct and motivate subordinates; train, counsel, and communicate with subordinates.
	Liaison	Maintain information links both inside and outside the organization; use mail, phone calls, and meetings.
Informational	Monitor	Seek and receive information, scan periodicals and reports, and maintain personal contacts.
	Disseminator	Forward information to other organization members; send memos and reports, and make phone calls.
	Spokesperson	Transmit information to outsiders through speeches, reports, and memos.
Decisional	Entrepreneur	Initiate improvement projects; identify new ideas and delegate idea responsibility to others.
	Disturbance handler	Take corrective action during disputes or crises; resolve conflicts among subordinates; adapt to environmental crises.
	Resource allocator	Decide who gets resources; scheduling, budgeting, and setting priorities.
	Negotiator	Represent department during negotiation of union contracts, sales, purchases, and budgets; represent departmental interests.

SOURCE: Adapted from Henry Mintzberg, "Managerial Work: Analysis from Observation," *Management Science* 18 (1971), pp. B97–B110.

Interpersonal roles
The activities of managers that involve performing symbolic duties; motivating, counseling, and supporting workers; and acting as liaisons to the larger firm and the outside world on behalf of employees.

Informational roles
The activities of managers that involve monitoring the activities of the business, disseminating information through reports and memos, and acting as spokespersons for the business.

Decisional roles
The activities of managers that involve making decisions about new products, handling disturbances in the business, allocating resources, and negotiating among persons with different points of view.

- **Interpersonal roles:** Here managers are expected to act like human beings with a full set of emotions. They are expected to perform symbolic duties like attending birthday parties and giving out employee awards; they are expected to motivate, counsel, and support employees, and they are expected to act as liaisons to the larger firm and outside world on behalf of employees. In the traditional view, these roles were all considered "leadership."

- **Informational roles:** Managers are expected to monitor the activities of the business, disseminate information through reports and memos, and act as a spokesperson for the business. In the traditional theories, these informational roles were poorly understood and subsumed under all categories.

- **Decisional roles:** Managers are, of course, supposed to make decisions. They are expected to make decisions about new products, which involves acting like entrepreneurs; to handle disturbances in the business; and to allocate resources by budgeting, scheduling, and setting priorities. Additionally, managers are expected to be able to negotiate among individuals with different points of view.

The behavioral perspective gives us a much more realistic and complex view of what managers do. The managerial role clearly involves much more than simply planning, organizing, leading, and controlling. Managers are also expected to nurture, care, inform, motivate, and decide.

MANAGERS AND INFORMATION

Actual studies of managers have found that they spend most of their time talking with other people—not analyzing statements, calculating results, or reading formal reports (see Figure 16.3). More than half of a manager's time is spent in meetings—in some businesses, this occupies 75 percent of a manager's time.[7]

What this means is that the vast majority of information that an executive takes in comes through the grapevine in the form of comments, opinions, gossip, and short stories. Only a very small part of a manager's total information comes through formal information systems or message systems.

To some extent, this situation is changing. Prior to the advent of business information systems, there were only manual systems of information collection and distribution. With the advent of computers, formal information systems, telecommunications systems such as electronic mail, subscriber databases like Compuserve, and presentation systems like electronic blackboards, information technology is playing a much larger role than in the past and will play a still larger role in the future.

THE REALISTIC SETTING: CULTURE, POLITICS, AND BUREAUCRACY

Complicating the behavioral picture described above, but making it even more realistic, are the features of business discussed in Chapter 2. To a large extent, managers are not free agents (see Figure 16.4). They must work within a given culture (certain basic business assumptions) and within a political environment in which other managers compete for limited resources. Furthermore, they must thoroughly understand the rules, regulations, and day-to-day procedures of how the business works (the bureaucracy) before they can accomplish their agendas. The following story gives some idea of the situation:

FIGURE 16.3

Managers and Information

Research on how managers obtain information shows that for the most part they get it from other people. A hefty 75 percent of a manager's time is spent in meetings—50 percent planned but 25 percent unplanned. Another 10 percent of the day is spent either making or receiving telephone calls, and 5 percent passes in clerical work. This leaves a scant 10 percent of a manager's time devoted to analysis: reading reports and research, making calculations, analyzing statements.

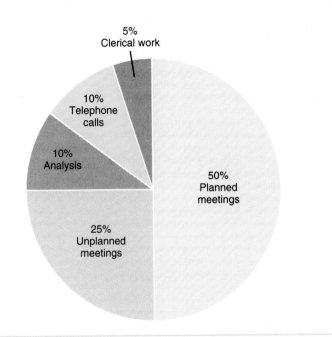

Ten years ago last summer, I resigned as an editor at *Fortune* magazine and went to work for Ford Motor Co. in Detroit. My new job was to communicate company positions on regulatory issues.

At the time I felt I was on a wonderful adventure of learning and personal fulfillment. In retrospect it was a shattering experience. At first I loved working at Ford because as a kid I was insecure and I wanted jobs that made me feel and appear important. At Ford I felt I was in the big time of world capitalism—I had finally hit the jackpot. I loved the view from my office, the panelling in the office, and the elegant Ford logo with its huge curving engraving.

I liked the people with whom I worked, but ultimately I could not take the politics of the office, the politics of the corporation. The corporation often took public positions not because it believed them but because they improved relationships with customers, suppliers, or competitors.

Inside the company there was a constant battle for turf control among the key players and their staffs. There was a tremendous amount of time spent advocating this position or that simply because it served some special group in the company. People often did not want to take responsibility for decisions. One person I know would reject papers from his staff that were too clear-cut and forced him to make a decision. This executive actually wanted to remain fuzzy on the issues rather than come to a decision.[8]

The behavioral view reminds us that managers ultimately are people.

FIGURE 16.4

A Realistic View of a Manager's Environment

Managers do not operate in a vacuum. They must deal with, and sometimes surmount, three factors within a firm. One is the company's culture, the framework of assumptions and acceptable behaviors that are expected of employees in general and managers in particular. Another is the company's politics, often arising from competition with other managers for valuable resources. A third factor is bureaucracy: the day-to-day rules and procedures governing the firm's operations. Any of these factors can affect a manager's ability to do the job.

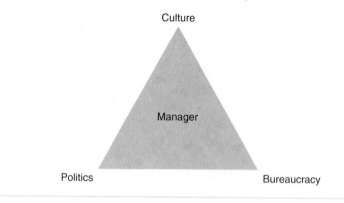

MANAGERS AND INFORMATION TECHNOLOGY

We can use the behavioral view of managers to get a good idea of how information technology might actually help managers. Table 16.2 relates the ten managerial roles to the actual use of information systems. As you can see, information technology is currently not very helpful in many managerial roles. For instance, there really are no information systems that directly assist a manager's figurehead or leader roles. Moreover, systems do not directly assist the manager as entrepreneur or negotiator (although certain decision support systems are helpful, as we describe later).

Nevertheless, in many areas information technology can be of direct assistance in the solution of management problems. The Focus on People illustrates how systems for coordinating and communicating can help executives on the go. Management information systems (described in the next section) directly help the manager monitor and control the business. This is a very powerful role. Decision support systems are central to a manager's decision-making roles and are especially helpful in allocating resources, as we will see in Section 16.4. In addition, recent DSS are being developed to handle crisis situations and to assist negotiators in selected situations. Executive support systems are beginning to affect how leaders actually perform their leadership roles and are being used to support the spokesperson function as well, as we will see in Section 16.5.

16.3 MANAGEMENT INFORMATION SYSTEMS

Management information systems (MIS) provide managers with reports on the firm's performance, both past and present. They serve the managers' informational role by helping to monitor actual business performance and predict future performance, thus per-

TABLE 16.2

How Information Systems Help Managers

Information technology can assist business managers in many, but not all, of the roles that Mintzberg defined. Management information systems (MIS) are helpful in the informational role, as managers assess a firm's performance and attempt to predict its future. An MIS can also help a manager handle conflicts or problems. A decision support system (DSS) can help clarify decisions regarding resource allocations. However, we do not yet have information technologies that directly assist other key managerial roles such as "figurehead," "leader," "entrepreneur," and "negotiator."

Role	Management Support Systems
Interpersonal roles	
Figurehead------------------------>	None exist
Leader----------------------------->	None exist
Liaison---------------------------->	Electronic communication systems
Informational roles	
Nerve center---------------------->	MIS
Disseminator----------------------->	Mail office systems
Spokesperson---------------------->	Office and professional systems Workstations
Decisional roles	
Entrepreneur---------------------->	None exist
Disturbance handler--------------->	MIS helpful
Resource allocator---------------->	DSS
Negotiator------------------------>	None exist

SOURCE: Adapted from Henry Mintzberg, "Managerial Work: Analysis from Observation," *Management Science* 18 (1971).

mitting managers to intervene when things are not going well; hence, they assist in controlling the business.

MIS are generally dependent on underlying transaction processing systems for their data. In other words, MIS summarize and report on the basic operations of the company. The system compresses the basic transaction data by summarization and presents

Computerized cash registers can capture daily sales data such as the quantity and type of product sold and the time of sale for use in management analysis and reporting. Well-designed management information systems can analyze this basic sales transaction data to determine profits, losses, sales trends, labor input, and inventory utilization.

SOURCE: © Bob Daemmrich, Stock, Boston.

FOCUS ON PEOPLE

SUPPORTING EXECUTIVES ON THE GO

If you've traveled by air recently, you've probably seen them—men and women who make five business calls, return three-page messages, and use their laptop computers to write eight memos and a sales report. They might even walk through the terminal and hail a cab without taking their cellular phones from their ears. They're called perpetual motion executives, or PMXs. PMXs travel a great deal and must perform their corporate executive duties on the road. To the deskbound, they seem incredibly productive. What are the special needs of this group? Let's look at two members.

As AT&T's managing director of consumer products, Harriet Donnelly travels worldwide to market her company's interactive network services and products. Each Monday she leaves her New Jersey home for the airport at 5:30 a.m. to travel to her other offices in California, Japan, or Europe. Once she arrives, she's in meetings all day,

returning to her hotel room around 9:00 or 10:00 p.m. Donnelly totes with her an NCR Safari 3170 notebook computer with a built-in fax modem, a SkyWord alphanumeric pager, and an AT&T cellular phone. The computer contains a personal organizer, E-mail software, a word processor, and a graphics package. The total equipment weight is only 6 pounds.

Arthur J. Marks, a general partner of New Enterprise Associates, a venture capital firm in San Francisco with investments in 16 companies, is on the road four of every five days visiting his companies. He carries a laptop computer, a cellular phone, and a pager. He uses fax machines in airline executive clubs and makes calls in airports and from airplanes. He also uses overnight mail a great deal. Marks emphasizes that Patricia Sutula, his secretary at his home office in Baltimore, Maryland, is central to his ability to work on the road because she directs his schedule, controls access to him, and makes many key decisions. They talk several times each day.

What are the technical problems of on-the-road management? Donnelly does not carry a lightweight printer—too many added pounds. When she needs hard copy, she makes a local phone call to the hotel and faxes the document to herself at the hotel's business center. Marks complains that current technology prevents him from receiving phone calls during a flight. Some executives find that to avoid untimely interruptions, they give their page telephone number only to immediate family members and to their secretaries. Many find that it is critical to find an appropriate hotel to support their needs. Marks tries to stay at hotels that have two telephone lines in his guest room so that he can talk on one line while using his modem or fax on the other. Most business travelers want hotels that have business centers that offer a range of technology, including faxes, printers, copying machines, and computers. However, executives on the road tend to work evenings as well as days and often find that the business center is closed for the night when they need it. Marks is irritated when his laptop battery runs low during a flight because planes offer no way to recharge batteries. Some travelers carry a spare battery with them (a solution Donnelly might find unacceptable).

FOCUS Question:

What other portable technology do you think would be helpful to support the work of mobile managers and executives?

SOURCES: Michael S. Malone, "Tethered to the Office Only by Technology," *The New York Times,* November 7, 1993, and Alison L. Sprout, "Saving Time Around the Clock," *Fortune,* Autumn 1993.

the information in long reports, which are usually produced on a regularly scheduled basis and answer structured, routine questions. Figure 16.5 shows how a typical MIS transforms raw data from transaction processing systems in order inventory, production, and accounting into MIS files. Managers can access the MIS files by using the MIS software.

Perhaps the best way to see how an MIS works is to look at a real-world, or in this case, a cookie world, MIS. As you read the following case study, ask yourself these questions: Where does an MIS obtain its data? What does it actually do with the data? What management and business problems does this system solve? What difference does the MIS make for the firm?

FIGURE 16.5

An MIS Helps Managers Access Transaction-Level Data

A management information system (MIS) provides routine summary reports on the firm's performance. Generally, an MIS obtains its data from the company's transaction processing systems, the systems that perform the firm's basic business procedures. As this diagram shows, raw transaction-level data from three functional areas—order inventory, production, and accounting—are funneled through each department's transaction processing system to be collected as data in MIS files. Managers can use the MIS software to access these data.

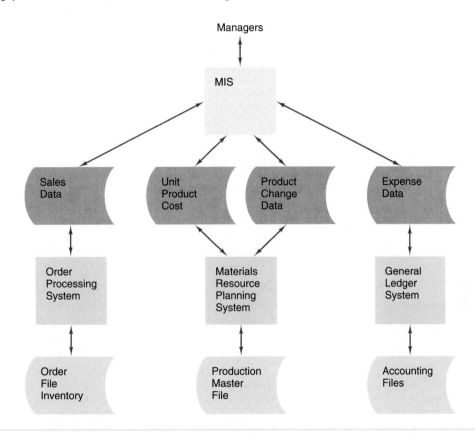

LEADING-EDGE APPLICATION: MRS. FIELDS COOKIES

Who would pay 75 cents for a cookie? Several million Americans, Europeans, and Japanese, that's who. When Debbie Fields started Mrs. Fields Cookies in 1984, no one expected her to make much money. Bankers turned her down, and she built the corporation one store at a time. By 1989, Mrs. Fields Cookies had gross revenues of $170 million.[9]

Each night after business closes, the managers of Mrs. Fields 500 cookie stores, 120 La Petite Boulangerie bakery-cafes, and 15 combination shops turn on their microcomputers, which automatically dial the company's headquarters in Park City, Utah, via an 800 number. The local managers have already loaded into a fixed corporate report form that records the day's transactions, including the following information:

- How many of each kind of cookie were sold.

- How many of each type were sold in each hour of the business day.

- How many workers were employed.

- How much inventory of what type is on hand.

- Time cards of employees who worked.

- New employee applications.

- How much money was deposited in the bank.

- Any other free text messages to Debbie Fields or her husband and manager, Randy Fields, who developed the system.

The information is rapidly uploaded via a local modem to headquarters, where it is stored on a minicomputer.

In the early morning at headquarters in Park City, a corporate manager called a store controller uses a microcomputer to call up the information from the 50 to 75 stores he or she monitors. The store controllers look for things like the following:

- Expected versus actual sales (exceptions from plan).

- Expected versus actual production.

- Expected versus actual labor costs per unit.

- Excess or insufficient inventory.

- Unexpected deviations from typical bank deposits.

The store controllers then intervene based on their analysis of sales and other data.

Through in-store information management, La Ruche Picarde, operators of Mammouth hypermarkets in France, ensures that perishables like fish are always fresh. Using NCR hardware, store and department managers have sales and inventory data available in any format that is needed to monitor business performance and predict future performance.

SOURCE: Courtesy of NCR Corporation.

The local store managers can request the central system to provide a production schedule, a labor force schedule (who should work when), skills testing of potential employees, inventory control (when to order new inventory and supplies), production tool parts and problem diagnosis, and even payroll. Each local store manager can decide which of these central services are desirable. The local managers retain control over hiring and firing and the mix of products to sell. Still, many managers prefer to have the central system take as much of the administrative burden as possible.

The philosophy upon which Randy Fields built the system was that financial accounting does not make the company any money—it just tells you how much money you made. What makes money is getting information from the field as fast as possible and changing to meet market demands. Fields also wanted to do away with as much paper as possible by putting all corporate forms on the computer. "Each paper form costs us 2 cents just to file at headquarters," notes Fields. Eliminating forms from the system has saved $700,000 each year.

The Fields realize now that they bet the future of their company on the MIS they call a Retail Operations Intelligence (ROI) System. In 1986 the Fields' operation almost collapsed; they had 135 stores and only 20 people at headquarters. The old sales tracking system required local store managers to keypunch in the daily sales data by using Touch-Tone phones. When Mrs. Fields Cookies expanded by adding 70 new stores in the Northeast, the new system was designed simply because the old one no longer worked.

The development of the MIS allows the company to monitor more stores with a reduced corporate staff. As Mrs. Fields Cookies expands into other retail food operations, the ROI system will be the backbone of the company. ROI has been so successful that Randy Fields has established a subsidiary, "Fields Software Group," to market the ROI system to other food retailers.

This case study is a leading-edge example of how personal computers, mini-computers, and telecommunications can be used to create a very powerful management information system. Let's go back and examine our list of questions, which should reveal a little more clearly just what an MIS actually does:

- **Where does an MIS obtain its data?** Like Mrs. Fields' ROI, most MIS obtain the raw data from transaction processing systems (TPS) like those described in Chapter 13. In the case of Mrs. Fields' MIS, the cash register captures sales data on time and type of product sold and summarizes this for inclusion into the local store's microcomputer.

- **What does an MIS actually do with the data?** Most MIS perform simple, repetitive summaries of transaction data and report exceptions or deviations from a plan. For instance, Mrs. Fields' MIS summarizes daily sales, labor input, and inventory use. In addition, the central headquarters has a plan that describes expected average output, cost, and inventory for each store. When a local store deviates from this corporate plan, central headquarters managers are alerted that something may be wrong. Thus, this exception or deviation report signals management that efforts may be needed to change local store procedures.

  But Mrs. Fields' ROI system is a leading-edge system, and it provides a good deal more than simple summary and exception reports. In many respects, it functions like a decision support system (described in Section 16.4) because it provides recommendations for production schedules, labor schedules, and the like.

- **What management and business problems does this system solve?** In general, MIS are good at handling routine, repetitive kinds of problems that are well structured—that is, for which there is an accepted methodology for arriving at an answer. For instance, in answer to the question, "How many people should I employ?" the Mrs. Fields' MIS can make a good estimate based on the number of predicted sales and the long historical experience that is captured in the system.

  The system would not handle less-structured problems, such as "Given that there has been a snow storm, that it is Christmas time with increased traffic indoors, and that there has been a large sales campaign for Mrs. Fields Cookies, what is an optimal hourly labor force for a specific store?" Answering these less-structured questions is more the province of sophisticated decision support systems, which are described in the next section.

  In general, from a management perspective, MIS are critical to the operational control of the business. Because such systems report and summarize basic transactions and compare them with a plan, they are vital in providing managers with the right information in a timely fashion. In the case of Mrs. Fields, the ROI system provides headquarters and central management with a bird's-eye view of how the company performs each day.

  From a business perspective, MIS help solve the problem of size by reducing coordination costs. As businesses grow and increase the scale of their operations, it is critical to achieve economies of scale. Ideally, as businesses grow, they should be able to make products more cheaply because they buy and sell in volume and have larger production runs. On the other hand, as Mrs. Fields found out with its old sales order system, coordination costs grow as the firm expands, and potentially they can prevent a business from reaping the benefits of large scale. MIS help reduce the costs of growth and make it possible for businesses to operate on a large scale with only minimal increases in coordination and management costs.

- **What difference does this MIS make for the firm?** Mrs. Fields' MIS really had strategic consequences for the firm because it permitted the company to expand from 160 stores to over 500 stores. Because the competition probably did not have such a powerful MIS, you could say that the MIS provided a temporary but important strategic competitive advantage. Furthermore, the MIS experience gained in building the ROI system has become a salable product and is being sold to other firms. In this sense, Mrs. Fields' MIS had a strategic consequence because it led to new products.

As we have seen, MIS are good at handling structured, repetitive problems; when a more interactive and flexible approach is desired, decision support systems, described in the next section, can be used.

16.4 INDIVIDUAL AND GROUP DECISION SUPPORT SYSTEMS

Although just about any computer that delivers information might be called a "decision support system," DSS are conceptually very different from MIS or TPS. Decision support systems (DSS) generally take less time and money to develop than MIS, are interactive in the sense that the user interacts with the data directly, and are useful for solving semistructured problems. As we noted earlier, a semistructured problem is one in which only parts of the problem have a clear-cut answer provided by a well-accepted methodology. Figure 16.6 summarizes major differences between an MIS and a DSS. Based on these characteristics, we can arrive at a working definition of a DSS: it is an interactive system under user control that provides data and models to support the discussion and solution of semistructured problems.

The generic DSS has three components. Figure 16.7 illustrates a DSS serving the same three business functions shown in Figure 16.5. The database of a DSS is a collection

FIGURE 16.6

Differences between an MIS and a DSS

Although these two concepts can overlap (see the example of Mrs. Fields Cookies), there are several basic differences. An MIS usually reports summaries of basic business transactions and notes exceptions from expected performance; its output is usually routine reports. It uses relatively simple analytical tools such as averages and summations to solve structured problems. A DSS, on the other hand, uses more sophisticated analytical and data modeling tools to solve semistructured problems. It provides data to support management decision making on issues that are less routine than those handled by an MIS.

MIS	DSS
• Reports summaries of basic transactions and exceptions from plan	• Provides data and models for decision making
• Uses simple analytical tools	• Uses sophisticated analysis and modeling tools
• Solves structured, repetitive problems	• Solves semi-structured problems
• Produces routine reports	• Provides interactive answers to nonroutine questions

FIGURE 16.7

Three Components of a DSS: Database, Model Base, and Easy-to-Use Software System

Here we see a DSS that serves the same three functional areas shown in Figure 16.5: order processing, production, and accounting/finance. Like an MIS, the DSS draws its data from the firm's transaction processing systems. However, the DSS model base contains much more sophisticated analytical and modeling tools than would be found in an MIS. The DSS software system allows users with little computer experience to access these data, often on-line.

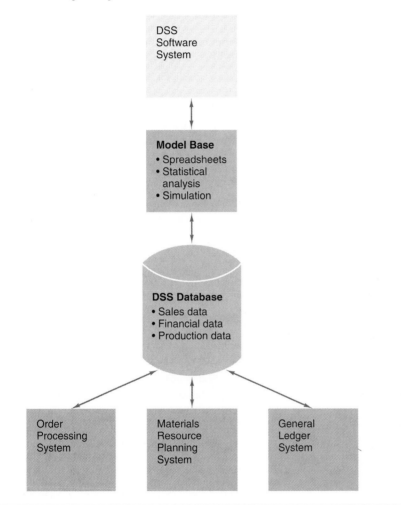

of information often taken from the firm's own internal transaction systems. Generally, this transaction information is summarized and transmitted to the DSS so that its database, unlike an MIS, contains data from inventory, production, and accounting.

A second element of a DSS is a **model base,** or the analytical tools used by the system. Perhaps this is the critical difference between an MIS and a DSS. As we noted in the preceding section, MIS generally have very simple analytical tools—averages, summations, deviations from plan, and the like. DSS, however, usually have very sophisticated analytical and modeling tools, such as built-in spreadsheets, statistical analysis, and simulation.

Model base

The analytical tools used by an information system; in a decision support system, it will include very sophisticated tools such as built-in spreadsheets, statistical analysis, and simulation.

The third element of a DSS is a software system that permits easy interaction between users of the system (who often have no computer expertise) and the database and model base.

The Focus on Problem Solving describes how DSS data analysis and presentation capabilities can help governments expose difficult to detect price collusion.

Distinguishing between an MIS and a DSS is not always easy. Generally, MIS produce routine reports on a batch basis with a regular schedule—every day, week, or month. DSS produce such reports, but they also permit the user to ask new and unanticipated questions and to intervene directly on-line to change the manner in which the data are presented. Sometimes, as illustrated in the following case, DSS have some MIS features. Once again, as you read the description of Redstone Advisors, keep the following questions in mind: Where does the DSS obtain its data? What does the DSS actually do with the data? What management and business problems does this system solve? What difference does the DSS make for the firm?

LEADING-EDGE APPLICATION: REDSTONE ADVISORS

Money management is a giant industry, with many firms each managing hundreds of millions or billions of dollars. Redstone Advisors manages $500 million in taxable and tax-exempt fixed income securities such as bonds. By the very nature of its work, money management requires the continuous collection and analysis of an enormous amount of data. Redstone must track a range of complex financial instruments and continually analyze both individual investments and overall market trends in swiftly changing markets.

Redstone managers hold monthly policy meetings to evaluate their company's investment strategy and determine its investment portfolio plan for the coming month. At these meetings, they set general guidelines for the managers, including establishing targets for the percentage of cash for portfolios and the weight of each business sector in the portfolio (for example, determining that 20 percent of their bonds should be in government treasury bills, 10 percent in tax-free municipals, 10 percent in banking bonds, 5 percent in mining company bonds, and so on). They also establish guidelines for the duration of the portfolios (that is, how many years out, on average, the bonds ought to go).

Once the policy meeting is completed, Redstone money managers make trades to bring their portfolios into line with the new guidelines for the coming month. The main task of the managers is first to identify appropriate financial instruments and then to determine if purchasing those instruments will bring their portfolios into accord with the new guidelines. To support them in this task, they use a software package called PORTIA.

PORTIA, a product of Thomson Financial Services of Boston and London, is a LAN-based portfolio management system. Traders use the system first as a decision support system and then as a system through which they can execute their trades. PORTIA is a DSS because it includes a simulation capability. Using this capability, traders first enter their proposed trades as if they were real trades. The system simulator treats them as real trades and evaluates the overall portfolio with these changes, thus giving the portfolio manager a preview of the proposed new portfolio. The manager then enters additional changes to attempt to bring the portfolio closer to the guidelines, and receives new feedback from PORTIA. This process is repeated iteratively until the manager is satisfied, at which point the remaining simulated trades are entered for real and actually executed. The portfolio's cash balances and holdings are also updated.

FOCUS ON PROBLEM SOLVING

DETECTING PRICE COLLUSION WITH A DSS

Price collusion and bid rigging are illegal in the United States, but such actions are secretive and detecting them can be difficult. Various state agencies have been finding the task a little easier with the help of information systems that detect subtle statistical relationships.

Price collusion usually leaves barely visible footprints but can often be spotted through careful statistical analysis. James McClave, president of Information Technology Co. (Info Tech), claims his collusion detection software uses 20 statistical tests to detect such activity. Patterns that lead to suspicion in supposedly competitive markets include:

- Market share that does not change significantly over time. In competitive markets, aggressive marketing and business practices cause fluctuations in market shares. Companies in bid-rigging cartels show much more stability.

- Product prices that do not vary significantly in relation to the distance of the supplier from the buyer.

- Long-term price stability. In a competitive market, prices tend to fall slowly over time as bidders become more competitive. In rigged markets, prices tend to remain stable or to rise.

- Bid prices that are clustered too closely together. For example, a bid of 14 cents per half-pint and another of 14.05 cents per half-pint are suspiciously close.

Collusion detection software finds patterns and displays them graphically. Analysts examine these patterns and draw conclusions wherever possible.

Info Tech got into the collusion-detection business in the late 1970s when the Florida attorney general asked the company to help develop an automated tool for spotting suspicious patterns in highway construction bidding. The tool, known as the Bid Analysis and Management System (BAMS), was successful and is now licensed by the American Association of State Highway and Transportation Officials to 30 state departments of transportation. Info Tech then went on to work with Florida officials to try to detect public school milk contract bid rigging. Until Info Tech's software was used, collusion over milk prices was not even suspected. Florida officials looked into public school milk only because it resembled other markets in which collusion thrives: a high dollar–volume commodity with a small number of suppliers and stable prices. After examining 18 months of school milk bid data, Info Tech uncovered annual losses to Florida of $33.5 million.

Statistical tests are not conclusive proof of price collusion. However, the evidence in the first milk case was strong enough that McClave relates that "within two weeks, they had witnesses talking." The federal government now uses the software and so far has obtained 43 milk price bid-rigging convictions and guilty pleas in 15 states.

FOCUS Question:
What features of DSS are illustrated by BAMS?

SOURCE: Gary H. Anthes, "Stat Tool Weeds Out Bid-Rigging Companies," *Computerworld,* July 5, 1993.

PORTIA has proven a popular product, currently being used by 1,000 firms to manage over $750 billion in assets. It is popular partially because of its simulation models. However, like many quality DSS, it also performs many functions found in an MIS system. It performs ongoing, routine analysis, including, in this case, determining for the Redstone traders the actual cash percentage, the weight by sector, and the portfolio duration. The system includes routine status and performance reporting. It also acts as a TPS, performing key order processing, including submission of buy and sell orders, electronic linkages to the brokers who will execute the orders, and automatic updating of the Redstone database once the orders have been completed. It even contains all the generic accounting that is standard to money management firms. Finally, PORTIA's value to money management firms is enhanced because it offers the broad functionality Redstone and many other portfolio managers require. For example, fixed-income security firms are interested in multicurrency capabilities because they often trade in foreign bonds, and this facility is a strength of PORTIA. Moreover, PORTIA is available in a Microsoft Windows version, making it easy for traders to use[10] (see Figure 16.8).

Now let's return to the questions we raised at the beginning of this case study by looking at the DSS capabilities of PORTIA:

- **Where does the DSS obtain its data?** In this case, the data come from a number of sources. Redstone must purchase daily market data from a data service such as Reuters or Dow Jones in order to be up-to-date in today's financial markets. Redstone is also the source of some of the data itself, such as the guidelines for evaluating the portfolios and the orders to buy and sell. Data also come from the systems of the brokerage firms that execute Redstone orders.

- **What does the DSS actually do with the data?** Routine reporting tools inform managers of the current value and composition of each portfolio as well as other analytical data Redstone requires. The DSS takes the current data and the simulation input from the trader and performs "what if" analysis and feedback. Managers can determine the effects of their proposed trades on the portfolio before actually entering the trades, and they can see the effects of various decisions on different currencies.

- **What management and business problems does this system solve?** The central management problem involves establishing monthly strategy guidelines to maximize returns on complex investments when market conditions are rapidly changing. The DSS gives Redstone's traders the ability to plan their trades in advance and to make trades that meet those guidelines. Through its on-line reporting capabilities, it also gives management the ability to monitor and control the activities of its portfolio managers and to measure performance.

- **What difference does the DSS make for the firm?** More than anything else, it allows management to manage their business the way they want despite the fast pace of the money management industry and the overwhelming amount of data the firm needs to handle. Senior management strategies can be executed and monitored. The system has other value in addition. Errors are reduced and productivity increased because of the automated links with the brokers and the accounting systems. In an industry in which changes are as rapid as they are in the financial markets, this system also offers traders speedy analysis as well as fast execution and reporting. A less tangible, although critical benefit provided by the system is its flexibility in international markets. Using PORTIA, Redstone and other firms can take advantage of the opportunities that are becoming available as the globalization of the world's economy continues.

FIGURE 16.8

A DSS for the Financial Industry

PORTIA is a portfolio management system that can be used to develop DSS for the financial services industry. Using PORTIA, money managers can simulate model portfolios under a variety of assumptions and currencies to guide their buying and selling decisions. This sample screen is used for creating reports.

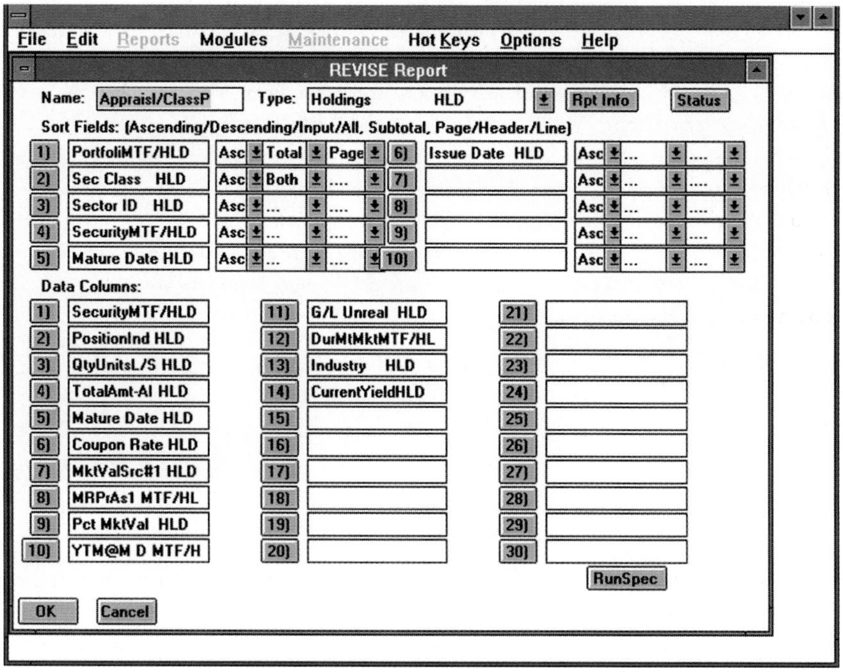

SOURCE: Courtesy of Thomas Financial Services.

GROUP DECISION SUPPORT SYSTEMS

DSS are primarily oriented toward the work of individuals. But many decisions are made by managers working together in groups. Special systems called **group decision support systems (GDSS)** have been developed to support managers. A GDSS is an interactive computer-based system to facilitate the solution of unstructured problems by a set of decision makers working together as a group.[11]

In recent years organizations have placed increased emphasis on group decision making. More and more meetings are held in order to broaden the expertise available for decision making and thereby to improve the quality of the decisions reached. But as meetings have multiplied, it has become clear that they can be both expensive and unproductive. New ways must be found to improve the group decision–making process in meetings.

Group decision support system (GDSS)

Interactive computer-based system to help a set of decision makers working together as a group solve unstructured problems.

Problems Posed by Group Meetings   Before considering how to assist and improve the group decision–making process, we need to be aware of problems that arise when people work together in meetings. Some of the main problems include:

- **Too many attendees.** Studies indicate that the optimal size of traditional meetings is between four and five individuals. As meetings grow larger, some attendees are unable to contribute. Others choose not to participate, preferring to be

Staff of the Ventana Corporation discuss the features of its GroupSystems for Windows meeting support software, which is designed to help teams work together for better and faster decisions. Participants interact through a network of PCs whenever and wherever they need to work together in meetings, between offices, across the country, or around the world. The software features special tools to help them create, share, record, organize, and evaluate ideas.

SOURCE: Courtesy of Ventana Corporation.

lost in the crowd (known as "free riding"). In larger meetings, one or two individuals can more easily dominate the discussion. The result is an expensive loss of time combined with a failure to elicit potentially valuable input.

- **Meeting atmospheres may not encourage individual participation.** Two related problems have emerged. First, many employees are hesitant to participate openly when their managers or others higher up the corporate ladder are present because they fear being judged. Second, many do not contribute their ideas for fear both their ideas and they personally will be criticized. The result, again, is an undesirable conformity and a fruitless attempt to engender new ideas.

- **Ideas may not be evaluated objectively.** Such fears are not unfounded. Too frequently ideas are evaluated on the basis of the source of the idea rather than on the merit of the idea itself. Moreover, in traditional meetings, it is standard practice to find reasons why a suggested line of action will not work rather than looking for ways to make it work. As a result, too many good ideas are rejected and too many poor ones are adopted. When setting priorities and making decisions, ways should be found to encompass the thinking of all the attendees and to evaluate input more objectively.

- **Meetings may be poorly documented.** Attendees often do not have the documentation they need to follow up on decisions made. Moreover, without adequate documentation organizational memory is lost—those who do not attend a specific meeting, such as staff at other sites, may not have the information they need to work on a project.

- **Too much time can be wasted arguing over facts or searching for information needed to make a decision.** The lack of availability of corporate and external information prevents factual disagreements from being settled quickly and thus makes meetings longer and less productive.

Characteristics of Group Decision Support Systems   Some of these problems can be solved by using group decision support systems. GDSS-guided meetings take place in conference rooms that contain special hardware and software tools to facilitate group decision making. The hardware includes computer and networking equipment, overhead projectors, and display screens. Special electronic meeting software can collect, rank, document, and store the ideas offered in a decision-making meeting. The more elaborate GDSS systems require a professional facilitator and support staff. The facilitator selects the software tools and helps to organize and run the meeting.

How GDSS Enhance Decision Making   A sophisticated GDSS will provide each attendee with a dedicated desktop computer under his or her individual control. No one will be able to see what individuals do on their computers until and unless they are ready to share the information, at which time they transmit it via a network to a central network server that makes the information available to all on the meeting network. Data can also be projected on a large screen or screens in the meeting room.

Let us look once again at the meeting problems listed above and see how GDSS contribute solutions.

- **Too many attendees.** Using GDSS hardware and software, meeting size can be increased significantly while at the same time productivity is increased because individuals can contribute simultaneously rather than one at a time. For example, during a brainstorming session, rather than going around the room and taking input one at a time from attendees, all prepare their input simultaneously and transmit the results to the group. The meeting can thus be both shorter and more productive. Studies indicate that GDSS meeting attendees believe the quality of participation in these meetings is much higher than in traditional meetings.

- **Meeting atmospheres may not encourage individual participation.** Using a GDSS, individuals contribute their ideas anonymously—when input is transmitted by an individual to the server, the source of the input is neither displayed nor even recorded, so that no one can determine who offered which ideas. In this way attendees do not need to fear criticism from their managers or be concerned that other attendees will criticize them rather than evaluate their ideas. Anonymity establishes an atmosphere in which even unconventional and novel ideas can and will be submitted, often to the benefit of the organization. Studies show that in this environment, not only are more ideas generated, but that the attendees are more satisfied with the ideas.

- **Ideas may not be evaluated objectively.** Again, anonymity prevents evaluating ideas based on their source and instead focuses attention on the ideas themselves. With a trained facilitator, attendees will also be asked to generate (again, anonymously) ideas on how to make the idea work rather than on why it won't work.

- **Meetings may be poorly documented.** All contributions, at each stage of the meeting, are transmitted to a network server that stores the data for future use by both attendees and others in the organization.

- **Too much time can be wasted arguing over facts or searching for information needed to make a decision.** In many GDSS meetings, the network is connected

COMPUTERS MAKE MEETINGS MORE PRODUCTIVE

Holding meetings is probably the most expensive and inefficient thing a company can do. Talkers drone on, daydreamers dream, and everyone leaves feeling nothing was accomplished. Yet the typical manager spends 35 to 70 percent of the day in meetings. Now electronic meeting software can help to make meetings more productive.

Typically, a computerized meeting begins with participants tapping out ideas for half an hour. As people write, their ideas appear on a large screen in the front of the meeting room. Participants then categorize and rank the anonymously contributed ideas. Participants can deal with issues and materials more rapidly than they could in a conventional meeting. For problems with issues that people like to discuss endlessly, computerized ranking is a way to quickly list and make priorities. The computer also helps meeting leaders stick to the agenda, because people tend to digress less with a keyboard than when they speak. Some computerized meetings let participants vote on issues secretly by using

numerical keypads connected to their terminals.

Jay Nunamaker, who studied and developed electronic meeting systems as a professor of MIS at the University of Arizona, points out that a typical hour-long meeting with 15 people allows each person an average of only 4 minutes to speak. In contrast, computerized meeting software gives everyone the potential to "speak" for 60 minutes. Nunamaker is also CEO of the Ventana Corp., which markets electronic meeting systems based on his work.

By using a computerized meeting room, the Boeing Corp. reduced the time required to complete a wide range of team projects by a remarkable 91 percent. In one case, a group of

SOURCES: David Kirkpatrick, "Here Comes the Payoff from PCs," *Fortune,* March 23, 1993, and William M. Bulkeley, "Computerizing Dull Meetings Is Touted As an Antidote to the Mouth That Bored," *The Wall Street Journal,* January 28, 1992.

to needed organizational databases in the same way as are individual DSS. In some cases, the network can be connected to external sources as well to aid in decision making.

GDSS are still relatively new and expensive. Their effectiveness depends heavily on how well the meeting is planned and conducted. Nonetheless, studies and the experiences of organizations described in the Focus on Organizations indicate that GDSS allow managers to be more productive and to use time more efficiently by producing the desired results in fewer meetings.

16.5 EXECUTIVE SUPPORT SYSTEMS

Special systems called executive support systems (ESS) have been developed to serve the information needs of managers at the highest organizational levels. They combine data from both internal and external sources to help senior management solve unstructured problems. ESS differ from MIS and DSS in several ways. Characteristically, ESS

- Are designed explicitly for the purposes of senior management.
- Are used by senior management without technical intermediaries.
- Require a greater proportion of information from outside the business.
- Contain both structured and unstructured data.
- Use state-of-the-art integrated graphics, text, and communications technology.

engineers, designers, machinists, and manufacturing managers used IBM's TeamFocus software (a version of Ventana's system) to design a standardized control system for complex machine tools in several plants. They completed the assignment with 15 electronic meetings in 35 days. Normally this project would take over a year. In another project, Boeing used Team-Focus to sharpen its identification of customer needs and to set a strategic direction. This process, which would normally have taken 6 weeks, was finished in two half-day electronic meetings. Boeing studied 64 meetings with 1,000 participants and found that computerization saved an average of $6,700 per meeting, mainly in employee time.

Other companies report similar results with electronic meeting software. When seven executives from one of Marriott's large Washington-area hotels participated in their first electronic meeting using VisionQuest, another type of electronic meeting software, they generated 139 ideas in only 25 minutes. Their challenge was to find new ways of improving guest satisfaction. They then rated each idea on a scale of one to five, first according to its likely effect on guests and then according to what each idea would probably cost. They emerged with a consensus that more thorough training of hotel employees was essential.

The financial firm of J. P. Morgan regularly uses its 13-seat electronic meeting room equipped with Team-Focus for meetings on strategic planning, organizational changes, auditing, and employee surveys. According to Lynn Reed, a vice-president in the firm's global technology and operations group, the software works best for meetings that last an hour or less and that are intended to achieve a group decision. Electronic meeting software is not useful for status-checking meetings in which each participant makes a report or for meetings with a single speaker.

FOCUS Question:
What people, organization, and technology factors would you consider when deciding whether to install an electronic meeting system?

One can think of ESS as generalized computing, telecommunications, and graphics systems that, like a zoom lens, can be focused quickly on detailed problems or retracted for a broad view of the company.

Contemporary ESS usually fall into one of three types. Some ESS focus on executive communications and office work. These systems begin by building powerful electronic mail networks and then expand outward to include new officelike functions, such as document processing, scheduling of executives' time, and so forth. A second type of ESS simply provides a more convenient interface to corporate data. Such systems deliver more business performance data faster than a typical MIS can and usually present the data in a graphic mode. A third type of ESS focuses on developing elaborate scenarios, applying sophisticated statistical models to company forecasts, and using other tools that are designed to expand a senior manager's ability to plan for the future.[12] Figure 16.9 shows a generic model for an ESS, which obtains data from the order processing, materials resource planning, and general ledger systems (transaction processing systems). In addition to these internal sources, data enter from external databases, are manipulated in the ESS database and model base, and are accessed through ESS software.

You might ask, "Haven't senior managers been using computers all along? Who uses all the MIS and DSS, not to mention the personal computers?" The answer to the first question is "no." Until very recently, senior managers generally did not believe it was appropriate for them to operate a keyboard, a skill they identified with clerical work. Senior managers generally left it to assistants and clerical workers to find and present data. Virtually all MIS and DSS are designed for corporate professional staff, both professional knowledge workers and middle managers. ESS are the only systems explicitly designed for senior executives.

In the next section, we present an example of a real-world ESS being used at Pratt & Whitney, a multibillion dollar subsidiary of United Technologies and a leading

FIGURE 16.9

An ESS Accesses Data from Both Internal and External Sources

An ESS (executive support system) is an information system geared to the needs of senior management. Since senior-level executives must plan long-term business strategies, they need to consider not only information from internal sources but data from external sources as well. Here we illustrate a generic ESS that includes a database and a model base. Its data come both from internal transaction processing systems and from outside databases (Dow Jones News or Dialog, perhaps). The ESS software uses integrated graphics, communications, and text to provide an easy-to-use interface for senior managers, who often have little experience with computers.

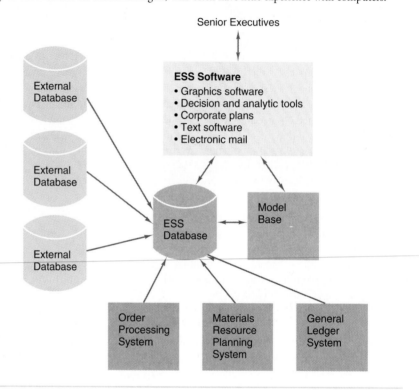

manufacturer of jet aircraft engines. They are headquartered in East Hartford, Connecticut. In response to growing market competition, executives at Pratt & Whitney's Commercial Engine Business (CEB) division recently developed a strategic plan to increase their market share by improving the quality of both their products and their customer service. As part of the implementation of that plan, they developed an ESS.

As you read about Pratt & Whitney, keep in mind our now-familiar questions: Where does the ESS obtain its data? What does the ESS actually do with the data? What management and business problems does this system solve? What difference does the system make for the firm?

LEADING-EDGE APPLICATION: PRATT & WHITNEY'S CEB EXECUTIVE SUPPORT SYSTEM

Pratt & Whitney's CEB management considers the quality of its customer service and the performance of its products as the heart of its business. CEB wanted software that would allow senior managers to monitor and analyze these critical success factors more closely. The software needed certain characteristics. First, it had to be interactive. Second, it needed to be heavily graphic so that senior managers could quickly and easily grasp the information presented. In addition, because senior management had not been significant users of computers, any system would have to be not only easy to learn, but one that could be learned intuitively rather than by instruction (corporate executives are not known for being willing to sit still for computer education). Finally, because Pratt & Whitney was changing from centralized mainframe computing to a networked desktop environment, the system needed to be flexible. Their new ESS had to handle cooperative processing so that tasks could be run on either a microcomputer or the larger host computer, depending on which was more suited to a particular task. They settled on Commander EIS software from Comshare.

The first system Pratt & Whitney decided to develop with Commander EIS was a system to track key quality and reliability measures of each jet engine model. The ESS drew data from three production systems and included such data as the reliability of each engine model, the availability of spare engines, and the availability of spare parts for each engine. This data could be examined either by engine model or by customer. The system also included data from customers, including such critical (to the customer) data as flight delays and cancellations due to engine problems. The system made available to senior management three types of information: product quality indicators, marketing information, and customer-specific information, including critical issues for each customer.

One of the users of the new system is Selwyn Berson, president of CEB. Berson and other executives can confirm the reliability of the engine models in operation and the status of engine orders for each of their customers. Senior executives can also respond to customer questions about new product and service delivery dates. They can discuss with customers not only current policy on engine quality but also the results of that policy by using information available on steps taken to improve engine reliability.

Executives are also able to track data by engine model number, determining how often the engines are brought into the shop and the sources of the problems. Thus, through the ESS, they are able to monitor engine performance and reliability over time. With this information quite literally at their fingertips, senior management can modify corporate plans and procedures to keep the new, two-track strategy on target.

In 1992 about 25 senior executives from various areas (including Human Resources and Finance) used the ESS. CEB executives predict that in time more than 200 executives and managers will use the system, and that its use will help highlight what is important to the whole organization so that all managers and executives will work toward a common goal.[13]

Now let's return to the questions we posed at the beginning of this case study:

- **Where does the ESS obtain its data?** The data are collected both internally and externally. Much of the data come from three existing production systems that carry data on product and part availability, repair records, and even customer service. The external data—maintenance issues and needs, flight delays and cancellations—come from customers.

- **What does the ESS actually do with the data?** The CEB ESS compresses and summarizes detailed data and presents them in a graphic format. This particular application provides little complex statistical analysis. Executives can examine the data to get more detailed information about specific customers or problems.

- **What management and business problems does this system solve?** By providing data on product quality and performance to senior managers, the new system helps the organization to identify problems at the highest level. Senior managers can easily see what areas of the business need immediate and long-term improvement and use this information to make organization-wide changes that are essential to the continuing success of the company. They have access to timely data on new engine and replacement part availability, reported engine problems and repairs, and customer service. Because data on company performance are directly available to them, without the technical assistance of others, senior managers have better control over the company.

The system addresses several key issues for management. Customer service should be improved because of management's new ability to be involved in and knowledgeable about this function. Moreover, by combining information specific to an individual customer with company-wide information about an engine model, customer relations is able to better understand and handle engine problems for individual customers. Senior management, in turn, can take a more strategic look at how customer support representatives can improve product availability. Management also believes that easy access to knowledge about how engine failure affects the customer's ability to fly should result in a heightened Pratt & Whitney sensitivity to the need to improve customer service.

The new system also gives management the ability to track, analyze, and ultimately deal with internal problems. They use the system to ensure that spare parts are always available. They monitor management of engines in the field. Through the information they access, they are able to assess engineering and research investments. They can determine engine problem trends, product or part shortages, even engine repair times. By accessing and analyzing such data, management will be able to identify problems earlier and deal with them more quickly and effectively than in the past. In addition, they expect to be able to plan better for the future.

- **What difference does the ESS make for the firm?** Walt Dempsey, from CEB's Business Management and Planning department and a strong supporter of the new ESS, believes it has created an organizational focus and alignment within the company that encourages executives to work toward common goals. He thinks that all functions within CEB will demonstrate an increased ability to contribute to the company's profitability by giving everyone better insight into what the company does and why they do the way they do. He expects the various departments to identify business processes that need changing so that the company can better serve its customers.

16.6 THE CHALLENGE OF BUILDING MANAGEMENT SUPPORT SYSTEMS

As this chapter suggests, building information systems that adequately support what managers do is a complex matter. To illustrate this complexity, it might be useful to contrast building a management support system (MSS) with building a bridge across a river—a typical civil engineering project. In the case of the bridge, landmasses evolve slowly over centuries and can be counted on not to change much. The materials and technology of building generally do not change within a decade or so. Demand for the bridge's services is more difficult to predict, but in the short term of, say, 5 years, demand can be predicted with some accuracy.

None of these features obtain for MSS. What managers want in terms of information can change radically in a few months. The technology can easily change within

2 years. Actual demand for service can mushroom or plummet in a short span, depending on the utility of the system and environmental demands.

Rather than thinking of MSS as civil engineering projects, it may be more useful to think in terms of living entities like gardens. The problem is how to build an information system that, like a garden, will be adaptable to changing weather patterns, productive, and easy to work with.[14] Here we briefly describe some of the people, organizational, and technology challenges that firms face in building robust, adaptable MSS.

PEOPLE CHALLENGES

One challenge in building an MSS is finding out exactly what kinds of information managers really want and need. You might think that managers could easily identify the information they need, but this has proved not to be so. In different situations, different information is needed. Some information is constant, but as situations change, the information needs also change. To some extent, this challenge can be solved by developing systems in an evolutionary manner over long periods of time.

A second people challenge is presented by the many different levels of computer skills in the business, which make it difficult for system builders to know what kinds of skills users have. As more and more management students learn computer skills in college, MSS can become more sophisticated. In the future, system builders will be able to assume that users are computer literate.

ORGANIZATIONAL CHALLENGES

We have said little in this chapter about costs. A system like Pratt & Whitney's ESS, however, can easily cost a million dollars over its lifetime of approximately 5 years. It is difficult to determine the lifetimes of systems because they change so much over time. Managers did not cost justify the system—they simply built it because they believed they needed it. But not all business organizations can afford this attitude. In any event, the question arises, "Are these expenditures worth it?" Answers are difficult to find because the benefits of these systems are intangible; that is, they cannot be given a precise monetary value. For instance, it is hard to place a dollar value on "more rapid decision making." Nor can "faster response to customers" be quantified.

A second organizational challenge presented by MSS is that a significant amount of organizational change may be required before a firm can build and install an MSS. It may be necessary to redesign the business before the computer databases can be integrated into a system like Pratt & Whitney's ESS. Various departments may use different definitions of the fiscal year, may have different measures of success, and may not want to share their data with other organizational units.

TECHNOLOGY CHALLENGES

Perhaps the most difficult technological challenge in building an MSS is establishing compatibility with existing systems in the business (see the Focus on Technology). When you want to build a new capability such as an ESS, you always have the problem of establishing compatibility with existing systems. In the case of Mrs. Fields' MIS, this was not a problem because the entire transaction reporting system was redesigned. In larger companies, this is not possible.

ACCESSING DATA THROUGH ESS

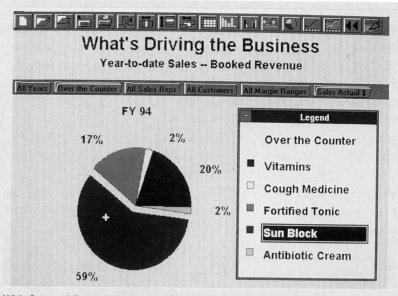

With Cognos' PowerPlay Business Intelligence software, managers can probe and explore data in graphical or numerical format, producing key reports on factors that drive the business.

SOURCE: Courtesy of Cognos.

The use of ESS (executive support systems) is growing rapidly. Sales of microcomputer-based ESS, which were about $5 million in 1985, reached $125 million in 1992 and are projected to top $325 million in 1996. Two reasons account for their growing popularity. First, they combine disparate data that are stored in separate systems, often on separate computers. Joining such diverse data as customer, sales, marketing, and product information has obvious value to the analyst and strategic planner. Second, ESS display the data in easy-to-understand graphic formats. While these systems were developed for executives, they are becoming popular with others who can benefit from their special facilities.

The growth in power of desktop computers combined with client/server computing have made ESS technically feasible. Desktop computers now provide individual users with powerful data analysis packages that also contain rich graphics features that can easily communicate the messages culled from the data. Meanwhile, client/server technology has made possible the collection of disparate data from mainframes, minicomputers, and other microcomputers, allowing the analyst to access and combine previously unconnected data. The largest technical challenge slowing the growth of ESS, according to Howard Dresner, an analyst with the Gartner Group in Stamford, Connecticut, is that of data

preparation. Locating the needed data, making sense of them, and relating them to data in other databases is difficult and time consuming. Additional problems arise when system-builders try to actually access the needed data and make them available to the ESS. This last problem has two aspects: security and compatibility.

Cort Jacobsen, a vice-president in Chemical Bank's securities trading department, is concerned about the security of his production data (the data that are actually used for ongoing operations). He fears that allowing analysts to query active trading databases would slow database operations and delay the posting of critical market information. Others are concerned that access to production data by people not authorized to update these systems could result in the corruption of that data. Charles Smith, general manager of a beer distributor in Kingston,

Massachusetts, has firsthand experience with the second problem, compatibility. His ESS uses LightShip (Pilot Software, Boston, Massachusetts), a general package that does not recognize the data format of VIP Beverages, the industry-specific database management software (DBMS) his company uses; LightShip simply cannot read data stored in the VIP Beverage database.

Smith solved his problem with a program that extracts the needed data from VIP Beverage, converts it to a file format for microcomputer DBMS that LightShip can read, and then stores the data in a desktop computer. By using this approach, known as data-staging, data are extracted periodically from the production database and stored in an intermediate database that can be accessed by ESS. Data-staging is growing in popularity not only because it makes separate systems compatible but because it allows increased secu-

SOURCE: Randall D. Cronk, "EISes Mine Your Data," *Byte,* June 1993.

Headcount Analysis by Job Type
Corporate Headcount
Divisional Headcount
Note shift in Admin Managers to Divisions

| YEARS | DIVISIONS | FUNCTIONS | JOB TYPES | CLASSES | Measures |

ADMIN MANAGER   Layer 2/11

| HEADS | Jan 94 | Feb 94 | Mar 94 | Apr 94 | May 94 | Jun 94 | Jul 94 | Aug 94 | Sep 94 | Oct 94 | Nov 94 | Dec 94 |

Cognos' PowerPlay Business Intelligence software makes it possible for managers and executives to quickly understand what's happening in their area of responsibility.

SOURCE: Courtesy of Cognos.

rity. Jacobsen at Chemical adopted data-staging to protect the integrity and functionality of his trading database. ESS users seldom need up-to-the-minute data—after all, their work is more strategic. Using data-extract programs, ESS databases can be updated weekly, or nightly if necessary. ESS users then submit their queries against the ESS database rather than against the production database.

When disparate data are needed, extraction programs are developed for each type of source. Using client/server technology, the data from the various sources are then collected on one server and often combined in a single database. The users of the ESS use computers that are joined to the network as clients, giving their ESS software full access to all the data stored on the server. With current graphical user interfaces, users find the access easy and do not need to be familiar with the complex preparations that are required to make the data available.

Both Smith and Jacobsen needed to have their IS departments build workaround programs (programs that will "work around" the problem) to extract the data into an ESS database. However, the developers of ESS software are becoming increasingly aware of this problem. More ESS vendors are including with their software "data providers" that will extract data from a wide range of database formats so that purchasers do not have to write their own workarounds. This technical/marketing development is one of the reasons for the increasing popularity of ESS.

FOCUS Questions:
What problems arise when providing data from ESS? How effective are the solutions described here?

This Year's Best Sellers
Top 5 Products Worldwide ($000's)
Highlighting on Net Change (+/-)

	This Year Sales	This Year Rank	Last Year Sales	This Year Rank	Net Change (+/-)
Vitamins	$45,747	1	$49,896	1	($4,149)
Multi-Vitamins	$44,241	2	$47,102	2	($2,861)
HiLife Adult	$39,081	3	$8,324	4	$30,757
Prolog Regular	$16,622	4	$9,958	3	$6,664
HiLife Liquid	$10,614	5	$1,890	8	$8,724

Managers must be able to easily navigate the data representing their organization, quickly distinguishing or separating each entity and its impact on the bottom line.

SOURCE: Courtesy of Cognos.

A second technology challenge concerns obsolescence. In the few years that the concept of ESS has existed, specialized software and hardware companies have sprung up to provide answers. Many software firms now offer executive support and MIS software products to help solve these problems. For example, Commander EIS, an ESS software package, incorporates internal and external databases; it also allows the information to be tailored to each executive's needs and offers powerful graphics along with touch-screen reporting (for executives who are reluctant to use a keyboard). Essentially, such products promise to do much of the work for you: they will help you to determine what information executives need to see, how to train them, and how to operate the systems in diverse machine environments.

One problem facing businesses is whether to be a leader or a follower. If you are a leader, you will have the capability first but will suffer the disadvantage of having to develop it yourself at great cost. Moreover, whatever you build will be rapidly outdated. If you are a follower, you can adopt commercial off-the-shelf solutions at a lower cost. As a follower, however, you will have the capability last and perhaps not find all that you want on the shelf.

RUNNING CASE PART 4

MACY'S STAGES A COMEBACK

Macy's new chief executive officer, Myron E. Ullman III, came up with a new five-year plan designed to put Macy's back on track. The plan aimed at cutting operating expenses from 37 percent to 32 percent of sales. Macy's would slash its advertising budget and stage fewer one-day sales to focus on frequent promotions and more attention to its frequent credit-card users. It would scale back on private-label goods and stock more name brands. It would increase customer service in departments such as designer apparel and luggage, while cutting back in areas such as junior sportswear. With sharper merchandising, more focused customer service, and closer attention to costs, the Macy's plan was designed to restore profits as the store gradually increased sales.

To stock and distribute merchandise more efficiently, Macy's installed a new computerized inventory management system called BPS, for buying, planning, and selling, that was developed by Federated Department Stores, Inc. (Federated's chains include Bloomingdale's, Stern's, and Burdines.) The system uses a point-of-sale system to capture data about what is actually sold at the checkout counter. The data captured at the point of sale are then transmitted to a central computer. At the end of each day the central computer sends the data to 100 national planners assigned to various product groups, such as men's apparel. The planners examine the sales data on their computer screens to determine what is selling and where. Armed with this information, they call store managers to investigate what's behind the numbers, and they instruct Macy's national buyers to ship specific items to specific stores. The planners also advise each store how much of each item to stock.

For example, when national planner Patti McCluskey found sales data showing a strong demand for knit shirts at the Macy's in Bridgewater, New Jersey, she notified Mark Owens, the men's apparel buyer, to allocate more knits and twills to that store. She also called Neal Goldberg, the Bridgewater store manager, and found out that the store's clientele favored golf. She then called Owens again to suggest other ways to increase sales, such as sending the store more V-necked tennis sweaters (customers who play golf at country clubs are likely to play tennis as well).

The new system increases Macy's chances of selling more and making those sales more profitable. In 1992, 46 percent of Macy's customers who shopped at the store left without buying anything, and 56 percent of them left empty-handed because the store did not have what they came in to purchase. After the new plan and system were implemented, a similar survey showed that only 23 percent of shoppers left Macy's without making a purchase and that only 29 percent of them could not find what they wanted.

Under this new system, Macy's has increased its business 15 percent on 25 percent less inventory. Although the system added 100 national planners, it cut the number of buyers from 425 to 180. With a direct computer link between Macy's and key suppliers, orders that used to take up to seven weeks to fill can now be completed within nine days.

Macy's is also developing information systems to support a more democratic company culture, in which employees are encouraged to learn as much as they can and to share their ideas with management. A new satellite network connects suppliers with salespeople in stores. Fashion designer Donna Karan can stage a teleconference with Macy's sales staff on how to best coordinate her clothing and accessories for the customer and answer sales staff questions. The network also lets Macy's executives brief employees on store performance, sales promotions, or other issues. Macy's is also planning to launch a 24-hour home shopping cable television channel that could bring in $250 million in sales within four years at a startup cost of $50 million.

Some critics wonder whether the new plan is enough to solidly turn the tide for Macy's. Getting employees to accept new computers and new ways of doing business takes years. Some store managers and buyers resent giving up some of their decision making to the national planners. Macy's needs to see whether it can recapture sales in the mid-price range, a segment of the business it neglected in the 1980s, without losing its pizzazz and upscale fashion image. The public needs to be convinced that Macy's is the place to shop once again.

As Macy's emerged from bankruptcy protection, its top executives agreed to merge with Federated Department Stores, Inc., Macy's longtime rival. Federated acquired a portion of Macy's debt and put forth its own reorganization plan for Macy's. The Federated plan would merge the two retail giants to create the largest department store retail chain in the United States. The combined company would have enormous clout in dealing with suppliers, but probably would accelerate the closing of weak stores. Wall Street, creditors, customers, and employees are closely watching Macy's to see how successfully it fares under this new management.

SOURCES: Stephanie Strom, "Macy Executives Approve Merger with Federated," *The New York Times*, July 14, 1994 and "Courting Analysts, Macy Looks Beyond Bankruptcy," *The New York Times*, June 2, 1994; Susan Caminiti, "A High-Priced Game of Catch-Up," *Fortune*, September 6, 1993; and Stephanie Strom, "A Key for a Macy Comeback," *The New York Times*, November 1, 1992.

RUNNING CASE Questions

1. How did Macy's try to solve its problems? What were the people, organizational, and technological dimensions of its solution?

2. How successful was Macy's solution? What recommendations would you make?

3. How important were Macy's new information systems to solving its problems? What kinds of problems could these systems solve for Macy's? What problems couldn't be solved by these systems?

SUMMARY

- The three major types of management support systems (MSS) found in business firms are MIS, DSS, and ESS. These systems serve different groups and interests in the firm. In order to understand how these systems work, you need to know something about what managers do.

- In the traditional view, managers plan, organize, lead, and control.

- In the contemporary behavioral view, managers perform three major types of roles: interpersonal, informational, and decisional.

- Managers receive most of their information from group and interpersonal, informal communications. But the information they receive from formal systems can be decisive.

- Information systems can be of most help in decisional and informational roles.

- MIS (management information systems) are routine reporting systems used to monitor and control businesses.

- DSS (decision support systems) are interactive systems under user control that are used in solving semistructured problems. A DSS has three components: a database, a model base, and an easy-to-use software system.

- GDSS (group decision support systems) facilitate the solution of unstructured problems for decision makers working together as a group.

- ESS (executive support systems) are graphics-oriented systems designed for senior management that provide generalized computing and telecommunication facilities for monitoring and controlling a business.

- Builders of MSS have discovered that determining exactly what information managers want in MSS is not always easy and that the skills of managers change rapidly.

- Businesses may have to reorganize themselves before they can build powerful MSS. Moreover, the benefits of MSS are difficult to quantify.

- It is difficult for businesses to develop new MSS that are compatible with existing systems. Early innovators in MSS find their systems can become obsolete unless substantial investments are made in technology.

KEY TERMS

Management information systems (MIS)

Decision support systems (DSS)

Semistructured problem

Structured problem

Executive support systems (ESS)

Traditional theories of management

Managing

Behavioral theories of management

Interpersonal roles

Informational roles

Decisional roles

Model base

Group decision support system (GDSS)

REVIEW QUESTIONS

1. What is the traditional view of management? What are the major functions of management?

2. How do behavioral descriptions of management differ from traditional views?

3. What are the behavioral characteristics of modern management?

4. What are the three categories of management roles discovered by behavioral scientists?

5. In which of these roles can information technology make an important contribution? In which role is the contribution of information technology not large?

6. What can managers do to change corporate culture, politics, and bureaucracy?

7. What is a management information system? Where does it get its information, what does it do to that information, and what difference does it make for the firm?

8. What is a decision support system? How does it differ from an MIS?

9. What is a group decision support system (GDSS)? How does it differ from a DSS?

10. Describe several problems that GDSS can help solve.

11. What is an executive support system? How does it differ from an MIS and a DSS?

12. List and briefly describe three challenges to building management support systems.

DISCUSSION QUESTIONS

1.   Your boss has asked you to come up with some alternative ideas about how computers can be used to support the decision-making needs of top management. What kinds of systems would you recommend? Which would you recommend first?

2.   How will hiring a large number of computer-literate, recent college graduates affect the use of systems in a business firm?

3.   In what ways could a management support system of any kind help a manager perform his or her leadership roles?

PROBLEM-SOLVING EXERCISES

1.   *Group exercise:* Divide the class into groups. Have each group find a description of a senior manager of a corporation in *Business Week, Forbes, Fortune,* or other business magazines. Have each group write a description of the kinds of decisions the manager has to make and suggest an executive support system or a decision support system that might be useful for this executive. Encourage each group to draw a diagram of its proposed system and present its finding to the class.

2.   Interview a manager at a local business or corporation. Write an analysis of his or her daily activities and the information required for these activities. What information systems does the manager currently use? What additional information systems would you suggest to help the manager with his or her work?

3.   *Hands-on exercise:* Prime Plastics is a small manufacturer of plastic parts used to package medical supplies. The following income statement shows its income, expenses, and net profit for 1994. (The net profit can be calculated by subtracting the firm's total expenses from total income.) Prime's management would like to find the impact on profits if the company could increase sales by 10 percent a year while limiting increases in

expenditures to only 5 percent a year. (Income from interest would remain the same each year.) Use appropriate software to develop an application that would project Prime's income, expenditures, and profits for the next 3 years.

Prime Plastics Income Statement: Year Ending 12/31/94

Income	
Sales	$1,300,000
Interest	110,000
Total income	$1,410,000
Expenses:	
Operating expenses	$490,000
Wages	450,000
Taxes	210,000
Total expenses	$1,150,000
Net Profit	$260,000

NOTES

1. James A. Stoner and Charles Wankel, *Management,* 3d ed. (Englewood Cliffs, N.J.: Prentice-Hall, 1986).

2. Peter F. Drucker, *Management: Tasks, Responsibilities, Practices* (New York: Harper & Row, 1974).

3. For an excellent contemporary introduction to management, see Richard L. Draft, *Management,* 3rd ed. (Fort Worth, Texas: Dryden Press, 1994)

4. John T. Kotter, "What Effective General Managers Really Do," *Harvard Business Review* (November-December 1982).

5. Henry Mintzberg, "Managerial Work: Analysis from Observation," *Management Science* 18 (October 1971). See also Kotter, "What Managers Do."

6. Kotter, "What Managers Do."

7. Margrethe Olson, "Manager or Technician? The Nature of the Information Systems Manager's Job," *MIS Quarterly* (December 1981).

8. Paul Weaver, "Life among Motown's Machiavellis," *The New York Times,* October 2, 1988. See also Paul Weaver, *The Suicidal Corporation.*

9. "MIS Holds Together a Crumbling Cookie," *InformationWEEK,* March 13, 1989 and Paula Klein, "New Fields? Park City's Ready," *InformationWEEK,* November 5, 1993.

10. Karen Corcell, "Portia Keeps The Faith," *Wall Street and Technology* 11, no. 11 (March 1994); "Fixed Income Money Manager Boosts Efficiency with Flexible, Comprehensive System," *Wall Street and Technology* 10, no. 9 (April 1993); Sheila O'Henry, "The Portfolio Management and Accounting Supermarket," *Wall Street and Technology* 11, no. 5 (November 1993).

11. Geraldine DeSanctis, and R. Brent Gallupe, "A Foundation for the Study of Group Decision Support Systems," *Management Science* 33, no. 5 (May 1987).

12. John F. Rockart, "Executive Support Systems and the Nature of Executive Work," working paper, Management in the 1990s Project, CISR WP #135 (MIT Sloan School, April 1986).

13. "The New Role for Executive Information Systems," *I/S Analyzer,* January 1992.

14. Kenneth C. Laudon and Jane P. Laudon, "How You Can Manage Very Large Scale System Projects," National Science Foundation working paper (New York University Center for Research on Information Systems, April 1989). See also Omar A. El Sawy and Burt Nanus, "Toward the Design of Robust Information Systems," *Journal of Management Information Systems* 5:4 (Spring 1989).

PROBLEM -SOLVING CASE

MANAGING PROFITABILITY FOR THE LONG HAUL

The $160 billion U.S. trucking industry is dominated by companies whose business strategy focuses on becoming the "core carrier" for a steadfast group of large shippers.

The theory is that stable, reliable relationships mean stable, reliable business, which in turn translates into steady profits. Many of these companies obtain 20 to 30 percent of their revenue from just one company. Only independent truckers rely on the "spot market," picking up jobs as they go, usually by relying on brokers who supply spot customers for a fee. OTR Express, Inc., of Olathe, Kansas, is a maverick that follows a strategy similar to that of independent truckers, but without using the brokers. In the process it has found both its business and its profits steadily increasing. In order to succeed, Bill Ward, the founder and head of OTR and a former programmer, relies heavily on information technology. Ward looked at industry practices and noticed that being the core carrier for a large shipper often means driving an empty truck one way in order to carry a load from one of its core customers to a location where there is no return load. These trucking firms average 12 percent empty (nonrevenue) runs. They maintain the loyalty of the large shippers by guaranteeing the availability of a truck for pickup, which forces them to own and maintain extra rigs to meet this guarantee. By relying on the spot market of intermittent shippers rather than regular shippers, Ward has managed to reduce his nonrevenue runs to about 6 percent. In addition, because he makes no commitments in advance, he does not need to own or maintain extra equipment.

Critics claim that trucking firms cannot survive through the spot market. How then does 6-year-old OTR do it? The key is a database of past and potential intermittent customers. The concept is simple—when OTR knows it has a truck delivering in a specific area, dispatchers call potential customers in that area until a shipment is found. In this way, the truck leaves the area where the delivery is made with a new load to be delivered elsewhere. In addition, Ward considers his drivers to be managers. They can earn up to $50,000 per year, compared with an industry average of about $30,000. In exchange Ward expects his drivers to work efficiently, conserve fuel, and stay out of accidents (thus lowering OTR's insurance premiums). He also hires only experienced drivers.

Ward readily states that the key to success has been OTR's customer database and its reliance on information technology. "We attribute our success to software," Ward says. At the heart of the technology is a straightforward database of information on potential customers. To locate a customer in the region where a load will be dropped off, dispatchers scan the database. OTR has developed software that divides their shipping areas into 120 regions and enables the dispatchers to anticipate business in what otherwise appears to be a random spot market. The system prioritizes customers within each geographic region based on the likelihood that a potential customer will need their services and the possibility and profitability of a run for that customer. The software looks at freight carried for each customer

Road Star OTR Express is trucking more miles and making more money

	1992	1991	1990	1989	1988
Total miles	22,195	16,948	14,328	9,897	5,529
Revenue per mile	$.936	$.924	$.936	$.899	$.904
Miles per week per truck	2,247	2,271	2,333	2,247	2,314
Empty miles	6.1%	6.5%	6.2%	6.2%	6.9%
Miles per load	1,460	1,460	1,408	1,347	1,266

SOURCE: "In for the Long Haul: OTR Express's Customer and Fleet Systems Drive a Maverick Business Model," *InformationWEEK*, May 31, 1993.

within the past 30 days, and factors in the probable value of the next load, the type and destination of the load, the price of fuel, and other elements. The goal is not only to find a customer quickly but also to increase revenue potential by finding the best customers. Once potential customers in a region have been culled from the database and prioritized, the dispatcher begins calling from the top of the list until a load is found. Drivers call in to the voice mail system for their next assignment.

OTR uses 45 Macintosh microcomputers linked in a LAN to a Macintosh Quadra 950 file server plus several IBM-compatible microcomputers to run a program that calculates mileage between cities. OTR uses its networked Macintosh desktop computers and its two programmers for other tasks as well. As Ward expressed it, OTR has "an insatiable demand for information." They track such information as truck fuel economy and individual driver financial performance, offering truckers financial incentives based on the data. Their programmers have developed a system that calculates mileage between cities. OTR also uses fleet management software to track the location of all trucks in order to make certain the trucks are dispersed geographically in a way that will optimize OTR's ability to take advantage of the ever-changing freight market. The company's system determines if there are too many or too few trucks in a region, the profitability of shipments from a state or region, and the number of OTR trucks headed in that direction.

Communications technology has become very popular in the trucking industry. For example, a number of companies use the government's global positioning system (GPS) to keep track of the location of all trucks in their fleets. Other companies use such wireless technology as cellular phones to communicate directly with their truckers. OTR has rejected this technology for the immediate future. Ward does not see the GPS as cost-effective, saying, "We haven't automated just for the sake of automation." He will invest in cellular phone technology when the whole nation is covered. "Cellular phones aren't much use to us with the present gaps in coverage," he claims.

These strategies have paid off for OTR. Founded in 1988, the customer database has grown steadily, and results reflect that growth. Sales in 1992 were up 30 percent over 1991, and earnings increased during the same period by more than 400 percent to $546,000. At the same time, book value rose 38 percent.

SOURCE: Chuck Appelby, "In for the Long Haul," *InformationWEEK*, May 31, 1993.

CASE STUDY QUESTIONS

1.   What problems do each of the systems described in this case study solve?

2.   Classify each of these systems as MIS, DSS, ESS, or none of these types, and explain your classification for each system.

3.   Develop and show an example of a management report for one of the OTR systems.

4.   What useful information for a manager is provided by the chart illustrated here? How could the chart be modified to create a management report that might be even more valuable to OTR managers?

5.   Evaluate each of the OTR management systems described above and determine if they can be used for operational purposes, and if so, how and by whom.

⊹ ILLUSTRATED CASE ⊹

REENGINEERING CIGNA WITH TECHNOLOGY

Cigna Corporation is a giant insurance company with 1993 revenues of nearly $19 billion and 1994 earnings estimated at $5 per share. It has also been a company in trouble in recent years. More than half its revenue comes from its property/casualty and health care insurance business. The property/casualty (p/c) business has been losing money for a number of years, reaching a loss of more than $600 million in 1993. P/c expenses have been far too high for Cigna to be able to charge competitively and still cover its costs. Health care has been very profitable in past years, but these profits are seriously threatened by the massive health care changes that are coming in the United States. Both units urgently need to find ways to cut costs. As with many insurance companies, one area of huge

costs at Cigna has been paper handling—in both the sales and customer service functions.

Cigna actually started to address its problems in the late 1980s, when the corporation began to plan a new strategy and its IS group formed the Systems Re-Engineering Group. To support this strategy, Cigna built a new headquarters at Two Liberty Plaza, Philadelphia. Like most other large corporations over the past 30 years, Cigna had been automating its business functions without a companywide plan for integrating its systems and maximizing their efficiency. The inability to share information in this worldwide giant was a serious impediment to improved productivity. J. Raymond Caron, president of the Cigna systems division, saw the new headquarters

The insurance industry is very paper intensive. Cigna Corporation distributes and uses 35,000 different forms. Before converting to electronic forms, Cigna had to keep track of tens of millions of sheets of paper each year.

SOURCE: © Mel Lindstrom.

building as an opportunity to establish companywide standards. In the 58-story building, Cigna installed what IBM described as "the world's largest LAN under one roof," a fiber optics–based token-ring LAN that connects about 4,000 users. John Clark, the assistant director of Cigna's headquarters LAN team, claims that the new network has more power in MIPs (millions of instructions per second) than all three of Cigna's mainframe data centers combined.

This unique network is the centerpiece of CignaLink, Cigna's emerging worldwide network. With the building of CignaLink and the desire by business staff throughout the company to connect to that network, Caron has been able to begin enforcing new standards on the company for all new information systems development and new computer equipment purchases. The standards include IBM PS/2 micro-

computers as the desktop computer, DOS, OS/2, or Windows as the operating system, and IBM's LAN Server network operating system. Caron's standards also include WordPerfect as the standard word processor and Lotus 1-2-3 as the standard spreadsheet.

Through CignaLink the new headquarters building is linked to Cigna's other Philadelphia office buildings, including One Liberty Plaza, which houses Cigna's executive suite. It is also connected to Cigna's major data centers in Voorhees, New Jersey, Windsor, Connecticut, and Thornton, Colorado, using IBM's Systems Network Architecture (SNA), as well as to 1,500 other locations and 470 LANs within the country. Cigna installed an E-mail network on CignaLink using Microsoft's Network Courier domestically and General Electric Information Systems Company's E-mail network interna-

---

FIGURE 1

A Simplified View of CignaLink

Each office runs PCs over a token-ring network. The token rings "talk" to an IBM mainframe. The several mainframes are connected via an IBM SNA network using T1- and T3-grade leased telephone lines.

Anatomy of Cigna-Link

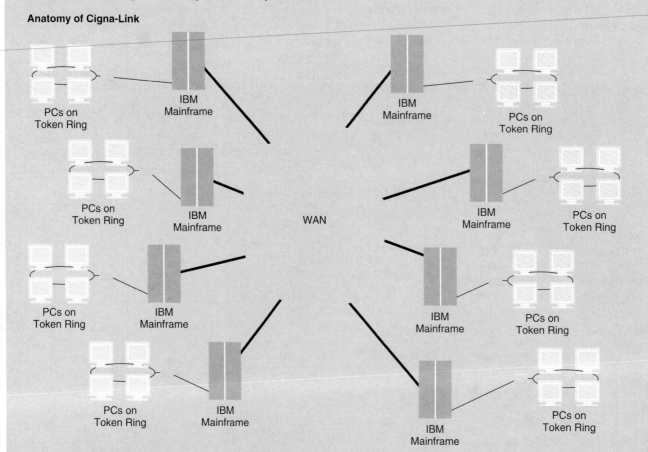

tionally. CignaLink runs 24 hours per day, as does its help-desk service. See Figure 1 for a high-level diagram of CignaLink.

The new network, and the standards that have accompanied it, have been used in a number of ways in the company to help reengineer the way it works. For example, CignaLink has allowed Cigna to move many applications from mainframes to a client/server architecture. Using this new technology, Cigna made available to its customer service staff previously isolated data from customer service, billing, claims, and other related systems. In the past, customer service representatives had to check with other departments, such as billing, to answer inquiries. Now customer service handles most customer calls directly, a major organizational change. During the first year the new organization and technology were in operation, customer service representatives were able to process 35 percent more inquiries than in the previous year, a dramatic

FIGURE 2

Traditional versus Electronic Forms Processing

Electronic forms make shorter work out of forms processing. For example, traditional typesetting and printing are unnecessary; physical distribution and storage are much more efficient; and centers that process the data on the forms do not have to rekey data from the paper-based form because the data retains its electronic format throughout the process.

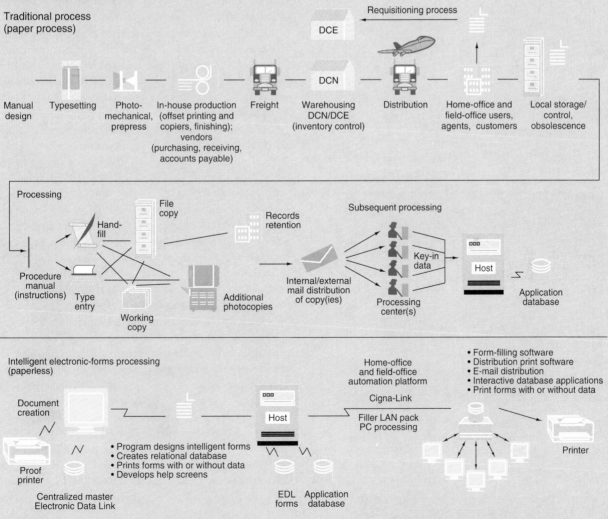

productivity improvement. At the same time, "first-call satisfaction" levels, which had hovered at around 75 percent, rose to greater than 90 percent, well above industry rates. Cigna expects these numbers to climb even higher after the installation of Windows-based software from Easel Corporation that allows the customer service representative to toggle instantly among the various systems.

Cigna's commitment to reengineering, the existence of new standards, and the operation of CignaLink changed the organization in a number of other ways, perhaps the most significant being the impact that is coming from its move to electronic forms. Cigna, through its agents and corporate clients, distributes and uses more than 35,000 different forms, representing tens of millions of sheets of paper per year. Printing, warehousing, and distributing these tens of millions of blank forms costs the company many millions of dollars every year. Once filled out, the forms then must be processed manually—a time-consuming and expensive serial process. They then must be warehoused, and, when needed, retrieved manually in a slow and expensive procedure. This is an enormous function in a large insurance company. The upper portion of Figure 2 illustrates the traditional paper handling process.

The move to electronic forms is radically revamping Cigna's workflow. With the new system, blank forms are designed and stored on the computer. Agents and customers print a copy only when needed, and the printing is done on the desktop printer of the individual who needs it. (See the lower portion of Figure 2.) Thus, separate printing, storage, and distribution costs are eliminated. A forms revision no longer results in an expensive scrapping of obsolete forms. Forms can be filled out on-line with automated routines for validating entries and with routing and tracking information, eliminating errors and the costly paper handling of completed documents (see Figure 3). Processing of these documents is sped up because they can be accessed on-line by anyone who needs them. Moreover, processors can access the same document simultaneously, eliminating most of the need to process serially.

The basic software Cigna used for this project is JetForm. JetForm-Design facilitates the creation of both a screen and a paper version of the documents. This software also includes the ability to transfer forms from one place to another automatically, a key facility given the scattered location of the form users. The newly created forms are automatically E-mailed to each site and installed onto each of the 25,000 target computers. JetForms-Filler enables a predesigned form to be filled in on-line, after which it is printed locally only if needed. JetForm for E-mail sends the completed electronic document through CignaLink to designated destinations. Such forms often need authorization signatures, and Cigna was dissatisfied with the security of JetForm's solution to the problem of automating signatures. However, JetForm and Cigna together worked out a way to use Microsoft Mail to give them the security they needed.

Cigna made the organizational changes to implement this system in several stages. First, Cigna phased in the number of electronic documents slowly, beginning with a pilot program of 120 forms. Second, the process itself was gradually phased in, as illustrated in Figure 4. Next, Cigna implemented design, information entry, and printing functions. Then, it installed the ability to E-mail the blank and filled-in forms. Finally, it eliminated the use of paper in the process by having each document stored in a database. The benefits of the whole project are described in Figure 4. By the end of 1993, Cigna had automated 1,800 forms and had fully rolled 30 of them out through all three phases of implementation. Cigna believes that it can save 80 percent of the cost of handling internal forms, saving millions of dollars through cost reductions.

FIGURE 3

Elements of an Electronic Form

An electronic form can help prevent errors by validating entries and save time by filling in parts of the form automatically. The form can also carry routing and tracking information.

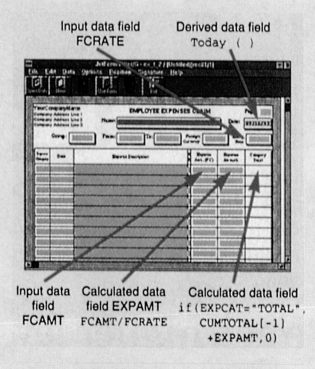

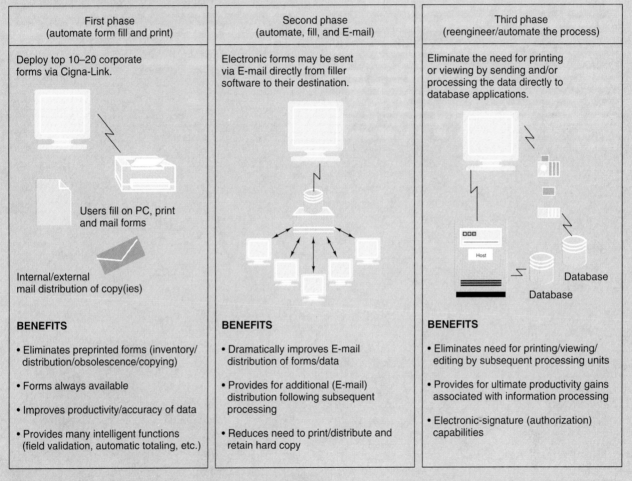

FIGURE 4

Cigna's Three-Phase Approach to Electronic Forms Adoption
The first phase transfers 10–20 forms onto PCs, where users fill them out, print them, and mail them through traditional mail. The second phase incorporates routing of the forms through E-mail. The third phase adds a data-processing component with electronic signatures and direct data transfer to database applications.

A Three-Phase Approach to Electronic Forms

First phase (automate form fill and print)	Second phase (automate, fill, and E-mail)	Third phase (reengineer/automate the process)
Deploy top 10–20 corporate forms via Cigna-Link.	Electronic forms may be sent via E-mail directly from filler software to their destination.	Eliminate the need for printing or viewing by sending and/or processing the data directly to database applications.
Users fill on PC, print and mail forms		
Internal/external mail distribution of copy(ies)		Database / Database

BENEFITS

First phase:
- Eliminates preprinted forms (inventory/distribution/obsolescence/copying)
- Forms always available
- Improves productivity/accuracy of data
- Provides many intelligent functions (field validation, automatic totaling, etc.)

Second phase:
- Dramatically improves E-mail distribution of forms/data
- Provides for additional (E-mail) distribution following subsequent processing
- Reduces need to print/distribute and retain hard copy

Third phase:
- Eliminates need for printing/viewing/editing by subsequent processing units
- Provides for ultimate productivity gains associated with information processing
- Electronic-signature (authorization) capabilities

It believes customer service will continue to improve, given the faster processing of forms and the ease of retrieval of electronic documents.

Both Cigna employees and outside observers stress that Cigna has been able to install this giant forms system and reengineer its organization for two reasons. First, the company had already established CignaLink, a single network link among all affected employees throughout the world, and second, Cigna had only one E-mail system running worldwide on CignaLink.

All is not coming up roses at Cigna despite these reengineering projects. Technology and reengineering cannot address all the issues negatively impacting Cigna profits. Wilson H. Taylor, Cigna's Chairman and Chief Executive, believes that part of the problem is the sheer size of Cigna. Much of the high cost, he believes, is related to Cigna's long-standing commitment to supplying a broad range of insurance services, and Cigna is now examining the possibility of getting out of some of its insurance lines altogether. Cigna can no longer be all things to all people.

The underlying problem is that the insurance market itself has changed. In the past, big corporate customers bought most or all of their insurance from one giant insurance company, such as Cigna. Today, a large number of small, specialty insurance providers are competing successfully with companies like Cigna in specific market niches. Because the costs of these smaller companies are lower and they are more agile than their larger counterparts, they are taking a great deal of business from Cigna and other insurance giants.

SOURCES: Chris Roush, "Cigna Seizes the Shears," *Business Week,* February 21, 1994; Thomas Hoffman, "Re-engineering Pays Off at Cigna," *Computerworld,* August 9, 1993; "Client/Server Setup Boosts Underwriter Productivity 25%," *Client/Server Journal,* August 11, 1993; Ben Smith and Howard Eglowstein, "In Good Electronic Form," *Byte,* November, 1993; Alan J. Ryan, "Cigna Re-engineers Itself," *Computerworld,* July 8, 1991; and Bob Violino, "Building a High-Tech Strategy," *InformationWeek,* December 2, 1991, and "Cigna Committed To New View Of IS," *InformationWeek,* October 26, 1992.

CASE QUESTIONS

1.   What human, organizational, and technological factors contributed to Cigna's problems?

2.   How did Cigna try to solve these problems? How successful was its solution?

3.   Describe and analyze the relationship between technology and organization in Cigna's reengineering project.

4.   Describe the ways CignaLink contributed to the changes at Cigna. List other ways you think the network will help this multinational insurance company.

Building Your Portfolio

Problem-solving exercises for portfolios are identified with a circuitry bar. Look for the circuitry bar in each chapter.

By using *Information Systems: A Problem-Solving Approach,* you developed valuable problem-solving skills that will help you excel in your future career and in your remaining courses in college. The projects and exercises in the text are very similar to the types of problems you are likely to encounter in your job. They can be used to create a structured portfolio demonstrating your mastery of analytical, writing, presentation, application development, and software skills that will be of great interest to prospective employers. Your portfolio also shows that you are meeting the American Assembly of Collegiate Schools of Business (AACSB) recommendation for skill building.

If you answered the case studies, worked through the problem-solving exercises (identified by a circuitry bar), and completed the solution design projects in Chapter 10, here are some of the skills and competencies you would be able to demonstrate:

Analytical, writing, and presentation skills: The group and individual problem-solving exercises and chapter case studies demonstrate that you can research a specific topic, analyze a problem, think creatively, suggest a solution, and prepare a clear written or oral presentation of your solution, working either individually or with others as a group.

Application development skills: The solution design exercises concluding Chapter 10 show employers that you can analyze a problem, design an application solution, and select appropriate software and hardware to implement the solution. These projects also demonstrate your skill in using spreadsheet or database software to implement the solution.

Software skills: The Hands-on exercises concluding each chapter demonstrate that you can select appropriate software to solve a problem and use your spreadsheet and database software skills to develop small real-world applications.

Keep your answers to the problem-solving exercises, solution design exercises, and case studies that you did for the course. You can then select the projects that you feel best demonstrate your capabilities and create a portfolio of your problem-solving and information systems skills to present with your résumé when you are job-hunting. Following are some of the projects in the text that might be of special interest to future employers:

1. Analytical, Writing, and Presentation Skills

Application	Chapter
Evaluating microcomputer software packages	11
Designing controls for a mainframe mortgage processing application	12
Developing Equal Opportunity Affairs compliance reports	13
Making recommendations for office automation and workflow redesign	14
Evaluating microcomputer operating system software	6
Developing a computer hardware recommendation plan	4
Designing a university database	7

Application	Chapter
Designing a network for an appliance retail chain	8
Analyzing business failures	9
Making recommendations for executive support systems	16

2. Application Development Skills

Skill	Chapter
Developing a marketing database for a video rental company	10
Developing a student housing referral database	10
Developing a DSS for estimating construction project costs	10

3. Software Skills

Application	Software Skill	Chapter
Sales commission projections	Spreadsheet	3
Portfolio planning	Spreadsheet	9
Income statement projections	Spreadsheet	16
Graphing incidence of production defects	Spreadsheet	13
Developing a personnel database	Database	2, 7
Employee skills inventory	Database	14
Waste management analysis	Database or spreadsheet	6
Bank loan credit authorization	Database or spreadsheet	15

You may find additional exercises and projects to include in your portfolio, It's up to you! You've worked hard, learned a great deal, and now have a portfolio to demonstrate what you have accomplished.

Glossary

Accountability The ability to trace actions to identify individuals responsible for making decisions to take those actions.

Accounts payable systems Accounting systems that keep track of amounts owed by a firm to its creditors.

Accounts receivable systems Accounting systems that keep track of amounts owed to the firm.

Ada A programming language developed for the Department of Defense to be portable across diverse brands of hardware; it also has nonmilitary applications and can be used for business problems.

Address The particular location in primary storage where data or program instructions are stored.

Analog signal A continuous sine wave form over a certain frequency range, with a positive voltage representing a 1 and a negative charge representing a 0; used for voice transmissions.

Applicant tracking systems Human resources systems that maintain data about applicants for jobs at a firm and provide reports to satisfy federal, state, and local employment regulations.

Application controls Manual and automated procedures to ensure that the data processed by a particular application remain accurate, complete, and valid throughout the processing cycle.

Application generator Software that can generate entire information system applications without customized programming; The end-user specifies what needs to be done, and the generator creates the appropriate program code.

Application software Programs designed to handle the processing for a particular computer application.

Application solution The use of an information system to solve a problem.

Applications software package A prewritten, precoded, commercially available program that handles the processing for a particular computer application (e.g., spreadsheet or database software for a personal computer).

Arithmetic-logic unit (ALU) The component of the CPU that performs arithmetic and logical operations on data.

Artificial intelligence (AI) The study and creation of machines that exhibit humanlike qualities, including the ability to reason.

Artificial intelligence shell The programming environment of an artificial intelligence system.

ASCII A seven- or eight-bit binary coding scheme used in data transmission, microcomputers, and some larger computers; stands for American Standard Code for Information Interchange.

Assembler A program that translates assembly language into machine code so it can be used by the computer.

Assembly language A programming language used for second-generation software; it consists of natural language-like acronyms and words such as add, sub(tract), and load and is considered a symbolic language.

Asynchronous transfer mode (ATM) Protocol for transmitting voice, data, and images over LANs and wide-area networks using computers from different vendors by parceling information into uniform cells of 53 groups of 8 bits.

Asynchronous transmission A method of transmitting one character or byte at a time when data are communicated between computers with each string of bits comprising a character framed by control bits.

Attribute A characteristic or quality of a particular entity.

Backward reasoning A strategy for searching the rules in a knowledge base in which the inference engine begins with a hypothesis and proceeds by asking the user questions about selected facts until the hypothesis is either confirmed or disproved.

Bandwidth The range of frequencies that can be accommodated on a particular telecommunications medium.

Bar code Specially designed bar characters that can be read by OCR scanning devices; used primarily on price tags and supermarket items.

BASIC A programming language frequently used for teaching programming and for microcomputers; although it is easy to learn, it does not easily support sound programming practices.

Basic business system A system that serves the most elementary day-to-day activities of an organization; it supports the operational level of the business and also supplies data for higher-level management decisions.

Batch input and processing An approach to input and processing in which data are grouped together as source documents before being input; once the data are input, they are stored as a transaction file before processing, which occurs some time later.

Baud A change in voltage from positive to negative and vice versa. The baud rate at lower speeds corresponds to a telecommunications transmission rate of bits per second. At higher speeds the baud rate is less than the bit rate because more than one bit at a time can be transmitted by a single signal change.

Behavioral theories of management Views of management that stress three roles—interpersonal, informational, and decisional.

Benefits systems Human resources systems that maintain data about employees' life insurance, health insurance, pensions, and other benefits, including changes in beneficiaries and benefits coverage.

Bit A binary digit that can have only one of two states, represented by zero or one.

Bit mapping A technology often used for displaying graphics on a video display terminal; it allows each pixel on the screen to be addressed and manipulated by the computer.

Bottom-up approach An approach to intelligent machines that concentrates on trying to build a physical analog to the human brain.

Business environment The aggregate conditions in which a business organization operates; the general environment includes government regulations, economic and political conditions, and technological developments, while the task environment includes persons or entities with which the firm is more directly involved, such as customers, suppliers, and competitors.

Business functions   The various tasks performed in a business organization—for example, manufacturing and production, sales and marketing, finance and accounting, and human resources activities.

Business organization   A complex, formal organization established for the purpose of producing products or services for a profit.

Business process   A set of related activities performed to achieve a defined outcome, such as the processing of a sales order.

Bus network   A network in which a number of computers are linked by a single loop circuit made of twisted wire, cable, or optical fiber; all messages are transmitted to the entire network and can flow in either direction, with special software identifying which component receives each message.

Bus width   The number of bits that can be moved at one time between the CPU and the other devices of a computer.

Byte   A single character of data made up of a combination of bits that a computer processes or stores as a unit; the unit in which computer storage capacity is measured.

C   A programming language with tight control and efficiency of execution like assembly language; it is portable across different microprocessors and is easier to learn than assembly language.

Case-based reasoning   Artificial intelligence technology that represents knowledge as a series of cases stored in a database.

Cash management systems   Financial systems that keep track of the receipt and disbursement of cash by a firm; they may also forecast the firm's cash flow.

CD-ROM   An optical disk system which is a form of read-only storage in that data can only be read from it, not written to it; stands for Compact Disk/Read-Only Memory.

Cellular telephones   Telephones working in a system that uses radio waves to transmit voice and data to radio antennas placed in adjacent geographic areas.

Central processing unit (CPU)   A hardware component of a computer system which processes raw data and controls other parts of the computer system.

Channel   A link by which voices or data are transmitted in a communications network.

Character printer   A printer that prints one character at a time; such printers are very slow, outputting 40 to 200 characters per second.

Client/server computing   Model of computing that divides processing tasks between "clients" and "servers" on a network, with each machine assigned the functions it performs best.

Coaxial cable   A transmission medium consisting of thickly insulated copper wire; it can transmit a larger volume of data than twisted wire and is faster and more interference-free; cannot be used for analog phone conversations.

COBOL   A programming language with English-like statements designed for processing large data files with alphanumeric characters; the predominant programming language for business applications; stands for COmmon Business Oriented Language.

Combinatorial explosion   The difficulty that arises when a problem requires a computer to test a very large number of rules to reach a solution; even a very fast computer cannot search through all the possibilities in a reasonable amount of time.

Communications satellite   Satellite orbiting above the earth that acts as a relay station for transmitting microwave signals.

Communications software   Software used in transmitting data via telecommunications links between computer systems and computer terminals.

Compiler   A language translator program that translates an entire higher-level language program into machine language.

Computer   Physical device that takes data as input, transforms these data by executing a stored program, and outputs information to a number of devices.

Computer-aided design   Automation of the creation and revision of designs using sophisticated graphics software.

Computer crime   The deliberate theft or criminal destruction of computerized data or services; the use of computer hardware, software, or data for illegal activities; or the illegal use of computers.

Computer dependance   The state of relying on computers to provide vital services; in a computer-dependent society, the malfunc-

tioning of computers may cause extensive damage to lives and/or property.

Computer hardware   The physical equipment used for the input, processing, and output work in an information system.

Computer literacy   Knowledge about the use of information technology equipment; it involves knowing about hardware, software, telecommunications, and information storage techniques.

Computer mouse   A hand-held device that can be moved on a desk top to control the position of the cursor on a video display screen.

Computer software   Preprogrammed instructions that coordinate the work of computer hardware components and perform the business processes required by each business information system.

Computer virus   A rogue software program that spreads rampantly through computer systems, destroying data or causing the systems to become congested and malfunction.

Concentrator   A device that collects and temporarily stores messages from terminals in a buffer or temporary storage area and sends bursts of signals to the host computer.

Controller   A device that supervises communications traffic between the CPU and peripheral devices such as terminals and printers.

Controls   The specific technology, policies, and manual procedures used to protect the assets, accuracy, and reliability of information systems.

Control totals   A manual or automated count of the number of transactions processed during input, processing, or output or critical quantities, such as order amounts; this count is then compared manually or by computer to a second count; discrepancies in the counts signal errors.

Control unit   The component of the main processor that controls and coordinates the other components of the computer.

Conversion strategies   Plans and methods for changing from an old system to a new system; include parallel conversion, direct cutover, pilot study, and phased approach.

Cooperative processing   The division of processing work for transaction-based applications among mainframes and personal computers.

Cost-effectiveness   Being economical in terms of providing benefits that exceed costs; measured by cost-benefit analysis.

Critical thinking   The sustained suspension of judgment with an awareness of multiple perspectives and alternatives.

CRT   An electronic tube that shoots a beam of electrons that illuminate pixels, or tiny dots, on a video display screen; stands for cathode ray tube.

Customization   The modification of a software package to meet a firm's unique requirements.

Cylinder   Represents circular tracks on the same vertical line within a disk pack.

Data   Raw facts that can be shaped and formed to create information.

Database   A group of related files; more specifically, a collection of data organized so they can be accessed and utilized by many different applications.

Database management system (DBMS)   Software that serves as an interface between a common database and various application programs; it permits data to be stored in one place yet be made available to different applications.

Data definition language   The part of a database management system that defines each data element as it appears in the database before it is translated into the form required by various application programs.

Data dictionary   The component in a database management system that stores definitions and other characteristics of data elements; it identifies what data reside in the database, their structure and format, and their business usage.

Data flow   The movement of data within an information system; a data flow can consist of a single data element or multiple data elements grouped together and can be manual or automated.

Data flow diagram   A graphic diagram that shows both how data flow to, from, and within an information system and the various processes that transform the data; used for documenting the logical design of an information system.

Data management software   Software that is used for such applications as creating and manipulating lists, creating files and databases to store data, and combining information.

Data manipulation language   A special tool in a database management system that manipulates the data in the database.

Data redundancy   The presence of duplicate data in multiple data files.

Data security   A control aimed at preventing the unauthorized use of data and ensuring that data are not accidentally altered or destroyed.

Data work   Work that primarily involves the processing, use, or dissemination of information.

Decisional roles   The activities of managers that involve making decisions about new products, handling disturbances in the business, allocating resources, and negotiating among persons with different points of view.

Decision making   The process of debating objectives and feasible solutions and choosing the best option; the third step of problem solving.

Decision support systems (DSS)   Interactive systems under user control that are used in solving semi-structured problems.

Demodulation   The process of converting analog signals into digital form.

Desktop publishing   Applications for producing documents that combine high-quality type and graphics with a variety of layout options, allowing users to produce professional-quality reports and documents.

Development methodology   A proven method of accomplishing the tasks of systems development to provide standards for guiding the activities of a systems development project.

Digital signal   A discrete flow in which data are coded as 0-bits and 1-bits and transmitted as a series of on-and-off electrical pulses; used for communication between computers and by some telephone systems.

Digitizing tablet   Input device that allows people to read, write, or trace designs on a pressure-sensitive tablet using an electronic stylus or puck. Used for graphics work and computer-aided design.

Direct-access storage device (DASD)   Magnetic disks, including both hard and floppy disks; called *direct access* because in this technology the computer can proceed immediately to a specific record without having to read all the preceding records.

Direct cutover   A conversion strategy in which the old system is replaced entirely with the new system on an appointed day; no system is available if the new system fails.

Disaster recovery plan   A plan that enables a firm to recover from an emergency in which all or part of its information system is destroyed; provides for immediate access to alternative computer hardware and the restoration of software program, data, and telecommunications facilities.

Disk access time   The speed at which data can be located on magnetic disks and loaded into primary storage or written onto a disk device.

Distributed database   A complete database or portions of a database that are maintained in more than one location.

Distributed processing   The distribution of processing among multiple computers linked by a communications network.

Documentation   A control that involves establishing and maintaining a clear-cut explanation of how an information system works from both a business and a technical standpoint; includes system, user, and operational documenting.

Document management technology   Information technology that is used for producing and managing the flow of documents in an organization; includes word processing, desktop publishing, and optical disk storage.

DOS   An operating system for 16-bit microcomputers; PC-DOS is used with the IBM Personal Computer; MS-DOS is used with other 16-bit microcomputers that function like the IBM PC.

Dot-matrix printer   An impact printer that uses a print head composed of many small hammers or pins that strike an inked ribbon as the print mechanism moves from side to side; such printers are usually faster than letter-quality printers but produce lower-quality output.

Double-sided disk   A floppy disk on which data can be stored on both sides.

Downloading   The process of extracting data from mainframes, reformatting these data, and placing them in a microcomputer.

Downsizing   The process of moving problem-solving applications from large computers, such as mainframes or minicomputers, to smaller computers, such as microcomputers.

Due process   The right to be treated fairly in accordance with established legal procedures, including such things as the right to appeal and the right to an attorney.

EBCDIC   An 8-bit binary coding scheme used in IBM and other mainframe computers; stands for Extended Binary Coded Decimal Interchange Code.

Electronic data interchange (EDI)   The direct computer-to-computer exchange of standard business transaction documents, such as invoices, bills of lading, and purchase orders, between two separate organizations.

Electronic mail   The computer-to-computer exchange of messages.

Entity   A person, place, or thing on which information is maintained.

EPROM   A memory device in which the memory chips can be erased and reprogrammed with new instructions; stands for erasable programmable read-only memory.

Ethics   Principles of right and wrong that can be used to guide the behavior of free moral agents who make choices.

Execution cycle   The portion of a machine cycle in which the required data are located, the instruction is executed, and the results are stored.

Executive support systems (ESS)   Graphic-oriented systems designed for senior management that provide generalized computing and telecommunications facilities and combine internal and external information; used for long-term planning.

Expert systems   Software applications that seek to capture expertise in limited domains of knowledge and experience and apply this expertise to solving problems.

External knowledge base   A knowledge base that is outside the organization, such as libraries of articles, collections of scientific or legal findings, and links to other professionals in universities or other businesses.

Fault-tolerant computer systems   Systems with extra hardware, software, and power as backups against system failure.

Fax (facsimile) machine   A machine that can transmit documents containing both text and graphics over telephone lines; the sending machine digitizes and transits the image, which is reproduced as a facsimile (fax) by the receiving machine.

Feasibility   The quality of being suitable, given a firm's internal and external constraints, including financial resources.

Feedback   Output that is returned to appropriate members of the organization to help them refine or correct the input phase.

Fiber optics   A transmission medium consisting of strands of clear glass fiber bound into cables through which data are transformed into beams of light and transmitted by a laser device; it is faster, lighter, and more durable than wire media but also more expensive and harder to install.

Field   A grouping of characters into a word, a group of words, or a complete number.

File   A group of related records.

File server   A computer with a large hard disk whose function is to allow other devices to share files and programs.

Finance and accounting function   The division of a business organization that manages the firm's financial assets (finance) and maintains the firm's financial records (accounting).

Flat panel display   A technology that uses charged chemicals or gases sandwiched between panes of glass to display output on a screen; used in lightweight, portable computers.

Flop   Stands for *floating point operations per* second. A floating point operation is a basic arithmetic operation on numbers that include a decimal point.

Floppy disks   Flexible, inexpensive disks used as a secondary storage medium; primarily used with microcomputers.

Formal systems   Information systems that rely on mutually accepted and relatively fixed definitions of data and procedures for collecting, storing, processing, and disseminating information.

FORTRAN   A programming language developed in 1954 for scientific, mathematical, and engineering applications; stands for FORmula TRANslator.

Forward reasoning   A strategy for searching the rules in a knowledge base in which the inference engine begins with information entered by the user and searches the rule base to arrive at a conclusion.

Fourth-generation development   The construction of information systems with little or no formal assistance from technical specialists, useful for smaller, informal systems and personal computer applications.

Fourth-generation language   Programming languages that are less proce-

dural than conventional languages (i.e., they need only specify what is to be done rather than provide the details of how to do it) and contain more English language–like commands; they are easier for nonspecialists to learn and use than conventional languages.

Frame relay   Network technology that organizes data into packets without error correction routines to transmit data over networks faster and cheaper than packet switching.

Frames   A way of organizing knowledge based on shared characteristics; an object is defined by its characteristics and can be related to any other object in the database that shares those characteristics.

Freedom   The ability to act and think without constraint.

Freedom of information   The right of citizens to have access to information stored by government and private organizations in order to be informed participants in the political process and to protect themselves from government abuse.

Front-end processor   A computer that manages communications for a host computer to which it is attached; the front-end processor is largely responsible for collecting and processing input and output data to and from terminals and performing such tasks as formatting, editing, and routing for the host computer.

Full-duplex transmission   A form of transmission over communication lines in which data can be sent in both directions simultaneously.

Fuzzy logic   A variety of concepts and techniques in AI for using rules to represent knowledge that is imprecise, uncertain, or unreliable.

General controls   Organization-wide controls, both manual and automated, that affect overall activities of computerized information systems.

General Problem Solver   A model of human problem solving that attempted to avoid the combinatorial explosion by reducing the number of rules through which a computer would have to search; useful for restricted areas, such as chess, but not for general problem solving.

Geographic information systems   Software used in producing maps or performing geographic modeling; such systems may be two dimensional or three dimensional.

Gigabyte   A measure of computer storage capacity; equals 1,073,741,824 bytes.

Graphical user interface   The feature of a microcomputer operating system that uses graphical symbols, or icons; rather than typing in commands, the user moves the cursor to the appropriate icon by rolling a mouse on a desk top.

Graphics language   A fourth-generation language for displaying computerized data in graphical form.

Group decision support system (GDSS) Interactive computer-based system to help a set of decision makers working together as a group solve unstructured problems.

Groupware   Software that attempts to expedite all the functions of a typical work group (e.g., tracking the calendars of all or related individuals in an office, scheduling meetings, and sharing ideas and documents).

Hacker   A person who gains unauthorized access to a computer network for profit, criminal mischief, or personal reasons.

Half-duplex transmission   A form of transmission over communication lines in which data can move in both directions, but not simultaneously.

Hard disk   A thin steel platter about the size of a phonograph record with an iron oxide coating; generally several are mounted together on a vertical shaft.

Hierarchical database model   The organization of data in a database in a top-down, treelike manner; each record is broken down into multilevel segments, with one root segment linked to several subordinate segments in a one-to-many, parent-child relationship.

Hierarchy   The arrangement of persons in a business organization according to rank and authority. Persons at the bottom of the hierarchy report to those on the next level who have more authority; these persons, in turn, report to the next level and so on, up to senior management.

High-level language   A programming language that consists of statements that, to some degree, resemble natural languages, such as English.

Host computer   The main computer in a network.

Human resources function   The division of a business organization that concentrates on attracting and maintaining a stable work force for the firm; it identifies potential employees, maintains records on existing employees, and creates training programs.

Hypermedia database   Organization of data as a network of nodes linked in any pattern established by the user.

Imaging   Systems and software that convert documents into digital form so that they can be stored, accessed, and manipulated by the computer.

Impact printer   A printer that forms characters by pressing a typeface device, such as a print wheel or cylinder, against paper and inked ribbon.

Implementation   The process of putting the solution of a problem into effect and evaluating the results and performance in order to make improvements; the fifth, and last, step of problem solving.

Index   A list, for a file or database, of the key field of each record and its associated storage location.

Indexed sequential-access method (ISAM)   A way of storing records sequentially on a direct-access storage device that also allows individual records to be accessed in any desired order using an index of key fields.

Inference engine   The process of searching through the rule base in an expert system; either a forward reasoning strategy or a backward reasoning strategy is used.

Informal structure   A network of personal relationships within a formal business organization.

Information   Data that have been shaped or formed by humans into a meaningful and useful form.

Informational roles   The activities of managers that involve monitoring the activities of the business, disseminating information through reports and memos, and acting as spokespersons for the business.

Information and knowledge economy An economy in which the majority of new wealth (gross national product) is produced by creating or processing information.

Information center   A facility that provides training, tools, standards, and expert support for solution design by end-users.

Information system   A set of interrelated components working together to collect, retrieve, process, store, and disseminate information for the purpose of facilitating planning, control, coordination, and decision making in businesses and other organizations.

Information systems literacy   Knowledge and hands-on facility with information technologies, together with a broadly based understanding of business organizations and individuals from a behavioral perspective and a similar understanding of how to analyze and solve business problems.

Information work   Work that primarily involves the creation or processing of information.

Ink-jet printer   A printer that produces an image by spraying electrically charged ink particles against paper through holes in the printhead.

Input   The capture or collection of raw data resources from within a business or from its external environment.

Input controls   Applications controls that ensure the accuracy and completeness of data entering the information system.

Input/output bus width   The number of bits that can be moved at one time between the CPU and the other devices of a computer.

Instruction cycle   The portion of a machine cycle in which an instruction is retrieved from primary storage and decoded.

Integrated Services Digital Network (ISDN)   An emerging international standard for extending common carrier digital service (sharing voice messages, digital information, and video pictures) to homes and offices from central telephone company centers.

Integrated software package   A software package that provides two or more applications, such as spreadsheets and word processing, allowing for easy transfer of data between them.

Intelligent database search machine   A "master" machine that can direct a search of a very large database by giving the target pattern to many machines that search simultaneously; when a machine finds a possible match, it sends it to the controller machine, which makes the final assessment.

Intelligent machines   Physical devices or computers that mimic the way people think.

Interpersonal roles   The activities of managers that involve performing symbolic duties; motivating, counseling, and supporting workers; and acting as liaisons to the larger firms and the outside world on behalf of employees.

Interpreter   Anguage translator program that translates a higher-level language program into machine code by translating one statement at a time and executing it.

Key field   A field in a record that uniquely identifies that record so that it can be retrieved, updated, or sorted.

Keypunch   An early form of inputting data in which data were coded onto 80-column cards, with each location on the card representing a character.

Key-to-tape/key-to-disk   A form of inputting in which data are keyed directly onto magnetic tape or magnetic disks.

Kilobyte   The usual measure of micro-computer storage capacity; equals 1,024 bytes.

Knowledge   The stock of conceptual tools and categories used by humans to create, collect, store, and share information.

Knowledge and data workers   The employees in a business organization who create and/or disseminate knowledge (e.g., engineers) or data (e.g., clerical workers) to solve business problems.

Knowledge- and information-intensive products   Products that require a great deal of learning and knowledge to create and often require information technologies to deliver in a timely fashion.

Knowledge base   A model of human knowledge used by artificial intelligence systems; consists of rules, semantic nets, or frames.

Knowledge engineer   Specialist trained in eliciting information and expertise from other professionals in order to translate the knowledge into a set of production rules, frames, or semantic nets.

Knowledge systems   Information systems used by knowledge workers in business organizations to solve questions requiring knowledge and technical expertise.

Knowledge work   Work that (1) is based on a codified body of findings and results; (2) can be taught in a school as principles, procedures, and methods; (3) is certified by the state or a university; and (4) is regulated by a professional body that sets standards.

Knowledge workers' roles in business   Business positions that involve interpreting the firm's external knowledge base; playing an active role as advisers and internal business consultants; and initiating, promoting, and evaluating new projects that incorporate new developments and changes into the firm.

Laser printer   A printer that produces an image by scanning a laser beam across a light-sensitive drum; the toner that adheres to the charged portions of the drum is then pulled off onto the paper.

Letter-quality printer   An impact printer that produces a high-quality image by pressing the image of a fully formed character against inked ribbon.

Liability   The idea that people may be obligated by law to compensate those they have injured in some way; liability is established by laws that set out legal remedies for proscribed behavior.

Light pen   An input device with light-sensitive photoelectric cells in its tip that is used to input data by "writing" on a video display device; usually used for graphics.

Line printer   A printer that prints an entire line at a time; can reach speeds of 3,000 lines per minute.

Local area network (LAN)   A transmission network encompassing a limited area, such as a single building or several buildings in close proximity; widely used to link personal computers so that they can share information and peripheral devices.

Logical design   The part of a solution design that provides a description of the general level of resources, the operational process, and the nature of outputs that the solution should require, it describes what the solution will do, not how it will work physically.

Logic Theorist   Software developed by Herbert Simon and Alan Newell that mimicked deductive logic; that is, it selected correct rules and postulates in order to create a coherent logical chain from premises to conclusion.

Logical view   The presentation of data as they would be perceived by end-users or business specialists.

Machine cycle   The series of operations involved in executing a single instruction.

Machine language   The programming language used in the first la generation of computer software; consists of strings of binary digits (0 and 1).

Magnetic disk   The most popular secondary storage medium; data are stored by means of magnetized spots on hard or floppy disks.

Magnetic ink character recognition (MICR)   A form of source data automation in which an MICR reader identifies characters written in magnetic ink; used primarily for check processing.

Magnetic tape   A secondary storage medium in which data are stored by means of magnetized and nonmagnetized spots on tape; it is inexpensive and relatively stable but also is relatively slow and can store information only sequentially.

Mainframe   A large computer, generally having 50 megabytes to over 1 gigabyte of RAM.

Management controls   A type of general control that provides appropriate management supervision and accountability for information systems (e.g., establishing formal written policies and procedures and segregating job functions to minimize error and fraud).

Management information systems (MIS)   Management support systems that provide routine summary reports on the firm's performance; used to monitor and control the business and predict future performance.

Managing   The process of using business resources to accomplish goals, coordinate the work of many workers, and establish criteria for measuring progress toward the established goals.

Manual system   An information system that uses only paper and pencil technology and does not rely on computers.

Manufacturing and production function   The division of a business organization that produces the firm's goods or services.

Massively parallel processing   Computer processing in which a very large number of inexpensive processor chips are chained together to work on a single computing problem simultaneously.

Megabyte   A measure of computer storage capacity; equals 1,048,576 bytes.

Megahertz   A measure of clock speed, or the pacing of events in a computer; equals one million cycles per second.

Microcomputer   A small, desktop or portable computer, generally have 256 kilobytes to 16 megabytes of RAM.

Microfilm and microfiche   Media that record output as microscopic filmed images that can be stored compactly.

Microprocessor   A silicon chip containing an entire CPU; used in microcomputers.

Microsecond   A measure of machine cycle time; equals one one-millionth of a second.

Microwave   A transmission medium in which high-frequency radio signals are sent through the atmosphere; used for high-volume, long-distance, point-to-point communication.

Middle management   The persons in the middle of the hierarchy in a business organization; they carry out the programs and plans of senior management by supervising employees.

Millisecond   A measure of machine cycle time; equals one one-thousandth of a second.

Microcomputer security   The policies, procedures, and technical tools used to safeguard microcomputers from unauthorized access; usually less formal than the controls for mainframes and minicomputers.

Minicomputer   A medium-sized computer, generally having 10 to 100 megabytes of RAM.

Mobile data networks   Radio-based networks for two-way transmission of digital data.

Model base   The analytical tools used by an information system; in a decision support system, it will include very sophisticated tools, such as built-in spreadsheets, statistical analysis, and simulation.

Modem   A device used to translate digital signals into analog signals and vice versa, a necessity when computers communicate through analog lines; stands for MOdulation and DEModulation.

Modulation   The process of converting digital signals into analog form.

Module   A logical way of partitioning or subdividing a program so that each component (i.e., module) performs a limited number of related tasks.

Multimedia   Technologies that facilitate the integration of two or more types of media, such as text, graphics, sound, voice, full-motion video, and/or animation into a computer-based application.

Multinational   Approach to organizing a business in which financial management and control are maintained out of a central home office, while production, sales, and marketing are located in other countries.

Multiplexer   A device that enables a single communications channel to carry data

transmission from multiple sources simultaneously.

Multiprocessing   The simultaneous use of two or more CPUs under common control to execute different instructions for the same program or multiple programs.

Multiprogramming   The concurrent use of a computer by several programs; one program uses the CPU while the others use other components, such as input and output devices.

Multitasking   The multiprogramming capability of single-user operating systems, such as those for microcomputers; it enables the user to run two or more programs at once on a single computer.

Nanosecond   A measure of machine cycle time; equals one one-billionth of a second.

Natural languages   Languages, including idioms, which are used by humans (examples: English, Russian, French).

Network database model   The organization of data in a database so that each data element or record can be related to several other data elements or records in a many-to-many relationship.

Network gateway   The network software that links a local area network to another network, such as the public telephone system or another corporate network.

Network topology   The shape or configuration of a network; the most common topologies are the star, bus, and ring.

Neural network   Hardware or software that emulates the physiology of animal or human brains.

Nonimpact printer   A printer, such as a laser, ink-jet, or thermal-transfer printer, that does not form characters by pressing a typeface device against ribbon and paper.

Nonvolatile   Property of memory that means that its contents will not be lost if electric power is disrupted or the computer is turned off.

Object code   The machine-language version of source code after it has been translated into a form usable by the computer.

Objectives   The goals of an organization.

Object-oriented database   Organization of data and the procedures acting on the data as objects that can automatically be retrieved and shared.

Object-oriented programming   A programming method that combines data and

the specific instructions acting on that data into one "object" that can be used in other programs.

Office activities   The activities performed by an office in an organization, consisting of (1) managing documents, (2) scheduling individuals and groups, (3) communicating with individuals and groups, (4) managing data on individuals and groups, and (5) managing projects.

Office data management technology   Information technology that centers around desktop databases for client or customer tracking, project tracking, calendar information, and other information required for office jobs.

Office roles   The functions played by an office in an organization, consisting of (1) coordinating and managing people and work, (2) linking diverse organizational units and projects, and (3) coupling the organization to the external environment.

Office scheduling technology   Information technology used to coordinate individual and group calendars, such as electronic calendars.

On-line database   A service that supplies information external to the firm, such as stock market quotations, general news and information, or specific legal and business information.

On-line input   An input approach in which data are input into the computer as they become available rather than being grouped as source documents.

On-line real-time processing   A type of processing in which data are processed as soon as they are input into the system rather than being stored for later processing.

On-line transaction processing (OLTP)   A transaction processing mode in which transactions entered on-line are immediately processed by the CPU.

Open Systems Interconnect (OSI)   Model of network protocols enabling any computer connected to a network to communicate with any other computer on the same network or a different network, regardless of the manufacturer.

Operating system   The systems software that manages and controls the activities of the computer.

Operational systems   Information systems used in monitoring the day-to-day activities of a business organization.

Optical character recognition (OCR)   A form of source data automation in which optical scanning devices read specially designed data off source documents and translate the data into digital form for the computer; bar codes are an example of OCR technology.

Optical disk   A disk on which data are recorded by laser beams rather than by magnetic means; such disks can store data at densities much greater than magnetic disks.

Order processing systems   Sales and marketing systems that record and process sales orders, track the status of orders, produce invoices, and often produce data for sales analysis and inventory control.

Organizational structure   The number of different levels, the type of work, and the distribution of power in an organization.

Organization perspective   A way of viewing a problem in which emphasis is placed on the firm's formal rules and procedures, production process, management, politics, bureaucracy, and culture as sources of its problems and the way in which they can contribute to a solution.

OS/2   An operating system that supports multitasking and multiple users in networks and that is used with 32-bit IBM microcomputers.

Output   The transfer of processed information to the people or business activities that will use it.

Output controls   Application controls that ensure that the results of computer processing are accurate, complete, and properly distributed.

Outsourcing   Using an external vendor of computer services to develop or operate an organization's information systems.

Packet switching   The breaking up of a block of text into packets of data approximately 128 bytes long; a value-added network gathers data from its subscribers, divides the data into packets, and sends the packets on any available communications channel.

Page printer   A printer that can print an entire page at a time; can reach speeds of more than 20,000 lines per minute.

Paging system   Wireless system for notifying users of telephone calls that can also be used to transmit short alphanumeric messages.

Parallel conversion   A conversion strategy in which the old system and the new system run in tandem until it is clear that the new system is working correctly.

Parallel processing   A type of processing in which more than one instruction is processed at a time; used in supercomputers.

Parallel sensor systems   A system in which each node continually receives information from lower-level sensors, evaluates the information, requests more if needed, and reports to higher-level machines.

Partitioned database   A database that is subdivided so that each location has only the portion of the database that serves its local needs.

Pascal   A programming language that consists of smaller subprograms, each of which is a structured program in itself; it is used on microcomputers and for teaching programming but is not well suited for business applications.

Pen-based input   Input devices that accept handwritten input by allowing users to print directly on a sensitized screen using a pen-like stylus.

People challenge   The problems posed by the interrelationship of technology and humans; refers both to the problems rapid changes in technology present for individuals and businesses and to the need to design systems individuals can control and understand.

People perspective   A way of viewing a problem in which emphasis is placed on the firm's employees as individuals and their interrelationships as sources of its problems and the way in which they can contribute to a solution.

Perceptive systems   Sensing devices used in robots that can recognize patterns in streams of data.

Perceptron   A machine devised by Frank Rosenblatt that could perceive letters or shapes and could be taught, or corrected, when it made mistakes; an example of the bottom-up approach to artificial intelligence.

Personal communications services   Systems for wireless transmission of voice and data sending low-power, high-frequency radio waves to closely spaced microcells.

Personal digital assistant (PDA)   Pen-based hand-held computer with built-in communication and organizational capabilities.

Phased approach   A conversion strategy in which a new system is introduced in steps.

Physical design   The part of a solutions design that translates the abstract logical system model into specifications for equipment, hardware, software, and other physical resources.

Physical view   The presentation of data as they are actually organized and structured on physical storage media.

Picosecond   A measure of machine cycle time; equals one one-trillionth of a second.

Pilot study   A conversion strategy in which a new system is introduced to only a limited part of an organization; if the system is effective there, it is installed throughout the rest of the organization.

PL/1   A programming language developed in 1964 by IBM for business and scientific applications; not as widely used as COBOL or FORTRAN.

Plotter   A device that is used for outputting high-quality graphics; pen plotters move in various directions to produce straight lines, whereas electrostatic plotters use electrostatic charges to produce images from tiny dots on treated paper.

Point-of-sale systems   Sales and marketing systems that capture sales data at the actual point of sale through the cash register or hand-held laser scanners.

Positions systems   Human resources systems that maintain information about positions (slots in a firm's organization chart); they maintain data about filled and unfilled positions and track changes in positions and job assignments.

Postimplementation   The use and evaluation of a new system after it is installed; the last stage of the traditional systems life cycle.

Primary storage   The component of the CPU that temporarily stores program instructions and the data being used by these instructions.

Privacy   The right of individuals and organizations to be left alone and to be secure in their personal papers.

Privacy Act of 1974   A federal statute that defines citizens' right in regard to, and management's responsibilities for, federal government records; sets out some of the principles for regulating computer technology in order to protect people's privacy.

Private branch exchange (PBX)   A central private switchboard that handles a firm's voice and digital communications needs.

Problem analysis   The consideration of the dimensions of a problem to determine what kind of problem it is and what general kinds of solutions may be appropriate; the first step in problem solving.

Problem understanding   The investigation—fact gathering and analysis—of a problem, leading to better understanding; the second step of problem solving.

Process control systems   Manufacturing and production systems that use computers to monitor the ongoing physical production processes.

Processing   The conversion of raw input into a more appropriate and useful form.

Processing controls   Application controls that ensure the accuracy and completeness of data during updating.

Process specifications   The logical steps for performing a process; they appear in documents accompanying lower-level data flow diagrams to show the various steps by which data are transformed.

Production workers   The employees in a business organization who actually produce or create the firm's products.

Productivity challenge   The need to increase U.S. productivity and bring it into line with the growth in computing power.

Program   A series of statements or instructions to the computer.

Program/data dependency   The close relationship between data stored in files and the specific software programs required to update and maintain those files, whereby any change in data format or structure requires a change in all the programs that access the data.

Programmed edit check   An application control technique for checking input data for errors before the data are processed; it uses a computerized checking procedure.

Project definition   The process of investigating a perceived problem to determine whether a problem actually exists and, if so, whether it requires further analysis and research; the first stage of the traditional systems life cycle.

Project management technology   Software that helps managers track and plan projects.

PROM   A memory device in which the memory chips can be programmed only once and are used to store instructions entered by the purchaser; stands for programmable read-only memory.

Protocol   The set of rules governing transmission between two components in a telecommunications network.

Prototyping   Building an experimental, or preliminary, system or part of a system for business specialists to try out and evaluate.

Pseudocode   A method of documenting the logic followed by program instructions in which English-like statements are used to describe processing steps and logic.

Quality control systems   Manufacturing and production systems that monitor the production process to identify variances from established standards so that defects can be corrected.

Quality of work life   The degree to which jobs are interesting, satisfying, and physically safe and comfortable.

Query language   A higher-level, easy-to-use, fourth-generation language for accessing data stored in databases or files.

RAID (Redundant Array of Inexpensive Disks)   High-performance disk storage technology that can deliver data over multiple paths simultaneously by packaging more than 100 smaller disk drives with a controller chip and specialized software in a single large box.

RAM   A memory device used for the short-term storage of data or program instructions; stands for random-access memory.

Random file organization   A way of storing data records so that they can be accessed in any sequence, regardless of their physical order; used with magnetic disk technology.

Read/write head   An electromagnetic device that reads or writes the data stored on magnetic disks.

Record   A grouping of related data fields, such as person's name, age, and address.

Recording density   The number of bits per inch that can be written on the surface of a floppy disk.

Reduced instruction set computing (RISC)   Technology for increasing microprocessor speed by embedding only the most frequently used instructions on a chip.

Reengineering   The rethinking and radical redesign of business processes to significantly improve cost, quality, service, and speed and to maximize the benefits of information technology.

Register   A storage location in the ALU or control unit; it may be an instruction register, an address register, or a storage register, depending on what is stored in it.

Relational database model   The organization of data in a database in two-dimensional tables called relations; a data element in any one table can be related to any piece of data in another table as long as both tables share a common data element.

Removable-pack disk system   Hard disks stacked into an indivisible unit called a pack that can be mounted and removed as a unit.

Repetition construct   A series of statements that repeats an instruction as long as the results of a conditional test are true; one of three basic control constructs in structured programming.

Replicated database   A central database that is duplicated at all other locations.

Report generator   A software tool that extracts data from files or databases to create customized reports that are not routinely produced by existing applications.

Request for Proposal (RFP)   A detailed list of questions for software vendors to answer as part of the process of evaluating a software package; the questions are designed to determine the extent to which the software package meets the requirements specified during the solution design process.

Responsibility   The idea that individuals, organizations, and societies are free moral agents who act willfully and with intentions, goals, and ideas; consequently, they can be held accountable for their actions.

Ring network   A network in which a number of computers are linked by a loop of wire, cable, or optical fiber in a manner that allows data to be passed along the loop in a single direction from computer to computer.

Robotics   The study of physical systems that can perform work normally done by humans, especially in hazardous or lethal environments.

ROM   A memory device used for the permanent storage of program instructions; stands for read-only memory.

Sales and marketing function   The diversion of a business organization that sells the firm's product or service.

Scanner   An electronic device that reads text or graphics and inputs the information into a computer automatically without human typing.

Schema   The logical description of an entire database; it lists all the data items and the relationships among them.

Secondary storage   The relatively long-term storage of data outside the CPU.

Sector method for storing data   A method of storing data on floppy disks in which the disk is divided into pie-shaped pieces, or sectors; each sector has a unique number that becomes part of the address.

Security   All of the policies, procedures, and technical tools used to safeguard information systems from unauthorized access, alteration, theft, and physical damage.

Selection construct   A series of statements that tests a condition; depending on whether the results of the test are true or false, one of two alternative instructions will be executed; one of three basic control constructs in structured programming.

Semantic nets   A way of representing knowledge when the knowledge is composed of easily identified objects with interrelated characteristics; objects are classified according to the principle of inheritance so that the objects in lower levels the net "inherit" all the general characteristics of the objects above them.

Semiconductor chip   A silicon chip upon which hundreds of thousands of circuit elements can be etched.

Semistructured problem   A problem in which only parts have a clear-cut answer provided by a well-accepted methodology.

Senior management   The persons at the top of the hierarchy in a business organization; they have the most authority and make long-range decisions for the organization.

Sensors   Devices that collect data directly from the environment for input into the computer.

Sequence construct   A series of statements that are executed in the order in which they appear, with control passing unconditionally from one statement to the next; one of three basic control constructs in structured programming.

Sequential file organization   A way of storing data records so that they must be retrieved in the physical order in which they are stored; the only file organization method that can be used with magnetic tape.

Simplex transmission   A form of transmission over communications lines in which data can travel in only one direction at all times.

Single-sided disk   A floppy disk on which data can be stored on only one side.

Social impacts   The effects of computers on society, including both political issues, such as the effect of computers on freedom and privacy, and social issues, such as their effect on crime, demography, and education.

Sociotechnical perspective   An approach to information systems that involves the coordination of technology, organizations, and people; in this approach, information technology, organizations, and individuals go through a process of mutual adjustment and discovery as systems are developed.

Solution design   The development of a solution to a problem, including both logical and physical design; the fourth step of problem solving.

Source code   The higher-level language translated by operating system software into machine language so that the higher-level programs can be executed by the computer.

Source data automation   Advanced forms of data input technology that generate machine-readable data at their point of origin; includes optical character recognition, magnetic ink character recognition, digitizers, and voice input.

Specialization   The division of work in a business organization so that each employee focuses on a specific task.

Spreadsheet software   Software that provides the user with financial modeling tools; data are displayed on a grid and numerical data can easily be recalculated to permit the evaluation of several alternatives.

Star network   A network in which a central host computer is connected to several smaller computers and/or terminals; all communications between the smaller computers or terminals must pass through the host computer.

Storage technology   Physical media for storing data (e.g., magnetic disks or tapes) and the software governing the organization of data on these media.

Stored-program concept   The concept that a program cannot be executed unless it is stored in the computer's primary storage along with the required data.

Strategic business challenge   The need for businesses to develop the ability to change quickly in response to changes in the external environment, technology, or markets.

Strategic information systems   Information systems that focus on solving problems related to the firm's long-term prosperity and survival; in particular, they are used to help a firm maintain its competitive advantage.

Strategic-level systems   Information systems used in solving a business organization's long-range, or strategic, problems.

Structured design   A software design principle according to which a program is supposed to be designed from the top down as a hierarchical series of modules, with each module performing a limited number of functions.

Structured problem   A routine, repetitive problem for which there is an accepted methodology for arriving at an answer.

Structured program flowchart   A method of documenting the logic followed by program instructions; uses graphic symbols to depict the steps that processing must take in a specific program, using the three control structures of structured programming.

Structured programming   A way of writing program code that simplifies control paths so that programs can be easily understood and modified by others; it relies on three basic control constructs—the sequence construct, the selection construct, and the repetition construct.

Structured Query Language (SQL)   A data manipulation language for relational database management systems that is an emerging business standard.

Subschema   The specific set of data from a database that each application program requires.

Supercomputer   A very sophisticated and powerful computer that can perform complex computations very rapidly.

Synchronous transmission   The transmission of characters in blocks framed by header and trailer bytes called flags; allows large volumes of data to be transmitted at high speeds between computers because groups of characters can be transmitted as blocks, with no start and stop bits between characters as in asynchronous transmission.

System 7   Operating system for the Macintosh microcomputer with multitasking, graphics, and multimedia capabilities.

System flowchart   A diagram that documents the sequence of processing steps that take place in an entire system; most useful for physical design in which such diagrams show the sequence of processing events and the files used by each processing step.

Systems analysis   The study and analysis of problems of existing information systems; it includes the identification of both the organization's objectives and its requirements for the solution of the problems.

Systems design   A model or blueprint for an information system solution to a problem; it shows in detail how the technical, organizational, and people components of the system will fit together.

Systems software   Generalized software that manages computer resources such as the CPU, printers, terminals, communications links, and peripheral equipment.

Systems study   The process of describing and analyzing problems of existing systems, specifying solution objectives, describing potential solutions, and evaluating various solution alternatives; the second stage of the traditional systems life cycle.

Tactical systems   Information systems used in solving a business organization's short-term, or tactical, problems, such as how to achieve goals and how to evaluate the process of achieving goals.

Technology challenge   The gap that has developed between the rapid advances in computer hardware and our ability to write useful software for it; also, the gap between the changes in both hardware and software and businesses' ability to understand and apply them.

Technology perspective   A way of viewing a problem in which emphasis is place on information technology hardware, software, telecommunications, and database as sources of business problems and how they can contribute to a solution.

Telecommunication technology   Physical media and software that support communication by electronic means, usually over some distance.

Telecommuting   Working at home on a computer tied into corporate networks and databases.

Teleconferencing   The use of telecommunications technology to enable people to meet electronically; can be accomplished via telephone or electronic mail.

Telemarketing systems   Sales and marketing systems that track the use of the telephone for contacting customers, offering products, and following up sales.

Thermal-transfer printer   A printer that produces high-quality images by transferring ink from a wax-based ribbon onto chemically treated paper.

Time-sharing   A technique in which many users share computer resources simultaneously (e.g., one CPU with many terminals); the computer spends a fixed amount of time on each program before proceeding to the next.

Top-down approach   An approach to intelligent machines that concentrates on trying to develop a logical analog to the human brain.

Top-down design   A principle of software design according to which the design should first consider the program's main functions, subdivide these functions into component modules, and then subdivide each component module until the lowest level of detail has been reached.

Total quality management   Concept that makes quality improvement the responsibility of all members of an organization.

Touch screen   A sensitized video display screen that allows data to be input by touching the screen surface with a finger or pointer.

Track   A concentric circle on a hard disk on which data are stored as magnetized spots; each track can store thousands of bytes.

Traditional file environment   The storage of data so that each application has its own separate data file or files and software programs.

Traditional systems life cycle   The oldest methodology for building an information system; consists of six stages (project definition, systems study, design, programming, installation, and post-implementation) that must be completed sequentially.

Traditional theories of management   Views of management that see its primary functions as being planning, organizing, leading, and controlling.

Training and skills systems   Human resources systems that maintain records of employees' training and work experience so that employees with appropriate skills for special assignments or job requirements can be identified.

Transaction   A record of an event to which a business must respond.

Transaction processing system   A basic business system that keeps track of the transactions necessary to conduct a business and uses these transactions to update the firm's records. Another name for basic business systems.

Transborder data flow   The movement of information in any form from one country to another.

Transformation of the American economy   The shift in the American economy from the production of manufactured goods toward the production of information and knowledge products and services.

Transmission Control Protocol/Internet Protocol (TCP/IP)   Network reference model used by the U.S. Department of Defense and widely used in the United States.

Transnational   Approach to organizing a business in which sales and production activities are managed from a global perspective without reference to national borders.

Turing test   A test devised by Alan Turing to determine if a machine is intelligent. A computer and a human are placed in separate rooms connected by a communications link; if the human is not aware that he or she is communicating with a machine, the machine is intelligent.

Twisted wire   The oldest transmission medium, consisting of strands of wire twisted in pairs, it forms the basis for the analog phone system.

Universal Product Code   A coding scheme in which bars and the width of space between them represent data that can be read by OCR scanning devices; frequently used in bar codes.

UNIX   A machine-independent operating system for microcomputers, minicomputers, and mainframes; it is interactive ad supports multiuser processing, multitasking, and networking.

Value-added network (VAN)   A multimedia, multipath network managed by a private firm that sets up the network and charges other firms a fee to use it.

Value chain   The viewing of a business firm as a series of basic activities that add value to the firm's services or products.

Very-high-level programming language   A programming language that produces program code with far fewer instructions than conventional languages; used primarily by professional programmers.

Video display terminal   A screen on which output can be displayed; varieties include monochrome or color, and text or text/graphics.

Videoconferencing   Teleconferencing in which participants can see each other on video screens.

Virtual storage   The division of programs into small fixed- or variable-length portions; only a small portion is stored in primary memory at one time so that programs can be used more efficiently by the computer.

Voice mail   A telecommunications system in which the spoken message of the sender is digitized, transmitted over a telecommunications network, and stored on disk until the recipient is ready to listen; at this time the message is reconverted to audio form.

Voice output   Output that emerges as spoken words rather than as a visual display.

Volatile   Property of memory that means that its contents will be lost if electric power is disrupted or the computer is turned off.

Wide area network (WAN)   A telecommunications network covering a large geographical distance; provided by common carriers that are licensed by the government.

Winchester disk system   A hermetically sealed unit of hard disks that cannot be removed from the disk drive.

Windows   A GUI shell that runs in conjunction with the DOS operating system.

Windows NT   A powerful operating system for use with 32-bit microprocessors in networked environments; supports multitasking and multiprocessing and can be used with Intel and some other types of microprocessors.

Word length   The number of bits that a computer can process together as a unit.

Word processing software   Software that handles such applications as electronic editing, formatting, and printing of documents; may include advanced features to correct spelling errors, check grammar, and offer a thesaurus for synonyms and antonyms.

Workstation   A desktop computer with powerful graphics and mathematical processing capabilities as well as the ability to perform several tasks at once.

WORM   An optical disk system in which data can be recorded only once on the disk by users and cannot be erased; stands for Write Once, Read Many.

Name Index

Organization Index

Subject Index